Network Algorithmics

Network Algorithmics

An Interdisciplinary Approach to Designing Fast Networked Devices

Second Edition

George Varghese
UCLA Department of Computer Science
Los Angeles, CA, United States

Jun Xu
School of Computer Science
Georgia Institute of Technology
Atlanta, GA, United States

MORGAN KAUFMANN PUBLISHERS

ELSEVIER   AN IMPRINT OF ELSEVIER

Morgan Kaufmann is an imprint of Elsevier
50 Hampshire Street, 5th Floor, Cambridge, MA 02139, United States

Notices

Knowledge and best practice in this field are constantly changing. As new research and experience broaden our understanding, changes in research methods, professional practices, or medical treatment may become necessary.

Practitioners and researchers must always rely on their own experience and knowledge in evaluating and using any information, methods, compounds, or experiments described herein. In using such information or methods they should be mindful of their own safety and the safety of others, including parties for whom they have a professional responsibility.

To the fullest extent of the law, neither the Publisher nor the authors, contributors, or editors, assume any liability for any injury and/or damage to persons or property as a matter of products liability, negligence or otherwise, or from any use or operation of any methods, products, instructions, or ideas contained in the material herein.

ISBN: 978-0-12-809927-8

For information on all Morgan Kaufmann and Elsevier publications
visit our website at https://www.elsevier.com/books-and-journals

Publisher: Mara Conner
Editorial Project Manager: Lindsay C. Lawrence
Production Project Manager: Manchu Mohan
Cover Designer: Matthew Limbert

Typeset by VTeX

For Aju and Tim and Andrew, who made all this possible...

Contents

Preface to the second edition

Unless otherwise stated, this preface is written by author Xu, who is referred to as "I" in the following. Author Varghese is referred to as "George" in the following.

When George invited me in 2015 to write the second edition and become a co-author of this legendary book, I felt both humbled and honored. I also felt a deep sense of mission, as the bulk of my research and teaching had been on network algorithmics since the mid-1990s and still is.

When I signed the new edition contract with the publisher, I was originally committed to significantly revising only three chapters: Chapter 13 (Switching), Chapter 14 (Scheduling packets), and Chapter 16 (Measuring network traffic). In August 2020, at the suggestion of George, I agreed to add two sections, on EarlyBird (Section 17.6) and Carousel (Section 17.7) respectively, to Chapter 17 (Network security), and one section on d-Left approach (Section 10.3.3), to Chapter 10 (Exact-match lookups).

I have made the following major revisions to Chapter 13 (Switching). First, I have made the use of virtual output queueing (VOQ) in switching a separate section (Section 13.7) instead of an integral part of the parallel iterative matching (PIM) algorithm (Section 13.7 in the first edition), since the concept of VOQ was introduced a few years earlier than PIM. Sections 13.11 through 13.16 are entirely new, in which a few more single-crossbar switching algorithms, including Sample-and-Compare, SERENA, QPS, SB-QPS, and SW-QPS, are introduced. This addition is critical, because PIM–iSLIP was the only single-crossbar switching algorithm "series" described in the first edition, which did not show readers any alternative way of designing such switching algorithms. These newly added algorithms provide such an alternative viewpoint. Each of them was selected (to be included in this book) for their conceptual simplicity, low computational and communication complexity, and elegance. In Section 13.17, I have described the combined input and output queueing (CIOQ) proposal that advocates combining switching with packet scheduling for providing QoS guarantees. Finally, I have added a short section (13.18.5) on load-balanced switching, a research topic that just emerged when the first edition went into print. A few other sections have been updated with "modern materials." For example, in Section 13.18.3 (Clos networks for medium-size routers), I have added a few paragraphs describing how a 3-stage Clos network can be used for data center networking and switching.

I have made the following major revisions to Chapter 14 (Scheduling packets). In Section 14.3, I have added approximate fair dropping (AFD), a low-complexity technique for fair bandwidth allocation. In Sections 14.8 through 14.14, I have added GPS, WFQ, WF2Q, QFQ, and an efficient ($O(\log n)$ time complexity per packet) algorithm, called the shape data structure (published in 2004), for tracking the GPS clock, which makes WFQ and WF^2Q efficiently implementable (also with $O(\log n)$ time complexity per packet). The fact that WFQ, an algorithm that is known to provide very strong fairness guarantees, is efficiently implementable using the shape data structure is extremely important since WFQ has been widely believed to be not efficiently implementable (with a time complexity of $O(n)$ per packet), even to this day. In Section 14.15, I have described two research proposals towards making packet scheduling reprogrammable in switches and routers.

I have made the following major revisions to Chapter 16 (Measuring network traffic). I have added a third SRAM/DRAM hybrid counter array scheme in Section 16.3 to the two such schemes described in Section 16.2. The former is very different than the latter two, as the former is randomized, whereas the latter two are both deterministic. However, all three counter schemes are passive in the sense they allow fast increments but do not allow fast reads. Hence, in Sections 16.4 and 16.5, I introduce an active counter array scheme called BRICK and a flow-state lookup scheme (that by definition has to be active) called RIH. Finally, in Sections 16.15 through 16.19, I provide a crash course on network data streaming and sketching (DSS). DSS, which originated first in the area of databases, has evolved over the past two decades into a booming research subtopic of network measurement and monitoring. For example, in the past decade or so, SIGCOMM and NSDI together accept several network DSS papers almost every year.

George has made significant updates to Chapters 5 (Copying data); 6 (Transferring control); 7 (Maintaining timers); 11 (Prefix-match lookups); 12 (Packet classification); 15 (Routers as distributed systems); and 18 (Conclusions).

My work in writing this edition has been supported in part by US National Science Foundation through grants NeTS-1423182, CNS-1909048, and CNS-2007006. I have reported my effort and progress every year in the annual or final project reports.

A special thanks to my current and former editors, Lindsay Lawrence and Brian Romer and Todd Green; to my co-author George, who came up with the ingenious term "network algorithmics" that defined the bulk of my research in the past 25 years; to my Ph.D. advisor, Mukesh Singhal, who taught me how to write research papers; to all my collaborators on various network algorithmics topics, especially to Bill Lin; to many colleagues at Georgia Tech, especially to Mostafa Ammar and Ellen Zegura; to former and current School Chairs Lance Fortnow and Vivek Sarkar who gave me a reduced service load for this book-writing effort; to former and current Ph.D. students who adventured in the field of network algorithmics with me and who helped me with drawing figures and tables, proofreading, and fixing 100+ "book bugs" in the first edition collected by George; to anonymous reviewers of this book; to my parents and my brother; to my wife Linda; and to my daughter Ellie.

Preface

Computer networks have become an integral part of society. We take for granted the ability to transact commerce over the Internet and that users can avail themselves of a burgeoning set of communication methods, which range from file sharing to Web logs. However, for networks to take their place as part of the fundamental infrastructure of society, they must provide performance guarantees.

We take for granted that electricity will flow when a switch is flicked and that telephone calls will be routed on Mother's Day. But the performance of computer networks such as the Internet is still notoriously unreliable. While there are many factors that go into performance, one major issue is that of network bottlenecks. There are two types of network bottlenecks: *resource bottlenecks* and *implementation bottlenecks*.

Resource bottlenecks occur when network performance is limited by the speed of the underlying hardware; examples include slow processors in server platforms and slow communication links. Resource bottlenecks can be worked around, at some cost, by buying faster hardware. However, it is quite often the case that the underlying hardware is perfectly adequate but that the real bottleneck is a design issue in the implementation. For example, a Web server running on the fastest processors may run slowly because of redundant data copying. Similarly, a router with a simple packet classification algorithm may start dropping packets when the number of ACL rules grows beyond a limit, though it keeps up with link speeds when classification is turned off. This book concentrates on such network implementation bottlenecks, especially at servers and routers.

Beyond servers and routers, new breeds of networking devices that introduce new performance bottlenecks are becoming popular. As networks become more integrated, devices such as storage area networks (SANs) and multimedia switches are becoming common. Further, as networks get more complex, various special-purpose network appliances for file systems and security are proliferating. While the first generation of such devices justified themselves by the new functions they provided, it is becoming critical that future network appliances keep up with link speeds.

Thus the objective of this book is to provide a set of techniques to overcome implementation bottlenecks at *all* networking devices and to provide a set of principles and models to help overcome current and *future* networking bottlenecks.

Audience

This book was written to answer a need for a text on efficient protocol implementations. The vast majority of networking books are on network protocols; even the implementation books are, for the most part, detailed explanations of the protocol. While protocols form the foundation of the field, there are just a handful of fundamental network infrastucture protocols left, such as TCP and IP. On the other hand, there are many implementations as most companies and start-ups customize their products to gain competitive advantage. This is exacerbated by the tendency to place TCP and IP everywhere, from bridges to SAN switches to toasters.

Thus there are many more people implementing protocols than designing them. *This is a textbook for implementors, networking students, and networking researchers, covering ground from the art of building a fast Web server to building a fast router and beyond.*

To do so, this book describes a collection of efficient implementation techniques; in fact, an initial section of each chapter concludes with a Quick Reference Guide for implementors that points to the most useful techniques for each topic. However, the book goes further and distills a fundamental method of crafting solutions to new network bottlenecks that we call *network algorithmics*. This provides the reader tools to design different implementations for specific contexts and to deal with new bottlenecks that will undoubtedly arise in a changing world.

Here is a detailed profile of our intended audience.

- *Network Protocol Implementors:* This group includes implementors of endnode networking stacks for large servers, PCs, and workstations and for network appliances. It also includes implementors of classic network interconnection devices, such as routers, bridges, switches, and gateways, as well as devices that monitor networks for measurement and security purposes. It also includes implementors of storage area networks, distributed computing infrastructures, multimedia switches and gateways, and other new networking devices. This book can be especially useful for implementors in start-ups as well as in established companies, for whom improved performance can provide an edge.
- *Networking Students:* Undergraduate and graduate students who have mastered the basics of network protocols can use this book as a text that describes how protocols should be implemented to improve performance, potentially an important aspect of their future jobs.
- *Instructors:* Instructors can use this book as a textbook for a one-semester course on network algorithmics.
- *Systems Researchers:* Networking and other systems researchers can use this text as a reference and as a stimulus for further research in improving system performance. Given that distributed operating systems and distributed computing infrastructures (e.g., the Grid) rely on an underlying networking core whose performance can be critical, this book can be useful to general systems researchers.

What this book is about

Chapter 1 provides a more detailed introduction to network algorithmics. For now, we informally define network algorithmics as interdisciplinary systems approach to streamlining network implementations. Network algorithmics is *interdisciplinary*, because it requires techniques from diverse fields such as architecture, operating systems, hardware design, and algorithms. Network algorithmics is also a *systems* approach, because routers and servers are systems in which efficiencies can be gained by moving functions in time and space between subsystems.

In essence, this book is about three things: fundamental networking implementation bottlenecks, general principles to address new bottlenecks, and techniques for specific bottlenecks that can be derived from the general principles.

Fundamental bottlenecks for an endnode such as a PC or workstation include data copying, control transfer, demultiplexing, timers, buffer allocation, checksums, and protocol processing. Similarly, fundamental bottlenecks for interconnect devices such as routers and SAN switches include exact and prefix lookups, packet classification, switching, and the implementation of measurement and security primitives. Chapter 1 goes into more detail about the inherent causes of these bottlenecks.

The fundamental methods that encompass network algorithmics include implementation models (Chapter 2) and 15 implementation principles (Chapter 3). The implementation models include models of operating systems, protocols, hardware, and architecture. They are included because the world of network protocol implementation requires the skills of several different communities, including operating system experts, protocol pundits, hardware designers, and computer architects. The implementation models are an attempt to bridge the gaps between these traditionally separate communities.

On the other hand, the implementation principles are an attempt to abstract the main ideas behind many specific implementation techniques. They include such well-known principles as "Optimize the expected case." They also include somewhat less well-known principles, such as "Combine DRAM with SRAM," which is a surprisingly powerful principle for producing fast hardware designs for network devices.

While Part 1 of the book lays out the methodology of network algorithmics, Part 2 *applies* the methodology to specific network bottlenecks in endnodes and servers. For example, Part 2 discusses copy avoidance techniques (such as passing virtual memory pointers and RDMA) and efficient control transfer methods (such as bypassing the kernel, as in the VIA proposal, and techniques for building event-driven servers).

Similarly, Part 3 of the book applies the methodology of Part 1 to interconnect devices, such as network routers. For example, Part 3 discusses efficient prefix-lookup schemes (such as multibit or compressed tries) and efficient switching schemes (such as those based on virtual output queues and bipartite matching).

Finally, Part 4 of the book applies the methodology of Part 1 to new functions for security and measurement that could be housed in either servers or interconnect devices. For example, Part 4 discusses efficient methods to compress large traffic reports and efficient methods to detect attacks.

Organization of the book

This book is organized into four overall parts. Each part is made as self-contained as possible to allow detailed study. Readers that are pressed for time can consult the index or Table of Contents for a particular topic (e.g., IP lookups). More importantly, the opening section of each chapter concludes with a Quick Reference Guide that points to the most important topics for implementors. The Quick Reference Guide may be the fastest guide for usefully skimming a chapter.

Part 1 of the book aims to familiarize the reader with the rules and philosophy of network algorithmics. It starts with Chapter 2, which describes simple models of protocols, operating systems, hardware design, and endnode and router architectures. Chapter 3 describes in detail the 15 principles used as a cornerstone for the book. Chapter 4 rounds out the first part by providing 15 examples, drawn for the most part from real implementation problems, to allow the reader a first opportunity to see the principles in action on real problems.

Part 2 of the book, called "Playing with Endnodes," shows how to build fast endnode implementations, such as Web servers, that run on general-purpose operating systems and standard computer architectures. It starts with Chapter 5, which shows how to reduce or avoid extra data copying. (Copying often occurs when network data is passed between implementation modules) and how to increase cache efficiency. Chapter 6 shows how to reduce or avoid the overhead of transferring control between implementation modules, such as the device driver, the kernel, and the application. Chapter 7 describes how to efficiently manage thousands of outstanding timers, a critical issue for large servers. Chapter 8 describes how to efficiently demultiplex data to receiving applications in a single step, allowing innovations such as user-level networking. Chapter 9 describes how to implement specific functions that often recur in specific protocol implementations, such as buffer allocation, checksums, sequence number bookkeeping, and reassembly. An overview of Part 2 can be found in Fig. 1.1.

Part 3 of the book, called "Playing with Routers," shows how to build fast routers, bridges, and gateways. It begins with three chapters that describe state lookups of increasing complexity. Chapter 10 describes exact-match lookups, which are essential for the design of bridges and ARP caches. Chapter 11 describes prefix-match lookups, which are used by Internet routers to forward packets. Chapter 12 describes packet classification, a more sophisticated form of lookup required for security and quality of service. Chapter 13 describes how to build crossbar switches, which interconnect input and output links of devices such as routers. Finally, Chapter 14 describes packet-scheduling algorithms, which are used to provide quality-of-service, and Chapter 15 discusses routers as distributed systems, with examples focusing on performance and the use of design and reasoning techniques from distributed algorithms. While this list of functions seems short, one can build a fast router by designing a fast lookup algorithm, a fast switch, and fast packet-scheduling algorithms. Part 4, called "Endgame," starts by speculating on the potential need for implementing more complex tasks in the future. For example, Chapter 16 describes efficient implementation techniques for measurement primitives, while Chapter 17 describes efficient implementation techniques for security primitives. The book ends with a short chapter, Chapter 18, which reaches closure by distilling the unities that underly the many different topics in this book. This chapter also briefly presents examples of the use of algorithmics in a canonical router (the Cisco GSR) and a canonical server (the Flash Web server). A more detailed overview of Parts 3 and 4 of the book can be found in Fig. 1.2.

Features

The book has the following features that readers, implementors, students, and instructors can take advantage of.

Intuitive introduction: The introductory paragraph of each chapter in Parts 2, 3, and 4 uses an intuitive, real-world analogy to motivate each bottleneck. For example, we use the analogy of making multiple photocopies of a document for data copying and the analogy of a flight database for prefix lookups.

Quick Reference Guide: For readers familiar with a topic and pressed for time, the opening section of each chapter concludes with a Quick Reference Guide that points to the most important implementation ideas and the corresponding section numbers.

Chapter organization: To help orient the reader, immediately after the Quick Reference Guide in each chapter is a map of the entire chapter.

Summary of techniques: To emphasize the correlation between principles and techniques, at the start of each chapter is a table that summarizes the techniques described, together with the corresponding principles.

Consistent use of principles: After a detailed description in Chapter 3 of 15 principles, the rest of the book consistently uses these principles in describing specific techniques. For reference, the principles are summarized inside the front cover. Principles are referred to consistently by number—for example, **P9** for Principle 9. Since principle numbers are hard to remember, three aids are provided. Besides the inside front cover summary and the summary at the start of each chapter, the first use of a principle in any chapter is accompanied by an explicit statement of the principle.

Exercises: Chapter 4 of the book provides a set of real-life examples of applying the principles that have been enjoyed by past attendees of tutorials on network algorithmics. Every subsequent chapter through Chapter 17 is followed by a set of exercises. Brief solutions to these exercises can be found in an instructor's manual obtainable from Elsevier.

Additional Teacher and Student Resources: Helpful ancillaries have been prepared to aid learning and teaching.

- For students, resources are available here: https://www.elsevier.com/books-and-journals/book-companion/9780443136795.
- For qualified professors, instructor-only teaching materials (including Lecture slides in PDF for most chapters) can be requested here: https://educate.elsevier.com/book/details/9780128099278.

Usage

This book can be used in many ways.

Textbook: Students and instructors can use this book as the basis of a one-semester class. A semester class on network algorithmics can include most of Part 1 and can sample chapters from Part 2 (e.g., Chapter 5 on copying, Chapter 6 on control overhead) and from Part 3 (e.g., Chapter 11 on prefix lookups, Chapter 13 on switching).

Implementation guide: Implementors who care about performance may wish to read all of Part 1 and then sample Parts 2 and 3 according to their needs.

Reference book: Implementors and students can also use this book as a reference book in addition to other books on network protocols.

Why this book was written

The impetus for this book came from my academic research into efficient protocol implementation. It also came from three networking products I worked on with colleagues: the first bridge, the Gigaswitch, and the Procket 40 Gbps router. To prove itself against detractors, the first bridge was designed to operate at wire speed, an idea that spread to routers and the entire industry. My experience watching the work of Mark Kempf on the first bridge (see Chapter 10) led to a lasting interest in speeding up networking devices.

Next, the DEC Gigaswitch introduced me to the world of switching. Finally, the Procket router was designed by an interdisciplinary team that included digital designers who had designed processors, experts who had written vast amounts of the software in core routers, and some people like myself who were interested in algorithms. Despite the varied backgrounds, the team produced innovative new ideas, which convinced me of the importance of interdisciplinary thinking for performance breakthroughs. This motivated the writing of Chapter 2 on implementation models, an attempt to bridge the gaps between the different communities involved in high-performance designs.

For several years, I taught a class that collected together these techniques. The 15 principles emerged as a way to break up the techniques more finely and systematically. In retrospect, some principles seem redundant and glib. However, they serve as part of a first attempt to organize a vast amount of material.

I have taught five classes and three tutorials based on the material in this book, and so this book has been greatly influenced by student responses and ideas.

Acknowledgments

A special thanks to my editors: Karen Gettman and Rick Adams and Karyn Johnson; to all my advisors, who taught me so much: Wushow Chou, Arne Nillson, Baruch Awerbuch, Nancy Lynch; to all my mentors: Alan Kirby, Radia Perlman, Tony Lauck, Bob Thomas, Bob Simcoe, Jon Turner; to numerous colleages at DEC and other companies, especially to Sharad Merhotra, Bill Lynch, and Tony Li of Procket Networks, who taught me about real routers; to students who adventured in the field of network algorithmics with me; to numerous reviewers of this book and especially to Jon Snader, Tony Lauck, Brian Kernighan, Craig Partridge, and Radia Perlman for detailed comments; to Kevin D'Souza, Stefano Previdi, Anees Shaikh, and Darryl Veitch for their reviews and ideas; to my family, my mother, my wife's father and mother, and my sister; and, of course, to my wife, Aju, and my sons, Tim and Andrew.

I'd like to end by acknowledging my heroes: four teachers who have influenced me. The first is Leonard Bernstein, who taught me in his lectures on music that a teacher's enthusiasm for the material can be infectious. The second is George Polya, who taught me in his books on problem solving that the process of discovery is as important as the final discoveries themselves. The third is Socrates, who taught me through Plato that it is worth always questioning assumptions. The fourth is Jesus, who has taught me that life, and indeed this book, is not a matter of merit but of grace and gift.

15 principles used to overcome network bottlenecks

Number	Principle	Used In/Networking Example
P1	Avoid obvious waste	Zero-copy interfaces
P2	Shift computation in time	
P2a	Precompute	Application device channels
P2b	Evaluate lazily	Copy-on-write
P2c	Share expenses, batch	Integrated layer processing
P3	Relax system requirements	
P3a	Trade certainty for time	Stochastic fair queueing
P3b	Trade accuracy for time	Switch load balancing
P3c	Shift computation in space	IPv6 fragmentation
P4	Leverage off system components	
P4a	Exploit locality	Locality-driven receiver
P4b	Trade memory for speed	Processing; Lulea IP lookups
P4c	Exploit existing hardware	Fast TCP checksum
P5	Add hardwareg	
P5a	Use memory interleaving and pipelinin	Pipelined IP lookups
P5b	Use wide word parallelism	Shared memory switches
P5c	Combine DRAM and SRAM effectively	Maintaining counters
P6	Create efficient specialized routines	UDP checksums
P7	Avoid unnecessary generality	Fbufs
P8	Don't be tied to reference implementation	Upcalls
P9	Pass hints in layer interfaces	Packet filters
P10	Pass hints in protocol headers	Tag switching
P11	Optimize the expected case	Header prediction
P11a	Use caches	Fbufs
P12	Add state for speed	Active VC list
P12a	Compute incrementally	Recomputing CRCs
P13	Optimize degrees of freedom	IP trie lookups
P14	Use bucket sorting, bitmaps	Timing wheels
P15	Create efficient data structures	Level-4 switching

The rules of the game

"Come, Watson, come!" he cried. "The game is afoot!"
—Arthur Conan Doyle in *The Abbey Grange*

The first part of this book deals with specifying the rules of the network algorithmics game. We start with a quick introduction where we define network algorithmics and contrast it to algorithm design. Next, we present models of protocols, operating systems, processor architecture, and hardware design; these are the key disciplines used in the rest of the book. Then we present a set of 15 principles abstracted from the specific techniques presented later in the book. Part 1 ends with a set of sample problems together with solutions obtained using the principles. Implementors pressed for time should skim the Quick Reference Guides directly following the introduction to each chapter.

Introducing network algorithmics

What really makes it an invention is that someone decides not to change the solution to a known problem, but to change the question.

—Dean Kamen

Just as the objective of chess is to checkmate the opponent and the objective of tennis is to win matches, the objective of the network algorithmics game is to battle networking implementation bottlenecks.

Beyond specific techniques, this book distills a fundamental way of crafting solutions to internet bottlenecks that we call *network algorithmics*. This provides the reader tools to design different implementations for specific contexts and to deal with new bottlenecks that will undoubtedly arise in the changing world of networks.

So what is network algorithmics? Network algorithmics goes beyond the design of efficient algorithms for networking tasks, though this has an important place. In particular, network algorithmics recognizes the primary importance of taking an interdisciplinary systems approach to streamlining network implementations.

Network algorithmics is an *interdisciplinary* approach because it encompasses such fields as architecture and operating systems (for speeding up servers), hardware design (for speeding up network devices such as routers), and algorithm design (for designing scalable algorithms). Network algorithmics is also a *systems* approach, because it is described in this book using a set of 15 principles that exploit the fact that routers and servers are systems, in which efficiencies can be gained by moving functions in time and space between subsystems.

The problems addressed by network algorithmics are fundamental networking performance *bottlenecks*. The solutions advocated by network algorithmics are a set of fundamental *techniques* to address these bottlenecks. Next, we provide a quick preview of both the bottlenecks and the methods.

1.1 The problem: network bottlenecks

The main problem considered in this book is how to make networks *easy to use* while at the same time realizing the *performance* of the raw hardware. Ease of use comes from the use of powerful network abstractions, such as socket interfaces and prefix-based forwarding. Unfortunately, without care, such abstractions exact a large performance penalty when compared to the capacity of raw transmission links such as optical fiber. To study this performance gap in more detail, we examine two fundamental categories of networking devices, *endnodes* and *routers*.

Network Algorithmics. https://doi.org/10.1016/B978-0-12-809927-8.00006-3

1.1.1 Endnode bottlenecks

Endnodes are the endpoints of the network. They include personal computers and workstations as well as large servers that provide services. Endnodes are specialized toward computation, as opposed to networking, and are typically designed to support *general-purpose* computation. Thus endnode bottlenecks are typically the result of two forces: structure and scale.

- *Structure:* To be able to run arbitrary code, personal computers and large servers typically have an operating system that mediates between applications and the hardware. To ease the software development, most large operating systems are carefully structured as *layered software*; to protect the operating system from other applications, operating systems implement a set of *protection mechanisms*; finally, core operating systems routines, such as schedulers and allocators, are written using *general mechanisms* that target as wide a class of applications as possible. Unfortunately, the combination of layered software, protection mechanisms, and excessive generality can slow down networking software greatly, even with the fastest processors.
- *Scale:* The emergence of large servers providing Web and other services causes further performance problems. In particular, a large server such as a Web server will typically have thousands of concurrent clients. Many operating systems use inefficient data structures and algorithms that were designed for an era when the number of connections was small.

Fig. 1.1 previews the main endnode bottlenecks covered in this book, together with causes and solutions. The first bottleneck occurs because conventional operating system structures cause packet data *copying* across protection domains; the situation is further complicated in Web servers by similar copying with respect to the file system and by other manipulations, such as checksums, that examine all the

Bottleneck	Chapter	Cause	Sample Solution
Copying	5	Protection, structure	Copying many data blocks without OS intervention (e.g., RDMA)
Context switching	6	Complex scheduling	User-level protocol implementations Event-driven Web servers
System calls	6	Protection, structure	Direct channels from applications to drivers (e.g., VIA)
Timers	7	Scaling with number of timers	Timing wheels
Demultiplexing	8	Scaling with number of endpoints	BPF and Pathfinder
Checksums/ CRCs	9	Generality Scaling with link speeds	Multibit computation
Protocol code	9	Generality	Header prediction

FIGURE 1.1

Preview of endnode bottlenecks, solutions to which are described in Part 2 of the book.

packet data. Chapter 5 describes a number of techniques to reduce these overheads while preserving the goals of system abstractions, such as protection and structure. The second major overhead is the *control overhead* caused by switching between threads of control (or protection domains) while processing a packet; this is addressed in Chapter 6.

Networking applications use timers to deal with failure. With a large number of connections, the timer overhead at a server can become large; this overhead is addressed in Chapter 7. Similarly, network messages must be demultiplexed (i.e., steered) on receipt to the right end application; techniques to address this bottleneck are addressed in Chapter 8. Finally, there are several other common protocol processing tasks, such as buffer allocation and checksums, which are addressed in Chapter 9.

1.1.2 Router bottlenecks

Though we concentrate on Internet routers, almost all the techniques described in this book apply equally well to any other network devices, such as bridges, switches, gateways, monitors, and security appliances, and to protocols other than IP, such as FiberChannel.

Thus throughout the rest of the book, it is often useful to think of a *router* as a "generic network interconnection device." Unlike endnodes, these are special-purpose devices devoted to networking. Thus there is very little structural overhead within a router, with only the use of a very lightweight operating system and a clearly separated forwarding path that often is completely implemented in hardware. Instead of structure, the fundamental problems faced by routers are caused by *scale* and *services*.

- *Scale:* Network devices face two areas of scaling: *bandwidth scaling* and *population scaling*. Bandwidth scaling occurs because optical links keep getting faster, as the progress from 1-Gbps to 40-Gbps links shows, and because Internet traffic keeps growing due to a diverse set of new applications. Population scaling occurs because more endpoints get added to the Internet as more enterprises go online.
- *Services:* The need for speed and scale drove much of the networking industry in the 1980s and 1990s as more businesses went online (e.g., Amazon.com) and whole new online services were created (e.g., eBay). But the very success of the Internet requires careful attention in the next decade to make it more effective by providing guarantees in terms of performance, security, and reliability. After all, if manufacturers (e.g., Dell) sell more online than by other channels, it is important to provide *network guarantees*—delay in times of congestion, protection during attacks, and availability when failures occur. Finding ways to implement these new services at high speeds will be a major challenge for router vendors in the next decade.

Fig. 1.2 previews the main router (bridge/gateway) bottlenecks covered in this book, together with causes and solutions.

First, all networking devices forward packets to their destination by looking up a forwarding table. The simplest forwarding table lookup does an exact match with a destination address, as exemplified by bridges. Chapter 10 describes fast and scalable exact-match lookup schemes. Unfortunately, population scaling has made lookups far more complex for routers. To deal with large Internet populations, routers keep a single entry called a *prefix* (analogous to a telephone area code) for a large group of stations. Thus routers must do a more complex *longest-prefix-match* lookup. Chapter 11 describes solutions to this problem that scale to increasing speeds and table sizes.

Bottleneck	Chapter	Cause	Sample Solution
Exact lookups	10	Link speed scaling	Parallel hashing
Prefix lookups	11	Link speed scaling Prefix database size scaling	Compressed multibit tries
Packet classification	12	Service differentiation Link speed and size scaling	Decision tree algorithms Hardware parallelism (CAMs)
Switching	13	Optical-electronic speed gap Head-of-line blocking	Crossbar switches Virtual output queues
Fair queueing	14	Service differentiation Link speed scaling Memory scaling	Weighted fair queueing Deficit round robin DiffServ, Core Stateless
Internal bandwidth	15	Scaling of internal bus speeds	Reliable striping
Measurement	16	Link speed scaling	Juniper's DCU
Security	17	Scaling in number and intensity of attacks	Traceback with bloom filters Extracting worm signatures

FIGURE 1.2

Preview of router bottlenecks, solutions to which are described in Parts 3 and 4 of the book.

Many routers today offer what is sometimes called *service differentiation*, where different packets can be treated differently in order to provide service and security guarantees. Unfortunately, this requires an even more complex form of lookup called *packet classification*, in which the lookup is based on the destination, source, and even the services that a packet is providing. This challenging issue is tackled in Chapter 12.

Next, all networking devices can be abstractly considered as switches that shunt packets coming in from a set of input links to a set of output links. Thus a fundamental issue is that of building a high-speed switch. This is hard, especially in the face of the growing gap between optical and electronic speeds. The standard solution is to use parallelism via a *crossbar switch*. Unfortunately, it is nontrivial to schedule a crossbar at high speeds, and parallelism is limited by a phenomenon known as *head-of-line blocking*. Worse, population scaling and optical multiplexing are forcing switch vendors to build switches with a large number of ports (e.g., 256), which exacerbates these other problems. Solutions to these problems are described in Chapter 13.

While the previous bottlenecks are caused by scaling, the next bottleneck is caused by the need for new services. The issue of providing performance guarantees at high speeds is treated in Chapter 14, where the issue of implementing so-called QoS (quality of service) mechanisms is studied. Chapter 15 briefly surveys another bottleneck that is becoming an increasing problem: the issue of bandwidth within a router. It describes sample techniques, such as striping across internal buses and chip-to-chip links.

The final sections of the book take a brief look at emerging services that must, we believe, be part of a well-engineered Internet of the future. First, routers of the future must build in support for measurement, because measurement is the key to engineering networks to provide guarantees. While routers today provide some support for measurement in terms of counters and NetFlow records, Chapter 16 also considers more innovative measurement mechanisms that may be implemented in the future.

Chapter 17 describes security support, some of which is already being built into routers. Given the increased sophistication, virulence, and rate of network attacks, we believe that implementing security features in networking devices (whether routers or dedicated intrusion prevention/detection devices) will be essential. Further, unless the security device can keep up with high-speed links, the device may miss vital information required to spot an attack.

1.2 **The techniques: network algorithmics**

Throughout this book, we will talk of many specific techniques: of interrupts, copies, and timing wheels; of Pathfinder and Sting; of why some routers are very slow; and whether Web servers can scale. But what underlies the assorted techniques in this book and makes it more than a recipe book is the notion of *network algorithmics*. As said earlier, network algorithmics recognizes the primary importance of taking a *systems* approach to streamlining network implementations.

While everyone recognizes that the Internet is a system consisting of routers and links, it is perhaps less obvious that every networking device, from the Cisco GSR to an Apache Web server, is also a system. A system is built out of interconnected subsystems that are instantiated at various points in time. For example, a core router consists of line cards with forwarding engines and packet memories connected by a crossbar switch. The router behavior is affected by decisions at various time scales, which range from manufacturing time (when default parameters are stored in NVRAM) to route computation time (when routers conspire to compute routes) to packet-forwarding time (when packets are sent to adjoining routers).

Thus one key observation in the systems approach is that one can often design an efficient subsystem by moving some of its functions in *space* (i.e., to other subsystems) or in *time* (i.e., to points in time before or after the function is apparently required). In some sense, the practitioner of network algorithmics is an unscrupulous opportunist willing to change the rules at any time to make the game easier. The only constraint is that the functions provided by the overall system continue to satisfy users.

In one of Mark Twain's books, a Connecticut Yankee is transported back in time to King Arthur's court. The Yankee then uses a gun to fight against dueling knights accustomed to jousting with lances. This is an example of changing system assumptions (replacing lances by guns) to solve a problem (winning a duel).

Considering the constraints faced by the network implementor at high speeds—increasingly complex tasks, larger systems to support, small amounts of high-speed memory, and a small number of memory accesses—it may require every trick, every gun in one's arsenal, to keep pace with the increasing speed and scale of the Internet. The designer can throw hardware at the problem, change the system assumptions, design a new algorithm—whatever it takes to get the job done.

This book is divided into four parts. The first part, of which this is the first chapter, lays a foundation for applying network algorithmics to packet processing. The second chapter of the first part outlines models, and the third chapter presents general principles used in the remainder of the book.

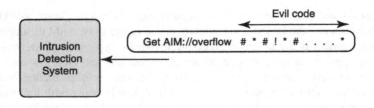

FIGURE 1.3

Getting wind of an evil packet by noticing the frequency of unprintable characters.

One of the best ways to get a quick idea about what network algorithmics is about is to plunge right away into a warm-up example. While the warm-up example that follows is in the context of a device within the network where new hardware can be designed, note that Part 2 is about building efficient servers using only software design techniques.

1.2.1 Warm-up example: scenting an evil packet

Imagine a front-end network monitor (or intrusion detection system) on the periphery of a corporate network that wishes to flag suspicious incoming packets—packets that could contain attacks on internal computers. A common such attack is a *buffer overflow* attack, where the attacker places machine code C in a network header field F.

If the receiving computer allocates a buffer too small for header field F and is careless about checking for overflow, the code C can spill onto the receiving machine's stack. With a little more effort, the intruder can make the receiving machine actually execute evil code C. C then takes over the receiver machine. Fig. 1.3 shows such an attack embodied in a familiar field, a destination Web URL (uniform resource locator). How might the monitor detect the presence of such a suspicious URL? A possible way is to observe that URLs containing evil code are often too long (an easy check) and often have a large fraction of unusual (at least in URLs) characters, such as #. Thus the monitor could mark such packets (containing URLs that are too long and have too many occurrences of such unusual characters) for a more thorough examination.

It is worth stating at the outset that the security implications of this strategy need to be carefully thought out. For example, there may be several innocuous programs, such as CGI scripts, in URLs that lead to false positives. Without getting too hung up in overall architectural implications, let us assume that this was a specification handed down to a chip architect by a security architect. We now use this sample problem, suggested by Mike Fisk, to illustrate algorithmics in action.

Faced with such a specification, a chip designer may use the following design process, which illustrates some of the principles of network algorithmics. The process starts with a strawman design and refines the design using techniques such as designing a better algorithm, relaxing the specification, and exploiting hardware.

1.2.2 Strawman solution

The check of overall length is straightforward to implement, so we concentrate on checking for a prevalence of suspicious characters. The first strawman solution is illustrated in Fig. 1.4. The chip

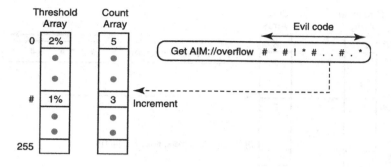

FIGURE 1.4

Strawman solution for detecting an evil packet by counting occurrences of each character via a count array (middle) and then comparing in a final pass with an array of acceptable thresholds (left).

maintains two arrays, T and C, with 256 elements each, one for each possible value of an 8-bit character. The threshold array, T-, contains the acceptable percentage (as a fraction of the entire URL length) for each character. If the occurrences of a character in an actual URL fall above this fraction, the packet should be flagged. Each character can have a different threshold.

The count array, C, in the middle, contains the current count $C[i]$ for each possible character i. When the chip reads a new character "i" in the URL, it increments $C[i]$ by 1. $C[i]$ is initialized to 0 for all values of i when a new packet is encountered. The incrementing process starts only after the chip parses the HTTP header and recognizes the start of a URL.

In HTTP, the end of a URL is signified by two newline characters; thus one can tell the length of the URL only after parsing the entire URL string. Thus, after the end of the URL is encountered, the chip makes a final pass over the array C. If $C[j] \geq L \cdot T[j]$ for any j, where L is the length of the URL, the packet is flagged.

Assume that packets are coming into the monitor at high speed and that we wish to finish processing a packet before the next one arrives. This requirement, called *wire-speed processing*, is very common in networking; it prevents processing backlogs even in the worst case. To meet wire-speed requirements, ideally the chip should do a small constant number of operations for every URL byte. Assume the main step of incrementing a counter can be done in the time to receive a byte.

Unfortunately, the two passes over the array, first to initialize it and then to check for threshold violations, make this design slow. Minimum packet sizes are often as small as 40 bytes and include only network headers. Adding 768 more operations (1 write and 1 read to each element of C, and 1 read of T for each of 256 indices) can make this design infeasible.

1.2.3 Thinking algorithmically

Intuitively, the second pass through the arrays C and T at the end seems like a waste. For example, it suffices to alarm if *any* character is over the threshold. So why check all characters? This suggests keeping track only of the largest character count c; at the end, perhaps the algorithm needs to check only whether c is over threshold with respect to the total URL length L.

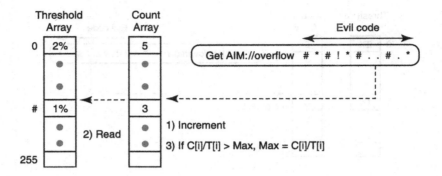

FIGURE 1.5

Avoiding the final loop through the threshold array by keeping track only of *Max*, the highest counter encountered so far relative to its threshold value.

This does not quite work. A nonsuspicious character such as "e" may well have a very high occurrence count. However, "e" is also likely to be specified with a high threshold. Thus if we keep track only of "e" with, say, a count of 20, we may not keep track of "#" with, say, a count of 10. If the threshold of "#" is much smaller, the algorithm may cause a *false negative*: The chip may fail to alarm on a packet that should be flagged.

The counterexample suggests the following fix. The chip keeps track in a register of the highest counter relativized to the threshold value. More precisely, the chip keeps track of the highest relativized counter *Max* corresponding to some character k, such that $C[k]/T[k] = Max$ is the highest among all characters encountered so far. If a new character i is read, the chip increments $C[i]$. If $C[i]/T[i] > Max$, then the chip replaces the current stored value of *Max* with $C[i]/T[i]$. At the end of URL processing, the chip alarms if $Max \geq L$.

Here's why this works. If $Max = C[k]/T[k] \geq L$, clearly the packet must be flagged, because character k is over threshold. On the other hand, if $C[k]/T[k] < L$, then for any character i, it follows that $C[i]/T[i] \leq C[k]/T[k] < L$. Thus if *Max* falls below threshold, then no character is above threshold. Thus there can be no false negatives. This solution is shown in Fig. 1.5.

1.2.4 Refining the algorithm: exploiting hardware

The new algorithm has eliminated the loop at the end but still has to deal with a divide operation while processing each byte. Divide logic is somewhat complicated and worth avoiding if possible—but how?

Returning to the specification and its intended use, it seems likely that thresholds are not meant to be exact floating-point numbers. It is unlikely that the architect providing thresholds can estimate the values precisely; one is likely to approximate 2.78% as 3% without causing much difference to the security goals. So why not go further and approximate the threshold by some power of 2 less than the exact intended threshold? Thus if the threshold is 1/29, why not approximate it as 1/32?

Changing the specification in this way requires negotiation with the system architect. Assume that the architect agrees to this new proposal. Then a threshold such as 1/32 can be encoded compactly as

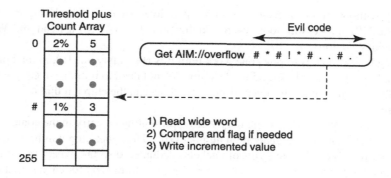

FIGURE 1.6

Using a wide word and a coalesced array to combine 2 reads into one.

the corresponding power of 2—i.e., 5. This threshold *shift* value can be stored in the threshold array instead of a fraction.

Thus when a character j is encountered, the chip increments $C[j]$ as usual and then shifts $C[j]$ to the left—dividing by $1/x$ is the same as multiplying by x—by the specified threshold. If the shifted value is higher than the last stored value for *Max*, the chip replaces the old value with the new value and marches on.

Thus the logic required to implement the processing of a byte is a simple shift-and-compare. The stored state is only a single register to store *Max*. As it stands, however, the design requires a Read to the Threshold array (to read the shift value), a Read to the Count array (to read the old count), and a Write to the Count array (to write back the incremented value).

Now reads to memory—1–2 nsec even for the fastest on-chip memories but possibly even as slow as 10 nsec for slower memories—are slower than logic. Single gate delays are only in the order of picoseconds, and shift logic does not require too many gate delays. Thus the processing bottleneck is the number of memory accesses.

The chip implementation can combine the 2 Reads to memory into 1 Read by coalescing the Count and Threshold arrays into a single array, as shown in Fig. 1.6. The idea is to make the memory words wide enough to hold the counter (say, 15 bits to handle packets of length 32K) and the threshold (depending on the precision necessary, no more than 14 bits). Thus the two fields can easily be combined into a larger word of size 29 bits. In practice, hardware can handle much larger words sizes of up to 1000 bits. Also, note that extracting the two fields packed into a single word, quite a chore in software, is trivial in hardware by routing wires appropriately between registers or by using multiplexers.

1.2.5 Cleaning up

We have postponed one thorny issue to this point. The terminal loop has been eliminated while leaving the initial initialization loop. To handle this, note that the chip has spare time for initialization after parsing the URL of the current packet and before encountering the URL of the next packet.

Unfortunately, packets can be as small as 50 bytes, even with an HTTP header. Thus even assuming a slack of 40 non-URL bytes other than the 10 bytes of the URL, this still does not suffice to initialize a 256-byte array without paying $256/40 = 6$ more operations per byte than during the processing of a URL. As in the URL processing loop, each initialization step requires a Read and Write of some element of the coalesced array.

A trick among lazy people is to postpone work until it is absolutely needed, in the hope that it may never be needed. Note that, strictly speaking, the chip does not need to initialize a $C[i]$ until character i is accessed for the first time in a subsequent packet. But how can the chip tell that it is seeing character i for the first time?

To implement lazy evaluation, each memory word representing an entry in the coalesced array must be expanded to include, say, a 3-bit generation number $G[i]$. The generation number can be thought of as a value of clock time measured in terms of packets encountered so far, except that it is limited to 3 bits. Thus, the chip keeps an additional register g, besides the extra $G[i]$ for each i, that is 3 bits long; g is incremented mod 8 for every packet encountered. In addition, every time $C[i]$ is updated, the chip updates $G[i]$ as well to reflect the current value of g.

Given the generation numbers, the chip need not initialize the count array after the current packet has been processed. However, consider the case of a packet whose generation number is h, which contains a character i in its URL. When the chip encounters i while processing the packet, the chip reads $C[i]$ and $G[i]$ from the Count array. If $G[i] \neq h$, this clearly indicates that entry i was last accessed by an earlier packet and has not been subsequently initialized. Thus the logic will write back the value of $C[i]$ as 1 (initialization plus increment) and set $G[i]$ to h. This is shown in Fig. 1.7.

The careful reader will immediately object. Since the generation number is only 3 bits, once the value of g wraps around, there can be aliasing. Thus if $G[i]$ is 5 and entry i is not accessed until eight more packets have gone by, g will have wrapped around to 5. If the next packet contains i, $C[i]$ will not be initialized and the count will (wrongly) accumulate the count of i in the current packet together with the count that occurred eight packets in the past.

The chip can avoid such aliasing by doing a separate "scrubbing" loop that reads the array and initializes all counters with outdated generation numbers. For correctness, the chip must guarantee one complete scan through the array for every eight packets processed. Given that one has a slack of (say) 40 non-URL bytes per packet, this guarantees a slack of 320 non-URL bytes after eight packets, which suffices to initialize a 256-element array using one Read and one Write per byte, whether the byte is a

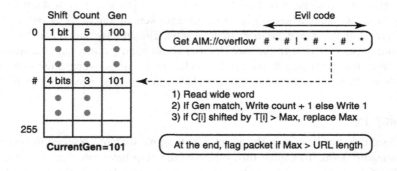

FIGURE 1.7

The final solution with generation numbers to finesse an initialization loop.

URL or a non-URL byte. Clearly, the designer can gain more slack, if needed, by increasing the bits in the generation number, at the cost of slightly increased storage in the array.

The chip, then, must have two states: one for processing URL bytes and one for processing non-URL bytes. When the URL is completely processed, the chip switches to the "Scrub" state. The chip maintains another register, which points to the next array entry s to be scrubbed. In the scrub state, when a non-URL character is received, the chip reads entry s in the coalesced array. If $G[s] \neq g$, $G[s]$ is reset to g and $C[s]$ is initialized to 0.

Thus the use of 3 extra bits of generation number per array entry has reduced initialization processing cycles, trading processing for storage. Altogether a coalesced array entry is now only 32 bits, 15 bits for a counter, 14 bits for a threshold shift value, and 3 bits for a generation number. Note that the added initialization check needed during URL byte processing does not increase memory references (the bottleneck) but adds slightly to the processing logic. In addition, it requires two more chip registers to hold g and s, a small additional expense.

1.2.6 Characteristics of network algorithmics

The example of scenting an evil packet illustrates three important aspects of network algorithmics.

a. **Network algorithmics is interdisciplinary:** Given the high rates at which network processing must be done, a router designer would be hard pressed not to use hardware. The example exploited several features of hardware: It assumed that wide words of arbitrary size were easily possible; it assumed that shifts were easier than divides; it assumed that memory references were the bottleneck; it assumed that a 256-element array contained in fast on-chip memory was feasible; it assumed that adding a few extra registers was feasible; and finally it assumed that small changes to the logic to combine URL processing and initialization were trivial to implement.

For the reader unfamiliar with hardware design, this is a little like jumping into a game of cards without knowing the rules and then finding oneself finessed and trumped in unexpected ways. A contention of this book is that mastery of a few relevant aspects of hardware design can help even a software designer understands at least the feasibility of different hardware designs. A further contention of this book is that such interdisciplinary thinking can help produce the best designs.

Thus Chapter 2 presents the rules of the game. It presents simple models of hardware that point out opportunities for finessing and trumping troublesome implementation issues. It also presents simple models of operating systems. This is done because end systems such as clients and Web servers require tinkering with and understanding operating system issues to improve performance, just as routers and network devices require tinkering with hardware.

b. **Network algorithmics recognizes the primacy of systems thinking:** The specification was relaxed to allow approximate thresholds in powers of 2, which simplified the hardware. Relaxing specifications and moving work from one subsystem to another is an extremely common systems technique, but it is not encouraged by current educational practice in universities, in which each area is taught in isolation.

Thus today, one has separate courses in algorithms, in operating systems, and in networking. This tends to encourage "black box" thinking instead of holistic or systems thinking. The example alluded to other systems techniques, such as the use of *lazy evaluation* and *trading memory for processing* in order to scrub the Count array.

Thus a feature of this book is an attempt to distill the system's principles used in algorithmics into a set of 15 principles, which are cataloged inside the front cover of the book and are explored in detail in Chapter 3. This book attempts to explain and dissect all the network implementations described in this book in terms of these principles. The principles are also given numbers for easy reference, though for the most part, we will use both the number and the name. For instance, take a quick peek at the inside front cover and you will find that relaxing specification is principle **P3** and lazy evaluation is **P2b**.

c. **Network algorithmics can benefit from algorithmic thinking:** While this book stresses the primacy of systems thinking to finesse problems wherever possible, there are many situations where systems constraints prevent any elimination of problems. In our example, after attempting to finesse the need for algorithmic thinking by relaxing the specification, the problem of false positives led to considering keeping track of the highest counter relative to its threshold value. As a second example, Chapter 11 shows that despite attempts to finesse Internet lookups using what is called *tag switching*, many routers resort to efficient algorithms for lookup.

It is worth emphasizing, however, that because the models are somewhat different from standard theoretical models, it is often insufficient to blindly reuse existing algorithms. For example, Chapter 13 discusses how the need to schedule a crossbar switch in 8 nsec leads to considering simpler maximal matching heuristics, as opposed to more complicated algorithms that produce optimal matchings in a bipartite graph.

As a second example, Chapter 11 describes how the BSD implementation of lookups blindly reused a data structure called a Patricia trie, which uses a skip count, to do IP lookups. The resulting algorithm requires complex backtracking.[1] A simple modification that keeps the actual bits that were skipped (instead of the count) avoids the need for backtracking. But this requires some insight into the black box (i.e., the algorithm) and its application.

In summary, the uncritical use of standard algorithms can miss implementation breakthroughs because of inappropriate *measures* (e.g., for packet filters such as BPF, the insertion of a new classifier can afford to take more time than search), inappropriate *models* (e.g., ignoring the effects of cache lines in software or parallelism in hardware), and inappropriate *analysis* (e.g., order-of-complexity results that hide constant factors crucial in ensuring wire-speed forwarding).

Thus another purpose of this book is to persuade implementors that insight into algorithms and the use of fundamental algorithmic techniques such as divide-and-conquer and randomization is important to master. This leads us to the following.

Definition. Network algorithmics is the use of an interdisciplinary systems approach, seasoned with algorithmic thinking, to design fast implementations of network processing tasks at servers, routers, and other networking devices.

Part 1 of the book is devoted to describing the network algorithmics approach in more detail. An overview of Part 1 is given in Fig. 1.8.

---

[1] The algorithm was considered to be the state of the art for many years and was even implemented in hardware in several router designs. In fact, a patent for lookups issued to a major router company appears to be a hardware implementation of BSD Patricia tries with backtracking. Any deficiencies of the algorithm can, of course, be mitigated by fast hardware. However, it is worth considering that a simple change to the algorithm could have simplified the hardware design.

Focus	Chapter	Motivation	Sample Topic
Models	2	Understand simple models for OS, hardware, networks	Memory technology techniques (interleaving, mixing SRAM/DRAM)
Strategies	3	Learn systems principles for overcoming bottlenecks	Pass hints, evaluate lazily Add state, exploit locality
Problems	4	Practice applying principles on simple problems	Designing a lookup engine for a network monitor

FIGURE 1.8

Preview of network algorithmics. Network algorithmics is introduced using a set of models, strategies, and sample problems, which are described in Part 1 of the book.

    While this book concentrates on networking, the general algorithmics approach holds for the implementation of any computer system, whether a database, a processor architecture, or a software application. This general philosophy is alluded to in Chapter 3 by providing illustrative examples from the field of computer system implementation. The reader interested only in networking should rest assured that the remainder of the book, other than Chapter 3, avoids further digressions beyond networking.

    While Parts 2 and 3 provide specific techniques for important specific problems, the main goal of this book is to allow the reader to be able to tackle *arbitrary* packet-processing tasks at high speeds in software or hardware. Thus the implementor of the future may be given the task of speeding up XML processing in a Web server (likely, given current trends) or even the task of computing the chi-square statistic in a router (possible because chi-square provides a test for detecting observed abnormal frequencies for tasks such as intrusion detection). Despite being assigned a completely unfamiliar task, the hope is that the implementor would be able to craft a new solution to such tasks using the models, principles, and techniques described in this book.

1.3 Exercise

1. **Implementing chi-square:** The chi-square statistic can be used to find if the overall set of observed character frequencies are unusually different (as compared to normal random variation) from the expected character frequencies. This is a more sophisticated test, statistically speaking, than the simple threshold detector used in the warm-up example. Assume that the thresholds represent the expected frequencies. The statistic is computed by finding the sum of

$$\left(ExpectedFrequency\,[i] - ObservedFrequency\,[i]\right)^2 / ExpectedFrequency\,[i]$$

   for all values of character i. The chip should alarm if the final statistic is above a specified threshold. (For example, a value of 14.2 implies that there is only a 1.4% chance that the difference is due to chance variation.) Find a way to efficiently implement this statistic, assuming once again that the length is known only at the end.

Network implementation models

2

A rather small set of key concepts is enough. Only by learning the essence of each topic, and by carrying along the least amount of mental baggage at each step, will the student emerge with a good overall understanding of the subject.

—Carver Mead and Lynn Conway

To improve the performance of endnodes and routers, an implementor must know the rules of the game. A central difficulty is that network algorithmics encompasses four separate areas: protocols, hardware architectures, operating systems, and algorithms. Networking innovations occur when area experts work together to produce synergistic solutions. But can a logic designer understand protocol issues, and can a clever algorithm designer understand hardware trade-offs, at least without deep study?

A useful dialog can begin with *simple models* that have explanatory and predictive power but without unnecessary detail. At the least, such models should define terms used in the book; at best, such models should enable a creative person *outside* an area to play with and create designs that can be checked by an expert *within* the area. For example, a hardware chip implementor should be able to suggest software changes to the chip driver, and a theoretical computer scientist should be able to dream up hardware matching algorithms for switch arbitration. This is the goal of this chapter.

The chapter is organized as follows. Starting with a model for protocols in Section 2.1, the implementation environment is described in bottom-up order. Section 2.2 describes relevant aspects of hardware protocol implementation, surveying logic, memories, and components. Section 2.3 describes a model for endnodes and network devices such as routers. Section 2.4 describes a model for the relevant aspects of operating systems that affect performance, especially in endnodes. To motivate the reader and to retain the interest of the area expert, the chapter contains a large number of networking examples to illustrate the application of each model.

Quick reference guide

Hardware designers should skip most of Section 2.2, except for Example 3 (design of a switch arbitrator), Example 4 (design of a flow ID lookup chip), Example 5 (pin count limitations and their implications), and Section 2.2.5 (which summarizes three hardware design principles useful in networking). Processor and architecture experts should skip Section 2.3 except for Example 7 (network processors).

Implementors familiar with operating systems should skip Section 2.4, except for Example 8 (receiver livelock as an example of how operating system structure influences protocol implementations). Even those unfamiliar with an area such as operating systems may wish to consult these sections if needed after reading the specific chapters that follow.

Network Algorithmics. https://doi.org/10.1016/B978-0-12-809927-8.00007-5

2.1 Protocols

Section 2.1.1 describes the transport protocol TCP and the IP routing protocol. These two examples are used to provide an abstract model of a protocol and its functions in Section 2.1.2. Section 2.1.3 ends with common network performance assumptions. Readers familiar with TCP/IP may wish to skip to Section 2.1.2.

2.1.1 Transport and routing protocols

Applications subcontract the job of reliable delivery to a transport protocol such as the Transmission Control Protocol (TCP). TCP's job is to provide the sending and receiving applications with the illusion of two shared data queues in each direction—despite the fact that the sender and receiver machines are separated by a lossy network. Thus whatever the sender application writes to its local TCP send queue should magically appear in the same order at the local TCP receive queue at the receiver, and vice versa. TCP implements this mechanism by breaking the queued application data into segments and retransmitting each segment until an acknowledgment (ack) has been received. A more detailed description of TCP operation can be found in Section A.1.1.

If the application is (say) a videoconferencing application that does not want reliability guarantees, it can choose to use a protocol called UDP (User Datagram Protocol) instead of TCP. Unlike TCP, UDP does not need acks or retransmissions because it does not guarantee reliability.

Transport protocols such as TCP and UDP work by sending segments from a sender node to a receiver node across the Internet. The actual job of sending a segment is subcontracted to the Internet routing protocol IP.

Internet routing is broken into two conceptual parts, called *forwarding* and *routing*. Forwarding is the process by which packets move from source to destination through intermediate routers. A *packet* is a TCP segment together with a routing header that contains the destination Internet address.

While forwarding must be done at extremely high speeds, the forwarding tables at each router must be built by a routing protocol, especially in the face of topology changes, such as link failures. There are several commonly used routing protocols, such as distance vector (e.g., RIP), link state (e.g., OSPF), and policy routing (e.g., BGP). More details and references to other texts can be found in Section A.1.2 in Appendix.

2.1.2 Abstract protocol model

A protocol is a state machine for all nodes participating in the protocol, together with interfaces and message formats. A model for a protocol state machine is shown in Fig. 2.1. The specification must describe how the state machine changes state and responds (e.g., by sending messages, setting timers) to interface calls, received messages, and timer events.

For instance, when an application makes a connect request, the TCP sender state machine initializes by picking an unused initial sequence number, goes to the so-called SYN-SENT state, and sends a SYN message. As a second example, a link-state routing protocol like OSPF has a state machine at each router; when a link state packet (LSP) arrives at a router with a higher sequence number than the last LSP from the source, the new LSP should be stored and sent to all neighbors. While the LSP is very different from TCP, both protocols can be abstracted by the state machine model shown in Fig. 2.1.

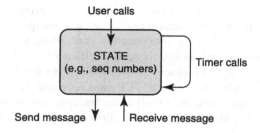

FIGURE 2.1

Abstract model of the state machine implementing a protocol at a node participating in a protocol.

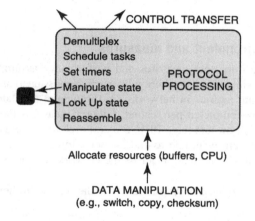

FIGURE 2.2

Common protocol functions. The small shaded black box to the lower left represents the state table used by the protocol.

This book is devoted to protocol implementations. Besides TCP and IP, this book will consider other protocols, such as HTTP. Thus, it is worth abstracting out the *generic and time-consuming functions* that a protocol state machine performs based on our TCP and routing examples. Such a model, shown in Fig. 2.2, will guide us through this book.

First, at the bottom of Fig. 2.2, a protocol state machine must receive and send data packets. This involves *data manipulations*, or operations that must read or write every byte in a packet. For instance, a TCP must copy received data to application buffers, while a router has to switch packets from input links to output links. The TCP header also specifies a checksum that must be computed over all the data bytes. Data copying also requires the allocation of resources such as buffers.

Second, at the top of Fig. 2.2, the state machine must *demultiplex* data to one of many clients. In some cases, the client programs must be activated, requiring potentially expensive control transfer. For instance, when a receiving TCP receives a Web page, it has to demultiplex the data to the Web browser application using the port number fields and may have to wake up the process running the browser.

Fig. 2.2 also depicts several generic functions shared by many protocols. First, protocols have a crucial state that must be looked up at high speeds and sometimes manipulated. For instance, a received TCP packet causes TCP to *look up* a table of connection state, while a received IP packet causes IP to look up a forwarding table. Second, protocols need to efficiently set *timers*, for example, to control retransmission in TCP. Third, if a protocol module is handling several different clients, it needs to *schedule* these clients efficiently. For instance, TCP must schedule the processing of different connections, while a router must make sure that unruly conversations between some pair of computers do not lock out other conversations. Many protocols also allow large pieces of data to be fragmented into smaller pieces that need *reassembly*.

One of the major theses of this book is that though such generic functions are often expensive, their cost can be mitigated with the right techniques. Thus each generic protocol function is worth studying in isolation. Therefore after Part 1 of this book, the remaining chapters address specific protocol functions for endnodes and routers.

2.1.3 Performance environment and measures

This section describes some important measures and performance assumptions. Consider a system (such as a network or even a single router) where jobs (such as messages) arrive and, after completion, leave. The two most important metrics in networks are throughput and latency. *Throughput* roughly measures the number of jobs completed per second. *Latency* measures the time (typically the worst case) to complete a job. System owners (e.g., ISPs, routers) seek to maximize throughput to maximize revenues, while users of a system want end-to-end latencies lower than a few hundred milliseconds. Latency also affects the speed of computation across the network, as, for example, in the performance of a remote procedure call.

The following performance-related observations about the Internet milieu are helpful when considering implementation trade-offs.

- *Link Speeds:* Backbone links are upgrading to 10 Gbps and 40 Gbps, and local links are upgrading to gigabit speeds. However, wireless and home links are currently orders of magnitude slower.
- *TCP and Web Dominance:* Web traffic accounts for over 70% of traffic in bytes or packets. Similarly, TCP accounts for 90% of traffic in a recent study (Braun, 1998).
- *Small Transfers:* Most Web documents accessed are small; for example, a SPEC (Carlton, 1996) study shows that 50% of accessed files are 50 kilobytes (KB) or less.
- *Poor Latencies:* Real round-trip delays exceed speed-of-light limitations; measurements in Crovella and Carter (1995) report a mean of 241 msec across the United States compared to speed-of-light delays of less than 30 msec. Increased latency can be caused by efforts to improve throughput, such as batch compression at modems and pipelining in routers.
- *Poor Locality:* Backbone traffic studies (Thompson et al., 1997) show 250,000 different source–destination pairs (sometimes called *flows*) passing through a router in a very short duration. More recent estimates show around a million concurrent flows. Aggregating groups of headers with the same destination address or other means does not reduce the number of header classes significantly. Thus locality, or the likelihood of computation invested in a packet being reused on a future packet, is small.
- *Small Packets:* Thompson et al. (1997) also show that roughly half the packets received by a router are minimum-size 40-byte TCP acknowledgments. To avoid losing important packets in a stream

of minimum-size packets, most router- and network-adaptor vendors aim for "wire-speed forwarding"—this is the ability to process minimum-size (40-byte) packets at the speed of the input link.[1]

- *Critical Measures:* It is worth distinguishing between *global* performance measures, such as end-to-end delay and bandwidth, and *local* performance measures, such as router lookup speeds. While global performance measures are crucial to overall network performance, this book focuses only on local performance measures, which are a key piece of the puzzle. In particular, this book focuses on forwarding performance and resource (e.g., memory, logic) measures.

- *Tools:* Most network management tools, such as HP's `OpenView`, deal with global measures. The tools needed for local measures are tools to measure performance within computers, such as profiling software. Examples include Rational's `Quantify` (http://www.rational.com) for application software, Intel's `VTune` (www.intel.com/software/products/vtune/), and even hardware oscilloscopes. Network monitors such as `tcpdump` (www.tcpdump.org) are also useful.

Case Study 1: SANs and iSCSI

This case study shows that protocol features can greatly affect application performance. Many large data centers connect their disk drives and computers together using a *storage area network (SAN)*. This allows computers to share disks. Currently, storage area networks are based on Fiber-Channel (Benner, 1995) components, which are more expensive than, say, Gigabit Ethernet. The proponents of iSCSI (Internet storage) (Satran et al., 2001) protocols seek to replace FiberChannel protocols with (hopefully cheaper) TCP/IP protocols and components.

SCSI is the protocol used by computers to communicate with local disks. It can also be used to communicate with disks across a network. A single SCSI command could ask to read 10 megabytes (MB) of data from a remote disk. Currently, such remote SCSI commands run over a FiberChannel transport protocol implemented in the network adaptors. Thus a 10-MB transfer is broken up into multiple FiberChannel packets, sent, delivered, and acknowledged (acked) without any per-packet processing by the requesting computer or responding disk.

The obvious approach to reduce costs is to replace the proprietary FiberChannel transport layer with TCP and the FiberChannel network layer with IP. This would allow us to replace expensive FiberChannel switches in SANs with commodity Ethernet switches. However, this has three implications. First, to compete with FiberChannel performance, TCP will probably have to be implemented in hardware. Second, TCP sends and delivers a byte stream (see Fig. A.1 in Appendix if needed). Thus multiple sent SCSI messages can be merged at the receiver. Message boundaries must be recovered by adding another iSCSI header containing the length of the next SCSI message.

The third implication is trickier. Storage vendors (Satran et al., 2001) wish to process SCSI commands out of order. If two independent SCSI messages C1 and C2 are sent in order but the C2 data arrives before C1, TCP will buffer C2 until C1 arrives. But the storage enthusiast wishes to steer C2 directly to a preallocated SCSI buffer and process C2 out of order, a prospect that makes the TCP purist cringe. The length field method described earlier fails for this purpose

---

[1] The preoccupation with wire-speed forwarding in networking is extremely different from the mentality in computer architecture, which is content with optimizing typical (and not worst-case) performance as measured on benchmarks.

because a missing TCP segment (containing the SCSI message length) makes it impossible to find later message boundaries. An alternate proposal suggests having the iSCSI layer insert headers at periodic intervals in the TCP byte stream, but the jury is still out.

2.2 Hardware

As links approach 40-gigabit/sec OC-768 speeds, a 40-byte packet must be forwarded in 8 nsec. At such speeds, packet forwarding is typically directly implemented in hardware instead of on a programmable processor. You cannot participate in the design process of such hardware-intensive designs without understanding the tools and constraints of hardware designers. And yet, a few simple models can allow you to understand and even play with hardware designs. Even if you have no familiarity with and have a positive distaste for hardware, you are invited to take a quick tour of hardware design, full of networking examples to keep you awake.

Internet lookups are often implemented using combinational logic, Internet packets are stored in router memories, and an Internet router is put together with components such as switches and lookup chips. Thus our tour begins with logic implementation, continues with memory internals, and ends with component-based design. For more details, we refer the reader to the classic VLSI text (Mead and Conway, 1980), which still wears well despite its age, and the classic computer architecture text (Hennessey and Patterson, 1996).

2.2.1 Combinatorial logic

Section A.2.1 in Appendix describes very simple models of basic hardware gates, such as NOT, NAND, and NOR, that can be understood by even a software designer who is willing to read a few pages. However, even knowing how basic gates are implemented is not required to have some insight into hardware design.

The first key to understanding logic design is the following observation. Given NOT, NAND, and NOR gates, Boolean algebra shows that any Boolean function $f(I_1, \ldots, I_n)$ of n inputs can be implemented. Each bit of a multibit output can be considered a function of the input bits. Logic minimization is often used to eliminate redundant gates and sometimes to increase speed. For example, if $+$ denotes OR and $\cdot$ denotes AND, then the function $O = I_1 \cdot I_2 + I_1 \cdot \overline{I_2}$ can be simplified to $O = I_1$.

Example 1. Quality of Service and Priority Encoders: Suppose we have a network router that maintains n output packet queues for a link, where queue i has higher priority than queue j if $i < j$. This problem comes under the category of providing quality of service (QoS), which is covered in Chapter 14. The transmit scheduler in the router must pick a packet from the first nonempty packet queue in priority order. Assume the scheduler maintains an N-bit vector (bitmap) I such that $I[j] = 1$ if and only if queue j is nonempty. Then the scheduler can find the highest-priority nonempty queue by finding the smallest position in I in which a bit is set. Hardware designers know this function intimately as a *priority encoder*. However, even a software designer should realize that this function is feasible for hardware implementation for reasonable n. This function is examined more closely in Example 2.

2.2.2 Timing and power

To forward a 40-byte packet at OC-768 speeds, any networking function on the packet must complete in 8 nsec. Thus the maximum signal transmission delay from inputs to outputs on any logic path must not exceed 8 nsec.[2] To ensure this constraint, a model of signal transmission delay in a transistor is needed.

Roughly speaking, each logic gate, such as a NAND or NOT gate, can be thought of as a set of capacitors and resistors that must be charged (when input values change) in order to compute output values. Worse, charging one input gate can cause the outputs of later gates to charge further inputs, and so on. Thus for a combinatorial function, the delay to compute the function is the sum of the charging and discharging delays over the worst-case path of transistors. Such path delays must fit within a minimum packet arrival time. Besides the time to charge capacitors, another source of delay is wire delay. More details can be found in Section A.2.2.

It also takes energy to charge capacitors, where the energy per unit time (power) scales with the square of the voltage, the capacitance, and the clock frequency at which inputs can change; $P = CV^2 f$. While new processes shrink voltage levels and capacitance, higher-speed circuits must increase clock frequency. Similarly, parallelism implies more capacitors being charged at a time. Thus many high-speed chips dissipate a lot of heat, requiring nontrivial cooling techniques such as heat sinks. ISPs and colocation facilities are large consumers of power. While our level of abstraction precludes understanding power trade-offs, it is good to be aware that chips and routers are sometimes power limited. Some practical limits today are 30 watts per square centimeter on a single die and 10,000 watts per square foot in a data center.

Example 2. Priority Encoder Design: Consider the problem of estimating timing for the priority encoder of Example 1 for an OC-768 link using 40-byte packets. Thus the circuit has 8 nsec to produce the output. Assume the input I and outputs O are N-bit vectors such that $O[j] = 1$ if and only if $I[j] = 1$ and $I[k] = 0$ for all $k < j$. Notice that the output is represented in unary (often called 1-hot representation) rather than binary. The specification leads directly to the combinational logic equation $O[j] = \overline{I[1]} \ldots \overline{I[j-1]} I[j]$ for $j > 0$.

This design can be implemented directly using N AND gates, one for each output bit, where the N gates take a number of inputs that range from 1 to N. Intuitively, since N input AND gates take $O(N)$ transistors, we have a design, Design 1, with $O(N^2)$ transistors that appears to take $O(1)$ time.[3] Even this level of design is helpful, though one can do better.

A more area-economical design is based on the observation that every output bit $O[j]$ requires the AND of the complement of the first $j - 1$ input bits. Thus we define the partial results $P[j] = \overline{I[1]} \ldots \overline{I[j-1]}$ for $j = 2 \ldots N$. Clearly, $O[j] = I[j]P[j]$. But $P[j]$ can be constructed recursively using the equation $P[j] = P[j-1]\overline{I[j-1]}$, which can be implemented using N two-input AND gates, connected in series. This produces a design, Design 2, that takes $O(N)$ transistors but takes $O(N)$ time.

Design 1 is fast and fat, and Design 2 is slow and lean. This is a familiar time–space trade-off and suggests we can get something in between. The computation of $P[j]$ in Design 2 resembles an unbalanced binary tree of height N. However, it is obvious that $P[N]$ can be computed using a fully

---

[2] Alternatively, parts of the function can be parallelized/pipelined, but then each part must complete in 8 nsec.

[3] A more precise argument, due to David Harris, using the method of Sutherland et al. (1999), shows the delay scales as $\log(N \log N)$ because of the effort required to charge a tree of N transistors in each AND gate.

balanced binary of 2-input AND gates of height $\log N$. A little thought then shows that the partial results of the binary tree can be combined in simple ways to get $P[j]$ for all $j < N$ using the same binary tree (Wang and Huang, 2000).

For example, if $N = 8$, to compute $P[8]$ we compute $X = \overline{I[0]} \ldots \overline{I[3]}$ and $Y = \overline{I[4]} \ldots \overline{I[7]}$ and compute the AND of X and Y at the root. Thus, it is easy to calculate $P[5]$, for instance, using one more AND gate by computing $X \cdot \overline{I[4]}$. Such a method is very commonly used by hardware designers to replace apparently long $O(N)$ computation chains with chains of length $2 \log N$. Since it was first used to speed up carry chains in addition, it is known as *carry look-ahead* or simply *look-ahead*. While look-ahead techniques appear complex, even software designers can master them because, at their core, they use divide-and-conquer.

2.2.3 Raising the abstraction level of hardware design

Hand designing each transistor in a network chip design consisting of 1 million transistors would be time consuming. The design process can be reduced to a few months using building blocks. A quick description of building block technologies, such as PLAs, PALs, and standard cells, can be found in Section A.2.5.

The high-order bit, however, is that just as software designers reuse code, so also hardware designers reuse a repertoire of commonly occurring functions. Besides common computational blocks, such as adders, multipliers, comparators, and priority encoders, designs also use decoders, barrel shifters, multiplexers, and demultiplexers. It is helpful to be familiar with these "arrows" in the hardware designer's quiver.

A decoder converts a $\log N$-bit binary value to an N-bit unary encoding of the same value; while binary representations are more compact, unary representations are more convenient for computation. A barrel shifter shifts an input I by s positions to the left or right, with the bits shifted off from an end coming around to the other end.

A *multiplexer* (mux) connects one of several inputs to a common output, while its dual, the *demultiplexer*, routes one input to one of several possible outputs. More precisely, a multiplexer (mux) connects one of n input bits I_j to the output O if a $\log n$-bit select signal S encodes the value j in binary. Its dual, the demultiplexer, connects input I to output O_j if the signal S encodes the value j in binary.

Thus the game becomes one of decomposing a complex logic function into instances of the standard functions, even using recursion when needed. This is exactly akin to reduction and divide-and-conquer and is easily picked up by software designers. For example, Fig. 2.3 shows the typical Lego puzzle faced by hardware designers: Build a 4-input multiplexer from 2-input multiplexers. Start by choosing one of I_0 and I_1 using a 2-input mux and then choosing one of I_2 and I_3 by another 2-input mux. Clearly, the outputs of the 2-input muxes in the first stage must be combined using a third 2-input mux; the only cleverness required is to realize that the select signal for the first two muxes is the least significant bit S_0 of the 2-bit select signal, while the third mux chooses between the upper and lower halves and so uses S_1 as the select bit.

The following networking example shows that reduction is a powerful design tool for designing critical networking functions.

Example 3. Crossbar Scheduling and Programmable Priority Encoders: Examples 1 and 2 motivated and designed a fast priority encoder (PE). A commonly used router arbitration mechanism uses an

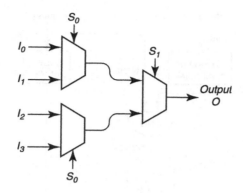

FIGURE 2.3

Building a 4-input mux with select bits S_0 and S_1 from three 2-input muxes. The figure uses the standard trapezoidal icon for a mux.

enhanced form of priority encoder called a programmable priority encoder (PPE). There is an N-bit input I as before, together with an additional $\log N$-bit input P. The PPE circuit must compute an output O such that $O[j] = 1$, where j is the first position beyond P (treated as a binary value) that has a nonzero bit in I. If $P = 0$, this reduces to a simple priority encoder.

PPEs arise naturally in switch arbitration (see Chapter 13 for details). For now, suppose a router connects N communication links. Suppose several input links wish to transmit a packet at the same time to output link L. To avoid contention at L, each of the inputs sends a request to L in the first time slot; L chooses which input link to grant a request to in the second slot; the granted input sends a packet in the third time slot.

To make its grant decision, L can store the requests received at the end of Slot 1 in an N-bit request vector R, where $R[i] = 1$ if input link i wishes to transmit to L. For fairness, L should remember the last input link P it granted a request to. Then, L should confer the grant to the first input link beyond P that has a request. This is exactly a PPE problem with R and P as inputs. Since a router must do arbitration for each time slot and each output link, a fast and area-efficient PPE design is needed. Even a software designer can understand and possibly repeat the process (Gupta and McKeown, 1999b) used to design the PPE found in the Tiny Tera, a switch built at Stanford and later commercialized. The basic idea is reduction: reducing the design of a PPE to the design of a PE (Example 2).

The first idea is simple. A PPE is essentially a PE whose highest-priority value starts at position P instead of at 0. A barrel shifter can be used to shift I first to the left by P bits. After this, a simple PE can be used. Of course, the output-bit vector is now shifted; we recover the original order by shifting the output of the PE to the right by P bits. A barrel shifter for N-bit inputs can be implemented using a tree of 2-input multiplexers in around $\log N$ time. Thus two barrel shifters and a PE take around $3 \log N$ gate delays.

A faster design used in Gupta and McKeown (1999b), which requires only $2 \log N$ gate delays, is as follows. Split the problem into two parts. If the input has some bit set at position P or greater, then the result can be found by using a PE operating on the original input after setting to zero all input bits

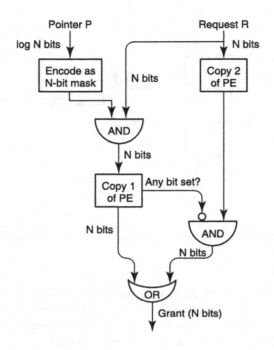

FIGURE 2.4

The Tiny Tera PPE design uses copy 1 of a priority encoder to find the highest bit set, if any, of all bits greater than P using a mask encoding of P. If such a bit is not found, the output of a second copy of a priority encoder is enabled using the bottom AND gate. The results of the two copies are then combined using an N-input OR gate.

with positions less than P.[4] On the other hand, if the input has no bit set at a position P or greater, then the result can be found by using a PE on the original input with no masking at all. This results in the design of Fig. 2.4, which, when tested on a Texas Instrument Cell Library, was nearly twice as fast and took three times less area than the barrel shifter design for a 32-port router.

The message here is that the logic design used for a time-critical component of a very influential switch design can be achieved using simple reductions and simple models. Such models are not beyond the reach of those of us who do not live and breathe digital design.

2.2.4 Memories

In endnodes and routers, packet forwarding is performed using combinational logic, but packets and forwarding state are stored in *memories*. Since memory access times are significantly slower than logic delays, memories form major bottlenecks in routers and endnodes.

---

[4] This can be done by ANDing the input with P encoded as a mask; such a mask is commonly known in the hardware community as a *thermometer* encoding of P.

Further, different subsystems require different memory characteristics. For example, router vendors feel it is important to buffer 200 msec—an upper bound on a round-trip delay—worth of packets to avoid dropping packets during periods of congestion. At, say, 40 Gbit/sec per link, such packet buffering requires an enormous amount of memory. On the other hand, router lookups require a smaller amount of memory, which is accessed randomly. Thus it helps to have simple models for different memory technologies. Next, we describe registers, SRAMs, DRAMs, and interleaved memory technology. Simple implementation models of these memory components can be found in Section A.2.4 in Appendix.

Registers

A *flip-flop* is a way of connecting two or more transistors in a feedback loop so that (in the absence of Writes and power failures) the bit stays indefinitely without "leaking" away. A *register* is an ordered collection of flip-flops. For example, most modern processors have a collection of 32- or 64-bit on-chip registers. A 32-bit register contains 32 flip-flops, each storing a bit. Access from logic to a register on the same chip is extremely fast, around 0.5–1 nsec.

SRAM

A static random access memory (SRAM) contains N registers addressed by $\log N$ address bits A. SRAM is so named because the underlying flip-flops refresh themselves and so are "static." Besides flip-flops, an SRAM also needs a decoder that decodes A into a unary value used to select the right register. Accessing an SRAM on-chip is only slightly slower than accessing a register because of the added decode delay. At the time of writing, it was possible to obtain on-chip SRAMs with 0.5-nsec access times. Access times of 1–2 nsec for on-chip SRAM and 5–10 nsec for off-chip SRAM are common.

Dynamic RAM

An SRAM bit cell requires at least five transistors. Thus SRAM is always less dense or more expensive than memory technology based on dynamic RAM (DRAM). The key idea is to replace the feedback loop (and extra transistors) used to store a bit in a flip-flop with an output capacitance that can store the bit; thus the charge leaks, but it leaks slowly. Loss due to leakage is fixed by refreshing the DRAM cell externally within a few milliseconds. Of course, the complexity comes in manufacturing a high capacitance using a tiny amount of silicon.

DRAM chips appear to quadruple in capacity every 3 years (Fromm et al., 1997) and are heading towards 1 gigabit on a single chip. Addressing these bits, even if they are packed together as 4- or even 32-bit "registers," is tricky. Recall that the address must be decoded from (say) 20 bits to (say) one of 2^{20} values. The complexity of such decode logic suggests divide-and-conquer. Why not decode in two stages?

Fig. 2.5 shows that most memories are internally organized two-dimensionally into rows and columns. The upper address bits are decoded to select the row, and then the lower address bits are used to decode the column. More precisely, the user first supplies the row address bits and enables a signal called RAS (row address strobe); later, the user supplies the column address bits,[5] and enables

---

[5] Many DRAM chips take advantage of the fact that row and column addresses are not required at the same time to multiplex row and column addresses on the same set of pins, reducing the pin count of the chip.

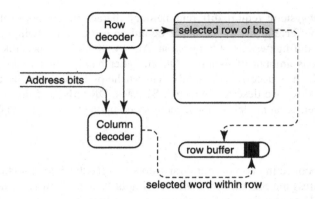

FIGURE 2.5

Most large memories are organized two-dimensionally in terms of rows and columns. Selecting a word consists of selecting first the row and then the column within the row.

a signal called CAS (column address strobe). After a specified time, the desired memory word can be read out. Assuming equal-size rows and columns, this reduces decode gate complexity from $O(N)$ to $O(\sqrt{(N)})$ at the expense of one extra decode delay. Besides the required delay between RAS and CAS, there is also a *precharge* delay between successive RAS and CAS invocations to allow time for capacitors to charge.

The fastest off-chip DRAMs take around 40–60 nsec to access (latency), with longer times, such as 100 nsec, between successive reads (throughput) because of precharge restrictions. Some of this latency includes the time to drive the address using external lines onto the DRAM interface pins; recent innovations allow on-chip DRAM with lower access times of around 30 nsec. It seems clear that DRAM will always be denser but slower than SRAM.

Page-mode DRAMs

One reason to understand DRAM structure is to understand how function can follow form. A classic example is a trick to speed up access times called *page mode*. Page mode is beneficial for access patterns that exhibit spatial locality, in which adjacent memory words are successively accessed. But having made a row access in Fig. 2.5, one can access words within the row without incurring additional RAS and precharge delays. Video RAMs exploit the same structure by having a row read into an SRAM, which can be read out serially to refresh a display at high speed. Besides page mode and video RAMS, perhaps there are other ideas that exploit DRAM structure that could be useful in networking.

Interleaved DRAMs

While memory latency is critical for computation speed, memory throughput (often called *bandwidth*) is also important for many network applications. Suppose a DRAM has a word size of 32 bits and a cycle time of 100 nsec. Then the throughput using a single copy of the DRAM is limited to 32 bits every 100 nsec. Clearly, throughput can be improved using access to multiple DRAMs. As in Fig. 2.6, multiple DRAMs (called *banks*) can be strung together on a single bus. The user can start a Read to

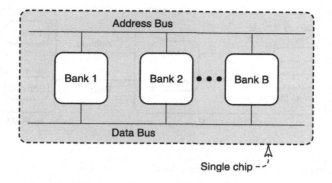

Single chip --'

FIGURE 2.6

The idea behind RAMBUS, SDRAM, and numerous variants is to create a single chip containing multiple DRAM parallel memories to gain memory bandwidth while using only one set of address and data lines.

Bank 1 by placing the address on the address bus. Assume each DRAM bank takes 100 nsec to return the selected data.

Instead of idling during this 100-nsec delay, the user can place a second address for Bank 2, a third for Bank 3, and so on. If the placing of each address takes 10 nsec, the user can "feed" 10 DRAM banks before the answer to the first DRAM bank query arrives, followed 10 nsec later by the answer to the second DRAM bank query, and so on. Thus the net memory bandwidth in this example is 10 times the memory bandwidth of a single DRAM, as long as the user can arrange to have consecutive accesses touch different banks.

While using multiple memory banks is a very old idea, it is only in the last 5 years that memory designers have integrated several banks into a single memory chip (Fig. 2.6), where the address and data lines for all banks are multiplexed using a common high-speed network called a *bus*. In addition, page-mode accesses are often allowed on each bank. Memory technologies based on this core idea abound, with different values for the DRAM sizes, the protocol to read and write, and the number of banks. Prominent examples include SDRAM with two banks and RDRAM with 16 banks.

Example 4. Pipelined Flow ID Lookups: A flow is characterized by source and destination IP addresses and TCP ports. Some customers would like routers to keep track of the number of packets sent by each network flow, for accounting purposes. This requires a data structure that stores a counter for each flow ID and supports the two operations of *Insert (FlowId)* to insert a new flow ID, and *Lookup (FlowId)* to find the location of a counter for a flow ID. Lookup requires an exact match on the flow ID—which is around 96 bits—in the time to receive a packet. This can be done by any exact-matching algorithm, such as hashing.

However, if, as many router vendors wish to do, the worst-case lookup time must be small and bounded, binary search (Cormen et al., 1990) is a better idea. Assume that flow ID lookups must be done at wire speeds for worst-case 40-byte packets at 2.5 Gbits/sec or OC-48 speeds. Thus the chip has 128 nsec to look up a flow ID.

To bound lookup delays, consider using a balanced binary tree, such as a B-tree. The logic for tree traversal is fairly easy. For speed, ideally the flow IDs and counters should be stored in SRAM.

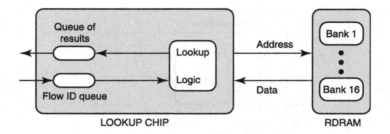

FIGURE 2.7

Solving the flow ID lookup problem by using a pipelined lookup chip that works on up to 16 concurrent flow ID lookups, each of which accesses an independent bank of the RDRAM. The lookup chip returns an index to, say, a network processor that updates the flow ID counter.

However, current estimates in core routers (Thompson et al., 1997) show around a million concurrent flows. Keeping state for a million flows in SRAM is expensive. However, plain DRAM using a binary tree with a branching factor of 2 would require $\log_2 1,000,000 = 20$ memory accesses. Even assuming an optimistic DRAM cycle time of 50 nsec, the overall lookup time is 1 usec, which is too slow.

A solution is to use pipelining, as shown in Fig. 2.7, where the pipelined logic accesses flow IDs stored in an RDRAM with 16 banks of memory, as shown in Fig. 2.6. All the nodes at height i in the binary tree are stored in Bank i of the RDRAM. The lookup chip works on 16 flow ID lookups (for 16 packets) concurrently. For example, after looking at the root node for Packet 1 in Bank 1, the chip can look up the second-level tree node for Packet 1 in Bank 2 and (very slightly after that) look up the root for Packet 2 in Bank 1. When Packet 1's lookup "thread" is accessing Bank 16, Packet 16's lookup thread is accessing Bank 1. Since direct RDRAM runs at 800 MHz, the time between address requests to the RAMBUS is small compared with the read access time of around 60 nsec. Thus while a single packet takes around $16 * 60$ nsec to complete, processing 16 packets concurrently allows a throughput of one flow ID lookup every 60 nsec.

Unfortunately, a binary tree with 16 levels allows only $2^{16} = 64$ K flow IDs, which is too small. Fortunately, RAMBUS allows a variation of page mode where 8 data words of 32 bits can be accessed in almost the same time as 1 word. This allows us to retrieve two 96-bit keys and three 20-bit pointers in one 256-bit memory access. Thus a tree with 3-way branching can be used, which allows potentially 3^{16}, or potentially 43 million, flow IDs.

2.2.5 Memory subsystem design techniques

The flow ID lookup problem illustrates three major design techniques commonly used in memory subsystem designs for networking chips.

- **Memory Interleaving and Pipelining:** Similar techniques are used in IP lookup, classification, and in scheduling algorithms that implement QoS. The multiple banks can be implemented using several external memories, a single external memory like a RAMBUS, or on-chip SRAM within a chip that also contains processing logic.

- **Wide Word Parallelism:** A common theme in many networking designs, such as the Lucent bit vector scheme (Chapter 12), is to use wide memory words that can be processed in parallel. This can be implemented using DRAM and exploiting page mode or by using SRAM and making each memory word wider.

- **Combining DRAM and SRAM:** Given that SRAM is expensive and fast and that DRAM is cheap and slow, it makes sense to combine the two technologies to attempt to obtain the best of both worlds. While the use of SRAM as a cache for DRAM databases is classical, there are many more creative applications of the idea of a memory hierarchy. For instance, the exercises explore the effect of a small amount of SRAM on the design of the flow ID lookup chip. Chapter 16 describes a more unusual application of this technique to implement a large number of counters, where the low-order bits of each counter are stored in SRAM.

It is more important for a novice designer to understand these design techniques (than to know memory implementation details) in order to produce creative hardware implementations of networking functions.

2.2.6 Component-level design

The methods of the last two subsections can be used to implement a *state machine* that implements arbitrary computation. A state machine has a current state stored in memory; the machine processes inputs using combinatorial logic that reads the current state and possibly writes the state. An example of a complex state machine is a Pentium processor, whose state is the combination of registers, caches, and main memory. An example of a simpler state machine is the flow ID lookup chip of Fig. 2.7, whose state is the registers used to track each of 16 concurrent lookups and the RDRAM storing the B-tree.

While a few key chips may have to be designed to build a router or a network interface card, the remainder of the design can be called component-level design: organizing and interconnecting chips on a board and placing the board in a box while paying attention to form factor, power, and cooling. A key aspect of the component-level design is understanding pin-count limitations, which often provide a quick "parity check" on feasible designs.

Example 5. Pin-Count Implications for Router Buffers: Consider a router that has forty 10 Gb/sec links. The overall buffering required is 200 msec * 400 Gb/sec, which is 80 gigabits. For cost and power, we use DRAM for packet buffers. Since each packet must go in and out of the buffer, the overall memory bandwidth needs to be twice the bandwidth into the box—i.e., 800 Gb/sec. Assuming 100% overhead for internal packet headers, links between packets in queues, and wasted memory bandwidth, it is reasonable to aim for 1600-Gb/sec memory bandwidth.

Using a single direct 64-bit-wide RDRAM with 16 banks, specifications show peak memory bandwidth of 1.28 GB/sec,[6] or 10.24 Gb/sec. Accessing each RDRAM requires 64 interface pins for data and 25 other pins for address and control, for a total of roughly 90 pins. A 1600-Gbps memory bandwidth requires 160 RDRAMs, which require 14400 pins in total. A conservative upper bound on the number of pins on a chip is around 1000. This implies that even if the router vendor were to build an

---

[6] Assuming the DRAM takes 100 ns between reads, if the width is 64 bits (8 bytes), with a single bank we can read 8 bytes every 100 ns (as mentioned on page 28), or 0.08 GB/sec.

extremely fast custom-designed packet-forwarding chip that could handle all packets at the maximum box rate, one would still need at least one more chip to drive data in and out of the RAMBUS packet buffers. Our message is that pin limitations are a key constraint in partitioning a design between chips.

2.2.7 Final hardware lessons

If all else is forgotten in this hardware design section, it is helpful to remember the design techniques of Section 2.2.5. Knowledge of the following parameter values is also useful to help system designers quickly weed out infeasible designs without detailed knowledge of hardware design. Unfortunately, these parameters are a moving target, and the following numbers were written based on technology available in 2004.

- **Chip Complexity Scaling:** The number of components per chip appears to double every 2 years. While 0.13-micron processes are common, 90-nm technology is ramping up, and 65-nm technology is expected after that. As a result, current ASICs can pack several million gate equivalents (that's a lot of combinatorial logic) plus up to 50 Mbits (at the time of writing, using half a 12-mm/side die) of on-chip SRAM on an ASIC.[7] Embedded DRAM is also a common option to get more space on-chip at the cost of larger latency.
- **Chip Speeds:** As feature sizes go down, on-chip clock speeds of 1 GHz are becoming common, with some chips even pushing close to 3 GHz. To put this in perspective, the clock cycle to do a piece of computation on a 1-GHz chip is 1 nsec. By using parallelism via pipelining and wide memory words, multiple operations can be performed per clock cycle.
- **Chip I/O:** The number of pins per chip grows, but rather slowly. While there are some promising technologies, it is best to assume that designs are pin limited to around 1000 pins.
- **Serial I/O:** Chip-to-chip I/O has also come a long way, with 10-Gbit serial links available to connect chips.
- **Memory Scaling:** On-chip SRAM with access times of 1 nsec are available, with even smaller access times being worked on. Off-chip SRAM with access times of 2.5 nsec are commonly available. On-chip DRAM access times are around 30 nsec, while off-chip DRAM of around 60 nsec is common. Of course, the use of interleaved DRAM, as discussed in the memory subsection, is a good way to increase memory subsystem throughput for certain applications. DRAM costs roughly 4–10 times less than SRAM per bit.
- **Power and Packaging:** The large power consumption of high-speed routers requires careful design of the cooling system. Finally, most ISPs have severe rack space limitations, and so there is considerable pressure to build routers that have small form factors.

These parameter values have clear implications for high-speed networking designs. For instance, at OC-768 speeds, a 40-byte packet arrives in 3.2 nsec. Thus it seems clear that all states required to process the packet must be in on-chip SRAM. While the amount of on-chip SRAM is growing, this memory is not growing as fast as the number of flows seen by a router. Similarly, with 1-nsec SRAMs, at most, three memory accesses can be made to a *single* memory bank in a packet arrival time.

Thus the design techniques of Section 2.2.5 must be used within a chip to gain parallelism using multiple memory banks and wide words and to increase the usable memory by creative combinations

---

[7] FPGAs are more programmable chips that can only offer smaller amounts of on-chip SRAM.

that involve off- and on-chip memory. However, given that chip densities and power constraints limit parallelism to, say, a factor of at most 60, the bottom line is that all packet-processing functions at high speeds must complete using at most 200 memory accesses and limited on-chip memory.[8] Despite these limitations, a rich variety of packet-processing functions have been implemented at high speeds.

2.3 **Network device architectures**

Optimizing network performance requires optimizing the path of data through the internals of the source node, the sink node, and every router. Thus it is important to understand the internal architecture of endnodes and routers. The earlier part of this chapter argued that logic and memory can be combined to form state machines. In essence, both routers and endnodes are state machines. However, their architectures are optimized for different purposes: endnode architectures (Section 2.3.1) for general *computation* and router architectures (Section 2.3.2) for Internet *communication*.

2.3.1 **Endnode architecture**

A processor such as a Pentium is a state machine that takes a sequence of instructions and data as input and writes output to I/O devices, such as printers and terminals. To allow programs that have a large state space, the bulk of the processor state is stored externally in cheap DRAM. In PCs, this is referred to as *main memory* and is often implemented using 1 GB or more of interleaved DRAM, such as SDRAM. However, recall that DRAM access times are large, say, 60 nsec. If the processor state were stored only in DRAM, an instruction would take 60 nsec to read or write to memory.

Processors gain speed using *caches*, which are comparatively small chunks of SRAM that can store commonly used pieces of state for faster access. Some SRAM (i.e., the L1 cache) is placed on the processor chip, and some more SRAM (i.e., the L2 cache) is placed external to the processor. A cache is a hash table that maps between memory address locations and contents. CPU caches use a simple hash function: They extract some bits from the address to index into an array and then search in parallel for all the addresses that map into the array element.[9] When a memory location has to be read from DRAM, it is placed in the cache, and an existing cache element may be evicted. Commonly used data is stored in a *data cache*, and commonly used instructions in an *instruction cache*.

Caching works well if the instructions and data exhibit temporal locality (i.e., the corresponding location is reused frequently in a small time period) or spatial locality (i.e., accessing a location is followed by access to a nearby location). Spatial locality is taken advantage of as follows. Recall that accessing a DRAM location involves accessing a row R and then a column within the row. Thus reading words within row R are cheaper after R is accessed. A Pentium takes advantage of this observation by prefetching 128 (*cache line size*) contiguous bits into the cache whenever 32 bits of data are accessed. Access to the adjoining 96 bits will not incur a cache miss penalty.

---

[8] Of course, there are ways to work around these limits, for instance, by using multiple chips, but such implementations often do badly in terms of cost, complexity, and power consumption.

[9] The number of elements that can be searched in parallel in a hash bucket is called the *associativity* of the cache. While router designers rightly consider bit extraction to be a poor hash function, the addition of associativity improves overall hashing performance, especially on computing workloads.

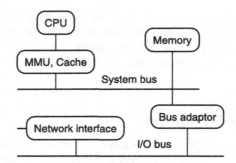

FIGURE 2.8

Model of a workstation.

Many computing benchmarks exhibit temporal and spatial locality; however, a stream of packets probably exhibits only spatial locality. Thus improving endnode protocol implementations often requires paying attention to cache effects.

The foregoing discussion should set the stage for the endnode architecture model shown in Fig. 2.8. The processor, or CPU—e.g., a Pentium or an Alpha—sits on a bus. A bus can be thought of as a network like an Ethernet, but optimized for the fact that the devices on the bus are close to each other. The processor interacts with other components by sending messages across the bus.

The input–output (I/O) devices are typically *memory mapped*. In other words, even I/O devices like the network adaptor and the disk look like pieces of memory. For example, the adaptor memory may be mapped to 100–200 in the memory address space. This allows uniform communication between the CPU and any device by using the same conventions used to interact with memory. In terms of networking, a Read (or Write) can be thought of as a message sent on the bus addressed to the memory location. Thus a Read 100 is sent on the bus, and the device that owns memory location 100 (e.g., the adaptor) will receive the message and reply with the contents of location 100.

Modern machines allow direct memory access (DMA), where devices such as the disk or the network adaptor send Reads and Writes directly to the memory via the bus without processor intervention. However, only one entity can use the bus at a time. Thus the adaptor has to contend for the bus; any device that gets hold of the bus "steals cycles" from the processor. This is because the processor is forced to wait to access memory while a device is sending messages across the bus.

In Fig. 2.8, also notice that the adaptor actually sits on a different bus (system bus or memory bus) from the bus on which the network adaptor and other peripherals (I/O bus) sit. The memory bus is designed for speed and is redesigned for every new processor; the I/O bus is a standard bus (e.g., a PCI bus) chosen to stay compatible with older I/O devices. Thus the I/O bus is typically slower than the memory bus.

A big lesson for networking in Fig. 2.8 is that the throughput of a networking application is crucially limited by the speed of the slowest bus, typically the I/O bus. Worse, the need for extra copies to preserve operating system structure causes every packet received or sent by a workstation to traverse the bus multiple times. Techniques to avoid redundant bus traversals are described in Chapter 5.

Modern processors are heavily pipelined with instruction fetch, instruction decode, data reads, and data writes split into separate stages. *Superscalar* and *multithreaded* machines go beyond pipelining

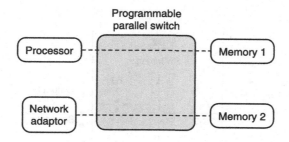

FIGURE 2.9

Using parallel connections within an endnode architecture to allow concurrent processing and network traffic via a parallel switch.

by issuing multiple instructions concurrently. While these innovations (see, for example, the classic reference on endnode architecture [Hennessey and Patterson, 1996]) remove computation bottlenecks, they do little for data-movement bottlenecks. Consider the following speculative architecture instead.

Example 6. Endnode Architecture Using a Crossbar Switch: Fig. 2.9 shows the endnode bus being replaced by a programmable hardware switch, as is commonly used by routers. The switch internally contains a number of parallel buses so that any set of disjoint endpoint pairs can be connected in parallel by the switch. Thus in the figure, the processor is connected to Memory 1, while the network adaptor is connected to Memory 2. Thus packets from the network can be placed in Memory 2 without interfering with the processor's reading from Memory 1. If the processor now wishes to read the incoming packet, the switch can be reprogrammed to connect the processor to Memory 2 and the adaptor to Memory 1. This can work well if the queue of empty packet buffers used by the adaptor alternates between the two memories.

There are recent proposals for Infiniband switch technology to replace the I/O bus in processors (Chapter 5). The ultimate message of this example is not that architectures such as Fig. 2.9 are necessarily good but that simple architectural idea to improve network performance, such as Fig. 2.9, are not hard for even protocol designers to conceive, given simple models of hardware and architecture.

2.3.2 Router architecture

A router model that covers both high-end routers (such as Juniper's M-series routers) and low-end routers (such as the Cisco Catalyst) is shown in Fig. 2.10. Basically, a router is a box with a set of input links, shown on the left, and a set of output links, shown on the right; the task of the router is to switch a packet from an input link to the appropriate output link based on the destination address in the packet. While the input and output links are shown separately, the two links in each direction between two routers are often packaged together. We review three main bottlenecks in a router: lookup, switching, and output queuing.

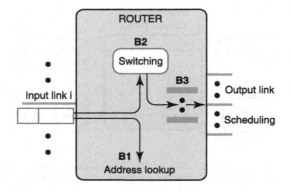

FIGURE 2.10

A model of a router labeled with the three main bottlenecks in the forwarding path: address lookup (**B1**), switching (**B2**), and output scheduling (**B3**).

Lookup

A packet arrives on, say, the left link, input link *i*. Every packet carries a 32-bit Internet Protocol (IP) address.[10] Assume that the first six bits of the destination address of a sample packet are 100100. A processor in the router inspects the destination address to determine where to forward the packet.

The processor consults a forwarding table to determine the output link for the packet. The forwarding table is sometimes called a *FIB*, for *forwarding information base*. The FIB contains a set of *prefixes* with corresponding output links. The reason for prefixes will be explained in Chapter 11; for now, think of prefixes as variable-length "area codes" that greatly reduce the FIB size. A prefix like 01*, where the * denotes the usual "don't care" symbol, matches IP addresses that start with 01. Assume that prefix 100* has associated output link 6, while prefix 1* has output link 2. Thus our sample packet, whose destination address starts with 100100, matches *both* prefixes 100* and 1*. The disambiguating rule that IP routers use is to match an address to the *longest matching prefix*. Assuming no longer matching prefixes, our sample packet should be forwarded to output link 6.

The processor that does the lookup and basic packet processing can be either shared or dedicated and can be either a general processor or a special-purpose chip. Early router designs used a shared processor (or processors), but this proved to be a bottleneck. Later designs, including Cisco's GSR family, use a dedicated processor per input link interface. The earliest designs used a standard CPU processor, but many of the fastest routers today, such as Juniper's M-160, use a dedicated chip (ASIC) with some degree of programmability. There has been a backlash to this trend toward ASICs, however, with customers asking routers to perform new functions, such as Web load balancing. Thus some new routers use *network processors* (see Example 7), which are general-purpose processors optimized for networking.

---

[10] Recall that while most users deal with domain names, these names are translated to an IP address by a directory service, called DNS, before packets are sent.

Algorithms for prefix lookups are described in Chapter 11. Many routers today also offer a more complex lookup called *packet classification* (Chapter 12), where the lookup takes as input the destination address *as well as* source address and TCP ports.

Switching

After address lookup in the example of Fig. 2.10, the processor instructs an internal switching system to transfer the packet from link i to output link 6. In older processors, the switch was a simple bus, such as shown in Fig. 2.8. This proved to be a major bottleneck because, if the switch has N input links running at B bits per second, the bus would have to have a bandwidth of $B \cdot N$. Unfortunately, as N increases, electrical effects (such as the capacitive load of a bus) predominate, limiting the bus speed.

Thus the fastest routers today internally use a parallel switch of the sort shown in Fig. 2.9. The throughput of the switch is increased by using N *parallel* buses, one for each input and one for each output. An input and an output are connected by turning on transistors connecting the corresponding input bus and output bus. While it is easy to build the data path, it is harder to schedule the switch, because multiple inputs may wish to send to the same output link at the same time. The switch-scheduling problem boils down to matching available inputs and outputs every packet arrival time. Algorithms for this purpose are described in Chapter 13.

Queuing

Once the packet in Fig. 2.10 has been looked up and switched to output link 6, output link 6 may be congested, and thus the packet may have to be placed in a queue for output link 6. Many older routers simply place the packet in a first-in-first-out (FIFO) transmission queue. However, some routers employ more sophisticated output scheduling to provide fair bandwidth allocation and delay guarantees. Output scheduling is described in Chapter 14.

Besides the major tasks of lookups, switching, and queuing, there are a number of other tasks that are less time-critical.

Header validation and checksums

The version number of a packet is checked, and the header-length field is checked for options. Options are additional processing directives that are rarely used; such packets are often shunted to a separate route processor. The header also has a simple checksum that must be verified. Finally, a time-to-live (TTL) field must be decremented and the header checksum recalculated. Chapter 9 shows how to incrementally update the checksum. Header validation and checksum computation are often done in hardware.

Route processing

Section A.1.2 describes briefly how routers build forwarding tables using routing protocols. Routers within domains implement RIP and OSPF, while routers that link domains also must implement BGP.[11]

---

[11] It is possible to buy versions of these protocols, but the software must be customized for each new hardware platform. A more insidious problem, especially with BGP and OSPF, is that many of the first implementations of these protocols vary in subtle ways from the actual specifications. Thus a new implementation that meets the specification may not interoperate with existing routers. Thus ISPs are reluctant to buy new routers unless they can trust the "quality" of the BGP code, in terms of its ability to interoperate with existing routers.

These protocols are implemented in one or more route processors. For example, when a LSP is sent to the router in Fig. 2.10, lookup will recognize that this is a packet destined for the router itself and will cause the packet to be switched to the route processor. The route processor maintains the link-state database and computes shortest paths; after computation, the route processor loads the new forwarding databases in each of the forwarding processors through either the switch or a separate out-of-band path.

In the early days, Cisco won its spurs by processing not just Internet packets but also other routing protocols, such as DECNET, SNA, and AppleTalk. The need for such multiprotocol processing is less clear now. A much more important trend is multi-protocol-label switching (MPLS), which appears to be de rigeur for core routers. In MPLS, the IP header is augmented with a header containing simple integer indices that can be looked up directly without a prefix lookup; Chapter 11 provides more details about MPLS.

Protocol processing

All routers today have to implement the simple network management protocol (SNMP) and provide a set of counters that can be inspected remotely. To allow remote communication with the router, most routers also implement TCP and UDP. In addition, routers have to implement the Internet control message protocol (ICMP), which is basically a protocol for sending error messages, such as "time-to-live exceeded."

Fragmentation, redirects, and ARPs

While it is clear that route and protocol processing is best relegated to a route processor on a so-called "slow path," there are a few router functions that are more ambiguous. For example, if a packet of 3000 bytes is to be sent over a link with a maximum packet size (MTU) of 1500 bytes, the packet has to be fragmented into two pieces.[12] While the prevailing trend is for sources, instead of routers, to do fragmentation, some routers do fragmentation in the fast path. Another such function is the sending of Redirects. If an endnode sends a message to the wrong router, the router is supposed to send a Redirect back to the endnode. A third such function is the sending of address resolution protocol (ARP) requests, whose operation is explored in the exercises.

Finally, routers today have a number of other tasks they may be called on to perform. Many routers within enterprises do content-based handling of packets, where the packet processing depends on strings found in the packet data. For example, a router that fronts a Web farm of many servers may wish to forward packets with the same Web URL to the same Web server. There are also the issues of accounting and traffic measurement. Some of these new services are described in Chapter 16.

Example 7. Network Processors: Network processors are general-purpose programmable processors optimized for network traffic. Their proponents say that they are needed because the unpredictable nature of router tasks (such as content-based delivery) makes committing router forwarding to silicon a risky proposition. For example, the Intel IXP1200 network processor evaluated in Spalink et al. (2000) internally contains six processors, each running at 177 MHz with a 5.6-nsec clock cycle. Each processor receives packets from an input queue; packets are stored in a large DRAM; after the processor has looked up the packet destination, the packet is placed on the output queue with a tag describing the output link it should be forwarded to.

---

[12] Strictly speaking, since each fragment adds headers, there will be *three* pieces.

The biggest problem is that the processors are responsible for moving packets in and out of DRAM. In the IXP1200, moving 32 bytes from the queue to the DRAM takes 45 clock cycles, and moving from the DRAM to the queue takes 55 cycles. Since a minimum-size packet is at least 40 bytes, this requires a total of 200 cycles = 1.12 usec, which translates to a forwarding rate of only around 900 K packets/second. The IXP1200 gets around this limit by using six parallel processors and an old architectural idea called *multithreading*. The main idea is that each processor works on multiple packets, each packet being a thread; when the processing for one packet stalls because of a memory reference, processing for the next thread is resumed. Using fast context switching between threads, and four contexts per processor, the IXP1200 can theoretically obtain 6 * 4 * 900 K = 21.6 M packets/second.

Network processors also offer special-purpose instructions for address lookup and other common forwarding functions. Some network processors also streamline the movement of data packets by having hardware engines that present only the header of each data packet to the processor. The remainder of the data packet flows directly to the output queue. The processor(s) read the header, do the lookup, and write the updated header to the output queue. The hardware magically glues together the updated header with the original packet and keeps all packets in order. While this approach avoids the movement of the remainder of the packet through the processor, it does nothing for the case of minimum-size packets.

Case Study 2: Buffering and optical switching

As fiber-optic links scale to higher speeds, electronics implementing combinational logic and memories in core routers becomes a bottleneck. Currently, packets arrive over fiber-optic links with each bit encoded as a light pulse. Optics at the receiver convert light to electrical pulses; the packet is then presented to forwarding logic implemented electronically. The packet is then queued to an outbound link for transmission, upon which the transmitting link optics convert electrical bits back to light. The electronic bottleneck can be circumvented by creating an all-optical router without any electro-optical conversions.

Unfortunately, doing IP lookups optically, and especially building dense optical packet memories, seems hard today. But switching light between several endpoints is feasible. Thus the numerous start-ups in the buzzing optical space tend to build optical *circuit switches* that use electronics to set up the circuit switch. A circuit switch connects input X to output Y for a large duration, as opposed to the duration of a single packet as in a packet switch. Such circuit switches have found use as a flexible "core" of an ISP's network to connect conventional routers. If traffic between, say, routers $R1$ and $R2$ increases, an ISP operator can (at a large time scale of, say, minutes) change the circuit switches to increase the bandwidth of the $R1$-to-$R2$ path. However, the wastefulness of reserving switch paths for small flow durations makes it likely that packet-switched routers will continue to be popular in the near future.

2.4 Operating systems

An operating system is a software that sits above hardware in order to make life easier for application programmers. For most Internet routers, time-critical packet forwarding runs directly on the hardware (Fig. 2.10) and is *not* mediated by an operating system. Less time-critical code runs on a router oper-

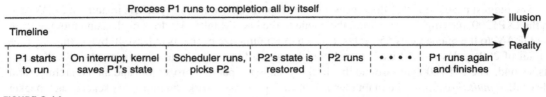

FIGURE 2.11

The programmer sees the illusion of an uninterrupted timeline shown above, while the real processor timeline may switch back and forth between several processes.

ating system that is stripped down, such as Cisco's IOS. However, to improve end-to-end performance for, say, Web browsing, an implementor needs to understand the costs and benefits of operating systems.

Abstractions are idealizations or illusions we invent to deal with the perversity and irregularity of the real world. To finesse the difficulties of programming on a bare machine, operating systems offer abstractions to application programmers. Three central difficulties of dealing with raw hardware are dealing with interrupts, managing memory, and controlling I/O devices. To deal with these difficulties, operating systems offer the abstractions of *uninterrupted computation*, *infinite memory*, and *simple I/O*.

A good abstraction increases programmer productivity but has two costs. First, the mechanism implementing the abstraction has a price. For example, scheduling processes can cause overhead for a Web server. A second, less obvious cost is that the abstraction can hide power, preventing the programmer from making optimal use of resources. For example, operating system memory management may prevent the programmer of an Internet lookup algorithm from keeping the lookup data structure in memory in order to maximize performance. We now provide a model of the costs and underlying mechanisms of the process (Section 2.4.1), virtual memory (Section 2.4.2), and I/O (Section 2.4.3) abstractions. More details can be found in Tanenbaum (1992).

2.4.1 Uninterrupted computation via processes

A program may not run very long on the processor before being interrupted by the network adaptor. If application programmers had to deal with interrupts, a working 100-line program would be a miracle. Thus operating systems provide programmers with the abstraction of uninterrupted, sequential computation under the name of a *process*.

The process *abstraction* is realized by three *mechanisms*: context switching, scheduling, and protection, the first two of which are depicted in Fig. 2.11. In Fig. 2.11, Process P1 has the illusion that it runs on the processor by itself. In reality, as shown on the timeline below, Process P1 may be interrupted by a timer interrupt, which causes the OS scheduler program to run on the processor. Displacing P1 requires the operating system to save the state of P1 in memory. The scheduler may run briefly and decide to give Process P2 a turn. Restoring P2 to run on the processor requires restoring the state of P2 from memory. Thus the actual time line of a processor may involve frequent context switches between processes, as orchestrated by the scheduler. Finally, *protection* ensures that incorrect or malicious behavior of one process cannot affect other processes.

As agents of computation, "processes" come in three flavors—interrupt handlers, threads, and user processes—ranked in order of increasing generality and cost. *Interrupt handlers* are small pieces of

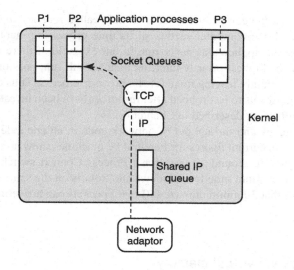

FIGURE 2.12

The processing of a received Internet packet in BSD is divided between the network adaptor, the kernel, and the destined process.

computation used to service urgent requests, such as the arrival of a message to the network adaptor; interrupt handlers use only a small amount of state, typically a few registers. *User processes* use the complete state of the machine, such as memory as well as registers; thus, it is expensive to switch between user processes as directed by the scheduler. Within the context of a single process, threads offer a cheaper alternative to processes. A *thread* is a lightweight process that requires less state, because threads within the same process share the same memory (i.e., same variables). Thus context switching between two threads in the same process is cheaper than switching processes, because memory does not have to be remapped. The following example shows the relevance of these concepts to endnode networking.

Example 8. Receiver Livelock in BSD Unix: In BSD UNIX, as shown in Fig. 2.12, the arrival of a packet generates an interrupt. The interrupt is a hardware signal that causes the processor to save the state of the currently running process, say, a Java program. The processor then jumps to the interrupt handler code, bypassing the scheduler for speed. The interrupt handler copies the packet to a kernel queue of IP packets waiting to be consumed, makes a request for an operating system thread (called a *software interrupt*), and exits. Assuming no further interrupts, the interrupt exit passes control to the scheduler, which is likely to cede the processor to the software interrupt, which has higher priority than user processes.

The kernel thread does TCP and IP processing and queues the packet to the appropriate application queue, called a *socket* queue (Fig. 2.12). Assume that the application is a browser such as Netscape. Netscape runs as a process that may have been asleep waiting for data and is now considered for being run on the processor by the scheduler. After the software interrupt exits and control passes back to the scheduler, the scheduler may decide to run Netscape in place of the original Java program.

Under high network load, the computer can enter what is called *receiver livelock* (Mogul and Ramakrishnan, 1997), in which the computer spends all its time processing incoming packets, only to discard them later because the applications never run. In our example, if there is a series of back-to-back packet arrivals, only the highest-priority interrupt handler will run, possibly leaving no time for the software interrupt and certainly leaving none for the browser process. Thus either the IP or socket queues will fill up, causing packets to be dropped after resources have been invested in their processing. Methods to mitigate this effect are described in Chapter 6.

Notice also that the latency and throughput of network code in an endnode depend on "process" activation times. For example, current figures for Pentium IV machines show around 2 μsec of interrupt latency for a null interrupt call, around 10 μsec for a Process Context switch on a Linux machine with two processes, and much more time for Windows and Solaris on the same machine. These times may seem small, but recall that 30 minimum-size (40-byte) packets can arrive in 10 μsec on a Gigabit Ethernet link.

2.4.2 Infinite memory via virtual memory

In virtual memory (Fig. 2.13), the programmer works with an abstraction of memory that is a linear array into which a compiler assigns variable locations. Variable X could be stored in location 1010 in this imaginary (or virtual) array. The virtual memory abstraction is implemented using the twin mech-

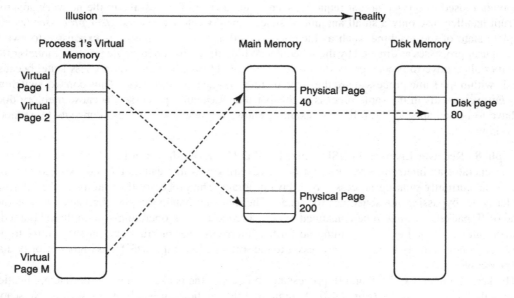

FIGURE 2.13

The programmer sees the illusion of contiguous virtual memory, which is, in reality, mapped to a collection of main memory and disk memory pages via page tables.

anisms of page table mapping and demand paging. Both these mechanisms are crucial to understand in order to optimize data transfer costs in an endnode.

Any virtual address must be mapped to a physical memory address. The easiest mapping is to use an offset into physical memory. For example, a virtual array of 15,000 locations could be mapped into physical memory from, say, 12,000 to 27,000. This has two disadvantages. First, when the program runs, a block of 15,000 contiguous locations has to be found. Second, the programmer is limited to using a total memory equal to the size of physical memory.

Both problems can be avoided by a mapping based on table lookup. Since it takes too much memory to implement a mapping from any virtual location to *any* physical location, a more restricted mapping based on *pages* is used. Thus for any virtual address, let us say that the high-order bits (e.g., 20 bits) form the page number and that the low-order bits (e.g., 12 bits) form the location within a page. All locations within a virtual page are mapped to the same relative location, but individual virtual pages can be mapped to arbitrary locations. Main memory is also divided into physical pages, such that every group of 2^{12} memory words is a physical page.

To map a virtual into a physical address, the corresponding virtual page (i.e., high-order 20 bits) is mapped to a physical page number while retaining the same location within the page. The mapping is done by looking up a page table indexed by the virtual page number. A virtual page can be located on any physical memory page. More generally, some pages (e.g., Virtual Page 2 in Fig. 2.13) may not be memory resident and can be marked as being on disk. When such a page is accessed, the hardware will generate an exception and cause the operating system to read the page from the disk page into a main memory page. This second mechanism is called *demand paging*.

Together, page mapping and demand paging solve the two problems of storage allocation and bounded memory allocations. Instead of solving the harder variable size storage allocation problem, the OS needs only to keep a list of fixed size free pages and to assign some free pages to a new program. Also, the programmer can work with an abstraction of memory whose size is bounded only by the size of the disk and the number of instruction address bits.

The extra mapping can slow down each instruction considerably. A Read to virtual location X may require two main memory accesses: a page table access to translate X to physical address P, followed by a Read to address P. Modern processors get around this overhead by caching the most recently used mappings between virtual and physical addresses in a *translation look-aside buffer* (TLB), which is a processor-resident cache. The actual translation is done by a piece of hardware called the *memory management unit* (MMU), as shown in Fig. 2.8.

The page table mapping also provides a mechanism for protection between processes. When a process makes a Read to virtual location X, unless there is a corresponding entry in the page table, the hardware will generate a page fault exception. By ensuring that only the operating system can change page table entries, the operating system can ensure that one process cannot read from or write to the memory of another process in an unauthorized fashion.

While router forwarding works directly on physical memory, all endnode and server networking code works on virtual memory. While virtual memory is a potential *cost* (e.g., for TLB misses), it also reflects a possible *opportunity*. For example, it offers the potential for packet copying between the operating system and the application (see Example 8) to be done more efficiently by manipulating page tables. This idea is explored further in Chapter 5.

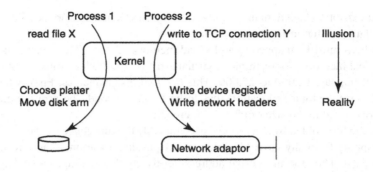

FIGURE 2.14

The programmer sees devices as disparate as a disk and a network adaptor as pieces of memory that can be read and written using system calls, but in reality, the kernel manages a host of device-specific details.

2.4.3 Simple I/O via system calls

Having an application programmer be aware of the variety and complexity of each I/O device would be intolerable. Thus operating systems provide the programmer with the abstraction of the devices as a piece of memory (Fig. 2.14) that can be read and written.

The code that maps from a simple I/O interface call to the actual physical Read (with all parameters filled in) to the device is called a *device driver*. If abstraction were the only concern, the device driver code could be installed in a library of commonly available code that can be "checked out" by each application. However, since devices such as disks must be shared by all applications, if applications directly control the disk, an erroneous process could crash the disk. Instead, secure operating system design requires that only the buggy application fail.

Thus it makes sense for the I/O calls to be handled by device drivers that are in a secure portion of the operating system that cannot be affected by buggy processes. This secure portion, called the *kernel*, provides a core of essential services, including I/O and page table updates, that applications cannot be trusted to perform directly.

Thus when a browser such as Netscape wants to make a disk access to read a Web page, it must make a so-called *system call* across the application–kernel boundary. System calls are a protected form of a function call. The hardware instruction is said to "trap" to a more privileged level (kernel mode), which allows access to operating system internals. When the function call returns after the I/O completes, the application code runs at normal privilege levels. A system call is more expensive than a function call because of the hardware privilege escalation and the extra sanitizing checks for incorrect parameter values. A simple system call may take a few microseconds on modern machines.

The relevance to networking is that when a browser wishes to send a message over the network (e.g., Process 2 in Fig. 2.14), it must do a system call to activate TCP processing. A few microseconds for a system call may seem small, but it is really very high overhead on a fast Pentium. Can applications speed up networking by bypassing the system call? If so, does OS protection get tossed out of the window? Answers to these tantalizing questions are postponed to Chapter 6.

2.5 Summary

This chapter is best sampled based on the reader's needs. Structurally, the chapter works its way through four abstraction levels that affect performance: hardware, architecture, operating systems, and protocols. Viewing across abstraction levels is helpful because packet-processing speeds can be limited by transistor paths implementing packet processing, by architectural limits such as bus speeds, by OS abstraction overheads such as system calls, and finally, even by protocol mechanisms. Several examples, which look ahead to the rest of the book, were described to show that performance can be improved by understanding each abstraction level.

Designers that consider all four abstraction levels for each problem will soon be lost in detail. However, there are a *few* important performance issues and major architectural decisions for which simultaneous understanding of all abstraction levels is essential. For example, the simple models given in this chapter can allow circuit designers, logic designers, architects, microcoders, and software protocol implementors to work together to craft the architecture of a world-class router. They can also allow operating system designers, algorithm experts, and application writers to work together to design a world-class Web server. As link speeds cross 40 Gbps, such interdisciplinary teams will become even more important. This need is alluded to by Raymond Kurzweil in a different context (Kurzweil, 2001):

> There's another aspect of creativity. We've been talking about great individual contributors, but when you're creating technology it's necessarily a group process, because technology today is so complex that it has to be interdisciplinary ... And they're all essentially speaking their own languages, even about the same concepts. So we will spend months establishing our common language ... I have a technique to get people to think outside the box: I'll give a signal-processing problem to the linguists, and vice versa, and let them apply the disciplines in which they've grown up to a completely different problem. The result is often an approach that the experts in the original field would never have thought of. Group process gives creativity a new dimension.

With fields like hardware implementation and protocol design replacing signal processing and linguistics, Kurzweil's manifesto reflects the goal of this chapter.

2.6 Exercises

1. **TCP Protocols and Denial-of-Service Attacks:** A common exploit for a hacker is to attempt to bring down a popular service, such as Yahoo, by doing a denial-of-service (DOS) attack. A simple DOS attack that can be understood using the simple TCP model of Fig. A.1 is TCP *Syn-Flooding*. In this attack, the hacker sends a number of SYN packets to the chosen destination D (e.g., Yahoo) using randomly chosen source addresses. D sends back a SYN-ACK to the supposed source S and waits for a response. If S is not an active IP address, then there will be no response from S. Unfortunately, state for S is kept in a pending connection queue at D until D finally times out S. By periodically sending bogus connection attempts pretending to be from different sources, the attacker can ensure that the finite pending connection queue is always full. Thereafter, legitimate connection requests to D will be denied.

   - Assume there is a monitor that is watching all traffic. What algorithm can be used to detect denial-of-service attacks? Try to make your algorithm as fast and memory-efficient as possible

so that it can potentially be used in real-time, even in a router. This is a hard problem, but even starting to think about the problem is instructive.
- Suppose the monitor realizes a TCP flood attack is underway. Why might it be hard to distinguish between legitimate traffic and flood traffic?

2. **Digital Design:** Multiplexers and barrel shifters are very useful in networking hardware, so working on this problem can help even a software person to build up hardware intuition.

- First, design a 2-input multiplexer from basic gates (AND, OR, NOT).
- Next, generalize the idea shown in the chapter to design an N-input multiplexer from $N/2$ input multiplexers. Use this to describe a design that takes $\log N$ gate delays and $O(N)$ transistors.
- Show how to design a barrel shifter using a reduction to multiplexers (i.e., use as many muxes as you need in your solution). Based on your earlier solutions, what are the gate and time complexities of your solution?
- Try to design a barrel shifter directly at the transistor level. What are its time and transistor complexities? You can do better using direct design than the simple reduction earlier.

3. **Thermometer Encoding:** Spell out the digital logic of the following 4-bit-input digital-to-analog converter (a.k.a. thermometer encoding), a wider slight variant of which is used in Fig. 2.4 for generating an N-bit mask. The inputs are i_1 (the least significant bit), i_2, i_3, and i_4. The outputs are $j_1, j_2, \cdots, j_{15}$. If the binary number $(i_4 i_3 i_2 i_1)_2$ has value k, then $j_1 = j_2 = \cdots = j_k = 1$ and the rest is 0. You need to spell out the formula for each j_l ($1 \leq l \leq 15$) as a logic function of the inputs. Please use notations $\vee$ (for OR), $\wedge$ (for AND), and $\neg$ (for NOT).

4. **Memory Design:** For the design of the pipelined flow ID lookup scheme described earlier, draw the timing diagrams for the pipelined lookups. Use the numbers described in the chapter, and clearly sketch a sample binary tree with 15 leaves and show how it can be looked up after four lookups on four different banks. Assume a binary tree, not a ternary tree. Also, calculate the number of keys that can be supported using 16 banks of RAMBUS if the first k levels of the tree are cached in on-chip SRAM.

5. **Memories and Pipelining Trees:** This problem studies how to pipeline a heap. A heap is important for applications like QoS, where a router wishes to transmit the packet with the earliest timestamp first. Thus it makes sense to have a heap ordered on timestamps. To make it efficient, the heap needs to be pipelined in the same fashion as the binary search tree example in the chapter, though doing so for a heap is somewhat harder. Fig. 2.15 shows an example of a P-heap capable of storing 15 keys. A P-heap (Bhagwan and Lin, 2000) is a full binary tree, such as a standard heap, except that nodes anywhere in the heap can be empty as long as all children of the node are also empty (e.g., nodes 6, 12, 13).

For the following explanations consult Fig. 2.15 and Fig. 2.16. Consider adding key 9 to the heap. Assume every node N has a count of the number of empty nodes in the subtree rooted at N. Since 9 is less than the root value of 16, 9 must move below. Since both the left and right children have empty nodes in their subtrees, we arbitrarily choose to add 9 to the left subtree (node 2). The index, value, and position values shown on the left of each tree are registers used to show the state of the current operation. Thus in Fig. 2.15, part (b), when 9 is added to the left subtree, the index represents the depth of the subtree (depth 2) and the position is the number of the node (i.e., node 2) that the value 9 is being added to.

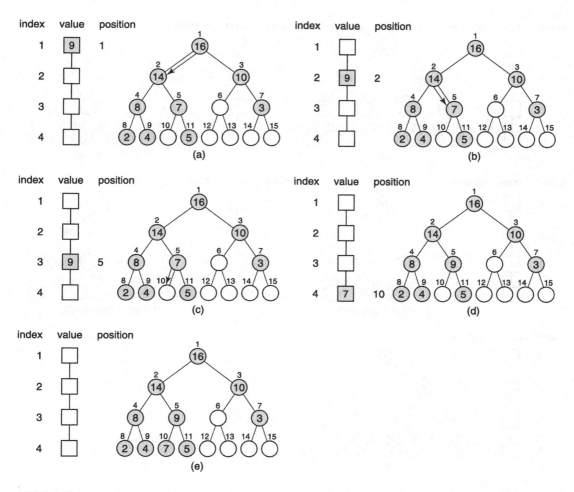

FIGURE 2.15

An enqueue example in five snapshots to be read from left to right and then top-down. In each snapshot, the index represents the depth of the subtree, and the position is the number of the node that the value is being added to.

Next, since 9 is less than 14 and since only the right child has space in its subtree, 9 is added to the subtree rooted at node 5. This time 9 is greater than 7, so 7 is replaced with 9 (in node 5) and 7 is pushed down to the empty node, 10. Thus in Fig. 2.15, part (d), the index value is 4 (i.e., operation is at depth 4) and the position is 10. Although in Fig. 2.15 only one of the registers at any index/depth has nonempty information, keeping separate registers for each index will allow pipelining.

Consider next what is involved in removing the largest element (dequeue). Remove 16 and try to push down the hole created until an empty subtree is created. Thus in Step 3, the hole is moved to node 2 (because its value, 14, is larger than its sibling, with value 10), then to node 4, and finally to

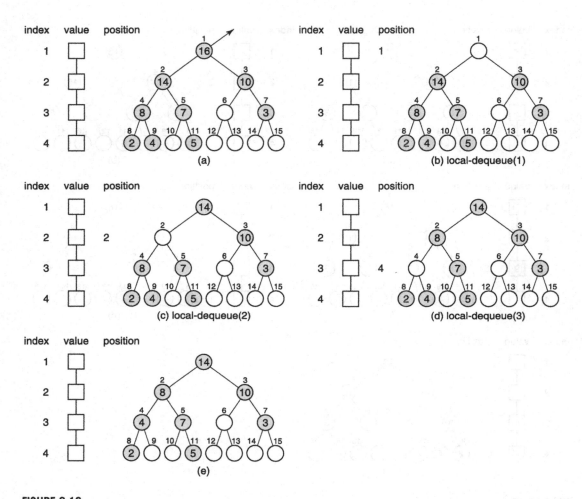

FIGURE 2.16

Dequeue example.

node 9. Each time a hole is moved down, the corresponding nonempty value from below replaces the old hole.

- In order to make the enqueue operation work correctly, the count of empty subtree nodes must be maintained. Explain briefly how the count should be maintained for each enqueue and dequeue operation (the structure will be pipelined in a moment, so make sure the count values respect this goal).
- A logical thing to do is to pipeline by level, as we did for the binary tree in the chapter. However, here we have a problem. At each level (say, inserting 9 at the root), the operation has to consult the two children at the next level as well. Thus when the first operation moves down to level 2,

one cannot bring in a second operation to level 1 or there will be memory contention. Clearly, waiting till one operation finishes completely will work, but this reduces to sequential processing of operations. What is the fastest rate you can pipeline the heap?
- Consider the operations "Enqueue 9; Enqueue 4.5; Dequeue" pipelined as you have answered earlier. Show six consecutive snapshots of the tree supporting these three operations.
- Assume that each level memory is an on-chip SRAM that takes 5 nsec for a memory access. Assume that you can read and write the value and count fields together in one access. Remember that some of the memories can be queried in parallel. What is the steady-state throughput of the heap, in operations per second?
- Could one improve the number of memory references by using a wider memory access and laying out the tree appropriately?
- Before this design, previous designs used a memory element for each heap element as well as logic for each element. Thus the amount of logic required scaled directly with heap size, which scales poorly in terms of density and power. In this design, the memory scales with the number of heap elements and thus scales with SRAM densities and power, but the logic required scales much better. Explain.

6. **Architecture, Caches, and Fast Hash Functions:** The L1 cache in a CPU provides essentially a fast hash function that maps from a physical memory address to its contents via the L1 cache. Suppose that one wants to teach an old dog (the L1 cache) a new trick (to do IP lookups) using a method suggested in Chiueh and Pradhan (1999). The goal is to use the L1 cache as a hash table to map 32-bit IP addresses to 7-bit port numbers. Assume a 16-KB L1 cache, of which the first 4 KB are reserved for the hash table, and a 32-byte cache block size. Assume a byte-addressable machine, a 32-bit virtual address, and a page size of 4 KB. Thus there are 512 32-byte blocks in the cache. Assume the L1 cache is directly indexed (called *direct mapped*). Thus bits 5 through 13 of a virtual address are used to index into one of 512 blocks, with bits 0 through 4 identifying the byte within each block.

- Given pages of size 4 KB and that the machine is byte addressable, how many bits in a virtual address identify the virtual page? How many bits of the virtual page number intersect with bits 5 through 13 used to index into the L1 cache?
- The only way to ensure that the hash table is not thrown out of the L1 cache when some other virtual pages arrive is to mark any pages that could map into the same portion of the L1 cache as uncacheable at start-up (this can be done). Based on your previous answer and the fact that the hash table uses the first 4 KB of L1 cache, precisely identify which pages must be marked as uncacheable.
- To do a lookup of a 32-bit IP address, first convert the address to a virtual address by setting to 0 all bits except bits 5 through 11 (bits 12 and 13 are zero because only the top quarter of the L1 cache is being used). Assume this is translated to the exact same physical address. When a Read is done to this address, the L1 cache hardware will return the contents of the first 32-bit word of the corresponding cache block. Each 32-bit word will contain a 25-bit tag and a 7-bit port number. Next, compare all bits in the IP address, other than bits 5 through 11, with the tag, and keep doing so for each 32-bit entry in the block. How many L1 cache accesses are required in the worst case for a hash lookup? Why might this be faster than a standard hash lookup in software?

7. **Operating Systems and Lazy Receiver Processing:** Example 8 described how BSD protocol processing can lead to receiver livelock. Lazy receiver processing (Druschel and Banga, 1996) combats this problem via two mechanisms.

   - The first mechanism is to replace the single shared IP processing queue by a separate queue per destination socket. Why does this help? Why might this not be easy to implement?
   - The second mechanism is to implement the protocol processing at the priority of the receiving process and as part of the context of the received process (and not a separate software interrupt). Why does this help? Why might this not be easy to implement?

Fifteen implementation principles

3

Instead of computing, I had to think about the problem, a formula for success that I recommend highly.

—Ivan Sutherland

After understanding how queens and knights move in a game of chess, it helps to understand basic strategies, such as castling and the promotion of pawns in the endgame. Similarly, having studied some of the rules of the protocol implementation game in the last chapter, you will be presented in this chapter with implementation strategies in the form of 15 principles. The principles are abstracted from protocol implementations that have worked well. Many good implementors *unconsciously* use such principles. The point, however, is to articulate such principles so that they can be *deliberately* applied to craft efficient implementations.

This chapter is organized as follows. Section 3.1 motivates the use of the principles using a ternary CAM problem. Section 3.2 clarifies the distinction between algorithms and algorithmics using a network security forensics problem. Section 3.3 introduces 15 implementation principles; Section 3.4 explains the differences between *implementation* and *design* principles. Finally, Section 3.5 describes some cautionary questions that should be asked before applying the principles.

Quick reference guide

The reader pressed for time should consult the summaries of the 15 principles found in Figs. 3.1–3.3. Two networking applications of these principles can be found in a ternary CAM update problem (Section 3.1) and a network security forensics problem (Section 3.2).

3.1 Motivating the use of principles—updating ternary content-addressable memories

Call a string *ternary* if it contains characters that are either 0, 1, or *, where * denotes a wildcard that can match both a 0 and a 1. Examples of ternary strings of length 3 include S1 = 01* and S2 = *1*; the actual binary string 011 matches both S1 and S2, while 111 matches only S2. A ternary content-addressable memory (CAM) is a memory containing ternary strings of a specified length together with associated information; when presented with an input string, the CAM will search all its memory locations in parallel to output (in one cycle) the lowest memory location whose ternary string matches the specified input key.

Network Algorithmics. https://doi.org/10.1016/B978-0-12-809927-8.00008-7

Number	Principle	Used In
P1	Avoid obvious waste	Zero-copy interfaces
P2 P2a P2b P2c	Shift computation in time Precompute Evaluate lazily Share expenses, batch	Application device channels Copy-on-write Integrated layer processing
P3 P3a P3b P3c	Relax system requirements Trade certainty for time Trade accuracy for time Shift computation in space	Stochastic fair queueing Switch load balancing IPv6 fragmentation
P4 P4a P4b P4c	Leverage off system components Exploit locality Trade memory for speed Exploit existing hardware	Locality-driven receiver Processing; Lulea IP lookups Fast TCP checksum
P5 P5a P5b P5c	Add hardware Use memory interleaving and pipelining Use wide word parallelism Combine DRAM and SRAM effectively	Pipelined IP lookups Shared memory switches Maintaining counters

FIGURE 3.1

Summary of Principles 1–5—systems thinking.

Number	Principle	Networking Example
P6	Create efficient specialized routines	UDP checksums
P7	Avoid unnecessary generality	Fbufs
P8	Don't be tied to reference implementation	Upcalls
P9	Pass hints in layer interfaces	Packet filters
P10	Pass hints in protocol headers	Tag switching

FIGURE 3.2

Summary of Principles 6–10—recovering efficiency while retaining modularity.

Fig. 3.4 shows an application of ternary CAMs to the longest-matching prefix problem for Internet routers. For every incoming packet, each Internet router must extract a 32-bit destination IP address from the incoming packet and match it against a forwarding database of IP prefixes with their corresponding next hops. An IP prefix is a ternary string of length 32 where all the wildcards are at the end. We will change notation slightly and let * denote any number of wildcard characters, so 101* matches 10100 and not just 1010.

Number	Principle	Networking Example
P11 P11a	Optimize the expected case Use caches	Header prediction Fbufs
P12 P12a	Add state for speed Compute incrementally	Active VC list Recomputing CRCs
P13	Optimize degrees of freedom	IP trie lookups
P14	Use bucket sorting, bitmaps	Timing wheels
P15	Create efficient data structures	Level-4 switching

FIGURE 3.3

Summary of Principles 11–15—speeding up key routines.

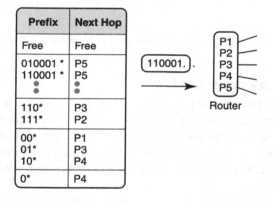

FIGURE 3.4

Example of using a ternary CAM for prefix lookups.

Thus in Fig. 3.4 a packet sent to a destination address that starts with 010001 matches the prefixes 010001* and 01* but should be sent to Port P5 because Internet forwarding requires that packets be forwarded using the longest match. We will have more to say about this problem in Chapter 11. For now, note that if the prefixes are arranged in a ternary CAM such that all longer prefixes occur before any shorter prefixes (as in Fig. 3.4), the ternary CAM provides the matching next hop in one memory cycle.

While ternary CAMs are extremely fast for message forwarding, they require that longer prefixes occur before shorter prefixes. But routing protocols often add or delete prefixes. Suppose in Fig. 3.4 that a new prefix, 11*, with next hop Port 1 must be added to the router database. The naive way to do insertion would make space in the group of length-2 prefixes (i.e., create a hole before 0*) by pushing up by one position all prefixes of length 2 or higher.

Unfortunately, for a large database of around 100,000 prefixes kept by a typical core router, this would take 100,000 memory cycles, which would make it very slow to add a prefix. We can obtain a

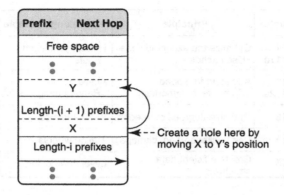

FIGURE 3.5

Finding a spot for the new prefix by moving X to Y's position recursively requires us to find a spot to move Y.

better solution systematically by applying the following two principles (described later in this chapter as principles **P13** and **P15**).

Understand and exploit degrees of freedom

In looking at the forwarding table on the left of Fig. 3.4 we see that all prefixes of the same length are arranged together and all prefixes of length i occur after all prefixes of length $j > i$. However, in the figure all prefixes of the same length are also sorted by value. Thus 00* occurs before 01*, which occurs before 10*. But it is unnecessary for the CAM to correctly return longest matching prefixes: We only require ordering between prefixes of *different* lengths; we do not require ordering between prefixes of the *same* length.

In looking at the more abstract view of Fig. 3.4 shown in Fig. 3.5, we see that if we are to add an entry to the start of the set of length-i prefixes, we have to create a hole at the end of the length-$(i + 1)$ set of prefixes. Thus we have to move the entry X, already at this position, to another position. If we move X one step up, we will be forced into our prior inefficient solution.

However, our observation about degrees of freedom says that we can place X *anywhere* adjacent to the other length-$(i + 1)$ prefixes. Thus, an alternative idea is to move X to the position held by Y, the last length-$(i + 2)$ prefix. But this forces us to find a new position for Y. How does this help? We need a second principle.

Use algorithmic techniques

Again, recursion suggests itself: We solve a problem by reducing the problem to a "smaller" instance of the same problem. In this case, the new problem of assigning Y a new position is "smaller" because the set of length-$(i + 2)$ prefixes is closer to the free space at the top of the CAM than the set of length-$(i + 1)$ prefixes. Thus we move Y to the end of the length-$(i + 3)$ set of prefixes, etc.

While recursion is a natural way to think, a better implementation is to unwind the recursion by starting from the top of the CAM and working downward by creating a hole at the end of the length-1 prefixes,[1] creating a hole at the end of the length-2 prefixes, etc., until we create a hole at the end of the length-i prefixes. Thus the worst-case time is $32 - i$ memory accesses, which is around 32 for small i.

Are we done? No, we can do better by further exploiting degrees of freedom. First, in Fig. 3.5 we *assumed* that the free space was at the *top* of the CAM. But the free space could be placed anywhere. In particular, it can be placed after the length-16 prefixes. This reduces the worst-case number of memory accesses by a factor of 2 (Shah and Gupta, 2001).

A more sophisticated degree of freedom is as follows. So far, the specification of the CAM insertion algorithm required that "a prefix of length i must occur before a prefix of length j if $i > j$." Such a specification is *sufficient* for correctness but is not *necessary*. For example, 010* can occur before 111001* because there is no address that can match both prefixes!

Thus a less exacting specification is "if two prefixes P and Q can match the same address, then P must come before Q in the CAM if P is longer than Q." This is used in Shah and Gupta (2001) to further reduce the worst-case number of memory accesses for insertion for some practical databases.

While the last improvement is not worth its complexity, it points to another important principle. We often divide a large problem into subproblems and hand over the subproblem for a solution based on a specification. For example, the CAM hardware designer may have handed over the update problem to a microcoder, specifying that longer prefixes be placed before shorter ones.

But, as before, such a specification may not be the only way to solve the original problem. Thus changes to the specification (principle **P3**) can yield a more efficient solution. Of course, this requires curious and confident individuals who understand the big picture or who are brave enough to ask dangerous questions.

3.2 Algorithms versus algorithmics

It may be possible to argue that the previous example is still essentially algorithmic and does not require system thinking. One more quick example will help clarify the difference between algorithms and algorithmics.

Security forensics problem

In many intrusion detection systems, a manager often finds that a flow (defined by some packet header, for example, a source IP address) is likely to be misbehaving based on some probabilistic check. For example, a source doing a port scan may be identified after it has sent 100,000 packets to different machines in the attacked subnet.

While there are methods to identify such sources, one problem is that the evidence (the 100,000 packets sent by the source) has typically disappeared (i.e., been forwarded from the router) by the time the guilty source is identified. The problem is that the probabilistic check requires accumulating some state (in, say, a suspicion table) for every packet received *over some period of time* before a source can be deemed suspicious. Thus if a source is judged to be suspicious after 10 seconds, how can one go back in time and retrieve the packets sent by the source during those 10 seconds?

---

[1] For simplicity, this description has assumed that the CAM contains prefixes of all lengths; it is easy to modify the algorithm to avoid this assumption.

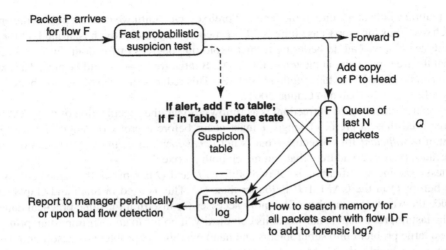

FIGURE 3.6

Keeping a queue of the last 100,000 packets that contains forensic information about what suspicious flows have been sent in the past.

To accomplish this, in Fig. 3.6 we keep a queue of the last 100,000 packets that were sent by the router. When a packet is forwarded, we also add a copy of the packet (or just keep a pointer to the packet) to the head of the queue. To keep the queue bounded, when the queue is full, we delete from the tail as well.

The main difficulty with this scheme is that when a guilty flow is detected, there may be lots of the flow's packets in the queue (Fig. 3.6). All of these packets must be placed in the forensic log for transmission to a manager. The naive method of searching through a large DRAM buffer is very slow.

The textbook algorithms approach would be to add some index structure to search quickly for flow IDs. For example, one might maintain a hash table of flow IDs that maps every flow to a list of pointers to all packets with that flow ID in the queue. When a new packet is placed in the queue, the flow ID is looked up in the hash table and the address of the new packet in the queue is placed at the end of the flow's list. Of course, when packets leave the queue, their entries must be removed from the list, and the list can be long. Fortunately, the entry to be deleted is guaranteed to be at the head of the queue for that flow ID.

Despite this, the textbook scheme has some difficulties. It adds more space to maintain these extra queues per flow ID, and space can be at a premium for a high-speed implementation. It also adds some extra complexity to packet processing to maintain the hash table and requires reading out all of a flow's packets to the forensic log before the packet is overwritten by a packet that arrives 100,000 packets later. Instead, the following "systems" solution may be more elegant.

Solution

Do not attempt to immediately identify all of a flow *F*'s packets when *F* is identified, but *lazily* identify them as they reach the end of the packet queue. This is shown in Fig. 3.7. When we add a packet to the head of the queue, we must remove a packet from the end of the queue (at least when the queue is full).

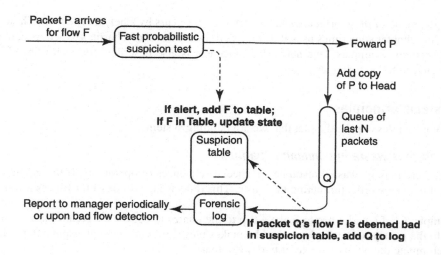

FIGURE 3.7

Keeping a queue of the last 100,000 packets that contains forensic information about what suspicious flows have been sent in the past.

If that packet (say, Q, see Fig. 3.6) belongs to flow F that is in the Suspicion Table and flow F has reached some threshold of suspicion, we then add packet Q to the forensic log. The log can be sent to a manager. The overhead of this scheme is significant but manageable; we have to do two packet-processing steps, one for the packet being forwarded and one for the packet being removed from the queue. But these two packet-processing steps are also required in the textbook scheme; on the other hand, the elegant scheme requires no hashing and uses much less storage (no pointers between the 100,000 packets).

3.3 Fifteen implementation principles—categorization and description

The two earlier examples and the warm-up exercise in Chapter 1 motivate the following 15 principles, which are used in the rest of the book. They are summarized inside the front cover. To add more structure, they are categorized as follows:

- **Systems Principles:** Principles 1–5 take advantage of the fact that a system is constructed from subsystems. By taking a systemwide rather than a black-box approach, one can often improve performance.
- **Improving Efficiency While Retaining Modularity:** Principles 6–10 suggest methods for improving performance while allowing complex systems to be built modularly.
- **Speeding It Up:** Principles 11–15 suggest techniques for speeding up a key routine considered by itself.

Amazingly, many of these principles have been used for years by Chef Charlie at his Greasy Spoon restaurant. This chapter sometimes uses illustrations drawn from Chef Charlie's experience, in addition to computer systems examples. One networking example is also described for each principle, though details are deferred to later chapters.

3.3.1 Systems principles

The first five principles exploit the fact that we are building systems.

P1: Avoid obvious waste in common situations

In a system, there may be wasted resources in special sequences of operations. If these patterns occur commonly, it may be worth eliminating the waste. This reflects an attitude of thriftiness toward system costs.

For example, Chef Charlie has to make a trip to the pantry to get the ice cream maker to make ice cream and to the pantry for a pie plate when he makes pies. But when he makes pie à la mode, he has learned to eliminate the obvious waste of two separate trips to the pantry.

Similarly, optimizing compilers look for obvious waste in terms of repeated subexpressions. For example, if a statement calculates $i = 5.1 * n + 2$ and a later statement calculates $j := (5.1 * n + 2) * 4$, the calculation of the common subexpression $5.1 * n + 2$ is wasteful and can be avoided by computing the subexpression once, assigning it to a temporary variable t, and then calculating $i := t$ and $j := t * 4$. A classic networking example, described in Chapter 5, is avoiding making multiple copies of a packet between the operating system and user buffers.

Notice that each operation (e.g., walk to pantry, line of code, single packet copy) considered by itself has no obvious waste. It is the sequence of operations (two trips to the pantry, two statements that recompute a subexpression, two copies) that have obvious waste. Clearly, the larger the exposed context, the greater the scope for optimization. While the identification of certain operation patterns as being worth optimizing is often a matter of designer intuition, optimizations can be tested in practice using benchmarks.

P2: Shift computation in time

Systems have an aspect in space and time. The space aspect is represented by the subsystems, possibly geographically distributed, into which the system is decomposed. The time aspect is represented by the fact that a system is instantiated at various time scales, from fabrication time to compile time to parameter-setting times to run time. Many efficiencies can be gained by shifting computation in time. Here are three generic methods that fall under time-shifting.

- *P2a: Precompute.* This refers to computing quantities before they are actually used, to save time at the point of use. For example, Chef Charlie prepares crushed garlic in advance to save time during the dinner rush. A common systems example is table-lookup methods, where the computation of an expensive function f in run time is replaced by the lookup of a table that contains the value of f for every element in the domain of f. A networking example is the precomputation of IP and TCP headers for packets in a connection; because only a few header fields change for each packet, this reduces the work to write packet headers (Chapter 9).
- *P2b: Evaluate Lazily.* This refers to postponing expensive operations at critical times, hoping that either the operation will not be needed later or a less busy time will be found to perform the opera-

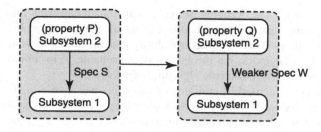

FIGURE 3.8

Easing the implementation of Subsystem 1 by weakening its specification from S to, say, W, at the cost of making Subsystem 2 do more work.

tion. For example, Chef Charlie postpones dishwashing to the end of the day. While precomputation is computing before the need, lazy evaluation is computing only when needed.

A famous example of lazy evaluation in systems is *copy-on-write* in the Mach operating system. Suppose we have to copy a virtual address space A to another space, B, for process migration. A general solution is to copy all pages in A to B to allow for pages in B to be written independently. Instead, copy-on-write makes page table entries in B's virtual address space point to the corresponding page in A. When a process using B writes to a location, then a separate copy of the corresponding page in A is made for B, and the write is performed. Since we expect the number of pages that are written in B to be small compared to the total number of pages, this avoids unnecessary copying.

A simple networking example occurs when a network packet arrives at an endnode X in a different byte order than X's native byte order. Rather than swap all bytes immediately, it can be more efficient to wait to swap the bytes that are actually read.

- *P2c: Share Expenses.* This refers to taking advantage of expensive operations done by other parts of the system. An important example of expense sharing is *batching*, where several expensive operations can be done together more cheaply than doing each separately. For example, Charlie bakes several pies in one batch. Computer systems have used batch processing for years, especially in the early days of mainframes, before time sharing. Batching trades latency for throughput. A simple networking example of expense sharing is timing wheels (Chapter 7), where the timer data structure shares expensive per-clock-tick processing with the routine that updates the time-of-day clock.

P3: Relax system requirements

When a system is first designed top-down, functions are partitioned among subsystems. After fixing subsystem requirements and interfaces, individual subsystems are designed. When implementation difficulties arise, the basic system structure may have to be redone, as shown in Fig. 3.8.

As shown in Chapter 1, implementation difficulties (e.g., implementing a divide) can sometimes be solved by relaxing the specification requirements for, say, Subsystem 1. This is shown in the figure by weakening the specification of Subsystem 1 from, say, S to W, but at the cost of making Subsystem 2 obey a stronger property, Q, compared to the previous property, P.

Three techniques that arise from this principle are distinguished by how they relax the original subsystem specification.

- *P3a: Trade Certainty for Time.* Systems designers can fool themselves into believing that their systems offer deterministic guarantees, when in fact we all depend on probabilities. For example, quantum mechanics tells us there is some probability that the atoms in your body will rearrange themselves to form a hockey puck, but this is clearly improbable.[2] This opens the door to consider randomized strategies when deterministic algorithms are too slow.

    In systems, randomization is used by millions of Ethernets worldwide to sort out packet-sending instants after collisions occur. A simple networking example of randomization is Cisco's NetFlow traffic measurement software: If a router does not have enough processing power to count all arriving packets, it can count random samples and still be able to statistically identify large flows. A second networking example is stochastic fair queuing (Chapter 14), where, rather than keep track exactly of the networking conversations going through a router, conversations are tracked probabilistically using hashing.

- *P3b: Trade Accuracy for Time.* Similarly, numerical analysis cures us of the illusion that computers are perfectly accurate. Thus it can pay to relax accuracy requirements for speed. In systems, many image compression techniques, such as MPEG, rely on lossy compression using interpolation. Chapter 1 used approximate thresholds to replace divides by shifts. In networking, some packet-scheduling algorithms at routers (Chapter 14) require sorting packets by their departure deadlines; some proposals to reduce sorting overhead at high speeds suggest approximate sorting, which can slightly reduce quality-of-service bounds but reduce processing.

- *P3c: Shift Computation in Space.* Notice that all the examples given for this principle relaxed requirements: Sampling may miss some packets, and the transferred image may not be identical to the original image. However, other parts of the system (e.g., Subsystem 2 in Fig. 3.8) have to adapt to these looser requirements. Thus we prefer to call the general idea of moving computation from one subsystem to another ("robbing Peter to pay Paul") *shifting computation in space.* In networking, for example, the need for routers to fragment packets has recently been avoided by having end systems calculate a packet size that will pass all routers.

P4: Leverage off system components

A black-box view of system design is to decompose the system into subsystems and then to design each subsystem in isolation. While this top-down approach has a pleasing modularity, in practice performance-critical components are often constructed partially bottom-up. For example, algorithms are designed to fit the features offered by the hardware. Here are some techniques that fall under this principle.

- *P4a: Exploit Locality.* Chapter 2 showed that memory hardware offers efficiencies if related data is laid out contiguously, e.g., same sector for disks, or same DRAM page for DRAMs. Disk-search algorithms exploit this fact by using search trees of high radix, such as B-trees. IP-lookup algorithms (Chapter 11) use the same trick to reduce lookup times by placing several keys in a wide word, as did the example in Chapter 1.

- *P4b: Trade Memory for Speed.* The obvious technique is to use more memory, such as lookup tables, to save processing time. A less obvious technique is to *compress* a data structure to make it more likely to fit into cache, because cache accesses are cheaper than memory accesses; in this case,

---

[2] Quote due to Tony Lauck.

both memory and speed may be improved. The Lulea IP-lookup algorithm described in Chapter 11 uses this idea by using sparse arrays that can still be looked up efficiently using space-efficient bitmaps.

- *P4c: Exploit Hardware Features.* Compilers use *strength reduction* to optimize away multiplications in loops; for example, in a loop where addresses are 4 bytes and the index i increases by 1 each time, instead of computing $4 * i$, the compiler calculates the new array index as being 4 higher than its previous value. This exploits the fact that multiplies are more expensive than additions on many modern processors. Similarly, it pays to manipulate data in multiples of the machine word size, as we will see in the fast IP-checksum algorithms described in Chapter 9.

If this principle is carried too far, the modularity of the system will be in jeopardy. Two techniques alleviate this problem. First, if we exploit other system features only to improve performance, then changes to those system features can only affect performance and not correctness. Second, we use this technique only for system components that profiling has shown to be a bottleneck.

P5: Add hardware to improve performance

When all else fails, goes the aphorism, use brute force. Adding new hardware,[3] such as buying a faster processor, can be simpler and more cost effective than using clever techniques. Besides the brute-force approach of using faster infrastructure (e.g., faster processors, memory, buses, links), there are cleverer hardware–software trade-offs. Since hardware is less flexible and has higher design costs, it pays to add the minimum amount of hardware needed.

Thus baking at the Greasy Spoon was sped up using microwave ovens. In computer systems, dramatic improvements each year in processor speeds and memory densities suggest doing key algorithms in software and upgrading to faster processors for speed increases. But computer systems abound with cleverer hardware–software trade-offs.

For example, in a multiprocessor system, if a processor wishes to write data, it must inform any "owners" of cached versions of the data. This interaction can be avoided if each processor has a piece of hardware that watches the bus for write transactions by other processors and automatically invalidates the cached location when necessary. This simple hardware snoopy cache controller allows the remainder of the cache-consistency algorithm to be efficiently performed in software.

Decomposing functions between hardware and software is an art in itself. Hardware offers several benefits. First, there is no time required to fetch instructions: Instructions are effectively hardcoded. Second, common computational sequences (which would require several instructions in software) can be done in a single hardware clock cycle. For example, finding the first bit set in, say, a 32-bit word may take several instructions on a RISC machine but can be computed by a simple priority encoder, as shown in the previous chapter.

Third, hardware allows you to explicitly take advantage of parallelism inherent in the problem. Finally, hardware manufactured in volume may be cheaper than a general-purpose processor. For example, a Pentium may cost $100, while an ASIC in volume with similar speeds may cost $10.

---

[3] By contrast, Principle **P4** talks about exploiting existing system features, such as the existing hardware. Of course, the distinction between principles tends to blur and must be taken with a grain of salt.

On the other hand, a software design is easily transported to the next generation of faster chips. Hardware, despite the use of programmable chips, is still less flexible. Despite this, with the advent of design tools such as VHDL synthesis packages, hardware design times have decreased considerably. Thus in the last few years chips performing fairly complex functions, such as image compression and IP lookups, have been designed.

Besides specific performance improvements, new technology can result in a complete paradigm shift. A visionary designer may completely redesign a system in anticipation of such trends. For example, the invention of the transistor and fast digital memories certainly enabled the use of digitized voice in the telephone network.

Increases in chip density have led computer architects to ponder what computational features to add to memories to alleviate the processor-memory bottleneck. In networks, the availability of high-speed links in the 1980s led to the use of large addresses and large headers. Ironically, the emergence of laptops in the 1990s led to the use of low-bandwidth wireless links and to a renewed concern for header compression. Technology trends can seesaw!

The following specific hardware techniques are often used in networking ASICs and are worth mentioning. They were first described in Chapter 2 and are repeated here for convenience.

- **P5a: Use Memory Interleaving and Pipelining.** Similar techniques are used in IP lookup, in classification, and in scheduling algorithms that implement QoS. The multiple banks can be implemented using several external memories, a single external memory such as a RAMBUS, or on-chip SRAM within a chip that also contains processing logic.
- **P5b: Use Wide Word Parallelism.** A common theme in many networking designs, such as the Lucent bit vector scheme (Chapter 12), is to use wide memory words that can be processed in parallel. This can be implemented using DRAM and exploiting page mode or by using SRAM and making each memory word wider.
- **P5c: Combine DRAM and SRAM.** We have explained in Chapter 2 and will explain in Chapter 16 two clever applications of this principle.

3.3.2 Principles for modularity with efficiency

An engineer who had read Dave Clark's classic papers (e.g., Clark [1985]) on the inefficiencies of layered implementations once complained to a researcher about modularity. The researcher (Radia Perlman) replied, "But that's how we got to the stage where we could complain about something." Her point, of course, was that complex systems like network protocols could only have been engineered using layering and modularity. The following principles, culled from work by Clark and others, show how to regain efficiencies while retaining modularity.

P6: Create efficient specialized routines by replacing inefficient general-purpose routines

As in mathematics, the use of abstraction in computer system design can make systems compact, orthogonal, and modular. However, at times the one-size-fits-all aspect of a general-purpose routine leads to inefficiencies. In important cases, it can pay to design an optimized and specialized routine.

A systems example can be found in database caches. Most general-purpose caching strategies would replace the least recently used record to disk. However, consider a query-processing routine processing a sequence of database tuples in a loop. In such a case, it is the most recently used record that will be used furthest in the future, so it is the ideal candidate for replacement. Thus many database applications replace the operating system caching routines with more specialized routines. It is best to do such specialization only for key routines, to avoid code bloat. A networking example is the fast UDP processing routines that we describe in Chapter 9.

P7: Avoid unnecessary generality

The tendency to design abstract and general subsystems can also lead to unnecessary or rarely used features. Thus, rather than building several specialized routines (e.g., **P6**) to replace the general-purpose routine, we might remove features to gain performance.[4]

Of course, as in the case of **P3**, removing features requires users of the routine to live with restrictions. For example, in RISC processors, the elimination of complex instructions such as multiplies required multiplication to be emulated by firmware. A networking example is provided by *Fbufs* (Chapter 5), which provides a specialized virtual memory service that allows efficient copying between virtual address spaces.

P8: Don't be tied to reference implementations

Specifications are written for clarity, not to suggest efficient implementations. Because abstract specification languages are unpopular, many specifications use imperative languages such as C. Rather than precisely describe *what* function is to be computed, one gets code that prescribes *how* to compute the function. This has two side effects.

First, there is a strong tendency to overspecify. Second, many implementors copy the reference implementation in the specification, which is a problem when the reference implementation was chosen for conceptual clarity and not efficiency. As Clark (1985) points out, implementors are free to change the reference implementation as long as the two implementations have the same external effects. In fact, there may be other structured implementations that are efficient as well as modular.

For example, Charlie knows that when a recipe tells him to cut beans and then to cut carrots, he can interchange the two steps. In the systems world, Clark originally suggested the use of upcalls (Clark, 1985) for operating systems. In an upcall, a lower layer can call an upper layer for data or advice, seemingly violating the rules of hierarchical decomposition introduced in the design of operating systems. Upcalls are commonly used today in network protocol implementations.

P9: Pass hints in module interfaces

A hint is information passed from a client to a service that, if correct, can avoid expensive computation by the service. The two key phrases are *passed* and *if correct*. By *passing* the hint in its request, a service can avoid the need for the associative lookup needed to access a cache. For example, a hint can be used to supply a direct index into the processing state at the receiver. Also, unlike caches, the hint is not guaranteed to be correct and hence must be checked against other certifiably correct information. Hints improve performance if the hint is correct most of the time.

This definition of a hint suggests a variant in which information is passed that is guaranteed to be correct and hence requires no checking. For want of an established term, we will call such information a *tip*. Tips are harder to use because of the need to ensure the correctness of the tip.

---

[4] Butler Lampson, a computer scientist and Turing Award winner, provides two quotes: *When in doubt, get rid of it* (anonymous) and *Exterminate Features* (Thacker).

As a systems example, the Alto File system (Lampson, 1989) has every file block on disk carry a pointer to the next file block. This pointer is treated as only a hint and is checked against the file name and block number stored in the block itself. If the hint is incorrect, the information can be reconstructed from disk. Incorrect hints must not jeopardize system correctness but result only in performance degradation.

P10: Pass hints in protocol headers

For distributed systems, the logical extension to Principle **P9** is to pass information such as hints in message headers. Since this book deals with distributed systems, we will make this a separate principle. For example, computer architects have applied this principle to circumvent inefficiencies in message-passing parallel systems such as the Connection Machine.

One of the ideas in active messages (Chapter 5) is to have a message carry the address of the interrupt handler for fast dispatching. Another example is tag switching (Chapter 11), where packets carry additional indices besides the destination address to help the destination address to be looked up quickly. Tags are used as hints because tag consistency is not guaranteed; packets can be routed to the wrong destination, where they must be checked.

3.3.3 Principles for speeding up routines

While the previous principles exploited system structure, we now consider principles for speeding up system routines considered in isolation.

P11: Optimize the expected case

While systems *can* exhibit a range of behaviors, the behaviors often fall into a smaller set called the "expected case" (Hennessey and Patterson, 1996). For example, well-designed systems should mostly operate in a fault- and exception-free regime. A second example is a program that exhibits *spatial locality* by mostly accessing a small set of memory locations. Thus it pays to make common behaviors efficient, even at the cost of making uncommon behaviors more expensive.

Heuristics such as optimizing the expected case are often unsatisfying for theoreticians, who (naturally) prefer mechanisms whose benefit can be precisely quantified in an average or worst-case sense. In defense of this heuristic, note that every computer in existence optimizes the expected case (see Chapter 2) at least a million times a second.

For example, with the use of paging, the worst-case number of memory references to resolve a PC instruction that accesses memory can be as bad as four (read instruction from memory, read first-level page table, read second-level page table, fetch operand from memory). However, the number of memory accesses can be reduced to 0 using caches. In general, caches allow designers to use modular structures and indirection, with gains in flexibility, and yet regain performance in the expected case. Thus it is worth highlighting caching.

P11a: Use caches

Besides caching, there are subtler uses of the expected-case principle. For example, when you wish to change buffers in the EMACS editor, the editor offers you a default buffer name, which is the last buffer you examined. This saves typing time in the expected case when you keep moving between two buffers. The use of header prediction (Chapter 9) in networks is another example of optimizing the expected case: The cost of processing a packet can be greatly reduced by assuming that the next packet received is closely related to the last packet processed (for example, by being the next packet in sequence) and requires no exception processing.

Note that determining the common case is best done by measurements and by schemes that automatically learn the common case. However, it is often based on the designer's intuition. Note that the expected case may be incorrect in special situations or may change with time.

P12: Add or exploit state to gain speed

If an operation is expensive, consider maintaining additional but redundant state to speed up the operation. For example, Charlie keeps track of the tables that are busy so that he can optimize waiter assignments. This is not absolutely necessary, for he can always compute this information when needed by walking around the restaurant.

In database systems, a classic example is the use of secondary indices. Bank records may be stored and searched using a primary key, say, the customer's Social Security number. However, if there are several queries that reference the customer name (e.g., "Find the balance of all Cleopatra's accounts in the Thebes branch"), it may pay to maintain an additional index (e.g., a hash table or B-tree) on the customer name. Note that maintaining additional state implies the need to potentially modify this state whenever changes occur.

However, sometimes this principle can be used without adding state by exploiting the existing state. We call this out as Principle **P12a**.

P12a: Compute incrementally

When a new customer comes in or leaves, Charlie increments the board on which he notes waiter assignments. As a second example, strength reduction in compilers (see example in **P4c**) incrementally computes the new loop index from the old using additions instead of computing the absolute index using multiplication. An example of incremental computation in networking is the incremental computation of IP checksums (Chapter 9) when only a few fields in the packet change.

P13: Optimize degrees of freedom

It helps to be aware of the variables that are under one's control and the evaluation criteria used to determine good performance. Then the game becomes one of optimizing these variables to maximize performance. For example, Charlie first used to assign waiters to tables as they became free, but he realized he could improve waiter efficiency by assigning each waiter to a set of contiguous tables.

Similarly, compilers use coloring algorithms to do register assignment while minimizing register spills. A networking example of optimizing degrees of freedom is multibit trie IP lookup algorithms (Chapter 11). In this example, a degree of freedom that can be overlooked is that the number of bits used to index into a trie node can vary, depending on the path through the trie, as opposed to being fixed at each level. The number of bits used can also be optimized via dynamic programming (Chapter 11) to demand the smallest amount of memory for a given speed requirement.

P14: Use special techniques for finite universes such as integers

When dealing with small universes, such as moderately sized integers, techniques like bucket sorting, array lookup, and bitmaps are often more efficient than general-purpose sorting and searching algorithms.

To translate a virtual address into a physical address, a processor first tries a cache called the TLB. If this fails, the processor must look up the page table. A prefix of the address bits is used to index into the page table directly. The use of table lookup avoids the use of hash tables or binary search, but it requires large page table sizes. A networking example of this technique is timing wheels (Chapter 7), where an efficient algorithm for a fixed timer range is constructed using a circular array.

P15: Use algorithmic techniques to create efficient data structures

Even where there are major bottlenecks, such as virtual address translation, systems designers finesse the need for clever algorithms by passing hints, using caches, and performing table lookup. Thus a major system designer is reported to have told an eager theoretician: "I don't use algorithms, son."

This book *does not* take this somewhat antiintellectual position. Instead, it contends that, in context, efficient algorithms can greatly improve system performance. In fact, a fair portion of the book will be spent describing such examples. However, there is a solid kernel of truth to the "I don't use algorithms" putdown. In many cases, Principles **P1** through **P14** need to be applied before any algorithmic issues become bottlenecks.

Algorithmic approaches include the use of standard data structures as well as generic algorithmic *techniques*, such as divide-and-conquer and randomization. The algorithm designer must, however, be prepared to see his clever algorithm become obsolete because of changes in system structure and technology. As described in the introduction, the real breakthroughs may arise from applying algorithmic *thinking* as opposed to merely reusing existing algorithms.

Examples of the successful use of algorithms in computer systems are the Lempel–Ziv compression algorithm employed in the UNIX utility *gzip*, the Rabin–Miller primality test algorithm found in public key systems, and the common use of B-trees (due to Bayer–McCreight) in databases (Cormen et al., 1990). Networking examples studied in this text include the Lulea IP-lookup algorithm (Chapter 11) and the RFC scheme for packet classification (Chapter 12).

3.4 Design versus implementation principles

Now that we have listed the principles used in this book, three clarifications are needed. First, conscious use of general principles does not eliminate creativity and effort but instead channels them more efficiently. Second, the list of principles is necessarily incomplete and can probably be categorized in a different way; however, it is a good place to start.

Third, it is important to clarify the difference between system *design* and *implementation* principles. Systems designers have articulated principles for system *design*. Design principles include, for example, the use of hierarchies and aggregation for scaling (e.g., IP prefixes), adding a level of indirection for increased flexibility (e.g., mapping from domain names to IP addresses allows DNS servers to balance the load between instances of a server), and virtualization of resources for increased user productivity (e.g., virtual memory).[5]

A nice compilation of design principles can be found in Lampson's article (Lampson, 1989) and Keshav's book (Keshav, 1997). Besides design principles, both Lampson and Keshav include a few

---

[5] The previous chapter briefly explains these terms (IP prefixes, DNS, and virtual memory).

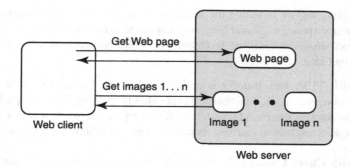

FIGURE 3.9

Retrieval of a Web page with images typically requires one request to get the page that specifies the needed images and more requests to retrieve each specified image. Why not have the Web server download the images directly?

implementation principles (e.g., "use hints" and "optimize the expected case"). This book, by contrast, assumes that much of the network design is already given, and so we focus on principles for efficient protocol *implementation*. This book also adds several principles for efficient implementation not found in Keshav (1991) or Lampson (1989).

On the other hand, Bentley's book on "efficient program design" (Bentley, 1982) is more about optimizing small code segments than the large systems that are our focus; thus many of Bentley's principles (e.g., fuse loops, unroll loops, reorder tests) are meant to speed up critical loops rather than speed up systems as a whole.

3.5 Caveats

Performance problems cannot be solved only through the use of Zen meditation.
—Paraphrased from Jeff Mogul, a computer scientist at HP Labs

The best of principles must be balanced with wisdom to understand the important metrics, with profiling to determine bottlenecks, and with experimental measurements to confirm that the changes are really improvements. We start with two case studies to illustrate the need for caution.

> **Case study 1: Reducing page download times**
> Fig. 3.9 shows that in order for a Web client to retrieve a Web page containing images, it must typically send a GET request for the page. If the page specifies inline images, then the client must send separate requests to retrieve the images before it can display the page. A natural application of principle **P1** is to ask why separate requests are needed. Why can't the Web server automatically download the images when the page is requested instead of waiting for a separate request? This should reduce page download latency by at least half a round trip delay.

To test our hypothesis, we modified the server software to do so and measured the resulting performance. To our surprise, we found only minimal latency improvement.

Using a network analyzer based on tcpdump, we found two reasons why this seeming improvement was a bad idea.

- **Interaction with TCP:** Web transfer is orchestrated by TCP as described in Chapter 2. To avoid network congestion, TCP increases its rate slowly, starting with one packet per round-trip, then to two packets per round trip delay, increasing its rate when it gets acks. Since TCP had to wait for acks anyway to increase its rate, waiting for additional requests for images did not add latency.
- **Interaction with Client Caching:** Many clients already cache common images, such as .gif files. It is a waste of bandwidth to have the Web server unilaterally download images that the client already has in its cache. Note that having the client request the images avoids this problem because the client will only request images it does not already have.

A useful lesson from this case study is the difficulty of improving part of a system (e.g., image downloading) because of interactions with other parts of the system (e.g., TCP congestion control).

Case study 2: Speeding up signature-based intrusion detection

As a second example, many network sites field an intrusion detection system, such as Snort (2001), that looks for suspicious strings in packet payloads that are characteristics of hacker attacks. An example is the string "perl.exe," which may signify an attempt to execute perl and then to execute arbitrary commands on a Web server. For every potentially matching rule that contains a string, Snort searches for each such string separately using the Boyer–Moore algorithm (Cormen et al., 1990). The worst case happens to be a Web packet that matches 310 rules. Simple profiling using gprof reveals (Fisk and Varghese, 2001) that 30% of the overhead in Snort arises from string searching.

An obvious application of **P1** seemed to be the following: Instead of separate searches for each string, use an integrated search algorithm that searches for all possible strings in a single pass over the packet. We modified Boyer–Moore to a set Boyer–Moore algorithm that could search for all specified strings in one pass. Implemented in a library, the new algorithm performed better than the Snort algorithm by a factor of 50 for the full Snort database. Unfortunately, when we integrated it into Snort, we found almost no improvement on packet traces (Fisk and Varghese, 2001). We found two reasons for this.

- **Multiple string matching is not a bottleneck for the trace:** For the given trace, very few packets matched multiple rules, each of which contained separate strings. When we used a trace containing only Web traffic (i.e., traffic with destination port 80), a substantial improvement was found.
- **Cache Effects:** Integrated string searching requires a data structure, such as a trie, whose size grows with the number of strings being searched. The simplest way to do integrated set searching is to place the strings contained in all rules in a single trie. However, when the number

of strings went over 100, the trie did not fit in cache, and performance suffered. Thus the system had to be reimplemented to use collections of smaller sets that took into account the hardware (**P4**).

A useful lesson from this case study is that purported improvements may not really target the bottleneck (which in the trace appears to be single-string matching) and can also interact with other parts of the system (the data cache).

3.5.1 Eight cautionary questions

In the spirit of the two case studies, here are eight cautionary questions that warn against the injudicious use of the principles.

Q1: Is it worth improving performance?

If one were to sell the system as a product, is performance a major selling strength? People interested in performance improvement would like to think so, but other aspects of a system, such as ease of use, functionality, and robustness, may be more important. For example, a user of a network management product cares more about features than performance. Thus, given limited resources and implementation complexity, we may choose to defer optimizations until needed. Even if performance is important, which performance metric (e.g., latency throughput, memory) is important?

Other things being equal, simplicity is best. Simple systems are easier to understand, debug, and maintain. On the other hand, the definition of simplicity changes with technology and time. Some amount of complexity is worthwhile for large performance gains. For example, years ago image compression algorithms such as MPEG were considered too complex to implement in software or hardware. However, with increasing chip densities, many MPEG chips have come to market.

Q2: Is this really a bottleneck?

The 80–20 rule suggests that a large percentage of the performance improvements comes from optimizing a small fraction of the system. A simple way to start is to identify key bottlenecks for the performance metrics we wish to optimize. One way to do so is to use profiling tools, as we did in Case Study 2.

Q3: What impact does the change have on the rest of the system?

A simple change may speed up a portion of the system but may have complex and unforeseen effects on the rest of the system. This is illustrated in Case Study 1. A change that improves performance but has too many interactions should be reconsidered.

Q4: Does the initial analysis indicate significant improvement?

Before doing a complete implementation, a quick analysis can indicate how much gain is possible. Standard complexity analysis is useful. However, when nanoseconds are at stake, constant factors are important. For software and hardware, because memory accesses are a bottleneck, a reasonable first-pass estimate is the number of memory accesses.

For example, suppose analysis indicates that address lookup in a router is a bottleneck (e.g., because there are fast switches to make data transfer not a bottleneck). Suppose the standard algorithm takes an average of 15 memory accesses while a new algorithm indicates a worst case of 3 memory accesses. This suggests a factor of 5 improvement, which makes it interesting to proceed further.

Q5: Is it worth adding custom hardware?

With the continued improvement in the price–performance of general-purpose processors, it is tempting to implement algorithms in software and ride the price–performance curve. Thus if we are considering a piece of custom hardware that takes a year to design, and the resulting price–performance improvement is only a factor of 2, it may not be worth the effort. On the other hand, hardware design times are shrinking with the advent of effective synthesis tools. Volume manufacturing can also result in extremely small costs (compared to general-purpose processors) for a custom-designed chip. Having an edge for even a small period such as a year in a competitive market is attractive. This has led companies to increasingly place networking functions in silicon.

Q6: Can protocol changes be avoided?

Through the years there have been several proposals denouncing particular protocols as being inefficient and proposing alternative protocols designed for performance. For example, in the 1980s, the transport protocol TCP was considered "slow" and a protocol called XTP (Chesson, 1989) was explicitly designed to be implemented in hardware. This stimulated research into making TCP fast, which culminated in Van Jacobson's fast implementation of TCP (Clark et al., 1989) in the standard BSD (Berkeley software distribution) release. More recently, proposals for protocol changes (e.g., tag and flow switching) to finesse the need for IP lookups have stimulated research into fast IP lookups.

Q7: Do prototypes confirm the initial promise?

Once we have successfully answered all the preceding questions, it is still a good idea to build a prototype or simulation and actually test to see if the improvement is real. This is because we are dealing with complex systems; the initial analysis rarely captures all effects encountered in practice. For example, understanding that the Web-image-dumping idea does not improve latency (see Case Study 1) might come only after a real implementation and tests with a network analyzer.

A major problem is finding a standard set of benchmarks to compare the standard and new implementations. For example, in the general systems world, despite some disagreement, there are standard benchmarks for floating-point performance (e.g., Whetstone) or database performance (e.g., debit–credit). If one claims to reduce Web transfer latencies using differential encoding, what set of Web pages provides a reasonable benchmark to prove this contention? If one claims to have an IP lookup scheme with small storage, which benchmark databases can be used to support this assertion?

Q8: Will performance gains be lost if the environment changes?

Sadly, the job is not quite over even if a prototype implementation is built and a benchmark shows that performance improvements are close to initial projections. The difficulty is that the improvement may be specific to the particular platform used (which can change) and may take advantage of properties of a certain benchmark (which may not reflect all environments in which the system will be used). The improvements may still be worthwhile, but some form of sensitivity analysis is still useful for the future.

For example, Van Jacobson performed a major optimization of the BSD networking code that allowed ordinary workstations to saturate 100-Mbps FDDI (Fiber Distributed Data Interface) rings. The optimization, which we will study in detail in Chapter 9, assumes that in the normal case the next packet is from the same connection as the previous packet, P, and has sequence number one higher than P. Will this assumption hold for servers that have thousands of simultaneous connections to clients? Will it hold if packets get sent over parallel links in the network, resulting in packet reordering? Fortunately, the code has worked well in practice for a number of years. Despite this, such questions alert us to possible future dangers.

3.6 Summary

This chapter introduced a set of principles for efficient system implementation. A summary can be found in Figs. 3.1–3.3. The principles were illustrated with examples drawn from compilers, architecture, databases, algorithms, and networks to show broad applicability to computer systems. Chef Charlie's examples, while somewhat tongue in cheek, show that these principles also extend to general systems, from restaurants to state governments. While the broad focus is on performance, cost is an equally important metric. One can cast problems in the form of finding the fastest solution for a given cost. Optimization of other metrics, such as bandwidth, storage, and computation, can be subsumed under the cost metric.

A preview of well-known networking applications of the 15 principles can be found in Figs. 3.1–3.3. These applications will be explained in detail in later chapters. The first five principles encourage systems thinking. The next five principles encourage a fresh look at system modularity. The last five principles point to useful ways to speed up individual subsystems.

Just as chess strategies are boring until one plays a game of chess, implementation principles are lifeless without concrete examples. The reader is encouraged to try the following exercises, which provide more examples drawn from computer systems. The principles will be applied to networks in the remaining chapters. In particular, the next chapter seeks to engage the reader by providing a set of 15 self-contained networking problems to play with.

3.7 Exercises

1. **Batching, Disk Locality, and Logs:** Most serious databases use log files for performance. Because writes to disk are expensive, it is cheaper to update only a memory image of a record. However, because a crash can occur at any time, the update must also be recorded on disk. This can be done by directly updating the record location on disk, but random writes to disk are expensive (see **P4a**). Instead, information on the update is written to a sequential log file. The log entry contains the record location, the old value (undo information), and the new value (redo information).

   • Suppose a disk page of 4000 bytes can be written using one disk I/O and that a log record is 50 bytes. If we apply batching (**2c**), what is a reasonable strategy for updating the log? What fraction of a disk I/O should be charged to a log update?
   • Before a transaction that does the update can commit (i.e., tell the user it is done), it must be sure the log is written. Why? Explain why this leads to another form of batching, *group commit*, where multiple transactions are committed together.

- If the database represented by the log gets too far ahead of the database represented on disk, crash recovery can take too long. Describe a strategy to bound crash recovery times.

2. **Relaxing Consistency Requirements in a Name Service:** The Grapevine system (Birell et al., 1982) offers a combination of a name service (to translate user names to inboxes) and a mail service. To improve availability, Grapevine name servers are replicated. Thus any update to a registration record (e.g., Joe → MailSlot3) must be performed on all servers implementing replicas of that record. Standard database techniques for distributed databases require that each update be atomic; that is, the effect should be as if updates were done simultaneously on all replicas. Because atomic updates require that all servers be available, and registration information is not as important as, say, bank accounts, Grapevine provides only the following loose semantics (**P3**): All replicas will *eventually* agree if updates stop. Each update is timestamped and passed from one replica to the other in arbitrary order. The highest timestamped update wins.

  - Give an example of how a user could detect inconsistency in Joe's registration during the convergence process.
  - If Joe's record is deleted, it should eventually be purged from the database to save storage. Suppose a server purges Joe's record immediately after receiving a Delete update. Why might Add updates possibly cause a problem? Suggest a solution.
  - The rule that the latest timestamp wins does not work well when two administrators try to create an entry with the same name. Because a later creation could be trapped in a crashed server, the administrator of the earlier creation can never know for sure that his creation has won. The Grapevine designers did not introduce mechanisms to solve this problem but relied on "some human-level centralization of name creation." Explain their assumption clearly.

3. **Replacing General-Purpose Routines with Special-Purpose Routines and Efficient Storage Allocators:** Consider the design of a general storage allocator that is given control of a large contiguous piece of memory and may be asked by applications for smaller, variable-size chunks. A general allocator is quite complex: As time goes by, the available memory fragments and time must be spent finding a piece of the requested size and coalescing adjacent released pieces into larger free blocks.

  - Briefly sketch the design of a general-purpose allocator. Consult a textbook such as Horowitz and Sahni (1978) for examples of allocators.
  - Suppose a profile has shown that a large fraction of the applications ask for 64 bytes of storage. Describe a more efficient allocator that works for the special case (**P6**) of allocating just 64-byte quantities.
  - How would you optimize the expected case (**P11**) and yet handle requests for storage other than 64 bytes?

4. **Passing Information in Interfaces**: Consider a file system that is reading or writing files from disk. Each random disk Read/Write involves positioning the disk over the correct track (seeking). If we have a sequence of, say, three Reads to Tracks 1, 15, and 7, it may pay to reorder the second and third Reads to reduce waste in terms of seek times. Clearly, as in **P1**, the larger the context of the optimization (e.g., the number of Reads or Writes considered for reordering), the greater the potential benefits of such *seek optimization*.

A normal file system only has an interface to open, read, and write a single file. However, suppose an application is reading multiple files and can pass that information (**P9**) in the file system call.

- What information about the pattern of file accesses would be useful for the file system to perform seek optimization? What should the interface look like?
- Give examples of applications that process multiple files and could benefit from this optimization. For more details, see the paper by Patterson et al. (1995). They call this form of tip a *disclosure*.

5. **Optimizing the Expected Case, Using Algorithmic Ideas, and Scavenging Files:** The Alto computer used a scavenging system (Lampson, 1989) that scans the disk after a crash to reconstruct file system indexes that map from file names and blocks to disk sectors. This can be done because each disk sector that contains a file block also contains the corresponding file identifier. What complicates matters is that the main memory is not large enough to hold information for every disk sector. Thus a single scan that builds a list in memory for each file will not work. Assume that the information for a single file will fit into memory. Thus a way that will work is to make a single scan of the disk for each file, but that would be obvious waste (**P1**) and too slow.

Instead, observe that in the expected case, most files are allocated contiguously. Thus suppose File X has pages 1–1000 located on disk sectors 301–1300. Thus the information about 1000 sectors can be compactly represented by three integers and a file name. Call this a run node.

- Assume the expected case holds and that all run nodes can fit in memory. Assume also that the file index for each file is an array (stored on disk) that maps from file block number to disk sector number. Show how to rebuild all the file indexes.
- Now suppose the expected case does not hold and that the run nodes *do not* all fit into memory. Describe a technique, based on the algorithmic idea of divide-and-conquer (**P15**), that is guaranteed to work (without reverting to the naive idea of building the index for one file at a time unless strictly necessary).

Principles in action

4

System architecture and design, like any art, can only be learned by doing. . . . The space of possibilities unfolds only as the medium is worked.

—Carver Mead and Lynn Conway

Having rounded up my horses, I now set myself to put them through their paces.

—Arnold Toynbee

The previous chapter outlined 15 principles for efficient network protocol implementation. Part 2 of the book begins a detailed look at specific network bottlenecks such as data copying and control transfer. While the principles are used in these later chapters, the focus of these later chapters is on the specific bottleneck being examined. Given that network algorithmics is as much a way of thinking as it is a set of techniques, it seems useful to round out Part 1 by seeing the principles in action on small, self-contained, but nontrivial network problems.

Thus this chapter provides examples of applying the principles in solving specific networking problems. The examples are drawn from real problems, and some of the solutions are used in real products. Unlike subsequent chapters, this chapter is not a collection of new material followed by a set of exercises. Instead, this chapter can be thought of as an extended set of exercises.

In Sections 4.1 to 4.15 15 problems are motivated and described. Each problem is followed by a hint that suggests specific principles, which is then followed by a solution sketch. There are also a few exercises after each solution. In classes and seminars on the topic of this chapter, the audience enjoyed inventing solutions by themselves (after a few hints were provided), rather than directly seeing the final solutions.

Quick reference guide

In an ideal world, each problem should have something interesting for every reader. For those readers pressed for time, however, here is some guidance. Hardware designers looking to sample a few problems may wish to try their hand at designing an Ethernet monitor (Section 4.4) or doing a binary search on long identifiers (Section 4.14). Systems people looking for examples of how systems thinking can finesse algorithmic expertise may wish to tackle a problem on application device channels (Section 4.1) or a problem on compressing the connection table (Section 4.11). Algorithm designers may be interested in the problem of identifying a resource hog (Section 4.10) and a problem on the use of protocol design changes to simplify an implementation problem in link state routing (Section 4.8).

Network Algorithmics. https://doi.org/10.1016/B978-0-12-809927-8.00009-9

4.1 Buffer validation of application device channels

Usually, application programs can only send network data through the operating system kernel, and only the kernel is allowed to talk to the network adaptor. This restriction prevents different applications from (maliciously or accidentally) writing or reading each other's data. However, communication through the kernel adds overhead in the form of system calls (see Chapter 2). In application device channels (ADCs), the idea is to allow an application to send data to and from the network by *directly* writing to the memory of the network adaptor. Refer to Chapter 5 for more details. One mechanism to ensure protection, in lieu of kernel mediation, is to have the kernel set up the adaptor with a set of valid memory pages for each application. The network adaptor must then ensure that the application's data can only be sent and received from memory in the valid set.

In Fig. 4.1, for example, application P is allowed to send and receive data from a set of valid pages $X, Y, \ldots, L, A$. Suppose application P queues a request to the adaptor to receive the next packet for P into a buffer in page A. Since this request is sent directly to the adaptor, the kernel cannot check that this is a valid buffer for P. Instead, the adaptor must validate this request by ensuring that A is in the set of valid pages. If the adaptor does not perform this check, application P could supply an invalid page belonging to some other application, and the adaptor would write P's data into the wrong page. The need for a check leads to the following problem.

Problem

When application P does a Receive, the adaptor must validate whether the page belongs to the valid page set for P. If the set of pages is organized as a linear list (Druschel et al., 1994), then validation can cost $O(n)$, where n is the number of pages in the set. For instance, in Fig. 4.1, since A is at the end of the list of valid pages, the adaptor must traverse the entire list before it finds A. If n is large, this can be expensive and can slow down the rate at which the adaptor can send and receive packets. How can the

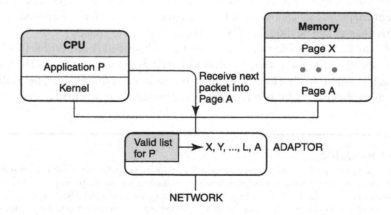

FIGURE 4.1

In application device channels, the network adaptor is given a set of valid pages (X, Y, L, A, etc.) for a given application P. When application P makes a request to receive data into page A, the adaptor must check if A is in the valid list before allowing the receive.

validation process be sped up? Try thinking through the solution before reading the hint and solutions that follow.

Hint: A good approach to reduce the complexity of validation is to use a better data structure than a list (**P15**). Which data structure would you choose? However, one can improve worst-case behavior even further and get smaller constant factors by using system thinking and by passing hints in interfaces (**P9**).

　　An algorithmic thinker will immediately consider implementing the set of valid pages as a *hash table* instead of a *list*. This provides an $O(1)$ average search time. Hashing has two disadvantages: (1) good hash functions that have small collision probabilities are expensive computationally; (2) hashing does not provide a good worst-case bound. Binary search does provide logarithmic worst-case search times, but this is expensive (it also requires keeping the set sorted) if the set of pages is large and packet transmission rates are higher. Instead, we replace the hash table lookup by an indexed array lookup, as follows (try using **P9** before you read on).

Solution

The adaptor stores the set of valid pages for each application in an array, as shown in Fig. 4.2. This array is updated only when the kernel updates the set of valid pages for the application. When the application does a Receive into page *A*, it also passes to the adaptor a handle (**P9**). The handle is the index of the array position where *A* is stored. The adaptor can use this to quickly confirm whether the page in the Receive request matches the page stored in the handle. The cost of validation is a bounds check (to see if the handle is a valid index), one array lookup, and one compare.

Exercises

- Is the handle a hint or a tip? Let's invoke principle **P1**: If this is a handle, why pass the page number (e.g., *A*) in the interface? Why does removing the page number speed up the confirmation task slightly?

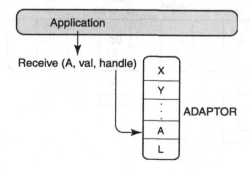

FIGURE 4.2

Finessing the need for a hash table lookup by passing a handle across the interface between the application and adaptor.

- To find the array corresponding to application P normally requires a hash table search using P as the key. This weakens the argument for getting rid of the hash table search to check if the page is valid—unless, of course, the hash search of P can be finessed as well. How can this be done?

4.2 Scheduler for asynchronous transfer mode flow control

In asynchronous transfer mode (ATM), an ATM adaptor may have hundreds of simultaneous virtual circuits (VCs) that can send data (called cells). Each VC is often flow controlled in some way to limit the rate at which it can send. For example, in rate-based flow control, a VC may receive credits to send cells at fixed time intervals. On the other hand, in credit-based flow control (Kung et al., 1994; Ozveren et al., 1994), credits may be sent by the next node in the path when buffers free up.

Thus in Fig. 4.3 the adaptor has a table that holds the VC state. There are four VCs that have been set up (1, 3, 5, 7). Of these, only VCs 1, 5, and 7 have some cells to send. Finally, only VCs 1 and 7 have credits to send cells. Thus the next cell to be sent by the adaptor should be from either one of the eligible VCs: 1 or 7. The selection from the eligible VCs should be done fairly, for example, in round-robin fashion. If the adaptor chooses to send a cell from VC 7, the adaptor would decrement the credits of VC 7 to 1. Since there are no more cells to be sent, VC 7 now becomes ineligible. Choosing the next eligible VC leads to the following problem.

Problem

A naive scheduler may cycle through the VC array looking for a VC that is eligible. If many of the VCs are ineligible, this can be quite inefficient, for the scheduler may have to step through several VCs that are ineligible to send one cell from an eligible VC. How can this inefficiency be avoided?

Hint: Consider invoking **P12** to add some extra state to speed up the scheduler main loop. What state can you add to avoid stepping through ineligible VCs? How would you maintain this state efficiently?

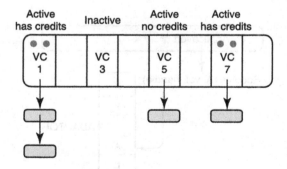

FIGURE 4.3

An ATM VC is eligible to send data if it is active (has some outstanding cells to send in the queue shown below the VC) and has credits (shown by gray dots above the VC). The problem is to select the next eligible VC in some fair manner without stepping through VCs that are ineligible.

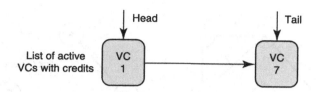

FIGURE 4.4

Maintaining a list of eligible VCs to speed up the scheduler main loop.

Solution

Maintain a list (Fig. 4.4) of eligible VCs in addition to the VC table of Fig. 4.3. The only problem is to efficiently *maintain* this state. This is the major difficulty in using **P12**. If the state is too expensive to maintain, the added state is a liability and not an asset. Recall that a VC is eligible if it has both cells to send and has credits. Thus a VC is removed from the list after service if VC becomes inactive or has no more credits; if not, the VC is added to the tail of the list to ensure fairness. A VC is added to the tail of the list either when a cell arrives to an empty VC cell queue and this (empty) queue also has credits or when the VC has no credits and receives a credit update.

Exercises

- How can you be sure that a VC is not added multiple times to the eligible list?
- Can this scheme be generalized to allow some VCs to get more opportunities to send than other VCs based on a weight assigned by a manager?

4.3 Route computation using Dijkstra's algorithm

How does a router S decide how to route a packet to a given destination D? Every link in a network is labeled with a cost, and routers like S often compute the shortest (i.e., lowest-cost) paths to destinations within a local domain. Assume the cost is a small integer. Recall from Chapter 2 that the most commonly used routing protocol within a domain is OSPF (Open Shortest Path First) based on link state routing.

In link state routing, every router in a subnet sends a link state packet (LSP) that lists its links to all of its neighbors. Each LSP is sent to every other router in the subnet. Each router sends its LSP to other routers using a primitive flooding protocol (Perlman, 1992). Once every router receives an LSP from every router, then every router has a complete map of the network. Assuming the topology remains stable, each router can now calculate its shortest path to every other node in the network using a standard shortest-path algorithm, such as Dijkstra's algorithm (Cormen et al., 1990).

In Fig. 4.5 source S wishes to calculate a shortest-path tree to all other nodes (A, B, C, D) in the network. The network is shown on the left frame in Fig. 4.5 with links numbered with their costs. In Dijkstra's algorithm S begins by placing only itself in the shortest-path tree. S also updates the cost to reach all its direct neighbors (e.g., B, A). At each iteration, Dijkstra's algorithm adds to the current

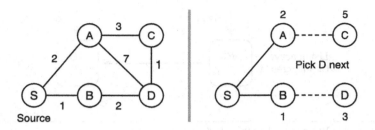

FIGURE 4.5

In Dijkstra's algorithm the source S builds a shortest-path tree rooted at S. At each stage, the closest node not in the tree is added to the tree.

tree the node that is closest to the current tree. The costs of the neighbors of this newly added node are updated. The process repeats until all nodes in the network belong to the tree.

For instance, in Fig. 4.5, after adding S, the algorithm picks B and then picks A. At this iteration, the tree is as shown on the right in Fig. 4.5. The solid lines show the existing tree, and the dotted lines show the best current connections to nodes that are not already in the tree. Thus since A has a cost of 2 and there is a link of cost 3 from A to C, C is labeled with 5. Similarly, D is labeled with a cost of 3 for the path through B. At the next iteration, the algorithm picks D as the least-cost node not already in the tree. The cost to C is then updated using the route through D. Finally, C is added to the tree in the last iteration.

This textbook solution requires determining the node with the least cost that is not already in the tree at each iteration. The standard data structure to keep track of the minimum-value element in a dynamically changing set is a priority queue. This leads to the following problem.

Problem

Dijkstra's algorithm requires a priority queue at each of N iterations, where N is the number of network nodes. The best general-purpose priority queues, such as heaps (Cormen et al., 1990), take $O(\log N)$ cost to find the minimum element. This implies a total running time of $O(N \log N)$ time. For a large network, this can result in slow response to failures and other network topology changes. How can route computation be speeded up?

Hint: Consider exploiting the fact that the link costs are small integers (**P14**) by using an array to represent the current costs of nodes. How can you efficiently, at least in an amortized sense, find the next minimum-cost node to include in the shortest-path tree?

Solution

The fact that the link costs are small integers can be exploited to construct a priority queue based on bucket sorting (**P14**). Assume that the largest link cost is *MaxLinkCost*. Thus the maximum cost of a path can be no more than $Diam * MaxLinkCost$, where $Diam$ is the diameter of the network. Assume $Diam$ is also a small integer. Thus one could imagine using an array with a location for every possible cost c in the range $1 \ldots Diam * MaxLinkCost$. If during the course of Dijkstra's algorithm the current

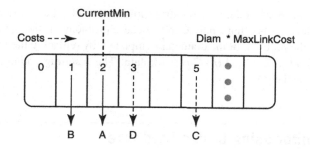

FIGURE 4.6

Using a priority queue based on bucket sorting to speed up Dijkstra's algorithm.

cost of a node X is c, then node X can be placed in a list pointed to by element c of the array (Fig. 4.6). This leads to the following algorithm.

Whenever a node X changes its cost from c to c', node X is removed from the list for c and added to the list for c'. But how is the minimum element to be found? This can be done by initializing a pointer called *CurrentMin* to 0 (which corresponds to the cost of S). Each time the algorithm wishes to find the minimum-cost node not in the tree, *CurrentMin* is incremented by 1 until an array location is reached that contains a nonempty list. Any node in this list can then be added to the tree. The algorithm costs $O(N + Diam * MaxLinkCost)$ because the work done in advancing *CurrentMin* can at most be the size of the array. This can be significantly better than $N \log N$ for large N and small values of *Diam* and *MaxLinkCost*.

A crucial factor in being able to efficiently use a bucket sort priority queue of the kind described earlier is that the node costs are always ahead of the value of *CurrentMin*. This is a monotonicity condition. If it were not true, the algorithm would start checking for the minimum from 1 at each iteration, instead of starting from the last value of *CurrentMin* and never backing up. The monotonicity condition is fairly obvious for Dijktra's algorithm because the costs of nodes not already in the tree have to be larger than the costs of nodes that are already in the tree.

Fig. 4.6 shows the state of the bucket sort priority queue after A has been added to the tree. This corresponds to the right frame of Fig. 4.5. At this stage, *CurrentMin* $= 2$, which is the cost of A. At the next iteration, *CurrentMin* will advance to 3, and D will be added to the tree. This will result in the C's cost being reduced to 4. We thus remove C from the list in position 5 and add it to the empty list in position 4. *CurrentMin* is then advanced to 4, and C is added to the tree.

Exercises

- The algorithm requires a node to be removed from a list and added to another, earlier list. How can this be done efficiently?
- In Fig. 4.6 how can the algorithm know that it can terminate after adding C to the tree instead of advancing to the end of the long array?
- In networks that have failures, the concept of diameter is a highly suspect one because the diameter could change considerably after a failure. Consider a wheel topology where all N nodes have diam-

eter 2 through a central spoke node; if the central spoke node fails, the diameter goes up to $N/2$. In actual practice the diameter is often small. Can this cause problems in sizing the array?

- Can you circumvent the problem of the diameter completely by replacing the linear array of Fig. 4.6 with a circular array of size $MaxLinkCost$? Explain. The resulting solution is known as Dial's algorithm (Ahuja et al., 1993).

4.4 Ethernet monitor using bridge hardware

Alyssa P. Hacker is working for Acme Networks and knows of the Ethernet bridge invented at Acme. A bridge (see Chapter 10) is a device that can connect Ethernets together. To forward packets from one Ethernet to another, the bridge must look up the 48-bit destination address in an Ethernet packet at high speeds.

Alyssa decides to convert the bridge into an Ethernet traffic monitor that will passively listen to an Ethernet and produce statistics about traffic patterns. The marketing person tells her that she needs to monitor traffic between arbitrary source–destination pairs. Thus for every active source–destination pair, such as A, B, Alyssa must keep a variable $P_{A,B}$ that measures the number of packets sent from A to B since the monitor was started. When a packet is sent from A to B, the monitor (which is listening to all packets sent on the cable) will pick up a copy of the packet. If the source is A and the destination is B, the monitor should increment $P_{A,B}$. The problem is to do this in 64 μsec, the minimum interpacket time on the Ethernet. The bottleneck is the lookup of the state $P_{A,B}$ associated with a pair of 48-bit addresses A, B.

Fortunately, the bridge hardware has a spiffy lookup hardware engine that can look up the state associated with a *single* 48-bit address in 1.4 μsec. A call to the hardware can be expressed as $Lookup(X, D)$, where X is the 48-bit key and D is the database to be searched. The call returns the state associated with X in 1.4 μsec for databases of less than 64,000 keys. What Alyssa must solve is the following problem.

Problem

The monitor needs to update state for AB when a packet from A to B arrives. The monitor has a lookup engine that can look up only *single* addresses and not address *pairs*. How can Alyssa use the existing engine to look up address pairs? The problem is illustrated in Fig. 4.7.

Hint: The problem requires using **P4c** to exploit the existing bridge hardware. Since 1.4 μsec is much smaller than 64 μsec, the design can afford to use more than one hardware lookup. How can a 96-bit lookup be reduced to a 48-bit lookup using three lookups?

A naive solution is to use two lookups to convert source A and destination B into smaller (<24-bit) indices I_A and I_B. The indices I_A and I_B can then be used to look up a two-dimensional array that stores the state for AB. This requires only two hardware lookups plus one more memory access, but it can require large amounts of memory. If there are 1000 possible sources and 1000 possible destinations, the array must contain a million entries. In practice, there may be only 20,000 active source–destination pairs. How could you make the required amount of memory proportional to the number of actual source–destination pairs?

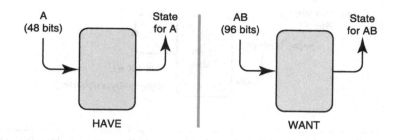

FIGURE 4.7

Adapting an engine that does destination lookups to doing source-destination lookups.

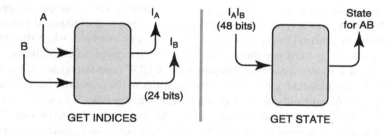

FIGURE 4.8

Converting a 96-bit lookup into a 48-bit lookup by first converting each 48-bit address into a 24-bit index and concatenating the indices.

Solution

As before, first use one lookup each to convert source A and destination B into smaller ($<$24-bit) indices I_A and I_B. Then use a third lookup to map from $I_A I_B$ to AB state. The solution is illustrated in Fig. 4.8. The third lookup effectively compresses the two-dimensional array of the naive solution. This solution is due to Mark Kempf and Mike Soha.

Exercises

- Can this problem be solved using only two bridge hardware lookups without requiring extra memory?
- The set of active source–destination pairs may change with time because some pairs of addresses stop communicating for long periods. How can this be handled without keeping the state for every possible address pair that has communicated since the monitor was powered on?

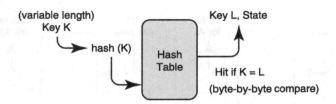

FIGURE 4.9

Demultiplexing in the x-kernel is done by hashing the protocol identifier K and (potentially) using a byte-by-byte comparison with the key L stored at the hash table entry.

4.5 Demultiplexing in the x-kernel

The x-kernel (Hutchinson and Peterson, 1991) provides a software infrastructure for protocol implementation in hosts. The x-kernel system provides support for a number of required protocol functions. One commonly required function is protocol *demultiplexing*. For example, when the Internet routing layer IP receives a packet, it must use the protocol field to determine whether the packet should be subsequently sent to TCP (transmission control protocol) or UDP (user datagram protocol).

Most protocols do demultiplexing based on some identifier in the protocol header. These identifiers can vary in length in different protocols. For example, Ethernet-type fields can be 5 bytes while TCP port numbers are 2 bytes long. Thus the x-kernel allows demultiplexing based on variable-length protocol identifiers. When the system is initialized, the protocol routine can register the mapping between the identifier and the destination protocol with the x-kernel. At run time, when a packet arrives the protocol routine can extract the protocol identifier from the packet and query the x-kernel demultiplexing routine for the destination protocol. Since packets can arrive at high speeds, the demultiplexing routine should be fast. This leads to the following problem.

Problem

On average, the fastest way to do a lookup is to use a hash table. As shown in Fig. 4.9, this requires computing some hash function on the identifier K to generate a hash index, using this index to access the hash table, and comparing the key L stored in the hash table entry with K. If there is a match, the demultiplexing routine can retrieve the destination protocol associated with key L. Assume that the hash function has been chosen to make collisions infrequent.

However, since the identifier length is an arbitrary number of bytes, the comparison routine that compares the two keys must, in general, do byte-by-byte comparisons. However, suppose the most common case is 4-byte identifiers, which is the machine word size. In this case, it is much more efficient to do a word comparison. Thus the goal is to exploit efficient word comparisons (**P4c**) to optimize the expected case (**P11**). How can this be done while still handling arbitrary protocols?

Hint: Notice that if the x-kernel has to demultiplex a 3-byte identifier, it has to use a byte-by-byte comparison routine; if the x-kernel has to demultiplex a 4-byte identifier and 4 bytes are the machine word size, it can use a word compare. The first degree of freedom that can be exploited is to have different comparison routines for the most common cases (e.g., word compares, long-word compares) and a default comparison routine that uses byte comparisons. Doing so trades some extra space for time (**P4b**). For correctness, however, it is important to know which comparison routine to use for each protocol. Consider invoking principles **P9** to pass hints in interfaces and **P2a** to do some precomputation.

Solution

Each protocol has to declare its identifier and destination protocol to the x-kernel when the system initializes. When this happens, each protocol can predeclare its identifier length, so the x-kernel can use a specialized comparison routine for each protocol. Effectively, information is being passed between the client protocol and the x-kernel (**P9**) at an earlier time (**P2a**). Assume that the x-kernel has a separate hash table for each client protocol and that the x-kernel knows the context for each client in order to use code specialized for thatclient.

Exercises

- Code up byte-by-byte and word comparisons on your machine and do a large number of both types of comparisons and compare the overall time taken for each.
- In the earlier ADC solution, the hash table lookup was finessed by passing an index (instead of the identifier length as earlier). Why might that solution be difficult in this case?

4.6 **Tries with node compression**

A *trie* is a data structure that is a tree of nodes, where each node is an array of M elements. Fig. 4.10 shows a simple example with $M = 8$. Each array can hold either a key (e.g., KEY 1, KEY 2, or KEY 3 in Fig. 4.10) or a pointer to another trie node (e.g., the first element in the topmost trie node of Fig. 4.10, which is the root). The trie is used to search for exact matches (and longest-prefix matches) with an input string. Tries are useful in networking for such varied tasks as IP address lookups (Chapter 11), bridge lookups (Chapter 10), and demultiplexing filters (Chapter 8).

Trie Node (space not used by pointers is wasted)

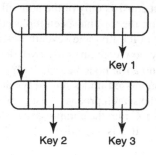

FIGURE 4.10

Trie storing three keys. Notice the wasted space in the trie nodes.

The exact trie algorithms do not concern us here. All one needs to know is how a trie is searched. Let $c = \log_2 M$ be the chunk size of a trie. To search the trie, search first breaks the input string into chunks of size c. Search uses successive chunks, starting from the most significant, to index into nodes of the trie, starting with the root node. When search uses chunk j to index into position i of the current trie node, position i could contain either a pointer or a key. If position i contains a nonnull pointer to node N, the search continues at node N with chunk $j + 1$; otherwise, the search terminates.

To summarize, each node is an array of pointers or keys, and the search process needs to index into these arrays. However, if many trie nodes are sparse, there is considerable wasted space (**P1**). For example, in Fig. 4.10, only 4 out of 16 locations contain useful information. In the worst case, each trie node could contain 1 pointer or key and there could be a factor of M in wasted memory. Assume $M \leq 32$ in what follows. Even if M is this small, a 32-fold increase in memory can greatly increase the cost of the design.

An obvious approach is to replace each trie node by a linear list of pairs of the form (i, val), where val is the nonempty value (either pointer or key) in position i of the node. For example, the root trie node in Fig. 4.10 could be replaced by the list $(1, ptr1)$; $(7, KEY1)$, where $ptr1$ is the pointer to the bottom trie node. Unfortunately, this can slow down trie search by a factor of M, because the search of each trie node may now have to search through a list of M locations, instead of a single indexing operation. This leads to the following problem.

Problem

How can trie nodes be compressed to remove null pointers without slowing down search by more than a small factor?

Hint: Despite compressing the nodes, array indexing needs to be efficient. If the nodes are compressed, how might information about which array elements are removed be represented? Consider leveraging off the fact that M is small by following **P14** (exploit the small integer size) and **P4a** (exploit locality).

Solution

Since $M < 32$, a bitmap of size 32 can easily fit into a computer word (**P14** and **P4a**). Thus null pointers are removed after adding a bitmap with zero bits indicating the original positions of null pointers. This is shown in Fig. 4.11. The trie node can now be replaced with a bitmap and a compressed trie node. A compressed trie node is an array that consists only of the nonnull values in the original node. Thus in Fig. 4.11, the original root trie node (on the top) has been replaced with the compressed trie node (on the bottom). The bitmap contains a 1 in the first and seventh positions, where the root node contains nonnull values. The compressed array now contains only two elements, the first pointer and KEY 3. This still begs the question: How should a trie node be searched?

Since both uncompressed and compressed nodes are arrays and the search process starts with an index I into the uncompressed node, the search process must consult the bitmap to convert the uncompressed index I into a compressed index C into the compressed node. For example, if I is 1 in Fig. 4.11, C should be 1; if I is 7, C should be 2. If I is any other value, C should be 0, indicating that there is only a null pointer.

Fortunately, the conversion from I to C can be accomplished easily by noting the following. If position I in the bitmap contains a 0, then $C = 0$. Otherwise, C is the number of 1's in the first I bits of the bitmap. Thus if $I = 7$, then $C = 2$, since there are two bits set in the first seven bits of the bitmap.

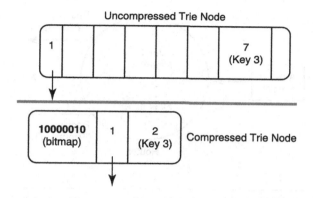

FIGURE 4.11

Compressing a trie node using a bitmap and bit counting to efficiently translate from an uncompressed index to a compressed index.

This computation requires at most two memory references: one to access the bitmap (because the bitmap is small [**P4a**]) and one to access the compressed array. The calculation of the number of bits set in a bitmap can be done using internal registers (in software) or combinatorial logic (in hardware). Thus the effective slowdown is slightly more than a factor of 2 in software and exactly 2 in hardware.

Exercises

- How could you use table lookup (**P14, P2a**) to speed up counting the number of bits set in software? Would this necessarily require a third memory reference?
- Suppose the bitmap is large (say, $M = 64$ K). It would appear that counting the number of bits set in such a large bitmap is impossibly slow in hardware or software. Can you find a way to speed up counting bits in a large bitmap (principles **P12** and **P2a**) using only one extra memory access? This will be extremely useful in Chapter 11.

4.7 **Packet filtering in routers**

Chapter 12 describes protocols that set up resources at routers for traffic, such as video, that needs performance guarantees. Such protocols use the concept of packet filters, sometimes called *classifiers*. Thus, in Fig. 4.12 each receiver attached to a router may specify a packet filter describing the packets it wishes to receive. For example, in Fig. 4.12 Receiver 1 may be interested in receiving NBC, which is specified by Filter 4. Each filter is some specification of the fields that describe the video packets that NBC sends. For example, NBC may be specified by packets that use the source address of the NBC transmitter in Germany and use a specified TCP destination and source port number.

Similarly, in Fig. 4.12 Receiver m may be interested in receiving ABC Sports and CNN, which are described by Filters 1 and 7, respectively. Packets arrive at the router at high speeds and must be sent

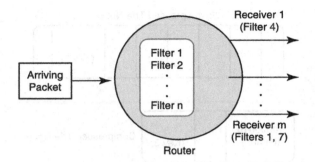

FIGURE 4.12

Packet filtering in a router may require a slow linear scan of all filters followed by making a copy of the packet for all filters that match.

to all receivers that request the packet. For example, Receivers 1 and 2 may both wish to receive NBC. This leads to the following problem.

Problem

Each receiving packet must be matched against all filters and sent to all receivers that match. A simple linear scan of all filters is expensive if the number of filters is large. Assume the number of filters is over a thousand. How can this expensive process be sped up?

Hint: One might think of optimizing the expected case by caching (**P11a**). However, why is caching difficult in this case? Consider adding a field (**P10**) to the packet header to make caching easier. Ideally, which protocol layer should this be added to? Adding a fixed well-known field for each possible video type is not a panacea because it requires global standardization, and filters can be based on other fields, such as the source address. Assume the field you add does not require globally standardized identifiers. What properties of this field must the source ensure?

Solution

Caching (**P11a**), the old workhorse of system designers, is not very straightforward in this problem. In general, a cache stores a mapping between an input a and some output $f(a)$. The cache then consists of a set of pairs of the form $(a, f(a))$. This set of pairs is stored as a database keyed by values of a. The database can be implemented as a hash table (in software) or a content-addressable memory (in hardware). Given input a and the need to calculate $f(a)$, the database is first checked to see if a is already in the database. If so, the fast path exits with the existing value of $f(a)$. If not, $f(a)$ is computed using some other (possibly expensive) computation and the pair $(a, f(a))$ is then inserted into the cache database. Subsequent inputs with value a can then be calculated very fast.

In the packet filtering problem, the goal is to calculate the set of receivers associated with a packet P. The problem is that the output is a function of a (potentially) large number of packet header fields of P. Thus to use caching, one has to store a large portion of the headers of P associated with the set of receivers for P. Storing a mapping between 64 bytes of packet header and an output set of receivers is an expensive proposition. It is expensive in time, since searching the cache can take longer because the

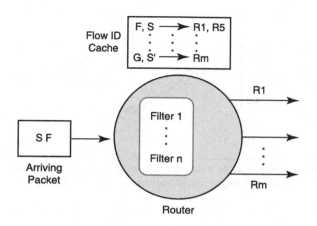

FIGURE 4.13

Adding a flow identifier (which is unique only with respect to a source) can speed up packet filtering.

keys are wide. It is also clearly expensive in storage. The larger storage needs in turn imply that fewer mappings can be cached for a given cache size, which leads to a poorer cache hit rate.

The ideal is to cache a mapping between one or two packet fields and the output receiver set. This would speed up cache search time and improve the cache hit rate. These fields should also preferably be in the routing header, which routers examine anyway. The problem is that there may be no such field that uniquely fingerprints packet P.

However, suppose we are system designers designing the routing protocol. We can add a field to the routing header. The problem might seem trivial if we could assign each possible stream of packets a unique global identifier. For example, if we could assign NBC identifier 1, ABC identifier 2, and CNN identifier 3, then we could cache using the identifier as the key. Such a solution would require some form of global standards committee responsible for naming every application stream. Even if that could be done, the receiver filter might ask for all NBC packets from a given source, and the filter could depend on other packet fields. This leads to the following final idea.

Change the routing header to add a flow identifier F (Fig. 4.13), whose meaning depends on the source. In other words, different sources can use the same flow identifier because it is the combination of the source and the flow identifier that is unique. Thus there is no need for global standardization (or other global coordination) of flow identifiers. A flow identifier is only a local counter maintained by the source. The idea is that a sending application at the sender can ask the routing layer for a flow identifier. This identifier is added to the routing header of all the packets for this application.

As usual, when the application packet first arrives, the router does a (slow) linear search to determine the set of receivers associated with the packet header. Because identifiers are not unique across sources, the router caches the mapping using the concatenation of the packet source address *and* the flow identifier as the key. Clearly, correctness depends on the sender application's not changing fields that could affect a filter without also changing the flow identifier in the packet.

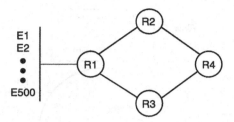

FIGURE 4.14

The LSP of router $R1$ (with even 500 endnode neighbors) may be too large to fit into a data link frame. Without a clever idea, this would require inefficient fragmentation and reassembly of the LSP at every hop.

Exercises

- What can go wrong if the source crashes and comes up again without remembering which identifiers it has assigned to different applications? What can go wrong when a receiver adds a new filter? How can these problems be solved?
- In the current solution, the flow identifier is used as a tip (Chapter 3) and not as a hint. What additional costs would be incurred if the flow identifier-source address pair is treated as a hint and not as a tip?

4.8 Avoiding fragmentation of LSPs

The following problem actually arose during the design of the OSI and OSPF (Perlman, 1992) link state routing protocols. This problem is about protocol design, as opposed to protocol implementation once the design is fixed. Despite this, it illustrates how design choices can greatly affect implementation performance.

Chapter 2 and Section 4.3 described link state routing. Recall that in link state routing, a router must send an LSP listing all its neighbors. The link state protocol consists of two separate processes. The first is the update process that sends LSPs reliably from router to router using a flooding protocol that relies on a unique sequence number per LSP. The sequence number is used to reject duplicate copies of an LSP. Whenever a router receives a new LSP numbered x from source S, the router will remember number x and will reject any subsequent LSPs received from S with sequence number x. After the update process does its work, the decision process at every router applies Dijkstra's algorithm to the network map formed by the LSPs.

While a router may have a small number of router neighbors, a router may have a large number of host computers (endnodes) that are connected directly to the router on the same LAN. For example, in Fig. 4.14 router $R1$ has 500 endnode neighbors $E1 \ldots E500$. Large LANs may even have a larger number of endnodes. This leads to the following problem.

Problem

At 8 bytes per endnode (6 bytes to identify the endnode and 2 bytes of cost information), the LSP can be very large (40,000 bytes for 5000 endnodes). This is much too huge for the LSP to fit into a maximum-size frame on many commonly used data links. For example, Ethernet has a maximum size of 1500 bytes and FDDI specifies a maximum of 4500 bytes. This implies that the large LSP must be fragmented into many data link frames on each hop and reassembled at each router before it can be sent onward. This requires an expensive reassembly process at each hop to determine whether all the pieces of a LSP have been received.

It also increases the latency of link state propagation. Suppose that each LSP can fit in M data link frames, that the diameter of the network is D, and that the time to send a data link frame over a link is 1 time unit. Then with hop-by-hop reassembly, the propagation time of an LSP can be $D \cdot M$. If a router did not have to wait to reassemble each LSP at each hop, the propagation delay would be only $M + D$. When the link state protocol was being designed, these problems were discovered by implementors reviewing the initial specification.

On the other hand, it seems impossible to propagate the fragments independently because the LSP carries a single sequence number that is crucial to the update process. Simply copying the sequence number into each fragment will not help because that will cause the later fragments to be rejected, since they have the same sequence number as the first fragment. The problem is to make the impossible possible by shifting computation around in space to avoid the need for hop-by-hop fragmentation. Changes to the LSP routing protocol are allowed.

Hint: Does the information about all 5000 endnodes have to be in the same LSP? Consider invoking **P3c** to shift computation in space.

Solution

If the individual fragments of the original LSP of $R1$ are to be propagated independently without hop-by-hop reassembly, then each fragment must be a separate LSP by itself, with a separate sequence number. This crucial observation leads to the following elegant idea.

Modify the link state routing protocol to allow any router $R1$ to be multiple pseudorouters $R1_a$, $R1_b$, $R1_c$ (see Fig. 4.15). The original set of endnodes are divided among these pseudorouters, so the LSP of each pseudorouter can fit into most data link frames *without* the need for fragmentation. For example, if most data link sizes are at least 576 bytes, roughly 72 endnodes can fit within a data link frame.

How is this concept of a pseudorouter actually realized? In the original LSP propagation, each router had a 6-byte ID that is placed in all LSPs sent by the router. To allow for pseudorouters, we change the protocol to have LSPs carry a 7-byte ID (6-byte router ID + 1-byte pseudorouter ID). The pseudorouter ID can be assigned by the actual router that houses all the pseudorouters. By allowing 256 pseudorouters per router, roughly 18,000 endnodes can be supported per router.

While the LSP propagation treats pseudorouters separately, it is crucial that route computation treat the separate pseudorouters as one router. After all, the endnodes are all directly connected to $R1$ in our example. But this is easily done because all the LSPs with the same first 6 bytes can be recognized as being from the same router.

In summary, the main idea is to shift computation in space (**P3c**) by having the source fragment the original LSP into independent LSPs instead of having each data link do the fragmentation. This is a

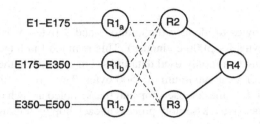

FIGURE 4.15

Avoiding hop-by-hop fragmentation by dividing a large router into pseudorouters.

good example of systems thinking. Needless to say, the implementors liked this solution (invented by Radia Perlman) much better than the original approach.

Exercises

- How can a router assign endnodes to pseudorouters? What happens if a router initially has a lot of endnodes (and hence a lot of pseudorouters) and then most of the endnodes die? This can leave a lot of pseudorouters, each of which has only a few endnodes. Why is this bad, and how can it be fixed?
- As in the relaxed-consistency examples described in Chapter 3, this solution can lead to some un-expected (but not very serious) temporary inconsistencies. Assuming a solution to the previous exercise, describe a scenario in which a given router, say, $R2$, can find (at some instant) that its LSP database shows the same endnode (say, E1) belonging to two pseudorouters, $R1_a$ and $R1_c$. Why is this no worse than ordinary LSP routing?

4.9 Policing traffic patterns

Some network protocols require that sources never send data faster than a certain rate. Instead of merely specifying the average rate over long periods of time, the protocol may also specify the maximum amount of traffic, B, in bits a source can send in any period of T seconds. This does limit the source to an average rate of B/T bits per second. However, it also limits the "burstiness" of the users' traffic to at most one burst of size B every T units of time. For example, choosing a small value of the parameter T limits the traffic burstiness considerably. Burstiness causes problems for networks because periods of high traffic and packet loss are followed by idle periods.

If every source meets its contract (i.e., sends no more than the specified amount in the specified period), the network can often guarantee performance and ensure that no traffic is dropped and that all traffic is delivered in timely fashion. Unfortunately, this is like saying that if everyone follows the rules of the road, traffic will flow smoothly. Most people do follow the rules: some because they feel it is the right thing to do, and many because they are aware of penalties that they have to pay when caught by traffic police. Thus policing is an important part of an ordered society.

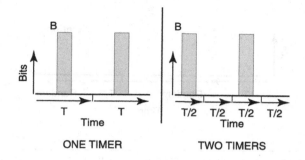

FIGURE 4.16

The naive use of a single or multiple timers (to check whether a flow sends no more than B every T seconds) does not catch all violations.

For the same reason, many designers advocate that the network should periodically police traffic to look for offenders that do not meet their contracts. Without policing, the offenders can get an unfair share of network bandwidth.

Assume that a traffic flow is identified by the source and destination addresses and the traffic type. Thus each router needs to ensure that a particular traffic flow sends no more than B bits in any period of T seconds. The simplest solution is for the router to use a single timer that ticks every T seconds and to count the number of bits sent in each period using a counter per flow. At the end of each period, if the counter exceeds B, the router has detected a violation.

Unfortunately, the single timer can police only some periods. For example, assume without loss of generality that the timer starts at time 0. Then the only periods checked are the periods $[0, T], [T, 2T], [2T, 3T], \ldots$. This *does not* ensure that the source flow does not violate its contract in a period like $[T/2, 3T/2]$, which overlaps the periods that are policed. For example, on the left side of Fig. 4.16, the flow sends a burst of size B just before the timer ticks at time T and sends a second burst of size B just after the timer ticks at time T.

One attempt to fix this problem is for the router to use multiple timers and counters. For example, as shown on the right of Fig. 4.16, the router could use one timer that starts at 0 and a second timer that starts at time $T/2$. Unfortunately, the flow can still violate its contract by sending no more than B in each policed period but sending more than B in some overlapping period.

For instance, in the right frame of Fig. 4.16 an offending flow sends a first burst of B at the end of the first period and a second burst of B at the start of the third period, sending $2B$ within a period slightly greater than $T/2$. Unfortunately, neither of the timers will detect the flow as being a violator. This leads to the following problem.

Problem

Multiple timers are expensive and do not guarantee that the flow will not violate its traffic contract. It is easy to see that with even a single timer, the flow can send no more than $2B$ in any period of T seconds. One approach is simply to assume that a factor-of-2 violation is not worth the effort to police. However, suppose that bandwidth is precious on a transcontinental link and that a factor-of-2 violation is serious. How could a violating flow still be caught using only a single timer?

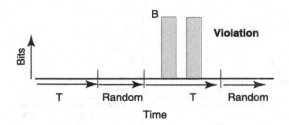

FIGURE 4.17

Picking a random gap of T seconds between policing intervals allows the router to catch a violating flow with high probability.

Hint: Consider exploiting a degree of freedom (**P13**) that has been assumed to be fixed in the naive solution. Do the policing intervals have to start at fixed intervals? Also consider using **P3a**.

Solution

As suggested in the hints, the policing intervals need not be fixed. Thus there can be an arbitrary gap between policing intervals. How should the gap be picked? Since a violating flow can pick its violating period of T to start at any instant, a simple idea is to invoke **P3a** to yield the following idea (Fig. 4.17).

The router uses a single timer of T units and a single counter, as before. A policing interval ends with a timer tick; if the counter is greater than B, a violation is detected. Then a flag is set indicating that the timer is now used only for inserting a random gap. Then the timer is restarted for a random time interval between 0 and T. When the timer ticks, the flag is cleared and the counter is initialized, and the timer is reset for a period of T to start policing again.

Exercises

- Suppose the counter is initialized and maintained during the gap period as well as during policing periods. Can the router make any valid inference during such a period, even if the gap period is less than T units?
- (Open Problem): Suppose the flow is adversarial. What is a good strategy for the flow to consistently violate the contract by as high a margin as possible and still elude the randomized detector described earlier? The flow strategy can be randomized as well. A good answer should be supported by a probabilistic analysis.

4.10 Identifying a resource hog

Suppose a device wishes to keep track of resources, like the packet memory allocated to various sources in a router. The device wants a cheap way to find the source consuming the most memory so that the device can grab memory back from such a resource hog. Fig. 4.18 shows five sources with their present resource consumption of 1, 9, 30, 24, and 7 units, respectively. The resource hog is S3.

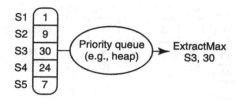

FIGURE 4.18

Finding the source that is a resource hog.

A simple solution to identify the resource hog is to use a heap. However, if the number of sources is a thousand or more, this may be too expensive at high speeds. Assume that the numbers that describe resource usage are integers in the range from 1 to 8000. Thus bucket sort techniques won't work well because we may have to search 8000 entries to find the resource hog.

Suppose, instead, that the device does not care about the exact maximum as long as the result comes within a factor of 2 (perfect fairness is unimportant as in **P3b**). For example, in the figure, assume it is fine to get an answer of 24 instead of 30. This leads to the following problem.

Problem

A software or hardware module needs to keep track of resources required by various users. The module needs a cheap way to find the user consuming the most resources. Since ordinary heaps are too slow, the device designers are willing to relax the system requirements (**P3b**) to be off by a factor of 2. Can this relaxation in accuracy requirements be translated into a more efficient algorithm?

Hint: Consider using three principles: trading accuracy for computation (**P3b**), using bucket sorting (**P14**), and using table lookups (**P4b, P2a**).

Solution

Since the answer can be off by a factor of 2, it makes sense to aggregate users whose resources are within a factor of 2 into the same "resource usage group." This can be a win if the resulting number of groups is much smaller than the original number of users; finding the largest group then will be faster than finding the largest user. This is roughly the same idea behind aggregation in hierarchical routing, where a number of destinations are aggregated behind a common prefix; this can make routing less accurate but reduces the number of routing entries. This leads to the following idea (try to work out the details before you read further).

Binomial bucketing can be used, as shown in Fig. 4.19, where all users are grouped into buckets according to resource consumption, where bucket i contains all users whose resource consumption lies between 2^i and $2^{i+1} - 1$. In Fig. 4.19, for instance, users S3 and S4 are both in the range $[16, 31]$ and hence are in the same bucket.

Each bucket contains an unsorted list of the resource records of all the users that fall within that bucket range. Thus in Fig. 4.19, S3 and S4 are in the same list. The data structure also contains a bitmap, with one bit for every bucket, that is set if the corresponding bucket list is nonempty (Fig. 4.19). Thus in Fig. 4.19 the bits corresponding to buckets $[1,1]$, $[4,7]$, $[8,15]$, and $[16,31]$ are set, while the bit corresponding to $[2,3]$ is clear.

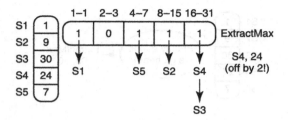

FIGURE 4.19

Aggregating users with resource consumption within a factor of 2 leads to a small number of aggregates whose membership can be represented using a bitmap.

Thus to find the resource hog, the algorithm simply looks for the bit position i corresponding to the rightmost bit set in the bitmap. The algorithm then returns the user at the head of the bucket list corresponding to position i. Thus in Fig. 4.19 the algorithm would return S4 instead of the more accurate S3.

Exercises

- How is this data structure maintained? What happens if the resources in a user (e.g., S3) are reduced from 30 to 16? What kind of lists is needed for efficient maintenance?
- How large is each bitmap? How can finding the rightmost bit set be done efficiently?

4.11 Getting rid of the TCP open connection list

A transport protocol such as TCP (Stevens, 1994) in computer X keeps state for every concurrent conversation that X has with other computers. Recall from Chapter 2 that the technical name for the shared state between the two endpoints of a conversation is a *connection*. Thus if a user wishes to send mail from X to another workstation, Y, the mail program in X must first establish a connection (shared state) to the mail program in Y. A busy server like a Web server may have lots of concurrent connections.

The state in a connection consists of things like the numbers of packets sent by X that have not been acknowledged by Y. Any packets that have not been acknowledged for a long time must be retransmitted by X. To do retransmission, transport protocols typically have a periodic timer that triggers the retransmission of any packets whose acknowledgments have been outstanding for a while.

The freely available BSD TCP code (Stevens, 1994) keeps a list of open connections (Fig. 4.20) to examine on timer ticks in order to perform any needed retransmissions. However, when a packet arrives at X, TCP at X must also quickly determine which connection the packet belongs to in order to update the state for the connection. Each connection is identified by a connection identifier that is carried in every packet.

Relying on the list to determine the connection for a packet would require searching the entire list, in the worst case; this could be slow for servers with large numbers of connections. Thus the x-kernel

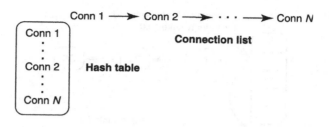

FIGURE 4.20

The x-kernel implementation uses a hash table mapping connections to state (for packet dispatching) as well as a linked list of connections (for timer processing). The redundant state causes dilution of the data cache.

implementation (Hutchinson and Peterson, 1991) added a hash table to the BSD implementation (**P15**) to efficiently map from connection identifiers in packets to the corresponding state for the connection. The hash table is an array of pointers indexed by hash value that points to lists of connections that hash to the same value. In addition, the original linked list of connections was retained for timer processing, while the hash table was supposed to speed up packet processing.

Oddly enough, measurements of the new implementation actually showed a slowdown! Careful measurements traced the problem to the fact that information about connections was stored redundantly, and this reduced the efficiency of the data cache when implemented on modern processors (see Chapter 2 for a model of a modern processor). This illustrates question **Q3** in Chapter 3, where an obvious improvement to one part of the system can affect other parts of the system. Note that while main memory may be cheap, fast memory such as the data cache is often limited. Commonly used structures such as the connection list should float into the data cache as long as they are small enough to fit.

The obvious solution is to avoid redundancy. The hash table is needed for fast lookups. The timer routine must also periodically and efficiently scan through all connections. This leads to the following problem.

Problem

Can you get rid of the waste caused by the explicit connection list while retaining the hash table? It is reasonable to add a small amount of extra information to the hash table. When doing so, observe that the original connection list was made doubly linked to allow easy deletion when connections terminate. But this adds storage and dilutes the data cache. How can a singly linked list be used *without slowing down deletion*?

Hint: The first part is easy to fix by linking the valid hash table entries in a list. The second part (avoiding the doubly linked list, which would require two pointers per hash table entry) is a bit harder.

A connection list consists of nodes, each of which contains a connection ID (96 bits for IP) plus two pointers (say, 32 bits each) for easy deletion. Since the hash table is needed for fast demultiplexing, the connection list can be removed if the valid hash table entries are linked together as shown in Fig. 4.21 and a pointer is kept to the head of the list. On a timer tick, the retransmit routine will periodically scan this list. Scanning the complete hash table is less efficient because the hash table may have many empty locations.

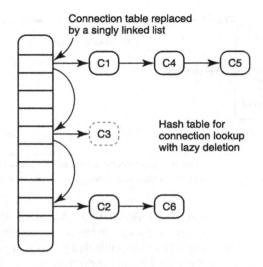

Connection table replaced by a singly linked list

Hash table for connection lookup with lazy deletion

FIGURE 4.21

Linking the valid hash table entries using forward pointers and lazy deletion. The dashed lines imply connection records that have been marked as deleted but that will be processed only in the next iteration.

The naive solution would add two pointers to each valid hash table entry to implement a doubly linked list. Since these pointers can be hash table indexes instead of arbitrary pointers to memory, the indexes need not be larger than the size of the hash table: Even the largest hash table storing connections should require no more than 16 bits, often much less. The naive solution does well, adding at most 32 bits per entry instead of 160 bits per entry, savings of 128 bits. However, it is possible to do better and to add only 16 bits per entry. Consider using lazy evaluation (**P2b**) and relaxing the specification (**P3**).

Solution

A doubly linked list is useful only for efficient deletions. When a connection (say, Connection $C3$ in Fig. 4.21) is terminated, the delete routine would ideally like to find the previous valid entry (i.e., the list containing Connection $C1$ in Fig. 4.21) in order to link the previous list to the next list (i.e., the list containing $C2$). This would require each hash table entry to store a pointer to the previous valid entry in the list.

Instead, consider principle **P3**, which asks whether the system requirements can be relaxed. Normally, one assumes that when a connection terminates, its storage must be reclaimed immediately. To reclaim storage, the hash table entry should be placed in a free list, where it can be used by another connection. However, if the hash table is a little larger than strictly necessary, it is not essential that the storage used by a terminated connection be reused immediately.

Given this relaxation of requirements, the implementation can *lazily* delete the connection state. When a connection is terminated, the entry must be marked as unused. This requires an extra bit of state, as in **P12**, but is cheap. The actual deletion of unused hash table entry E involves linking the entry before E to the entry after E and also requires returning E to a free list. However, this deletion can be done on the next list traversal when the traversal encounters an unused entry.

Exercises

- Write pseudocode for the addition of a new connection, the termination of a connection, and the timer-based traversal.
- How can we get away with singly linked lists for the lists of connections in each hash table list?
- Hugh Hopeful is always interested in clever tricks that he never thinks through completely. He suggests a way to avoid back pointers in any doubly linked list. Suppose a node X needs to be deleted. Normally, the deletion routine is passed a handle to retrieve X, which is typically a pointer to node X. Instead, Hugh suggests that the handle be a pointer to the node *before* X in the linked list (except when X is the head of the list when the handle is a null pointer). Hugh claims that this allows his implementation to efficiently locate both the node prior to X and the node after X using only forward pointers. Present a counter-example to stop Hugh before he writes some buggy code.

4.12 Acknowledgment withholding

Transport protocols such as TCP ensure that data is delivered to the destination by requiring that the destination send an acknowledgment (ack) for every piece of received data. This is analogous to certified mail. Packets and acks are numbered. Acks are often cumulative; an ack for a packet numbered N implicitly acknowledges all packets with numbers less than or equal to N.

Cumulative acks allow the receiver the flexibility of not sending an ack for every received packet. Instead, acks can be batched (**P2c**). For example, in Fig. 4.22 a file transfer program is sending file blocks, one in every packet. Blocks 1 and 2 are individually acknowledged, but blocks 3 and 4 are acknowledged with a single ack for block 4.

Reducing acks is a good thing for the sender and receiver. Although acks are small, they contain headers that must be processed by every router and the source and the destination. Further, each received packet, however small, can cause an interrupt at the destination computer, and interrupts are expensive. Thus, ideally, a receiver should batch as many acks as possible. But what should the receiver batching policy be? This leads to the following problem.

Problem

Ack withholding is difficult at a receiver that is not clairvoyant. In Fig. 4.22, for example, if block 3 arrives first and is processed quickly, how long should the receiver wait for block 4 before sending the ack for block 3? If block 4 never arrives (because the sender has no more data to send), then withholding the ack for block 3 would cause incorrect behavior. The classical solution is to set an ack-withholding timer; when the timer expires, a cumulative ack is sent. This limits the time that an ack can be withheld.

However, the withholding timer also causes problems. Some applications are sensitive to latency. Adding an ack-withholding timer can increase latency in cases where the sender has no more data to send. If the transport protocol could be modified, what information could be added to avoid unnecessary latency and yet allow acks to be effectively batched?

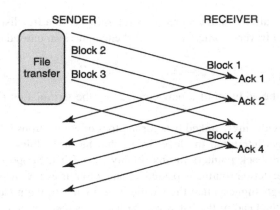

SENDER   RECEIVER

FIGURE 4.22

The use of cumulative acks allows the receiver to acknowledge several packets with one ack (e.g., blocks 3 and 4) but introduces the problem of determining a good receiver ackpolicy.

Hint: In an application such as FTP, which software module knows that there is more data to be sent? For ack withholding, which software module would ideally like to know that there is more data to be sent? Now consider using **P9** and **P10**.

Solution

In an application such as file transfer, the sender *application* knows that there is more data to be sent (e.g., there will be a block 4 after block 3). The sending application may also be willing to tolerate the latency due to batching of acks. However, it is the transport module at the receiver that needs to know this information. This observation leads to a simple proposal.

The sender application passes a bit to the sender transport (in the application–transport interface) that is set when the application has more data to send. Assume that the transport protocol can be modified to carry a withhold bit. The sending transport can use the information passed by the application to set a withhold bit w in every packet that it sends; w is cleared when the sender wants an immediate ack. The moral, of course, is that it is better for the sender to telegraph his intentions than for the receiver to make guesses about the future!

For example, in Fig. 4.23 the sender transport is informed by the sending file transfer application that there are four blocks to be sent. Thus the sender transport sets the withhold bit on the first three packets and clears the bit in the fourth packet. The receiver acts on this information to send one ack instead of four. On the other hand, an application that is latency sensitive can choose not to pass any information about data to be sent. Note also that the withhold bit is a hint; the receiver can choose to ignore this information and send an ack anyway. Despite its apparent cleverness, this solution is a bad idea in today's TCP. See the exercises for details.

Exercises

- Another technique for reducing acks is to piggyback acks on data flowing from the receiver to the sender. To support this, most transport protocols, such as TCP, have extra fields in data packets to

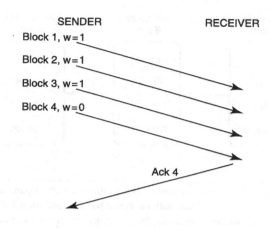

FIGURE 4.23

Telegraphing the sender's intentions using a withhold bit w.

convey reverse ack information. However, piggybacking has the same classical trade-off between latency and piggybacking efficiency. How long should the receiver transport wait for reverse data? On the other hand, there are common applications where the sender application knows this information. How could the solution outlined earlier be extended to support piggybacking as well as ack batching?

- Recall that Chapter 3 outlined a set of cautionary questions for evaluating purported improvements. For example, **Q3** asks whether a change can affect the rest of the system. Why might aggressive ack withholding interact with other aspects of the transport protocol, such as flow and congestion control (Stevens, 1994)?

4.13 Incrementally reading a large database

Suppose a user continuously reads a large database stored on a Website. The Web page can change and the reader only wants the incremental (**P12a**) updates since the last read of the database. Thus in Fig. 4.24 there is a database of highly popular food items that is being read constantly by readers around the world who wish to keep up with culinary fashion. Fortunately, food fashions change slowly.

Thus a reader that last read at 2 p.m. and reads again at 6 p.m. only wants the differences: Coke to Pepsi, and Wheaties to Cheerios. If, on the other hand, a different user reads at 3 p.m. and then at 6 p.m., she, too, only wants the difference: Wheaties to Cheerios. This leads to the following problem.

Problem

Find a way for the database to efficiently perform such incremental queries. One solution is to have the database remember what each user has previously read. However, it is unreasonable for the database to remember what each user has previously read, since there may be millions of users. Find another solution that is less burdensome for the database program.

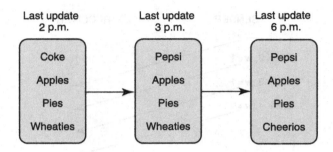

FIGURE 4.24

A slowly changing database of food items shown at three different times: 2 p.m., 3 p.m., and 6 p.m. Notice that only the soft drink has changed from 2 to 3 p.m. and that only the cereal has changed from 3 to 6 p.m. Thus a reader who is constantly monitoring the database wishes to find only the differences from the last time the database was read.

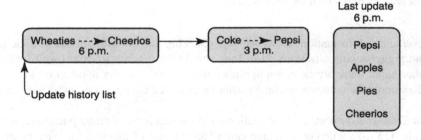

FIGURE 4.25

Solving the incremental-update problem using an update history list.

Hint: If the database does not store any information about the last Read performed by a user, then it follows that user Read requests must pass some information (**P10**) about the last Read request made by the same user. Passing the entire details of the last Read would be overkill and inefficient. What simple piece of information can succinctly characterize the user's last request? Now consider adding redundant state (**P12**) at the database that can easily be indexed using the information passed by the user to facilitate efficient incremental query processing.

Solution

As said earlier, user Read requests must pass some information (**P10**) about the last Read request made by the same user. The most succinct and relevant piece of information about the last user request is the *time* at which it was made. If user requests pass the time of the last Read, then the database needs to be organized to efficiently compute all updates after any given time. This can be done by storing copies of the database at all possible earlier times. This is clearly inefficient and can be avoided by storing only the incremental changes (**P12a**). This leads to the following algorithm.

Add an update history list to the database, with most recent updates closer to the head of the list. Read requests carry the time T of the last Read, so a Read request can be processed by scanning the update list from the head to find all updates after T.

For example, in Fig. 4.25 the head of the update history list has the latest change (compare with Fig. 4.24) at 6 p.m. from Wheaties to Cheerios and the next earliest change at 3 p.m. from Coke to Pepsi. Consider a Read request that has a last Read time of 5 p.m. In this case, when scanning the list from the head, the request processing will find the 6 p.m. update and stop when it reaches the 3 p.m. update because $3 < 5$. Thus the Read request will return only the first update.

Exercises

- If a single entry changes multiple times, a single entry change can be stored redundantly in the list, which costs space and time. What principle can you use to avoid this redundancy? Assume the database is just a collection of records and that you want each record to appear at most once in the incremental list.
- If the number of records is large or the foregoing trick is not adopted, the incremental list size will grow very big. Suggest a sensible policy for periodically reducing the size of the incremental list.

4.14 **Binary search of long identifiers**

The next-generation Internet (IPv6) plans to use larger, 128-bit addresses to accommodate more Internet endpoints. Suppose the goal is to look up 128-bit addresses. Assume the algorithm works on a machine whose natural word size is 32 bits. Then each comparison of two 128-bit numbers will take $128/32 = 4$ operations to compare each word individually. In general, suppose each identifier in the table is W words long. In our example, $W = 4$. Naive binary search will take $W \cdot \log N$ comparisons, which is expensive. Yet this seems obviously wasteful. If all the identifiers have the same first $W - 1$ words, then clearly $\log N$ comparisons are sufficient. The problem is to modify binary search to take $\log N + W$ comparisons. The strategy is to work in columns, starting with the most significant word and doing binary search in that column until equality is obtained in that column. At that point, the algorithm moves to the next word to the right and continues the binary search where it left off.

Thus in Fig. 4.26, which has $W = 3$, consider a search for the three-word identifier BMW. Pretend each character is a word. Start by comparing in the leftmost column in the middle element, as shown by the arrow labeled 1.[1] Since the B in the search string matches the B at the arrow labeled 1, the search moves to the right (not shown) to compare the M in BMW with the N in the middle location of the second column. Since $N < M$, the search performs the second probe at the quarter position of the second column. This time the two M's match and the search moves rightward and finds W, but (oops!) the search has found AMW, not BMW as desired. This leads to the following problem.

---

[1] Many implementors implement binary search to pick the fourth element from the top (i.e., the first B) as the middle and not the fifth element as we have done. Keep this somewhat unusual convention in mind while following the example.

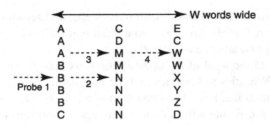

FIGURE 4.26

Binary search of long identifiers can result in a multiplicative factor of W, the number of words in an identifier. The naive method of reducing this to an additive factor by moving to the right on equality fails.

```
        A           C           E
        A           D           C
        A ----3---> M ----4---> W
        B           M           W
  ----> B ----2---> N ----5---> X
 Probe 1 B           N           Y
        B           N           Z
        C           N           D
```

FIGURE 4.27

Adding a guard range to every element in a column to allow binary search to work correctly when switching columns.

Problem

Find some state that can be added to each element in each column that can fix this algorithm to work correctly in $\log N + W$ comparisons.

Hint: The problem is caused by the fact that when the search moved to the quarter position in column 2, it assumed that all elements in the quarter of the second column begin with B. This assumption is false in general. What state can be added to avoid making this false assumption, and how can the search be modified to use this state?

Solution

The trick is to add state to each element in each column, which can constrain the binary search to stay within a guard range. This is shown in Fig. 4.27. In the figure, for each word like B in the leftmost (most significant) column, add a pointer to the range of all other words that also contain B in this position. Thus the first probe of the binary search for BMW starts with the B in BNX. On equality, the search moves to the second column, as before. However, search also keeps track of the guard range corresponding to the B's in the first column. The figure shows that the guard range includes only rows 4 through 7. This guard range is stored with the first B compared (see arrows in Fig. 4.27).

Thus when the search moves to column 2 and finds that M in BMW is less than the N in BNX, it attempts to halve the range as before and to try a second probe at the third entry (the M in AMW). However, the third entry is lower than the high point of the current guard range (4 through 7, assuming the first element is numbered 1). So without doing a compare, the search tries to halve the binary search range again. This time the search tries entry 4, which is in the guard range. The search finds equality, moves to the right, and finds BMW, as desired.

In general, every multiword entry $W_1, W_2, \ldots, W_n$ will store a precomputed guard range. The range for W_i points to the range of entries that have $W_1, W_2, \ldots, W_i$ in the first i words. This ensures that on a match with W_i in the ith column, the binary search in column $i + 1$ will search only in this guard range. For example, the N entry in BNY (second column) has a guard range of 5–7, because these entries all have BN in the first two words.

The resulting search strategy takes $\log_2 N + W$ probes if there are N identifiers. The cost is the addition of two 16-bit pointers to each word. Since most word sizes are at least 32 bits, this results in adding 32 bits of pointer space for each word, which can at most double memory usage. Besides adding state, a second dominant idea is to use precomputation (**P2a**) to trade a slower insertion time for a faster search. The idea is due to Butler Lampson.

Exercise

- (This is harder than the usual exercises.) The naive method of updating the binary search data structure requires rebuilding the entire structure (especially because of the precomputed ranges) when a new entry is added or deleted. However, the whole scheme can be elegantly represented by a binary search tree, with each node having the usual > and < pointers but also an = pointer, which corresponds to moving to the next column to the right, as shown earlier. The subtree corresponding to the = pointer naturally represents the guard range. The structure now looks like a trie of binary search trees. Use this observation and standard update techniques for balanced binary trees and tries to obtain logarithmic update times.

4.15 Video conferencing via asynchronous transfer mode

In ATM, the network first sets up a VC through a series of switches before data can be sent. Standard ATM allows one-to-many VCs, where a VC can connect a single source to multiple receivers. Any data sent by the source is replicated and sent to every receiver in the one-to-many VC.

Although it is not standardized, it is also easy to have many-to-many VCs, where every endpoint can be both a source and a receiver. The idea is that when any source sends data, the switches replicate the data to every receiver. Of course, the main problem in many-to-many VCs is that if two sources talk at the same time, then the data from the two sources can be arbitrarily interleaved at the receivers and cause confusion. This is possibly why many-to-many VCs are not supported by standards, though it is often easy for switch hardware to support many-to-many VCs.

Fig. 4.28 shows a simple topology consisting of an ATM switch that connects N workstations. To showcase the bandwidth of the switch, the system designers have designed a videoconferencing application. The conferencing application can allow users at any of the N workstations to have a videoconference with each other. The application should bring up a screen (on every workstation in the conference) that displays at least the current speaker and also plays the speech of the current speaker. In addition, in the event of a conversation, it is desirable to see the expressions of the participants. The designers soon run into the following problem.

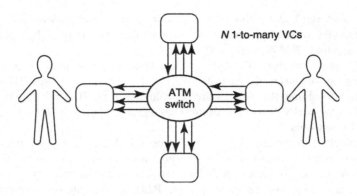

FIGURE 4.28

A videoconferencing system that uses an ATM switch with the ability to support many-to-many VCs.

Problem

The naivest solution would use up to N^2 point-to-point connections between every pair of participating workstations. A better solution is shown in Fig. 4.28. It uses up to N many-to-many VCs between each participating workstation and the other workstations. The video and speech of each workstation is connected by a one-to-many VC to every other participating workstation. Thus every participating workstation gets the video output of all participants and the application can choose which one (or ones) to display. Unfortunately, the ATM switch requires that bandwidth on the switch be statically divided among the N one-to-many VCs. Given a minimum bandwidth for video quality of B_{min} and a total switch bandwidth of B, this limits the number of participating workstations to be less than B/B_{min}. Is there a more scalable solution?

Hint: Consider exploiting the switch hardware's ability to support many-to-many VCs (**P4c**). However, to prevent confusion, only one source should transmit at a time in any many-to-many VC. Instead of developing a complex protocol to ensure such a constraint, what hardware can be added (**P5**) to ensure this constraint?

Solution

As suggested in the hint, the designers chose to exploit the many-to-many VC capability of the switch to replace N one-to-many VCs with a constant number of many-to-many VCs. This allowed the fixed switch bandwidth to scale to a large number of participants. However, this generic idea requires elaboration. How many many-to-many VCs should be used? How is the potential confusion caused by many-to-many VCs resolved? Here are the details of a solution worked out by Jon Turner at Washington University.

First, consider the use of a *single* many-to-many VC named C. A naive solution to the confusion problem entails a protocol (say, a round-robin protocol) that ensures that only one workstation at a time connects its video output to C. Such protocols require coordination, and the coordination adds latency and expense. Instead, as systems thinkers, the designers observed that, at a minimum, only the current speaker needs to be displayed.

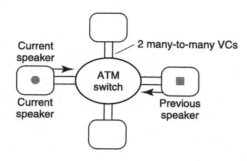

FIGURE 4.29

Replacing N one-to-many VCs with two many-to-many VCs through the use of a speech detector and a simple hardware state machine at each input.

Thus the designers added extra hardware (**P5**) in the form of a speech detector to the input at each workstation. If the detector detects significant speech activity at a workstation X, then the detector connects the video input of X to C; otherwise, the video input of X is not connected to C. Since this hardware was quite cheap, the extra scalability came at a reasonable price.

Next, the designers observed that keeping a video image of the last speaker provides visual continuity in the expected case when there is a dialog between two participants. Thus instead of one many-to-many VC, they used *two* many-to-many VCs, C and L, one for the current speaker and one for the last speaker, as shown in Fig. 4.29.

Exercises

- Write pseudocode (using some state variables) for the hardware at each workstation to update its connections to C and L. Assume the speech detector output is a function.
- What happens if more than one user speaks at one time? What could you add to the hardware state machine so that the application displays something reasonable? For instance, it would be unreasonable for the images of the two speakers to be morphed together in this case.

Playing with endnodes 2

The supreme accomplishment is to blur the line between work and play.
—**Arnold Toynbee**

The second part of the book deals with endnode algorithmics. This is the application of network algorithmics to building fast protocol implementations at endnodes, especially at servers. If you like, you can think of it as a systematic collection of techniques for building fast servers. The techniques are applied mostly in a software setting. Much of it has to do with getting around operating system structure to enable high-speed data transfers. We study how to reduce the overhead incurred by copying, control transfer, demultiplexing, timers, and other generic protocol-processing tasks.

Playing with endnodes

2

Copying data

Copy from one, it's plagiarism; copy from two, it's research.
—**Wilson Mizner**

Imagine an office where every letter received is first sent to shipping and receiving. Shipping and receiving opens the letter, figures out which department it is meant for, and makes a photocopy for their records. They then hand it to the security department, which pores over every line of the letter, looking for signs of industrial espionage. To maintain an audit trail for possible later use, the security department also makes a photocopy of the letter for good measure. Finally, the letter, somewhat the worse for wear, reaches the intended recipient in personnel.

You would probably think this a pretty ludicrous state of affairs, worthy to be featured in a Charlie Chaplin movie. But then you might be surprised to learn that early Web servers and computers routinely made a number of extra copies of received and sent messages. Unlike photocopies, which take up only a small amount of paper, power, and time, extra copying in a computer consumes two precious resources: memory bandwidth and memory itself. Ultimately, if there are k copies involved in processing a message in a Web server, the throughput of the Web server can be k times slower.

Thus this chapter will focus on removing the obvious waste (**P1**) involved in such unnecessary copies. A copy is unnecessary if it is not imposed by the hardware. For example, the hardware does require copying bits received by an adaptor to the computer memory. However, as we shall see, there is no essential reason (other than those imposed by conventional operating system structuring) for copying between application and operating system buffers. Eliminating redundant copies allows the software to come closer to realizing the potential of the hardware, one of the goals of network algorithmics.

This chapter will also briefly talk about other operations (such as checksumming and encryption) that touch all the data in the packet and other techniques to more closely align protocol software to hardware constraints, such as bus bandwidths and caches. While we will briefly repeat some of the relevant operating systems and architectural facts, it will help the reader to be familiar with endnode architecture and operating system models of Chapter 2. In summary this chapter surveys techniques for reducing the costs of data manipulation without sacrificing modularity and without major changes to operating system design.

This chapter is organized as follows. Section 5.1 describes why and how extra data copies occur. Section 5.2 describes a series of techniques to avoid copies by local restructuring of the operating system and network code at an endnode. Section 5.3 shows how to avoid both copy and control overhead for large transfers using remote direct memory access (DMA) techniques that involve protocol changes.

Section 5.4 broadens the discussion to consider the file system in, say, a Web server and it shows how to avoid wasteful copies between the file cache and the application. Section 5.5 broadens the discussion to consider other operations that touch all the data, such as checksumming and encryption,

Network Algorithmics. https://doi.org/10.1016/B978-0-12-809927-8.00011-7

Table 5.1 Techniques for copy avoidance and cache efficiency that are discussed in this chapter, together with the corresponding principles.

Number	Principle	Used in
P13	Memory location (on adaptor) as degree of freedom	Afterburner
P2b	Lazy copying using copy-on-write	Mach
P11a	Cache VM mappings per path	Solaris fbufs
P7	Uniform fbuf space across processes	
P10	Pass buffer name and offset in packet	RDMA systems
P4	VM mapping to avoid copies in cache and application	Flash
P11a	Cache VM mappings per path	Flash-lite
	Buffer sequence numbers enable checksum caching	
P6	New system call that splices I/O	Sendfile()
P1	Avoid repeated memory access across manipulations	ILP
P13	Layout code to minimize I-cache misses	x-kernel
P13	Layer processing order as degree of freedom	LDRP

and introduces a well-known technique called *integrated layer processing*. Section 5.6 broadens the discussion beyond copying to show that without careful consideration of cache effects, performance can suffer.

The world has changed since the first edition of this book and this chapter reflects some of these changes. The changes include the emergence of servers with multicore CPUs with NUMA (non-uniform memory access, where groups of cores share an L3 cache), the rapid emergence of 100 Gbps links, the ubiquity of solid state disks (NVM) that can saturate network links, and recent trends in remote DMA techniques such as the popular RoCE (RDMA over converged Ethernet). We will fit these trends into our framework, showing that the main ideas of the first edition still hold.

Although this is the first chapter of the book that is devoted to techniques for overcoming a specific bottleneck, the techniques are based on the principles described in Part I of the book. The techniques and the corresponding principles are summarized in Table 5.1.

Quick reference guide

The most useful sections for an implementor today are as follows. Section 5.3.1 on remote direct memory access (RDMA) describes techniques to avoid memory copying overheads in computing and storage clusters and modern incarnations of the idea like RoCE and Fibre Channel. RDMA is only useful for some applications, and so the remaining sections concentrate on avoiding copying overheads in general purpose operating systems. Section 5.2.5 summarizes the current thinking on zero-copy networking and some modern proposals in Linux that could benefit from a form of precomputation called *fbufs* that is introduced in Section 5.2.3. Section 5.4.3 describes a less radical but effective method called *I/O splicing* to directly connect I/O subsystems and send a file without copying. Finally, Section 5.6.1 describes techniques to improve cache performance.

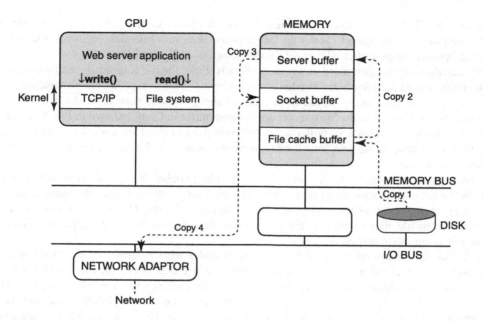

FIGURE 5.1

Redundant copies involved in handling a GET request at a server.

5.1 Why data copies

In Fig. A.1 in the Appendix we describe how TCP works in the context of a Web server. Fig. A.1 only shows the sending of the GET request for a file, followed by the file data itself in two TCP segments. What Fig. A.1 does not show is how the Web server processes the GET request. In this chapter we ignore the control transfer required to transfer the request to some application server process. Instead, Fig. 5.1 shows the sequence of data transfers involved in reading file data from the disk (in the worst case) to the sending of the corresponding segments via the network adaptor.

The main hardware players in Fig. 5.1 are the CPU, the memory bus, the I/O bus, the disk, and the network adaptor. The main software players are the Web server application and the kernel. There are two main kernel subsystems involved, the file system and the networking system. For simplicity, the picture shows only one CPU in the server (many servers are multiprocessors and particularly multicore machines) and focuses only on requests for static content (many requests are for dynamic content that is served by a Common Gateway Interface (CGI) process).[1]

Intuitively, the story is simple. The file is read from disk into the application buffer via, say, a *read()* system call. The combination of the HTTP response and the application buffer is then sent to the

---

[1] The picture makes it appear that the code for the file system and the TCP/IP code is on the processor. In reality the code is also stored in memory and is fetched by the processor. However, the portion of the code that fits into the processor instruction cache indeed can be considered to be in the processor.

network over the TCP connection to the client by, say, a *write()* system call. The TCP code in the network subsystem of the kernel breaks up the response data into bite-size segments and transmits them to the network adaptor after adding a TCP checksum to each segment.

In practice the story is often more messy in the details. First, the file is typically read into a piece of kernel memory, called the *file cache*, in what we call Copy 1. This is a good idea because subsequent requests to a popular file can be served from main memory without slow disk I/O. The file is then copied from the file cache into the Web server application buffer in Copy 2 shown in Fig. 5.1. Since the application buffer and the file cache buffer are in different parts of main memory, this copy can only be done by the CPU's reading the data from the first memory location and writing into the second location across the memory bus.

The Web server then does a *write()* to the corresponding socket. Since the application can freely reuse its buffer (or even deallocate it) at any time after the *write()*, the network subsystem in the kernel cannot simply transmit out of the application buffer. In particular the TCP software may need to re-transmit part of the file after an unpredictable amount of time, by which time the application may wish to use the buffer for other purposes.

Thus UNIX (and many other operating systems) provides what is known as *copy* semantics. The application buffer specified in the *write()* call is copied to a socket buffer (another buffer within the kernel, at a different address in memory than either the file cache or the application buffer). This is called Copy 3 in Fig. 5.1. Finally, each segment is sent out to the network (after IP and link headers have been pasted) by copying the data from the socket buffer to memory within the network adaptor. This is called Copy 4.

In between, before transmission to the network, the TCP software in the kernel must make a pass over the data to compute the TCP checksum. Techniques for efficiently implementing the TCP checksum are described in Chapter 9, but for now it suffices to think of the TCP checksum as essentially computing the sum of 16-bit words in each TCP segment's data.

Each of the four copies and the checksum consume resources. All four copies and the checksum calculation consume bandwidth on the memory bus. The copies between memory locations (Copies 2 and 3) are actually worse than the others because they require one Read and one Write across the bus for every word of memory transferred. The TCP checksum requires only one Read for every word and a single Write to append the final checksum. Finally, Copies 1 and 4 can be as expensive as Copies 2 and 3 if the CPU does the heavy lifting for the copy (so-called programmed I/O); however, if the devices themselves do the copy (so-called DMA), the cost is only a single Read or Write per word across the bus.

The copies also consume I/O bus bandwidth and ultimately memory bandwidth itself. A memory that supplies a word of size W bits every x nanoseconds has a fundamental limit on throughput of W/x bits per nanosecond. For example, even assuming DMA, these copies ensure that the memory bus is used seven times for each word in the file sent out by the server. Thus the Web server throughput cannot exceed $T/7$, where T is the smaller of the speed of the memory and the memory bus.

Second, and more basically, the extra copies consume *memory*. The same file (Fig. 5.1) could be stored in the file cache, the application buffer, and the socket buffer. While memory seems to be cheap and plentiful (especially when buying a PC!), it does have some limits, and Web servers would like to use as much as possible for the file cache to avoid slow disk I/O. Thus triply replicating a file can reduce the file cache by a factor of 3, which in turn can dramatically reduce the cache hit rate and, hence, overall server performance.

In summary redundant copies hurt performance in two fundamental and orthogonal ways. First, by using more bus and memory bandwidth than strictly necessary, the Web server runs slower than bus speeds, even when serving documents that are in memory. Second, by using more memory than it should, the Web server will have to read an unduly large fraction of files from disk instead of from the file cache.

Note also that we have only described the scenario in which static content is served. In reality the SPECweb benchmarks assume that 30% of the requests are for dynamic content. Dynamic content is often served by a separate CGI process (other than the server application) that communicates this content to the server via some interprocess communication mechanism, such as a UNIX pipe, which often involves another copy.

Ideally, all these pesky extra bus traversals should be removed. Clearly, Copy 1 is not required if the data is in cache and so we can ignore it. If it's not in cache, the server runs at disk speed, which is too slow anyway (though the use of fast non-volatile memory changes this equation). Copy 2 seems unnecessary. Why can't the data be sent directly from the file cache memory location to the network? Similarly, Copy 3 seems unnecessary. Copy 4 is unavoidable.

5.2 Reducing copying via local restructuring

Before tackling the full complexity of eliminating all redundant copies in Fig. 5.1, this section starts by concentrating on Copy 3, the fundamental copy made from the application to kernel buffers (or vice versa) when a network message is sent (received). This is a fundamental issue for networking, independent of file system issues. It also turns out that general solutions that eliminate all redundant I/O copies (Section 5.4) build on the techniques developed in this section.

This section assumes that the protocol is fixed but the local implementation (at least the kernel) can be restructured. The goal, of course, is to perform minimal restructuring in order to continue to leverage the vast amount of investment in existing kernel and application software. Section 5.2.1 describes techniques based on exploiting adaptor memory. Section 5.2.2 describes the core idea behind copy avoidance (by remapping shared physical pages) and its pitfalls. Section 5.2.3 shows how to optimize page remapping using precomputation and caching based on I/O streams; however, this technique involves changing the application programming interface (API). Finally, Section 5.2.4 describes another technique, one that uses virtual memory (VM) but does not change the API.

5.2.1 Exploiting adaptor memory

The simple idea here is to exploit a degree of freedom (**P13**) by realizing that memory can be located *anywhere* on the bus in a memory-mapped architecture. Recall from Chapter 2 that memory mapping means that the CPU talks to all devices, such as the adaptor and the disk, by reading and writing to a portion of the physical memory space that is located on the device.

Thus while kernel memory is often resident on the memory subsystem, there is no reason why part of the kernel memory cannot be on the adaptor itself, which typically contains some memory. By leveraging off the existing adaptor memory (**P4**) and utilizing this degree of freedom in terms of placement of kernel memory, we can place kernel memory on the adaptor. The net result is that once

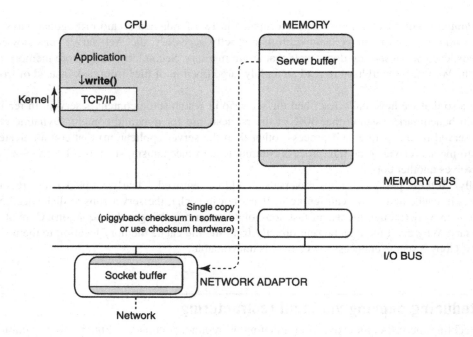

FIGURE 5.2

The Witless (Afterburner) approach eliminates the need for the kernel-to-adaptor copy by placing kernel buffers in the adaptor.

the data is copied from application to kernel memory it is already in the adaptor and so does not need to be copied again for transmission to the network. This is shown in Fig. 5.2.

Compare Fig. 5.2 with Fig. 5.1. Notice that Fig. 5.2 ignores any disk-to-memory transfer. Essentially, the useless Copy 3 in Fig. 5.1 is now combined with the essential Copy 4 in Fig. 5.1 to form a single copy in Fig. 5.2.

What about the checksum? We will see this in more general form in Section 5.5, but the main idea is to use principle **P2c**, expense sharing. When data is being moved from the application buffer to the adaptor resident kernel memory by the processor (using so-called programmed I/O, or PIO, which is I/O under processor control), the CPU is reading every word of the packet anyway. Since such bus reads are expensive, the CPU might as well piggyback the checksum computation with the copy process by keeping a register that accumulates the running sum of words that are transferred.

This idea, first espoused by Van Jacobson and called the Witless (or simple-minded) approach, was never built. Later this approach was used by Banks and Prudence (1993) at Hewlett-Packard labs and called the Afterburner adaptor. In the Afterburner approach, the CPU did not transfer data from memory to the adaptor. Instead, the adaptor did so, using so-called direct memory access, or DMA. Thus since the CPU is no longer involved in the copy process, the adaptor should do the checksum. The Afterburner adaptor had special (but simple) checksum hardware that checksummed words as the DMA transfer took place.

While the idea is a good one, it has three basic flaws. First, it implies that the network adaptor needs lots of memory to provide support for many high-throughput TCP connections (which require large window sizes); the memory required may make the adaptor more expensive than one wishes. Second, in the Witless approach, where the checksum is calculated by the CPU, doing the checksum while copying a received packet to the application buffer can imply that corrupted data can be written to application buffers. Though this can be discovered at the end, when the checksum does not compute, it does cause some awkwardness to prevent applications from reading incorrect data. A third problem with delayed acknowledgments is explored in the exercises.

5.2.2 Using copy-on-write

While the basic idea in the Witless approach can be considered to be eliminating the kernel-to-adaptor copy, the alternate idea pursued in the next three subsections is to eliminate the application-to-kernel copy (in most cases) using VM remappings. Recall that one reason for the separate copy was the possibility that the application would modify the buffer and hence violate TCP semantics. A second reason is that the application and kernel use different virtual address spaces.

Some operating systems (notably Mach) offer a facility called copy-on-write (COW) that allows a process to replicate a virtual page (VP) in memory at low cost. The idea is to make the copy point to the original physical page P from which it was copied. This only involves updating a few descriptors (a few words of memory) instead of copying a whole packet (say, 1500 bytes of data). However, the nice thing about COW is that if the original owner of the data modifies the data, the OS will detect this condition automatically and generate two separate physical copies, P and P'. The original owner now points to P and can make modifications on P; the owner of the copied page points to the old copy, P'. This works fine if the vast majority of times pages are not modified (or only a few pages are modified) by the original owner.

Thus in a COW system, the application could make a COW copy for the kernel. In the hopefully rare event that the application modifies its buffer, the kernel makes a (expensive) physical copy. However, that should be uncommon. Clearly, we are using lazy evaluation (**P2b**) to minimize overhead in the expected case (**P11**). Finally, in Fig. 5.3 the checksum can be piggybacked either with the copy to or from adaptor memory or by using CRC hardware on the adaptor.

Unfortunately, many operating systems, such as UNIX[2] and Windows, do not offer COW. However, much of the same effect can be obtained by understanding the basis behind the COW service, which is the use of VM.

Implementing copy-on-write

Recall from Chapter 2 that most modern computers use VM. Recall that the programmer works with an abstraction of infinite memory that is a linear array into which she (or more accurately her compiler) assigns variable locations, so, say, location X would be location 1010 in this imaginary (or virtual) array. These virtual addresses are then mapped into physical memory (which can reside on disk or in main memory) using a page table (Chapter 2).

---

[2] System V UNIX does implement COW when a process is forked. The pages shared between the child and the parent process are shared with the COW bit set.

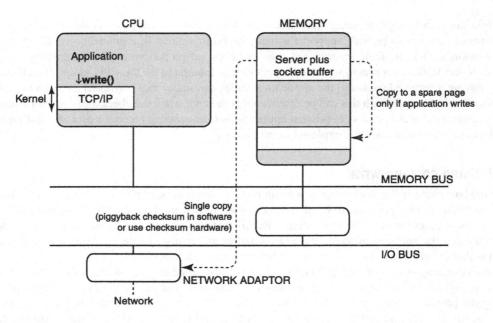

FIGURE 5.3

Using COW.

For any virtual address, the high-order bits (e.g., 20 bits) form the page number, and the low-order bits (e.g., 12 bits) form the location within a page. Main memory is also divided into physical pages such that (say) every group of 2^{12} memory words is a physical page. Recall that a virtual address is mapped to a physical address by mapping the corresponding VP to a physical page number by looking up a page table indexed by the VP number. If the desired page is not memory resident, the hardware generates an exception that causes the operating system to read the page from disk into main memory. Recall also that the overhead of reading page tables from memory can be avoided in the common case using a TLB (translation look-aside buffer), which is a processor resident cache.

Looking under the hood, VM is the basis for the COW scheme. Suppose virtual page X is pointing to a physical memory–resident page P. Suppose that the operating system wishes to replicate the contents of X onto a new VP, Y. The hard way to do this would be to allocate a new physical page, P', to copy the contents of P to P', and then to point Y to P' in the page table. The simpler way, embodied in COW, is to *map* the new VP, Y, back to the old physical page, P, by changing a page table entry. Since most modern operating systems use large page sizes, changing a page table entry is more efficient than copying from one physical page to another.

In addition, the kernel also sets a COW protection bit as part of the page table entry for the original VP, X. If the application tries to write to page X, the hardware will access the page table for X, notice the bit set, and generate an exception that calls the operating system. At this point the operating system will copy the physical page, P, to another location, P', and then make X point to P', after clearing the COW bit. Y continues to point to the old physical page, P. While this is every bit as expensive as

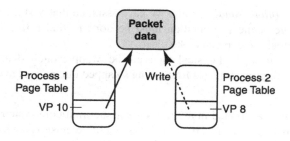

FIGURE 5.4

Basic operations involved in making a copy of a page using VM.

physical page copying, the point is that this expense is incurred only in the (hopefully) rare case when an application writes to a COW page.

The explanation of how COW works should present the following opportunity. While operating systems such as UNIX and Windows do not offer COW, they still offer VM. VM presents a level of indirection that can be exploited by changing page table entries to finesse physical copying. Thus much of the core idea behind Fig. 5.3 can be reused in most operating systems. All that remains is to find an alternate way to protect against application Writes in place of COW protection.

5.2.3 Fbufs: optimizing page remapping

Even ignoring the aspect of protecting against application writes, Fig. 5.4 implies that a large buffer can be transferred from application to kernel (or vice versa) with a Write to the page table. This simplistic view of page remapping is somewhat naive and misleading.

Fig. 5.4 shows a concrete example of page remapping. Suppose the operating system wishes to make a fast copy of data of Process 1 (say, the application) in VP 10 to some virtual page (e.g., VP 8) in the page table of Process 2's (say, the kernel). Naively, this seems to require only changing the page table entry corresponding to VP 8 in Process 2 to point to the packet data to which that VP table entry 10 in Process 1 already points. However, there are several additional pieces of overhead that are glossed over by this simple description.

- *Multiple-level page tables:* Most modern systems use multiple levels of page table mappings because it takes too much page table memory to map from, say, 20 bits of a VP. Thus the real mapping may require changing mappings in at least a first- and a second-level page table. For portability, there are also both machine-independent and machine-dependent tables. Thus there are several Writes involved, not just one.
- *Acquiring locks and modifying page table entries:* Page tables are shared resources and thus must be protected using locks that must be acquired and released.
- *Flushing translation look-aside buffers (TLBs):* As we said earlier, to save translation time, commonly used page table mappings are cached in the TLB. When a new VP location for VP 8 is written, any TLB entries for VP 8 must be found and flushed (i.e., removed) or corrected.

- *Allocating VM in destination domain:* While we have assumed that VM location 8 was the location for the destination page, some computation must be done to find a free page table entry in the destination process before the copy can take place.
- *Locking the corresponding pages:* Physical pages can be swapped out to disk to make room for other VPs currently on disk. To prevent pages from being swapped out, pages have to be locked, which is additional overhead.

All these overheads are exacerbated in multiprocessor and multicore systems. The net result is that while the page table mapping can seem very good (the mapping seems to take a constant time, independent of the size of the packet data), the constant factors (see **Q4** in the discussion of caveats) are actually a big overhead. This was experimentally demonstrated by experiments performed by Druschel and Peterson (1993) in the early 1990s. In the decade that followed, if anything, page mapping overheads have only increased.

Druschel and Peterson, however, did not stop with the experiments but invented an operating system facility called *fbufs* (short for "fast buffers"), which actually removes most or all of the four sources of page remapping overhead. Their idea can be described as follows in terms of the principles used in this book.

Fbufs

The main idea in fbufs is to realize that if an application is sending a lot of data packets to the network through the kernel, then a buffer will probably be reused multiple times, and thus the operating system can precompute (**P2a**) all the page mapping information for the buffer ahead of time and then avoid much of the page mapping overhead during the actual data transfer. Alternatively, the mappings can be computed lazily (**P2b**) when the data transfer is first started (causing high overhead for the first few received packets) but can be cached (**P11a**) for the subsequent packets. In this version page remapping overheads are eliminated in the common case.

The simplest way to do this would be to use what is called *shared memory*. Map a number of pages $P_1, \ldots, P_n$ into the VM tables of the kernel as well as all sending applications $A_1, \ldots, A_k$. However, this is a bad idea, because we now can have (say) application A_1 reading the packets sent by application A_2.[3] This would violate security and fault-isolation goals.

A more secure notion would be to reserve (or lazily establish) mapped shared pages for each application-to-kernel transfer and vice versa. For example, there could be one set of buffers (pages) for FTP, one set for HTTP, and so on. More generally, some operating systems define multiple security subsystems besides kernel and application. Thus the fbuf designers call a path a sequence of security domains. For our simple examples described earlier, it suffices to think of a path as either kernel, application or application, kernel (e.g., FTP, kernel or kernel, HTTP). We will see why paths are unidirectional—that is, why each application needs two paths in both directions—in a minute.

Fig. 5.5 shows a more complex example of paths, where the Ethernet software is implemented as a kernel-level driver, the TCP/IP stack is implemented as a user-level security domain, and, finally, the Web application is implemented at the application layer. Each security domain has its own set of page tables. The receiving paths are Ethernet, TCP/IP, Web and Ethernet, OSI, FTP.

---

[3] It is worth knowing that the VM hardware normally enforces this security constraint by making sure that any accesses by A_2 can access only physical pages mapped into the page tables of A_2.

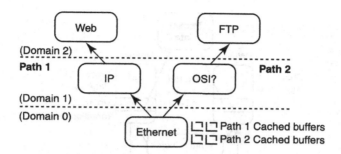

FIGURE 5.5

Premapping or lazily establishing buffer pages into the page tables of each domain in a path avoids the expense of page remapping in the real-time path, after the initial setup.

To implement the fbuf idea the operating system could take some number of physical pages $P_1, \ldots, P_k$ and premap them onto the page tables of the Ethernet driver, the TCP/IP code, and the Web application. The same operation could be performed with a different set of physical pages for Ethernet, OSI, and FTP. Thus we are using principle **P2a** to precompute mappings. Reserving physical pages for each path could be wasteful because traffic is bursty; instead, a better idea is to lazily establish (**P2b**) such mappings when a path becomes busy.

Lazy establishment avoids the overheads of updating multiple levels of page tables, acquiring locks, flushing TLBs, and allocating destination VM after the first few data packets arrive and are sent. Instead, all this work is done once, when the transfer first starts. To make fbufs work, it is crucial that when a packet arrives, the lowest-level driver (or even the adaptor itself) be able to quickly figure out what the complete path the packet will be mapped to when receiving a packet from the network. This function, called *early demultiplexing*, is described in detail in Chapter 8. Intuitively, in Fig. 5.5 this is done by examining all the packet headers to determine (for instance) that a packet with an Ethernet, IP, and HTTP header belongs to Path 1.

The driver (or the adaptor) will then have a list of free buffers for that path, which will be used by the adaptor to write the packet to; when the adaptor is done it will pass the buffer descriptor to the next application in the path. Note that a buffer descriptor is only a pointer to a shared page, not the page itself. When the last application in the path finishes with the page, it passes it back to the first application in the path, where it again becomes a free buffer, and so on.

At this point, the reader may wonder why paths are unidirectional. Paths are made unidirectional because the first process on each path is assumed to be a writer and the remaining processes are assumed to be readers. This can be enforced during the premapping by setting a write-allowed bit for the first application in its page table entry, and a read-only bit in the page table entries of all the other applications. Clearly, this is asymmetric in both directions and requires unidirectional paths. But this does ensure some level of protection.

This is shown in Fig. 5.6 with just two domains in a path. Note that the writer writes packets into buffers described by a queue of free fbufs and then puts the written descriptor onto a queue of written fbufs that are read by the next application (only one is shown in Fig. 5.6).

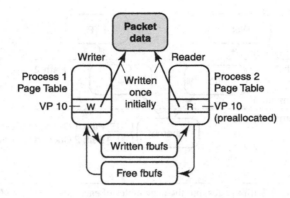

FIGURE 5.6

The single writer optimization.

So far, it is possible that premapped page 8 in the first application on a path is mapped to page 10 in the second application. This is painful because when the second application reads a descriptor for page 8, it must somehow know that it corresponds to its own VP 10. Instead, the designers used the principle of avoiding unnecessary generality (**P7**) and insisted that the fbuf get mapped to the *same* VP in all applications on the path. This can be done by reserving some number of initial pages in the VM of all processes to be fbuf pages.

At this point, we may feel that we are finished, but there are still a few thorny problems. To achieve protection, we allowed only a single writer and had multiple readers. However, that means that pages are *immutable*; only the writer can touch them. But what about adding headers when one goes down the stack. The solution to this problem is shown in Fig. 5.7, where a packet is really an aggregate data structure with pointers to individual fbufs so that headers can be added by adding an ordinary buffer or an fbuf to the aggregate.

This is not as big a deal as it sounds because the commonly used UNIX mbufs (see Chapter 9) are also composites of buffers strung together.[4]

So far, the fbuf scheme has used the underlying VM mapping ideas in Fig. 5.3 except that it has made them more efficient by amortizing the mapping costs over (hopefully) a large number of packet transfers. Page table updates are removed in the common case. This can be done in ordinary operating systems. In fact, after the fbufs paper, Thadani and Khalidi (1995) extended the idea and implemented it in Sun's Solaris operating system. But this begs the question: How are standard copy semantics preserved? What if the application does a Write? A standard operating system such as UNIX cannot depend on COW as in Fig. 5.3.

The ultimate answer in fbufs is that *standard copy semantics are not preserved*. The API is changed. Application writers must be careful not to write to an fbuf when it has been handed to the kernel until the fbuf is returned by the kernel in a free list. To protect against buggy or malicious code, the kernel

---

[4] To be precise, UNIX mbufs are strung together in a linear topology, while buffer aggregates form a more general tree topology, but the performance costs due to chaining and indexing are similar.

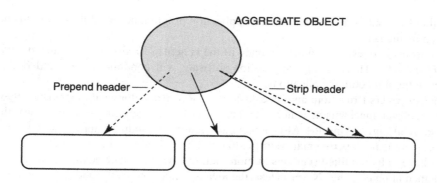

FIGURE 5.7

Using aggregate objects to allow adding layers to add headers while allowing only a single writer.

can briefly toggle the write-enable bit when an fbuf is transferred from the application to the kernel; the bit is set again when the fbuf is given back. If the application does a Write when it does not have write permission, an exception is generated and the application crashes, leaving other processes unaffected.

Since the toggling of the write-enable bits requires some of the overhead that fbufs worked hard to avoid, the fbuf facility also allows another form of fbufs, called *volatile*. Observe that if the writer is a trusted entity (such as the kernel), then there is no point enforcing write protection. If the kernel has a bug that causes it to make unexpected writes, the whole system will crash anyway.

Changing the API in this way sounds dramatic. Does this mean that the huge amount of existing UNIX application software (which uses the networking stack) must be rewritten? Since this is infeasible, there are several ways out. First, the existing API can be augmented with new system calls. For example, the Solaris extensions in Thadani and Khalidi (1995) add a *uf_write()* call in addition to the standard *write()* call. Applications interested in performance can be rewritten using these new calls.

Second, the extensions can be used in implementing common I/O substrates (such as the UNIX *stdio* library) that are a part of several applications. Applications that are linked to this library do not need to be changed and yet can potentially benefit in performance.

Eventually, the pragmatic consideration is not whether the API changes but how hard it is to modify applications to benefit from the API changes. The experiences described in Thadani and Khalidi (1995) and Pai et al. (1999b) for a number of applications indicate that the changes required in an application to migrate to an fbuf-like API are small and localized.

5.2.4 Transparently emulating copy semantics

One reaction to the new fbuf API is simply to modify applications to gain performance. It is worth pointing out that while the changes may be simple and localized, the mental model that a programmer has of a buffer changes in a fairly drastic way. In the standard UNIX API the application assigns buffer addresses; in fbufs, the buffers are assigned by the kernel from the fbuf address space. In the standard UNIX API the programmer can design the buffer layout anyway he pleases, including the use of contiguous buffers. In fbufs data received from the network can be arbitrarily scattered into pieces linked together by a buffer aggregate, and the application programmer must deal with this new buffer model chosen by the kernel.

Thus a reasonable question is whether many of the benefits of fbufs can be realized *without modifying the UNIX API*. Theoretically, application software will continue to run, and one might get performance without recoding applications.

In a series of papers Brustoloni and Steenkiste (e.g., Ref. Brustoloni and Steenkiste, 1996) showed that there is a clever mechanism, which they call *TCOW* (for transient copy-on-write), that makes this possible. While preserving the API theoretically allows unmodified applications to enjoy better performance, there is no experimental confirmation of this possibility. Thus in practice, it is likely that applications have to be modified (perhaps in more intuitive ways) to take advantage of the underlying kernel implementation changes. Nevertheless, the idea is simple and clever and worth pointing out.

Recall that the standard API requires allowing an application to write or deallocate a buffer passed to the kernel at any time. The fbuf design changes the API by making it illegal for an application to do this. Instead, to preserve the API while doing only VM mappings, the operating system must deal with these two potential threats, application writes and application deallocates, during the period the buffer is being used by the kernel to send or retransmit a packet. In the Genie system (Brustoloni and Steenkiste, 1996) VM mapping is used, as in fbufs, but these two threats are dealt with as follows.

Countering Write Threats by Modifying the VM Fault Manager: First, when an application does a Write, the buffer is marked specially, as Read Only. Thus if the application does a Write, the VM fault manager is invoked. Normally, this should cause an exception. But, of course, if the OS is preserving copy semantics, this should not be an error. Thus Genie modifies the exception handler as follows. First, for each such page/buffer, Genie keeps track of whether there are outstanding sends (sends to the network) using a simple counter that is incremented when the Send starts and decremented when the Send completes. Second, the fault handler is modified to make a separate copy of the page for the application (which incorporates the new Write) if there is an outstanding Send. Of course, this makes performance suffer, but it does preserve the standard copy semantics of APIs such as UNIX. This technique, called transient copy-on-write protection, is invoked only when needed—when the buffer is also being read out by the network subsystem.

Countering Deallocate Threats by Modifying the Pageout Daemon: In a standard VM system, there is a process that is responsible for putting deallocated pages into a free list from which pages may be written to disk. This pageout daemon can be modified not to deallocate a page when the page is being used to send or receive packets.

Interestingly these two ideas are both instances of principle **P3c**, shifting computation in space. The work of checking for unexpected writes is moved to the VM fault handler, and the work of dealing with deallocates is moved to the page deallocation routine.

These two ideas are sufficient for *sending* a packet but not for receiving. On receiving, Genie needs to depend, like fbufs, on hardware support[5] in the adaptor to split a packet's headers into one buffer and the remaining data into a page-size buffer that can be swapped to the application's buffer.

---

[5] Hardware support for parsing in the adaptor is the simplest alternative proposed by the Genie system; there are a number of more baroque mechanisms proposed as part of the Genie system to get around this hardware requirement, but they seem too complicated and full of side effects to be useful in practice.

To do so without a physical copy, the kernel's data buffer must start at the same offset within the page as the application's receive buffer. For a large buffer, the first and last pages (which can be partially filled) are probably most efficiently handled by a physical copy; however, the intermediate pages that are full can simply be swapped from the kernel to the application by the right page table mappings. There is a cute optimization called *reverse copyout* that is explored in the exercises.

Given the complexity that underlies page table remapping, it is unclear how page remapping is done efficiently in Genie. One possibility is that Genie uses the same fbuf idea of caching VM mappings on a path basis[6] to avoid the overhead of TLB flushing, dealing with multiple page tables, and so on.

When all is said and done, can the TCOW idea benefit legacy applications? There is no experimental confirmation of this in Brustoloni and Steenkiste (1996) and Brustoloni (1999) because the experiments use a simple copy benchmark and not an existing application such as a Web server. Fundamentally, it seems hard for an existing legacy application to benefit from the new kernel implementation of the existing API.

Consider an application running over TCP that supplies a buffer to TCP. Since there is no feedback to the application (unlike fbufs), the application does not know when it can safely reuse the buffer. If the application overwrites the buffer too early while TCP is holding the buffer for retransmission, then safety is not compromised, but performance is compromised because of the physical copy involved in COW. It appears improbable that an unmodified application could choose the times to modify buffers in accordance with TCP sending times and would have aligned its buffers well enough to allow page swapping to work well.

Thus applications do need to be modified to take full advantage of the Genie system. Even if they do, there is still the hard problem of knowing when to reuse a buffer because of the lack of feedback. The application could monitor TCOW faults and accordingly modify its reuse pattern. But if applications need to be modified in subtle ways to take full advantage of the new kernel, it is unclear what benefit was gained from preserving the API. Nevertheless, the ideas in Genie are fun to study, and they fall nicely within the general area of network algorithmics.

5.2.5 Are zero copies used today?

Much has transpired since the first edition, and the general consensus so far has been that, at least for general purpose operating systems like Linux, zero copy implementations are not worthwhile. The overhead of page mapping seems too much compared to simply copying data from the application to the kernel (A reworked TCP zero-copy receive API, 2018) for the same reasons that Druschel and Peterson found many years ago. This is particularly true because early studies found that the major overhead was protocol processing.

However, things may be changing. A paper (Cai et al., 2021) shows that as we move to 100 Gbps after doing all the major optimizations (e.g., large MTU sizes called jumbo frames and a form of batching called segmentation offload we will study in the next chapter), throughput for the Linux network stack saturates at around 42 Gbps per core. *The major bottleneck that remains is the data copy* from the kernel to user space and vice versa. The same paper (Cai et al., 2021) suggests that the time may be ripe

---

[6] The Genie experiments were done on an ATM network, where the virtual circuit identifier can provide a quick mapping to the path.

to reconsider recent zero-copy implementation proposals via page table mappings in Linux, both at the receive side (A reworked TCP zero-copy receive API, 2018) and at the sender side (sendmsg, 2022).

A sender side proposal for zero-copy by De Bruijn (sendmsg) uses the ideas described earlier in this chapter. Once again, the assumption is that the application must lock and take care not to reuse a buffer that is mapped while the kernel is using the buffer. The application can tell when it is safe to reuse the buffer pages by a notification message that the kernel places in the error queue associated with the socket, with sequence numbers allowing notifications to be matched to completed send calls.

The proposed receive side fix is more complicated because the kernel must place the received packet in a general buffer, determine the application it is destined for, and then map the buffer to the application's user space. As we have seen before in this chapter, this requires a network adaptor or NIC to separate the headers from the data, and place the data aligned with a page. Dumazet's patch (A reworked TCP zero-copy receive API, 2018) sets the MTU to 61,512—this allows fifteen 4096-byte pages of data, together with 40 bytes for IPv6 and 32 bytes for TCP. The interesting general idea in this patch is that rather than using memory mapping (mmap()) for a file, it implements mmap() for TCP sockets. Benchmarking in a controlled setting shows a potential reduction of 3X in the processing time per Mbyte (A reworked TCP zero-copy receive API, 2018).

Note that none of these recent proposals use the further optimizations suggested in this chapter such as fbufs to amortize the cost of page mapping over a sequence of calls. Further, they are only being considered, with no serious deployment at the time of writing. Zero-copy mechanisms are, however, widely deployed today as part of two other more specialized techniques. The first is the DPDK (Data Plane Data Kit) (2018) method for kernel bypass we will study in the next chapter. The second is systems that incorporate remote DMA as we will study next.

5.3 Avoiding copying using remote DMA

While fbufs provide a reasonable solution to the problem of avoiding redundant application-to-kernel copies, there is a more direct solution that also removes an enormous amount of control overhead. Normally, if a 1-MB file is transferred between two workstations on an Ethernet, the file is chopped up into 1460-byte pieces. The CPU is involved in processing each of these 1460-byte pieces to do TCP processing and copying each packet (possibly via a zero-copy interface such as fbufs) to application memory.

On the other hand, recall from Chapter 2 how a CPU orchestrates a DMA operation between, say, disk and memory for, say, a 1-MB transfer. The CPU sets up the DMA, tells the disk the range of addresses into which the data must be written, and goes about its business. One megabyte of data later, the disk interrupts the CPU to essentially say, "Master, your job is done." Note that the CPU does not micromanage every piece of this transfer, unlike in the earlier case of the corresponding network transfer.

This analogy suggests the vision of doing DMA across the network, or RDMA as it is sometimes called. In fact, it is hardly surprising that this networking feature was first proposed in VAX Clusters by a group of computer architects (Kronenberg et al., 1986). It is said that breakthroughs often come via outsiders to an area. There is an apocryphal story about how one of the inventors of VAX Clusters came to the networking people at DEC and asked to learn about networking. They laughed at him and gave him a copy of the standard undergraduate text at that time. He came back 6 months later with the RDMA design.

The intent is that data should be transferred between two memories in two computers across the network without per-packet mediation by the two CPUs. Instead, the two adaptors conspire to read from one memory and to write to the other: DMA across the network. To realize this vision two problems must be solved: (1) how the receiving adaptor knows where to place the data—it cannot ask the host for help without defeating the intent; (2) how security is maintained. The possibility of rogue packets coming over the network and overwriting key pieces of memory should make one pause.

This section starts by describing this very early idea and then moves on to describe modern incarnations of this idea in the Fibre Channel, Infiniband and iSCSI proposals.

5.3.1 Avoiding copying in a cluster

In the last few years clusters of workstations have become accepted as a cheaper and more effective substitute for large computers. Thus many Web servers are really server farms. While this appears to be recent technology, 20 years ago Digital Equipment Corporation (DEC) introduced a successful commercial product called VAX Clusters to provide a platform for scalable computing for, say, database applications. The heart of the system was a 140-Mbit network called the computer interconnect, or CI, which used an Ethernet-style protocol. To this interconnect, customers could connect a number of VAX computers and network-attached disks. The issue of efficient copying was motivated by the need to transfer large amounts of data between the remote disk and the memory of a VAX. RDMA was born from this need.

RDMA requires that packet data containing part of a large file go into its final destination when it gets to the destination adaptor. This is trickier than it sounds. In traditional networking when the packet arrives the processor is involved in at least examining the packet and deciding where the packet is to go. Even if the CPU looks at headers, it can only tell based on the destination application which queue of receive buffers to use.

Suppose the receiving application queues Pages 1, 2, and 3 to the receiving adaptor for Application 1. Suppose the first packet arrives and is sent to Page 1, the third packet arrives out of order and is put in Page 2 instead of Page 3. Assume that Pages 1, 2, and 3 should store the receiving file. The CPU can always remap pages at the end, but remapping all the pages at the end of the transfer for a large file can be painful. Out-of-order arrival can always happen, even on a FIFO link, because of packet loss.

Instead, the idea in VAX Clusters is first to have the destination application lock a number of physical pages (such as Pages 11 and 16 in Fig. 5.8) that comprise the destination memory for the file transfer. The logical view presented, however, is a buffer of consecutive logical pages (e.g., Pages 1 and 2 in Fig. 5.8) called, say, *B*. This buffer name *B* is passed to the sending application.

The source now passes (**P10**, pass information in protocol headers) the buffer name and offset with each packet it sends. Thus when sending Packet 3 out of order in our last example, Packet 3 will contain *B* and Page 3 and so can get stored in Page 3 of the buffer even though it arrives before Packet 2. Thus after all packets arrive there is no need for any further page remapping. This is an example of **P10**: passing information, such as a buffer name, in message headers.

To realize the ideal of not bothering the processor on every packet arrival, there are several additional requirements. First, the adaptor must implement the transport protocol (and do all the checking for duplicates, etc.), as in TCP processing. Second, the adaptor must be able to determine where the data begins and where the headers stop so as only to copy the data into the destination buffer.

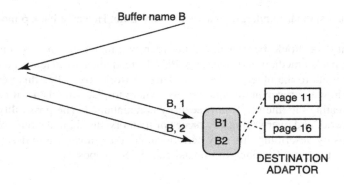

FIGURE 5.8

Doing DMA across the network.

Finally, it is somewhat cavalier to allow any packet carrying a buffer ID from the network to be written directly into memory. This could be a security hole. To mitigate against this, the buffer IDs contain a random string that is hard to guess. More importantly, VAX Clusters are used only between trusted hosts in a cluster. It is more difficult to imagine scaling this approach to Internet data transfers.

5.3.2 Modern-day incarnations of RDMA

VAX Clusters introduced a very early *storage area network*. Storage area networks (SANs) are back-end networks that connect many computers to shared storage, in terms of network-attached disks. There are several successors to VAX Clusters that provide SAN technology today. These range from the venerable Fiber Channel (Benner, 1995) technology to modern upstarts such as Infiniband (Infiniband Trade Association, 2001) and iSCSI (Satran et al., 2001).

Fiber channel

In 1988 the American National Standards Institute (ANSI) Task Group X3T11 began work on a standard called Fibre Channel (Benner, 1995). One of the goals of Fibre Channel was to take the standard SCSI (small computer system interface) between a workstation and a local disk and extend it over larger distances. Thus in many Fibre Channel installations, SCSI is still used as the protocol that runs over Fiber Channel.

Fibre Channel goes further than VAX Clusters in the underlying network, using modern network technology such as point-to-point fiber links connected with switches. This allows speeds of up to 64 Gbps and allows a larger distance span than in the Vax Cluster network. Switches can even be remotely connected, allowing a trading firm to have backup storage of all trades at a remote site. The use of switches requires attention to such issues as credit flow control, which is done very carefully to avoid dropping packets where possible to maintain the illusion of a lossless computer bus over the network.

Fibre Channel also makes slightly more concession to security than VAX Clusters. In VAX Clusters any device with the right name can overwrite the memory of any other device. Fiber Channel allows the network to be virtualized into zones. Nodes in a zone cannot access the memory of nodes in other zones. Some recent products go even further and propose techniques based on authentication.

However, other than these differences in the underlying technology, the underlying ideas are the same. RDMA via named buffers is still a key enabling idea. While Fibre Channel has had much recent competition from Ethernet based RDMA methods such as RoCE (Guo et al., 2016) (see below), it has still been the mainstay of storage area networks (SANs) for two decades and shows no signs of disappearing.

One reason for its continued popularity (The State of Fibre Channel, 2022) may be the popularity of solid state disks or NVM (Non Volatile Memory) especially over the PCI Express bus (NVMe). Fibre Channel latencies are particularly low. Thus despite the potential cost advantages of Ethernet solutions, the performance of Fibre Channel may explain its continued use in SANs.

Infiniband

Infiniband starts with the observation that the internal I/O bus used within many workstations and PCs, the PCI bus, is showing its age and needs replacement. With a maximum bandwidth of 533 MB/sec, the PCI bus is being overwhelmed by modern high-speed peripherals, such as Gigabit Ethernet interface cards. While there are some temporary alternatives, such as the PCI-X bus, the internal computer interconnect needs to scale in the same way as the external Internet has scaled from, say, 10-Mbit Ethernet to Gigabit Ethernet.

Also, observe that there are three separate networking technologies within a computer: the network interface (e.g., Ethernet), the disk interface (e.g., SCSI over Fibre Channel), and the PCI bus. Occam's razor suggests substituting these three with one network technology. Accordingly, Compaq, Dell, HP, IBM, and Sun banded together to form the Infiniband Trade Association.

The Infiniband specifications use many of the ideas in Fibre Channel's underlying network technology. The interconnect is also based on switches and point-to-point links. Infiniband has a few additional twists. It uses the proposal for 128-bit IP addresses in the next-generation Internet as a basis for addressing. It allows individual physical links to be virtualized into separate virtual links called *lanes*. It has features for quality of service and even multicast. Once again, RDMA is the key technology to avoid copies.

While Infiniband has not enjoyed the spurt in popularity of Ethernet based solutions described next or even that of Fibre Channel in Storage Area Networks, it is still widely used in supercomputing installations for high performance computing (SHARP, 2019). It is also used for speeding up large machine learning workloads using abstractions for in-network computing called SHARP that we describe in Section 5.5. For instance, it is used in two of the world's largest supercomputers in Oakridge and Los Alamos, with close to 10,000 Infiniband nodes each (SHARP, 2019).

iSCSI via iWarp and RoCE

Given that IP has invaded various other networking spaces, such as voice, TV, and radio, a natural consequence is to invade the storage space. This, the argument goes, should drive down prices (while also opening up new markets for network vendors). Further, Fibre Channel and Infiniband are being extended to connect remote data centers over the Internet. This involves using transport protocols that are not necessarily compatible with TCP in terms of reacting to congestion. Why not just adapt TCP for this purpose instead of trying to modify these other protocols to be TCP friendly?

For the purposes of this chapter, the most interesting thing about iSCSI is the way it must emulate RDMA over standard IP protocols. In particular recall that in all RDMA implementations, the host adaptor implements the transport protocol in hardware. There are two common solutions, iWarp and RoCE, with the latter popular in data centers.

iWarp: In the Internet world the transport protocol is TCP. Thus adaptors must implement TCP in hardware. This is not too hard, and chips that perform TCP offload are available.

The harder parts are as follows. First, as we saw in Case Study 1 of Chapter 2, TCP is a streaming protocol. The application writes bytes to a queue, and these bytes are arbitrarily segmented into packets. The RDMA idea, on the other hand, is based on messages, each of which has a named buffer field. Second, RDMA over TCP requires a header to hold named buffers.

The iWarp (RDMA Consortium, 2001) proposal solves both these problems by logically layering three protocols over TCP. The first protocol, MPA, adds a header that defines message boundaries in the byte stream. The second and third protocols implement the RDMA header fields but are separated as follows. Notice that when a packet carries data, all that is needed is a buffer name and offset. Thus this header is abstracted out into a so-called DDA (for direct data access) header together with a command verb (such as READ or WRITE).

The iWarp RDMA protocol that is layered over DDA adds a header with a few more fields. For example, for an RDMA remote READ, the initial request must specify the remote buffer name (to be read) and the local name (to be written to). One of these two buffer names can be placed in the DDA header, but the other must be placed in the RDMA header. Thus, except for control messages such as initiating a READ, all data carries only a DDA header and not an RDMA header.

During the evolution from VAX Clusters to the RDMA proposal, one interesting generalization was to replace a *named* buffer with an *anonymous* buffer. In this case the DDA header contains a queue name, and the packet is placed in a buffer corresponding to the buffer at the head of the free queue at the receiver.

RoCE: In response to the perceived complexity of iWarp, RoCE or RDMA over Converged Ethernet (Guo et al., 2016) was introduced. Recall that RDMA in Infiniband runs over networks that use credit-based flow control to make the network lossless. Because packet drops are rare in such clusters, the RDMA Infiniband transport (as implemented on the NIC) was not designed to *efficiently* recover from packet losses. When the receiver receives an out-of-order packet, it discards it and sends a NACK; this causes the sender to retransmits all packets in the window.

The central idea in RoCE is to run over UDP, not TCP, but to use a crude form of flow control at switches called PFC (for Priority Flow Control) to prevent packet drops due to congestion, believed to be the most common cause of loss in the network. The idea is that when a downstream switch is congested it sends a signal to the upstream switch to make it "pause" before the downstream switch has to drop packets. This crude form of flow control (compared to credit based flow control in Infiniband) is easy to implement, but has many potential disadvantages: unfairness cause by head-of-line blocking, and extreme failure modes such as "pause spreading" and network deadlocks (Guo et al., 2016).

Despite these disadvantages of RoCE, its perceived simplicity, latency and cost has made RoCE very popular in data centers. A paper (Mittal et al., 2018) comparing RoCE and iWarp for example suggests that at the time of comparison, iWarp had a latency that was three times worse, and a throughput that was four times lower, than RoCE. To be fair, the same paper (Mittal et al., 2018) argues that the cost-performance disadvantages of iWarp are not fundamental and can be mitigated with a cleverer implementation, but these ideas have not penetrated to the market to the best of our knowledge.

5.4 Broadening to file systems

So far this chapter has concentrated only on avoiding redundant copies that occur while sending data between an application (such as a Web server) and the network. However, Fig. 5.1 shows that even after removing all redundant overhead due to network copying, there are still redundant copies involving the file system. Thus in this section, we will cast our net more widely. We leverage our intellectual investment by extending the copy-avoidance techniques discussed so far to the file system.

Recall from Fig. 5.1 that to process a request for File X, the server may have to read X from disk (Copy 1) into a kernel buffer (representing the file cache) and then make a copy from the file cache to the application buffer (Copy 2). Copy 1 goes out of the picture if the file is already in cache, a reasonable assumption for popular files in a server with sufficient memory. The main goal is to remove Copy 2. Note that in a Web server unnecessarily doubling the number of copies not only halves the effective bus bandwidth but potentially halves the size of the server cache. This in turn reduces server performance by causing a larger miss rate, which implies that a larger fraction of documents is served at disk speeds and not bus speeds.

This section surveys three techniques for removing the redundant file system copy (Copy 2). Section 5.4.1 describes a technique called *shared memory mapping* that can reduce Copy 2 but is not well integrated with the network subsystem. Section 5.4.2 describes IO-Lite, essentially a generalization of fbufs to include the file system. Finally, Section 5.4.3 describes a technique called *I/O splicing* that is used by many commercial Web servers.

5.4.1 Shared memory

Modern UNIX variants (Stevens, 1998) provide a convenient system call known as *mmap()* to allow an application such as a server to map a file into its VM address space. Other operating systems provide equivalent functions. Conceptually, when a file is mapped into an application's address space, it is as if the application has cached a copy of the file in its memory. This seems redundant because the file system also maintains cached files. However, using the magic of VM (**P4**, leverage off system components), the cached file is really only a set of mappings, so other applications and the file server cache can gain common access to one set of physical pages for the file.

The Flash Web server (Pai et al., 1999a) avoids Copy 1 and Copy 2 in Fig. 5.1 by having the server application map frequently used files into memory. Given that there are limits on the number of physical pages that can be allocated to file pages and limits on page table mappings, the Flash Web server has to treat these mapped files as a cache. Instead of caching whole files, it caches segments of files and uses an LRU (least recently used) policy to unmap files that have not been used for a while.

Note that such cache maintenance functions are duplicated by the file system cache (which has a more precise view of resources such as free pages because it is kernel resident). However, this can be looked on as a necessary evil to avoid Copies 1 and 2 in Fig. 5.1. While Flash uses *mmap()* to avoid file system copying, it runs over the UNIX API. Hence, Flash is constrained to make an extra copy in the network subsystem (Copy 3 in Fig. 5.1). Just when progress is being made to eliminate Copy 2, pesky Copy 3 reappears again!

Copy 3 can be avoided by combining emulated copying using TCOW (Brustoloni and Steenkiste, 1996) with *mmap()*. However, this has some of the disadvantages of TCOW mentioned earlier. It is also not a complete solution that generalizes to avoid copying for interaction with a CGI process via a UNIX pipe.

5.4.2 IO-lite: A unified view of buffering

While combining emulated copy with *mmap()* does away with all redundant copying, it still has some missing optimizations. First, it does nothing to avoid the copying between any CGI application generating dynamic content and the Web server. Such an application is typically implemented as a separate process[7] that sends dynamic content to the server process via a UNIX pipe. But pipes and other similar interprocess communication typically involve copying the content between two address spaces.

Second, notice that none of our schemes so far has done anything about the TCP checksum, an expensive operation. But if the same file keeps hitting in the cache, other than the first response containing the HTTP header, all subsequent packets that return the file contents stay the same for every request. Why can't the TCP checksums be cached? However, that requires a cache that can somehow map from packet contents to checksums. This is inefficient in a conventional buffering scheme.

This section describes a buffering scheme called IO-Lite (Pai et al., 1999b) that generalizes the fbuf ideas to include the file system. IO-Lite not only eliminates all redundant copies in Fig. 5.1, but also eliminates redundant copying between the CGI process and the server. It also has a specialized buffer-numbering scheme that lets a subsystem (such as TCP) efficiently realize that it is resending an earlier packet.

IO-Lite is the intellectual descendant of fbufs, though integration with the file system adds significantly more complexity. It is first worth noting that fbufs cannot be combined with *mmap*, unlike TCOW, which is combined with *mmap* in Brustoloni (1999). This is because in *mmap* the application picks the address and format of an application buffer, while in fbufs the kernel picks the address and format of a fast buffer. Thus if the application has mapped a file using a buffer in the application virtual address space, the buffer cannot be sent using an fbuf (kernel address space) without a physical copy.

Since fbufs cannot be combined with *mmap*, IO-Lite generalizes fbufs to include the file system, making *mmap* unnecessary. Also, IO-Lite is implemented in a general-purpose operating system (UNIX), as opposed to fbufs. But setting aside these two differences, IO-Lite borrows all the main ideas from fbufs: the notion of read-only sharing via immutable buffers (called *slices* in IO lite), the use of composite buffers (called *buffer aggregates*), and the notion of a lazily created cache of buffers for a path (called an *I/O stream* in IO-Lite).

Despite the core similarities, IO-Lite requires solving difficult problems to integrate with the file system. First, IO-Lite must deal with complex sharing patterns, where several applications may have buffers pointing to the IO-Lite buffer together with the TCP code and the file server. Second, an IO-Lite page can be both a VM page (backed up by the paging backup file on disk) and at the same time a file page (backed up by the actual disk copy of the file). Thus IO-Lite has to implement a complex replacement policy that integrates both the standard page replacement rules together with file cache replacement policies (Pai et al., 1999b). Third, the goal of running over UNIX requires careful thought to find a clean way to integrate IO-Lite without major surgery throughout UNIX.

Fig. 5.9 shows the steps in responding to the same GET request pictured in Fig. 5.1. When the file is first read from disk into the file system cache, the file pages are stored as IO-Lite buffers. When the

---

[7] Because of the overhead of copying data between a CGI process generating dynamic content and the server process, some vendors have proposed merging the CGI code within the server process. However, that makes the system more brittle because faulty third-party content-generation software can crash the server. Better solutions, such as Windows ASP, propose incorporating safe languages into Web pages such that the server executes the code and puts the result in the page it serves. Thus, despite the references to CGI processes in this chapter, CGI may well be obsolete.

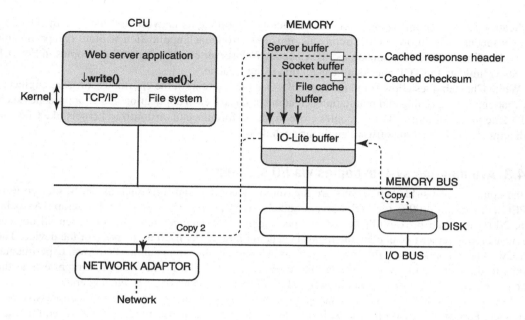

FIGURE 5.9

IO-Lite removes all the redundant copying in Fig. 5.1 by effectively passing around pointers (via VM mappings) to a single IO-Lite buffer. Assuming the file, the TCP checksum, and the HTTP response are all cached, the Web server only has to transmit these cached values in a single copy to the network interface.

application makes a call to read the file, no physical copy is made, but a buffer aggregate is created with a pointer to the IO-Lite buffer. Next, when the application sends the file to TCP for transmission, the network system gets a pointer to the same IO-Lite pages. To prevent errors, the IO-Lite system keeps a reference count for each buffer and reallocates a buffer only when all users are done.

Fig. 5.9 also shows two more optimizations. The application keeps a cache of HTTP responses for common files and can often simply append the standard response with minimal modifications. Second, every buffer is given a unique number (**P12**, add redundant state) by IO-Lite, and the TCP module keeps a cache of checksums indexed by buffer number. Thus when a file is transmitted multiple times, the TCP module can avoid calculating the checksum after the first time. Notice that these changes eliminate all the redundancy in Fig. 5.1, which speeds up the processing of a response.

IO-Lite can also be used to implement a modified pipe program that eliminates copying. When this IPC mechanism is used between the CGI process and the server process, all copying is eliminated without compromising the safety and fault isolation provided by implementing the two programs as separate processes. IO-Lite can also allow applications to customize their buffer-caching strategy, allowing fancier caching strategies for Web servers based on both size and access frequency.

It is important to note that IO-Lite manages these performance feats without completely eliminating the kernel and without closely tying the application with the kernel. The Cheetah Web server (Engler et al., 1995) built over the Exokernel operating system takes a more extreme position, allowing each application (including the Web server) to completely customize its network and file system. The Exokernel mechanisms allow such extreme customization from each application without compromising safety. By dint of these customizations, the Cheetah Web server can eliminate all the copies in Fig. 5.1 and also eliminate the TCP checksum calculation using a cache.

While Cheetah does allow some further tricks (see the Exercises), the enormous software engineering challenge of designing and maintaining custom kernels for each application makes approaches such as IO-Lite more attractive. IO-Lite comes close to the performance of customized kernels like Cheetah with a much smaller set of software engineeringchallenges.

5.4.3 Avoiding file system copies via I/O splicing

In the commercial world Web servers are measured by commercial tests such as the SPECweb tests (SPEC consortium, 1999) for Web servers and the Web polygraph tests (Web Polygraph Association, 2001) for Web proxies. In the proxy space there is an annual cache-off, in which all devices are measured together to calculate the highest cache hit rate, normalized to the price of the device. The SPECweb benchmarks use a different system, in which manufacturers submit their own experimental results to the benchmark system, though these results are audited. In the Web polygraph tests at the time of writing, a Web server technology based on I/O-Lite ideas was among the leaders.

However, in the SPECweb benchmarks, a number of other Web servers also show impressive performance. Part of the reason for this is just faster (and more expensive) hardware. However, there are two simple ideas that can avoid the need for complete model shifts as is the case in IO-Lite.

The first idea is to push the Web server application completely into the kernel. Thus in Fig. 5.1 all copies can be eliminated because the application and the kernel are part of the same entity. The major problem with this approach is that such in-kernel Web servers have to deal with the idiosyncrasies of operating system implementation changes. For example, for a popular high-performance server that runs over Linux, every internal change to Linux can invalidate assumptions made by the server software and cause a crash. Note that a conventional user-space server does not have this problem because all changes to the UNIX implementation still preserve the API.

The second idea keeps the server application in user space but relies on a simple idea called *I/O splicing* to eliminate all the copying in Fig. 5.1. I/O splicing, shown in Fig. 5.10, was first introduced in Fall and Pasquale (1993). The idea is to introduce a new system call that *combines* the old call to read a file with the old call (**P6**, efficient specialized routines) to send a message to the network. By allowing the kernel to splice together these two hitherto-separate system calls, we can avoid all redundant copies. Many systems have system calls such as *sendfile()*, which are now used by several commercial vendors.

Despite the success of this mechanism, mechanisms based on *sendfile* do not generalize well to communication with say CGI processes.. Thus there is still a need for reducing copy overhead for data that is computed on the fly and not stored in a file as we saw earlier (A reworked TCP zero-copy receive API, 2018).

5.5 Broadening beyond copies

There are several data manipulations in the network beyond copying that can be made more effcient if done at the same time, avoiiding multiple passes over the data. This leverages the principle of avoiding

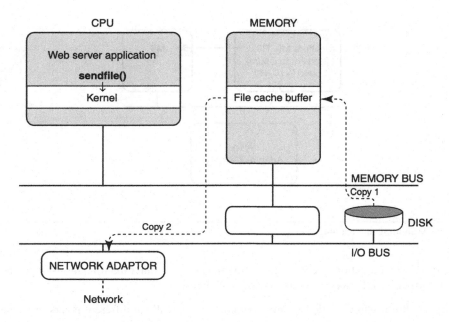

FIGURE 5.10

In I/O splicing, all the indirection caused by copying to and from user-space buffers is removed by a single system call that "splices" together the I/O stream from the disk with the I/O stream to the network. As always, Copy 1 can be removed for files in the cache.

obvious waste (**P1**), and expense sharing (**P2c**). We describe two such ideas, integrated layer processing (ILP) and in-network computing.

ILP: Clark and Tennehouse, in a landmark paper, suggested generalizing Van Jacobson's idea (described earlier) of integrating checksums and copying. In more detail the Jacobson idea is based on the following observation. When copying a packet word from a location (say, $W10$ in adaptor memory in Fig. 5.11) to a location in memory (say, $M9$ in memory in Fig. 5.11), the processor has to load $W10$ into a register and then store that register to $M9$. Typically, most RISC processors require that, between a load and a store, the compiler insert a so-called *delay slot*, or empty cycle, to keep the pipeline working correctly (never mind why!). That empty cycle can be used for other computation. For example, it can be used to add the word just read to a register that holds the current checksum. Thus with no extra cost the copy loop can often be augmented to be the checksum loop as well.

But there are other data-intensive manipulations, such as encrypting data and doing format conversions. Why not, Clark and Tennenhouse (1990) argued, integrate all such manipulations into the copy loop? For example, in Fig. 5.11 the CPU could read $W10$ and then decrypt $W10$ and write the decrypted word to $M9$ rather than have that done in another loop. They called this idea *integrated layer processing*, or ILP. The essential idea is to avoid obvious waste (**P1**), in terms of reading (and possibly) writing the bytes of a packet several times for multiple data-manipulation operations on the same packet.

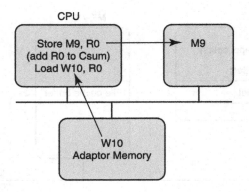

FIGURE 5.11

Integrating checksumming and copying.

Thus ILP is a generalization of copy-checksum integration to other manipulations (e.g., encryption, presentation formatting). However, it has several challenges.

- **Challenge 1:** Information needed for manipulations is typically at different layers (e.g., encryption is at the application layer, and checksumming is done at the TCP layer). Integrating the code from different layers without sacrificing modularity is hard.
- **Challenge 2:** Each manipulation may operate on different-size chunks and different portions of the packet. For example, TCP works in 16-bit quantities for a 16-bit checksum, while the popular DES encryption works in 64-bit quantities. Thus while working with one 32-bit word, the ILP loop has to deal with two TCP checksum words and half a DES word.
- **Challenge 3:** Some manipulations may be dependent on each other. For example, one should probably not decrypt a packet if the TCP checksum fails.
- **Challenge 4:** ILP can increase cache miss rate because it can reduce locality within a single manipulation. If we did TCP separately and DES separately instead of in a single loop, the code we'd use at each instant is smaller for the two single loops as opposed to the single loop. This makes it more likely that the code will be found in the instruction cache in the more naive implementation. Increasing integration beyond a certain point can destroy code locality so much that it may even have adverse effects. Some studies have shown this to be a major issue.

The first three challenges show that ILP is hard to do. The fourth challenge suggests that integrating more than a few operations can possibly even reduce performance. Finally, if the packet data is used multiple times, it could well reside in the data cache (even in a naive implementation), making all the bother about integrating loops unnecessary. Possibly for these reasons, ILP has remained a tantalizing idea. Beyond the copy–checksum combination, there has been little follow-up work in integrating other manipulations in academic or commercial systems.

In-Network Computing and SHARP: In contrast to in-network computing, recent Infiniband hardware (SHARP, 2019) has made the very old idea of in-network computing a practical reality at very high speeds. The idea is that many High Performance Computing applications synchronize multiple computations using mechanisms such as barriers and reduction, and reduce data using constructs such as

AllReduce. Further, many distributed machine learning algorithms need aggregate computations such as summing or finding the minimum of a large number of variables. If aggregate operations can be performed while data is travelling through the network, host computation can be saved. More importantly, in-network computing can reduce latency and even network bandwidth.

SHARP (2019) (Scalable Hierarchical Aggregation and Reduction Protocol) does precisely that. In some sense, SHARP does integrated processing of the application and network layers, a form of ILP. The problem of breaking layer abstraction is mitigated by the network offering a set of abstractions for these commonly used functions. SHARP technology has been incorporated into the classic MPI (Message Passing Interface for parallel computers), and is used in several supercomputers.

5.6 Broadening beyond data manipulations

So far this chapter has concentrated on reducing the memory (and bus) bandwidth caused by data-manipulation operations. First, we concentrated on removing redundant data copying between the network and the application. Second, we addressed redundant copying between the file system, the application, and the network. Third, we looked at removing redundant memory reads and writes using integrated layer processing when several data-manipulation operations operate over the same packet. What is common to all these techniques is an attempt to reduce pressure on the memory and the I/O bus by avoiding redundant reads and writes.

But once this is done, there are still other sources of pressure that appear within an endnode architecture as shown in Fig. 5.1. This is alluded to in the following excerpt from e-mail sent after the alpha release of a fast user-level Linux Web server (Riccardi, 2001):

> With zero-copy sendfile, data movement is not an issue anymore, asynchronous network IO allows for really inexpensive thread scheduling, and system call invocation adds a very negligible overhead in Linux. What we are left with now is purely wait cycles, the CPUs and the NICs are contending for memory and bus bandwidth.

In essence once the first-order effects (such as eliminating copies) are taken care of, performance can be improved only by paying attention to what might be thought of as second-order effects. The next two subsections discuss two such architectural effects that greatly impact the use of bus and memory bandwidth: the effective use of caches and the choice of DMA versus PIO.

5.6.1 Using caches effectively

The architectural model of Fig. 5.1 avoids two important details that were described in Chapter 2. Recall that the processor keeps one or more data caches (D-caches), and one or more instruction caches (I-caches). The data cache is a table that maps from memory addresses to data contents; if there are repeated reads and writes to the same location L in memory and L is cached, then these reads and writes can be served directly out of the data cache without incurring bus or memory bandwidth. Similarly, recall that programs are stored in memory; every line of code executed by the CPU has to be fetched from main memory unless it is cached in the instruction cache.

Data Cache Optimization

Now, one might think packet data benefits little from a data cache, for there is little reuse of the data and copying involves writing to a *new* memory address, as opposed to repeated reads and writes from the *same* memory address. However, what if when packet data is received into memory by DMA, it is also sent to the processor cache? This is not as hard to do as it seems because the bus is a broadcast bus and the cache can "snoop" on transactions on the bus (Huggahalli et al., 2005). But if the data is already in the processor cache, then the copy from the socket buffer to application memory becomes a cache access. There is also a reduction in memory bandwidth and bus bandwidth.

But the presence of modern multicore machines complicates direct cache access. Which processor cache should the packet be sent by DMA to? One possibility is to send the packet to the cache corresponding to the core on which the receive application is running. This is called Receive Flow Steering (RFS); if the mechanism can be done in hardware it is referred to as aRFS (for accelerated Receive Flow Steering) (Cai et al., 2021).

Direct Cache Access (DCA) is standard in many processors and is often enabled by default (Cai et al., 2021). Unfortunately, the combination of high link speeds (100 Gbps) and increased end-to-end latencies implies that the number of bytes in flight (the so-called bandwidth delay product) is high. If this number is higher than the size of data cache, then cache can be overwritten before the application reads from the cache, negating the benefits of DCA, resulting in significant drop in the throughput per core (Cai et al., 2021). The same paper suggests that window size tuning in TCP should take into account cache sizes to avoid this effect.

There are two other items stored in memory that can benefit from caches. First, the program executing the protocol code to process a packet must be fetched from memory, unless it is stored in the I-cache. Second, the state required to process a packet (e.g., TCP connection state tables) must be fetched from memory, unless it is stored in the D-cache.

Of these two other possible contenders for memory bandwidth, the code to be executed is potentially a more serious threat. This is because the state, in bytes, required to process a packet (say, one connection table entry, one routing table entry) is generally small. However, for a small, 40-byte packet, even this can be significant. Thus avoiding the use of redundant state (which tends to pollute the D-cache) wherever possible can improve performance, as was described in Problem 11 of Chapter 4.

However, the code required to execute all of the networking stack (Data Link, TCP, IP, socket layer, and kernel entry and exit) can be much larger. For example, measurements in Blackwell (1996) show a total code size of 34 KB using a 1995 NetBSD TCP implementation. Given that even large packets on an Ethernet are at most 1.5 KB, the effort to load the code from memory can easily dwarf the effort to copy the packet multiple times.

In particular, if the I-cache is 8 KB (typical for older machines, such as the early Alpha machines used in Blackwell, 1996), this means that at most a quarter of the networking stack can fit in the cache. This in turn could imply that all or most of the code has to be fetched from memory every time a packet needs to be processed. Modern machines have not improved their I-cache sizes significantly. The Pentium III uses 16 KB. Thus effective use of the I-cache could be a key to improved performance, especially for small packets.

We now describe two techniques that can be used to improve I-cache effectiveness: code arrangement and locality-driven-layer processing.

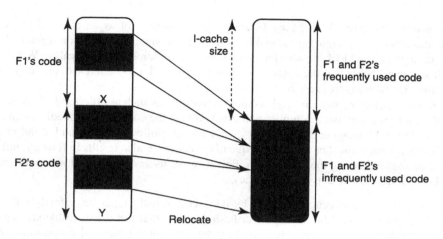

FIGURE 5.12

The figure on the left shows networking code that is laid out in memory so that frequently used (white) and infrequently used (black) code is arbitrarily intermixed. Using a direct-mapped cache of half the size of the total code can lead two frequently used instructions, such as X and Y, to collide. This problem can be avoided by relocating all frequently used code to be contiguous, as shown on the right.

Code arrangement

It is hard to realize when one is writing networking code that the actual layout of code in memory (and hence in the I-cache) is a degree of freedom that can be exploited (**P13**) with some effort. The key idea in code arrangement (Mosberger et al., 1996) is to lay out code in memory to optimize the common case (**P11**) such that commonly used code fits in the I-cache and the effort of loading the I-cache is not wasted.

At first glance, this seems to require no extra work. Since a cache should favor frequently used code over infrequently used code, this should happen automatically. Unfortunately, this is incorrect because of the following two aspects of the way I-caches are implemented.

- *Direct mapping:* An I-cache is a mapping of memory addresses to contents; the mapping is usually implemented by a simple hash function that optimizes for the case of sequential access. Thus most processors use direct-mapped I-caches, where the low-order bits of a memory address are used to index the I-cache array. If the high-order bits match, the contents are returned directly from cache; otherwise, a Read to memory is done across the bus, and the new data value and high-order bits are stored in the same location.

  Fig. 5.12 shows the effect of this implementation artifact. The figure on the left shows the memory layout of code for two networking functions, with black code denoting infrequently used code. Since the I-cache size is only half the total size of the code, it is possible for two frequently accessed lines of code (such as X and Y, with addresses that are the same modulo the I-cache size) to map to the same location in the I-cache. Thus if both X and Y are used to process every packet, they will keep evicting each other from the cache even though they are both frequently used.

- *Multiple instructions per block:* Many I-caches can be thought of as an array of blocks, where multiple instructions (say, eight) are stored in a block. Thus when an instruction is fetched, all eight instructions in the same block are also fetched on the assumption of spatial locality: With sequential access, it seems probable that the other seven instructions will also be fetched, and it is cheaper to read multiple instructions from memory at the same time.
Unfortunately, much of networking code contains error checks such as "If error E do X, else do Z." Z is hardly ever executed, but a compiler will often arrange the code for Z immediately after X. For example, in Fig. 5.12 imagine that code for Z immediately follows X. If X and Z fall in the same block of eight instructions, then fetching frequently accessed X also results in fetching infrequently used Z. This makes loading the cache less efficient (more useless work) and makes the cache less useful after loading (less useful code in cache).

Note that both of these effects are caused by the fact that real caches imperfectly reflect temporal locality. The first is caused by an imperfect hash function that can cause collisions between two frequently used addresses. The second is caused by the fact that the cache also optimizes for spatial locality.

Both effects can be mitigated by reorganizing networking code (Mosberger et al., 1996) so that all frequently used code is contiguous (see right of Fig. 5.12). For example, in the case "If error E do X, else do Z," the code for Z can be moved far away from X. This does require an extra jump instruction to be added to the code for Z so that it can jump back to the code that followed Z in the unoptimized version. However, this extra jump is taken only in the error case, and so it is not much of a cost.

This is an example of realizing that the memory location of code is a degree of freedom that can be optimized (**P13**) and an example of optimizing the expected case (**P11**) despite increasing the code path for infrequently used code.

Locality-driven layer processing

Code reorganization can help up to a point but fails if the working set (i.e., the set of instructions actually accessed for almost every packet) exceeds the I-cache size. For example, in Fig. 5.12, if the size of the white, frequently used instructions is larger than the I-cache, code reorganization will still help (fewer loads from memory are required because each load loads only useful instructions). However, every instruction will still have to be fetched from memory.

While the working set of the networking stack may fit into a modern I-cache (which is getting bigger), it is possible that more complicated protocols (that run over TCP/IP) may not. The idea behind locality-driven layer processing (Blackwell, 1996) is to be able to use the I-cache effectively as long as the code for each layer of the networking stack fits into the I-cache. By repeatedly processing the code for the same layer across multiple packets, the expense of loading the I-cache is shared (**P2c**) over multiple packets.

Consider the top timeline in Fig. 5.13. In a conventional processing timeline (shown from left to right in the figure), all the networking layers of packet $P1$ are processed before those of packet $P2$. Imagine that two packets $P1$ and $P2$ arrive at a server. In a conventional implementation, all the processing of $P1$ is finished, starting with the data link layer (e.g., Ethernet driver) and ending with the transport (e.g., TCP) layer. Only then is the processing of packet $P2$ started.

The main idea in locality-driven processing is to exploit another degree of freedom (**P13**) and to process all the layer code for as many received packets as possible before moving on to the next layer. Thus in the bottom timeline, after the data link layer code for $P1$ is finished, the CPU moves on to

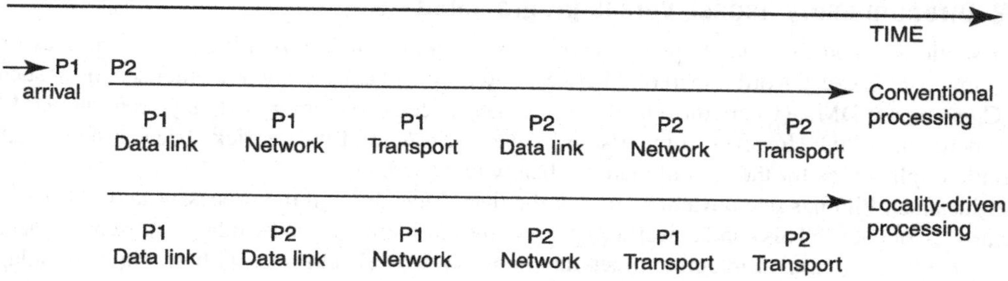

FIGURE 5.13

In a conventional processing timeline (shown from left to right), all the networking layers of packet $P1$ are processed before those of packet $P2$. In locality-driven receiver processing, each layer code is executed multiple times for multiple received packets (two in the picture) before moving on to the next layer.

execute the data link layer code for $P2$, *not* the network layer code for $P1$. This should not affect correctness because code for a layer should not depend on the state of lower layers. By contrast, integrated layer processing has more subtle dependencies and failure cases.

Thus if the code for each layer (e.g., the data link layer) fits into the I-cache while the code for all layers does not, then this optimization amortizes the cost of loading the I-cache over multiple packets. This is effectively using batch processing (**P2c**, expense sharing). The larger the size of the batch, the more effective the use of the I-cache.

The implementation can be made to tune the size of the batch dynamically (Blackwell, 1996). The code can batch-process up to, say, k packets from the queue of arrived packets, where k is a parameter that limits the latency. If the system is lightly loaded, then only one message at a time will be processed. On the other hand, if the system is heavily loaded, the batch size increases to make more effective use of memory bandwidth when it is most needed.

Software engineering considerations

Optimizations such as code restructuring (Fig. 5.12) and locality-driven processing (Fig. 5.13) also need to be evaluated by their effects on code modularity and maintenance. After all, one could rewrite the kernel and all applications using assembly language to more perfectly optimize memory bandwidth. But it would be difficult to get the code to work or be maintainable.

Code restructuring is best done by a compiler. For example, error-handling code can be annotated with hints (Mosberger et al., 1996) suggesting which branches are more frequently taken (generally obvious to the programmer), and a specially augmented compiler can restructure the code for I-cache locality. Algorithms for this purpose are described in Mosberger et al. (1996).

On the other hand, locality-driven processing preserves modularity within layers. Communication between layers must be changed as follows. If each layer code passes a packet to the code for a higher layer with a procedure call, this code must be modified to add packets to a *queue* for the higher layer. Similarly, when a layer is called, it removes packets from its read queue until the queue is exhausted; after processing each packet, it places it on the queue for its next-higher layer. This strategy works well when each layer can reuse buffers from other layers, as is the case for UNIX mbufs. Overall, the code changes may not be severe.

5.6.2 Direct memory access versus programmed I/O

Earlier sections stated that the Witless scheme uses programmed I/O, or PIO (i.e., the processor or CPU is involved in every word transferred between memory and adaptor), while other schemes, such as VAX Clusters, use DMA (where the adaptor copies data directly to memory). It may seem that DMA is always better than PIO. However, comparisons between DMA and PIO are tricky because each method has subtle implications for the overall memory bandwidth used.

For instance, PIO has one advantage in that the data flows through the processor and thus ends up in the processor cache. This can be useful to prevent loss of memory bandwidth for subsequent access. Also, with PIO it is easy to integrate other functions, such as checksums, without requiring adaptor hardware to do the same function.

However, some studies have shown that if data arrives and is used much later (e.g., one scheduling quantum later) by the application, then placing data in the D-cache too early is wasteful of the D-cache and lowers rather than raises D-cache hit rate. On the other hand, DMA can steal cycles from the CPU and also requires some careful cache invalidation when data is written into a memory location (that could also be cached). So the jury is still out. The choice between the two is best decided on a case-by-case basis, taking into account architectural considerations and the application at hand. A more detailed study of the issues involved can be found in Mogul and Ramakrishnan (1997).

5.7 Conclusions

As networks get faster, links today, such as Gigabit Ethernet, are often faster than the buses and memories within desktop computers and servers. Thus memory and bus bandwidth are crucial resources. This chapter describes techniques to optimize the use of memory and bus bandwidth for processing IP and Web packets, the dominant traffic streams found today on the Internet.

To this end, the chapter started by showing how to remove redundant copies involved in processing an IP packet using adaptor memory or VM remapping. We then showed how to remove redundant copies involved in processing Web requests at a server by generalizing VM remapping to include the file system or by combining file system and network I/O in a single system call. We then showed how to combine various data manipulations in one fell swoop. All of these techniques require changes to the application and kernel, but the changes are fairly localized and mostly preserve modularity.

It is important to state that all the performance problems involved in building a modern Web server have not been eliminated. Complex Web sites, such as amazon.com, often use several tiers of processing to respond to Web requests, including an application server, a Web server, and a database server. Such database-driven Web servers introduce new bottlenecks that may require new techniques beyond those described in this chapter. However, the underlying principles should hopefully remain the same.

Table 5.1 presents a summary of the techniques used in this chapter, together with the major principles involved. In terms of principles this chapter is about the repeated use of **P1**, avoiding obvious waste, where the waste is unnecessary reads and writes that consume precious memory and bus bandwidth. At first glance, principle **P1** seems vacuous or at best a cliché. What makes this principle deeper is that the waste is not apparent unless one broadens one's vision to see as much of the system as possible.

Within each local subsystem (e.g., application to kernel, kernel to network, disk to file system) there is no wasted memory bandwidth. It is only when one follows the adventures of a received packet that one discovers the redundancy between application-to-kernel and kernel-to-network copies. It is only when one broadens one's view even further to see the contortions involved in responding to a Web request that one notices the further redundancies involving the file system. Only when one broadens one's view further still does one see all the manipulations involved in processing a packet and the wasted reads to memory. Finally, it is only when one examines the loading of instructions that one sees the alarming possibility that the protocol code can be several times larger than the packet size.

Thus the use of the first principle of network algorithmics requires a synoptic eye, one that sees the whole system, from HTTP and its headers, to the file system, and down to the instruction caches. While this seems daunting in complexity, Chapter 2 has already argued that simple models of hardware, architecture, operating systems, and protocols can make such a holistic viewpoint possible. For example, I-caches have a number of complex variants, but a simple model of a direct-mapped I-cache with multiple instructions per block is not hard for an operating system designer to keep in mind.

Finally, compared to the beauty and complexity of theoretical techniques such as the ellipsoid algorithm for linear programming and the theory of rapidly mixing Markov chains, techniques in systems such as copy avoidance seem drab and shallow. However, one can argue that the complexity of systems is not in *depth* (i.e., the complexity of each component by itself) but in *breadth* (i.e., the complex relationships between components). Perhaps the breadth of understanding (HTTP, file system, networking code, instruction cache implementation) required to optimize memory bandwidth in a Web server provides some evidence for this thesis.

5.8 Exercises

1. **Data caches and copies:** A normal data cache is a mapping from a memory location address to a piece of content. If the content is frequently accessed, then the content can be accessed directly from the fast cache instead of making a memory access. Assuming the cache is a write-back cache, even writes can be written to the cache instead of memory and only written to memory when the cache is overwritten. A modern cache block is fairly large (128 bits), with a mapping from a 32-bit address to 128 bits of data starting at that address.

   We want to address the copying problem where various modules (including the network and file system) copy data via intermediate buffers that are soon overwritten (e.g., socket buffer, application buffer). The chapter did so with software changes. Here we consider whether changing the hardware architecture can help *without software changes* such as IO-Lite, fbufs, and mmap.

   - Even an ordinary data cache may help remove some of the overhead when copying data from location L to location M. Explain why. (Assume that location M is a temporary buffer that is soon overwritten, as in a socket buffer. Assume that if only a single word is written in a large cache block, the remaining words can be marked invalid.) Intuitively, this problem is asking whether there is an equivalent of COW (used to reduce copying between virtual address spaces) in the world of data caches.
   - Now assume a different data cache design, where a cache is a mapping from *one or more* addresses to the same content. Thus a cache has changed from a one-to-one mapping to a many-to-one mapping. For example, assume a cache where two locations can point to the same content. Thus a cache entry may be (L, M, C), where L and M are addresses and C is the common con-

tents of L and M. A memory access to *either* L or M will return C. What is the advantage over the previous scheme in the previous item?

- This is all very speculative and wild. Comment on the disadvantages of the idea in the previous item. In particular, many caches use a technique called *set associativity*, where a simple hash function (e.g., low-order bits) is used to select a small set of cache entries that the hardware searches in parallel. Why might the multiple address per cache entry interact poorly with the set associative search?

2. **Application-level optimizations for Web servers:** Operating systems such as the Exokernel (Engler et al., 1995) take an even more extreme viewpoint and allow the application to customize kernel features for its benefit without compromising safety for other applications. One interesting optimization is to combine the final TCP FIN with the read of the last data segment (an optimization allowed by TCP).

- Why does this optimization help small Web transfers (which are quite common)?
- Why is this optimization hard to do in a regular Web server, and why is it easier if the application is integrated with the kernel, as in the Exokernel?
- Explain how this optimization can be migrated to an ordinary Web server by passing information across the interface (**P9**) without compromising safety.

3. **Reverse copyout:** The emulated COW paper (Brustoloni and Steenkiste, 1996) describes an interesting degree of freedom (**P13**) for copying page-aligned data between two modules (say, system and application). Imagine that you wish to copy a *partial* page from an application page, X, to a system page, Y. If the page is full, assume that you can swap the two pages efficiently. Assume the partial page has useful data D and some remainder R.

- If the amount of data D is small compared to R, it is simpler to copy D to the destination page in Y. On the other hand, if D is large (say, almost all of the page) compared to R, devise a simple strategy to minimize copying. Note that if the destination page, Y, has some other data in the remainder of the page, that data must remain after the copy.
- What is a simple threshold you would use to choose between these two strategies?

Transferring control

Control thy passions, lest they take vengeance on thee.
—**Epictetus**

In a Scott Adams cartoon Dilbert complains to Dogbert that he is embarrassed to work at a company where even paying a simple invoice takes 6 months. The invoice first comes into the mail room for aging, spends some time at the secretary's desk, goes to the desk of the main decision maker, and finally ends up in accounts payable. When processing an invoice in Dilbert's company, the flow of control works its way through layers of command, each of which incurs significant overhead.

A management consultant might suggest that Dilbert's company streamline the processing of an invoice by eliminating mediating layers wherever possible and by making each layer as responsive as possible. However, each layer has some reason for existence. The mailroom aggregates mail delivery service for all departments in the company. The secretary protects the busy boss from interrupts and weeds out inappropriate requests. The boss must eventually decide whether the invoice is worth paying. Finally, the mundane details of disbursing cash are best left to accounts payable.

A modern CPU processing a network message also goes through similar layers of mediation. The device, for example, an Ethernet adaptor, interrupts the CPU, asking somewhat stridently for attention. Control is passed to the kernel. The kernel batches interrupt wherever possible, does the network layer processing for the packet, and finally schedule the application process (say, a Web server) to run. As always, the reception of a single packet provides too limited a picture of the overall processing context. For instance, a Web server will parse the request (such as a GET) in the network packet, look for the file, and institute proceedings to retrieve the file from disk. When the file gets read into memory, a response containing the requested file is sent back, prepended with an HTTP header.

While Chapter 5 concentrated on reducing the overhead of operations that touch the *data* in a packet (e.g., copying, checksumming), this chapter concentrates on reducing the *control* overheads involved in processing a packet. As in Chapter 5, we start by examining the control overheads involved in sending or receiving a packet. We then broaden to our canonical network application, a Web server.

As we said in the introduction to Chapter 5, there have been changes in the underlying technologies, but not the principles, since the first edition. The most relevant for the purposes of reducing control overheads are as follows. First, as described in Chapter 5 multicore CPUs are the norm. However, the issue that concerns us more in this chapter is *affinity*. How do modern CPUs make sure that that network processing occurs in the same CPU (or on CPUs that share the same L3 cache) that runs the application? We describe packet steering mechanisms to affinitize packet processing.

Second, hypervisors and virtual switches are standard in data centers to improve server utilization. This adds another layer of control overhead. Thus, new solutions like SRIOV (2018) (Single Root I/O Virtualization, see later for details) have emerged to bypass these overheads. Third, in the first edition, the major industry standard for kernel bypass to avoid system calls was called VIA (Buonadonna et al., 2002). VIA has largely been subsumed by a new standard called DPDK (2018) (Data Plane Development Kit) that we describe at the end of Section 6.5.

Fourth, warehouse scale computing (Barroso et al., 2017) has become the de facto standard for processing user requests in clouds like Amazon, Azure, and Google. In response to the slowing down of Moore's Law, such clouds often serve a request (e.g., a Search or Shopping request) by farming out a query to thousands of servers and collecting the response. Since the response is gated by the response of the slowest server, there is a new focus on the *tail latency* of requests, seeking to reduce this latency to microseconds. Further, compared to High Performance Computing (Barroso et al., 2017), warehouse scale computing is less interested in merely higher performance, but in the highest performance *per dollar*. Thus, dedicating cores to a networking function may be unacceptable in the interests of maximizing resource utilization (Marty et al., 2019).

We are grateful to Amy Ousterhout, Jeff Mogul, and Sylvia Ratnasamy for pointers to recent work; any errors or omissions, of course, are completely our responsibility.

This chapter is organized as follows. Section 6.1 starts by describing the control flow costs involved in a computer: interrupt overheads (involved when a device asks asynchronously for attention), system calls (involved when a user asks the kernel for service, thus moving the flow of control across a protection boundary), and process-context switching (allowing a new process to run when the current process is stymied waiting for some resource or has run too long). Thus the rest of this chapter is organized around reducing these control overhead costs, from the largest (context switching) to the smallest (interrupt overhead).

Accordingly, Section 6.2 concentrates on reducing process-context switching by describing how to structure *networking* code (e.g., TCP/IP) to avoid context switching. Section 6.3 then describes how to structure *application code* (e.g., a Web server) to reduce context-switching costs. Sections 6.4 and 6.5 focus on reducing or eliminating system call overhead. Section 6.4 shows how to reduce overhead in the implementation of a crucial system call used by event-driven Web servers to decide which of the connections they are handling are ready to be serviced. Section 6.5 goes further and describes user-level networking that bypasses the kernel in the common case of sending and receiving a packet. Section 6.6 describes more recent and forward looking research in fundamentally restructuring operating systems to reduce network control overhead. Finally, Section 6.7 briefly describes simple ideas to avoid interrupt overhead.

The techniques described in this chapter (and the corresponding principles invoked) are summarized in Table 6.1.

Quick reference guide

The most useful sections for an implementor today are as follows. Section 6.3 describes how to structure *application code* (e.g., a Web server) to reduce context-switching costs, presenting alternatives to event-driven Web servers. Section 6.4 focuses on reducing the overhead of the select() system call (or similar calls in other operating systems) used by event-driven servers to decide which client to service next, and the use of the epoll() systems call in Linux. Section 6.5 shows how to eliminate system call overhead using techniques such as DPDK (Data Plane Development Kit) and SRIOV (Single Root I/O Virtualization). Section 6.6 describes radical restructuring of operating systems towards reducing network control overheads. Section 6.7 describes NAPI polling in Linux to prevent receive livelock.

Table 6.1 Techniques for reducing control overhead that are discussed in this chapter, together with the corresponding principles.

Number	Principle	Used in
P8	Go beyond downcalls used in specifications	Upcalls
P8	Process per message, not per layer	x-Kernel
P13	Link protocol implementation with user code	Mach variants
P13	Process per disk access	Flash
P13	Modularize by task, not clients	Haboob Web server
P4	VM mapping to avoid copies in cache and application	Flash
P15	Bitmap tree	Fast ufalloc()
P12a	Incrementally compute interest vector	Fast select()
P9	Pass hints from protocol to select ()	
P12	Remember interest across calls	
P3c	Move protection from kernel to adaptor	ADCs
P2	Have kernel authorize adaptor on initialization	
P13	Batch process interrupts	Most OSs
P2b	Execute protocol in the context of the receive process	LRP (lazy receiver processing)

6.1 Why control overhead?

Chapter 5 started with a review of the *copying* overhead involved in a Web server by showing the potential copies (Fig. 5.1) involved in responding to a GET request at a server. By contrast, Fig. 6.1 shows the potential *control* overhead involved in a large Web server that handles many clients. Note that in comparison with Fig. 5.1 for Web copies, Fig. 6.1 ignores all aspects of data transfer. Thus Fig. 6.1 uses a simplified architectural picture that concentrates on the control interplay between the network adaptor and the CPU (via interrupts), between the application and the kernel (via system calls), and between various application-level processes or threads (via scheduler invocations). The reader unfamiliar with operating systems may wish to consult the review of operating systems in Chapter 2. For simplicity, the picture shows only one CPU in the server (many servers are multiprocessors) and a single disk (some servers use multiple disks and disks with multiple heads). Assume that the server can handle a large number (say, thousands) of concurrent clients.

For the purposes of understanding the possible control overhead involved in serving a GET request, the relevant aspects of the story are slightly different from that in Chapter 5. First, assume the client has sent a TCP SYN request to the server that arrives at the adaptor from which it is placed in memory. The kernel is then informed of this arrival via an *interrupt*. The kernel notifies the Web server via the unblocking of an earlier *system call*; the Web server application will accept this connection if it has sufficient resources.

In the second step of processing some server process parses the Web request. For example, assume the request is GET File 1. In the third step the server needs to locate where the file is on disk, for example, by navigating directory structures that may also be stored on disk. Once the file is located, in the fourth step, the server process initiates a Read to the file system (another system call). If the file is in the file cache, the read request can be satisfied quickly; failing a cache hit, the file subsystem initiates

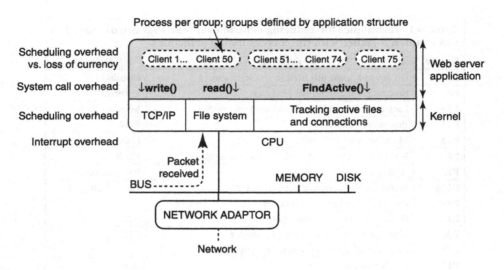

FIGURE 6.1

Control overhead involved in handling a GET request at a server.

a disk seek to read the data from disk. Finally, after the file is in an application buffer, the server sends out the HTTP response by writing to the corresponding connection (another system call).

So far the only control overhead appears to be that of system calls and interrupts. However, that is because we have not examined closely the structure of the networking and application code.

First, if the networking code is structured naively, with a single process per layer in the stack, then the process scheduling overhead (on the order of hundreds of microseconds) for processing a packet can easily be much larger than a single packet arrival time. This potential scheduling overhead is shown in Fig. 6.1 with a dashed line to the TCP/IP code in the kernel. Fortunately, most networking code is structured more monolithically, with minimal control overhead, although there are some clever techniques that can do even better.

Second, our description of Web processing has focused on a single client. Since we are assuming a large Web server that is working concurrently on behalf of thousands of clients, it is unclear how the Web server should be structured. At one extreme, if each client is a separate process (or thread) running the Web server code, *concurrency* is maximized (because when client 1 is waiting for a disk read, client 2 could be sending out network packets) at the cost of high *process scheduling* overhead.

On the other hand, if all clients are handled by a single event-driven process, then context-switching overhead is minimized, but the single process must internally schedule the clients to maximize concurrency. In particular, it must know when file reads have completed and when network data has arrived.

Many operating systems provide a *system call* for this purpose that we have generically called **FindActive()** in Fig. 6.1. For example, in UNIX the specific name for this generic routine is the *select()* system call. While even an empty system call is expensive because of the kernel-to-application boundary crossing, an inefficient *select()* implementation can be even more expensive.

Thus there are challenging questions as to how to structure both the networking and server code in order to minimize scheduling overhead and maximize concurrency. For this reason, Fig. 6.1 shows the clients partitioned into groups, each of which is implemented in a single process or thread. Note that placing all clients in a single group yields the event-driven approach, while placing each client in a separate group yields the process-per-client (or thread-per-client) approach.

Thus an unoptimized implementation can incur considerable process-switching overhead (hundreds of microseconds) if the application and networking code is poorly structured. Even if process-structuring overhead is removed, system calls can cost tens of microseconds, and interrupts can cost microseconds. To put these numbers in perspective, observe that on a 100-Gbps Ethernet link, a 40-byte packet can arrive at a PC every 3.2 nanoseconds.

Given that 100-Gbps links have already arrived, it is clear that careful attention has to be paid to control overhead. Note that as we have seen in Chapter 2, as CPUs get faster, historically the control overheads associated with context switching, system calls, and interrupts have not improved at the same rate. Some progress has been made with more efficient operating systems such as Linux, but the progress will not be sufficient to keep up with increasing link speeds.

We now begin attacking the bottlenecks described in Fig. 6.1.

6.2 Avoiding scheduling overhead in networking code

One of the major difficulties with implementing a protocol is to balance modularity (so you implement a big system in pieces and get each piece right, independent of the others) and performance (so you can get the overall system to perform well). As a simple example, consider how one might implement a networking stack. The "obvious modularity" would be to implement the transport protocol (e.g., TCP) as a process, the routing protocol (e.g., IP) as a process, and the applications as a separate process. If that were the case, however, every received packet would take at least two process-context switches, which are expensive. There are, however, a number of creative alternatives that allow modularity as well as efficiency. These were first pointed out by Dave Clark in a series of papers.

Fig. 6.2 provides an example that Clark (1985) used to illustrate his ideas. It consists of a simple application that reads data from a keyboard and sends it to the network using a reliable transport protocol. When the data is received by some receiver on the network, the data is displayed on the screen. The vertical slices show the various protocol layers, with the topmost slice (routines such as display-get-data and display-receive) being the application protocol, the second slice (routines such as transport-receive and transport-send) being the transport protocol, and the bottom slice (routines such as net-receive and net-dispatch) being the network protocol. The naive way to implement this protocol would be to have a process per slice, which would involve three processes and two full-scale context switches per received or sent packet.

Instead, Clark suggests using only two processes, each at the sender and two processes at the receiver (shown as boxed vertical sections), to implement the network protocol stack. In Fig. 6.2 the leftmost two sections correspond to receiver processes and the rightmost two sections correspond to sender processes. Thus the sender has a Keyboard Handler process that gathers data coming in from the keyboard and calls *transport-arm-to-send* when it has got some data. Notice that *transport-arm-to-send* is a transport-layer function that is exported to the Keyboard Handler process and is executed by the Keyboard Handler process. At this point the Keyboard Handler can suspend itself (a context switch). *Transport-arm-to-send* only tells the transport protocol that this connection wishes to send data; it does not transfer data.

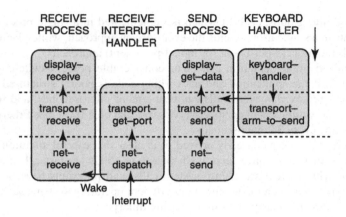

FIGURE 6.2

Implementing a protocol using upcalls.

However, the transport-send process may not send data immediately because of flow control limitations. When the flow control limits are removed (because of acks arriving), the Send Process will execute the *transport-send* routine for this connection. The *send* call will first upcall the application protocol, which exports a routine called *display-get-data* that actually provides the transport protocol with the data for the application. This is advantageous because the application may have received more keyboard data by the time the transport protocol is ready to send, and one might as well send as much data as possible in a packet. Finally, within the context of the same process, transport adds a transport-layer header and makes a call to the network protocol to actually send the packet.

At the receiving end, the packet is received by the receive interrupt handler using a network-layer routine called *net-dispatch* that needs to find which process to dispatch the received packet to. To find out, *net-dispatch* makes an upcall to transport-get-port. This is a routine exported by the transport layer that looks at port numbers in the header to figure out which application (e.g., FTP) must handle the packet. Then a context switch is made and the Receive Handler relinquishes control and wakes up the Receive Process, which executes network-layer functions, transport-layer functions, and finally the application-level code to display the data. Note that a single process is executing all the layers of protocol.

The idea was a bit unusual at the time because the conventional dogma until that point was that layers should only use services of layers below; thus calls between layers had, historically, been "downcalls." However, Clark pointed out that downcalls were perhaps required for protocol *specifications* but were not the only alternative for protocol *implementations*. In our example in particular, upcalls are used to obtain data (e.g., the upcall to *display-get-data*) and for advice from upper layers (upcall to *transport-get-port*).

While upcalls are commonly used in real implementations, there is probably no difference between an upcall and a standard procedure call except for its possible novelty in the context of a networking layered implementation. However, the more important idea, which is perhaps more lasting, is the idea of using only one or two processes to process a message, each process consisting of routines from two or more protocol layers. This idea found its way into systems like the x-kernel (Hutchinson and Peterson, 1991) and into user-level networking, which is described in the next section.

More generally, the idea of considering alternative implementation structures that preserve modularity without sacrificing performance is a classic example of Principle **P8**, which says that implementors should consider alternatives to reference implementations described in specifications. Notice that each protocol layer can still be implemented modularly but the upcalled routines can be registered by upper layers when the system starts up.

6.2.1 Making user-level protocol implementations real

Most modern machines certainly do not implement each protocol layer in a separate process. Instead, in UNIX or Linux, all the protocol code (transport, network, and data link) is handled as part of a single kernel "process" or a more lightweight process called a "thread". When a packet arrives via an interrupt, the interrupt handler notes the arrival of the packet, possibly queues it to memory, and then schedules a kernel thread (via what is sometimes called a *software interrupt*) to actually process the packet.

The kernel thread does the data link, network, and transport-layer code (using upcalls); by looking at the transport port numbers, the kernel process knows the application. It then wakes up the application. Thus every packet is processed using at least two context switches: one from the interrupt context to the kernel process doing protocol handling, and one from the kernel thread to the thread running the application code (e.g., the Web, FTP).

The idea behind user-level protocol implementation is to realize the aspect of Clark's idea shown in the receive process of Fig. 6.2, where the protocol handlers execute in the same process as the application and can communicate using upcalls. User-level implementations have two possible advantages: We can potentially bypass the kernel and go directly from the interrupt handler to the application, as in the Clark model, saving a context switch. Also, the protocol code can be written and debugged in user space, which is a far friendlier place to implement protocols (debugging tools work in user space and do not work well at all in the kernel).

One extreme way to do this was advocated in Mach, where all protocols were implemented in user space. Also, protocols were allowed to be significantly more general than in Clark's example of Fig. 6.2. Thus when a receiving interrupt handler received a packet, it had no way of easily telling to which process it should dispatch the packet (since the network-layer implementations done in the final process contained the demultiplexing code). In particular, one can't just call transport to examine the port number (as in Clark's example) since we can have lots of possible transport protocols and lots of possible network protocols.

A naive method was initially used, as shown in Fig. 6.3. This involved a separate demultiplexing process that received all packets and examined them to determine the final destination process, which they are then dispatched to. The naive method was quite inefficient years ago; it is less so now with multicore machines as we will see in the structuring of Google's Snap (Marty et al., 2019) system described later in this chapter. The inefficiency arises because context switches were expensive, and the new demultiplexing process actually adds back the missing context switch.

The simple idea used to remedy this situation is to pass extra information (**P9**) across the application–kernel interface so that each application can pass information about what kinds of packets it wants to process. This is shown in Fig. 6.4. For example, a mail application may wish for all packets whose Ethernet-type field is IP, whose IP number specifies TCP and whose TCP destination port number is 25.

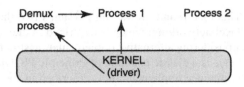

FIGURE 6.3

Demultiplexing a packet to the final destination process using an intermediate demultiplexing process is expensive.

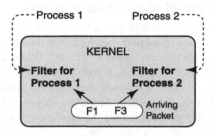

FIGURE 6.4

The packet filter approach to demultiplexing.

Recall that we are talking about the mail application implementing all of IP, TCP, and mail. To do so, the kernel defines an interface, which is typically some form of programming language. For example, the earliest one was the CSPF (CMU Stanford packet filter), which specifies the fields for packets using a stack-based programming language. A more commonly used language is BPF (Berkeley packet filter), which uses a stack-based language; a more efficient language is Pathfinder. These demultiplexing algorithms are described in Chapter 8.

Note that one has to be careful about passing information from an application to a kernel; any such information should be checked so that malicious or wrong applications cannot destroy the kernel. In particular, one has to prevent applications from providing arbitrary code to kernels, which then causes havoc. Fortunately, there are software technologies that can "sandbox" foreign code so that it can do damage only within its own allotted space of memory (its sandbox). For example, a stack-based language can be made to work on a specified size of stack that can be bounds checked at every point. This form of technology has culminated recently in execution of arbitrary Java applets received from the network.

Clearly, if packets are dispatched from the kernel interrupt handler (using the collection of packet filters) to the receiving process, the receiving process should implement the protocol stack. However, replicating the TCP/IP code in every application would cause a lot of code redundancy. Thus TCP/IP is generally (in such systems) implemented as a shared library that is linked in (a single copy is used to which the application has a pointer, but with the code written in a so-called *reentrant* way, to allow reuse).

This is not as easy as it looks because there is some TCP state that is common to all connections, though most are TCP state connection specific. There are other problems because the last write done by an application should be retransmitted by TCP, but the application may exit its process after its last write. However, these problems can be fixed. User-level implementations have been written (Maeda and Bershad, 1993; Thekkath et al., 1993) to provide excellent performance. Fundamentally, they exploit a degree of freedom (**P13**) in observing that protocols do not have to be implemented in the kernel.

6.3 Avoiding context-switching overhead in applications

The last section concentrated on removing process-scheduling overhead for processing a single packet received by the network by effectively limiting the processing to fielding one interrupt (which, as we discuss in Section 6.7, can also be removed or amortized over several packets) and dispatching the packet to the final process in which the application (that processes the packet) resides. If the destination process is currently running, then there is even no process-scheduling overhead. Thus after all optimizations there can be close to no control overhead for processing a packet.

This is analogous to Chapter 5, in which the first few sections showed how to process a received packet with zero copies. However, in that chapter after broadening one's viewpoint to see the complete application processing, it became apparent that there were further redundant copies caused by interactions with the file system.

In a similar fashion this section broadens beyond the processing of a single packet to consider how an application processes packets. Once again, as in Chapter 5, we consider a Web server (Fig. 6.1) because it is a canonical example of a server that needs to be made more efficient and because of its importance in practice.

In what follows, we will use a Web server as an example of a canonical server that may require the handling of a large number of connections. In another example Barile (2004) describes a TCP-to-UDP proxy server for a telephony server that can handle 100,000 concurrent connections.

How should a Web server be structured? Before tackling this question, it helps to understand the potential concurrency within a single Web server. Readers familiar with operating systems may wish to skim over the next three paragraphs. These are included for readers not as familiar with the secret life of a workstation.[1]

Even with a single CPU and a single disk head, there are opportunities for concurrency. For example, assume that in processing a read for File 1, File 1 is not in cache. Thus the CPU initiates a disk read. Since this may take a few milliseconds to complete, and the CPU can do an instruction almost every nanosecond, it is obvious waste to idle the CPU during this read. Thus a more sensible strategy is to have the CPU switch to processing another client while Client 1's disk read is in progress. This allows processing by the disk on behalf of Client 1 to be overlapped with processing by the CPU for Client 2.

A second example of concurrency between the CPU and a device (that is relevant to a Web server) is overlapping between network I/O (as performed by the adaptor) and the CPU. For example, after a server accepts a connection, it may do a Read to an accepted connection for Client 1. If the CPU waits for the Read to complete it may wait a long time, potentially also several milliseconds. This is

---

[1] Recall that the intent of network algorithmics and of this book is to allow all constituencies, for example, hardware designers, to understand the relevant issues.

because the remote client has to send a packet that has to make its way through the network and finally be written by the adaptor to the socket corresponding to Client 1 at the server.

By switching to another client, processing by the network on behalf of Client 1 is overlapped with processing by the CPU on behalf of some other client. Similarly, when doing a Write to the network, the Write may be blocked because of the lack of buffer space in the socket buffer. This buffer space may be released much later when acknowledgments arrive from the destination.

The last three paragraphs show that for a Web server to be efficient, every opportunity for concurrency must be exploited to increase effective throughput. Thus a CPU in a Web server must switch between clients when one client is blocked waiting for I/O. We now consider various ways to structure a server application and their effects on concurrency and scheduling overhead.

6.3.1 Process per client

In terms of programming, the simplest way to implement a Web server is to structure the processing of each client as a separate process. In other words, every client is in a separate group by itself in Fig. 6.1. In Chapter 2 we saw that the operating system scheduler juggles between processes, assigning a new process to a CPU when a current process is blocked. Most modern operating systems also can take into account multiple CPUs and schedule the CPUs such that all CPUs are doing useful work wherever possible.

Thus the Web server application need not do the juggling between clients; the *operating system* does this automatically on the application's behalf. For example, when Client 1 is blocked waiting for the disk controller, the operating system may save all the context for the Client 1 process to memory and allow the Client 2 process to run by restoring its context from memory.

This simplicity, however, comes at a cost. First, as we have seen, process-context switching and restoring is expensive. It requires reads and writes from memory to registers to save and restore context. Recall that the context includes changing the page tables being used (because page tables are per process); thus any virtual memory translations cached within the TLB (translation lookaside buffer) need to be cached. Similarly, the contents of the data cache and the instruction cache are likely to represent the tastes and preferences of the previously resident process; thus much of it may be useless to the new process. When all caches fail, the initial performance of the switched-in process can be very poor.

Further, spawning a new process when a new client comes in, as was done by some initial Web servers, is also expensive.[2] Fortunately, the overhead to create and destroy processes when clients come and go can be avoided by precomputation and/or lazy process deletion (**P2**, shifting computation in time). When a client finishes its request processing and the connection is terminated, rather than destroy the process, the process can be returned to a pool of idle processes. The process can then be assigned to the next new client that needs a process to shepherd its request through the server.

A second issue is the problem of matchmaking between new arriving clients and processes in the process pool. A naive way to do this is as follows. Each new client is handed to a well-known matchmaking process, which then hands off each new client to some available process in the pool. However, operating system designers have realized the importance of matchmaking. They have invented system

---

[2] While some of these early schemes may seem primitive in terms of the techniques in this book, they were probably very simple to program and maintain. It is difficult to quantify the trade-off between efficiency and ease of implementation and maintenance.

calls (for instance, the *Accept* call in UNIX) to do matchmaking at the cost of a system call invocation, as opposed to requiring a process-context switch.

When a process in the pool is done, it makes an *Accept* call and waits in line in a kernel data structure. When a new client comes in, its socket is handed off to the idle process that is first in line. Thus the kernel provides matchmaking services directly.

6.3.2 Thread per client

Even after removing the overheads of creating a process on demand and the overhead of matchmaking, processes are an expensive solution. Since the rate of arrivals to popular Web servers can easily exceed 10 Gbps, it is not unusual for a Web server to have 50000 concurrent clients citegooglecarousel being served at once.

As we have seen, even if the processes are already created, switching between processes incurs TLB and cache misses and requires effort to save and restore context. Further, each process requires memory to store context. This can take away from the memory needed by the file cache.

An intermediate stance is to use threads or lightweight processes. Note that threads generally trust each other, as is appropriate for all the threads processing different clients in a Web server. Thus in Fig. 6.5 we can replace the processing of each client with a separate thread per client, all within the protection of a single process. Note that the threads share the same virtual memory. Thus TLB entries do not have to be flushed between threads.

Further, the fact that threads can share memory implies that all threads can use a common cache to share file name translations and even files. Implementing a process per client, on the other hand, implies that file caches can often not be shared efficiently across processes, because each process uses a separate virtual memory space. Thus application caches for Web servers, as described in Chapter 5, will suffer in performance because files common to many clients are replicated.[3] Thus a classic Web server, the Apache Web server, was implemented using a thread per client in Windows.

However, when all is said and done, the overhead for switching between threads, while smaller than that for switching between processes, is still considerable. Fundamentally, the operating system must still save and restore per-thread context such as stacks and registers. Also, the memory required to store per-thread or per-process state takes away from the file cache, which then leads to potentially higher miss rates.

6.3.3 Event-driven scheduler

If a general-purpose operating system facility is too expensive, the simplest strategy is to avoid it completely. Thus while thread scheduling provides a facility for juggling between clients without further programming, if it is too expensive, the application may benefit from *doing the juggling itself*. Effectively, the application must implement its own internal scheduler that juggles the state of each client.

For example, the application may have to implement a state machine that remembers that Client 1 is in Stage 2 (HTTP processing) while Client 2 is in Stage 3 (waiting for disk I/O) and Client 3 is in Stage 4 (waiting for a socket buffer to clear up to send the next part of the response).

---

[3] However, this replication will not cost much *if* a system such as I/O-Lite, described in Chapter 5, is used. The problem is that historically many operating systems did not have such mechanisms to allow subsystems to share data.

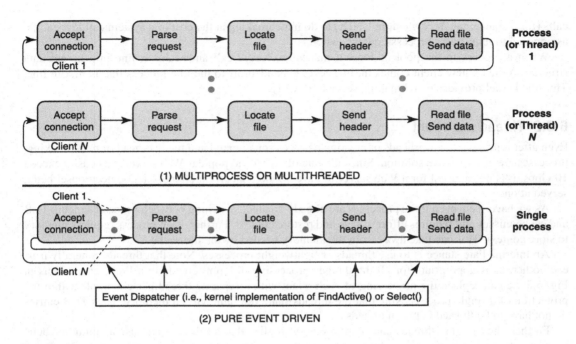

FIGURE 6.5

The two simplest alternatives for structuring a Web server: (1) the use of a single process (or thread) per client; (2) a single process implementation that uses an event manager to tell the process of the status of I/O for each client.

However, the kernel has an advantage over an application program because the kernel sees all I/O completion events. For example, if Client 1 is blocked waiting for I/O, in a per-thread implementation, when the disk controller interrupts the CPU to say that the data is now in memory, the kernel can now attempt to schedule the Client 1 thread.

Thus if the Web server application is to do its own scheduling between clients, the kernel must pass information (**P9**) across the API to allow a single-threaded application to view the completion of all I/O that it has initiated. Many operating systems provide such a facility, which we generically called *FindActive()* in Fig. 6.1. For example, Windows NT 3.5 has an I/O completion port (IOCP) mechanism, UNIX provides the *select()* system call, Linux provides the *epoll()* system call.

The main idea is that the application stays in a loop invoking the *FindActive()* call. Assuming there is always some work to do on behalf of some client, the call will return with a list of I/O descriptors (e.g., file 1 data is now in memory, connection 5 has received data) with pending work. When the Web server processes these active descriptors, it loops back to making another *FindActive()* call.

If there is always some client that needs attention (typically true for a busy server), there is no need to sleep and invoke the costs of context switching (e.g., scheduler overhead, TLB misses) when juggling between clients. Of course, such juggling requires that the application keeps a state machine that allows it to do its own context switching among the many concurrent requests. Such application-specific internal scheduling is more efficient than invoking the general-purpose, external scheduler. This is because the application knows the minimum set of context that must be saved when moving from client to client.

The Zeus server and the original Harvest/Squid proxy cache server use the single-process event-driven model. Fig. 6.5 contrasts the multiprocess (and multithreaded) server architectures with an event-driven architecture. The details of a generic event-driven implementation using a single process can be found in Barile (2004), together with pointers to source code. Barile (2004) describes generic code that is abstracted to work across platforms (a crucial requirement for today's server environments), including Windows and UNIX.

6.3.4 Event-driven server with helper processes

In principle, an event-driven server can extract as much concurrency from a stream of client operations as a multiprocess or multithreaded server. Unfortunately, many operating systems, such as UNIX, do not provide suitable support for nonblocking disk operations.

For example, if an event-driven server is not to waste opportunities to do useful work, then when it issues a *read()* to a file that is not in cache, we wish the *read()* to return immediately saying it is unavailable so that the *read()* is nonblocking. This allows the server to move on to other clients. Later, when the disk I/O completes, the application can find out using the next invocation of the *FindActive()* call. On the other hand, if the *read()* call is blocking, then the server main loop would be stuck waiting for the milliseconds required for disk I/O to complete.

The difficulty is that many operating systems, such as Solaris and UNIX, allow nonblocking *read()* and *write()* operations on network connections but may block when used on disk files. These operating systems do allow other asynchronous system calls for disk I/O, but these are not integrated with the *select()* call (i.e., the UNIX equivalent of *FindActive()*). Thus in such operating systems one must choose between the loss of concurrency incurred by blocking on disk I/O and going beyond the single-process model.

The Flash Web server (Pai et al., 1999a) goes beyond the single-process model to maximize concurrency. When a file is to be read, the main server process first tests if the file is already in memory using either a standard system call[4] or by locking down the file cache pages so that the server process always knows which files are in the cache.[5] If the file is not in memory, the main server process instructs a helper process to perform the potentially blocking disk read. When the helper is done, it communicates to the main server process via some form of interprocess communication such as a pipe.

Note that unlike the multiprocess model, helpers are needed only for each concurrent disk operation and not for each concurrent client request. In some sense, this model exploits a degree of freedom (**P13**) by observing that there are interesting alternatives between a single process and a process per client.

Besides file reads, helper processes can also be used to do directory lookups to locate the file on disk. While Flash maintains a cache that maps between directory path names and disk files, if there is a cache miss, then there is a need to search through on-disk directory structures. Since such directory lookups can also block, these are also relegated to helper processes. Increasing the pathname cache

---

[4] The original Flash Web server uses UNIX's *mincore()* command.
[5] If the virtual memory system could swap out cached files under the nose of the server, the server may think a file is in cache when it really is not.

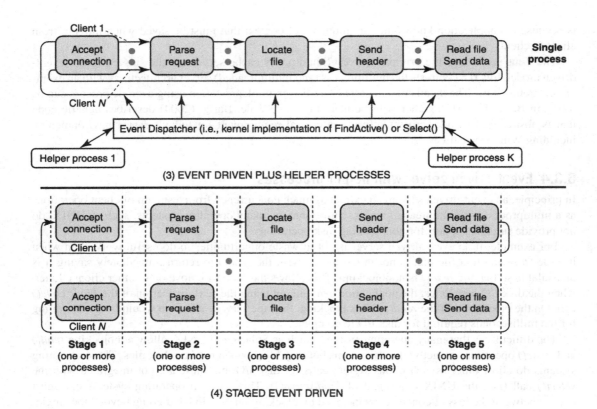

FIGURE 6.6

Two other proposals for Web architectures besides the two shown in Fig. 6.5: (3) event-driven plus helper processes; (4) staged event-driven architecture.

does increase memory consumption, but the reduced cache miss rate may reduce the number of helper processes required and so decrease memory overall.

Clearly, helper processes should be prespawned to avoid the latency of creating a process each time a helper process is invoked. How many helper processes should be spawned? Too few can cause concurrency loss, and too many results in wasted memory. The solution in Flash (Pai et al., 1999a) is to dynamically spawn and destroy helper processes according to load.

6.3.5 Task-based structuring

The top of Fig. 6.6 depicts the event-driven approach augmented with helper processes. Notice the similarity to the simple event-handler approach shown at the bottom of Fig. 6.5, except for the addition of helper processes.

There are some problems with the event-driven architecture with helper processes.

- **Complexity:** The application designer must manage the state machine for juggling client requests without help.
- **Modularity:** The code for the server is written as one piece. While Web servers are popular, there are many other Web services that may use some similar pieces of code (e.g., for accepting connections). A more modular approach could allow code reuse.
- **Overload control:** Production Web servers have to deal with wide variations of load from huge client populations. Thus it is crucial to continue to make some progress during overload (without thrashing) and to be as fair as possible across clients.

The main idea in the staged event-driven architecture (Welsh et al., 2001) is to exploit another degree of freedom (**P13**) in decomposing code. Instead of decomposing into threads *horizontally* by client, as in a multithreaded architecture, the server system is decomposed *vertically* by tasks within each client request cycle, as shown on the bottom of Fig. 6.5. Each stage can be handled by one or more threads. Thus the staged model can be considered a refinement of the simple event-driven model. This is because it assigns a main thread and a potential thread to each stage of server processing. Once that is done, the stages communicate via queues, and more refined overload control can be done at each stage.

As far as we can determine, event based web servers still rule the roost in most major web servers. Despite the potential advantages of the SEDA model, it has influenced server implementations without being directly used. Part of the reason is that the technology has changed since SEDA was proposed, as threading has become cheaper and multicore machines are standard. A retrospective on SEDA (2010) written ten years after the paper suggests that one advantage of SEDA compared to more standard approaches today is that task queues makes bottlenecks explicit. This allows more surgical and fairer handling of requests during overload conditions.

6.4 Scalable I/O Notification

To motivate the problem, Section 6.4.1 presents a mysterious performance problem found in the literature. Section 6.4.2 then describes the usage and implementation of the *select()* call in UNIX. Section 6.4.3 describes an analysis of the overheads and applies the implementation principles to suggest ideas for improvement. Based on the analysis, Section 6.4.4 describes an improvement, assuming that the API cannot change. Finally, Section 6.4.5 proposes an even better solution that involves a more dramatic change to the API that is reflected in the Linux *epoll()* system call that is commonly used.

6.4.1 A server mystery

The previous section suggested that avoiding process-scheduling overheads was important in a Web server. For example, an event-driven server completely reduces process scheduling overhead by using a single thread for all clients and then using a *FindActive()* call such as *select()*. Now, the CERN Web proxy used a process per client, and the Squid (formerly Harvest) Web server (Chankhunthod et al., 1996) used an event-driven implementation. Measurements done in a LAN (local area network) environment indeed showed (Chankhunthod et al., 1996) that the Squid Web proxy performed an order of magnitude better than the CERN server.

A year later another group repeated these tests in a WAN (i.e., wide area network) environment (Maltzahn et al., 1997) and found that in the WAN environment there was *no difference* in performance between the CERN and Squid servers. The problem is to elucidate this mystery.

The mystery was finally solved by Banga and Mogul (1998). A key observation is that given the same throughput (in terms of connections per second), the higher round-trip delays in a WAN environment lead to a *larger number of concurrent connections* in a WAN setting. For example, in a WAN environment with mean connection times of 2 seconds (Banga et al., 1999) and a Web server throughput of 3000 connections per second, Little's law (from queuing theory) predicts that the average number of concurrent connections is the product, or 6000.

On the other hand, in a LAN environment with a round-trip delay of 2 milliseconds, the average number of concurrent connections drops to six. Note that if the throughput stays the same, in the wide area setting a large fraction of the connections must be idle (waiting for replies) at any given time.

Given this, the two main causes of overhead were two system calls used by the event-driven server. The standard UNIX implementation of both these calls scales poorly with a large number of connections. The two calls were:

- *select()*: Event-driven servers running on UNIX use the *select()* call for the *FindActive()* call. Experiments by Banga and Mogul (1998) show that more than half of the CPU is used for kernel and user-level *select()* functions with 500 connections.
- *ufalloc():* The server also needs to allocate the lowest unallocated descriptor for new sockets or files. This seemingly simple call took around a third of the CPU time.

ufalloc() performance can easily be explained and fixed. Normally, finding a free descriptor can be efficiently implemented using a free list of descriptors. Unfortunately, UNIX requires choosing the *lowest unused* descriptor. For example, if the currently allocated descriptor list has the elements (in an unsorted order) 9, 1, 5, 4, 2, then one cannot determine that the lowest unallocated number is 3 without traversing the entire unsorted list. Fortunately, a simple change to the kernel implementation (**P15**, use efficient data structures) can reduce this overhead to nearly zero.[6]

6.4.2 Problems with implementations of *select()*

Assuming that *ufalloc()* overhead can easily be minimized by changing the kernel implementation, it is important to improve the remaining bottleneck caused by the *select()* implementation in an event-driven server. Because the causes of the problem are more complex, this section starts by reviewing the use and implementation of *select()* in order to understand the various sources of overhead.

Parameters

Select() is *called* as follows:

- *Input:* An application calls *select()* with three bitmaps (sets) of descriptors (one for descriptors it wishes to read from, one for those it wishes to write to, and one for those it wishes to hear exceptions from), a timeout value, and a parameter called *nfds* that is the highest-numbered file descriptor in

---

[6] While the reader familiar with algorithms will immediately think of a heap, a better solution, which exploits typical computer architectures, is explored in Exercise 3.

any of the three sets plus 1. The purpose of *nfds* is to save the kernel time by restricting the scope of its search for the bits that have value 1 in the three bitmaps.
- *Interim:* The application is blocked if there is no descriptor ready.
- *Output:* When something of interest occurs, the call returns with number of ready descriptors (passed by value as an integer) and the specific lists of descriptors of each category (passed by reference, by overwriting input bitmaps).

Usage in a Web server

Having understood the parameters of the *select()* call, it is important to understand how *select()* could be used by an event-driven Web server. A plausible use of *select()* is as follows (Banga and Mogul, 1998). The server application thread stays in a loop with three major components:

- *Initialize:* The application first zeroes out bitmaps and sets bits for descriptors of interest for read and write. For example, the server application may be interested in reading from file descriptors and writing and reading from network sockets open to clients.
- *Call:* The application then calls *select()* with bitmaps it built in the previous step, and it blocks if no descriptor is ready at the point of call; if a timeout occurs, the application does exception processing.
- *Respond:* After the call returns, the application linearly walks through returned bitmaps and invokes appropriate read and write handlers for descriptors corresponding to set bit positions.

Note that the costs of building the bitmaps in Step 1 and scanning the bitmaps in Step 3 are charged to the user, though they are directly attributable to the costs of preparing for and responding to a *select()* call.

Implementation

Having understood the parameters of the *select()* call, it is important to understand how *select()* is implemented in the kernel of a typical UNIX variant (Wright and Stevens, 1995). The kernel does the following (annotated with sources of overhead):

- *Prune:* The kernel starts by using the bitmaps passed as parameters to build a summary of descriptors marked in at least one bitmap (called the *selected* set).

  This requires a linear search through bitmaps of size N regardless of how many descriptors the application is currently interested in.

- *Check:* Next, for each descriptor in the selected set, the kernel checks if the descriptor is ready; if not, the kernel queues the application thread ID on the select queue of the descriptor. The kernel puts the calling application thread to sleep if no descriptors are ready.

  This requires investigation of all selected descriptors, independent of how many are actually ready. This step is more expensive than simply scanning a bitmap.

- *Resume:* When I/O occurs to make a descriptor ready (i.e., a packet arrives to a socket that the server is waiting for data from), the kernel I/O module checks its select queue and wakes up all threads waiting for a descriptor.

  This requires scheduler overhead, which seems fundamentally unavoidable without polling or busy waiting.

- *Rediscover:* Finally, *select()* rediscovers the list of ready descriptors by making a scan of all selected descriptors to see which have become ready between the time *select()* was put to sleep and was later awakened. This requires repeating the same expensive checks made in Step 2.

  They are repeated despite the fact that the I/O module knew which descriptors became ready but did not inform the *select()* implementation.

6.4.3 Analysis of *select()*

We start by describing opportunities for optimization in the existing *select()* implementation and then use our principles to suggest strategies to improve performance.

Obvious waste in select() implementation

Principle **P1** seeks to remove obvious waste. In order to apply Principle **P1**, it helps to catalog the sources of "obvious waste" in the *select()* implementations. With each source of waste, we also attach a *scapegoat* that can be blamed for the waste.

1. *Recreating interest on each call:* The same bitmap is used for input and output. This overloading causes the application to rebuild the bitmaps from scratch, though it maybe interested in most of the same descriptors across consecutive calls to *select()*. For example, if only 10 bits change in a bitmap of size 6000 on each call, the application still has to walk through 6000 bits, to set each if needed.

   Blame this on either the interface (API) or on the lack of incremental computing in the application.

2. *Rechecking state after resume:* No information is passed from a protocol module (that wakes up a thread sleeping on a socket) to the *select()* call that is invoked when the thread resumes. For example, if the TCP module receives data on socket 9, on which thread 1 is sleeping, the TCP module will ensure that thread 1 is woken up. However, no information is passed to thread 1 as to who woke up thread 1; thus thread 1 must again check all selected sockets to determine that socket 9 indeed has data. Clearly, the TCP module knew this when it woke up thread 1.

   Blame the kernel implementation.

3. *Kernel rechecks readiness for descriptors known not to be ready:* The Web server application is typically interested in a socket until connection failure or termination. In that case, why repeat tests for readiness if no change in state has been observed? For example, assume that socket 9 is a connection to a remote client with a delay of 1 second to send and receive network packets. Assume that at time t, a request is sent to the client on socket 9 and the server is waiting for a response, which arrives at $t + 1$ seconds. Assume that in the interval from t to $t + 1$, the server thread calls *select()* 15,000 times. Each time *select()* is called the kernel makes an expensive check of socket 9 to determine that no data has arrived. Instead, the kernel can infer this from the fact that the socket was checked at time t and no network packet has been received for this socket since time t. Thus 15,000 expensive and useless checks can be avoided; when the packet finally arrives at time $t + 1$, the TCP module can pass information to reinstate checking of this socket.

   Blame the kernel implementation.

4. *Bitmaps linear with descriptor size:* Both kernel and user have to scan bitmaps proportional to the size of possible descriptors, not to the amount of useful work returned. For example, if there are 6000 possible descriptors a Web server may have to deal with at peak load, the bitmaps are of length 6000. Suppose during some period there are 100 concurrent clients, of which only 10 are ready during each call to *select()*. Both kernel and application are scanning and copying bitmaps of size 6000, though the application is only interested in 200 bits and only 10 bits are set when each *select()* returns.

Blame the API.

Strategies and principles to fix select()

Given the sources of waste just listed, some simple strategies can be applied using our algorithmic principles.

- *Recreate interest on each call:* Consider changing the API (**P9**) to use separate bitmaps for input and output. Alternatively, preserve the API and use incremental computation (**P12a**).
- *Recheck state after resume:* Pass information between protocol modules that know when a descriptor is ready and the select module (**P9**).
- *Have kernel recheck readiness for descriptors known not to be ready:* Kernel keeps state across calls so that it does not recheck readiness for descriptors known not to be ready (**P12a**, use incremental computation).
- *Use bitmaps linear with ready size, not descriptor size:* Change the API in a fundamental way to avoid the need for state-based queries about all descriptors represented by bitmaps (**P9**).

6.4.4 Speeding up *select()* without changing the API

Banga and Mogul (Banga and Mogul, 1998) show how to eliminate the first three (of the four) elements of waste listed earlier.

1. *Avoid rebuilding bitmaps from scratch:* The application code is changed to use *two* bitmaps of descriptors it is interested in. Bitmap *A* is used for long-term memory, and bitmap *B* is used as the actual parameter passed by reference to *select()*. Thus between calls to *select()*, only the (presumably few) descriptors that have changed have to be updated in bitmap *A*. Before calling *select()*, bitmap *A* is copied to bitmap *B*. Because copy can proceed a word at a time, the copy is more efficient than a laborious bit-by-bit inspection of the bitmap. In essence, the new bitmap is being computed incrementally (**P12a**).
2. *Avoid rechecking all descriptors when select() wakes up:* To avoid this overhead, the kernel implementation is modified such that each thread keeps a hints set *H* that records sockets that have become ready since the last time the thread called *select()*. The protocol or I/O modules are modified such that when new data arrives (network packet, disk I/O completes), the corresponding descriptor index is written to the hints set of all threads that are on the select queue for that descriptor. Finally, after a thread wakes up in *select()*, only the descriptors in *H* are checked. The essence of this optimization is passing hints between layers (**P9**).
3. *Avoid rechecking descriptors known not to be ready:* The fundamental observation is that a descriptor that is waiting for data need not be checked until asynchronous notification occurs (e.g., the descriptor is placed in hints set *H* described earlier). Clearly, however, any newly arriving descrip-

tors (e.g., newly opened sockets) must be checked. A third, subtle point is that even after network data has arrived for a socket (e.g., 1500 bytes), the application may read only 200 bytes. Thus a descriptor must be checked for readiness even after data first arrives, until there is no more data left (i.e., application reads all data) to signify readiness.

To implement these ideas, besides the hints set H for each thread, the kernel implementation keeps two more sets. The first is an interest set I of all descriptors the thread is interested in. The second is a set of descriptors R that are known to be ready. The interest set I reflects long-term interest; for example, a socket is placed in I the first time it is mentioned in a *select()* call and is removed only when the socket is disconnected or reused. Let the set passed to *select()* be denoted by S. Then I is updated to $I_{new} = I_{old} \cup S$. Note that this incorporates newly selected descriptors without losing previously selected descriptors.[7]

Next, the kernel checks only those descriptors that are in I_{new} but are either (1) in the hints set H or (2) not in I_{old} or (3) in the old ready set R_{old}. Note that these three predicates reflect the three categories discussed two paragraphs back. They represent either recent activity, newly declared interest, or unconsumed data resulting from prior activity. The descriptors found by the check to be ready are recorded in R_{new}. Finally, the *select()* call returns to the user the elements in $R_{new} \cap S$. This is because the user only cares about the readiness of descriptors specified in the selecting set S. As an example, socket 15 may be checked when it is first mentioned in a *select()* call and so enters I; socket 15 may be checked next when a network packet of 500 bytes arrives, causing socket 15 to enter H; finally, socket 15 may be checked repeatedly as part of R until the application consumes all 500 bytes, at which point socket 15 leaves R. The basis of this optimization is **P12**, adding state for speed. The optimization maintains state across calls (**P12**) to reduce redundant checks.

6.4.5 Speeding up *select()* by changing the API

The technique described in Section 6.4.4 improves performance considerably by eliminating the first three (and chief) sources of overhead in *select()*. However, it does so by maintaining extra state (**P12**) in the form of three more sets of descriptors (i.e., H, I, and R) that are also maintained as bitmaps. This, taken together with the selection set S passed in each call, requires the scanning and updating of four separate bitmaps.

In a situation where a large number of connections are present but only a few are active at any instant, this fundamentally still requires paying some small overhead, proportional to the total number of connections as opposed to the number of active connections. This is the fourth source of "waste" enumerated earlier, and it appears unavoidable given the present API.

Further, as we saw earlier, even the modified fast *select()* potentially checks a descriptor multiple times for each event such as a packet arrival (if the application does not consume all the data at once). Such additional checks are unavoidable because *select()* provides the state of each descriptor.

If one looks closely at the interface, what the application fundamentally requires is to be notified of the stream of events (e.g., file I/O completed, network packet arrived) that causes changes in state. Event-based notifications appear, on the surface, to have some obvious drawbacks that may have prevented them from being used in the past.

---

[7] The reader may wonder whether it suffices to set $I = S$. The exercises explore some of the issues with this alternative implementation.

- *Asynchronous notification:* If the application is notified as soon as an event occurs, this can take excessive overhead and be difficult to program. For example, when an application is servicing socket 5, a packet to socket 12 may arrive. Interrupting the application to inform it of the new packet may be a bad idea.
- *Excessive event rate:* The application is interested in the events that cause state change and not in the raw event stream. For a large Web transfer, several packets may arrive to a socket and the application may wish to get one notification for a batch, and not one for every packet. The overhead for each notification is in terms of communication costs (CPU) as well as storage for each notification.

Principle **P6** suggests designing efficient specialized routines to overcome bottlenecks. In this spirit, Banga, Mogul, and Druschel (Banga et al., 1999) describe a new event-based API that avoids both these problems.

- *Synchronous inquiry:* As in the original *select()* call, the application can inquire for pending events. For example, in the previous example, the application continues to service socket 5 and all other active sockets before asking for (and being told about) events such as packet arrival on socket 12.
- *Coalescing of events:* If a second event occurs for a descriptor while a first event has been queued for notification, the second notification is omitted. Thus there can be at most one outstanding event notification per descriptor.

The use of this new API is straightforward and roughly follows the style in which applications use the old *select()* API. The application stays in a loop in which it asks synchronously for the next set of events and goes to sleep if there are none. When the call returns, the application goes through each event notification and invokes the appropriate read or write handlers. Implicitly, the setting up of a connection registers interest in the corresponding descriptor, while disconnection removes the descriptor from the interest list.

The implementation is as follows. Associated with each thread is a set of descriptors in which it is interested. Each descriptor (e.g., socket) keeps a reverse mapping list of all threads interested in the descriptor. On I/O activity (e.g., data arrival on a socket), the I/O module uses its reverse mapping list to identify all potentially interested threads. If the descriptor is in the thread's interest set, a notification event is added to a queue of pending events for that thread.

A simple per-thread bitmap, one bit per descriptor, is used to record the fact that an event is pending in the queue and is used to avoid multiple event notifications per descriptor. Finally, when the application asks for the next set of events, these are returned from the pending queue.[8]

Linux epoll() API: Event mechanisms like *select()* require the server to re-declare its interest set every time it wishes to retrieve events, since the kernel does not remember the interest sets from previous calls. In Linux, our prior discussion of (Banga et al., 1999) culminated in the *epoll()* (epoll(7)) API which actually uses three separate system calls to avoid the problems of *select()*. First, the *epoll_create* system call instructs the kernel to create an event data structure that can be used to track events on a number of descriptors. Thereafter, the *epoll_ctl* call is used to modify interest sets, while the *epoll_wait* call is used to retrieve events. The intellectual connection between the work in Banga et al. (1999) and *epoll()* is described in (Gammo et al., 2004).

---

[8] This simple description glosses over some tricky race conditions and overflow conditions.

As we have seen, a drawback of *select()* is that it does work proportional to the size of the interest set, rather than the number of events returned, which causes poor scaling. The *epoll* API, of course, avoids this issue. As described in Gammo et al. (2004), if the server has many idle connections, performance degrades badly when using *select()* but not when using *epoll()*. The advent of multicore CPUs complicated the design of *epoll()* since many applications scale by using multi-threading. This was not supported by early implementations of *epoll()* but was fixed later.

There are other subtleties. Imagine a socket descriptor shared across multiple operating system threads or processes. When an event happens all of the threads/processes must be woken up. This is sometimes called the "thundering herd" (epoll(7), 2022) problem. This is avoided by having a flag that ensures that the kernel wakes up just one of the waiting threads/processes.

6.5 Avoiding system calls or Kernel Bypass

For now, forget about the intervening discussion of *select()* and recall the discussion of user-level networking. We seem to have gotten the kernel out of the picture on the receipt or sending of a packet, but sadly that is not quite the case. When an application wants to send data, it must somehow tell the adaptor where the data is.

When the application wants to receive data, it must specify buffers where the received packet data should be written to. Today, in UNIX this is typically done using system calls, where the application tells the kernel about data it wishes to send and buffers it wishes to receive to. Even if we implement the protocol in user space, the kernel must service these system calls (which can be expensive; see Chapter 2) for every packet sent and received.

This appears to be required because there can be several applications sending and receiving data from a common adaptor; since the adaptor is a shared resource, it seems unthinkable for an application to write directly to the device registers of a network adaptor without kernel mediation to check for malicious or erroneous use. Or is it?

A simple analogy suggests that alternatives may be possible. In Fig. 6.7 we see that when an application wants to set the value of a variable X equal to 10, it does not actually make a call to the kernel. If this were the case, every read and write in a program would be slowed down very badly. Instead, the hardware determines the virtual page of X, translates it to a physical page (say, 10) via the TLB, and then allows direct access as long as the application has Page 10 mapped into its virtual memory.

If Page 10 is not mapped into the application's virtual memory, the hardware generates an exception and causes the kernel to intervene to determine why there is a page access violation. Notice that the kernel was involved in *setting up* the virtual memory for the application (only the kernel should be allowed to do so, for reasons of security) and may be involved if the application violates its page accesses that the kernel set up. However, the kernel is *not involved* in every access. Could we hope for a similar approach for application access to adaptor memory to avoid wasted system calls (**P1**)?

To see if this is possible, we need to examine more carefully what information an application sends and receives from an adaptor. Clearly, we must prevent incorrect or malicious applications from damaging other applications or the kernel itself. Fig. 6.8 shows an application that wishes to receive data directly from the adaptor. Typically, an application that does so must queue a *descriptor*. A descriptor is a small piece of information that describes the buffer in main memory where the data for the next

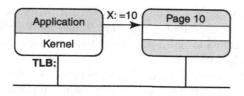

FIGURE 6.7

Reading and writing to memory is not mediated by the kernel.

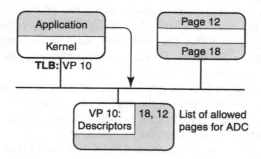

FIGURE 6.8

Application device channels.

packet (for this application) should be written to. Thus we should consider carefully and separately both descriptor memory as well as the actual buffer memory.

We can deal with descriptor memory quite easily by recalling that the adaptor memory is memory mapped. Suppose that the adaptor has 10,000 bytes of memory that is considered memory on the bus and that the physical page size of the system is 1000 bytes. This means that the adaptor has 10 physical pages. Suppose we allocate two physical pages to each of five high-performance applications (e.g., Web, FTP) that want to use the adaptor to transfer data. Suppose the Web application gets two physical pages, 9 and 10. Then the kernel maps the physical pages 9 and 10 into the Web application's page table and the physical pages 3 and 4 into the FTP application's page table.

Now the Web application can write directly to physical pages 9 and 10 without any danger; if it tries to write into pages 3 and 4, the virtual memory hardware will generate an exception. Thus we are exploiting existing hardware (**P4c**) in the form of the TLB to protect access to pages. So now let us assume that Page 10 is a sequence of free buffer descriptors written by the Web application; each buffer descriptor describes a page of main memory (assume this can be done using just 32 bits) that will be used to receive the next packet described for the Web application.

For example, Page 10 could contain the sequence 18, 12 (see Fig. 6.8). This means that the Web application has currently queued physical pages 18 and 12 for the next incoming packet and its successor. We assume that pages 18 and 12 are in main memory and are physically locked pages that were assigned to the Web application by the kernel when the Web application first started.

When a new packet arrives for the Web application, the adaptor will demultiplex the packet to the descriptor Page 10 using a packet filter, and then it will write the data of the packet (using DMA (direct memory access)) to Page 18. When it is done, the adaptor will write the descriptor 18 to a page of written page descriptors (exactly as in fbufs), say, Page 9, that the Web application is authorized to read. It is up to the Web application to finish processing written pages and periodically to queue new free buffer descriptors to the adaptor.

This sounds fine, but there is a serious security flaw. Suppose the Web application, through malice or error, writes the sequence 155, 120 to its descriptor page (which it can do). Suppose further that Page 155 is in main memory and is where the kernel stores its data structures. When the adaptor gets the next packet for the Web application it will write it to Page 155, overwriting the kernel data structures. This causes a serious problem, at least causing the machine to crash.

Why, you may ask, can't virtual memory hardware detect this problem? The reason is that virtual memory hardware (observe the position of the TLB in Fig. 6.7) only protects against unauthorized access by processes running on the CPU. This is because the TLB intercepts every Read (or Write) access done by the CPU and can do checks. However, devices like adaptors that do DMA bypass the virtual memory system and access memory directly.

This is not a problem in practice because applications cannot program the devices (such as disks, adaptors) to read or write to specific places at the application's command. Instead, access is always mediated by the kernel. If we are getting rid of the kernel, then we have to ensure that everything the application can instruct the adaptor to do is carefully scrutinized.

The solution used in the application device channel (ADC) (Druschel et al., 1994) solution promoted by Druschel, Davy, and Peterson is to have the kernel pass (**P9**, pass hints in interfaces) the adaptor a list of valid physical pages that each application using the adaptor can access directly. This can be done once when the application first starts and before data transfer begins. In other words, the time-consuming computation involved in authorizing pages is shifted in time (**P2**) from the data transfer phase to application initialization. For example, when the Web application first starts, it can ask the kernel for two physical pages, say, 18 and 12, and then ask the kernel to authorize the use of these pages to the adaptor.

The kernel is then bypassed for normal data operation. However, if now the Web application queues the descriptor 155 and a new packet arrives, the adaptor will first check the number 155 against its authorized list for the application (i.e., 18, 12). Since 155 is not in the list, the adaptor will not overwrite the kernel data structures (phew!).

In summary, ADCs are based on shifting protection functions in space (**P3c**) from the kernel to the adaptor, using some precomputed information (list of allowed physical pages, **P2a**) passed from the kernel to the adaptor (**P9**), and augmented with the normal virtual memory hardware (**P4c**).

The architecture community has, in recent years, been promoting the use of *active messages* (von Eicken et al., 1992a), for similar reasons. An active message is a message that carries the address of the user-level process that will handle the packet.[9]

An active message (such as the ADC approach) avoids kernel intervention and temporary buffering by using preallocated buffers or by using small messages that are responded to directly by the application, thus providing low latency. Low latency, in turn, allows computation and communication to overlap in parallel machines. The active messages implementation (von Eicken et al., 1992a) allowed

---

[9] This is a way of avoiding packet filters completely by passing more information in packets, but it is a bit scary in a networking environment because of the security risks; however, it is typically used only within clusters of machines that trust each other.

only small messages or (large) block transfer. The fast messages implementation (Pakin et al., 1997) goes further to combine user-level scatter–gather interfaces and flow control to enable uniform high performance for a continuum from short to long messages.

What are kernels good for?

It is important to consider this question because the ADC and active message approaches bypass the kernel. Kernels are good for protection (protecting the system and good users from malice or errors) and for scheduling resources among different applications. Thus if we remove the kernel from the run-time data path, it is up to the solution to provide these services in lieu of the kernel. For example, ADCs do protection using the virtual memory hardware (to protect descriptors) and adaptor enforcement (to protect buffer memory).

It also must multiplex the physical communication link (especially on the sending side) among the different ADCs and provide some sort of fairness. To do this in every device would require replicating traditional kernel code in every device; however, it can be argued that some devices, such as the disk and the network adaptor, are special in terms of their performance needs and are worth giving special treatment. The first commercial deployment of the ADC idea and the UUNET solution (similar to ADCs and proposed concurrently) advocated at Cornell (von Eicken et al., 1995) was known as the Virtual Interface Architecture (VIA). We briefly describe VIA and then move on to the modern version called DPDK (2018) that is widely deployed.

6.5.1 The virtual interface architecture proposal

VIA (Compaq, Intel, and Microsoft Corporations, 1997) was a commercial standard that advocated the ideas in ADCs. The term *virtual interface* makes sense because one can think of an ADC as providing each application with its own virtual interface that it can manipulate without kernel intervention. The virtual interfaces are, of course, multiplexed on a single physical interface. VIA was proposed by an industry consortium that includes Microsoft, Compaq, and Intel.

VIA uses the following terminology that can easily be understood based on the earlier discussion.

- **Registered Memory:** These are regions of memory that the application uses to send and receive data. These regions are authorized for the application to read and write from; they are also pinned down to avoid paging.
- **Descriptor:** To send or receive a packet, the application uses a user-level library (`libvia`) to construct a descriptor that is just a data structure with information about the buffer, such as a pointer. VIA allows a descriptor to refer to multiple buffers in registered memory (for scatter–gather) and allows different memory protection tags. Descriptors can be added to a descriptor queue.
- **Doorbells:** These represent an unspecified method to communicate descriptors to the network interface. This can be done via writing part of the interface card's memory or by triggering an interrupt on the card; it varies from implementation to implementation. Doorbells are pointers to descriptors, thus leading to a second level of indirection.

6.5.2 Data Plane Development Kit (DPDK)

While there have been other open source proposals for Kernel Bypass and user space network implementations such as netmap (Rizzo and Landi, 2011), the canonical kernel bypass mechanism is no longer VIA but DPDK (Data Plane Development kit) (DPDK, 2018). DPDK is a set of libraries that high performance applications can include to bypass the kernel to realize the Application Device Channel idea introduced earlier. However, DPDK goes further with several optimizations.

First, DPDK relies on polling instead of interrupts to receive packets, an idea that we will see again in Section 6.7. Second, DPDK does not use general purpose OS buffer mechanisms but preallocates packet buffers so as not to incur the overhead of allocation or deallocation of memory as packets are sent and received. Third, there is no copying of data between user and kernel memory spaces as a packet is copied once to memory via DMA by the NIC, and this memory location is used by DPDK and the applications—thus DPDK is also a zero-copy interface. Fourth, the overhead of processing packets can be amortized over batches of packets with one API call on reception and sending. Fifth, DPDK uses very large page table sizes (DPDK, 2018) (so-called "hugepages" of say 1GB in size) compared to classical memory pages (4K in many platforms). This reduces the load on the cache used to translate virtual to physical addresses—Translation Lookaside Buffers (TLBs). This in turn reduces TLB misses. There are also several other optimizations, for instance to align memory cache lines. In addition, DPDK has a host of libraries for network processing including for longest matching prefix and exact match.

Note that while DPDK is now part of the Linux Foundation and is an open-source Linux project, it is not the canonical Linux network stack analyzed in Cai et al. (2021). High performance applications must *choose* to bypass the Linux stack using DPDK. Note also that many of the ideas in DPDK and related schemes have flowed into the standard networking stack. For example, batching is done in Linux using various batching mechanisms on the sending and the receiving sides like GSO (Generic Sender Offload) (Ousterhout, 2021) where the transport protocol creates a single large packet to traverse the stack and reduce system call overhead. Similarly, the Linux networking stack now uses NAPI (New API) (Salim et al., 2001) to use some combination of polling and interrupts as we will see in Section 6.7.

DPDK is also used in the storage space to improve performance with the advent of fast non-volatile memories that have much lower latencies than classic disk storage. For such storage (e.g., SSDs or Solid State Disks) the kernel overhead consumes a large fraction of media latency. Thus the SPDK (Storage Processing Development Kit) (spdk, 2022) framework builds on DPDK to offer a set of storage specific libraries that leverage DPDK for fast storage processing and kernel bypass.

6.5.3 Single Root I/O Virtualization (SR-IOV)

As we said in the introduction to this chapter, the world has changed. Virtualization has become pervasive to improve physical server utilization and for other reasons. Thus many virtual machines (VMs) are safely multiplexed together in a single physical machine by the addition of another operating system layer called a hypervisor. To allow networking between virtual machines on the same physical server, the hypervisor must include a virtual switch. Unfortunately, the virtual switch adds another layer of overhead when VMs send networking packets to other VMs in other physical servers.

Just as kernel bypass mechanisms like DPDK bypass the *kernel*, the idea in Single Root I/O Virtualization (SR-IOV) is to add hardware protection mechanisms in the network interface to bypass the *virtual switch and hypervisor*. This is done by a hardware IOMMU (I/O Memory Mapping Unit) that helps the NIC translate device virtual addresses to physical addresses just as a MMU helps the CPU to do so for other virtual addresses. By having the hypervisor initially create these mappings for each VM, each VM gets protected access to the NIC without hypervisor mediation once the mappings have been created. This creates what SR-IOV calls a "virtual function" in which each VM sees a virtual NIC all to itself, in addition to the "physical function" which is the actual SR-IOV capable NIC. The term "Single Root" is confusing but refers to the the fact that in SR-IOV the PCI Express device is shared within a *single* computer.

If most communication is between VMs in the same physical server, DPDK should suffice; but if communication is between VMs in different servers, SR-IOV can improve performance by bypassing the hypervisor.

Despite its origins in the world of virtualization, SR-IOV is part of the PCIe standard and so is much more general than it may first appear. It does not require a hypervisor or even VMs to be used. This is exploited in some proposals such as Arrakis (Peter et al., 2015) to generalize the operating system to allow more streamlined I/O processing for other functions such as storage, and even in High Performance Computing. Arrakis refactors the classical operating system kernel to be merely the control plane, avoiding the need for kernels to be involved in the "data plane" for I/O operations to devices. This is similar to the way the control plane sets up forwarding tables in Software Defined Networks (SDN).

6.6 **Radical Restructuring of Operating Systems**

While we have already surveyed techniques like kernel bypass and the use of *epoll()* in Linux, these involve fairly *local restructuring* of the operating system to lubricate the flow of packets. DPDK, for instance, simply provides an interface for applications to safely bypass the kernel and *epoll()* is a new Linux API for scalable event notification. Another local restructuring proposal is Megapipe (Han et al., 2012) which suggests replacing the classic socket-based networking API with what they call lightweight sockets that remove the file related overheads of the classic socket interface. The API also allows for more aggressive batching to reduce (but not completely avoid) the cost of system calls.

In this section, we briefly survey several proposals for more *radical restructuring* of operating systems even beyond Arrakis (Peter et al., 2015), that seeks to reduce overhead for all I/O. None of these proposals except Google's Snap (Marty et al., 2019) is, as far as we know, deployed widely, but the ideas are stimulating. At the very least, they are helpful to understand the general issues, and may provoke further thought even among implementors constrained by current Operating Systems. At the very best, such operating systems may be needed in the immediate future as commodity operating systems like Linux are already hard pressed to reach 100 Gbps per core (Cai et al., 2021), and certainly find it hard to reduce say the 99-percentile latency of network operations to microseconds (Ousterhout, 2021) for warehouse scale computing (Barroso et al., 2017).

At the outset, it is worth clarifying what we hope to gain by radically restructuring operating systems for better networking performance besides higher raw throughput. These are well articulated in Belay et al. (2016). Besides throughput and protection which are already partly addressed by library OS methods such as DPDK (2018), three additional goals for warehouse scale computing (Barroso et al., 2017) are as follows. They seek to reduce the tail (often measure by 99th percentile) latency to microseconds, strive for good utilization in the face of varying data center load, and enable rapid deployment of new features.

All three of these additional goals are motivated by warehouse style "scale out" computing described in the chapter introduction, where multiple cheap commodity servers are used to serve a user request. Since the request cannot complete until the slowest response is received, this explains the sensitivity to tail latency. Further, as we have seen, the metric to improve is computation per dollar (Barroso et al., 2017); thus it is important to keep resources and cores fully utilized. Finally, most cloud vendors employ an army of programmers to work on different networking features; hence, it is important to create an environment in which new code can be rapidly debugged and deployed.

Of the approaches we survey, perhaps the least radical is Google's Snap (Marty et al., 2019). However, it is the most widely used as it is deployed widely in a large fraction of Google's fleet of servers. Snap advocates a microkernel approach like Mach (Rashid et al., 1989) where the networking code is pulled into a separate user level thread as opposed to a library called by the application thread. This approach, which was deprecated earlier, is now becoming much more feasible because of the availability of multiple cores and cheap inter-thread communication. In return for potential inter-thread IPC overhead, Snap decouples the release of networking code from application code, which are intertwined in library OS methods like DPDK. It also decouples networking code from kernel updates which are interwoven in classical network stacks like Linux (Cai et al., 2021). Further, Snap provides more central allocation of networking resources (as in a classical operating system like Linux) compared to library OS methods like DPDK; this helps improve core utilization. Snap allows several scheduling modes (Marty et al., 2019) including one that can dedicate cores for achieving better latency (as in DPDK), and also modes where load is balanced among cores to improve CPU utilization. Snap, however, is not optimal in reducing tail latency.

Next, ZygOS (Prekas et al., 2017) observes like Snap that data plane operating systems like Arrakis (Peter et al., 2015) and IX (Belay et al., 2016) reduce latency by avoiding shared processing of flows, but cannot handle load imbalances across cores. ZygOS addresses work imbalance by work stealing in which idle cores steal work from overloaded cores. On the other hand, Shenango (Ousterhout et al., 2019) uses a dedicated core to detect core congestion at microsecond time scales to do more fine grained core rebalancing across applications, as opposed to the balancing of load within an application across cores done in ZygOS. Finally, even more radical are proposals like Homa (Montazeri et al., 2018) that advocate completely changing the transport to reduce tail latency even further by even tackling network congestion at the edge. This is done by having the receiving transport protocol control priority queues (**P10**) in the network. The jury is still out, in terms of impact, on each of these proposals, with the exception of Snap which is widely deployed in Google (Marty et al., 2019).

6.7 Reducing interrupts

We have worked our way down the hierarchy of control overheads from process scheduling to select call implementations to system calls. At the bottom of the list is interrupt overhead. While involving less overhead than process scheduling or system calls, interrupt overhead can be substantial. Each time a packet arrives, fielding the corresponding interrupt from the device disrupts processor pipelines and requires some context switching to service the interrupt. There is no way to avoid interrupts completely. However, one can reduce interrupt overhead using the following tricks.

- **Interrupt only for significant events:** For example, in the ADC solution, the adaptor does not need to interrupt the processor on every packet reception but only for the first packet received in a stream of packets (we can assume the application will check for more packets received) and when the queue of free buffer descriptors becomes empty. This can reduce interrupt overhead to 1 in N

packets received, if N packets are received in a burst. This is just an application of batching or expense sharing (**P2c**).

Batching is very commonly used in operating systems today not just to reduce the overhead of interrupts but also to reduce system call overhead using such mechanisms as jumbo frames (large packet sizes), and sender and receiver offloads. More details of various batching/offload mechanisms used in Linux can be found in (Segmentation Offloads, 2022). These include mechanisms such as TSO (TCP segmentation offload), GSO (Generic Sender Offload) on the send side, and GRO (Generic Receiver Offload) on the receive side (Segmentation Offloads).

- **Polling:** The idea here is that the processor (CPU) keeps checking to see if packets have arrived and the adaptor never interrupts. This can be more overhead than interrupt-driven processing if the number of packets received is low, but it can become more efficient for high throughput data streams. Another variation is clocked interrupts (Smith and Traw, 2001): The CPU periodically polls when a timer fires.
- **Application controlled:** An even more radical idea, once proposed by Dave Clark, is that the sender be able to control when the receiver interrupts by passing a bit in the packet header. For example, a sending FTP could set the interrupt bit only for the last data packet in a file transfer. This is another example of **P10**, passing hints in protocol headers. It is probably too radical for use. However, a more recent paper (Dittia et al., 1997) proposes implementing a refinement of this idea in an ATM chip that was indeed fabricated.

In general, the use of batching works quite well in practice. However, in some implementations, such as the first bridge implementation (described in Chapter 10), the use of polling is also very effective. Thus more radical ideas, such as clocked or application-controlled interrupts, have become less useful. Note that the RDMA (remote direct memory access) ideas described in Chapter 5 also have the great potential advantage of removing the need for both per-packet system calls and per-packet interrupts for a large data transfer.

6.7.1 Avoiding receiver livelock

Besides inefficiencies due to the cost of handling interrupts, interrupts can interact with operating system scheduling to drive end-system throughput to zero, a phenomenon known as *receiver livelock*. Recall that in Example 8 of Chapter 2 we showed that in BSD UNIX the arrival of a packet generates an interrupt. The processor then jumps to the interrupt handler code, bypassing the scheduler, for speed. The interrupt handler copies the packet to a kernel queue of IP packets waiting to be consumed, makes a request for an operating system thread (called a *software interrupt*), and exits.

Recall also that under high network load, the computer can enter what is called *receiver livelock* (Mogul and Ramakrishnan, 1997), in which the computer spends all its time processing incoming packets, only to discard them later because the applications never run. If there is a series of back-to-back packet arrivals, only the highest-priority interrupt handler will run, possibly leaving no time for the software interrupt and certainly none for the browser process. Thus either the IP or socket queues will fill up, causing packets to be dropped after resources have been invested in their processing.

Many of these ideas are now part of the Linux NAPI processing framework (Salim et al., 2001). When the network adaptor or NIC receives a packet, it generates an Interrupt Request (IRQ) to the driver and selects a CPU core to process the new data using a *packet steering mechanism* that either distributes load using a hash of the TCP 4-tuple (Receive Packet Steering or RPS), or sends the packet to the core the application is running on (Receive Flow Steering or RFS). Receive Flow Steering helps improve data cache hit rate by steering received packets to the CPU that the application thread (that will consume the packet) is running on. Both steering mechanisms can be accelerated using NIC hardware (**P5**); the hardware version of RPS is called RSS, and the hardware version of RFS is called aRFS (Cai et al., 2021).

The driver then triggers NAPI polling (Salim et al., 2001) where the core polls until a certain number of frames are received or a timer expires. For example, the default parameters described in Cai et al. (2021) are 300 (frame limit) and 2 msec (timer). The originators of the NAPI framework explicitly cite (Salim et al., 2001) the early ideas of Mogul and Ramakrishnan (1997)

Another technique (Mogul and Ramakrishnan, 1997) is to turn off interrupts for a certain number of clock ticks so that some fraction of the CPU time is reserved for non-interrupt processing. This can be done by keeping track of how much time is spent in interrupt routines for a device and masking off that device if the fraction spent exceeds a specified percentage of total time. However, merely doing so can drop all packets that arrive during overload, including well-behaved and important packet flows.

A very nice solution to this problem is described by Druschel and Banga (1996),[10] who suggest combating this problem via two mechanisms. First, they suggest using a separate queue per destination socket instead of a single shared queue. When a packet arrives, early demultiplexing (Chapter 8) is used to place the packet in the appropriate per-socket queue. Thus if a single socket's queues fill up because its application is not reading packets, other sockets can still make progress.

The second mechanism is to implement the protocol processing at the priority of the receiving process and as part of the context of the received process (and not a separate software interrupt). First, this removes the unfair practice of charging protocol processing for application X to the application, Y, that was running when the packet for X arrives. Second, it means that if an application is running slowly, its per-socket queue fills up and its particular packets will be dropped, allowing others to progress. Third, and most importantly, since protocol processing is done at a lower priority (application processing), it greatly alleviates the livelock problem caused by the partial processing (i.e., protocol processing only) of many packets without the corresponding application processing required to remove these packets from the socket queue.

This mechanism, called *lazy receiver processing* (LRP), essentially uses lazy evaluation (**P2b**), not so much for efficiency but for fairness and to avoid livelock. Solutions that require less drastic changes are described in Mogul and Ramakrishnan (1997).

6.8 Conclusions

After the basic restructuring to avoid copying, control overhead is probably the next most important overhead to attack in a networking application. From reducing the overhead of process scheduling to limiting system calls to reducing interrupt overhead, fast server implementations must reduce unnecessary overheads due to these causes. Newer operating systems, such as Linux, are making giant strides toward reducing the inherent control overhead costs. However, modern architectures are getting faster in

---

[10] This solution was also explored in the Exercises for Chapter 2.

the processing of instructions using cached data without a commensurate speedup in context switching and interrupt processing.

This chapter started by surveying basic techniques for reducing process-scheduling overhead for networking code. These lessons have been taken to heart by the networking community. Hardly any implementor worth his or her salt will do something egregious, such as structuring each layer as a separate process, and not resorting freely to upcalls. However, the deeper lesson of Fig. 6.2 is not the seemingly arcane structure, but the implicit idea of user-level networking. User-level networking was not developed at the time Clark presented his paper, but is mainstream today. Note that user-level networking, together with ADCs, makes possible technologies such as DPDK (2018) which are pervasive.

On the other hand, the art of structuring processing in the application context, for example, a Web server, is still an open question. While event-driven servers (augmented with helper processes) satisfactorily balance the need to maximize concurrency and minimize context-switching overhead, the software engineering and debugging aspects of such designs still leave many questions unanswered. The staged event-driven approach is a step in this direction.

The event-driven approach also relies on the fast implementation of equivalents of the *select()* call. While the *select()* approaches has fundamental scalability problems, it is reassuring that the ideas for new event notification APIs described in the first edition (Banga et al., 1999) have now become mainstream in Linux with *epoll()*.

Allowing applications to communicate directly with network devices using a protected virtual interface is an idea that is here to stay with technologies such as DPDK (2018) and SPDK (spdk, 2022). Finally, while interrupts are fundamentally unavoidable, their nuisance value can be greatly mitigated by the use of batching and the use of polling in appropriate environments. Once again, it is reassuring to know that the fundamental ideas of avoiding receive livelock (Mogul and Ramakrishnan, 1997) described in the first edition are alive and well in modern technologies such as DPDK and Linux NAPI polling (Salim et al., 2001).

Some of the more radical operating system restructuring ideas described in this chapter may be needed in the near future, given the throughput and latency limits of even the best tuned network stacks in conventional operating systems. In terms of ideas, papers like Arrakis (Peter et al., 2015) and Shenango (Ousterhout et al., 2019) show that just as operating system ideas impact endnode networking (as in most of this chapter), the reverse can also be true. Arguably, Arrakis (Peter et al., 2015) is influenced by the data plane, control plane separation in telephone networks and Software Defined Networks. On the other hand, Shenango (Ousterhout et al., 2019) uses mechanisms to detect congestion in operating system queues that are arguably inspired by classic networking techniques—though the specifics are different.

Table 6.1 shows a list of the techniques used in this chapter, with the corresponding principles. In summary, while Epictetus urged his readers to control their passions, we feel it is equally important for implementors of networking code to be passionate about control.

6.9 Exercises

1. **Packet Filters and Upcalls:** In the description on upcalls (Fig. 6.2) we showed that the system figured out which application the packet was for by upcalling a transport routine. But if you can do that, who needs packet filters anyway? What hidden assumption is being made here?

2. **Comparing Web Server Structuring Models:** In the text we compared various server structuring mechanisms with respect to simple metrics such as scheduling efficiency and CPU concurrency. Consider the following other metrics for comparison.

   - *Disk Concurrency:* Some systems employ multiple disks and do disk scheduling. Why might the event-driven approach have problems in such an environment, compared to a multithreaded approach? Does the event-driven approach with helper processes have the same problems?
   - *Gathering Statistics:* Web servers need to keep statistics on usage patterns for accounting. Why might gathering statistics be more complex in process-per-client and thread-per-client architectures? Why is it simpler in an event-driven architecture?

3. **Algorithms versus Algorithmics in *ufalloc()* Reimplementation:** In this exercise we will consider how to efficiently reimplement *ufalloc()* to find the lowest unallocated descriptor.

   - First consider using a binary heap. For N identifiers, how many memory accesses are required? How much space is required, in bits?
   - Assume that the machine has a W-bit (e.g., for the Alpha, $W = 64$) word and that there is an efficient instruction (or set of instructions) to find the rightmost zero in a W-bit word. Suppose the allocated descriptors are represented as set bits in a large bitmap (**P14**) of size N. Show how to augment this bitmap with some extra state (**P12**) to efficiently compute the lowest unallocated descriptor.
   - What are the space and time costs of this scheme compared to a simple heap? Can a simple heap be made faster by the (standard) trick of increasing the radix of the heap to have $K > 1$ elements in every heap node?

4. **Modified Implementation of Fast *select()*:** The text explains how elements are *added* to the sets I, H, and R but does not specify completely how they are *removed*. Explain how elements are removed, especially with respect to the hints set H.

5. **Modified Implementation of Fast *select()*:** In the fast select implementation of Banga and Mogul (1998), consider changing the implementation as follows:
   (a) First, I_{new} is set equal to S (and not to $I_{old} \cup S$ as before).
   (b) R_{new} is computed as before.
   (c) What is returned to the user is R_{new} (and not $R_{new} \cap S$) as before.
   Answer the following questions.

   - Explain in words what is different from this implementation and the one proposed by Banga and Mogul.
   - Explain why this implementation may require one to be careful about how it removes elements from the hints set H in order not to miss state changes due to newly arriving packets.
   - Explain how this scheme can be inferior to the existing implementation, assuming no application changes. Find a worst-case scenario.
   - Explain why this implementation can sometimes be *better* than the existing implementation if the application is smart enough not to choose a socket in its selecting set as long as it still has unread data. (In other words, if a socket has unconsumed data, the application is smart enough not to select it until all data has been consumed.)

6. **Comparing the APIC Approach to the ADC Approach:** In the text we described the ADC approach to application-level networking, thereby bypassing the kernel and avoiding system calls. We want to compare this approach to an approach used in the APIC chip. First use a search engine to locate and print out a paper called "The APIC Approach to High-Performance Network Interface Design: Protected DMA and Other Techniques" (Dittia et al., 1997). Read the paper carefully, and then answer the following questions about its particular twists to the ADC design for a practical system.

- There are two types of memory the ADC approach protects: The device registers on the adaptor, and the buffer memory containing the data. The first is protected by overloading the virtual memory scheme; the second is protected by having the kernel hand the adaptor a list of pages that an application can read/write from. Contrast this to the APIC approach to protecting the device registers. Why is an access mask helpful? Why is each connection register mapped both into the application and kernel memory?
- In the APIC, the buffer memory is protected by having the APIC read (from memory) a kernel descriptor that contains validation information about the buffer. In the ADC approach, the validating information is already in the adaptor. Why add this extra complexity?
- In the APIC, there is a third kind of memory that needs to be protected: Buffer descriptors contain links to other descriptors, and this link memory needs to be validated. Why is this not needed in the ADC approach?
- A different way to do link notarization is to have the kernel create an array of pointers to real buffers, one for each application. Only the kernel can read or write this array. The applications queue buffer descriptors as offsets into this array. This is a standard approach in systems called *using one level of indirection.* Compare this approach to the APIC link notarization approach.
- A disadvantage of the APIC approach is that the adaptor has to do a number of Reads to main memory to do all its checks. How many such Reads are required in the worst case for a received packet? Why might this be insignificant?
- The paper describes splitting a packet into two pieces. Why is this needed? What assumption does this method make about protocols (that an approach based on packet filters does not need)?

Maintaining timers

7

That was, is, and shall be: Time's wheel runs back or stops.

—Robert Browning

A timer module in a system is analogous to a secretary who keeps track of all the appointments of a busy executive. The executive tells the secretary to schedule appointments and sometimes to cancel appointments before they occur. It is the secretary's job to interrupt the executive with a warning just before the scheduled time of an appointment. Many secretaries actually do this using a so-called *tickler file*, which is a moving window over the next N days. When the day's appointments are done, the tickler file is rolled to bypass the current day. We will find a strong analogy between a tickler file and a timing wheel, the main data structure of this chapter.

The chapter is organized as follows. Section 7.1 describes why timers are needed. Section 7.2 describes a model of a timer routine and the relevant parameters that are critical for performance. Section 7.3 describes the simplest techniques for maintaining timers, some of which are still appropriate in some cases. Section 7.4 introduces the main data structure, called *timing wheels*. This is followed by two specific instantiations of timing wheels called *hashed wheels* (in Section 7.5) and *hierarchical timing wheels* (in Section 7.6). The chapter ends with a technique called *soft timers* (Section 7.9) that reduces timer overhead by amortizing timer maintenance across other system calls. Table 7.1 summarizes the principles applied in the various timer schemes.

When compared to the first edition, probably the most notable change has been the hundreds of thousands of fine granularity timers (Saeed et al., 2017) that are now routinely used in hosts in clouds to provide bandwidth isolation for Virtual Machine traffic via traffic shaping, and for modern congestion control algorithms like BBR (Cardwell et al., 2017) that do fine-graining pacing to reduce packet drops. These new applications make a stronger case for the use of the main data structure in this chapter (timing wheels), and the need for even more streamlined timer implementations in multicore machines.

Quick reference guide

The most useful section for an implementor may be Section 7.5 on hashed timing wheels, versions of which have appeared in many operating systems, such as FreeBSD and in Google machines as part of the Carousel (Saeed et al., 2017) traffic shaping software. Linux used hierarchical timing wheels (Section 7.6) in early versions, as well as in a recent version that is more efficient but offers less precise timers (Corbet, 2015).

Table 7.1 Principles used by the timer schemes described in this chapter.

Number	Principle	Timer technique
P14	Use array to store bounded timers	Basic timing wheels
P2c, 4	Leverage off time-of-day update	
P15	Using hashing or hierarchies	Hashed, hierarchical timing wheels
P10	Pass handle to delete timer	Any timer scheme
P4	Leverage off system calls, etc.	Soft timers
P3	Relax need for accurate timers	
P11	Optimize for fast timers	

7.1 Why timers?

Why do systems need timers? Systems need timers for failure recovery and also to implement algorithms in which the notion of time or relative time is integral. Several kinds of failures cannot be detected asynchronously. Some can be detected by periodic checking (e.g., disk watchdog timers), and such timers always expire. Other failures can only be inferred by the lack of some positive action (e.g., message acknowledgment) within a specified period. If failures are infrequent, these timers rarely expire.

Many systems also implement algorithms that use time or relative time. Examples include algorithms that control the rate of production of some entity (e.g., rate-based flow control in networks) and *scheduling* algorithms. These timers almost always expire.

The performance of algorithms to implement a timer module becomes an issue when any of the following are true. First, performance becomes an issue if the algorithm is implemented by a processor that is interrupted each time a hardware clock ticks and the interrupt overhead is substantial. Second, it becomes an issue if fine-granularity timers are required. Third, it becomes an issue if the average number of active timers is large. All three factors are becoming increasingly critical in cloud servers running at 100 Gbps that do fine-grained traffic shaping of hundreds of thousands of flows (Saeed et al., 2017).

If the hardware clock interrupts the host every tick and the interval between ticks is on the order of microseconds, then the interrupt overhead is substantial. Most host operating systems offer timers of coarse granularity (milliseconds or seconds). Alternatively, in some systems finer-granularity timers reside in special-purpose hardware. In either case the performance of the timer algorithms will be an issue because they determine the latency incurred in starting or stopping a timer and the number of timers that can be simultaneously outstanding.

As an example, consider communications between members of a distributed system. Since messages can be lost in the underlying network, timers are needed at some level to trigger retransmissions. A host in a distributed system can have several timers outstanding. Consider, for example, a server with 50,000 connections and three timers per connection. Further, as networks scale to 100 gigabit speeds and beyond, both the required resolution and the rate at which timers are started and stopped will increase.

Some network implementations do not use a timer per packet; instead, only a few timers are used for the entire networking package. Such TCP implementation gets away with two timers because the

TCP implementation maintains its own timers for all outstanding packets and uses a single kernel timer as a clock to run its own timers. TCP maintains its packet timers in the simplest fashion: Whenever its single kernel timer expires, it ticks away at all its outstanding packet timers. For example, many TCP implementations use two timers: a 200-millisecond timer and a 500-millisecond timer.

The naive method works reasonably well if the granularity of timers is low and losses are rare. However, it is desirable to improve the resolution of the retransmission timer to allow speedier recovery. For example, the University of Arizona has a TCP implementation called TCP Vegas (Brakmo et al., 1994) that performs better than the commonly used TCP Reno. One of the reasons TCP Reno has bad performance when experiencing losses is the coarse granularity of the timeouts.

Besides faster error recovery, fine-granularity timers also allow network protocols to more accurately measure small intervals of time. For example, accurate estimates of round trip delay are important for the TCP congestion-control algorithm (Jacobson, 1988) and the SRM (scalable reliable multicast) framework (Floyd et al., 1995) that is implemented in the Web conferencing tool (McCanne, 1992).

More recently, beyond accurate round trip delay measurements, recent congestion algorithms have been using fine grained timers. Google's BBR algorithm (Cardwell et al., 2017), for instance, uses fine grained pacing to reduce packet drops in the network, especially for video.

Finally, many multimedia applications routinely use timers, and the number of such applications is increasing. An early example can be found in Siemens' CHANNELS run-time system for multimedia (Boecking et al., 1995), where each audio stream uses a timer with granularity that lies between 10 and 20 milliseconds. For multimedia and other real-time applications, it is important to have worst-case bounds on the processing time to start and stop timers.

Besides networking applications, process control and other real-time applications will benefit from large numbers of fine-granularity timers. Also, the number of users on a system may grow large enough to lead to a large number of outstanding timers. This is the reason cited for redesigning the timer facility by the developers of the IBM VM/XA SP1 operating system (Davison, 1989).

In the following sections we will describe a family of schemes for efficient timer implementations based on a data structure called a *timing wheel*. We will also survey some of the systems that have implemented timer packages based on the ideas in this chapter.

7.2 Model and performance measures

A timer module (Varghese and Lauck, 1987) has four component routines:

STARTTIMER (Interval, *RequestId*, *ExpiryAction*):   The client calls this routine to start a timer that will expire after "Interval" units of time. The client supplies a *RequestId* that is used to distinguish this timer from other timers the client has outstanding. Finally, the client can specify what action must be taken on expiry, for instance, calling a client-specified routine or setting an event flag.

STOPTIMER (*RequestId*):   This routine uses its knowledge of the client and *RequestId* to locate the timer and stop it.

PERTICKBOOKKEEPING: Let the granularity of the timer be T units. Then every T units, this routine checks whether any outstanding timers have expired; if so, it calls STOPTIMER, which in turn calls the next routine.

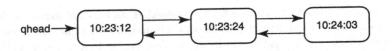

FIGURE 7.1

Timer queue example used to illustrate Scheme 2.

EXPIRYPROCESSING: This routine does the *ExpiryAction* specified in the STARTTIMER call.

The first two routines are activated on client calls; the last two are invoked on timer ticks. The timer is often an external hardware clock.

Two performance measures can be used to choose between algorithms described in the rest of this chapter. Both are parameterized by n, the average (or worst-case) number of outstanding timers. They are the space (*Space*) required for the timer data structures and the latency (*Latency*), or the time between the invoking of a routine in the timer module and its completion. Assume that the caller of the routine blocks until the routine completes. Both the average and worst-case latency are of interest.

7.3 Simplest timer schemes

The two simplest schemes for timer implementation are, in fact, commonly used. In the first scheme STARTTIMER finds a memory location and sets that location to the specified timer interval. Every T units, PERTICKBOOKKEEPING will decrement each outstanding timer; if any timer becomes zero, EXPIRYPROCESSING is called.

This scheme is extremely fast for all but PERTICKBOOKKEEPING. It also uses one record per outstanding timer, the minimum space possible. It is appropriate if there are only a few outstanding timers, if most timers are stopped within a few ticks of the clock, and if PERTICKBOOKKEEPING is done with suitable performance by special-purpose hardware.

Note that instead of doing a *Decrement*, we can store the absolute time at which timers expire and do a *Compare*. This option is valid for all timer schemes we describe; the choice between them will depend on the size of the time-of-day field, the cost of each instruction, and the hardware on the machine implementing these algorithms. In this chapter we will use the Decrement option, except when describing Scheme 2.

In a second simple scheme, used in older versions of UNIX, PERTICKBOOKKEEPING latency is reduced at the expense of STARTTIMER performance. Timers are stored in an ordered list. Unlike Scheme 1, we will store the absolute time at which the timer expires, not the interval before expiry. The timer that is due to expire at the earliest time is stored at the head of the list. Subsequent timers are stored in increasing order, as shown in Fig. 7.1. In Fig. 7.1 the lowest timer is due to expire at absolute time 10 hours, 23 minutes, and 12 seconds.

Because the list is sorted, PERTICKBOOKKEEPING need only increment the current clock time and compare it with the head of the list. If they are equal or if the time of day is greater, it deletes that list element and calls EXPIRYPROCESSING. It continues to delete elements at the head of the list until the expiry time of the head of the list is strictly less than the time of day. STARTTIMER searches the list to find the position to insert the new timer. In the example STARTTIMER will insert a new timer due to expire at 10:24:01, between the second and third elements.

The worst-case latency to start a timer is $O(n)$. The average latency depends on the distribution of timer intervals (from time started to time stopped) and on the distribution of the arrival process according to which calls to STARTTIMER are made.

STOPTIMER need not search the list if the list is doubly linked. When STARTTIMER inserts a timer into the ordered list, it can store a pointer to the element. STOPTIMER can then use this pointer to delete the element in $O(1)$ time from the doubly linked list. This can be used by any timer scheme. This is an application of **P9**, passing hints in layer interfaces. More precisely, the user passes a handle to the timer in the STOPTIMER interface.

If this scheme is implemented by a host processor, the interrupt overhead on every tick can be avoided if there is hardware support to maintain a single timer. The hardware timer is set to expire at the time at which the timer at the head of the list is due to expire. The hardware intercepts all clock ticks and interrupts the host only when a timer actually expires. Unfortunately, some processor architectures do not offer this capability.

As for *Space*, Scheme 1 needs the minimum space possible; Scheme 2 needs $O(n)$ extra space for the forward and back pointers between queue elements.

A linked list is one way of implementing a priority queue. For large n, tree-based data structures are better. These include unbalanced binary trees, heaps, postorder and end-order trees, and leftist trees (Cormen et al., 1990; Vaucher and Duval, 1975). They attempt to reduce the latency in Scheme 2 for STARTTIMER from $O(n)$ to $O(\log(n))$. In Myhrhaug (2001) it is reported that this difference is significant for large n and that unbalanced binary trees are less expensive than balanced binary trees.

Unfortunately, unbalanced binary trees easily degenerate into a linear list; this can happen, for instance, if a set of equal timer intervals is inserted. It would, however, be a good idea to compare the performance of timing wheels against an implementation using simple binary heaps. We will lump these algorithms together as Scheme 3: tree-based algorithms. Linux high resolution timers (hrtimers) use balanced (red-black) trees (Gleixner and Niehaus, 2006).

Thus the three simple schemes take the time that is least logarithmic in the number of timers for either STARTTIMER or PERTICKBOOKKEEPING. This is a problem for high-speed implementations. The next section shows how to do better.

7.4 Timing wheels

The design of the first scheme follows a common problem-solving paradigm:

First solve a simpler problem, and then use the insight to solve the more complex problem.

The simpler problem we tackle first is as follows. Suppose timers are all set for some small interval, say, MAXINTERVAL, and let the granularity of the timer be 1 unit. This suggests the use of **P4**, bucket-sorting techniques, instead of the sorting techniques suggested by Schemes 2 and 3. However, bucket sorting is really used for static sorting of a set of numbers. Here, new numbers keep being added and deleted, and we still want to maintain order. (In technical algorithmic terms the timer data structure must implement a priority queue that allows the operations of addition, deletion, and finding the smallest element.) What is the bucket-sorting equivalent of a priority queue?

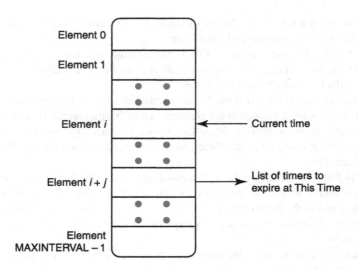

FIGURE 7.2

Array of lists used by Scheme 4 for timer intervals up to MAXINTERVAL.

Given this motivation, it is not hard to have the following picture (shown in Fig. 7.2) float into the reader's mind. Imagine that current time is represented by a pointer to an element in a circular array with dimensions [0, MAXINTERVAL − 1]. On every timer tick (for per-tick bookkeeping), we simply increment the pointer by 1 mod the size of the array.

To set a timer at j units past current time, we index (Fig. 7.2) into Element $i + j$ mod MAXINTERVAL and put the timer at the head of a list of timers that will expire at a time = $CurrentTime + j$ units. Each tick, we increment the current timer pointer (modMAXINTERVAL) and check the array element being pointed to. If the element is 0 (no list of timers waiting to expire), then no more work is done on that timer tick. But if it is nonzero, then we do EXPIRYPROCESSING on all timers that are stored in that list. Thus the latency for STARTTIMER is $O(1)$; PERTICKBOOKKEEPING is $O(1)$ except when timers expire, but this is the best possible. If the timer lists are doubly linked and, as before, we store a pointer to each timer record, then the latency of STOPTIMER is also $O(1)$.

We can describe this array somewhat more picturesquely as a *timing wheel*, where the wheel turns one array element every timer unit. For a secretary, this is similar to a tickler file. For sorting experts, this is similar to a bucket sort that trades off memory for processing. However, since the timers change value every time instant, intervals are entered as offsets from the current time pointer. It is sufficient if the current time pointer increases every time instant.

A bucket sort sorts N elements in $O(M)$ time using M buckets, since all buckets have to be examined. This is inefficient for large $M > N$. In timer algorithms, however, the crucial observation is that some entity needs to do $O(1)$ work per tick to update the current time; it costs only a few more instructions for the same entity to step through an empty bucket. This is a nice example of using Principles **P4** (leveraging system components) and **P2c** (expense sharing).

The system is already doing some work per tick to increment time. Thus what matters when figuring out the cost of the algorithm is only the *additional expense* caused by the algorithm, not the cost taken in isolation as is typically measured in algorithms classes. Note that this assumption would be false if the system did not do some work on every clock tick and, instead, relied on a piece of hardware to keep the time of day. What matters, unlike the sort, is not the total amount of work to sort N elements, but the average (and worst-case) part of the work that needs to be done per timer tick.

Still, memory is finite: It is difficult to justify 2^{32} words of memory to implement 32-bit timers. So how would you generalize this idea to larger timer values? If you haven't seen it before, try to come up with your own ideas before reading further.

One naive solution is to implement timers within some range using this scheme and the allowed memory. Timers greater than this value are implemented using, say, Scheme 2. Alternatively, this scheme can be extended in two ways to allow larger values of the timer interval with modest amounts of memory. The two techniques are motivated by two algorithmic techniques (**P15**): hashing and radix sort.

7.5 Hashed wheels

The design of the first extension follows a second common problem-solving paradigm:

Use analogies to derive techniques for the problem at hand from solutions to a different problem.

Many ideas first occur by analogy, even if the analogy is not always exact. The previous scheme has an obvious analogy to inserting an element in an array using the element value as an index. If there is insufficient memory, can we hash the element value to yield an index? For example, if the table size is a power of 2, an arbitrary-size timer can easily be divided by the table size; the remainder (low-order bits) is added to the current time pointer to yield the index within the array. The result of the division (high-order bits) is stored in a list pointed to by the index.

In Fig. 7.3 let the table size be 256 and the timer be a 32-bit timer. The remainder on division is the last 8 bits. Let the value of the last 8 bits be 20. Then the timer index is 10 (current time pointer) + 20 (remainder) = 30. The 24 high-order bits are then inserted into a list that is pointed to by the 30th element.

Other methods of hashing are possible. For example, any function that maps a timer value to an array index could be used. We will defend our choice at the end of Section 7.5. However, we now come to a fork in the road for our design. Whatever hash function we use, there are two ways to maintain each list.

The most straightforward way, which seems best until we look a little closer, is to do Scheme 2 within each bucket. This clearly generalizes Scheme 2 while improving its performance because each of the "little" lists should be smaller than a single list. Now for the details. Unfortunately, its performance depends on the hash function because STARTTIMER can be slow because the 24-bit quantity must be inserted into the correct place in the list. The worst-case latency for STARTTIMER is still $O(n)$.

Assuming that a worst-case STARTTIMER latency of $O(n)$ is unacceptable, we can maintain each time list as an unordered list instead of an ordered list. At first glance, this seems like a bad idea. We

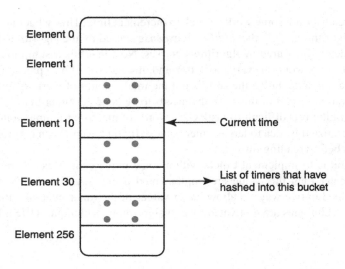

Element 0

Element 1

Element 10 ← Current time

Element 30 → List of timers that have hashed into this bucket

Element 256

FIGURE 7.3

Array of lists used by Schemes 5 and 6 for arbitrary-size timers: basically a hash table.

have certainly made STARTTIMER faster; but if lists are unordered, then it seems that per tick we will have to do a lot more work, seemingly a bad trade-off. Let us look a little closer, however.

Clearly, STARTTIMER now has a worst-case and average latency of $O(1)$. PERTICKBOOKKEEPING now does take longer. Every timer tick, we increment the pointer (mod $TableSize$); if there is a list there, we must decrement the high-order bits for every element in the array, exactly as in Scheme 1. However, if the hash table has the property described earlier, then the average size of the list will be $O(1)$.

We can make a stronger statement about the average behavior regardless of how the hash distributes. This is perhaps not quite so obvious. Notice that every $TableSize$ ticks, we decrement once all timers that are still living. Thus for n timers, we do $n/TableSize$ work on average per tick. If $n < TableSize$, then we do $O(1)$ work on average per tick. If all n timers hash into the same bucket, then every $TableSize$ ticks we do $O(n)$ work, but for intermediate ticks we do $O(1)$ work. What this means is that if we want to keep the per-tick work small and bounded, we simply arrange that the number of buckets is some factor larger than the maximum number of concurrent timers we support. We can even reduce this work as much as we want by increasing the number of buckets. This is an example of a result about *amortized complexity*, which is stronger than a result about *average complexity*.

Thus the hash distribution in Scheme 6 controls only the "burstiness" (variance) of the latency of PERTICKBOOKKEEPING, not the average latency. Since the worst-case latency of PERTICK-BOOKKEEPING is always $O(n)$ (all timers expire at the same time), we believe that the choice of hash function for Scheme 6 is insignificant. Obtaining the remainder after dividing by a power of 2 is cheap and, consequently, recommended. Further, using an arbitrary hash function to map a timer value into an array index would require PERTICKBOOKKEEPING to compute the hash on each timer tick, which would make it more expensive.

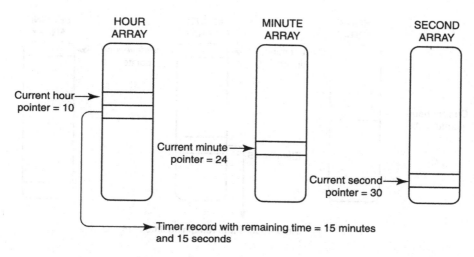

FIGURE 7.4

Hierarchical set of arrays of lists used by Scheme 7 to "map" time more efficiently.

7.6 **Hierarchical wheels**

The second extension of the basic scheme exploits the concept of hierarchy. To represent the number 1000000, we need only 7 digits instead of 1000000 because we represent numbers hierarchically in units of 1's, 10's, 100's, etc. Similarly, to represent all possible timer values within a 32-bit range, we do not need a 2^{32}-element array. Instead, we can use a number of arrays, each of different granularity. For instance, we can use four arrays as follows:

- A 100-element array in which each element represents a day
- A 24-element array in which each element represents an hour
- A 60-element array in which each element represents a minute
- A 60-element array in which each element represents a second

Thus instead of $100 * 24 * 60 * 60 = 8.64$ million locations to store timers up to 100 days, we need only $100 + 24 + 60 + 60 = 244$ locations.

As an example, consider Fig. 7.4. Let the current time be 11 days, 10 hours, 24 minutes, 30 seconds. Then to set a timer of 50 minutes and 45 seconds, we first calculate the absolute time at which the timer will expire, which is 11 days, 11 hours, 15 minutes, 15 seconds. Then we insert the timer into a list beginning 1 (11 − 10 hours) element ahead of the current hour pointer in the hour array. We also store the remainder (15 minutes and 15 seconds) in this location. We show this in Fig. 7.4, ignoring the day array, which does not change during the example.

The seconds array works as usual: Every time the hardware clock ticks we increment the second pointer. If the list pointed to by the element is nonempty, we do EXPIRYPROCESSING for elements in that list. However, the other three arrays work slightly differently.

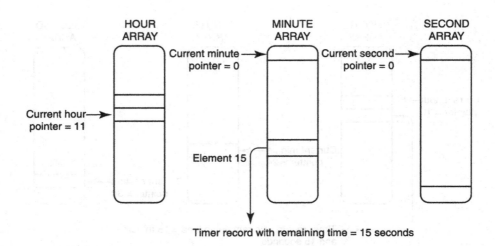

FIGURE 7.5

The previous example, but after the hour component of the timer expires (using Scheme 7).

Even if there are no timers requested by the user of the service, there will always be a 60-second timer that is used to update the minute array, a 60-minute timer to update the hour array, and a 24-hour timer to update the day array. For instance, every time the 60-second timer expires, we will increment the current minute timer, do any required EXPIRYPROCESSING for the minute timers, and reinsert another 60-second timer.

Returning to the example, if the timer is not stopped, eventually the hour timer will reach 11. When the hour timer reaches 11, the list is examined; EXPIRYPROCESSING will insert the remainder of the seconds (15) in the minute array, 15 elements after the current minute pointer (0). Of course, if the minutes remaining were zero, we could go directly to the second array. At this point, the table will look like Fig. 7.5.

Eventually, the minute array will reach the 15th element; as part of EXPIRYPROCESSING we will move the timer into the second array 15 seconds after the current value. Fifteen seconds later, the timer will actually expire, at which point the user-specified EXPIRYPROCESSING is performed.

The choice between Scheme 6 and Scheme 7 is tricky. For small values of T and large values of M, Scheme 6 can be better than Scheme 7 for both STARTTIMER and PERTICKBOOKKEEPING. However, for large values of T and small values of M, Scheme 7 will have a better average cost (latency) for PERTICKBOOKKEEPING but a greater cost for STARTTIMER latency.

Observe that if the timer precision is allowed to decrease with increasing levels in the hierarchy, then we need not migrate timers between levels. For instance, in our earlier example we would round off to the nearest hour and only set the timer in hours. When the hour timer goes off, we do the user-specified EXPIRYPROCESSING without migrating to the minute array. Essentially, we now have different timer modes, one for hour timers, one for minute timers, etc. This reduces PERTICKBOOKKEEPING overhead further, at the cost of a loss in precision of up to 50% (e.g., a timer for 1 minute and 30 seconds that is rounded to 1 minute). Alternatively, we can improve the precision by allowing just one migration between adjacent lists.

For Linux, currently the kernel has two different timer facilities for two different use cases we described at the start of this chapter. The high-resolution timer ("hrtimer") echanism gives users accurate timers that run to completion as for instance in rate control algorithms. The lower resolution timer is for timing out events and inferring failure. While the hrtimer uses balanced (red-black) trees (Gleixner and Niehaus, 2006), the lower resolution timer (Corbet, 2015) uses a hierarchical timer but, as pointed out in the prevous paragraph, chooses to limit timer migration (called "cascading" in Linux parlance (Corbet, 2015)) at the cost of precision. Earlier versions of Linux (first implemented in 1997 (Gleixner and Niehaus, 2006)) used only one approach—the hierarchical timing wheel with migration—that was called Cascading Timing Wheel (CTW).

7.7 BSD implementation

Adam Costello was the first to use hashed wheels to implement (Costello and Varghese, 1998) the BSD UNIX callout and timer facilities. The earlier BSD kernels took time proportional to the number of outstanding timers to set or cancel timers. The Costello implementation, which is based on Scheme 6, takes constant time to start, stop, and maintain timers; this led to a highly scalable design that could support thousands of outstanding timers without much overhead.

In the original BSD implementation each callout was represented by a CALLOUT structure containing a pointer to the function to be called (C_FUNC), a pointer to the function's argument (C_ARG), and a time (C_TIME) expressed in units of clock ticks. Outstanding callouts were kept in a linked list, sorted by their expiration times. The C_TIME member of each callout structure was differential, not absolute; the first callout in the list stores the number of ticks from now until expiration, and each subsequent callout in the list stores the number of ticks between its own expiration and the expiration of its predecessor.

In BSD UNIX callouts are set and canceled using TIMEOUT() and UNTIMEOUT(), respectively. TIMEOUT(FUNC, ARG, TIME) registers FUNC(ARG) to be called at the specified time. UNTIMEOUT(FUNC, ARG) cancels the callout with matching function and argument. Because the CALLTODO list was searched linearly, both operations originally took time proportional to the number of outstanding callouts. Interrupts were locked out for the duration of the search.

Adding new algorithms to an existing system can sometimes run into compatibility problems with existing interfaces. For example, the Costello implementation was based on Scheme 6. Costello found, however, that the TIMEOUT()/UNTIMEOUT() interface in BSD did not allow the passing of handles, which was used in all the schemes we described above to quickly cancel a timer. The Costello implementation used two solutions to this problem. For calls using the existing interface, a search for a callout given a function pointer and argument is done using a hash table. A second solution was also implemented: A new interface function was defined for removing a callout (UNSETCALLOUT()) that takes a handle as its only argument. This allowed existing code to use the old interface and new applications to use the new interface. The performance difference between these two approaches was slight, so the hash table approach was preferable.

In the Costello implementation, the timer routines were guaranteed to lock out interrupts only for a small, bounded amount of time. The Costello implementation also extended the SETITIMER() interface to allow a process to have multiple outstanding timers, thereby reducing the need for users to maintain their own timer packages. The changes to the BSD kernel were small (548 lines of code added, 80 removed). Details can be found in (Costello and Varghese, 1998); the written report contains several important implementation details that are not given here.

The advent of multicore machines required changes to the Costello implementation. An early change was that a single callwheel was replaced by a per-CPU callwheel to improve scalability and performance (Motin and Italiano, 2018). Motin and Italiano (Motin and Italiano, 2018) have recently introduced an updated version called Calloutng to address the following three drawbacks of the Costello implementation. First, intervals are rounded to the next tick resulting in a loss of accuracy; second, the CPU is woken up on every interrupt resulting in extra energy consumption; finally, one cannot defer and coalesce callouts which leads to extra interrupts. They considered using a balanced tree but decided to retain the wheel structure. The code was, however, updated to give more attention to accuracy, to allow aggregation, to use a new hash function to index into the wheel, and to carefully consider CPU cache affinity affects (Motin and Italiano, 2018).

7.8 Google Carousel implementation

Many years after the Costello implementation, Google built a scalable traffic shaping sytem called Carousel (Saeed et al., 2017) whose underlying data structure is a timing wheel that can handle hundreds of thousands of concurrent fine-grained timers. Because the speeds and scale are so much higher than the Costello implementation, we briefly review the new use cases that motivated this design.

The first use case is the use of fine grained pacing in rate-based congestion control algorithms like BBR (Cardwell et al., 2017). Recall that the TCP congestion control algorithm is based on reducing the window size (number of outstanding bytes that have not yet been acked) based on congestion signals like congestion-encountered bits set by congested routers and dropped packets. The problem with TCP's congestion control algorithm is that when a cumulative acknowledgement arrives for a large number of bytes, the sender can release a burst of traffic into the network, which can cause packets to be dropped in routers. Rate based congestion algorithms like BBR, by contrast, control the rate of packet sending based on congestion signals. The rate in turn is enforced by fine grained timers that control the time between sending of packets. The use of BBR is reported to greatly improve round trip delays around the world and Youtube Quality of Experience measures (Cardwell et al., 2017)

The second use case is Virtual Machine (VM) isolation in severs that hosts thousands of VMS each of which can communicate with hundreds of other VMs. Without iimits on the bandwidth used by each VM either in isolation or aggregate, if one VM misbehaves by sending at too high a rate, other VMs may be adversely affected because they share the same physical outgoing link. The third use case is similar in terms of the Incast problem (Saeed et al., 2017) in warehouse computing, where a request receives hundreds of responses from other servers that causes dropped packets in routers. Incast can be mitigated by having a busy receiver rate control the acks it sends back using fine grained pacing.

The second and third use cases are traditionally done by token bucket schemes which we will describe in the chapter on router QoS, Chapter 14. Briefly the idea is that each user is given a certain number of tokens to send bytes every timer tick. When the user has sent more bytes than it has tokens, the user's traffic is either dropped (in which case it is called a policer) or placed in a queue till more tokens arrive (in which case it is called a shaper). While such schemes have traditionally been implemented in routers, the three use cases above require token buckets in hosts. For example, Linux's

Qdisc (Components of Linux Traffic Control, 2022) supports various fair queuing disciplines including HTB (hierarchical token buckets).

Measurements on Google servers (Saeed et al., 2017) show that the use of existing Qdisc mechanisms in Linux resulting in either imperfect rate control or excessively high CPU overhead. Thus rather than rely on Linux timers, the Carousel designers (Saeed et al., 2017) use a large hashed timing wheel. Carousel is not, however, a timing facilty. It is instead a shaper/policer that scales to hundreds of thousands of flows. To avoid the problem in a shaper where the application keeps bursting packets that are queued in Carousel, the Carousel system also adds a second idea called *deferred completions*.

The idea in deferred completions is to not allow the system call to complete until any packets stored by Carousel are sent to the NIC by Carousel. This provides feedback that slows down an over-zealous sender. Deferred completions means that completions can arrive out of order—an application paced to a slow rate may receive a completion later than a faster rate application even though it send its request earlier. This requires a way to match completions and requests using a hash table (**P15**) but this added complexity is worthwhile. Deferred completions are thus a way to change the interface (**P9**).

Notice that unlike the traditional use cases where timers are used to trigger retransmission or detect failure, the Carousel timers always expire (unlike retransmission or failure timers that almost never expire), and thus some of the optimizations used in the Linux timer facilty (see Corbet, 2015) cannot be used. Instead, Carousel uses several other implementation tricks. Carousel uses one timing wheel per CPU to avoid lock contention and can use multiple cores if needed. It also uses pre-allocated buffers (**P2a**) to reduce the overhead of buffer allocation.

The net result is that Carousel shapes traffic 10 times more accurately for Google traffic (Saeed et al., 2017) while improving overall machine CPU utilization by 10% and reducing memory by two orders of magnitude when compared to the best earlier techiques for traffic shaping. This shows the utility of timing wheels when fundamentally integrated into a shaping algorithm (as opposed to being used solely as a timer facility) combined with innovations such as deferred completions.

7.9 Obtaining finer granularity timers

As networks grow faster, one might expect retransmission timers to grow smaller as round-trip delays to destinations decrease. If round-trip delays fall to microseconds, it makes sense to expect the retransmit timers to fall to microseconds as well. Unfortunately, with most operating systems, one is stuck with a millisecond timer even when round-trip delays fall to microseconds. The use of a timing wheel can allow finer-granularity retransmission timers. But the timers can still be no smaller than the granularity of the timer tick.

Now many CPUs provide a programmable hardware interrupt chip that can be programmed to interrupt the CPU at a desired frequency. Thus an apparently simple method to improve timer resolution is to increase the frequency of the clock interrupt. Together with the use of a timing wheel, this would appear to provide much finer timer granularities.

Unfortunately, there is a flaw in the argument. As we have argued in the model section, modern CPUs tend to keep a lot of state to speed up processing. This includes pipeline state, the use of a large number of registers, and caches and TLBs. An interrupt causes high overhead, because it involves the saving and restoring of CPU state, and can cause changes to locality patterns that result in cache and TLB misses after exiting the interrupt handler. Early measurements in Aron and Druschel (1999) showed the cost of an interrupt on a 300- or 500-Mhz Pentium was around 4.5 microseconds. Worse, as processors get faster, there is no indication that interrupt processing times will improve.

Thus having a more frequent hardware interrupt will result in too much overhead. As the problem is defined, considering the timer module as a black box leaves us no way out. However, systems thinking provides a solution to our dilemma by considering Principle **P4** again and leveraging off other system components. Observe that the life of a CPU is chock full of other kinds of transition events that involve state saving and restoring and changes in locality patterns. Such transition events include system calls (e.g., a call to a device handler), exceptions (e.g., a page fault), and hardware interrupts (e.g., an interrupt from the network adaptor).

If we place a check for expired timers as part of the code for such transition events, the overhead for state saving and locality changes is already part of the transition event and is not increased significantly by the timer handler. This is good. Unfortunately, unlike the hardware clock interrupt, the frequency of transition events is unpredictable. This is bad.

However, experiments over a wide range of benchmarks in Aron and Druschel (1999) show that the mean delay between transition events varies from 5 to 30 microseconds, depending on what the CPU is running, that delays over 100 microseconds occur in only 6% of the cases, and that the maximum delay never exceeded 1 millisecond.

The data suggests an interesting use of **P3**, relaxing system requirements. Instead of providing a "hard" timer facility that *always* provides microsecond timers, we provide a "soft" timer (Aron and Druschel, 1999) facility that *often* provides 10 microseconds timers. We can also bound the error of the soft timer facility by adding a hardware clock interrupt every 1 millisecond. Thus soft timers are useful for applications that can benefit from an expected case (**P11**) of tens of microseconds and a worst case of 1 millisecond.

Fortunately, a large fraction of applications that use timers can benefit from such approximate timers. Consider failure recovery, for example, fast retransmission. If most retransmissions are fast except for the occasional retransmission that takes 1 millisecond, failure performance will improve. Also, consider algorithms where the rate of production of some entity is being controlled. As long as the algorithm correctness can tolerate variability or jitter in the rate, performance should improve in the expected case. For example, Aron and Druschel (1999) show how a TCP connection can be rate controlled to send packets roughly every 12 microseconds. The finer rate control decreases the burstiness of the data, but deviations in the rate do not affect correctness.

Finally, perhaps the right way to handle microsecond, or even nanosecond, timers is to add hardware (**P5**). Such hardware could be in the form of a timer chip that completely handles all timers within the chip using timing wheels or a d-heap. Thus the chip has an internal hardware clock, and the hardware clock interrupt is fielded within the chip; the CPU is interrupted only when a timer expires. However, if timers are frequently canceled, there can be considerable overhead for the CPU to cancel timers by communicating with the chip.

7.10 Conclusions

This chapter describes two techniques for efficient timer implementation. The first technique, timing wheels, reduces the overhead of a timer implementation to constant time, regardless of the number of outstanding timers. This allows a timer facility to provide a very large number of timers, a useful feature for today's Internet servers, which sometimes service thousands of concurrent clients. The second technique, soft timers, reduces the operating system overhead incurred by PERTICKBOOKKEEPING. This allows a timer facility to provide fine-grained timers in the expected case, a useful feature as Internet link speeds increase. The principles used within these two schemes are summarized in Table 7.1.

When timing wheels were first described (Varghese and Lauck, 1987), they were generally considered as solving a useless problem. As one system designer put it at the time, "If it ain't broke, why fix it?"—a valid question. It helps, however, to think of schemes for problems that you project will appear in the future. The following information is paraphrased from Justin Gibbs, a key early implementor of FreeBSD, though its references to actual product use are dated.

Quoted in the first edition of this book, Gibbs said that (in those days) Yahoo! served all of its content through 500 FreeBSD servers distributed throughout the world. Also in those days, Hotmail, the largest provider of Web-based e-mail services, initially used FreeBSD for both e-mail routing and Web services. Further, thousands of ISPs, including two of the largest ISPs in the nation, Best Internet and USWest, relied on FreeBSD in that era to provide Internet news services, packet routing, Web hosting, and shell services for their users.

In the latter half of 1997 it became apparent, however, that the timer services used in the FreeBSD kernel would soon become a bottleneck for system throughput. Timer events were employed in several applications that require per-transaction, time-based, notifications. As the number and/or frequency of transactions was scaled higher, the load on the timer interface increased linearly. As an example, the FreeBSD kernel used to schedule a "watch dog" timer for every disk transaction, which, if fired, initiates error recovery actions. On a typical server machine, over 15% of the CPU was consumed by timer event scheduling under a modest load of 250 concurrent disk transactions. Analysis of the algorithms employed by the old timer interfaces showed that the CPU load would rise linearly with the number of concurrent transactions. System scalability was compromised.

After finding a bug in the Costello implementation that he fixed, Justin Gibbs implemented Hashed Wheels in FreeBSD. His implementation reduced timer overhead in the FreeBSD benchmarks to a fraction of a percent of total CPU usage. The Costello algorithm ensured near constant overhead regardless of the transactional load, guaranteeing that the timer facility scaled to many thousands of transactions with ease. While the BSD code was later updated for multicore machines and later by Motin and Italiano (Motin and Italiano, 2018), the basic use of a hashed wheel remains after twenty years.

Many other operating systems, such as Linux, now use timing wheels, as do most real-time operating systems, including ones used in routers. Note that Linux does offer two timer facilities: a coarse timer (Corbet, 2015) that uses hierarchical wheels but limits migration (cascading) between wheels, and a high resolution timer (Gleixner and Niehaus, 2006) that uses red-black trees. Finally, modern cloud operating systems that do scalable traffic shaping for hundreds of thousands of flows at very fine granularity also use hashed wheels because they allow more precise shaping with small CPU overhead (Saeed et al., 2017). Attention to algorithmics can bear fruit in the long run.

7.11 Exercises

1. **Better Hash Functions:** Currently hashed wheels use a very simple and primitive hash function (low-order bits). Find a way to use your favorite hash function to do hashed wheels. (*Hint*: Consider

working with absolute time and not relative time.) What particular aspect of performance of a timer module would a better hash function improve? (This idea is due to Travis Newhouse.)

2. **Hierarchical Wheels Versus Hashed Wheels and Heaps:** Current implementations of timing wheels use hashed wheels.

- What is one possible advantage of hierarchical wheels over hashed wheels? Can you quantify the difference precisely?
- Suppose we do hierarchical wheels by dividing a 32-bit timer into four chunks of 8 bits apiece. What is the difference between such a timing wheel and a 256-way *d*-heap? When might the heap be a better solution?

Demultiplexing

Biologically the species is the accumulation of the experiments of all its successful individuals since the beginning.

—**H.G. Wells**

A protocol, like a copy center or an ice cream parlor, should be able to serve multiple clients. The clients of a protocol could be end-users (as in the case of the file transfer protocol), software programs (for example, when the tool `traceroute` uses the Internet protocol), or even other protocols (as in the case of the email protocol SMTP, which uses TCP).

Thus when a message arrives, the receiving protocol must *dispatch* the received message to the appropriate client. This function is called *demultiplexing*. Demultiplexing is an integral part of data link, routing, and transport protocols. It is a fundamental part of the abstract protocol model of Chapter 2.

Traditionally, demultiplexing is done layer by layer using a demultiplexing field contained in each layer header of the received message. Called *layered demultiplexing*, this is shown in Fig. 8.1. For example, working from bottom to top in the picture, a packet may arrive on the Ethernet at a workstation. The packet is examined by the Ethernet driver, which looks at a so-called *protocol type field* to decide what routing protocol (e.g., IP, IPX) is being used. Assuming the type field specifies IP, the Ethernet driver may upcall the IP software.

After IP processing, the IP software inspects the protocol ID field in the IP header to determine the transport protocol (e.g., TCP or UDP?). Assuming it is TCP, the packet will be passed to the TCP software. After doing TCP processing, the TCP software will examine the port numbers in the packet to demultiplex the packet to the right client, say, to a process implementing HTTP.

Traditional demultiplexing is fairly straightforward because each layer essentially does an exact match on some field or fields in the layer header. This can be done easily, using, say, hashing, as we describe in Chapter 10. Of course, the lookup costs add up at each layer.

By contrast, this chapter concentrates on *early demultiplexing*, which is a much more challenging task at high speeds. Referring back to Fig. 8.1, early demultiplexing determines the entire *path* of protocols taken by the received packet in one operation when the packet first arrives. In the last example early demultiplexing would determine in one fell swoop that the path of the Web packet was Ethernet, IP, TCP, Web. A possibly better term is *layered demultiplexing*. However, this book uses the more accepted name of early demultiplexing.

What makes early demultiplexing hard in general is to also allow applications to *flexibly* specify the lower layer protocols they wish to run over or whose packets they wish to receive. This is particularly useful for traffic monitoring or security applications. However, if the early demultiplexing is confined to TCP connections that have become standard in the last 20 years, the problem is much simpler and

Network Algorithmics. https://doi.org/10.1016/B978-0-12-809927-8.00014-2

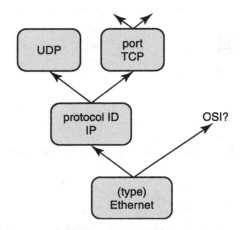

FIGURE 8.1

Traditional layered demultiplexing has each layer demultiplex a packet to the next layer software above using a field in the layer header.

can be done (as we showed in Chapter 6) by packet steering mechanisms that check if the protocol is TCP and IP (type field in Ethernet) and then demultiplexing based on the TCP 4-tuple.

Recall that Linux does "early demultiplexing" in one of two ways: either by distributing load using a hash of the TCP 4-tuple (Receive Packet Steering or RPS), or by sending the packet to the core the application is running on (Receive Flow Steering or RFS). RFS also uses a hash of the 4-tuple but uses it to index a table whose entry points to the core the packet should be steered to.

While this simple hash-based mechanism works very well for TCP and IP, it does not solve the problem of early demultiplexing for other protocols that the application can specify in real time such as is needed for a traffic monitoring application. This is the subject of this chapter.

This chapter is organized as follows. Section 8.1 delineates the reasons for early demultiplexing, and Section 8.2 outlines the goals of an efficient demultiplexing solution. The rest of the chapter studies various implementations of early demultiplexing. The chapter starts with the pioneering CMU/Stanford packet filter (CSPF) (Section 8.3), moves on to the commonly used Berkeley packet filter (BPF) (Section 8.4), and ends with more recent proposals, such as Pathfinder (Section 8.5) and DPF (Section 8.6).

The demultiplexing techniques described in this chapter (and the corresponding principles used) are summarized in Table 8.1.

Quick reference guide

The Berkeley packet filter (BPF) is freely available. However, other demultiplexing algorithms are more efficient. The implementor who wishes to design a demultiplexing routine should consider PathFinder, described in Section 8.5. While dynamic packet filter (DPF, see Section 8.6) is even faster, many implementors may find the need for dynamic code generation in DPF to be an obstacle. Recall also that early demultiplexing for TCP connections is now standard and is available in Linux under various steering mechanisms. Thus the techiques in this chapter are only useful for flexible demultiplexing for say traffic monitoring.

Table 8.1 Principles used in the various demultiplexing techniques discussed in this chapter.

Number	Principle	Used in
P9	Pass header specifications from user to kernel	CSPF
P1	Use CFG to avoid unnecessary tests	BPF
P4c	Use a register-based specification language	
P15	Factor common checks using a generalized trie	Pathfinder
P2	Specialize code when classifier is modified	DPF

8.1 Opportunities and challenges of early demultiplexing

Why is early demultiplexing a good idea? The following basic motivations were discussed in Chapter 6.

- *Flexible User-Level Implementations:* The original reason for early demultiplexing was to allow *flexible* user-level implementation of protocols without excessive context switching.
- *Efficient User-Level Implementations:* As time went on, implementors realized that early demultiplexing could also allow *efficient* user-level implementations by minimizing the number of context switches. The main additional trick was to structure the protocol implementation as a shared library that can be linked to application programs.

Note that with the advent of receive packet steering primitives for TCP packets, user level implementations can easily be done today for TCP. However, there are other advantages of early demultiplexing.

- *Prioritizing Packets:* Early demultiplexing allows important packets to be prioritized and unnecessary ones to be discarded quickly. For example, Chapter 6 shows that the problem of receiver livelock can be mitigated by early demultiplexing of received packets to place packets directly on a per-socket queue. This allows the system to discard messages for slow processes during overload while allowing better-behaved processes to continue receiving messages. More generally, early demultiplexing is crucial in providing quality-of-service guarantees for traffic streams via service differentiation. If all traffic is demultiplexed into a common kernel queue, then important packets can get lost when the shared buffer fills up in periods of overload. Routers today do packet classification for similar reasons (Chapters 12 and 14). Early demultiplexing allows explicit scheduling of the processing of data flows; scheduling and accounting can be combined to prevent anomalies such as priority inversion.
- *Specializing Paths:* Once the path for a packet is known, the code can be specialized to process the packet because the wider context is known. For example, rather than having each layer protocol check for packet lengths, this can be done just once in the spirit of **P1**, avoiding obvious waste. The philosophy of paths is taken to its logical conclusion in Mosberger and Peterson (1996), who describe an operating system in which paths are first-class objects.
- *Fast Dispatching:* This chapter and Chapter 6 have already described an instance of this idea using packet filters and user-level protocol implementations. Early demultiplexing avoids per-layer multiplexing costs; more importantly, it avoids the control overhead that can sometimes be incurred in delayered multiplexing.

8.2 Goals

If early demultiplexing is a good idea, is it easy to implement? Early demultiplexing is particularly easy to implement if each packet carries some information in the outermost (e.g., data link or network) header, which identifies the final endpoint. This is an example of **P14**, passing information in layer headers. For example, if the network protocol is a virtual circuit protocol such as ATM, the ATM virtual circuit identifier (VCI) can directly identify the final recipient of the packet.

However, protocols such as IP do not offer such a convenience. MPLS (multi-protocol label switching) does offer this convenience, but MPLS is generally used only between routers, as described in Chapter 11. Even using a protocol such as ATM, the number of available VCIs may be limited. In lieu of a single demultiplexing field more complex data structures are needed that we call *packet filters* or *packet classifiers*. Of course, as we have pointed out at the start, doing this just for TCP connections is easy using a hash of the TCP 4-tuple but the more general solutions require better data structures.

Such data structures take a complete packet header as input and map the input to an endpoint or path. Intuitively, the endpoint of a packet represents the receiving application process, while the path represents the sequence of protocols that need to be invoked in processing the packet prior to consumption by the endpoint. Before describing how packet filters are built, here are the goals of a good early-demultiplexing algorithm.

*   *Safety:* Many early-demultiplexing algorithms are implemented in the kernel based on input from user-level programs. Each user program P specifies the packets it wishes to receive. As with Java programs, designers must ensure that incorrect or malicious users cannot affect other users. This is particularly important even today for traffic monitoring.
*   *Speed:* Since demultiplexing is done in real time, the early-demultiplexing code should run quickly, particularly in the case where there is only a single filter specified.
*   *Composability:* If N user programs specify packet filters that describe the packets they expect to receive, the implementation should ideally compose these N individual packet filters into a single composite packet filter. The composite filter should have the property that it is faster to search through the composite filter than to search each of the N filters individually, especially for large N.

This chapter takes a mildly biological view, describing a series of packet filter species, with each successive adaptation achieving more of the goals than the previous one. Not surprisingly, the earliest species is nearly extinct, though it is noteworthy for its simplicity and historical interest.

8.3 CMU/Stanford packet filter: pioneering packet filters

The CMU/CSPF (Mogul et al., 1987) was developed to allow user-level protocol implementations in the Mach operating system. In the CSPF model application programs provide the kernel with a *program* describing the packets they wish to receive. The program supplied by A operates on a packet header and returns **true** if the packet should be routed to application A. Like the old Texas Instrument calculators, the programming language is a stack-based implementation of an *expression tree* model.

As shown in Fig. 8.2, the leaves of the tree represent simple test predicates on packet headers. An example of a test predicate is equality comparison with a fixed value; for example, in Fig. 8.2, ETHER.TYPE = ARP represents a check of whether the Ethernet type field in the received packet

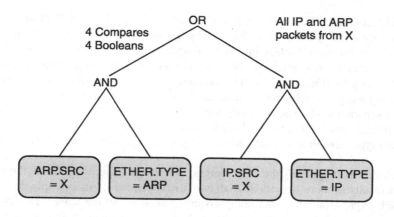

FIGURE 8.2

The CMU/CSPF allows applications to provide programs that specify an expression tree representing the packets they wish to receive. The tree shown here effectively asks for all IP and ARP packets sent by IP source address X.

matches the constant value specified for ARP (address resolution protocol) packets. The other nodes in the tree represent boolean operations such as AND and OR.

Thus the left subtree of the expression tree in Fig. 8.2 represents any ARP packet sent from source IP address X, while the right subtree represents any IP packet sent from source IP address X. Since the root represents an OR operation, the overall tree asks for all IP or ARP packets sent by a source X. Such an expression could be provided by a debugging tool to the kernel on behalf of a user who wished to examine IP traffic coming from source X.

While the expression tree model provides a *declarative* model of a filter, such filters actually use an *imperative* stack-based language to describe expression trees. To provide safety, CSPF provides stack instructions of limited power; to bound running times, there are no jumps or looping constructs. Safety is also achieved by checking program loads and stores in real time to eliminate wild memory references. Thus stack references are monitored to ensure compliance with the stack range, and references to packets are vetted to ensure they stay within the length of the packet being demultiplexed.

8.4 Berkeley packet filter: enabling high-performance monitoring

CSPF guarantees security by using instructions of limited power and by doing run-time bounds checking on memory accesses. However, CSPF is not composable and has problems with speed. The next mutation in the design of packet filters occurred with the introduction of the BPF (McCanne and Jacobson, 1993).

The BPF designers were particularly interested in using BPF as a basis for high-performance network-monitoring tools such as `tcpdump`, for which speed was crucial. They noted two speed problems with the use of even a single CSPF expression tree of the kind shown in Fig. 8.2.

- *Architectural Mismatch:* The CSPF stack model was invented for the PDP-11 and hence is a poor match to modern RISC architectures. First, the stack must be simulated at the price of an extra memory reference for each Boolean operation to update the stack pointer. Second, RISC architectures gain efficiency from storing variables in fast registers and doing computation directly from registers. Thus to gain efficiency in a RISC architecture, as many computations as possible should take place using a register value before it is reused. For instance, in Fig. 8.2, the CSPF model will result in two separate loads from memory for each reference to the Ethernet type field (to check equality with ARP and IP). On modern machines, it would be better to reduce memory references by storing the type field in a register and finishing all comparisons with the type field in one fell swoop.
- *Inefficient Model:* Even ignoring the extra memory references required by CSPF, the expression tree model often results in more operations than are strictly required. For example, in Fig. 8.2, notice that the CSPF expression takes four comparisons to evaluate all the leaves. However, notice that once we know that the Ethernet type is equal to ARP (if we are evaluating from left to right), then the extra check for whether the IP source address is equal to X is redundant (Principle **P1**, seek to avoid waste). The main problem is that in the expression tree model there is no way to "remember" packet parse state as the computation progresses. This can be fixed by a new model that builds a state machine.

CSPF had two other minor problems. It could only parse fields at fixed offsets within packet headers; thus it could not be used to access a TCP header encapsulated within an IP header because this requires first parsing the IP header-length field. CSPF also processes headers using only 16-bit fields; this doubles the number of operations required for 32-bit fields such as IP addresses.

The BPF fixes these problems as follows. First, it replaces the stack-based language with a register-based language, with an indirection operator that can help parse TCP headers. Fields at specified packet offsets are loaded into registers using a command such as "LOAD [12]," which loads the Ethernet type field, which happens to start at an offset of 12 bytes from the start of an Ethernet packet.

BPF can then do comparisons and jumps such as "JUMP_IF_EQUAL ETHERTYPE_IP, TARGET1, TARGET2." This instruction compares the accumulator register to the IP Ethernet type field; if the comparison is true, the program jumps to line number TARGET1; otherwise, it jumps to TARGET2. BPF allows working in 8-, 16-, and 32-bit chunks.

More fundamentally, BPF uses a *control flow graph* (CFG) model of computation, as illustrated in Fig. 8.3. This is basically a state machine starting with a root, whose state is updated at each node, following which it transitions to other node states, shown as arcs to other nodes. The state machine starts off by checking whether the Ethernet type field is that of IP; if true, it need only check whether the IP source field is X to return true. If false, it needs to check whether the Ethernet type field is ARP and whether the ARP source is X. Notice that in the left branch of the state machine we do not check whether the IP source address is X. Thus the worst-case number of comparisons is 3 in Fig. 8.3, compared to 4 in Fig. 8.2.

The BPF is used as a basis for a number of tools, including the well-known `tcpdump` tool by which users can obtain a readable transcript of TCP packets flowing on a link. BPF is embedded into the BSD kernel as shown in Fig. 8.4.

When a packet arrives on a network link, such as an Ethernet, the packet is processed by the appropriate link-level driver and is normally passed to the TCP/IP protocol stack for processing. However, if

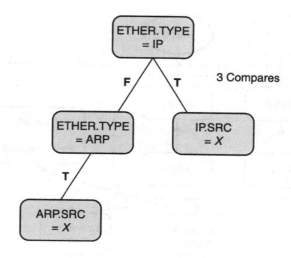

FIGURE 8.3

The BPF uses a state machine or CFG as its underlying model, which enables it to avoid redundant comparisons when compared to Fig. 8.2.

BPF is active, BPF is first called. BPF checks the packet against each currently specified user filter. For each matching filter, BPF copies as many bytes as are specified by the filter to a per-filter buffer. Notice that multiple BPF applications can cause multiple copies of the same packet to be buffered. The figure also shows another common BPF application besides tcpdump, the reverse ARP demon (rarpd).

There are two small features of BPF that are also important for high performance. First, BPF filters packets before buffering, which avoids unnecessary waste (**P1**) when most of the received packets are not wanted by BPF's applications. The waste is not just memory for buffers but also for the time required to do a copy (Chapter 5).

Second, since packets can arrive very fast and the read() system call is quite slow, BPF allows batch processing (**P2c**) and allows multiple packets to be returned to the monitoring application in one call. To handle this and yet allow packet boundaries to be distinguished, BPF adds a header to each packet that includes a timestamp and length. Users of tcpdump do not have to use this interface; instead, tcpdump offers a more user-friendly interface: interface commands are compiled to BPF instructions.

8.5 Pathfinder: factoring out common checks

BPF is a more refined adaptation than CSPF because it increases speed for a single filter. However, every packet must still be compared with each filter in turn. Thus the processing time grows with the number of filters. Fortunately, this is not a problem for typical BPF usage. For example, a typical tcpdump application may provide only a few filters to BPF.

However, this is not true if early demultiplexing is used to discriminate between a large number of packet streams or paths. In particular, each TCP connection may provide a filter, and the number

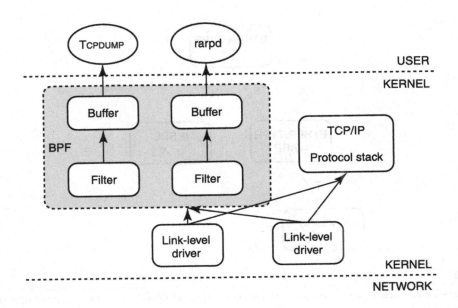

FIGURE 8.4

Packets arriving on a link are sent to both BPF (for potential logging) and the protocol stack (for normal protocol processing). BPF applies all currently specified filters and queues the packet to the appropriate buffer if the filter indicates a match.

of concurrent TCP connections in a busy server can be large. The need to deal with this change in environment (user-level networking) led to another successful mutation called *Pathfinder* (Bailey et al., 1994). Pathfinder goes beyond BPF by providing *composability*. This allows scaling to a large number of users.

To motivate the Pathfinder solution, imagine there are 500 filters, each of which is exactly the same (Ethernet type field is IP, IP protocol type is TCP) except that each specifies a different TCP port pair. Doing each filter sequentially would require comparing the Ethernet type of the packet 500 times against the (same) IP Ethernet type field and comparing the IP protocol field 500 times against the (same) TCP protocol value. This is wasteful (**P1**).

Next, comparing the TCP port numbers in the packet to each of the 500 port pairs specified in each of the 500 filters is not obvious waste. However, this is exactly analogous to a linear search for exact matching. This suggests that integrating all the individual filters into a single composite filter can considerably reduce unnecessary comparisons when the number of individual filters is large. Specifically, this can be done using hashing (**P15**, using efficient data structures) to perform an exact search; this can replace 500 comparisons with just a few comparisons.

As we have said repeatedly at the start of this chapter, if one only has TCP this notion of hashing is already implemented by receive packet steering mechanisms. A more complex data structure is needed if one wishes to do flexible demultiplexing of general protocols.

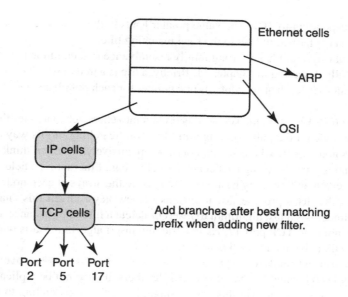

FIGURE 8.5

The Pathfinder data structure integrates several versions of the BPF CFG integrated into a composite structure. In the composite structure all the different field values specified in different filters for a given header field are placed in a single node. Rather than searching these values linearly, the header field values are placed in a hash table.

A data structure for this purpose is shown in Fig. 8.5. The basic idea is to superimpose the CFGs for each filter in BPF so that all comparisons on the same field are placed in a single node. Finally, each node is implemented as a hash table containing all comparison values to replace linear search with hashing.

Fig. 8.5 shows an example with at least four filters, two of which specify TCP packets with destination port numbers 2 and 5; for now, ignore the dashed line to TCP port 17, which will be used as an example of filter insertion in a moment. Besides the TCP filters, there are one or more filters that specify ARP packets and one or more filters that specify packets that use the OSI protocol.

The root node corresponds to the Ethernet type field; the hash table contains values for each possible Ethernet type field value used in the filters. Each node entry has a value and a pointer. Thus the ARP entry points to nodes that further specify what type of ARP packets must be received; the OSI entry does likewise. Finally, the Ethernet type field corresponding to IP points to a node corresponding to the IP protocol field.

In the IP protocol field node one of the values corresponding to TCP (which has value 6) will point to the TCP node. In the TCP node there are three values pointing to the three possible destination port values of 2 and 5 (recall that the 17 has not been inserted yet). When a TCP packet arrives, demultiplexing proceeds as follows.

Search starts at the root, and the Ethernet type field is hashed to find a matching value corresponding to IP. The pointer of this value leads to the IP node, where the IP protocol type field is hashed to find a matching value corresponding to TCP. The value pointer leads to the TCP node, where the destination port value in the packet is hashed to lead to the final matching filter.

The Pathfinder data structure has a strong family resemblance to a common data structure called a *trie*, which is more fully described in Chapter 11. Briefly, a trie is a tree in which each node contains an array of pointers to subtries; each array contains one pointer for each possible value of a fixed-character alphabet.

To search the trie for a keyword, the keyword is broken into characters, and the ith character is used to index into the ith node on the path, starting with the root. Searching in this way at node i yields a pointer that leads to node $i + 1$, where search continues recursively. One can think of the Pathfinder structure as generalizing a trie by using packet header fields (e.g., Ethernet type field) as the successive characters used for search and by using hash tables to replace the arrays at each node.

It is well known that tries provide fast insertions of new keys. Given this analogy, it is hardly surprising that Pathfinder has a fast algorithm to insert or delete a filter. For instance, consider inserting a new filter corresponding to TCP port 17. As in a trie, the insert algorithm starts with a search for the longest matching prefix (Chapter 11) of this new filter.

This longest match corresponds to the path `Ethernet Type = IP and IP Protocol = TCP`. Since this path has already been created by the other two TCP filters, it need not be replicated. The insertion algorithm only has to add branches (in this case a single branch) corresponding to the portion of the new filter beyond the longest match. Thus the hash table in the TCP node need only be updated to add a new pointer to the port 17 filter.

More precisely, the basic atomic unit in Pathfinder is called a *cell*. A cell specifies a field of bits in a packet header (using an offset, length, and a mask), a comparison value, and a pointer. For example, ignoring the pointer, the cell that checks whether the protocol field in the IP header is (`9, 1, 0xff, 6`)—the cell specifies that the tenth byte of the IP header should be masked with all 1's and compared to the value 6, which specifies TCP.

Cells of a given user are strung together to form a *pattern* for that user. Multiple patterns are superimposed to form the Pathfinder trie by not recreating cells that already exist. Finally, multiple cells that specify identical bit fields but different values are coalesced using a hash table.

Besides using hash tables in place of arrays, Pathfinder also goes beyond tries by making each node contain arbitrary code. In effect, Pathfinder recognizes that a trie is a specialized state machine that can be generalized by performing arbitrary operations at each node in the trie. For instance, Pathfinder can handle fragmented packets by allowing *loadable* cells in addition to the *comparison* cells described earlier. This is required because for a fragmented packet, only the first fragment specifies the TCP headers; what links the fragments together is a common packet ID described in the first fragment.

Pathfinder handles fragmentation by placing an additional loadable cell (together with the normal IP comparison cell specifying, say, a source address) that is loaded with the packet ID after the first fragment arrives. A cell is specified as loadable by not specifying the comparison value in a cell.

The loadable cell is not initially part of the Pathfinder trie but is instead an attribute of the IP cells. If the first fragment matches, the loaded cell is inserted into the Pathfinder trie and now matches subsequent fragments based on the newly loaded packet ID. After all fragments have been removed, this newly added cell can be removed. Finally, Pathfinder handles the case when the later fragments arrive before the first fragment by postponing their processing until the first fragment arrives.

Although Pathfinder has been described so far as a tree, the data structure can be generalized to a directed acyclic graph (DAG). A DAG allows two different filters to initially follow different paths through the Pathfinder graph and yet come together to share a common path suffix. This can be useful, for instance, when providing a filter for TCP packets for destination port 80 that can be fragmented or unfragmented. While one needs a separate path of cells to specify fragmented and unfragmented IP packets, the two paths can point to a common set of TCP cells.

Finally, Pathfinder also allows the use of OR links that lead from a cell. The idea is that each of the OR links specify a value, and each of the OR links is checked to find a value that matches and then that link is followed.

In order to prioritize packets during periods of congestion, as in Chapter 6, the demultiplexing routine must complete in the minimum time it takes to receive a packet. Software implementations of Pathfinder are fast but are typically unable to keep up with line speeds. Fortunately, the Pathfinder state machine can be implemented in hardware to run at line speeds. This is analogous to the way IP lookups using tries can be made to work at line speeds (Chapter 11).

The hardware prototype described in Bailey et al. (1994) trades functionality for speed. It works in 16-bit chunks and implements only the most basic cell functions; it does, however, implement fragmentation in hardware. The limited functionality implies that the Pathfinder *hardware* can only be used as a cache to speed up Pathfinder *software* that handles the less common cases. A prototype design running at 100 MHz was projected to take 200 nanoseconds to process a 40-byte TCP message, which is sufficient for 1.5 Gbps. The design can be scaled to higher wire speeds using faster clock rates, faster memories, and a pipelined traversal of the state machine.

8.6 Dynamic packet filter: compilers to the rescue

The Pathfinder story ends with an appeal to hardware to handle demultiplexing at high speeds. Since it is unlikely that most workstations and PCs today can afford dedicated demultiplexing hardware, it appears that implementors must choose between the *flexibility* afforded by early demultiplexing and the limited *performance* of a software classifier. Thus it is hardly surprising that high-performance TCP (Clark et al., 1989), active messages (von Eicken et al., 1992b), and remote procedure call (RPC) (Thekkath et al., 1993) implementations use hand-crafted demultiplexing routines.

Dynamic packet filter (DPF) (Engler and Kaashoek, 1996) attempts to have its cake (gain flexibility) and eat it (obtain performance) at the same time. DPF starts with the Pathfinder trie idea. However, it goes on to eliminate indirections and extra checks inherent in cell processing by *recompiling the classifier into machine code each time a filter is added or deleted*. In effect, DPF produces separate, optimized code for each cell in the trie, as opposed to generic, unoptimized code that can parse any cell in the trie.

DPF is based on *dynamic code generation* technology (Engler, 1996), which allows code to be generated at run time instead of when the kernel is compiled. DPF is an application of Principle **P2**, shifting computation in time. Note that by run time we mean *classifier update* time and not *packet processing* time.

This is fortunate because this implies that DPF must be able to recompile code fast enough so as not to slow down a classifier update. For example, it may take milliseconds to set up a connection, which in turn requires adding a filter to identify the endpoint at the same time. By contrast, it can take a few microseconds to receive a minimum-size packet at gigabit rates. Despite this leeway, submillisecond compile times are still challenging.

To understand why using specialized code per cell is useful, it helps to understand two generic causes of cell-processing inefficiency in Pathfinder:

- *Interpretation Overhead:* Pathfinder code is indeed compiled into machine instructions when kernel code is compiled. However, the code does, in some sense, "interpret" a generic Pathfinder cell. To see this, consider a generic Pathfinder cell C that specifies a 4-tuple: offset, length, mask, value. When a packet P arrives, idealized machine code to check whether the cell matches the packet is as follows:

```
LOAD R1, C(Offset); (* load offset specified in cell into register R1 *)
LOAD R2, C(length); (* load length specified in cell into register R2 *)
LOAD R3, P(R1, R2); (* load packet field specified by offset into R3 *)
LOAD R1, C(mask); (* load mask specified in cell into register R1 *)
AND R3, R1; (* mask packet field as specified in cell *)
LOAD R2, C(value); (* load value specified in cell into register R2 *)
BNE R2, R3; (* branch if masked packet field is not equal to value *)
```

Notice the extra instructions and extra memory references in Lines 1, 2, 4, and 6 that are used to load parameters from a generic cell in order to be available for later comparison.
- *Safety-Checking Overhead:* Because packet filters written by users cannot be trusted, all implementations must perform checks to guard against errors. For example, every reference to a packet field must be checked at run time to ensure that it stays within the current packet being demultiplexed. Similarly, references need to be checked in real time for memory alignment; on many machines, a memory reference that is not aligned to a multiple of a word size can cause a trap. After these additional checks, the code fragment shown earlier is more complicated and contains even more instructions.

By specializing code for each cell, DPF can eliminate these two sources of overhead by exploiting information known when the cell is added to the Pathfinder graph.

- *Exterminating Interpretation Overhead:* Since DPF knows all the cell parameters when the cell is created, DPF can generate code in which the cell parameters are directly encoded into the machine code as immediate operands. For example, the earlier code fragment to parse a generic Pathfinder cell collapses to the more compact cell-specific code:

```
LOAD R3, P(offset, length); (* load packet field into R3 *)
AND R3, mask; (* mask packet field using mask in instruction *)
BNE R3, value; (* branch if field not equal to value *)
```

Notice that the extra instructions and (more importantly) extra memory references to load parameters have disappeared, because the parameters are directly placed as immediate operands within the instructions.
- *Mitigating Safety-Checking Overhead:* Alignment checking can be reduced in the expected case (**P11**) by inferring at compile time that most references are word aligned. This can be done by examining the complete filter. If the initial reference is word aligned and the current reference (offset

plus the length of all previous headers) is a multiple of the word length, then the reference is word aligned. Real-time alignment checks need only be used when the compile time inference fails, for example, when indirect loads are performed (e.g., a variable-size IP header). Similarly, at compile time the largest offset used in any cell can be determined and a single check can be placed (before packet processing) to ensure that the largest offset is within the length of the current packet.

Once one is onto a good thing, it pays to push it for all it is worth. DPF goes on to exploit compile time knowledge in DPF to perform further optimizations as follows. A first optimization is to combine small accesses to adjacent fields into a single large access. Other optimizations are explored in the exercises.

DPF has the following potential disadvantages that are made manageable through careful design.

- *Recompilation Time:* Recall that when a filter is added to the Pathfinder trie (Fig. 8.5), only cells that were not present in the original trie need to be created. DPF optimizes this expected case (**P11**) by caching the code for existing cells and copying this code directly (without recreating them from scratch) to the new classifier code block. New code must be emitted only for the newly created cells. Similarly, when a new value is added to a hash table (e.g., the new TCP port added in Fig. 8.5), unless the hash function changes, the code is reused and only the hash table is updated.
- *Code Bloat:* One of the standard advantages of interpretation is more compact code. Generating specialized code per cell *appears* to create excessive amounts of code, especially for large numbers of filters. A large code footprint can, in turn, result in degraded instruction cache performance. However, a careful examination shows that the number of distinct code blocks generated by DPF is only proportional to the number of *distinct header fields* examined by all filters. This should scale much better than the number of filters. Consider, for example, 10,000 simultaneous TCP connections, for which DPF may emit only three specialized code blocks: one for the Ethernet header, one for the IP header, and one hash table for the TCP header.

The final performance numbers for DPF are impressive. DPF demultiplexes messages 13–26 times faster than Pathfinder on a comparable platform (Engler and Kaashoek, 1996). The time to add a filter, however, is only three times slower than Pathfinder. Dynamic code generation accounts for only 40% of this increased insertion overhead.

In any case, the larger insertion costs appear to be a reasonable way to pay for faster demultiplexing. Finally, DPF demultiplexing routines appear to rival or beat hand-crafted demultiplexing routines; for instance, a DPF routine to demultiplex IP packets takes 18 instructions, compared to an earlier value, reported in Clark (1985), of 57 instructions. While the two implementations were on different machines, the numbers provide some indication of DPF quality.

The final message of DPF is twofold. First, DPF indicates that one can obtain both performance and flexibility. Just as compiler-generated code is often faster than hand-crafted code, DPF code appears to make hand-crafted demultiplexing no longer necessary. Second, DPF indicates that hardware support for demultiplexing at line rates may not be necessary. In fact, it may be difficult to allow dynamic code generation on filter creation in a hardware implementation. Software demultiplexing allows cheaper workstations; it also allows demultiplexing code to benefit from processor speed improvements.

Technology changes can invalidate design assumptions

There are several examples of innovations in architecture and operating systems that were discarded after initial use and then returned to be used again. While this may seem like the whims of fashion ("collars are frilled again in 1995") or reinventing the wheel ("there is nothing new under the sun"), it takes a careful understanding of current technology to know when to dust off an old idea, possibly even in a new guise.

Take, for example, the core of the telephone network used to send voice calls via analog signals. With the advent of fiber optics and the transistor, much of the core telephone network now transmits voice signals in digital formats using the T1 and SONET hierarchies. However, with the advent of wavelength-division multiplexing in optical fiber, there is at least some talk of returning to analog transmission.

Thus the good system designer must constantly monitor available technology to check whether the system design assumptions have been invalidated. The idea of using dynamic compilation was mentioned by the CSPF designers in Mogul et al. (1987) but was not considered further. The CSPF designers assumed that tailoring code to specific sets of filters (by recompiling the classifier code whenever a filter was added) was too "complicated."

Dynamic compilation at the time of the CSPF design was probably slow and also not portable across systems; the gains at that time would have also been marginal because of other bottlenecks. However, by the time DPF was being designed, a number of systems, including VCODE (Engler, 1996), had designed fairly fast and portable dynamic compilation infrastructure. The other classifier implementations in DPF's lineage had also eliminated other bottlenecks, which allowed the benefits of dynamic compilation to stand out more clearly.

8.7 Conclusions

While it may be trite to say that necessity is the mother of invention, it is also often true. New needs drive new innovations; the lack of a need explains why innovations did not occur earlier. The CSPF filter was implemented when the major need was to avoid a process context switch; having achieved that, improved filter performance was only a second-order effect. BPF was implemented when the major need was to implement a few filters very efficiently to enable monitoring tools like `tcpdump` to run at close to wire speeds. Having achieved that, scaling to a large number of filters seemed less important.

Pathfinder was implemented to support user-level networking in the x-kernel (Hutchinson and Peterson, 1991), and to allow Scout (Mosberger and Peterson, 1996) to use paths as a first-class object that could be exploited in many ways. Having found a plausible hardware implementation, perhaps improved software performance seemed less important. DPF was implemented to provide high-performance networking together with complete application-level flexibility in the context of an extensible operating system (Engler et al., 1995). Table 8.1 presents a summary of the techniques used in this chapter, together with the major principles involved.

However, given the popularity of TCP/IP today and the availability of packet steering mechanisms in major operating systems, it seems unclear that Pathfinder and DPF are worth the extra complexity today. BPF continues to be useful for monitoring tools.

In terms of ideas, however, as in the H.G. Wells quote at the start of the chapter, each algorithm builds on the earlier algorithms. All filter implementations borrow from CSPF the intellectual leap of separating demultiplexing from packet processing, together with the notion that application demultiplexing specifications can be safely exported to the kernel. DPF and Pathfinder in turn borrow from BPF the basic notion of exploiting the underlying architecture using a register-based, state-machine model. DPF borrows from Pathfinder the notion of using a generalized trie to factor out common checks.

8.8 Exercises

1. **Other Uses of Early Demultiplexing:** Besides the uses of early demultiplexing already described, consider the following potential uses.

   - *Quality of Service:* Why might early demultiplexing help offer different qualities of service to different packets in an end system? Give an example.
   - *Integrated Layer Processing:* Integrated layer processing (ILP) was studied in Chapter 5. Discuss why early demultiplexing may be needed for ILP.
   - *Specializing Code:* Once the path of a protocol is known, one can possibly specialize the code for the path, just as DPF specializes the code for each node. Give an example of how path information could be exploited to create more efficient code.

2. **Further DPF Optimizations:** Besides the optimizations already described, consider the following other optimizations that DPF exploits.

   - *Atom Coalescing:* It often happens that a node in the DPF tree checks for two smaller field values in the same word. For example, the TCP node may check for a source port value and a destination port value. How can DPF do these checks more efficiently? What crucial assumption does this depend on, and how can DPF validate this assumption?
   - *Optimizing Hash Tables:* When DPF adds a classifier, it may update the hash table at the node. Unlike Pathfinder, the code can be specialized to the specific set of values in each hash table. Explain why this can be used to provide a more efficient implementation for small tables and for collision handling in some cases.

Protocol processing

9

Household tasks are easier and quicker when they are done by somebody else.

—James Thorpe

Our mental image of a musician is often associated with giving a recital, and our image of a researcher may involve his mulling over a problem. However, musicians spend more time in less glamorous tasks, such as practicing scales, and researchers spend more time than they wish on mundane chores, such as writing grants. Mastery of a vocation requires paying attention to many small tasks and not just to a few big jobs.

Similarly, tutorials on efficient protocol implementation often emphasize methods of avoiding data-touching overhead and structuring techniques to reduce control overhead. These, of course, were the topics covered in Chapters 5 and 6. This is entirely appropriate because the biggest improvements in endnode implementations often come from attention to such overhead.

However, having created a zero-copy implementation with minimal context switching—and there is strong evidence that modern implementations of network appliances have learned these lessons well—new bottlenecks invite scrutiny. In fact, a measurement study by Kay and Pasquale (1993) shows that these other bottlenecks can be significant.

There are a host of other protocol implementation tasks that can become new bottlenecks. Chapters 7 and 8 have already dealt with efficient timer and demultiplexing implementations. This chapter deals briefly with some of the common remaining tasks: buffer management, checksums, sequence number bookkeeping, reassembly, and generic protocol processing.

The importance of these protocol-processing "chores" may be increasing for the following reasons. First, link speeds in the local network are already at gigabit levels and are going higher. Second, market pressures are mounting to implement TCP, and even higher-level application tasks, such as Web services and XML, in hardware. Third, there is a large number of small packets on the Internet for which data manipulation overhead may *not* be the dominant factor.

This chapter is organized as follows. Section 9.1 delves into techniques for managing buffer, that is, techniques for fast buffer allocation and buffer sharing. Section 9.2 presents techniques for implementing cyclic redundancy checks (CRCs) (mostly at the link level) and checksums (mostly at the transport level). Section 9.3 deals with the efficient implementation of generic protocol processing, as exemplified by TCP and UDP. Finally, Section 9.4 covers the efficient implementation of packet reassembly.

The techniques presented in this chapter (and the corresponding principles) are summarized in Table 9.1.

Network Algorithmics. https://doi.org/10.1016/B978-0-12-809927-8.00015-4

Table 9.1 Principles used in the various protocol-processing techniques discussed in this chapter.

Number	Principle	Used in
P4b	Use linear buffers, not mbuf chains	Linux sk_buf
P4b	Buddy system without coalescing	BSD 4.2 malloc()
P2b	Sequential chunk allocation, lazy chunk creation	J-machine
P14	Efficient buffer stealing	SFQ
P13	Dynamic buffer thresholds	
P2a	CRC multiple bits at a time using table lookup	Many CRC chips
P2b	Lazy carry evaluation	Fast checksums
P12a	Recompute header checksum	RFC 1624
P4c	Compute data link and application CRC	Infiniband
P11	Predict next TCP header	BSD TCP
P3c	Shift fragmentation from router to source	Path MTU
P11	Fast fragment reassembly	
P6	Create efficient specialized routines	UDP checksums

Quick reference guide

The first part of Section 9.1 describes a number of buffering strategies, including UNIX mbufs and Linux sk_bufs, as well as a variety of efficient memory allocators, such as the Kingsley allocator. Implementors interested in fast cyclic redundancy check (CRC) algorithms should read Section 9.2.1; those interested in fast IP checksums should read Section 9.2.2. The first few pages of Section 9.3 describe the classic TCP processing optimization called *header prediction*.

9.1 Buffer management

All protocols have to manage buffers. In particular, packets travel up and down the protocol stack in buffers. The operating system must provide services to allocate and deallocate buffers. This requires managing free memory; finding memory of the appropriate size can be challenging, especially because buffer allocation must be done in real time. Section 9.1.1 describes a simple systems solution for doing buffer allocation at high speeds, even for requests of variable sizes.

If the free space must be shared between a number of connections or users, it may also be important to provide some form of fairness so that one user cannot hog all the resources. While static limits work, in some cases it may be preferable to allow dynamic buffer limits, where a process in isolation can get as many buffers as it needs but relinquishes extra buffers when other processes arrive. Section 9.1.2 describes two dynamic buffer-limiting schemes that can be implemented at high speeds.

9.1.1 Buffer allocation

The classical BSD UNIX implementation, called *mbufs*, allowed a single packet to be stored as a linear list of smaller buffers, where a buffer is a contiguous area of memory.[1] The motivation for this technique

---

[1] Craig Partridge attributes the invention of mbufs to Rob Gurwitz (Partridge et al., 2004).

is to allow the space allocated to the packet to grow and shrink (for example, as it passes up and down the stack). For instance, it is easy to grow a packet by prepending a new mbuf to the current chain of mbufs. For even more flexibility, BSD mbufs come in three flavors: two small sizes (100 and 108 bytes) and one large size (2048 bytes, called a *cluster*).

Besides allowing dynamic expansion of a packet's allocated memory, mbufs make efficient use of memory, something that was important around 1981, when mbufs were invented. For example, a packet of 190 bytes would be allocated two mbufs (wasting around 20 bytes), while a packet of 450 bytes would be allocated five mbufs (wasting around 50 bytes).

However, dynamic expansion of a packet's size may be less important than it sounds because the header sizes for important packet paths (e.g., Ethernet, IP, TCP) are well known and can be preallocated. Similarly, saving memory may be less important in workstations today than increasing the speed of packet processing. On the other hand, the mbuf implementation makes accessing and copying data much harder because it may require traversing the list.

Thus very early on, Van Jacobson designed a prototype kernel that used what we called *pbufs*. As Jacobson puts it in an email note (Jacobson, 1993): "There is exactly one, contiguous, packet per pbuf (none of that mbuf chain stupidity)."

While pbufs have sunk into oblivion, the Linux operating system currently uses a very similar idea (Cox, 1996) for network buffers called *sk_buf*. These buffers, like pbufs, are linear buffers with space saved in advance for any packet headers that need to be added later. At times, this will incur wasted space to handle the worst-case headers, but the simpler implementation makes this worthwhile. Both sk_bufs and pbufs relax the specification of a buffer to avoid unnecessary generality (**P7**) and trade memory for time (**P4b**).

Given that the use of linear buffer sizes, as in Linux, is a good idea, how do we allocate memory for packets of various sizes? Dynamic memory allocation is a hard problem in general because users (e.g., TCP connections) deallocate at different times, and these deallocations can fragment memory into a patchwork of holes of different sizes.

The standard textbook algorithms, such as First-Fit and Best-Fit (Wilson et al., 1995), effectively stroll through memory, looking for a hole of the appropriate size. Any implementor of a high-speed networking implementation, say, TCP, should be filled with horror at the thought of using such allocators. Instead, the following three allocators should be considered.

Segregated pool allocator

One of the fastest allocators, due to Chris Kingsley, was distributed along with BSD 4.2 UNIX. Kingsley's *malloc()* implementation splits all of memory into a set of segregated pools of memory in powers of 2. Any request is rounded up to its closest power of 2, a table lookup is done to find the corresponding pool list, and a buffer is allocated from the head of that list if available. The pools are said to be segregated because when a request of a certain size fails, there is no attempt made to carve up available larger buffers or to coalesce contiguous smaller buffers.

Such carving up and coalescing is actually done by a more classical scheme called the *buddy system* (see Wilson et al., 1995 for a thorough review of memory allocators). Refraining from doing so clearly wastes memory (**P4b**, trading memory for speed). If all the requests are for exactly one pool size, then the other pools are wasted. However, this restraint is not as bad as it seems because allocators using the buddy system have a far more horrible worst case.

Suppose, for example, that all requests are for size 1 and that every alternate buffer is then deallocated. Then, using the buddy system, memory degenerates into a series of holes of size 1 followed by an allocation of size 1. Half of the memory is unused, but no request of size greater than 2 can be satisfied. Notice that this example cannot happen with the Kingsley allocator because the size-1 requests will only deplete the size-1 pool and will not affect the other pools. Thus trafficking between pools may help improve the expected memory utilization but not the worst-case utilization.

Linux allocator

The Linux allocator (Chelf, 2001), originally written by Doug Lea, is sometimes referred to as *dlmalloc()*. Like the Kingsley allocator, the memory is broken into pools of 128 sizes. The first 64 pools contain memory buffers of exactly one size each, from 16 through 512 bytes in steps of 8. Unlike the case of power-of-2 allocation, this prevents more than 8 bytes of waste for the common case of small buffers. The remaining 64 pools cover the other, higher sizes, spaced exponentially.

The Linux allocator (Chelf, 2001) does merge adjacent free buffers and promotes the coalesced buffer to the appropriate pool. This is similar to the buddy system and hence is subject to the same fragmentation problem of any scheme in which the pools are not segregated. However, the resulting memory utilization is very good in practice.

A useful trick to tuck away in your bag of tricks concerns how pools are linked together. The naive way would be to create separate free lists for each pool using additional small nodes that point to the corresponding free buffer. But since the buffer is free, this is obvious waste (**P1**). Thus the simple trick, used in Linux and possibly in other allocators, is to store the link pointers for the pool free lists in the corresponding free buffers themselves, thereby saving storage.

The Lea allocator uses memory more efficiently than the Kingsley allocator but is more complex to implement. This may not be the best choice for a wire-speed TCP implementation that desires both speed and the efficient use of memory.

Batch allocator

One alternative idea for memory allocation, which has an even simpler hardware implementation than Kingsley's allocator, leverages batching (**P2c**). The idea, shown in Fig. 9.1, is for the allocator to work in large chunks of memory. Each chunk is allocated sequentially. A pointer *Curr* is kept to the point where the last allocation is terminated. A new request of size B is allocated after *Curr*, and *Curr* increases to *Curr* + B. This is extremely fast, handles variable sizes, and does not waste any memory—up to the point, that is, when the chunk is used up.

The idea is that when the chunk is used up, another chunk is immediately available. Of course, there is no free lunch, while the second chunk is being used, some spare chunk must be created in the background. The creation of this spare chunk can be done by software, while allocates can easily be done in hardware. Similar ideas were presented in the context of the MIT J-machine (Dally et al., 1987), which relied on an underlying fast messaging service.

Creating a spare chunk can be done in many ways. The problem, of course, is that deallocates may not be done in the same order as allocates, thus creating a set of holes in the chunks that need somehow to be coalesced. Three alternatives for coalescing present themselves. If the application knows that eventually all allocated buffers will be freed, then using some more spare chunks may suffice to ensure that before any chunk runs out, some chunk will be completely scavenged. However, this is a dangerous game.

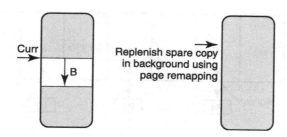

FIGURE 9.1

Sequentially allocating from a large chunk and using a spare chunk. The magic comes from using the time it takes to completely allocate a chunk to create a new chunk.

Second, if memory is accessed through a level of indirection, as in virtual memory, and the buffers are allocated in virtual memory, it is possible to use page remapping to gather together many scattered physical memory pages to appear as one contiguous virtual memory chunk. Finally, it may be worth considering compaction. Compaction is clearly unacceptable in a general-purpose allocator like UNIX, where any number of pieces of memory may point to a memory node. However, in network applications using buffers or other treelike structures, compaction may be feasible using simple local compaction schemes (Sikka and Varghese, 2000).

9.1.2 Sharing buffers

If buffer allocation was not hard enough, consider making it harder by asking also for a fairness constraint.[2] Imagine that an implementation wishes to fairly share a group of buffers among a number of users, each of whom may wish to use all the buffers. The buffers should be shared roughly equally among the active users that need these buffers. This is akin to what in economics is called *Pareto optimality* and also to the requirements for fair queuing in routers studied in Chapter 14. Thus it is not surprising that the following buffer-stealing algorithm was invented (McKenney, 1991) in the context of a stochastic fair queuing (SFQ) algorithm.

Buffer stealing

One way to provide roughly Pareto optimality among users is as follows. When all buffers are used up and a new user (whose allocated buffers are smaller than the highest current allocation) wishes one more buffer, *steal* the extra buffer from the highest buffer user. It is easy to see that even if one user initially grabs all the buffers when other users become active, they can get their fair share by stealing.

The problem is that a general solution to the problem of buffer stealing uses a heap. A heap has $O(\log n)$ cost, where n is the number of users with current allocations. How can this be made faster?

Once again, as is often the case in algorithmics versus algorithms, the problem is caused by reading too much into the specification. If allocations keep changing in *arbitrary* increments and the algorithm

---

[2] However, to make things easier in return, this section assumes constant-size buffer allocation with all its potential memory wastage.

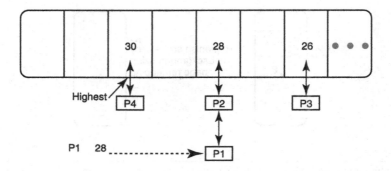

FIGURE 9.2

The McKenney algorithm for buffer stealing finesses the need for logarithmic heap overhead by relying on the fact that buffer values change by at most 1 on any operation.

wishes always to find the highest allocation, a logarithmic heap implementation is required. However, if we can relax the specification (and this seems reasonable in practice) to assume that a user steals one buffer at a time, then the allocated amounts change not in arbitrary amounts but only by +1 or −1. This observation results in a constant-time algorithm (the McKenney algorithm, Fig. 9.2), which also assumes that buffer allocations fall in a bounded set. For each allocation size i, the algorithm maintains a list of processes that have size exactly i. The algorithm maintains a variable called *Highest* that points to the highest amount allocated to any process.

When a process P wishes to steal a buffer, the algorithm finds a process Q with the highest allocation at the head of the list pointed to by *Highest*. While doing so, process P gains a buffer and Q loses a buffer. The books are updated as follows.

When process P gets buffer $i + 1$, P is removed from list i and added to list $i + 1$, updating *Highest* if necessary. When process Q loses buffer $i + 1$, Q is removed from list $i + 1$ and added to list i, updating *Highest* $= i$ if the *Highest* list becomes empty.

Notice this could become arbitrarily inefficient if P and Q could change their allocations by sizes larger than 1. If Q could reduce its allocation by, say, 100 and there are no other users with the same original allocation, then the algorithm would require stepping through 100 lists, looking for the next possible value of highest. Because the maximum amount an allocation can change by is 1, the algorithm moves through only one list. In terms of algorithmics, this is an example of the special opportunities created by the use of finite universes (**P14** suggests the use of bucket sorting and bitmaps for finite universes).

Dynamic thresholds

Limiting access by any one flow to a shared buffer is also important in shared memory switches (Chapter 13). In the context of shared memory switches Choudhury and Hahne describe an algorithm similar to buffer stealing that they call *Pushout*. However, even using the buffer-stealing algorithm due to McKenney (1991), Pushout may be hard to implement at high speeds.

Instead, Choudhury and Hahne (1998) propose a useful alternative mechanism called *dynamic buffer limiting*. They observe that maintaining a single threshold for every flow is either overly limiting (if the threshold is too small) or unduly dangerous (if the threshold is too high). Using a static value of threshold is no different from using a fixed window size for flow control. But TCP uses a *dynamic* window size that adapts to congestion. Similarly, it makes sense to exploit a degree of freedom (**P13**) and use *dynamic thresholds*.

Intuitively, TCP window flow control increases a connection's window size if there appears to be unused bandwidth, as measured by the lack of packet drops. Similarly, the simplest way to adapt to congestion in a shared buffer is to monitor the free space remaining and to increase the threshold proportional to the free space. Thus user i is limited to no more than cF bytes, where c is a constant and F is the current amount of free space. If c is chosen to be a power of 2, this scheme only requires the use of a shifter (to multiply by c) and a comparator (to compare with cF). This is far simpler than even the buffer-stealing algorithm.

Choudhury and Hahne recommend a value of $c = 1$. This implies that a single user is limited to taking no more than half the available bandwidth. This is because when the user takes half, the free space is equal to the user allocation and the threshold check fails. Similarly, if $c = 2$, any user is limited to no more than 2/3 of the available buffer space. Thus unlike buffer stealing, this scheme always holds some free space in reserve for new arrivals, trading slightly suboptimal use of memory for a simpler implementation.

Now suppose there are two users and that $c = 1$. One might naively think that since each user is limited to no more than half, two active users are limited to a quarter. The scheme does better, however. Each user can now take 1/3, leaving 1/3 free. Next, if two new users arrive and the old users do not free their buffers, the two new users can get up to 1/9 of the buffer space.

Thus, unlike buffer stealing, the scheme is not fair in a short-term sense. However, if the same set of users is present for sufficiently long periods, the scheme should be fair in a long-term sense. In the previous example after the buffers allocated to the first two users are deallocated, a fairer allocation should result.

9.2 Cyclic redundancy checks and checksums

Once a TCP packet is buffered, typically a check is performed to see whether the packet has been corrupted in flight or in a router's memory. Such checks are performed by either checksums or CRCs. In essence, both CRCs and checksums are hash functions H on the packet contents. They are designed so that if errors convert a packet P to corrupted packet P', then $H(P) \neq H(P')$ with high probability.

In practice, every time a packet is sent along a link, the data link header carries a link level CRC. But in addition, TCP computes a checksum on the TCP data. Thus a typical TCP packet on a wire carries *both* a CRC and a checksum. While this may appear to be obvious waste (**P1**), it is a consequence of layering. The data link CRC covers the data link header, which changes from hop to hop. Since the data link header must be recomputed at each router on the path, the CRC does not catch errors caused *within routers*. While this may seem unlikely, routers do occasionally corrupt packets (Stone and Partridge, 2000) because of implementation bugs and hardware glitches.

Given this, the CRC is often calculated in hardware by the chip (e.g., Ethernet receiver) that receives the packet, while the TCP checksum is calculated in software in BSD UNIX. This division of labor explains why CRC and checksum implementations are so different. CRCs are designed to be powerful error-detection codes, catching link errors such as burst errors. Checksums, on the other hand, are less adept at catching errors; however, they tend to catch common end-to-end errors and are much simpler to implement in software.

The rest of this section describes CRC and then checksum implementation. The section ends with a clever way, used in Infiniband implementations, to finesse the need for software checksums by using *two* CRCs in each packet, both of which can easily be calculated by the same piece of hardware.

9.2.1 Cyclic redundancy checks

The CRC "hash" function is calculated by dividing the packet data, treated as a number, with a fixed generator G. G is just a binary string of predefined length. For example, CRC-16 is the string 11000000000000101, of length 17; it is called CRC-16 because the remainder added to the packet turns out to be 16 bits long.

Generators are easier to remember when written in polynomial form. For example, the same CRC-16 in polynomial form becomes $x^{16} + x^{15} + x^2 + 1$. Notice that whenever x^i is present in the generator *polynomial*, position i is equal to 1 in the generator *string*. Whatever CRC polynomial is picked (and CRC-32 is very common), the polynomial is published in the data link implementation specification and is known in advance to both receiver and sender.

A formal description of CRC calculation is as follows. Let r be the number of bits in the generator string G. Let M be the message whose CRC is to be calculated. The CRC is simply the remainder c of $2^{r-1}M$ (i.e., M left-shifted by $r-1$ bits) when divided by G. The only catch is the division is mod-2 division, which is illustrated next.

Working out the mathematics slightly, $2^{r-1}M = k.G + c$. Thus $2^{r-1}M + c = k.G$ because addition is the same as subtraction in mod-2 arithmetic, a fact strange but true. Thus, even ignoring the preceding math, the bottom line is that *if we append the calculated CRC c to the end of the message, the resulting number divides the generator G.*

Any bit errors that cause the sent packet to change to some other packet will be caught as long as the resulting packet is not divisible by G. CRCs, like good hash functions, are effective because common errors based on flipping a few bits (random errors) or changing any bit in a group of contiguous bits (burst errors) are likely to create a packet that does not divide G. Simple analytical properties of CRCs are derived in Tanenbaum (1981).

For the implementor, however, what matters is not *why* CRC works but *how* to implement it. The main thing to learn is how to compute remainders using mod-2 division. The algorithm uses a simple iteration in which the generator G is progressively "subtracted" from the message M until the remainder is "smaller" than the generator G. This is exactly like ordinary division except that "subtraction" is now exclusive-OR, and the definition of whether a number is "smaller" depends on whether its most significant bit (MSB) is 0.

More precisely, a register R is loaded with the first r bits of the message. At each stage of the iteration, the MSB of R is checked. If it is 1, R is "too large" and the CRC string G is "subtracted" from R. Subtraction is done by exclusive-OR (EX-OR) in mod-2 arithmetic. Assuming that the MSB of the generator is always 1, this zeroes out the MSB of R. Finally, if the MSB of R is already 0, R is "small enough" and there is no need to EX-OR.

A single iteration completes by left-shifting R so that the MSB of R is lost, and the next message bit gets shifted in. The iterations continue until all message bits are shifted in, and the MSB of register R is 0. At this point, register R contains the required checksum.

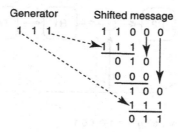

FIGURE 9.3

CRC is calculated by dividing the shifted message with the generator. The intent is to shift in all the message bits and to zero out any most significant bits that are set. Horizontal lines indicate EX-OR operations. Vertical lines denote shifting in the next message bit. Dashed lines show where the generator is brought down. The generator is used for the EX-OR when the MSB of the current result is 1; if not, zero is used.

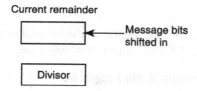

FIGURE 9.4

Naive hardware implementation requires three clock cycles per bit.

For example, let $M = 110$ and $G = 111$. Then $2^{r-1}M = 11000$. Then the checksum c is calculated as shown in Fig. 9.3. In the first step of Fig. 9.3 the algorithm places the first 3 bits (110) of the shifted message in R. Since the MSB of 110 is 1, the algorithm hammers away at R by EX-ORing R with the generator $G = 111$ to get 001. The first iteration completes by shifting out the MSB and (Fig. 9.3 topmost vertical arrow) shifting in the fourth message bit, to get $R = 010$.

In the second iteration the MSB of R is 0 and so the algorithm desists. This is represented in Fig. 9.3 by computing the EX-OR of R with 000 instead of the generator. As usual, the MSB of the result is shifted in, and the last message bit, also a zero, is shifted in to get $R = 100$. Finally, in the third iteration because the MSB of R is 1, the algorithm once again EX-ORs R with the generator. The algorithm terminates at this point because the MSB of R is 0. The resulting checksum is R without the MSB, or 11.

Naive implementation

Cyclic redundancy checks have to be implemented at a range of speeds from 1 Gbit/second to slower rates. Higher-speed implementations are typically done in hardware. The simplest hardware implementation would mimic the foregoing description and use a shift register that shifts in bits one at time. Each iteration requires three basic steps: checking the MSB, computing the EX-OR, and then shifting.

The naive hardware implementation shown in Fig. 9.4 would require three clock cycles to shift in a bit; doing a comparison for the MSB in one cycle and the actual EX-OR in another cycle and the shift

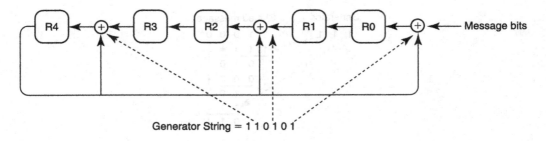

Generator String = 1 1 0 1 0 1

FIGURE 9.5

Linear feedback shift register implementation of a CRC remainder calculation. The EX-ORs are combined with a shift by placing EX-OR gates (the circles) to the right of some registers. Specifically, an EX-OR gate is placed to the right of register i if bit i in the generator string (see dashed lines) is set. The only exception is (what would have been) register $R5$. Such a register need not be stored because it corresponds to the MSB, which is always shifted out.

in the third cycle. However, a cleverer implementation can be used to shift in one bit every clock cycle by *combining* the test for MSB, the EX-OR, and the shift into a single operation.

Implementation using linear feedback shift registers

In Fig. 9.5 the remainder R is stored as five separate 1-bit registers, $R4$ through $R0$, instead of a single 5-bit register, assuming a 6-bit generator string. The idea makes use of the observation that the EX-OR needs to be done only if the MSB is 1; thus in the process of shifting left the MSB, we can feed back the MSB to the appropriate bits of the remainder register. The remaining bits are EX-ORed during their shift to the left.

Notice that in Fig. 9.5 an EX-OR gate is placed to the right of register i if bit i in the generator string (see dashed lines) is set. The reason for this rule is as follows. Compared to the simple iterative algorithm, the hardware of Fig. 9.5 effectively combines the left shift of iteration J together with the MSB check and EX-OR of iteration $J + 1$. Thus the bit that will be in position i in iteration $J + 1$ is in position $i - 1$ in iteration J.

If this is grasped (and this requires shifting one's mental pictures of iterations), the test for the MSB (i.e., bit 5) in iteration $J + 1$ amounts to checking MSB $- 1$ (i.e., bit 4 in $R4$) in iteration J. If bit 4 is 1, then an EX-OR must be performed with the generator. For example, the generator string has a 1 in bit 2, so $R2$ must be EX-ORed with a 1 in iteration $J + 1$. But bit 2 in iteration $J + 1$ corresponds to bit 1 in iteration J. Thus the EX-OR corresponding to $R2$ in iteration $J + 1$ can be achieved by placing an EX-OR gate to the right of $R2$: the bit that will be placed in $R2$ is EX-ORed during its transit from $R1$.

Notice that the check for MSB has been finessed in Fig. 9.5 by using the output of $R4$ as an input to all the EX-OR gates. The effect of this is that if the MSB of iteration $J + 1$ is 1 (recall that this is in $R4$ during iteration J), then all the EX-ORs are performed. If not, and if the MSB is 0, no EX-ORs are done, as desired; this is the same as EX-ORing with zero in Fig. 9.3.

The implementation of Fig. 9.5 is called a *linear feedback shift register* (LFSR), for obvious reasons. This is a classical hardware building block, which is also useful for the generation of random numbers for, say, QoS (Chapter 14). For example, random numbers using, say, the Tausworth implementation can be generated using three LFSRs and an EX-OR.

Faster implementations

The bottleneck in the implementation of Fig. 9.5 is the shifting, which is done one bit at a time. Even at one bit every clock cycle, this is very slow for fast links. Most logic on packets occurs after the bit stream arriving from the link has been deserialized[3] into wider words of, say, size W. Thus the packet-processing logic is able to operate on W bits in a single clock cycle, which allows the hardware clock to run W times slower than the interarrival time between bits.

Thus to gain speed, CRC implementations have to shift W bits at a time, for $W > 1$. Suppose the current remainder is r and we shift in W more message bits whose value as a number is, say, n. Then in essence the implementation needs to find the remainder of $(2^W \cdot r + n)$ in one clock cycle.

If the number of bits in the current remainder register is small, the remainder of $2^W \cdot r$ can be precomputed (**P2a**) for all r by table lookup. This is the basis of a number of software CRC implementations that shift in, say, 8 bits at a time. In hardware it is faster and more space efficient to use a matrix of XOR gates to do the same computation. The details of the parallel implementation can be found in Albertengo and Riccardo (1990), based on the original idea described by Sarwate (1988).

9.2.2 Internet checksums

Since CRC computation is done on every link on the Internet, it is done in hardware by link chips. However, the software algorithm, even shifting 8 bits at a time, is slow. Thus TCP chose to use a more efficient error-detection hash function based on summing the message bits. Just as accountants calculate sums of large sets of numbers by column and by row to check for errors, a *checksum* can catch errors that change the resulting sum.

It is natural to calculate the sum in units of the checksum size (16 bits in TCP), and some reasonable strategy must be followed when the sum of the 16-bit units in the message overflows the checksum size. Simply losing the MSB will, intuitively, lose information about 16-bit chunks computed early in the summing process. Thus TCP follows the strategy of an end-around carry. When the MSB overflows, the carry is added to the least significant bit (LSB). This is called one's *complement addition*.

The computation is straightforward. The specified portion of each TCP packet is summed in 16-bit chunks. Each time the sum overflows, the carry is added to the LSB. Thus the main loop will naively consist of three steps: Add the next chunk; test for carry; if carry, add to LSB. However, there are three problems with the naive implementation.

- *Byte swapping:* First, in some machines, the 16-bit chunks in the TCP message may be stored byte-swapped. Thus it may appear that the implementation has to reverse each pair of bytes before addition.
- *Masking:* Second, many machines use word sizes of 32 bits or larger. Thus the naive computation may require masking out 16-bit portions.
- *Check for carry:* Third, the check for carry after every 16-bit word is added can potentially slow down the loop as compared to ordinary summation.

---

[3] This is done by what is often called a *SERDES* chip, which stands for serializer–deserializer chip.

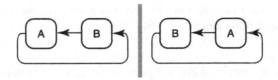

FIGURE 9.6

The 1's complement addition of two 16-bit quantities stays the same (except for byte reversal) when the quantities are represented in byte-reversed form. This is because carries from any bit position flow to the same next-bit position in both original and byte-reversed formats. Consider, for example, how the MSB of B flows to the LSB of A in both formats.

All three problems can be solved by not being tied to the reference implementation (**P8**) and, instead, by fitting the computation to the underlying hardware (**P4c**). The following ideas and Fig. 9.6 are taken from Partridge (1993).

- *Ignore byte order:* Fig. 9.6 shows that swapping every word before addition on a byte-reversed machine is obvious waste (**P1**). The figure shows that whether or not AB is stored byte reversed as BA, any carry from the MSB of byte B still flows to the LSB of byte A. Similarly, in both cases, any carry from the MSB of byte A flows to the LSB of byte B. Thus any 1's-complement addition done on the byte-reversed representation will have the same answer as in the original, except byte reversed. This in turn implies that it suffices to add in byte-reversed form and to do a final byte reversal only at the end.
- *Use natural word length:* If a machine has a 32- or 64-bit word, the most natural thing to do is to maintain the running sum in the natural machine word size. All that happens is that carries accumulate in the higher-order 16 bits of the machine word, which need to be added back to the lower 16 bits in a final operation.
- *Lazy carry evaluation:* Using a larger word size has the nice side effect of allowing lazy evaluation (**P2b**) of carry checking. For example, using a 32-bit word allows an unrolled loop that checks for carries only after every 16 additions (Stevens, 1994) because it takes 16 additions in the worst case to have the carry overflow from bit 32.

In addition, as noted in Chapter 5, the overhead of reading in the checksum data into machine registers can be avoided by piggybacking on the same requirement for copying data from the network device into user buffers, and vice versa.

Header checksum

Finally, besides the TCP and UDP checksums on the *data*, IP computes an additional 1's-complement checksum on just the IP *header*. This is crucial for network routers and other hardware devices that need to recompute Internet checksums.

Hardware implementations of header checksum can benefit from *parallel* and *incremental* computation. One strategy for parallelism is to break up the data being checksummed into W 16-bit words and to compute W different 1's-complement sums in parallel, with a final operation to fold these W sums into one 16-bit checksum. A complete hardware implementation of this idea with $W = 2$ is described in Touch and Parham (1996).

The strategy for incremental computation is defined precisely in RFC 1624 (Rijsinghani, 1994). In essence, if a 16-bit field m in the header changes to m', the header checksum can be recalculated by subtracting m and adding in m' to the older checksum value. There is one subtlety, having to do with the two representations of zero in 1's-complement arithmetic (Rijsinghani, 1994), that is considered further in the exercises.

9.2.3 Finessing checksums

The humble checksum's reason for existence, compared to the more powerful CRC, is the relative ease of checksum implementation in software. However, if there is hardware that already computes a data link CRC on every data link frame, an obvious question is: *Why not use the underlying hardware to compute another checksum on the data?* Doing otherwise results in extra computation by the receiving processor and appears to be obvious waste (**P1**). Once again, it is only obvious waste when looking across layers; at each individual layer (data link, transport), there is no waste.

Clearly, the CRC changes from hop to hop, while the TCP checksum should remain unchanged to check for end-to-end integrity. Thus if a CRC is to be used for both purposes, *two* CRCs have to be computed. The first is the usual CRC, and the second should be on some invariant portion of the packet that includes all the data and does not change from hop to hop.

One of the problems with exploiting the hardware (**P4c**) to compute the equivalent of the TCP checksum is knowing which portion of the packet must be checksummed. For example, TCP and UDP include some fields of the IP header[4] in order to compute the end-to-end checksum. The TCP header fields may also not be at a fixed offset because of potential TCP and IP options. Having a data link hardware device understand details of higher-layer headers seems to violate layering.

On the other hand, all the optimizations that avoid data copying and described in Chapter 5 also violate layering in a similar sense. Arguably, it does not matter what a single endnode does internally as long as the protocol behavior, as viewed externally by a black-box tester, meets conformance tests. Further, there are creative structuring techniques (**P8**, not being tied to reference implementations) of the endnode software that can allow lower layers access to this form of information.

The Infiniband architecture (Infiniband Specification, 2000) does specify that end system hardware compute two CRCs. The usual CRC is called the *variant* CRC; the CRC on the data, together with some of the header, is called the *invariant* CRC. Infiniband transport and network layer headers are simpler than those of TCP, and thus computing the invariant portion is fairly simple.

However, the same idea could be used even for a more complex protocol, such as TCP or IP, while preserving endnode software structure. This can be achieved by having the upper layers pass information about offsets and fields (**P9**) to the lower layers through layer interfaces. A second option to avoid passing too many field descriptions is to precompute the pseudoheader checksum/CRC as part of the connection state (Jacobson, 1993) and instead to pass the precomputed value to the hardware.

---

[4] These portions form what is called the TCP and UDP *pseudoheader* (Stevens, 1994).

9.3 **Generic protocol processing**

Section 9.1 described techniques for buffering a packet, and Section 9.2 described techniques to efficiently compute packet checksums. The stage is now set to actually process such a packet. The reader unfamiliar with TCP may wish first to consult the models in Chapter 2.

Since TCP accounts for 90% of traffic (Braun, 1998) in most sites, it is crucial to efficiently process TCP packets at close to wire speeds. Unfortunately, a first glance at TCP code is daunting. While the TCP sender code is relatively simple, Stevens (1994) says:

> TCP input processing is the largest piece of code that we examine in this text. The function `tcp_input` is about 1100 lines of code. The processing of incoming segments is not complicated, just long and detailed.

Since TCP appears to be complex, Greg Chesson and Larry Green formed Protocol Engines, Inc., in 1987, which proposed an alternative protocol called XTP (Chesson, 1989). XTP was carefully designed with packet headers that were easy to parse and streamlined processing paths. With XTP threatening to replace TCP, Van Jacobson riposted with a carefully tuned implementation of TCP in BSD UNIX that is well described in Stevens (1994). This implementation was able to keep up with even 100-Mbps links. As a result, while XTP is still used (Chesson, 1989), TCP proved to be a runaway success.

Central to Jacobson's optimized implementation is a mechanism called *header prediction* (Jacobson, 1993). Much of the complexity of the 1100 lines of TCP receive processing comes when handling rare cases. Header prediction provides a fast path through the thicket of exceptions by optimizing the expected case (**P11**).

TCP header prediction

The first operation on receiving a TCP packet is to find the protocol control block (PCB) that contains the state (e.g., receive and sent sequence numbers) for the connection of which the packet is a part. Assuming the connection is set up and that most workstations have only a few concurrent connections, the few active connection blocks can be cached. The BSD UNIX code (Stevens, 1994) maintains a one-behind cache containing the PCB of the last segment received; this works well in practice for workstation implementations.

After locating the PCB, the TCP header must be processed. A good way to motivate header prediction, found in Partridge (1993), comes from looking at the fields in the TCP header, as shown in Fig. 9.7.

After a connection is set up, the destination and source ports are fixed. Since IP networks work hard to send packets in order, the sequence number is likely to be the next in sequence after the last packet received. The control bits, often called flag bits, are typically off, with the exception of the ack bit, which is always set after the initial packet is sent. Finally, most of the time, the receiver does not change its window size, and the urgent pointer is irrelevant. Thus the only two fields whose information content is high are the ack number and checksum fields.

Motivated by this observation, header prediction identifies the expected case as one of two possibilities: receiving a pure acknowledgment (i.e., the received segment contains no data) or receiving a pure data packet (i.e., the received segment contains an ack field that conveys no new information). In addition, the packet should also reflect business as usual in the following precise sense: no unexpected TCP flags should be set, and the flow control window advertised in the packet should be no different from what the receiver had previously advertised. In pseudocode (simplified from Ref. Jacobson, 1993):

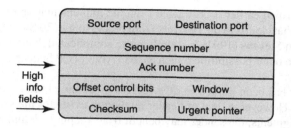

FIGURE 9.7

TCP header fields: the fields most likely to change are the checksum and the ack fields. The other fields carry very little information and can often be predicted from past values.

```
IF (No unexpected flags) AND (Window in packet is as before)
AND (Packet sequence number is the next expected) THEN
    IF (Packet contains only headers and no data)
    Do Ack Processing
/* Release acked bytes, stop timers, awaken process */
ELSE IF (Packet does not ack anything new) /* pure data */
    Copy data to user buffer while checksumming;
    Update next sequence number expected;
    Send Acks if needed and release buffer;
ENDIF
ELSE /* header prediction failed -\/- take long path */
...
```

Clearly, this code is considerably shorter than the complete TCP receive processing code. However, some of the checks can be made more efficient by leveraging off the fact that most machines can do efficient comparisons in units of a machine word size (**P4a**, exploit locality).

For example, consider the TCP flags contained in the control bits of Fig. 9.7. There are six flags, each encoded as a bit: SYN, FIN, RESET, PUSH, URG, ACK. If it is business as usual, all the flags must be clear, with the exception of ACK, which must be set, and PUSH, which is irrelevant. Checking for each of these conditions *individually* would require several instructions to extract and compare each bit.

Instead, observe that the flags field is the fourth word of the TCP header and that the window size is contained in the last 16 bits. In the header prediction code the sender precomputes (**P2a**) the expected value of this word by filling in all the expected values of the flag and using the last advertised value of the window size.

The expected value of the fourth TCP header word is stored in the PCB entry for the connection. Given this setup, the first two checks in the pseudocode shown earlier can be accomplished in one stroke by comparing the fourth word of the TCP header in the incoming packet with the expected value stored in the PCB. If all goes well, and tests indicate they often do, the expected value of the fourth field is computed only at the start of the connection. It is this test that explains the origin of the name *header prediction*: a portion of the header is being predicted and checked against an incoming segment.

The pseudocode described earlier is abstracted from the implementation by Jacobson in a research kernel (Jacobson, 1993) that claims to do TCP receiving processing in 30 Sun SPARC instructions! The BSD UNIX code given in Stevens (1994) is slightly more complicated, having to deal with mbufs and with the need to eliminate other possibilities, such as the PAWS (TCP Sequence number wrapping) test (Stevens, 1994).

The discussion so far has been limited to TCP receive processing because it is more complex than sending a TCP segment. However, a dual of header prediction exists for the sender side. If only a few fields change between segments, the sender may benefit from keeping a template TCP (and IP) header in the connection block. When sending a segment, the sender need only fill in the few fields that change into the template. This is more efficient if copying the TCP header is more efficient than filling in each field. Caching of sending packet headers is implemented in the Linux kernel.

Before finishing this topic, it is worth recalling Caveat **Q8** and examining how sensitive this optimization is to the system environment. Originally, header prediction was targeted at workstations. The underlying assumption (that the next segment is for the same connection and is one higher in sequence number than the last received segment) works well in this case.

Clearly, the assumption that the next segment is for the same connection works poorly in a server environment. This was noted as early as Jacobson (1993), who suggested using a hash of the port numbers to quickly locate the PCB. McKenney and Dove confirmed this by showing that using hashing to locate the PCB can speed up receive processing by an order of magnitude in an OLTP (online transaction processing) environment.

The FIFO (first in, first out) assumption is much harder to work around. While some clever schemes can be used to do sequence number processing for out-of-order packets, there are some more fundamental protocol mechanisms in TCP that build on the FIFO assumption. For example, if packets can be routinely misordered, TCP receivers will send duplicate acknowledgments. In TCP's fast retransmit algorithm (Stevens, 1994) TCP senders use three duplicate acknowledgments to infer a loss (see Chapter 14).

Thus lack of FIFO behavior can cause spurious retransmissions, which will lower performance more drastically as compared to the failure of header prediction. However, as TCP receivers evolve to do selective acknowledgment (Floyd et al., 1999), this could allow fast TCP processing of out-of-order segments in the future.

9.3.1 UDP processing

Recall that UDP is TCP without error recovery, congestion control, or connection management. As with TCP, UDP allows multiplexing and demultiplexing using port numbers. Thus UDP allows applications to send IP datagrams without the complexity of TCP. Although TCP is by far the dominant protocol, many important applications, such as videoconferencing, use UDP. Thus it is also important to optimize UDP implementations.

Because UDP is stateless, header prediction is not relevant: one cannot store past headers that can be used to predict future headers. However, UDP shares with TCP two potentially time-consuming tasks: demultiplexing to the right PCB, and checksumming, both of which can benefit from TCP-style optimizations (Partridge and Pink, 1993).

Caching of PCB entries is more subtle in UDP than in TCP. This is because PCBs may need to be looked up using wildcarded entries for, say, the remote (called *foreign*) IP address and port. Thus there may be PCB 1 that specifies local port L with all the other fields wildcarded, and PCB 2 that specifies local port L and remote IP address X. If PCB 1 is cached and a packet arrives destined for PCB 2, then the cache can result in demultiplexing the packet for the wrong PCB. Thus caching of wildcarded entries is not possible in general; address prefixes cannot be cached for purposes of route lookup (Chapter 11), for similar reasons.

Partridge and Pink (1993) suggest a simple strategy to get around this issue. A PCB entry, such as PCB 1, that can "hide" or match another PCB entry is never allowed to be cached. Subject to this restriction, the UDP implementation of Partridge and Pink (1993) caches both the PCB of the last packet *received* and the PCB of the last packet *sent*. The first cache handles the case of a train of received packets, while the second cache handles the common case of receiving a response to the last packet sent. Despite the cache restrictions, these two caches still have an 87% hit rate in the measurements of Partridge and Pink (1993).

Finally, Partridge and Pink (1993) also implemented a copy-and-checksum loop for UDP as in TCP. In the BSD implementation UDP's *sosend* was treated as a special case of sending over a connected socket. Instead, Partridge and Pink propose an efficient special-purpose routine (**P6**) that first calculates the header checksum and then copies the data bytes to the network buffer while updating the checksum. (Some of these ideas allowed Cray machines to vectorize the checksum loop in the early 1990s.) With similar optimizations used for receive processing, Partridge and Pink report that the checksum cost is essentially zero for CPUs that are limited by memory access time and not processing.

9.4 **Reassembly**

Both header prediction for TCP and even the UDP optimizations of Partridge and Pink (1993) assume that the received data stream has no unusual need for computation. For example, TCP segments are assumed not to contain window size changes or to have flags set that need attention. Besides these, an unstated assumption so far is that the IP packets do not need to be *reassembled*.

Briefly, the original IP routing protocol dealt with diverse links with different maximum packet sizes or maximum transmission units (MTUs) by allowing routers to slice up IP packets into fragments. Each fragment is identified by a packet ID, a start byte offset into the original packet, and a fragment length. The last fragment has a bit set to indicate it is the last. Note that an intermediate router can cause a fragment to be itself fragmented into multiple smaller fragments. IP routing can also cause duplicates, loss, and out-of-order receipt of fragments.

At the receiver, Humpty Dumpty (i.e., the original packet) can be put together as follows. The first fragment to arrive at the receiver sets up the state that is indexed by the corresponding packet ID. Subsequent fragments are steered to the same piece of state (e.g., a linked list of fragments based on the packet ID). The receiver can tell when the packet is complete if the last fragment has been received and if the remaining fragments cover all the bytes in the original packets length, as indicated by each fragment's offset. If the packet is not reassembled after a specified time has elapsed, the state is timed out.

While fragmentation allows IP to deal with links of different MTU sizes, it has the following disadvantages (Kent and Mogul, 1987). First, it is expensive for a router to fragment a packet because it involves adding a new IP header for fragment, which increases the processing and memory bandwidth needs. Second, reassembly at endnodes is considered expensive because determining when a complete packet has been assembled potentially requires sorting the received fragments. Third, the loss of a fragment leads to the loss of a packet; thus when a fragment is lost, transmission of the remaining fragments is a waste of resources.

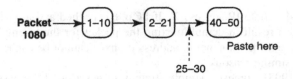

FIGURE 9.8

One data structure for reassembly is a linked list of fragments that is indexed by packet ID and sorted by the start byte offset (first field). The second field is the end offset. Thus the fragment that starts at offset 25 is inserted after the second list element.

The current Internet strategy (Kent and Mogul, 1987) is to shift the fragmentation computation in space (**P3c**) from the router and the receiver to the *sender*. The idea behind the so-called *path MTU* scheme is that the onus falls on the sender to compute a packet size that is small enough to pass through all links in the path from sender to receiver. Routers can now refuse to fragment a packet, sending back a control message to the receiver. The sender uses a list of common packet sizes (**P11**, optimizing the expected case) and works its way down this list when it receives a refusal.

The path MTU scheme nicely illustrates algorithmics in action by removing a problem by moving to another part of the system. However, a misconception has arisen that path MTU has completely removed fragmentation in the Internet. This is not so. Almost all core routers support fragmentation in hardware, and a significant amount of fragmented traffic has been observed (Shannon et al., 2001) on Internet backbone links many years after the path MTU protocol was deployed.

Note that the path MTU protocol requires the sender to keep state, typically in PCB, as to the best current packet size to use. This works well if the sender uses TCP, but not if the sender uses UDP, which is stateless. In the case of UDP path MTU can be implemented only if the application above UDP keeps the necessary state and implements path MTU (unless the path MTU is stored as a routing table entry like in an IBM AIX system). This is harder to deploy because it is harder to change many applications, unlike changing just TCP. Thus at the time of writing, shared file system protocols such as NFS, IP within IP encapsulation protocols, and many media player and game protocols run over UDP and do not support path MTU. Finally, many attackers compromise security by splitting an attack payload across multiple fragments. Thus intrusion detection devices must often reassemble IP fragments to check for suspicious strings within the reassembled data.

Thus it is worth investigating fast reassembly algorithms because common programs such as NFS do not support the path MTU protocol and because real-time intrusion detection systems must reassemble packets at line speeds to detect attacks hidden across fragments. The next section describes fast reassembly implementations at receivers.

9.4.1 Efficient reassembly

Fig. 9.8 shows a simple data structure, akin to the one used in BSD UNIX, for reassembling a data packet. Assume that three fragments for the packet with ID 1080 have arrived. The fragments are sorted in a list by their starting offset number. Notice that there are overlapping bytes because the first fragment contains bytes 1–10, while the second contains 2–21.

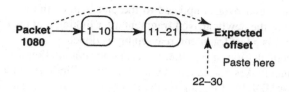

FIGURE 9.9

This implementation is similar to that of Fig. 9.8, except it optimizes for the case that the fragments are nonoverlapping and arrive in order.

Thus if a new fragment with packet ID 1080 arrives containing offsets 25–30, the implementation will typically search through the list, starting from the head, to find the correct position. The correct position is between start offsets 2 and 40 and so is after the second list item.

Each time a fragment is placed in the list, the implementation can check during list traversal if all required bytes have been received up to this fragment. If so, it continues checking to the end of the list to see if all bytes have been received and the last fragment has the last fragment bit set. If these conditions are met, then all required fragments have arrived; the implementation then traverses the list again, copying the data of each fragment into another buffer at the specified offset, potentially avoiding copying overlapping portions.

The resulting implementation is quite complex and slow and typically requires an extra copy. Note that to insert a fragment, one has to locate the packet ID's list and then search within the list. This requires two linear searches. Is IP reassembly fundamentally hard?

Oddly enough, there exists a counterexample reassembly protocol that has been implemented in hardware at gigabit speeds: the ATM AAL-5 cell reassembly protocol (Partridge, 1993), which basically describes how to chop up IP packets into 53-byte ATM cells while allowing reassembly at the cells into packets at the receiver. What makes the AAL-5 reassembly algorithm simple to implement in hardware is not the fixed-length cell (the implementation can be generalized to variable-length cells) but the fact that *cells can only arrive in FIFO order.*

If cells can arrive only in FIFO order, it is easy to paste each successive cell into a buffer just after where the previous cell was placed. When the last cell arrives carrying a last cell bit (just as in IP), the packet's CRC is checked. If the CRC computes, the packet is successfully reassembled. Note that ATM does not require any offset fields because packets arrive in order on ATM virtual circuits.

Unlike ATM cells, IP datagrams can arrive (theoretically) in any order because IP uses a datagram (post office) model as opposed to a virtual circuit (telephony) model. However, we have just seen that header prediction, and, in fact, the fast retransmission algorithm, depends crucially on the fact that in the expected case, IP segments arrive in order (**P11**, optimizing the expected case). Combining this observation with that of the AAL-5 implementation suggests that one can obtain an efficient reassembly algorithm, even in hardware, by optimizing for the case of FIFO arrival of fragments, as shown in Fig. 9.9.

Fig. 9.9 maintains the same sorted list as in Fig. 9.8 but also keeps a pointer to the end of the list. Optimizing for the case that fragments arrive in order and are nonoverlapping, when a fragment containing bytes 22–30 arrives, the implementation checks the ending byte number of the last received fragment (stored in a register, equal to 21) against the start offset of the new fragment. Since 22 is

$21 + 1$, all is well. The new end byte is updated to the end byte of the new fragment (30), and the pointer is updated to point to the newly arrived fragment after linking it at the end of the list. Finally, if the newly arriving fragment is a last fragment, reassembly is done.

Compared to the implementation in Fig. 9.8, the check for completion as well as the check to find out where to place a fragment takes constant and not linear time. Similarly, one can cache the expected packet ID (as in the TCP or UDP PCB lookup implementations) to avoid a list traversal when searching for the fragment list. Finally, using data structures such as pbufs instead of mbufs, even the need for an extra copy can be avoided by directly copying a received fragment into the buffer at the appropriate offset.

If the expected case fails, the implementation can revert to the standard BSD processing. For example, Chandranmenon and Varghese (1998) describe this expected-case optimization in which the code keeps two lists and directly reuses the existing BSD code (which is hard to get right!) when the expected case fails. The expected case is reported by Chandranmenon and Varghese (1998) as taking 38 SPARC instructions, which is comparable with Jacobson's TCP estimates.

As with header prediction, it is worth applying Caveat **Q8** and examining the sensitivity of this optimization of this implementation to the assumptions. Actually, it turns out to be pretty bad. This is because measurements indicate that many recent implementations, including Linux, have senders send out fragments in reverse order! Thus fragments arrive in reverse order 9% of the time (Shannon et al., 2001).

This seemingly eccentric behavior is justified by the fact that it is only the last fragment that carries the length of the entire packet; by sending it first the sender allows the receiver to know what length buffer to allocate after the first fragment is received, assuming the fragments arrive in FIFO order. Note that the FIFO assumption still holds true. However, Fig. 9.9 has a concealed but subtle additional assumption: that fragments will be sent in offset order. Before reading further, think how you might modify the implementation of Fig. 9.9 to handle this case.

The solution, of course, is to use the first fragment to decide which of two expected cases to optimize for. If the first fragment is the first fragment (offset 0), then the implementation uses the mode described in Fig. 9.9. If the first fragment is the last (last bit set), the implementation jumps to a different state, where it expects fragments in reverse order. This is just the dual of Fig. 9.9, where the next fragment should have its last byte number to be 1 less (as opposed to 1 more) than the start offset of the previous fragment. Similarly, the next fragment is expected to be pasted at the start of the list and not the end.

9.5 Conclusions

This chapter describes techniques for efficient buffer allocation, CRC and checksum calculation, protocol processing such as TCP, and finally reassembly.

For buffer allocation, techniques such as the use of segregated pools and batch allocation promise fast allocation with potential trade-offs: the lack of storage efficiency (for segregated pools) versus the difficulty of coalescing noncontiguous holes (for batch allocation). Buffer sharing is important to use memory efficiently and can be done by efficiently stealing buffers from large users or by using dynamic thresholds.

For CRC calculation, efficient multibit remainder calculation finesses the obvious waste (**P1**) of calculating CRCs one bit at a time, even using LFSR implementations. For checksum calculation, the main trick is to fit the computation to the underlying machine architecture, using large word lengths, lazy checks for carries, and even parallelism. The optimizations for TCP, UDP, and reassembly are all based on optimizing simple expected cases (e.g., FIFO receipt, no errors) that cut through a welter of corner cases that the protocol must check for but rarely occur. Table 9.1 presents a summary of the techniques used in this chapter together with the major principles involved.

Beyond the specific techniques, there are some general lessons to be gleaned. First, when considering the buffer-stealing algorithm, it is tempting to believe that finding the user with the largest buffer allocation requires a heap, which requires logarithmic time. However, as with timing wheels in Chapter 7, McKenney's algorithm exploits the special case that buffer sizes only increase and decrease by 1.

The general lesson is that for algorithmics, special cases matter. Theoreticians know this well; for example, the general problem of finding a Hamiltonian cycle (Cormen et al., 1990) is hard for general graphs but is trivial if the graph is a ring. In fact, the practitioner of algorithmics should look for opportunities to change the system to permit special cases that permit efficient algorithms.

Second, the dynamic threshold scheme shows how important it is to optimize one's degrees of freedom (**P13**), especially when considering *dynamic* instead of *static* values for parameters. This is a very common evolutionary path in many protocols: for example, collision-avoidance protocols evolved from using fixed backoff times to using dynamic backoff times in Ethernet; transport protocols evolved from using fixed window sizes to using dynamic window sizes to adjust to congestion; finally, the dynamic threshold scheme of this chapter shows the power of allowing dynamic buffer thresholds.

Third, the discussion of techniques for buffer sharing shows why algorithmics, at least in terms of abstracting common networking tasks and understanding a wide spectrum of solutions for these tasks, can be useful. For example, when writing this chapter, it became clear that buffer sharing is also part of many credit-based protocols, such as Ozveren et al. (1994) (see the protocol in Chapter 15), except that in such settings a sender is allocating buffer space at a distant receiver. Isolating the abstract problem is helpful because it shows, for instance, that the dynamic threshold scheme of Choudhury and Hahne can provide finer grain buffer sharing than the technique of Ozveren et al. (1994).

Finally, the last lesson from header prediction and fast reassembly is that attempts to design new protocols for faster implementation can often be countered by simpler implementations. In particular, arguing that a protocol is "complex" is often irrelevant if the complexities can be finessed in the expected case.

As a second example, a transport protocol (Sabnani and Netravali, 1989) was designed to allow efficient sequence number processing for protocols that used large windows and could handle out-of-order delivery. The protocol embedded concepts such as *chunks* of contiguous sequence numbers into the protocol for this purpose. Simple implementation tricks described in the patent (Thomas et al., 1992) can achieve much the same effect, using large words to effectively represent chunks without redesigning the protocol.

Thus history teaches that attempts to redesign protocols for efficiency (as opposed to more functionality) should be viewed with some skepticism.

9.6 Exercises

1. **Dynamic Buffer Thresholds and Credit-Based Flow Control:** Read the credit-based protocol described in Chapter 15. Consider how to modify the buffer-sharing protocol of Chapter 15 to use

dynamic thresholds. What are some of the possible benefits? This last question is ideally answered by a simulation, which would make it a longer-term class project.

2. **Incremental Checksum Computation:** RFC 1141 states that when an IP header with checksum H is modified by changing some 16-bit field value (such as the TTL field) m to a new value m', then the new checksum should become $H + m + m'$, where X denotes the 1's complement of X. While this works most of the time, the right equation, described in RFC 1624, is to compute $(H + m + m')$: this is slightly more inefficient but correct. This should show that tinkering with the computation can be tricky and requires proofs.

   To see the difference between these two implementations, consider an example given in RFC 1624 with an IP header in which a 16-bit field $m = 0x5555$ changes to $m' = 0x3285$. The 1's-complement sum of all the remaining header bytes is $0xCD7A$. Compute the checksum both ways and show that they produce different results. Given that these two results are really the same in 1's complement notation (different representations of zero), why might it cause trouble at the receiver?

3. **Parallel Checksum Computation:** Figure out how to modify checksum calculation in hardware so as to work on W chunks of the packet in parallel and finally to fold all the results.

4. **Hardware Reassembly:** Suppose the FIFO assumption is not true and fragments arrive out of order. In this problem your assignment is to design an efficient hardware reassembly scheme for IP fragments subject to the restrictions stated in Chapter 2. One idea you could exploit is to have the hardware DMA engine that writes the fragment to a buffer also write a control bit for every word written to memory. This only adds a bit for every 32 bits.

   When all the fragments have arrived, all the bits are set. You could determine whether all bits are set by using a summary tree, in which all the bits are leaves and each node has 32 children. A node's bit is set if all its children's bits are set. The summary tree does not require any pointers because all node bit positions can be calculated from child bit positions, as in a heap. Describe the algorithms to update the summary tree when a new fragment arrives. Consider hardware alternatives in which packets are stored in DRAM and bitmaps are stored in SRAM, as well as other creative possibilities.

Playing with routers

My work is a game, a very serious game.
—M.C. Escher

Part 1 dealt with models and principles and Part 2 dealt with applying these models and principles to endnodes. The third part of this book deals with router algorithmics. *This is the application of network algorithmics to building fast routers. However, many of the techniques apply to bridges, gateways, measurement devices, and firewalls. The techniques are applied mostly in a hardware setting, and much of it has to do with processing packets at wire speeds as links get faster. We study exact lookups, prefix lookups, packet classification, switching, and quality of service (QoS). We also study some other chores within a router, such as striping and flow control across chip-to-chip links within a router.*

Exact-match lookups

10

"Challenge-and-response" is a formula describing the free play of forces that provokes new departures in individual and social life. An effective challenge stimulates men to creative action.
—Arnold Toynbee

In Part 3, for simplicity of terminology, we will generically refer to interconnect devices as *routers*. Each chapter in Part 3 addresses the efficient implementation of a key function for such routers. In the simplest model of a router forwarding path the destination address of a packet is first looked up to determine a destination port; the packet is then switched to the destination port; finally, the packet is scheduled at the destination port to provide QoS (Quality of Service) guarantees. In addition, modern high-performance routers also subject packets to internal striping (to gain throughput) and to internal credit-based flow control (to prevent loss on chip-to-chip links). The chapters are arranged to follow the same order, from lookups to switching to QoS.

Thus the first three chapters concentrate on the surprisingly difficult problem of state lookup in routers. The story begins with the simplest exact match lookups in this chapter, progresses to longest-prefix lookups in Chapter 11, and culminates with the most complex classification lookups in Chapter 12.

What is an exact-match lookup? Exact-match lookups represent the simplest form of database query. Assume a database with a set of tuples; each tuple consists of a unique fixed-length key together with some state information. A query specifies a key K. The goal is to return the state information associated with the tuple whose key is K.

Now, exact-match queries are easily implemented using well-studied techniques, such as binary search and hash tables (Cormen et al., 1990). However, they are still worth studying in this book for two reasons. First, in the networking context the models and metrics for lookups are different from the usual algorithmic setting. Such differences include the fact that lookups must complete in the time to receive a packet, the use of memory references rather than processing as a measure of speed, and the potential use of hardware speedups. Exact-match lookups offer the simplest opportunity to explore these differences. A second reason to study exact-match lookups is that they are crucial for an important networking function, called *bridging*,[1] that is often integrated within a router.

We are grateful to Michael Mitzenmacher for proofreading Section 10.3.3 that describes the d-left scheme.

This chapter is organized around a description of the *history* of bridges. This is done for one chapter in the book, in the hope of introducing the reader to the *process* of algorithmics at work in a real

---

[1] A device commonly known as a LAN switch typically implements bridge functionality.

Network Algorithmics. https://doi.org/10.1016/B978-0-12-809927-8.00017-8

Table 10.1 Principles used in the various exact-match lookup techniques discussed in this chapter.

Number	Principle	Used in
P15	Use efficient data structures: binary search table	First bridge
P5	Hardware FPGA for lookup only	
P15	Use efficient data structure: perfect hashing	Gigaswitch
P2a	Precompute hash function with bounded collisions	FDDI bridge
P5	Pipeline binary search	

product that changed the face of networking. This chapter also describes some of the stimuli that lead to innovation and introduces some of the people responsible for it.

Arnold Toynbee (Toynbee and Caplan, 1972) describes history using a challenge–response theory, in which civilizations either grow or fail in response to a series of challenges. Similarly, the history of bridges can be described as a series of three challenges, which are described in the three sections of this chapter: Ethernets Under Fire (Section 10.1), Wire Speed Forwarding (Section 10.2), and Scaling Lookups to Higher Speeds (Section 10.3). The responses to these challenges led to what is now known as 802.1 spanning tree bridges (IEEE Media, 1997).

The techniques described in this chapter (and the corresponding principles) are summarized in Table 10.1.

Quick reference guide

The implementor interested in fast exact-match schemes should consider either parallel hashing techniques inspired by perfect hashing (Section 10.3.1) or d-left (Section 10.3.3), or pipelined binary search (Section 10.3.2).

10.1 Challenge 1: Ethernet under fire

The first challenge arose in the late 1980s. Ethernet, invented in the 1970s as a low-cost, high-bandwidth interconnect for personal computers, was attacked as behaving poorly at large loads and being incapable of spanning large distances. Recall that if two or more nodes on an Ethernet send data at the same time, a collision occurs on the shared wire. All senders then compute a random retransmission time and retry, where the randomization is chosen to minimize the probability of further collisions.

Theoretical analyses (e.g., Bux and Grillo, 1985) claimed that as the utilization of an Ethernet grew, the effective throughput of the Ethernet dropped to zero because the entire bandwidth was wasted on retransmissions. A second charge against Ethernet was its small distance limit of 1.5 km, much smaller than the limits imposed by, say, the IBM token ring.

While the limited-bandwidth charge turned out to be false in practice (Boggs et al., 1988), it remained a potent marketing bullet for a long time. The limited-distance charge was, and remains, a true limitation of a single Ethernet. In this embattled position network marketing people at Digital Equipment Corporation (DEC) around 1980 pleaded with their technical experts for a technical riposte to

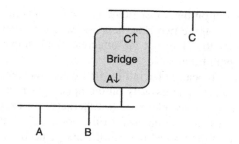

FIGURE 10.1

Toward designing a bridge connecting two Ethernets.

these attacks. Could not their bright engineers find a clever way to "extend" a single Ethernet such that it could become a longer Ethernet with a larger effective bandwidth?

First, it was necessary to discard some unworkable alternatives. Physical layer bit repeaters were unworkable because they did not avoid the distance and bandwidth limits of ordinary Ethernets. Extending an Ethernet using a router did, in theory, solve both problems but introduced two other problems. First, in those days routers were extremely slow and could hardly keep up with the speed of the Ethernet.

Second, there were at least six different routing protocols in use at that time, including IBM's SNA, Xerox's SNS, DECNET, and AppleTalk. Hard as it may be to believe now, the Internet protocols were then only a small player in the marketplace. Thus a router would have to be a complex beast capable of routing multiple protocols (as Cisco would do a few years later), or one would have to incur the extra cost of placing multiple routers, one for each protocol. Thus the router solution was considered a nonstarter.

Routers interconnect links using information in the routing header, while repeaters interconnect links based on physical-layer information, such as bits. However, in classical network layering there is an intermediate layer called the data link layer. For an Ethernet, the data link layer is quite simple and contains a 48-bit unique Ethernet destination address.[2] Why is it not possible, the DEC group argued, to consider a new form of interconnection based only on the data link layer? They christened this new beast a data link layer relay, or a *bridge*.

Let us take an imaginary journey into the mind of Mark Kempf, an engineer in the Advanced Development Group at DEC, who invented bridges in Tewksbury, MA, around 1980. Undoubtedly, he drew something like Fig. 10.1, which shows two Ethernets connected by a bridge; the lower Ethernet line contains stations A and B, while the upper Ethernet contains station C.

The bridge should make the two Ethernets look like one big Ethernet so that when A sends an Ethernet packet to C it magically gets to C without A's having to even know there is a bridge in the middle. Perhaps Mark reasoned as follows in his path to a final solution.

Packet Repeater: Suppose A sends a packet to C (on the lower Ethernet) with destination address C and source address A. Assume the bridge picks up the entire packet, buffers it, and waits for a

---

[2] Note that Ethernet 48-bit addresses have no relation to 32-bit Internet addresses.

transmission opportunity to send it on the upper Ethernet. This avoids the physical coupling between the collision-resolution processes on the two Ethernets that would be caused by using a bit repeater. Thus the distance span increases to 3 km, but the effective bandwidth is still that of one Ethernet because every frame is sent on both Ethernets.

Filtering Repeater: The frame repeater idea in Fig. 10.1 causes needless waste (**P1**) when A sends a packet to B by sending the packet unnecessarily on the upper Ethernet. This waste can be avoided if the bridge has a table that maps station addresses to Ethernets. For example, suppose the bridge in Fig. 10.1 has a table that maps A and B to the lower Ethernet and C to the upper Ethernet. Then on receipt of a packet from A to B on the lower Ethernet, the bridge need not forward the frame because the table indicates that destination B is on the same Ethernet the packet was received on. If, say, a fraction p of traffic on each Ethernet is to destinations on the same Ethernet (locality assumption), then the overall bandwidth of the two Ethernet systems becomes $(1 + p)$ times the bandwidth of a single Ethernet. This follows because the fraction p can be simultaneously sent on both Ethernets, increasing overall bandwidth by this fraction. Hence *both* bandwidth and distance increase. The only difficulty is figuring out how the mapping table is built.

Filtering Repeater With Learning: It is infeasible to have a manager build a mapping table for a large bridged network. Can the table be built automatically? One aspect of Principle **P13** (exploit degrees of freedom) is Polya's (Polya, 1957) problem-solving question: "Have you used all the data?" So far, the bridge has looked only at *destination addresses* to forward the data. Why not also look at *source addresses*? When receiving a frame from A to B, the bridge can look at the source address field to realize that A is on the lower Ethernet. Over time, the bridge will learn the ports through which all active stations can be reached.

Perhaps Mark rushed out after his insight, shouting "Eureka!" But he still had to work out a few more issues. First, because the table is initially empty, bridges must forward a packet, perhaps unnecessarily, when the location of the destination has not been learned. Second, to handle station movement, table entries must be timed out if the source address is not seen for some time period T. Third, the entire idea generalizes to more than two Ethernets connected together without cycles, to bridges with more than two Ethernet attachments, and to links other than Ethernets that carry destination and source addresses. But there was a far more serious challenge that needed to be resolved.

10.2 Challenge 2: wire speed forwarding

When the idea was first proposed, some doubting Thomas at DEC noticed a potential flaw. Suppose in Fig. 10.1 that A sends 1000 packets to B and that A then follows this burst by sending, say, 10 packets to C. The bridge receives the 1000 packets, buffers them, and begins to work on forwarding (actually discarding) them. Suppose the time that the bridge takes to look up its forwarding table is twice as long as the time it takes to receive a packet. Then after a burst of 1000 back-to-back packets arrive, a queue of 500 packets from A to B will remain as a backlog of packets that the bridge has not even examined.

Since the bridge has a finite amount of buffer storage for, say, 500 packets, when the burst from A to C arrives they may be dropped without examination because the bridge has no more buffer storage. This is ironic because the packets from A to B that are in the buffer will be dropped after examination, but the bridge has dropped packets from A to C that need to be forwarded. One can change the numbers used in this example but the bottom line is unchanged: If the bridge takes more time to forward a packet

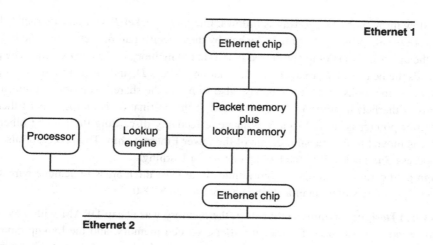

FIGURE 10.2

Implementation of the first Ethernet-to-Ethernet bridge.

than the minimum packet arrival time, there are always scenarios in which packets to be forwarded will be dropped because the buffers are filled with packets that will be discarded.

The critics were quick to point out that routers did not have this problem[3] because routers dealt only with packets addressed to the router. Thus if a router were used, the router–Ethernet interface would not even pick up packets destined for *B*, avoiding this scenario.

To finesse this issue and avoid interminable arguments, Mark proposed an implementation that would do *wire speed forwarding* between two Ethernets. In other words, the bridge would look up the destination address in the table (for forwarding) and the source address (for learning) in the time it took a minimum-size packet to arrive on an Ethernet. Given a 64-byte minimum packet, this left 51.2 microsecond to forward a packet. Since a two-port bridge could receive a minimum-size packet on each of its Ethernets every 51.2 microsecond, this actually translated into doing two lookups (destination and source) every 25.6 microsecond.

It is hard to appreciate today, when wire speed forwarding has become commonplace, how astonishing this goal was in the early 1980s. This is because in those days one would be fortunate to find an interconnect device (e.g., router, gateway) that worked at kilobit rates, let alone at 10 Mbit/sec. Impossible, many thoughts. To prove them wrong, Mark built a prototype as part of the Advanced Development Group in DEC. A schematic of his prototype, which became the basis for the first bridge, is shown in Fig. 10.2.

The design in Fig. 10.2 consists of a processor (the first bridge used a Motorola 68000), two Ethernet chips (the first bridge used AMD Lance chips), a lookup chip (which is described in more detail later), and a four-ported shared memory. The memory could be read and written by the processor, the Ethernet chips, and the lookup engine.

---

[3] Oddly enough, even routers have the same problem of distinguishing important packets from less important ones in times of congestion, but this was not taken seriously in the 1980s.

The data flow through the bridge was as follows. Imagine a packet P sent on Ethernet 1. Both Ethernet chips were set in "promiscuous mode," whereby they received all packets. Thus the bits of P are captured by the upper Ethernet chip and stored in the shared memory in a receive queue. The processor eventually reads the header of P, extracts the destination address D, and gives it to the lookup engine.

The lookup engine looks up D in a database also stored in the shared memory and returns the port (upper or lower Ethernet) in around 1.3 microsecond. If the destination is on the upper Ethernet, then the packet buffer pointer is moved to a free queue, effectively discarding the packet; otherwise, the buffer pointer is moved to the transmit queue of the lower Ethernet chip. The processor also provides the source address S in packet P to the lookup engine for learning.

His design paid careful attention to algorithmics in at least three areas to achieve wire speed forwarding at a surprisingly small manufacturing cost of around $1000.

- **Architectural Design:** To minimize the cost, the memory was cheap DRAM with a cycle time of 100 nanosecond that was used for packet buffers, scratch memory, and the lookup database. The four-port memory (including the separate connection from the lookup engine to the memory) and the buses were carefully designed to maximize parallelism and minimize interference. For example, while the lookup engine worked on doing lookups to memory, the processor continued to do useful work. Note that the processor has to examine the receive queues of both Ethernet chips in dovetailed fashion to check for packets to be forwarded from either the top or bottom Ethernets. Careful attention was paid to memory bandwidth, including the use of page mode (Chapter 2).
- **Data Copying:** The Lance chips used DMA (Chapter 5) to place packets in the memory without processor control. When a packet was to be forwarded between the two Ethernets, the processor only flipped a pointer from the receive queue of one Ethernet chip to the transmit queue of the other processor.
- **Control Overhead:** As with most processors, the interrupt overhead of the 68000 was substantial. To minimize this overhead, the processor used polling, staying in a loop after a packet interrupt and servicing as many packets that arrive, in order to reduce context-switching overhead (Chapter 6). When the receive queues are empty, the processor moves on to doing other chores, such as processing control traffic. The first data packet arrival after such an idle period interrupts the processor, but this interrupt overhead is spread over the entire batch of packets that arrive before another idle period begins.
- **Lookups:** Very likely, Mark went through the eight cautionary questions found in Chapter 3. First, to avoid any complaints, he decided to use binary search (**P15**, efficient data structures) for lookup because of its determinism. Second, having a great deal of software experience before he began designing hardware, he wrote some sample 68000 code and determined that software binary search lookup was the bottleneck (**Q2** in Chapter 3) and would exceed his packet processing budget of 25.6 microsecond. Eliminating the destination and source lookup would allow him to achieve wire speed forwarding (**Q3**). Recall that each iteration of binary search reads an address from the database in memory, compares it with the address that must be looked up, and uses this comparison to determine the next address to be read. With added hardware (**P5**), the comparison can be implemented using combinatorial logic (Chapter 2), and so a first-order approximation of lookup time is the number

of DRAM memory accesses. As the first product aimed for a table size of 8000,[4] this required $\log_2 8000$ memory accesses of 100-nanosecond each, yielding a lookup time of 1.3 microsecond. Given that the processor does useful work during the lookup, two lookups for source and destination easily fit within a 25.6 microsecond budget (**Q4**).

To answer **Q5** in Chapter 3 as to whether custom hardware is worthwhile, Mark found that the lookup chip could be cheaply and quickly implemented using a PAL (programmable array logic; see Chapter 2). To answer **Q7**, his initial prototype met wire speed tests constructed using logic analyzers. Finally, **Q8**, which asks about the sensitivity to environment changes, was not relevant to a strictly worst-case design like this.

The 68000 software, written by Bob Shelley, also had to be carefully constructed to maximize parallelism. After the prototype was built, Tony Lauck, then head of DECNET, was worried that bridges would not work correctly if they were placed in cyclic topologies. For example, if two bridges are placed between the same pair of Ethernets, messages sent on one Ethernet will be forwarded at wire speed in the loop between bridges. In response, Radia Perlman, then the DEC routing architect, invented her celebrated *spanning tree* algorithm. The algorithm ensures that bridges compute a loop-free topology by having redundant bridges turn off appropriate bridge ports.

While you can read up on the design of the spanning tree algorithm in Perlman's book (Perlman, 1992), it is interesting to note that there was initial resistance to implementing her algorithm, which appeared to be "complex" when compared to simple, fast bridge data forwarding. However, the spanning tree algorithm used control messages, called *Hellos*, that are not processed in real time.

A simple back-of-the-envelope calculation by Tony Lauck related the number of instructions used to process a hello (at most 1000), the rate of hello generation (specified at that time to be once every second), and the number of instructions per second of the Motorola 68000 (around 1 million). Lauck's vision and analysis carried the day, and the spanning tree algorithm was implemented in the final product.

Manufactured at a cost of $1000, the first bridge was initially sold at a markup of around eight, ensuring a handsome profit for DEC when sales initially climbed. In 1986 Mark Kempf was awarded US Patent 4,597,078, titled "Bridge circuit for interconnecting networks." DEC made no money from patent licensing, choosing instead to promote the IEEE 802.1 bridge interconnection standards process.

Together with the idea of self-learning bridges, the spanning tree algorithm has passed into history. Ironically, one of the first customers complained that the bridge did not work correctly; field service later determined that the customer had connected two bridge ports to the same Ethernet, and the spanning tree had (rightly) turned the bridge off! While features like autoconfigurability and provable fault tolerance have only recently been added to Internet protocols, they were part of the bridge protocols in the 1980s.

The success of Ethernet bridges led to proposals for several other types of bridges connecting other local area networks and even wide area bridges. The author even remembers working with John Hart (who went on to become CTO of 3Com) and Fred Baker (who went on to become a Cisco Fellow) on building satellite bridges that could link geographically distributed sites. While some of the initial enthusiasm to extend bridges to supplant routers was somewhat extreme, bridges found their most successful niche in cheaply interconnecting similar local area networks at wire speeds.

---

[4] This allows a bridged Ethernet to have only 8000 stations. While this is probably sufficient for most customer sites, later bridge implementations raised this figure to 16K and even 64K.

However, after the initial success of 10-Mbps Ethernet bridges, engineers at DEC began to worry about bridging higher-speed LANs. In particular, DEC decided, perhaps unwisely, to concentrate their high-speed interconnect strategy around 100-Mbps FDDI token rings (UNH Inter Operability Lab, 2001). Thus in the early 1990s engineers at DEC and other companies began to worry about building a bridge to interconnect two 100-Mpbs FDDI rings. Could wire speed forwarding, and especially exact-match lookups, be made 10 times faster?

10.3 Challenge 3: scaling lookups to higher speeds

First, let's understand why binary search forwarding *does not* scale to FDDI speeds. Binary search takes $\log_2 N$ memory accesses to look up a bridge database, where N is the size of the database. As bridges grew popular, marketing feedback indicated that the database size needed to be increased from 8 K to 64 K. Thus using binary search, each search would take 16 memory accesses. Doing a search for the source and destination addresses using 100-nanosecond DRAM would then take 3.2 microsecond.

Unlike Ethernet, where small packets are padded to ensure a minimum size of 64 bytes, a minimum-size packet consisting of FDDI, routing, and transport protocol headers could be as small as 40 bytes. Given that a 40-byte packet can be received in 3.2 microsecond at 100 Mbps, two binary search lookups would use up all of the packet-processing budget for a single link, leaving no time for other chores, such as inserting and removing from link chip queues.

One simple approach to meet the challenge of wire speed forwarding is to retain binary search but to use faster hardware (**P5**). In particular, faster SRAM (Chapter 2) could be used to store the database. Given a factor of 5–10 decrease in memory access time using SRAM in place of DRAM, binary search will easily scale to wire speed FDDI forwarding.

However, this approach is unsatisfactory for two reasons. First, it is more expensive because SRAM is more expensive than DRAM. Second, using faster memory gets us lookups at FDDI speeds but will not work for the next speed increment (e.g., Gigabit Ethernet). What is needed is a way to reduce the number of memory accesses associated with a lookup so that bridging can scale with link technology. Of the two following approaches to bridge-lookup scaling, one is based on hashing and the other on hardware parallelism.

10.3.1 Scaling via hashing

In the 1990s DEC decided to build a fast crossbar switch connecting up to 32 links, called the Gigaswitch (Souza et al., 1994). The switch-arbitration algorithms used in this switch will be described in Chapter 13. This chapter concentrates on the bridge-lookup algorithms used in the Gigaswitch. The vision of the original designers, Bob Simcoe and Bob Thomas, was to have the Gigaswitch be a switch connecting point-to-point FDDI links without implementing bridge forwarding and learning. Bridge lookups were considered to be too complex at 100-Mbps speeds.

Into the development arena strode a young software designer who changed the product direction. Barry Spinney, who had implemented an Ada compiler in his last job, was determined to do hardware design at DEC. Barry suggested that the Gigaswitch be converted to a bridge interconnecting FDDI local area networks. To do so, he proposed designing an FDDI-to-Gigaswitch network controller (FGC)

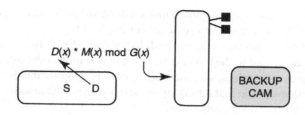

FIGURE 10.3

Gigaswitch hashing uses a hash function with a programmable multiplier, a small, balanced binary tree in every hash bucket, and a backup CAM to hold the rare case of entries that result in more than seven collisions.

chip on the line cards that would implement a hashing-based algorithm for lookups. The Gigaswitch article (Souza et al., 1994) states that each bridge lookup makes at most four reads from memory.

Now, every student of algorithms (Cormen et al., 1990) knows that hashing, on average, is much faster (constant time) than binary search (logarithmic time). However, the same student also knows that hashing is much slower in the worst case, potentially taking linear time because of collisions. How, then, can the Gigaswitch hash lookups claim to take at most four reads to memory in the worst case even for bridge databases of size 64K, whereas binary search would require 16 memory accesses?

The Gigaswitch trick has its roots in an algorithmic technique (**P15**) called *perfect hashing* (Dietzfelbinger et al., 1988; Belazzougui et al., 2009; Limasset et al., 2017). The idea is to use a parameterized hash function, where the hash function can be changed by varying some parameters. Then appropriate values of the parameters can be precomputed (**P2a**) to obtain a hash function such that the worst-case number of collisions is small and bounded.

While finding such a good hash function may take (in theory) a large amount of time, this is a good trade-off because this new station's addresses do not get added to local area networks at a very rapid rate. On the other hand, once the hash function has been picked, lookup can be done at wire speeds.

Specifically, the Gigaswitch hash function treats each 48-bit address as a 47-degree polynomial in the Galois field of order 2, GF(2). While this sounds impressive, this is the same arithmetic used for calculating CRCs; it is identical to ordinary polynomial arithmetic, except that all additions are done mod 2. A hashed address is obtained by the equation $A(X) * M(X) \mod G(X)$, where $G(X)$ is the irreducible polynomial $X^{48} + X^{36} + X^{25} + X^{10} + 1$, $M(X)$ is a nonzero, 47-degree programmable hash multiplier, and $A(X)$ is the address expressed as a 47-degree polynomial.

The hashed address is 48 bits. The bottom 16 bits of the hashed address is then used as an index into a 64K-entry hash table. Each hash table entry [see Fig. 10.3 as applied to the destination address lookup, with $D(x)$ being used in place of $A(x)$] points to the root of a balanced binary tree of height at most 3. The hash function has the property that it suffices to use only the remaining high-order 32 bits of the hashed address to disambiguate collided keys.

Thus the binary tree is sorted by these 32-bit values, instead of the original 48-bit keys. This saves 16 bits to be used for associated lookup information. Thus any search is guaranteed to take no more than four memory accesses, one to lookup the hash table and three more to navigate a height-3 binary tree.

It turns out that picking the multiplier is quite easy in practice. The coefficients of $M(x)$ are picked randomly. Having picked $M(x)$, it sometimes happens that a few buckets have more than seven colliding addresses. In such a case these entries are stored in a small hardware lookup database called a content addressable memory or CAM (studied in more detail in Chapter 11).

The CAM lookup occurs in parallel with the hash lookup. Finally, in the extremely rare case when several dozen addresses are added to the CAM (say, when new station addresses are learned that cause collisions), the central processor initiates a rehashing operation and distributes the new hash function to the line cards. It is perhaps ironic that rehashing occurred so rarely in practice that one might worry whether the rehashing code was adequately tested!

The Gigaswitch became a successful product, allowing up to 22 FDDI networks to be bridged together with other link technologies, such as ATM. Barry Spinney was assigned US patent 5,920,900, "Hash-based translation method and apparatus with multiple-level collision resolution." While techniques based on perfect hashing (Dietzfelbinger et al., 1988) have been around for a while in the theoretical community, Spinney's contribution was to use a pragmatic version of the perfect hashing idea for high-speed forwarding.

10.3.2 Using hardware parallelism

Techniques based on perfect hashing do not completely provide worst-case guarantees. While they do provide worst-case *search* times of three to four memory accesses, they cannot guarantee worst-case *update* times. It is conceivable that an update takes an unpredictably long time while the software searches for a hash function with the specified bound on the number of collisions.

One can argue that exactly the same guarantees are provided every moment by millions of Ethernets around the world and that nondeterministic update times are far preferable to nondeterministic search times. However, proving that long update times are rare in practice requires either considerable experimentation or good analysis. This makes some designers uncomfortable. It leads to a preference for search schemes that have bounded worst-case search and update times.

An alternate approach is to apply hardware parallelism (**P5**) to a deterministic scheme such as binary search. Binary search has deterministic search and update times; its only problem is that search takes a logarithmic number of memory accesses, which is too slow. We can get around this difficulty by *pipelining* binary search to increase lookup throughput (number of lookups per second) without improving lookup latency. This is illustrated in Fig. 10.4.

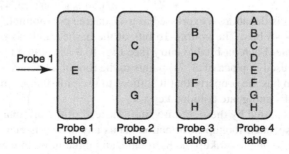

FIGURE 10.4

Pipeling binary search for a database with keys A through H.

The idea is to have a logarithmic number of processing stages, each with its own memory array. In Fig. 10.4 the keys are the characters A through H. The first array has only the root of the trie, the median element E. The second array corresponds to the quartile and third quartile elements C and G, which are the possible keys at the second probe of binary search, and so on. Search keys enter from the left and progress from stage to stage, carrying a pointer that identifies which key in the corresponding stage memory must be compared to the search key. The lookup throughput is nearly one per memory access because there can be multiple concurrent searches progressing through the stages in order.

Although the figure shows the elements in, say, Stage 2, C and G, as being separated by their spacing in the original table, they can be packed together to save memory in the stages. Thus the overall memory across all stages becomes equal to the memory in a nonpipelined implementation. Indexing into each stage memory becomes slightly more tricky.

Assume Stage i has passed a pointer j to Stage $j + 1$ along with search key S. Stage $j + 1$ compares the search key S to its jth array entry. If the answer is equal, the search is finished but continues flowing through the pipeline with no more changes. If the search key is smaller, the search key is passed to stage $i + 1$ with the pointer $j0$ (i.e., j concatenated with bit 0); if the search key is larger, the pointer passed is $j1$. For example, if the key searched for is F, then the pointer becomes 1 when entering Stage 2 and becomes 10 when entering Stage 3.

The author first heard of this idea from Greg Waters, who later went on to implement IP lookups for the core router company Avici. While the idea looks clever and arcane, there is a much simpler way of understanding the final solution. Computer scientists are well aware of the notion of a binary search tree (Cormen et al., 1990). Any binary search table can be converted into a fully balanced binary search tree by making the root the median element, and so on, along the lines of Fig. 10.4. Any tree is trivially pipelined by height, with nodes of height i being assigned to Stage i.

The only problem with a binary search tree, as opposed to a table, is the extra space required for pointers to children. However, it is well known that for a full binary search tree, such as a heap (Cormen et al., 1990), the pointers can be implicit and can be calculated based on the history of comparisons, as shown earlier. The upshot is that a seemingly abstruse trick can be seen as the combination of three simple and well-known facts from theoretical computer science.

10.3.3 The d-left approach

Now we introduce d-left, the state of art solution (Broder and Mitzenmacher, 2001) to the exact-match problem that has been used in Cisco switch products. The objective of this approach is similar to that of perfect hashing: to minimize the maximum number of objects hashed into any bucket in a hash table. However, when a random hash function is used, this maximum is known to be much larger than the average (Gonnet, 1981). More precisely, when n objects are hashed into n buckets, the expectation of this maximum is $(1 + o(1)) \log n / \log \log n$ (with high probability). As explained earlier, the objective of perfect hashing is to reduce this maximum to a small number (say 2 or 3) so that every bucket can fit into a memory block, using a hash function that is perfect for the set of keys to be inserted into the hash table; as a result, much precomputation is needed to find such a perfect hash function.

d-left is a variation of a slightly older idea called d-random that is now widely known as "the power of d choices" (Mitzenmacher, 1996). The original idea of d-random is to use $d > 1$ random hash functions (say $h_1, h_2, \cdots, h_d$) instead of one. Given a hash key x, there are d candidate hash buckets into which x can be inserted: buckets indexed by $h_1(x)$, $h_2(x)$, $\cdots$, $h_d(x)$ respectively. Among them, x is inserted into the bucket that is least occupied; ties are broken randomly (which gives the d-random scheme its name). The objective of such a greedy insertion strategy is to keep the number of objects inside each hash bucket as even as possible across the hash table, and as a result, to make the maximum number of objects in any bucket as small as possible. Indeed, it was shown in Broder and Mitzenmacher (2001) that, in d-random, given the same workload above of inserting n objects into a hash table with n buckets, the expectation of this maximum number is reduced to $(\log \log n / \log d) + O(1)$, from $(1 + o(1)) \log n / \log \log n$ when only a single random hash function is used.

There are only two slight differences between d-left and d-random. First, in d-left, the hash table is partitioned into d equal-sized (in number of buckets) logically independent subtables, each of which contains n/d buckets (with indices $1, 2, \cdots, n/d$); in comparison, there is no such partitioning in d-random. These d subtables are numbered $1, 2, \cdots, d$ and arranged from left to right, so that subtable 1 is the leftmost, subtable 2 is the second leftmost, and so on. When an object x is to be inserted, each of the d hash functions h_1, h_2, $\cdots$, h_d maps x to a hash value in the range $[1, n/d]$. The d candidate buckets where x can be inserted are the bucket indexed by $h_1(x)$ in subtable 1, the bucket indexed by $h_2(x)$ in the subtable 2, ..., and the bucket indexed by $h_d(x)$ in subtable d. As in d-random, among these d buckets, the one that is least occupied is where x should be inserted.

Second, in d-left, a tie is broken in a very different way. In d-left if there are more than one least occupied buckets among the d buckets where an object x should be inserted into, then x will be inserted into the leftmost one among them (i.e., the one in the leftmost subtable). This tie-breaking strategy of "going as left as possible" gives d-left its name.

It has been shown that this tie-breaking strategy outperforms, in terms of resulting in a stochastically smaller maximum (occupancy) number, other tie-breaking strategies such as the standard strategy of breaking ties (uniformly) randomly. This finding is perhaps counterintuitive, or even surprising, to some readers. In particular, how can an asymmetric strategy of "always going left" when there is a tie beat a symmetric strategy of breaking ties randomly? We refer readers to Broder and Mitzenmacher (2001) for an intuitive answer to this question, which is still quite subtle. Note that this "going left" tie-breaking strategy performs better only when the performance metric is the maximum occupancy of any bucket. For example, if the performance metric is instead the maximum total occupancy (number of objects in) of any subtable, the random tie-breaking strategy performs better.

Finally, we provide a brief comparison between d-left and perfect hashing. In practice, d-left can achieve a similar maximum occupancy (of any bucket) as perfect hashing. In doing so, d-left does not have to recompute the hash function from time to time (when the set of MAC addresses changes), whereas perfect hashing does. As this recomputation can take a long time for a large set of MAC addresses (e.g., minutes as reported in Broder and Mitzenmacher, 2001), perfect hashing may not be suitable for a LAN environment where the set of MAC addresses "attached" to a switch changes frequently, such as in a campus WiFi network. Compared to perfect hashing, the only obvious disadvantage of d-left is that, when searching for an object x, all the d buckets where x may possibly appear have to be probed. However, since these d buckets belong to logically independent subtables, the probing of these d buckets can be performed in a parallel or pipelined manner (**P5a**), if these d subtables are put in physically independent memory or cache modules.

10.4 Summary

This chapter on exact-match lookups is written as a story, the story of bridging. Three morals can be drawn from this story.

First, bridging was a direct response to the challenge of efficiently extending Ethernets without using routers or repeaters; wire speed forwarding was a direct response to the problem of potentially losing important packets in a flood of less important packets. At the risk of sounding like a self-help book, I hold that challenges are best regarded as opportunities and not as annoyances. The mathematician Felix Klein (Bell, 1986) used to say, "You must always have a problem; you may not find what you were looking for but you will find something interesting on the way." For example, it is clear that the main reason bridges were invented, that is, the lack of high-performance multiprotocol routers, is *not* the reason bridges are still useful today.

This brings us to the second moral. Today it is clear that bridges will never displace routers because of their lack of scalability using flat Ethernet addresses, lack of shortest-cost routing, etc. However, they remain interesting today because bridges are interconnect devices with better cost for performance and higher flexibility than routers for interconnecting a small number of similar local area networks. Thus bridges still abound in the marketplace, often referred to as *switches*. What many network vendors refer to as a *switch* is a crossbar switch, such as the Gigaswitch, that is capable of bridging on every interface. A few new features, notably virtual LANs (VLANs) (Perlman, 1992), have been added. But the core idea remains the same.

Third, the *techniques* introduced by the first bridge have deeply influenced the next generation of interconnect devices, from core routers to Web switches. Recall that Roger Bannister, who first broke the 4-minute-mile barrier, was followed in a few months by several others. In the same way, the first Ethernet bridge was quickly followed by many other wire speed bridges. Soon the idea began to flow to routers as well. Other important concepts introduced by bridges include the use of memory references as a metric, the notion of trading update time for faster lookups, and the use of minimal hardware speedups. All these ideas carry over into the study of router lookups in the next chapter.

In conclusion, the challenge of building the first bridge stimulated creative actions that went far beyond the first bridge. While wire speed router designs are fairly commonplace today, it is perhaps surprising that there are products still being announced that claim gigabit wire speed processing rates for such abstruse networking tasks as encryption and even XML transformations.

10.5 Exercise

1. **ARP Caches:** Another example of an exact-match lookup is furnished by ARP (address resolution protocol) caches in a router or endnode. In an Internet router when a packet first arrives at a destination, the router must store the packet and send an ARP request to the Ethernet containing the packet. The ARP request is broadcast to all endnodes on the Ethernet and contains the IP address of the destination. When the destination responds with an ARP reply containing the Ethernet address of the destination, the router stores the mapping in an ARP table and sends the stored data packet, with the destination Ethernet address filled in.

   - What lookup algorithms can be used for ARP caches?
   - Why might the task of storing data packets awaiting data translation result in packet reordering?

- Some router implementations get around the reordering problem by dropping all data packets that arrive to find that the destination address is not in the ARP table (however, the ARP request is sent out). Explain the pros and cons of such a scheme.

2. **Using CAM to Absorb Overflows From a Hash Table:** Suppose 1 million nodes are hashed into a hash table that contains 1 million buckets. On average, what is the total number of overflows if each bucket can hold at most 4 nodes (say in a memory line)? Calculating this number will help us determine the right size for the CAM. Here, you may assume that the hash function is strictly uniform (across the 1 million indices/buckets). You may also approximate the Binomial random variable you will encounter in this case by a Poisson random variable (since 1 million is a large enough number).

Prefix-match lookups

You can look it up.
—Traditional

Consider a flight database in London that lists flights to a thousand US cities. One alternative would be to keep a record specifying the path to each of the 1000 cities. Suppose, however, that most flights to America hub through Boston, except flights to California, which hub through Los Angeles. This observation can be exploited to reduce the flight database from a thousand entries to two prefix entries (USA* → Boston; USA.CA.* → LA).

A problem with this reduction is that a destination city like USA.CA.Fresno will now match both the USA* and USA.CA.* prefixes; the database must return the longest match (USA.CA.*). Thus prefixes have been used to compress a large database but at the cost of a more complex *longest-matching-prefix* lookup.

As described in Chapter 2 the Internet uses the same idea. In the year 2022 core routers stored only around 900,000 prefixes instead of potentially billions of entries for each possible Internet address. For example, to a core router, all the computers within a university, such as UCLA (University of California, Los Angeles), will probably be reachable by the same next hop. If all the computers within UCLA are given the same initial set of bits (the network number or prefix), then the router can store *one* entry for UCLA instead of thousands of entries for each computer in UCLA.

The world has changed significantly since the first edition as follows.

- *Prefix Growth:* Since the first edition, the core routing table has grown from around 150,000 in 2004 to around 900,000 prefixes in 2022.
- *IP v6:* When the first edition was written, 128-bit IPv6 was being talked about but did not penetrate significantly because of the prevalence of Network Address Translation (NAT) boxes. However, the popularity of mobile and Internet of Things (IoT) devices have led to rapid deployment of IPv6, with IPv6 availability of Google users at over 30% (Google, 2022).
- *DRAM versus SRAM:* Many router hardware lookups find it cheaper to use a small amount of on-chip memory and large low-latency external DRAM instead of SRAM.
- *Programmable Chips with TCAM:* Chips, such as Intel's Tofino-3 (Intel Corporation, 2022), have emerged that have a fairly large amount of TCAM and are programmable. While IP lookups can be done using TCAM, new data structures can use TCAM to scale to larger databases. Further, they can be programmed to do different IP lookup schemes using a new higher level language for router programming called P4 (P4 Open Source Programming Language, 2022).
- *Software Defined Networks (SDN):* The SDN movement allows the control plane (and with programmable chips, even the data plane) to be changed by a centralized controller. Each router simply

Network Algorithmics. https://doi.org/10.1016/B978-0-12-809927-8.00018-X

allows a set of match-action rules that can be used to implement bridge lookups, MPLS lookups, IP lookups, or other forms of lookup by simply changing the definition of a match.

- *Multicore Processors:* Processors have become faster and multicore. Thus software implementations of IP lookups at Gigabit speeds are feasible today.
- *Network Function Virtualization (NFV):* There is a growing trend among mobile carriers to replace complex middleboxes (that performed network functions such as longest matching prefix, firewalls, parental controls etc.) with flexible software realizations, a trend called Network Function Virtualization (NFV, 2022).

Despite these changes, the underlying algorithmic ideas have remained except for small variations that we will point out including fast software implementations such as DXR (2022) and algorithms optimized for large amounts of DRAM and small on-chip SRAM such as SAIL (Yang et al., 2014).

The entire chapter is organized as follows. Section 11.1 provides an introduction to prefix lookups. Section 11.2 describes attempts to finesse the need for IP lookups. Section 11.3 presents non-algorithmic techniques for lookup based on caching and parallel hardware. Section 11.4 describes the simplest technique based on unibit tries.

The chapter then transitions to describe seven more sophisticated schemes: multibit tries (Section 11.5), level-compressed tries (Section 11.6), Lulea-compressed tries (Section 11.7), Tree bitmap (Section 11.8), binary search on prefix ranges (Section 11.9) (with a modern manifestation called DXR), binary search on prefix lengths (Section 11.11), and linear search on prefix lengths (Section 11.12).

The chapter ends with Section 11.13 on memory allocation issues, Section 11.14 on fixed function lookup chips, and Section 11.15 on programmable chips, and the P4 language to program them. The techniques described in this chapter (and the corresponding principles) are summarized in Table 11.1.

Quick reference guide

The most important lookup algorithms in our opinion for an implementor today are as follows. At speeds up to 100 Gbps in hardware or software using DRAM technology, the simplest and most effective scheme is based on binary search on prefix ranges (DXR) (Section 11.9) and is unencumbered by patents. At faster speeds, especially using more expensive SRAM technology, the most effective algorithm described in this chapter is Tree bitmap (Section 11.8). On the other hand, a simple scheme using small on-chip SRAM and external DRAM is SAIL (Section 11.12). Finally, Section 11.15 describes the P4 language, and potential IP lookup implementations in programmable router chips like Tofino-3 (Intel Corporation, 2022) that leverage both CAM and RAM.

11.1 Introduction to prefix lookups

This section introduces prefix notation, explains why prefix lookup is used, and describes the main metrics used to evaluate prefix lookup schemes.

11.1.1 Prefix notation

Internet prefixes are defined using bits and not alphanumerical characters, of up to 32 bits in length. To confuse matters, however, IP prefixes are often written in dot-decimal notation. For example, at the

Table 11.1 Principles involved in the various prefix-lookup schemes described in this chapter.

Number	Principle	Lookup technique
P2a, P10	Precompute indices	Tag switching
P2a, P10	Pass indices computed at run time	IP switching
P4a	Exploit ATM switch hardware	
P11	Cache whole IP addresses	Lookup caches
P5	Hardware parallel lookup	CAMs
P4b	Expand prefixes to gain speed	Controlled expansion
P13	Strides as a degree of freedom	Variable-stride tries
P4b	Compress to gain speed	Lulea tries
P12, P2a	Precomputed count of bits set	
P15	Use efficient search	Binary search on prefix lengths
P12	Add marker state	
P2a	Precompute marker watch	
P2a	Precompute range to prefix matching	Binary search on prefixes

time of writing UCSD has a 16-bit prefix 132.239. Each of the decimal digits between dots represents a byte. Since in binary 132 is 10000100 and 239 is 11101111, the UCSD prefix in binary can also be written as 1000010011101111*, where the wildcard character * is used to denote that the remaining bits do not matter. UCSD hosts have 32-bit IP addresses beginning with these 16 bits.

Because prefixes can be variable length, a second common way to denote a prefix is by slash notation of the form A/L. In this case A denotes a 32-bit IP address in dot-decimal notation and L denotes the length of the prefix. Thus the UCSD prefix can also be denoted as 132.239.0.0/16, where the length 16 indicates that only the first 16 bits (i.e., 132.239) are relevant. A third common way to describe prefixes is to use a mask in place of an explicit prefix length. Thus the UCSD prefix can also be described as 128.239.0.0 with a mask of 255.255.0.0. Since 255.255.0.0 has 1's in the first 16 bits, this implicitly indicates a length of 16 bits.[1]

Of these three ways to denote a prefix (binary with a wildcard at the end, slash notation, and mask notation), the last two are more compact for writing down large prefixes. However, for pedagogical reasons, it is much easier to use small prefixes as examples and to write them in binary. Thus in this chapter we will use 01110* to denote a prefix that matches all 32-bit IP addresses that start with 01110. The reader should easily be able to convert this notation to the slash or mask notation used by vendors. Also, note that most prefixes are at least 8 bits in length; however, to keep our examples simple, this chapter uses smaller prefixes.

---

[1] The mask notation is actually more general because it allows noncontiguous masks where the 1's are not necessarily consecutive starting from the left. Such definitions of networks actually do exist. However, they are becoming increasingly uncommon and are nonexistent in core router prefix tables. Thus we will ignore this possibility in this chapter.

11.1.2 Why variable-length prefixes?

Before we consider how to deal with the complexity of variable-length-prefix matching, it is worth understanding why Internet prefixes are variable length. Given a telephone number such as 858-549-3816, it is a trivial matter to extract the first three digits (i.e., 858) as the area code. If fixed-length prefixes are easier to implement, what is the advantage of variable-length prefixes?

The *general* answer to this question is that variable-length prefixes make more efficient use of the address space. This is because areas with a large number of endpoints can be assigned shorter prefixes, while areas with a few endpoints can be assigned longer prefixes.

The *specific* answer comes from the history of Internet addressing. The Internet began with a simple hierarchy in which 32-bit addresses were divided into a network address and a host number; routers only stored entries for networks. For flexible address allocation, the network address came in variable sizes: Class A (8 bits), Class B (16 bits), and Class C (24 bits). To cope with the exhaustion of Class B addresses, the Classless Internet Domain Routing (CIDR) scheme (Rekhter and Li, 1996) assigns new organizations multiple contiguous Class C addresses that can be aggregated by a common prefix. This reduces core router table size.

Today, the potential depletion of the address space has led Internet registries to be very conservative in the assignment of IP addresses. A small organization may be given only a small portion of a Class C address, perhaps a /30, which allows only four IP addresses within the organization. Many organizations are coping with these sparse assignments by sharing a few IP addresses among multiple computers, using schemes such as network address translation, or NAT.

Thus, CIDR and NAT have helped the Internet handle exponential growth with a finite 32-bit address space. While adoption of IP with a 128-bit address (IPv6) is rapidly increasing (Google, 2022), the effectiveness of NAT in the short run and the complexity of rolling out a new protocol have made 32-bit IP addresses still dominant at the time of writing.

The bottom line is that the decision to deploy CIDR helped save the Internet, but it has introduced the complexity of longest-matching prefix lookup.

11.1.3 Lookup model

Recall the router model of Chapter 2. A packet arrives on an input link. Each packet carries a 32-bit Internet (IP) address.[2]

The processor consults a forwarding table to determine the output link for the packet. The forwarding table contains a set of *prefixes* with their corresponding output links. The packet is matched to the longest prefix that matches the destination address in the packet, and the packet is forwarded to the corresponding output link. The task of determining the output link, called *address lookup*, is the subject of this chapter, which surveys lookup algorithms and shows that lookup can be implemented at gigabit and terabit speeds.

Before searching for IP lookup solutions, it is important to be familiar with some basic observations about traffic distributions, memory trends, and database sizes, which are shown in Table 11.2. These in turn will motivate the requirements for a lookup scheme.

---

[2] While most users deal with domain names, recall again that these names are translated to IP addresses by a directory service called DNS before packets are sent.

Table 11.2 Some current data about the lookup problem and the corresponding implications for lookup solutions.

Observation	Inference
1. 250,000 concurrent flows in backbone	Caching works poorly in backbone routers
2. 50% are TCP acks	Wire speed lookup needed for 40-byte packets
3. Lookup dominated by memory accesses	Lookup speed measured by number of memory accesses
4. Prefix lengths from 8 to 32	Naive schemes take 24 memory accesses
5. 1 million prefixes today and multicast and host routes	With growth, require 500,000–1 million prefixes
6. Unstable BGP, multicast	Updates in milliseconds to seconds
7. Higher speeds need SRAM	Worth minimizing memory
8. IPv6, multicast delays	Both 32-bit and 128-bit lookups crucial today

First, a study of backbone traffic (Thompson et al., 1997) as far back as 1997 showed around 250,000 concurrent flows of short duration, using a fairly conservative measurement of flows. Measurement data shows that this number is only increasing to easily over a million concurrent TCP flows. This large number of flows means caching solutions do not work well.

Second, the same study (Thompson et al., 1997) showed that roughly half the packets received by a router are minimum-size TCP acknowledgments. Thus it is possible for a router to receive a stream of minimum-size packets. Hence, being able to prefix lookups in the time to forward a minimum-size packet can finesse the need for an input link queue, which simplifies system design. A second reason is simple marketing: Many vendors claim wire speed forwarding, and these claims can be tested. Assuming wire speed forwarding, forwarding a 40-byte packet should take no more than 32 nanoseconds at 10 Gbps (OC-192 speeds), and 8 nanoseconds at 40 Gbps (OC-768).

Clearly, the most crucial metric for a lookup scheme is lookup speed. The third observation states that because the cost of computation today is dominated by memory accesses, the simplest measure of lookup speed is the worst-case number of memory accesses. The fourth observation shows that backbone databases have all prefix lengths from 8 to 32, and so naive schemes will require 24 memory accesses in the worst case to try all possible prefix lengths.

The fifth observation states that while current databases are around 900,000 prefixes, the possible use of host routes (full 32-bit addresses) and multicast routes means that future backbone routers will have prefix databases of over 1 million prefixes.

The sixth observation refers to the speed of updates to the lookup data structure, for example, to add or delete a prefix. Unstable routing-protocol implementations can lead to requirements for updates on the order of milliseconds. Note that whether seconds or milliseconds, this is several orders of magnitude below the lookup requirements, allowing implementations the luxury of precomputing (**P2a**) information in data structures to speed up lookup, at the cost of longer update times.

The seventh observation comes from Chapter 2. While standard (DRAM) memory is cheap, DRAM access times are currently around 20–40 nanoseconds, and so higher-speed memory (e.g., off- or on-chip SRAM, 1–5 nanoseconds) may be needed at higher speeds. While DRAM memory is essentially unlimited, SRAM and on-chip memory are limited by expense or unavailability. Thus a third metric is memory usage, where memory can be expensive fast memory (cache in software, SRAM in hardware) as well as cheaper, slow memory (e.g., DRAM, SDRAM).

Note that a lookup scheme that does not do incremental updates will require two copies of the lookup database so that search can proceed in one copy while lookups proceed on the other copy. Thus it may be worth doing incremental updates simply to reduce high-speed memory by a factor of 2!

The eighth observation concerns prefix lengths. IPv6 requires 128-bit prefixes. Multicast lookups require 64-bit lookups because the full group address and a source address can be concatenated to make a 64-bit prefix. However, the full deployment of both IPv6 and multicast is still proceeding. Thus at the time of writing, it is important to be able to support both 32-bit and 128-bit IP lookups.

In summary, the interesting metrics, in order of importance, are lookup speed, memory, and update time. As a concrete example, a good on-chip design using 16 Mbits of on-chip memory may support any set of 1,000,000 prefixes, do a lookup in 8 nanoseconds to provide wire speed forwarding at terabit speeds, and allow prefix updates in 1 millisecond.

The following notations is used consistently in reporting the theoretical performance of IP lookup algorithms. N denotes the number of prefixes (e.g., 900,000 for large databases in 2022), and W denotes the length of an address (e.g., 32 for IPv4).

Finally, two additional observations can be exploited to optimize the expected case.

O1:   Almost all prefixes are 24 bits or less, with the majority being 24-bit prefixes and the next largest spike being at 16 bits. Some vendors use this to show worst-case lookup times only for 24-bit prefixes; however, the future may lead to databases with a large number of host routes (32-bit addresses) and integration of ARP caches.

O2:   It is fairly rare to have prefixes that are prefixes of other prefixes, such as the prefixes 00* and 0001*. In fact, the maximum number of prefixes of a given prefix in current databases is seven.

While the ideal is a scheme that meets worst-case lookup time requirements, it is desirable to have schemes that also utilize these observations to improve average storage performance.

11.2 Finessing lookups

The first instinct for a systems person is not to solve complex problems (like longest matching prefix) but to *eliminate* the problem.

Observe that in virtual circuit networks such as ATM, when a source wishes to send data to a destination, a call, analogous to a telephone call, is set up. The call number virtual circuit index [VCI] at each router is a moderate-size integer that is easy to look up. However, this comes at the cost of a round-trip delay for call setup before data can be sent.

In terms of our principles, ATM has a previous hop switch pass an index (**P10**, pass hints in protocol headers) into a next hop switch. The index is precomputed (**P2a**) just before data is sent by the previous hop switch (**P3c**, shifting computation in space). The same abstract idea can be used in datagram

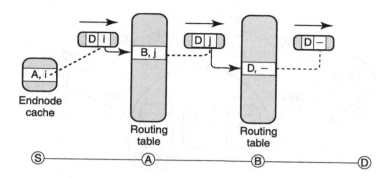

FIGURE 11.1

Replacing the need for a destination lookup in a datagram router by having each router pass an index into the next router's forwarding table.

networks such as the Internet to finesse the need for prefix lookups. We now describe two instantiations of this abstract idea: tag switching (Section 11.2.1) and flow switching (Section 11.2.2).

11.2.1 Threaded indices and tag switching

In threaded indices (Chandranmenon and Varghese, 1996), each router passes an index into the next router's forwarding table, thereby avoiding prefix lookups. The indexes are precomputed *by the routing protocol* whenever the topology changes. Thus in Fig. 11.1 source S sends a packet to destination D to the first router A as usual; however, the packet header also contains an index i into A's forwarding table. A's entry for D says that the next hop is router B and that B stores its forwarding entry for D at index j. Thus A sends the packet on to B, but first it writes j (Fig. 11.1) as the packet index. This process is repeated, with each router in the path using the index in the packet to look up its forwarding table.

The two main differences between threaded indices and VCIs are as follows. First, threaded indexes are per *destination* and not per active *source–destination pair* as in virtual circuit networks such as ATM. Second, and more importantly, threaded indexes are precomputed *by the routing protocol whenever the topology changes*. As a simple example, consider Fig. 11.2, which shows a sample router topology where the routers run the Bellman–Ford protocol to find their distances to destinations.

In Bellman–Ford (used, for example, in the intradomain protocol Routing Information Protocol [RIP] (Perlman, 1992)), a router R calculates its shortest path to D by taking the minimum of the cost to D through each neighbor. The cost through a neighbor such as A is A's cost to D (i.e., 5) plus the cost from R to A (i.e., 3). In Fig. 11.2 the best-cost path from R to D is through router B, with cost 7. R can compute this because each neighbor of R (e.g., A, B) passes its current cost to D to R, as shown in the figure. To compute indices as well, we modify the basic protocol so that *each neighbor reports its index for a destination in addition to its cost to the destination*. Thus in Fig. 11.2 A passes i and B passes j; thus when R chooses B, it also uses B's index j in its routing table entry for D. In summary, each router uses the index of the minimal-cost neighbor for each destination as the threaded index for that destination.

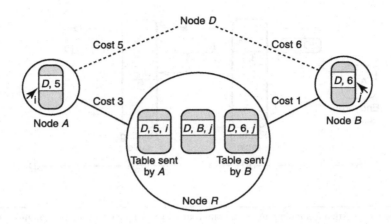

FIGURE 11.2

Setting up the threaded indexes or tags by modifying Bellman–Ford routing.

Cisco later introduced tag switching (Meiners et al., 2008), which is similar in concept to threaded indices, except tag switching also allows a router to pass a stack of tags (indices) for multiple routers downstream. Both schemes, however, do not deal well with hierarchies. Consider a packet that arrives from the backbone to the first router in the exit domain. The exit domain is the last autonomously managed network the packet traverses—say, the enterprise network in which the destination of the packet resides.

The only way to avoid a lookup at the first router, R, in the exit domain is to have some earlier router outside the exit domain pass an index (for the destination subnet) to R. But this is impossible because the prior backbone routers should have only one aggregated routing entry for the entire destination domain and can thus pass only one index for all subnets in that domain. The only solution is either to add extra entries to routers outside a domain (infeasible) or to require ordinary IP lookup at domain entry points (the chosen solution). Today tag switching is flourishing in a more general form called *multiprotocol label switching* (MPLS) (Meiners et al., 2008). However, neither tag switching nor MPLS completely avoids the need for ordinary IP lookups.

11.2.2 Flow switching

A second proposal to finesse lookups was called *flow switching* (Newman et al., 1997; Parulkar et al., 1995). Flow switching also relies on a previous hop router to pass an index into the next hop router. Unlike tag switching, however, these indexes are computed on demand when data arrives, and they are then cached.

Flow switching starts with routers that contain an internal ATM switch and (potentially slow) processors capable of doing IP forwarding and routing. Two such routers R1 and R2 are shown in Fig. 11.3. When R2 first sends an IP packet to destination D that arrives on the left input port of R1, the input port sends the packet to its central processor. This is the slow path. The processor does the IP lookup and switches the packet internally to output link L. So far nothing is out of the ordinary.

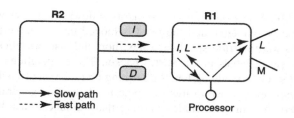

FIGURE 11.3

In IP switching, if R1 wishes to switch packets sent to D that are destined for output link L, R1 picks an idle virtual circuit I, places the mapping I, L in its input port, and then sends I back to R2. If R2 now sends packets to D labeled with VCI I, the packet will get switched directly to the output link without going through the processor.

Life gets more exciting if R1 decides to "switch" packets going to D. R1 may decide to do so if, for instance, there is a lot of traffic going to D. In that case R1 first picks an idle virtual circuit identifier I, places the mapping $I \rightarrow L$ in its input port hardware, and then sends I back to R2. If R2 now sends packets to D labeled with VCI I to the input port of R1, the input port looks up the mapping from I to L and switches the packet directly to the output link L without going through the processor.

Of course, R2 can repeat this switching process with the preceding router in the path, and so on. Eventually, IP forwarding can be completely dispensed with in the switched portion of a sequence of flow-switching routers.

Despite its elegance, flow switching seems likely to work poorly in the backbone. This is because backbone flows are short lived and exhibit poor locality. A contrarian opinion is presented in Molinero-Fernandez and McKeown (2002) where the authors argue for the resurrection of flow switching based on TCP connections. They claim that the current use of circuit-switched optical switches to link core routers, the underutilization of backbone links running at 10% of capacity, and increasing optical bandwidths all favor the simplicity of circuit switching at higher speeds.

Both IP and tag switching are techniques to finesse the need for IP lookups by passing information in protocol headers. Like ATM, both schemes rely on passing indices (**P10**). However, tag switching precomputes the index (**P2a**) at an earlier time scale (topology change time) than ATM (just before data transfer). On the other hand, in IP switching the indices are computed on demand (**P2c**, lazy evaluation) after the data begins to flow. However, neither tag nor IP switching completely avoids prefix lookups, and each adds a complex protocol. We now look afresh at the supposed complexity of IP lookups.

11.2.3 Status of tag switching, flow switching, and multiprotocol label switching

While tag switching and IP switching were originally introduced to speed up lookups, IP switching has died away. However, tag switching in the more general form of multi-protocol-label switchings (MPLS) (IETF MPLS Charter, 1997) has reinvented itself as a mechanism for providing flow differentiation to provide quality of service. Just as a VCI provides a simple label to quickly distinguish a flow, a label allows a router to easily isolate a flow for special service. In effect, MPLS uses labels to finesse the need for packet classification (Chapter 12), a much harder problem than prefix lookups. Thus although prefix matching is still required, MPLS is also de rigueur for a core router today.

Briefly, the required MPLS fast path forwarding is as follows. A packet with an MPLS header is identified, a 20-bit label is extracted, and the label is looked up in a table that maps the label to a forwarding rule. The forwarding rule specifies a next hop and also specifies the operations to be performed on the current set of labels in the MPLS packet. These operations can include removing labels ("popping the label stack") or adding labels ("pushing on to the label stack").

Router MPLS implementations have to impose some limits on this general process to guarantee wire speed forwarding. Possible limits include requiring that the label space be dense, supporting a smaller number of labels than 2^{20} (this allows a smaller amount of lookup memory while avoiding a hash table), and limiting the number of label-stacking operations that can be performed on a single packet.

11.3 Non-algorithmic techniques for prefix matching

In this section we consider two other systems techniques for prefix lookups that do not rely on algorithmic methods: caching and ternary CAMs. Caching relies on locality in address references, while CAMs rely on hardware parallelism.

11.3.1 Caching

Lookups can be sped up by using a cache (**P11a**) that maps 32-bit addresses to next hops. However, cache hit ratios in the backbone are poor (Newman et al., 1997) because of the lack of locality exhibited by flows in the backbone. The use of a large cache still requires the use of an exact-match algorithm for lookup. Some researchers have advocated a clever modification of a CPU cache lookup algorithm for this purpose (Chiueh and Pradhan, 1999). In summary, caching can help, but it does not avoid the need for fast prefix lookups.

11.3.2 Ternary content-addressable memories

Ternary content-addressable memories (CAMs) that allow "don't care" bits provide parallel search in one memory access. Today's CAMs can search and update in one memory cycle (e.g., 10 nanoseconds) and handle any combination of 100,000 prefixes. They can even be cascaded to form larger databases. CAMs, however, have the following issues.

- *Density Scaling:* One bit in a TCAM requires 10–12 transistors, while an SRAM requires 4–6 transistors. Thus TCAMs will also be less dense than SRAMs or take more area. Board area is a critical issue for many routers.
- *Power Scaling:* TCAMs take more power because of the parallel compare. CAM vendors are, however, chipping away at this issue by finding ways to turn off parts of the CAM to reduce power. Power is a key issue in large core routers.
- *Match Arbitration:* The match logic in a CAM requires all matching rules to arbitrate so that the highest match wins. Older-generation CAMs took around 10 nanoseconds for an operation, but this is no longer as much of an issue for modern TCAMs.
- *Extra Chips:* Given that many routers, such as the Cisco GSR and the Juniper M160, already have a dedicated Application Specific Integrated Circuit (ASIC) (or network processor) doing packet

```
P1 = 101*
P2 = 111*
P3 = 11001*
P4 = 1*
P5 = 0*
P6 = 1000*
P7 = 100000*
P8 = 100*
P9 = 110
```

FIGURE 11.4

Sample prefix database used for the rest of this chapter. Note that the next hops corresponding to each prefix have been omitted for clarity.

forwarding, it is tempting to integrate the classification algorithm with the lookup without adding CAM interfaces and CAM chips. Note that CAMs typically require a bridge ASIC in addition to the basic CAM chip and sometimes require multiple CAM chips.

- *Programmable Chips with built-in TCAM:* By contrast to the problem of extra chips cited by the last bullet (that is caused by separate CAM and packet forwarding chips), a game change in recent years has been the emergence of programmable chips capable of performing forwarding with TCAM built in. For example, Intel's Tofino-3 (Intel Corporation, 2022) contains 384 TCAM blocks of size 44×512 each, enough to support a large enterprise or data center but not enough for the backbone without some algorithmic tricks.

In summary, CAM technology is rapidly improving and is supplanting algorithmic methods in smaller routers. However, for larger core routers that may wish to have databases of a million routes in the future, it may be better to have solutions (as we describe in this chapter) that scale with standard memory technologies such as SRAM. SRAM is likely always to be cheaper, faster, and denser than CAMs. While it is clearly too early to predict the outcome of this war between algorithmic and TCAM methods, even semiconductor manufacturers have hedged their bets and provide *both* algorithmic and CAM-based solutions.

11.4 Unibit tries

It is helpful to start a survey of algorithmic techniques (**P15**) for prefix lookup with the simplest technique: a *unibit trie*. Consider the sample prefix database of Fig. 11.4. This database will be used to illustrate many of the algorithmic solutions in this chapter. It contains nine prefixes, called P1 to P9, with the bit strings shown in the figure.

In practice there is a next hop associated with each prefix omitted from the figure. To avoid clutter, prefix names are used to denote the next hops. Thus in the figure, an address D that starts with 1 followed by a string of 31 zeroes will match P4, P6, P7, and P8. The longest match is P7.

Fig. 11.5 shows a unibit trie for the sample database of Fig. 11.4. A unibit trie is based on the simple algorithmic technique (**P15**) of divide and conquer based on the bits in the destination address, starting

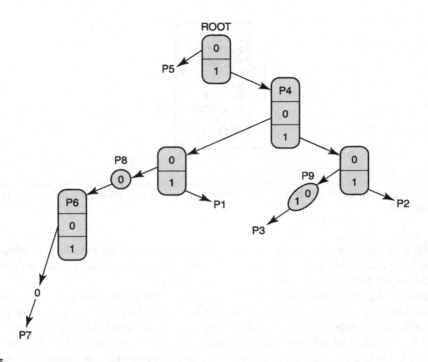

FIGURE 11.5

The one-bit trie for the sample database of Fig. 11.4.

with the most significant. A unibit trie is a tree in which each node is an array containing a 0-pointer and a 1-pointer. At the root all prefixes that start with 0 are stored in the subtrie pointed to by the 0-pointer and all prefixes that start with a 1 are stored in the subtrie pointed to by the 1-pointer.

Each subtrie is then constructed recursively in a similar fashion using the remaining bits of the prefixes allocated to the subtrie. For example, in Fig. 11.5 notice that P1 = 101 is stored in a path traced by following a 1-pointer at the root, a 0-pointer at the right child of the root, and a 1-pointer at the next node in the path.

There are two other fine points to note. In some cases, a prefix may be a substring of another prefix. For example, P4 = 1* is a substring of P2 = 111*. In that case, the smaller string, P4, is stored inside a trie node on the path to the longer string. For example, P4 is stored at the right child to the root; note that the path to this right child is the string 1, which is the same as P4.

Finally, in the case of a prefix such as P3 = 11001, after we follow the first three bits, we might naively expect to find a string of nodes corresponding to the last two bits. However, since no other prefixes share more than the first 3 bits with P3, these nodes would only contain one pointer apiece. Such a string of trie nodes with only one pointer each is called a one-way branch.

Clearly one-way branches can greatly increase wasted storage by using whole nodes (containing at least two pointers) when only a single bit suffices. (The exercises will help you quantify the amount of wasted storage.) A simple technique to remove this obvious waste (**P1**) is to compress the one-way branches.

In Fig. 11.5 this is done by using a text string (i.e. "01") to represent the pointers that would have been followed in the one-way branch. Thus in Fig. 11.5 two trie nodes (containing two pointers apiece) in the path to P3 have been replaced by a single text string of 2 bits. Clearly, no information has been lost by this transformation. (As an exercise, determine if there is another path in the trie that can similarly be compressed.)

To search for the longest matching prefix of a destination address D, the bits of D are used to trace a path through the trie. The path starts with the root and continues until search fails by ending at an empty pointer or at a text string that does not completely match. While following the path, the algorithm keeps track of the last prefix encountered at a node in the path. When search fails, this is the longest matching prefix that is returned.

For example, if D begins with 1110, the algorithm starts by following the 1-pointer at the root to arrive at the node containing P4. The algorithm remembers P4 and uses the next bit of D (a 1) to follow the 1-pointer to the next node. At this node, the algorithm follows the 1-pointer to arrive at P2. When the algorithm arrives at P2, it overwrites the previously stored value (P4) by the newer prefix found (P2). At this point search terminates because P2 has no outgoing pointers.

On the other hand, consider doing a search for a destination D' whose first 5 bits are 11000. Once again, the first 1 bit is used to reach the node containing P4. P4 is remembered as the last prefix encountered, and the 1 pointer is followed to reach the rightmost node at height 2.

The algorithm now follows the third bit in D' (a 0) to the text string node containing "01." Thus we remember P9 as the last prefix encountered. The fourth bit of D' is a 0, which matches the first bit of "01." However, the fifth bit of D' is a 0 (and not a 1 as in the second bit of "01"). Thus the search terminates with P9 as the longest matching prefix.

The literature on tries (Knuth, 1973) does not use *text strings* to compress one-way branches as in Fig. 11.5. Instead, the classical scheme, called a *Patricia trie*, uses a *skip count*. This count records the number of bits in the corresponding text string, not the bits themselves. For example, the text string node "01" in our example would be replaced with the skip count "2" in a Patricia trie.

This works fine as long as the Patricia trie is used for *exact* matches, which is what they were used for originally. When search reaches a skip count node, it skips the appropriate number of bits and follows the pointer of the skip count node to continue the search. Since bits that are skipped are not compared for a match, Patricia requires that a complete comparison between the searched key and the entry found by Patricia be done at the end of the search.

Unfortunately, this works very badly with prefix matching, an application that Patricia tries were *not* designed to handle in the first place. For example, in searching for D', whose first 5 bits are 11000 in the Patricia equivalent of Fig. 11.5, search would skip the last two bits and get to P3. At this point the comparison will find that P3 does not match D'.

When this happens, a search in a Patricia trie has to backtrack and go back up the trie searching for a possible shorter match. In this example, it may appear that search could have remembered P4. But if P4 was also encountered on a path that contains skip count nodes, the algorithm cannot even be sure of P4. Thus it must backtrack to check if P4 is correct.

Unfortunately, the BSD implementation of IP forwarding (Wright and Stevens, 1995) decided to use Patricia tries as a basis for best matching prefix. Thus the BSD implementation used skip counts; the implementation also stored prefixes by padding them with zeroes. Prefixes were also stored at the leaves of the trie, instead of within nodes, as shown in Fig. 11.5. The result is that prefix matching can, in the worst case, result in backtracking up the trie for a worst case of 64 memory accesses (32 down the tree and 32 up).

Given the simple alternative of using text strings to avoid backtracking, doing skip counts is a bad idea. In essence, this is because the skip count transformation does *not* preserve information, while the text string transformation does. However, because of the enormous influence of BSD, a number of vendors and even other algorithms (e.g., Ref. Nilsson and Karlsson, 1998) have used skip counts in their implementations.

11.5 Multibit tries

Most large memories use DRAM. DRAM has a large latency (say 30 nanoseconds) when compared to register access times (2 nanoseconds). Since a unibit trie may have to make 32 accesses for a 32-bit prefix, the worst-case search time of a unibit trie is at least 32 * 30 = 0.96 microseconds. This clearly motivates *multibit* trie search. The number of bits one can search at a time is a degree of freedom algorithmic techniques (**P13**) we can exploit.

To search a trie in *strides* of say 4 bits, the main problem is dealing with prefixes like 10101* (length 5), whose lengths are not a multiple of the chosen stride length, 4. If we search 4 bits at a time, how can we ensure that we do not miss prefixes like 10101*? *Controlled prefix expansion* solves this problem by transforming an existing prefix database into a new database with *fewer prefix lengths* but with potentially *more prefixes*. By eliminating all lengths that are not multiples of the chosen stride length, expansion allows faster multibit trie search, at the cost of increased database size.

For example, removing odd prefix lengths reduces the number of prefix lengths from 32 to 16 and would allow trie search 2 bits at a time. To remove a prefix like 101* of length 3, observe that 101* represents addresses that begin with 101, which in turn represents addresses that begin with 1010* or 1011*. Thus 101* (of length 3) can be replaced by two prefixes of length 4 (1010* and 1011*), both of which inherit the next hop forwarding entries of 101*.

However, the expanded prefixes may collide with an existing prefix at the new length. In that case, the expanded prefix is removed. The existing prefix is given priority because it was originally of longer length.

In essence, expansion trades memory for time (**P4b**). The same idea can be used to remove any chosen set of lengths except length 32. Since trie search speed depends linearly on the number of lengths, expansion reduces search time.

Consider the sample prefix database shown in Fig. 11.4, which has nine prefixes, P1 to P9. The same database is repeated on the *left* of Fig. 11.6. The database on the *right* of Fig. 11.6 is an equivalent database, constructed by expanding the original database to contain prefixes of lengths 3 and 6 only. Notice that of the four expansions of P6 = 1000* to 6 bits, one collides with P7 = 100000* and is thus removed.

11.5.1 Fixed-stride tries

Fig. 11.7 shows a trie for the same database as Fig. 11.6, using expanded tries with a fixed stride length of 3. Thus each trie node uses 3 bits. The replicated entries within trie nodes in Fig. 11.7 correspond

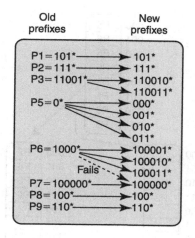

Old prefixes → New prefixes

P1=101* ——→ 101*
P2=111* ——→ 111*
P3=11001* ——→ 110010*
——→ 110011*
P5=0* ——→ 000*
——→ 001*
——→ 010*
——→ 011*
P6=1000* ——→100001*
——→100010*
Fails ---→100011*
P7=100000* ——→100000*
P8=100* ——→100*
P9=110* ——→110*

FIGURE 11.6

Controlled expansion of the original prefix database shown on the left (which has five prefix lengths, 1, 3, 4, 5, and 6) to an expanded database (which has only 2 prefix lengths, 3 and 6).

exactly to the expanded prefixes on the right of Fig. 11.6. For example, P6 in Fig. 11.6 has three expansions (100001, 100010, 100011).

These three expanded prefixes are pointed to by the 100 pointer in the root node of Fig. 11.7 (because all three expanded prefixes start with 100) and are stored in the 001, 010, and 011 entries of the right child of the root node. Notice also that the entry 100 in the root node has a stored prefix P8 (besides the pointer pointing to P6's expansions), because P8 = 100* is itself an expanded prefix.

Thus each trie node element is a record containing *two* entries: a stored prefix and a pointer. Trie search proceeds 3 bits at a time. Each time a pointer is followed, the algorithm remembers the stored prefix (if any). When search terminates at an empty pointer, the last stored prefix in the path is returned.

For example, if address D begins with 1110, search for D starts at the 111 entry at the root node, which has no outgoing pointer but a stored prefix (P2). Thus search for D terminates with P2. A search for an address that starts with 100000 follows the 100 pointer in the root (and remembers P8). This leads to the node on the lower right, where the 000 entry has no outgoing pointer but a stored prefix (P7). The search terminates with result P7. Both the pointer and stored prefix can be retrieved in one memory access using wide memories (**P5b**).

A special case of fixed-stride tries, described in Gupta et al. (1998), uses fixed strides of 24, 4, and 4. The authors observe that DRAMs with more than 2^{24} locations are becoming available, making even 24-bit strides feasible.

11.5.2 Variable-stride tries

In Fig. 11.7 the leftmost leaf node needs to store the expansions of P3 = 11001*, while the rightmost leaf node needs to store P6 (1000*) and P7 (100000*). Thus because of P7 the rightmost leaf node needs to examine 3 bits. However, there is no reason for the leftmost leaf node to examine more than

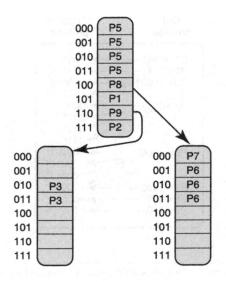

FIGURE 11.7

Expanded trie (which has two strides of 3 bits each) corresponding to the prefix database of Fig. 11.6.

2 bits because P3 contains only 5 bits, and the root stride is 3 bits. There is an extra degree of freedom that can be optimized (**P13**).

In a *variable-stride* trie, the number of bits examined by each trie node can vary, even for nodes at the same level. To do so, the stride of a trie node is encoded with the pointer to the node. Fig. 11.7 can be transformed into a variable-stride trie (Fig. 11.8) by replacing the leftmost node with a four-element array and encoding length 2 with the pointer to the leftmost node. The stride encoding costs 5 bits. However, the variable stride trie of Fig. 11.8 has four fewer array entries than the trie of Fig. 11.7.

Our example motivates the problem of picking strides to minimize the total amount of trie memory. Since expansion trades memory for time, why not minimize the memory needed by optimizing a degree of freedom (**P13**), the strides used at each node? To pick the variable strides, the designer first specifies the worst-case number of memory accesses. For example, with 40-byte packets at 1-Gbps and 80-nanosecond DRAM, we have a time budget of 320 nanoseconds, which allows only four memory accesses. This constrains the maximum number of nodes in any search path (four in our example).

Given this fixed height, the strides can be chosen *to minimize storage*. This can be done using dynamic programming (Srinivasan and Varghese, 1999) in a few seconds, even for large databases of 150,000 prefixes. A degree of freedom (the strides) is optimized to minimize the memory used for a given worst-case tree height.

A trie is said to be optimal for height h and a database D if the trie has the smallest storage among all variable-stride tries for database D, whose height is no more than h. It is easy to prove (see exercises) that the trie of Fig. 11.8 is optimal for the database on the left of Fig. 11.6 and height 2.

The general problem of picking an optimal stride trie can be solved recursively (Fig. 11.9). Assume the tree height must be h. The algorithm first picks a root with stride s. The $y = 2^s$ possible pointers in

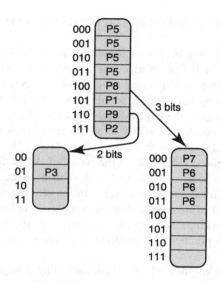

FIGURE 11.8

Transforming the fixed-stride trie of Fig. 11.7 into a variable-stride trie by encoding the stride of each trie node along with a pointer to the node. Notice that the leftmost leaf node now only contains four locations (instead of eight), thus reducing the number of locations from 24 to 20.

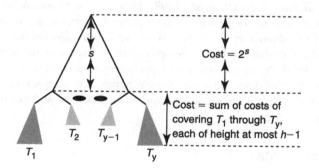

FIGURE 11.9

Picking an optimum variable-stride trie via dynamic programming.

the root can lead to y nonempty subtries $T_1, \ldots T_y$. If the s-bit pointer p_i leads to subtrie T_i, then all prefixes in the original database D that start with p_i must be stored in T_i. Call this set of prefixes D_i.

Suppose we could recursively find the optimal T_i for height $h - 1$ and database D_i. Having used up one memory access at the root node, there are only $h - 1$ memory accesses left to navigate each subtrie T_i. Let C_i denote the storage cost required, counted in array locations, for the optimal T_i. Then for a fixed root stride s, the cost of the resulting optimal trie $C(s)$ is 2^s (cost of root node in array locations) plus $\sum_{i=1}^{y} C_i$. Thus the optimal value of the initial stride is the value of s, where $1 \leq s \leq 32$, that minimizes $C(s)$.

A naive use of recursion leads to repeated subproblems. To avoid repeated subproblems, the algorithm first constructs an auxiliary 1-bit trie. Notice that any subtrie T_i in Fig. 11.9 must be a subtrie N of the 1-bit trie. Then the algorithm uses dynamic programming to construct the optimal cost and trie strides for each subtrie N in the original 1-bit trie for all values of height from 1 to h, building bottom-up from the smallest-height subtries to the largest-height subtries. The final result is the optimal strides for the root (of the 1-bit subtrie) with height h. Details are described in Srinivasan and Varghese (1999).

The final complexity of the algorithm is easily seen to be $O(N * W^2 * h)$, where N is the number of original prefixes in the original database, W is the width of the destination address, and h is the desired worst-case height. This is because there are $N * W$ subtries in the 1-bit trie, each of which must be solved for heights that range from 1 to h, and each solution requires a minimization across at most W possible choices for the initial stride s. Note that the complexity is linear in N (the largest number, around 150,000 at the time of writing) and h (which should be small, at most 8), but quadratic in the address width (currently 32). In practice, the quadratic dependence on address width is not a major factor.

For example, Srinivasan and Varghese (1999) show that using a height of 4, the optimized MAE-East database required 423 KB of storage, compared to 2003 KB for the unoptimized version. The unoptimized version uses the "natural" stride lengths 8, 8, 8, 8. The dynamic program took 1.6 seconds to run on a 300-MHz Pentium Pro. The dynamic program is even simpler for fixed-stride tries and takes only 1 milliseconds to run. However, the use of fixed strides requires 737 KB instead of 423 KB.

Clearly, 1.6 seconds are much too long to let the dynamic program be run for every update and still allow millisecond updates (Labovitz et al., 1997). However, backbone instabilities are caused by pathologies in which the same set of prefixes S are repeatedly inserted and deleted by a router that is temporarily swamped (Labovitz et al., 1997). Since we had to allocate memory for the full set, including S, anyway, the fact that the trie is suboptimal in its use of memory when S is deleted is irrelevant. On the other hand, the rate at which new prefixes get added or deleted by managers seems more likely to be on the order of days. Thus a dynamic program that takes several seconds to run every day seems reasonable and will not unduly affect worst-case insertion and deletion times while still allowing reasonably optimal tries.

11.5.3 Incremental update

Simple insertion and deletion algorithms exist for multibit tries. Consider the addition of a prefix P. The algorithm first simulates search on the string of bits in the new prefix P up to and including the last complete stride in prefix P. Search will terminate either by ending with the last (possibly incomplete) stride or by reaching a nil pointer. Thus for adding P10 = 1100* to the database of Fig. 11.7, search follows the 110-pointer and terminates at the leftmost leaf trie node X.

For the purposes of insertion and deletion, for each node X in the multibit trie, the algorithm maintains a corresponding 1-bit trie, with the prefixes stored in X. This auxiliary structure need not be in fast memory. Also, for each node array element, the algorithm stores the length of its present best match. After determining that P10 must be added to node X, the algorithm expands P10 to the stride of X. Any array element to which P10 expands (which is currently labeled with a prefix of a length smaller than P10) must be overwritten with P10.

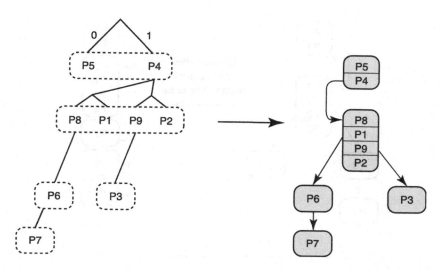

FIGURE 11.10

The level-compressed (LC) trie scheme decomposes the 1-bit trie recursively into full subtries of the largest size possible (*left*). The children in each full subtrie (shown by the dotted boxes) are then placed in a trie node to form a variable-stride trie that is specific to the database chosen.

Thus in adding P10 $= 1100*$, the algorithm must add the expansions of 0* into node X. In particular, the 000 and 001 entries in node X must be updated to be P10.

If the search ends before reaching the last stride in the prefix, the algorithm creates new trie nodes. For example, if the prefix P11 $= 1100111*$ is added, search fails at node X when a nil pointer is found at the 011 entry. The algorithm then creates a new pointer at this location that is made to point to a new trie node that contains P11. P11 is then expanded in this new node.

Deletion is similar to insertion. The complexity of insertion and deletion is the time to perform a search ($O(W)$) plus the time to completely reconstruct a trie node ($O(S)$, where S is the maximum size of a trie node). For example, using 8-bit trie nodes, the latter cost will require scanning roughly $2^8 = 256$ trie node entries. Thus to allow for fast updates, it is crucial to also limit the size of any trie node in the dynamic program described earlier.

11.6 Level-compressed (LC) tries

An LC trie (Nilsson and Karlsson, 1998) is a variable-stride trie in which every trie node contains no empty entries. An LC-trie is built by first finding the largest-root stride that allows no empty entries and then recursively repeating this procedure on the child subtries. An example of this procedure is shown in Fig. 11.10, starting with a 1-bit trie on the left and resulting in an LC trie on the right. Notice that P4 and P5 form the largest possible full-root subtrie—if the root stride is 2, then the first two array entries will be empty. The motivation, of course, is to avoid empty array elements, to minimize storage.

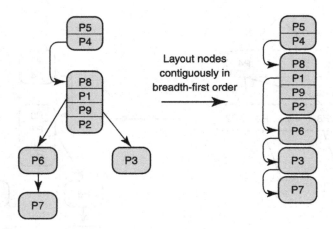

FIGURE 11.11

Array representation of LC tries.

However, general variable-stride tries are more tunable, allowing memory to be traded for speed. For example, the LC trie representation using a 1997 snapshot of MAE-East has a trie height of 7 and needs 700 KB of memory. By comparison, an optimal variable-stride trie (Srinivasan and Varghese, 1999) has a trie height of 4 using 400 KB. Recall also that the optimal variable-stride calculates the best trie for a given target height and thus would indeed produce the LC trie *if* the LC trie were optimal for its height.

In its final form, the variable-stride LC trie nodes are laid out in breadth-first order (first the root, then all the trie nodes at the second level from left to right, then third-level nodes, etc.), as shown on the right of Fig. 11.11. Each pointer becomes an array offset. The array layout and the requirement for full subtries make updates slow in the worst case. For example, deleting P5 in Fig. 11.10 causes a change in the subtrie decomposition. Worse, it causes almost every element in the array representation of Fig. 11.11 to be moved upward.

11.7 Lulea-compressed tries

Though LC tries and variable-stride tries attempt to compress multibit tries by varying the stride at each node, both schemes have problems. While the use of full arrays allows LC tries not to waste any memory because of empty array locations, it also increases the height of the trie, which cannot then be tuned. On the other hand, variable-stride tries can be tuned to have short height, at the cost of wasted memory because of empty array locations in trie nodes. The Lulea approach (Degermark et al., 1997), which we now describe, is a multibit-trie scheme that uses fixed-stride trie nodes of large stride but uses *bitmap* compression to reduce storage considerably.

We know that a string with repetitions (e.g., AAAABBAAACCCC) can be compressed using a bitmap denoting repetition points (i.e., 10001010010000) together with a compressed sequence (i.e.,

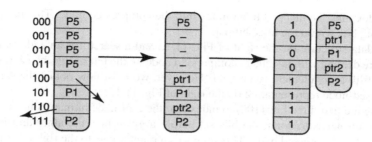

FIGURE 11.12

Compressing the root node of Fig. 11.7 (after leaf pushing) using the Lulea bitmap compression scheme.

ABAC). Similarly, the root node of Fig. 11.7 contains a repeated sequence (P5, P5, P5, P5) caused by expansion.

The Lulea scheme (Degermark et al., 1997) avoids this obvious waste by compressing repeated information using a bitmap and a compressed sequence without paying a high penalty in search time. For example, this scheme used only 160 KB of memory to store the MAE-East database. This allows the entire database to fit into expensive SRAM or on-chip memory. It does, however, pay a high price in insertion times.

Some expanded trie entries (e.g., the 110 entry at the root of Fig. 11.7) have two values, a pointer and a prefix. To make compression easier, the algorithm starts by making each entry have exactly one value by pushing prefix information down to the trie leaves. Since the leaves do not have a pointer, we have only next-hop information at leaves and only pointers at nonleaf nodes. This process is called *leaf pushing*.

For example, to avoid the extra stored prefix in the 110 entry of the root node of Fig. 11.7, the P9 stored prefix is pushed to all the entries in the leftmost trie node, with the exception of the 010 and 011 entries (both of which continue to contain P3). Similarly, the P8 stored prefix in the 100 root node entry is pushed down to the 100, 101, 110, and 111 entries of the rightmost trie node. Once this is done, each node entry contains either a stored prefix or a pointer but not both.

The Lulea scheme starts with a conceptual leaf-pushed expanded trie and replaces consecutive identical elements with a single value. A node bitmap (with 0's corresponding to removed positions) is used to allow fast indexing on the compressed nodes.

Consider the root node in Fig. 11.7. After leaf pushing, the root has the sequence P5, P5, P5, P5, ptr1, P1, ptr2, P2 (ptr1 is a pointer to the trie node containing P6 and P7, and ptr2 is a pointer to the node containing P3). After replacing consecutive values with the first value, we get P5, -, -, -, ptr1, P1, ptr2, P2, as shown in the middle frame of Fig. 11.12. The rightmost frame shows the final result, with a bitmap indicating removed positions (10001111) and a compressed list (P5, ptr1, P1, ptr2, P2).

If there are N original prefixes and pointers within an original (unexpanded) trie node, the number of entries within the compressed node can be shown never to be more than $2N + 1$. Intuitively, this is because N prefixes partition the address space into at most $2N + 1$ disjoint subranges and each subrange requires at most one compressed node entry.

Search uses the number of bits specified by the stride to index into the current trie node, starting with the root and continuing until a null pointer is encountered. However, while following pointers, an uncompressed index must be mapped to an index into the compressed node. This mapping is accomplished by counting bits within the node bitmap.

Consider the data structure on the right of Fig. 11.12 and a search for an address that starts with 100111. If we were dealing with just the uncompressed node on the left of Fig. 11.12, we could use 100 to index into the fifth array element to get ptr1. However, we must now obtain the same information from the compressed-node representation on the right of Fig. 11.12.

Instead, we use the first three bits (100) to index into the root-node bitmap. Since this is the second bit set (the algorithm needs to count the bits set before a given bit), the algorithm indexes into the second element of the compressed node. This produces a pointer ptr1 to the rightmost trie node. Next, imagine the rightmost leaf node of Fig. 11.7 (after leaf pushing) also compressed in the same way. The node contains the sequence P7, P6, P6, P6, P8, P8, P8, P8. Thus the corresponding bitmap is 11001000, and the compressed sequence is P7, P6, P8.

Thus in the rightmost leaf node, the algorithm uses the next 3 bits (111) of the destination address to index into bit 8. Since this bit is a 0, the search terminates: There is no pointer to follow in the equivalent uncompressed node. However, to retrieve the best matching prefix (if any) at this node, the algorithm must find any prefix stored before this entry.

This would be trivial with expansion because the value P8 would have been expanded into the 111 entry, but since the expanded sequence of P8 values has been replaced by a single P8 value in the compressed version, the algorithm has to work harder. Thus the Lulea algorithm *counts* the number of bits set before position 8 (which happens to be 3) and then indexes into the third element of the compressed sequence. This gives the correct result P8.

The Lulea paper (Degermark et al., 1997) describes a trie that uses fixed strides of 16, 8, and 8. But how can the algorithm efficiently count the bits set in a large bitmap, say of 64K bits in size, that a 16-bit stride needs to use? Before you read on, try to answer this question using principles **P12** (adding state for speed) and **P2a** (precomputation).

To speed up counting set bits, the algorithm accompanies each bitmap with a summary array that contains a cumulative count (*precomputed*) of the number of set bits associated with fixed-size chunks of the bitmap. Using 64-bit chunks, the summary array takes negligible storage. Counting the bits set up to position i now takes two steps. First, access the summary array at position j, where j is the chunk containing bit i. Then access chunk j and count the bits in chunk j up to position i. The sum of the two values gives the count.

While the Lulea paper uses 64-bit chunks, the example in Fig. 11.13 uses 8-bit chunks. The large bitmap is shown from left to right, starting with 10001001, as the second array from the top. Each 8-bit chunk has a summary count that is shown as an array above the bitmap. The summary count for chunk i counts the cumulative bits in the previous chunks of the bitmap (not including chunk i).

Thus the first chunk has count 0, the second has count 3 (because 10001001 has three bits set), and the third has count 5 (because 10000001 has two bits set, which added to the previous chunk's value of 3 gives a cumulative count of 5).

Consider searching for the bits set up to position X in Fig. 11.13, where X can be written as $J011$. Clearly, X belongs to chunk J. The algorithm first looks up the summary count array to retrieve $numSet[J]$. This yields the number of bits set up to but not including chunk J. The algorithm then retrieves chunk J itself (10011000) and counts the number of bits set until the third position of chunk J. Since the first three bits of chunk J are 100, this yields the value 1. Finally, the desired overall bit count is $numSet[J] + 1$.

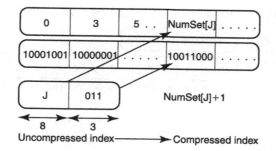

FIGURE 11.13

To allow fast counting of the bits set even in large bitmaps (e.g., 64 Kbits), the bitmap is divided into chunks and a summary count of the bits set before each chunk precomputed.

Notice that the choice of the chunk size is a trade-off between memory size and speed. Making a chunk equal to the size of the bitmap will make counting very slow. On the other hand, making a chunk equal to a bit will require more storage than the original trie node! Choosing a 64-bit chunk size makes the summary array size only 1/64 the size of the original node, but this requires counting the bits set within a 64-bit chunk. Counting can easily be done using special instructions in software and via combinational logic in hardware.

Thus search of a node requires first indexing into the summary table, then indexing into the corresponding bitmap chunk to compute the offset into the compressed node, and finally retrieving the element from the compressed node. This can take three memory references per node, which can be quite slow.

The final Lulea scheme also compresses entries based on their next-hop values (entries with the same next-hop values can be considered the same even though they match different prefixes). Overall the Lulea scheme has very compact storage. Using an early (1997) snapshot of the MAE-East database of around 40,000 entries, the Lulea paper (Degermark et al., 1997) reports compressing the entire database to around 160 KB, which is roughly 32-bits per prefix.

This is a very small number, given that one expects to use at least one 20-bit pointer per prefix in the database. The compact storage is a great advantage because it allows the prefix database to potentially fit into limited on-chip SRAM, a crucial factor in allowing prefix lookups to scale to OC-768 speeds.

Despite compact storage, the Lulea scheme has two disadvantages. First, counting bits requires at least one extra memory reference per node. Second, leaf pushing makes worst-case insertion times large. A prefix added to a root node can cause information to be pushed to thousands of leaves. The full tree bitmap scheme, which we study next, overcomes these problems by abandoning leaf pushing and using *two* bitmaps per node.

11.8 Tree bitmap

The tree bitmap (Eatherton et al., 2004) scheme starts with the goal of achieving the same storage and speed as the Lulea scheme, but it adds the goal of fast insertions. While we have argued that fast

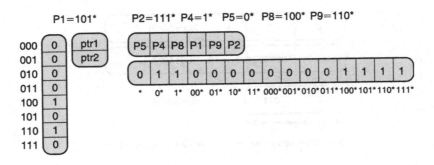

FIGURE 11.14

The tree bitmap scheme allows the compression of Lulea without sacrificing fast insertions by using *two* bitmaps per node. The first bitmap describes valid versus null pointers, and the second describes internally stored prefixes.

insertions are not as important as fast lookups, they clearly are desirable. Also, if the only way to handle an insertion or deletion is to rebuild the Lulea-compressed trie, then a router must keep two copies of its routing database, one that is being built and one that is being used for lookups. This can potentially double the storage cost from 32 bits per prefix to 64 bits per prefix. This in turn can halve the number of prefixes that can be supported by a chip that places the entire database in on-chip SRAM.

To obtain fast insertions and hence avoid the need for two copies of the database, the first problem in Lulea that must be handled is the use of leaf pushing. When a prefix of a small length is inserted, leaf pushing can result in pushing down the prefix to a large number of leaves, making insertion slow.

11.8.1 Tree bitmap ideas

Thus the first and main idea in the tree bitmap scheme is that there are *two* bitmaps per trie node, one for all the internally stored prefixes and one for the external pointers. Fig. 11.14 shows the tree bitmap version of the root node in Fig. 11.12.

Recall that in Fig. 11.12, the prefixes P8 = 100* and P9 = 110* in the original database are missing from the picture on the left side because they have been pushed down to the leaves to accommodate the two pointers (*ptr*1, which points to nodes containing longer prefixes such as P6 = 1000*, and *ptr*2, which points to nodes containing longer prefixes such as P3 = 11001*). This results in the basic Lulea trie node, in which each element contains either a pointer or a prefix but not both. This allows the use of a *single* bitmap to compress a Lulea node, as shown on the extreme right of Fig. 11.12.

By contrast, the same trie node in Fig. 11.14 is split into *two* compressed arrays, each with its own bitmap. The first array, shown vertically, is a *pointer array*, which contains a bitmap denoting the (two) positions where nonnull pointers exist and a compressed array containing the nonnull pointers, *ptr*1 and *ptr*2.

The second array, shown horizontally, is the *internal prefix array*, which contains a list of all the prefixes within the first 3 bits. The bitmap used for this array is very different from the Lulea encoding and has one bit set for every possible prefix stored within this node. Possible prefixes are listed lexicographically, starting from *, followed by 0* and 1*, and then on to the length-2 prefixes (00*, 01*,

10*, 11*), and finally the length-3 prefixes. Bits are set when the corresponding prefixes occur within the trie node.

Thus in Fig. 11.14, the prefixes P8 and P9, which were leaf pushed in Fig. 11.12, have been resurrected and now correspond to bits 12 and 14 in the internal prefix bitmap. In general, for an r-bit trie node, there are $2^{r+1} - 1$ possible prefixes of lengths r or less, which requires the use of a $(2^{r+1} - 1)$ bitmap. The scheme gets its name because the internal prefix bitmap represents a trie in a linearized format: Each row of the trie is captured top-down from left to right.

The second idea in the tree bitmap scheme is to keep the trie nodes as small as possible to reduce the required memory access size for a given stride. Thus a trie node is of fixed size and contains only a pointer bitmap, an internal prefix bitmap, and child pointers. But what about the next-hop information associated with any stored prefixes?

The trick is to store the next hops associated with the internal prefixes stored within each trie node in a separate array associated with this trie node. Putting next-hop pointers in a separate result array potentially requires two memory accesses per trie node (one for the trie node and one to fetch the result node for stored prefixes).

However, a simple lazy evaluation strategy (**P2b**) is *not* to access the result nodes until search terminates. Upon termination, the algorithm makes a final access to the correct result node. This is the result node that corresponds to the last trie node encountered in the path that contained a valid prefix. This adds only a single memory reference at the end, in addition to the one memory reference required per trie node.

The third idea is to use only *one* memory access per node, unlike Lulea, which uses at least two memory accesses. Lulea needs two memory accesses per node because it uses large strides of 8 or 16 bits. This increases the bitmap size so much that the only feasible way to count bits is to use an additional chunk array that must be accessed separately. The tree bitmap scheme gets around this by simply using smaller-stride nodes, say, of 4 bits. This makes the bitmaps small enough that the entire node can be accessed by a single wide access (**P4a**, exploit locality). Combinatorial logic (Chapter 2) can be used to count the bits.

11.8.2 Tree bitmap search algorithm

The search algorithm starts with the root node and uses the first r bits of the destination address (corresponding to the stride of the root node, 3 in our example) to index into the pointer bitmap at the root node at position P. If there is a 1 in this position, there is a valid child pointer. The algorithm counts the number of 1's to the left of this 1 (including this 1) and denotes this count by I. Since the pointer to the start position of the child pointer block (say, y) is known, as is the size of each trie node (say, S), the pointer to the child node can be calculated as $y + (I * S)$.

Before moving on to the child, the algorithm must also check the internal bitmap to see if there are one or more stored prefixes corresponding to the path through the multibit node to position P. For example, suppose P is 101 and a 3-bit stride is used at the root node bitmap, as in Fig. 11.14. The algorithm first checks to see whether there is a stored internal prefix 101*. Since 101* corresponds to the 13th bit position in the internal prefix bitmap, the algorithm can check if there is a 1 in that position (there is one in the example). If there was no 1 in this position, the algorithm would back up to check whether there is an internal prefix corresponding to 10*. Finally, if there is not a 10* prefix, the algorithm checks for the prefix 1*.

This search algorithm appears to require a number of iterations, proportional to the logarithm of the internal bitmap length. However, for bitmaps of up to 512 bits or so in hardware, this is just a matter of simple combinational logic. Intuitively, such logic performs all iterations in parallel and uses a priority encoder to return the longest matching stored prefix.

Once it knows there is a matching stored prefix within a trie node, the algorithm does not immediately retrieve the corresponding next-hop information from the result node associated with the trie node. Instead, the algorithm moves to the child node while remembering the stored-prefix position and the corresponding parent trie node. The intent is to remember the last trie node T in the search path that contained a stored prefix, and the corresponding prefix position.

Search terminates when it encounters a trie node with a 0 set in the corresponding position of the extending bitmap. At this point, the algorithm makes a final access to the result array corresponding to T to read off the next-hop information. Further tricks to reduce memory access width are described in Eatherton's MS thesis (Eatherton, 1995), which includes a number of other useful ideas.

Intuitively, insertions in a tree bitmap are very similar to insertions in a simple multibit trie without leaf pushing. A prefix insertion may cause a trie node to be changed completely; a new copy of the node is created and linked in atomically to the existing trie. Compression results in Eatherton et al. (2004) show that the tree bitmap has all the features of the Lulea scheme, in terms of compression and speed, along with fast insertions. The tree bitmap also has the ability to be tuned for hardware implementations ranging from the use of RAMBUS-like memories to on-chip SRAM.

11.8.3 PopTrie: an alternate bitmap algorithm

Many years after the initial Lulea and Tree bitmap algorithms, a new bitmap algorithm called Poptrie (Asai and Ohara, 2015) was proposed. The algorithm gets its name from the population count instruction (called *popcount*) that can count the number of bits set (in say a 64-bit machine word) on a modern CPU. The setting is for a software implementation, perhaps for Network Function Virtualization. The motivation is that since the Tree bitmap of stored prefixes is not a simple linear bitmap it cannot be calculated easily in software. The Poptrie paper (Asai and Ohara, 2015) describes some experiments to suggest that Tree bitmap is fairly slow in software, and suggests an alternative.

The alternative to Tree bitmap is again to use an aggressive form of leaf-pushing so insertion is again slow compared to Tree bitmap. In Poptrie, every leaf stores an associated prefix (corresponding to its most specific ancestor prefix). Thus every multibit trie element either is a null pointer with an associated leaf-pushed prefix, or contains a pointer to a descendant node. Thus each node has a basic bitmap where the 1's represent valid pointers to descendants and the 0's represent stored prefixes. Thus each trie node has the basic bitmap and two base pointers: the first base pointer (base0) points to the start of the stored prefix array, and the second (base1) to the start of the descendant pointer array.

Poptrie breaks an IP address into 6-bit chunks (a uniform stride of 6 bits) so each basic bitmap is 64 bits. During search, when indexing into the bitmap using the current chunk of the address, if the bit is 1, then there is a descendant node. In that case, search continues by counting the number of 1's and using the count to index into the compressed array of pointers whose start is base1. If the indexed bit is a 0, search terminates with a stored prefix. Search now ends by counting the number of 0's and indexing into the base0 array to retrieve the next hop associated with the longest match. Because Poptrie uses 64 bit bitmaps, the counting can be done efficiently in software by a popcount instruction in 1 cycle.

The basic scheme as described takes a tremendous amount of storage because of the very aggressive leaf pushing. But many of the consecutive entries have the same stored prefix. As in our description of

Lulea, one can do a form of run-length encoding using a second bitmap, called the LeafVector. Thus if there is a run of consecutive stored prefixes say P4, P4, P4, P5. ., in the base0 array this is replaced by one copy of P4 and a LeafVector bitmap 1001 ...

In summary, all three schemes use different but closely related semantics for bitmaps. Lulea uses a single bitmap and large strides, but uses a summary bitmap to recover speed. Tree bitmap does not do leaf pushing, but uses two bitmaps, one for compressing pointers and one Tree bitmap that represents the stored prefixes. Poptrie does aggressive leaf pushing, and uses two bitmaps: one that distinguishes pointers from prefixes, and one that compresses consecutive stored prefixes.

While the Poptrie paper shows better performance than Tree bitmap in software, there are two concerns. First, it is not clear that Lulea cannot simulate the forwarding performance of Poptrie with smaller (say 6-bit) strides and using the popcount instruction to count bits. Second, as we will see below, the current fastest method in software uses a different strategy, based on binary search on prefix ranges.

11.9 Binary search on ranges

So far, all our schemes (unibit tries, expanded tries, LC tries, Lulea tries, tree bitmaps) have been trie variants. Are there other algorithmic paradigms (**P15**) to the longest-matching-prefix problem? Now, exact matching is a special case of prefix matching. Both binary search and hashing (Cormen et al., 1990) are well-known techniques for exact matching. Thus we should consider generalizing these standard exact-matching techniques to handle prefix matching. In this section we examine an adaptation of binary search; in the next section we look at an adaptation of hashing.

In *binary search on ranges* (Lampson et al., 1998), each prefix is represented as a range, using the start and end of the range. Thus the range endpoints for N prefixes partition the space of addresses into $2N + 1$ disjoint intervals. The algorithm (Lampson et al., 1998) uses binary search to find the interval in which a destination address lies. Since each interval corresponds to a unique prefix match, the algorithm *precomputes* this mapping and stores it with range endpoints. Thus prefix matching takes $\log_2(2N)$ memory accesses.

Consider a tiny routing table with only two prefixes, P4 = 1* and P1 = 101*. This is a small subset of the database used in Fig. 11.6. Fig. 11.15 shows how the binary search data structure is built as a table (left) and as a binary tree (right).

The starting point for this scheme is to consider a prefix as a range of addresses. To keep things simple, imagine that addresses are 4 bits instead of 32 bits. Thus P4 = 1* is the range 1000 to 1111, and P1 = 101* is the range 1010 to 1011. Next, after adding in the range for the entire address space (0000 to 1111), the endpoints of all ranges are sorted into a binary search table, as shown on the left of Fig. 11.15.

In Fig. 11.15, the range endpoints are drawn vertically on the left. The figure also shows the ranges covered by each of the prefixes. Next, *two* next-hop entries are associated with each endpoint. The leftmost entry, called the > entry, is the next hop corresponding to addresses that are *strictly greater* than the endpoint but strictly less than the next range endpoint in sorted order. The rightmost entry, called the = entry, corresponds to addresses that are *exactly equal* to the endpoint.

For example, it should be clear from the ranges covered by the prefixes that any addresses greater than or equal to 0000 but strictly less than 1000 do not match any prefix. Hence the entries

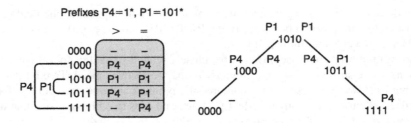

FIGURE 11.15

Binary search on values of a tiny subset of the sample database, consisting of only prefixes P4 = 1* and P1 = 101*.

corresponding to 0000 are −, to denote no next hop.[3] Similarly, any address greater than or equal to 1000 but strictly less than 1010 must match prefix P4 = 1*.

The only subtle case, which illustrates the need for two separate entries for > and =, is the entry for 1011. If an address is strictly greater than 1011 but strictly less than the next entry, 1111, then the best match is P4. Thus the > pointer is P4. On the other hand, if an address is exactly equal to 1011, its best match is P1. Thus the = pointer is P1.

The entire data structure can be built as a binary search table, where each table entry has three items, consisting of an endpoint, a > next-hop pointer, and a = next-hop pointer. The table has at most $2N$ entries, because each of N prefixes can insert two endpoints. Thus after the next-hop values are precomputed, the table can be searched in $\log_2 2N$ time using binary search on the endpoint values. Alternatively, the table can be drawn as a binary tree, as shown on the right in Fig. 11.15. Each tree node contains the endpoint value and the same two next-hop entries.

The description so far shows that binary search on values can find the longest prefix match after $\log_2 2N$ time. However, the time can be reduced using binary trees of higher radix, such as B-trees. While such trees require wider memory accesses, this is an attractive trade-off for DRAM-based memories, which allow fast access to consecutive memory locations (**P4a**).

Computational geometry (Preparata and Shamos, 1985) offers a data structure called a *range tree* for finding the narrowest range. Range trees offer fast insertion times as well as fast $O(\log_2 N)$ search times. However, there seems to be no easy way to increase the radix of range trees to obtain $O(\log_M N)$ search times for $M > 2$.

As described, this data structure can easily be built in linear time using a stack and an additional trie. It is not hard to see that even with a balanced binary tree (see exercises), adding a short prefix can change the > pointers of a large number of prefixes in the table. A trick to allow fast insertions and deletions in logarithmic time is described in Warkhede et al. (2001).

Naively done, binary search on prefix values is somewhat slow when compared to multibit tries. However, unlike the other trie schemes, all of which are subject to patents, binary search is free of such restrictions. Thus at least a few vendors have implemented this scheme into hardware. In hardware, the

---

[3] In a core router, no prefix match implies that the message should be dropped; in a router within a domain no prefix match is often sent to the so-called default route.

use of a wide memory access (to reduce the base of the logarithm) and pipelining (to allow one lookup per memory access) can make this scheme sufficiently fast.

The original paper (Lampson et al., 1998) written in 1998 suggests two optimizations to improve speed even in software. First, it suggests improving "the worst-case number of memory accesses of the basic binary search scheme with a precomputed table of best-matching prefixes for the first bits . . . if there are prefixes of longer length with that prefix the array element stores a pointer to a binary search table/tree that contains all such prefixes" (Lampson et al., 1998). The paper shows that this simple trick of using an array as a front-end reduces the maximum number of prefixes in each partitioned table from over 38000 to 336, reducing the worst case binary table size to 336, which makes binary search faster (10 memory accesses versus $\log_2 N + 1$ where N is the size of the original table). Second, it suggests using larger radixes instead of binary trees and exploiting the cache line size of a Pentium processor to make such k-way search efficient in software.

Best of all, a highly optimized form of the original binary search on prefix ranges paper with initial table lookup (Lampson et al., 1998) called DXR (Zec et al., 2012) first suggested in 2021 currently appears to offer the fastest software implementations of over 2.5 Billion IP lookups per second on a commodity CPU (AMD R7-1700) with 8 cores in 2022. This makes it a good building block for Network Function Virtualization devices. We now describe the new optimizations in DXR.

11.10 Binary search on ranges with Initial Lookup Table

The core idea in DXR (Zec et al., 2012) is still binary search on ranges with an initial table. Thus rather than have 1 binary search, if the root has N pointers there can be pointers to N different binary search tables. Once again, each prefix is converted to a range (start and end address).

DXR, however, goes beyond the original binary search on ranges idea with an initial table (Lampson et al., 1998) using multithreading and careful compression to fit into the cache hierarchy of a modern CPU in clever ways. First, they use a *multithreaded* implementation so the apparent cost of binary search can be hidden by increasing the number of hardware threads. Second, they use several compression ideas to reduce memory to make it more likely for the database to fit into the L2/L3 caches. Neighboring address ranges that resolve to the same next hop are merged. Next, the end address can be derived from the start of the next interval. Thus each entry only needs the start address (2 bytes, because the first 16 or more bits have already been resolved by direct lookup), and the next hop (1 or 2 bytes to index a next hop table). A further twofold compression can be achieved for chunks which reference only 8-bit next hop indices and correspond to prefix lengths up to 24 bits. For these, the range start can be compressed to 8 bits or less, which is a big savings. Finally, they experiment with initial table sizes beyond 2^{16} and find better numbers by using anywhere from 16 to 21 bits.

Using a 16 bit initial table, for instance, is compact and takes "less than 2 bytes per prefix, and exceeds 100 million lookups per second (Mlps) on a single commodity CPU core in synthetic tests with uniformly random queries" (DXR, 2022). Using 21 bits, allows "200 Mlps per CPU core at the cost of increased memory footprint, and deliver aggregate throughputs exceeding two billion lookups per second" (DXR, 2022) using 8 cores. A version of DXR merged in FreeBSD uses a two-stage trie with a 16-4 split before proceeding with binary search.

Note that partitioning (into multiple prefix search tables) also reduces the cost of updates because a prefix addition or the deletion of a prefix P does not affect all the partitioned tables, but affects only the tables that are pointed to by root entries that match P. This translates into a huge savings since a full build is much more costly than an incremental update: The cost of a full build for a 16-bit initial table is reported to be 70 msec and goes up to 300 msec for a 20-bit initial stride (Zec and Mikuc, 2017), whereas that of an incremental update is reported to be only 10s of microseconds on average for random tests (Zec et al., 2012).

There seems to be two fundamental reasons why DXR does so well. First, the bigger reason is that careful compression allows it to fit into the cache hierarchy; as the table size grows, the cache size of modern processors should also grow. Second, the seemingly long time taken for binary search seems to be hidden by thread parallelism. A recent updated Zec and Mikuc (2017) suggests that as CPUs scale to more hardware threads (say 36 threads) this could easily double the throughput of DXR.

Despite its success for IPv4, it is unlikely that DXR will work well as is for IPv6 because of 128-bit keys and a more sparse address space. However, it is worth pointing out that the original paper Lampson et al. (1998) suggests a multicolumn binary search for binary search of long identifiers (see the Exercise in this chapter on Multicolumn search). Multicolumn search with multithreading (and the compression ideas used in DXR) may be the basis for a fast software IPv6 implementation but more work is needed.

The code for DXR is available online and has been integrated into FreeBSD which allows it to be used as part of a Network Function Virtualization device based on FreeBSD.

11.11 Binary search on prefix lengths

In this section we adapt another classical exact-match scheme, hashing, to longest prefix matching. Binary search on prefix lengths finds the longest match using $\log_2 W$ hashes, where W is the maximum prefix length. This can provide a very scalable solution for 128-bit IPv6 addresses. For 128-bit prefixes, this algorithm takes only seven memory accesses, as opposed to 16 memory accesses using a multibit trie with 8-bit strides. To do so, the algorithm first segregates prefixes by length into separate hash tables. More precisely, it uses an array L of hash tables such that $L[i]$ is a pointer to a hash table containing all prefixes of length i.

Assume the same tiny routing table, with only two prefixes, P4 = 1* and P1 = 101*, of lengths 1 and 3, respectively, that was used in Fig. 11.15. Recall that this is a small subset of Fig. 11.6. The array of hash tables is shown horizontally in the top frame (A) of Fig. 11.16. The length-1 hash table storing P4 is shown vertically on the left and is pointed to by position 1 in the array; the length-3 hash table storing P1 is shown on the right and is pointed to by position 3 in the array; the length-2 hash table is empty because there are no prefixes of length 2.

Naively, a search for address D would start with the greatest-length hash table l (i.e., 3), would extract the first l bits of D into D_l, and then search the length-l hash table for D_l. If search succeeds, the best match has been found; if not, the algorithm considers the next smaller length (i.e., 2). The algorithm moves in decreasing order among the set of possible prefix lengths until it either finds a match or runs out of lengths.

The naive scheme effectively does *linear* search among the distinct prefix lengths. The analogy suggests a better algorithm: binary search (**P15**). However, unlike binary search on prefix *ranges*, this is binary search on prefix *lengths*. The difference is major. With 32 lengths, binary search on lengths takes five hashes in the worst case; with 32,000 prefixes, binary search on prefix ranges takes 16 accesses.

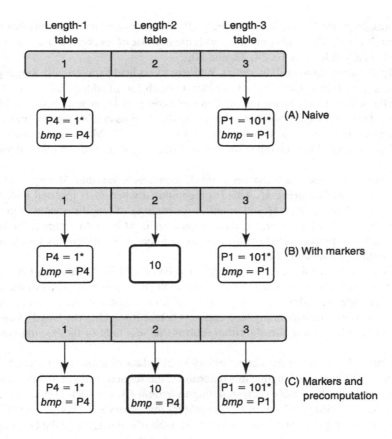

FIGURE 11.16

From naive linear search on the possible prefix lengths to binary search.

Binary search must start at the *median* prefix length, and each hash must divide the possible prefix lengths in half. A hash search gives only two values: *found* and *not found*. If a match is found at length *m*, then lengths strictly greater than *m* must be searched for a longer match. Correspondingly, if no match is found, search must continue among prefixes of lengths strictly less than *m*.

For example, in Fig. 11.16, part (A), suppose search begins at the median length-2 hash table for an address that starts with 101. Clearly, the hash search does not find a match. But there is a longer match in the length-3 table. Since only a match makes search move to the right half, an "artificial match," or *marker*, must be introduced to force the search to the right half when there is a potentially longer match.

Thus part (B) introduces a bolded marker entry 10, corresponding to the first two bits of prefix P1 = 101, in the length-2 table. In essence, state has been added for speed (**P12**). The markers allow probe failures in the median to rule out all lengths greater than the median.

Search for an address *D* that starts with 101 works correctly. Search for 10 in the length-2 table (in part (B) of Fig. 11.16) results in a match; search proceeds to the length-3 table, finds a match with

$P1$, and terminates. In general, a marker for a prefix P must be placed at all lengths that binary search will visit in a search for P. This adds only a logarithmic number of markers. For a prefix of length 32, markers are needed only at lengths 16, 24, 28, and 30.

Unfortunately, the algorithm is still incorrect. While markers lead to potentially longer prefixes, they can also cause search to follow false leads. Consider a search for an address D' whose first three bits are 100 in part (B) of Fig. 11.16. Since the median table contains 10, search in the middle hash table results in a match. This forces the algorithm to search in the third hash table for 100 and to fail. But the correct best matching prefix is at the first hash table – i.e., P4 = 1*. Markers can cause the search to go off on a wild goose chase! On the other hand, a backtracking search of the left half would result in linear time.

To ensure logarithmic time, each marker node M contains a variable $M.bmp$, where $M.bmp$ is the longest prefix that matches string M. This is precomputed when M is inserted into its hash table. When the algorithm follows marker M and searches for prefixes of lengths greater than M, and if the algorithm fails to find such a longer prefix, then the answer is $M.bmp$. In essence, the best matching prefix of every marker is precomputed (**P2a**). This avoids searching all lengths less than the median when a match is obtained with a marker.

The final version of the database containing prefixes P4 and P1 is shown in part (C) of Fig. 11.16. A *bmp* field has been added to the 10 marker that points to the best matching prefix of the string 10 (i.e., P4 = 1*). Thus when the algorithm searches for 100 and finds a match in the median length-2 table, it *remembers* the value of the corresponding *bmp* entry P4 before it searches the length-3 table. When the search fails (in the length-3 table), the algorithm returns the *bmp* field of the last marker encountered (i.e., P4).

A trivial algorithm for building the simple binary search data structure from scratch is as follows. First determine the distinct prefix lengths; this determines the sequence of lengths to search. Then add each prefix P in turn to the hash table corresponding to $length(P)$. For each prefix, also add a marker to all hash tables corresponding to lengths $L < length(P)$ that binary search will visit (if one does not already exist). For each such marker M, use an auxiliary 1-bit trie to determine the best matching prefix of M. Further refinements are described in Waldvogel et al. (1997).

While the search algorithm takes five hash table lookups in the worst case for IPv4, we note that in the expected case most lookups should take two memory accesses. This is because the expected case observation *O1* shows that most prefixes are either 16 or 24 bits (at least today). Thus doing binary search at 16 and then 24 will suffice for most prefixes.

The use of hashing makes binary search on prefix lengths somewhat difficult to implement in hardware. However, its scalability to large prefix lengths, such as IPv6 addresses, is notable.

11.12 **Linear search on prefix lengths with hardware assist**

The last section shows we can make binary search on prefix lengths work by adding markers and other mechanisms. Unfortunately, this adds complexity and makes insertion slow. The idea in this section is to revisit naive linear search on prefix lengths (that we discarded in the last section), but add some hardware assistance to make it practical.

Assume the setting is hardware with on-chip memory (with say 1 nsec access time) of a few Mbytes and a massive amount of slower DRAM (with say 50 nsec access time). How can we do IP Lookups with a small number (say 1 or 2) of sequential DRAM accesses? We can easily also afford up to to 32 on-chip memory accesses because the on-chip accesses are dwarfed by a single DRAM access. We will describe two such schemes, both based on using bitmaps to represent the stored prefixes at each length. Since these bitmaps are compact, they can be stored in on-chip memory; a corresponding hash table for each length is stored in off-chip DRAM using a scheme such as d-left (Broder and Mitzenmacher, 2001) (described in Section 10.3.3). For example, if there are just two prefixes $P4 = 1*$ and $P1 = 100*$. The length-1 bitmap would be 10 (first bit set corresponding to $P4$, the length-2 bitmap would be 0000, and the length-3 bit map would be 00010000 (fourth bit is set corresponding to $P1$).

The skeleton idea, then, is to search on-chip either sequentially or in parallel to find the longest matching *length*, say L. Then a hash table access is made to an off-chip DRAM hash table that stores all L bit prefixes using the first L bits of the address as a key to retrieve the next hop. Clearly, a naive use of indexed bitmaps does not work well because at prefix lengths such as 32 the corresponding bitmap is of size 2^{32} which is too large to fit into on-chip memory. We will describe two schemes that show how to deal with this memory explosion caused by larger length bitmaps.

11.12.1 Using Bloom Filters to compress prefix bitmaps

Observe that the bitmaps, especially at larger lengths will be very sparse. Thus each bitmap can be compressed by what is called a Bloom Filter (Bloom, 1970). In a Bloom Filter any entry x is hashed a small constant number of times (often 3 times) with independent hash functions (say $h_1(x) = i, h_2(x) = j, h_3(x) = k$, and bits i, j, k are set in the bitmap. Thus if there are N_L prefixes at length L, the theory shows that the N_L prefixes require cN_L bits, where c is a small constant.

While we will study Bloom filters later in this book when we survey techniques for measurement and security, for now it is worth noting that Bloom filters have no false negatives, but can have false positives. It may happen that when doing a lookup for entry y that is not present, the corresponding indices $h_1(y), h_2(y), h_3(y)$ are all set, leading search to incorrectly conclude that y exists in that Bloom Filter. However, if c is sufficiently large, the probability of a false positive is low.

A paper by Dharmapurikar et al. (2003) suggests using 32 Bloom Filters to compress all the stored prefixes stored at each length on-chip, followed by off-chip lookups. If i is the longest length Bloom Filter that matches, an off-chip access is made to off-chip Hash Table i. However, the Bloom filter may rarely have a false positive, in which case the chip will try the next smallest Bloom filter length that matched, and so on. While in the worst case there can be several DRAM accesseses (such pathological IP addresses can be cached), the expected number of DRAM accesses is close to 1. Nevertheless, this lack of deterministic performance leads to the next proposal called SAIL.

11.12.2 SAIL: Uncompressed Bitmaps up to a pivot level

SAIL (Yang et al., 2014) starts by observing that up to some length (which they refer to as a *pivot* length) one can easily store all the bitmaps without further compression. In particular, they suggest that storing all bitmaps up to 24 requires only $\Sigma_{i=1}^{24} 2^i = 32$ Mbits. Thus their implementation pivots at length 24, but this could be changed. While 4 Mbytes is large, it is feasible in on-chip SRAM. Better still, the amount of required on-chip memory remains constant even as the IPv4 database increases arbitrarily. They also observe that prefixes of length greater than 24 bits are rare: hence they use prefix expansion to store all such prefixes in 256 element multibit trie nodes indexed by their 24-bit prefix in off-chip DRAM. Note that we need 256 element trie nodes for these rare cases because the expansion of a 24-bit prefix results in up to 256 32-bit entries.

Because SAIL is also designed to work in software, SAIL starts lookup at length 24. SAIL first determines whether the longest match is exactly 24 bits, less than 24 bits, or possibly greater than 24 bits. If the match is 24 bits, SAIL terminates by a lookup into the 24-bit next hop table in DRAM. If the match is less than 24 bits, search continues sequentially from 23 to 1, trying each bitmap on-chip until the longest match length is found at say W; this is followed by a lookup to the W length hash table in DRAM. Finally, if the match is greater than 24 (this should occur rarely), SAIL uses the last 8 bits of the IP address to index into the corresponding multibit trie node in DRAM corresponding to the first 24-bits of the address.

The key mechanism then is to efficiently implement a predicate that determines whether the longest match is equal to 24, < 24, or possibly greater than 24. This is trickier than it may seem. Consider the conceptual unibit trie level corresponding to the pivot length 24. Let the first 24 bit prefix of the address being looked up be P.

There are four cases to consider. If there is no trie node corresponding to the path P, then the longest match must be less than 24. Second, if there is a trie node but it is a pure pointer, then search must continue at levels greater than 24. But Case 2 can fail as a match is not guaranteed to be found at longer lengths (as in binary search on prefix lengths). The third case is that the corresponding trie node is a stored prefix but not a pointer; but in this case search terminates with a 24-bit match). The fourth case is that the corresponding trie node is both a stored prefix and a pointer.

For example, consider a smaller version of our earlier database with $P4 = 1*$, $P2 = 101*$, $P3 = 11001*$, $P7 = 1000000*$ and a new prefix $P10 = 100*$. If we assume the pivot level is 3, Case 1 occurs say when the first bits of the address are 000, and Case 2 occurs when the first 3 bits are 110 (a pure pointer pointing to $P3$). Further, Case 3 occurs when the first 3 bits being matched are 101 (they match $P2$ and no longer prefix. Finally, Case 4 occurs when the first 3 bits being matched are 100 (they match $P10$ and also potentially the longer match $P7$.

A single bitmap at the pivot level cannot distinguish these four cases because a single indexed bit has only 2 possible values. Thus SAIL uses an idea called *pivot pushing* to reduce four cases to three cases. For example, case 4 (which should be rare) can be eliminated by pushing the stored prefix to length 25 by expansion; thus, the prefix can be stored in an off-chip multibit trie node. That still leaves 3 cases. Case 1 is distinguished by a corresponding 0 in the 24-bit on-chip bitmap. However, Case 2 and Case 3 both correspond to a 1 in the bitmap. They are distinguished by one more lookup to the corresponding next hop array of Length 24 bit prefixes. If there is a match (Case 3), search terminates with a 24-bit match.

If there is no match in the 24-bit next hop array and there is a 1 in the corresponding bit in the Length 24 bitmap, we are in Case 2 (pure pointer) and search must proceed to an off-chip multibit trie node. But as in binary search on prefix lengths this can cause us to hare off on a wild goose chase when the best match is actually at lengths less than 24. SAIL fixes this problem as usual using precomputation. The longest match corresponding to the pointer is pushed to Level 25 in case no other longer match works. Again just as in Case 4, such pushing should be done rarely, because prefixes greater than 24 are rare.

The overall performance of SAIL in a hardware model requires 2 DRAM accesses in the (rare) worst case for a match that is longer than 24-bits. This is because it requires a DRAM access into the

24-bit next hop table (to distinguish Case 2 and Case 3) followed by a lookup into the multibit trie node (for Case 2).

While SAIL was possibly designed in this way to make the software implementation fast, we have already seen that DXR is likely to outperform SAIL on modern CPUs because of its smaller cache footrpint. By contrast, SAIL requires 4 Mbytes of cache. Thus the SAIL ideas seem more relevant for hardware settings with on-chip memory and cheap and large off-chip DRAM. If that is indeed the setting, then SAIL can be simplified as follows.

First, we can segregate the DRAM into 2 separate parallel banks that can be looked up in parallel. The first DRAM bank can be used to store next hops for prefixes of all lengths strictly less than or equal to 24, while a second bank can contain all the multibit trie nodes for prefixes of lengths greater than 24. If these two lookups can be done in parallel in one DRAM access time there is no need for pivot pushing. The bit map corresponding to Length 24 is treated like the other bit maps of length < 24, with bits set only for valid prefixes of that length (and not for pointers to greater length prefixes as in vanilla SAIL). Instead, a hardware thread searches through all the bitmaps on-chip of lengths less than or equal to 24 looking for the longest match length; a second parallel thread looks up the multibit trie node (if it exists) corresponding to the full 32 bits, using the first 24 bits as a key. It is easy to combine all the results since Thread 2 results (if any) are more specific than Thread 1 results.

Finally, all the next hop tables can be indexed using say d-left hashing described in the chapter on exact matching (more specifically in Section 10.3.3). The resulting hardware requires less DRAM (at most the size of the prefix database instead of the indexed arrays used in the SAIL paper (Yang et al., 2014). It is also easier and faster to add and delete prefixes because the pivot pushing has been eliminated. This simplification was probably not considered in the SAIL paper (Yang et al., 2014) because of the need to do a software implementation. However, given the existence of DXR, a simplified SAIL seems most useful in a pure hardware setting with on-chip SRAM and off-chip DRAM.

11.13 **Memory allocation in compressed schemes**

With the exception of binary search and fixed-stride multibit tries, many of the schemes described in this chapter need to allocate memory in different sizes. Thus if a compressed trie node grows from two to three memory words, the insertion algorithm must deallocate the old node of size 2 and allocate a new node of size 3. Memory allocation in operating systems is a somewhat heuristic affair, using algorithms, such as best-fit and worst-fit, that do not guarantee worst-case properties.

In fact, all standard memory allocators can have a worst-case fragmentation ratio that is very bad. It is possible for allocates and deallocates to conspire to break up memory into a patchwork of holes and small allocated blocks. Specifically, if Max is the size of the largest memory allocation request, the worst-case scenario occurs when all holes are of size $Max - 1$ and all allocated blocks are of size 1. This can occur by allocating all of the memory using requests of size 1, followed by the appropriate deallocations. The net result is that only $\frac{1}{Max}$ of memory is guaranteed to be used, because all future requests may be of size Max.

The allocator's use of memory translates directly into the maximum number of prefixes that a lookup chip can support. Suppose that—ignoring the allocator—one can show that 20 MB of on-chip memory can be used to support 640,000 prefixes in the worst case. If one takes the allocator into account and $Max = 32$, the chip can guarantee supporting only 20,000 prefixes!

Matters are not helped by the fact that CAM vendors at the time of writing were advertising a worst-case number of 100,000 prefixes, with 10-nanoseconds search times and microsecond update times. Thus, given that algorithmic solutions to prefix lookup often compress data structures to fit into SRAM, algorithmic solutions *must* also design memory allocators that are fast and that minimally fragment memory.

There is an old result (Robson, 1974) that says that *no allocator* that does not compact memory can have a utilization ratio better than $\frac{1}{\log_2 Max}$. For example, this is 20% for $Max = 32$. Since this is unacceptable, *algorithmic solutions involving compressed data structures must use compaction.* Compaction means moving allocated blocks around to increase the size of holes.

Compaction is hardly ever used in operating systems for the following reason. If you move a piece of memory M, you must correct all pointers that point to M. Fortunately, most lookup structures are trees, in which any node is pointed to by at most one other node. By maintaining a *parent* pointer for every tree node, nodes that point to a tree node M can be suitably corrected when M is relocated. Fortunately, the parent pointer is needed only for updates and not for search. Thus the parent pointers can be stored in an off-chip copy of the database used for updates in the route processor, without consuming precious on-chip SRAM.

Even after this problem is solved, one needs a simple algorithm that decides when to compact a piece of memory. The existing literature on compaction is in the context of garbage collection (e.g., Refs. Wilson, 1992; Lai and Baker, 1996) and tends to use *global* compactors that scan through all of the memory in one compaction cycle. To bound insertion times, one needs some form of *local* compactor that compacts only a small amount of memory around the region affected by an update.

11.13.1 Frame-based compaction

To show how simple local compaction schemes can be, we first describe an extremely simple scheme that does minimal compaction and yet achieves 50% worst-case memory utilization. We then extend this to improve utilization to closer to 100%.

In *frame merging*, assume that all M words of memory are divided into $\frac{M}{Max}$ frames of size Max. Frame merging seeks to keep the memory utilization to at least 50%. To do so, all nonempty frames should be at least 50% full. Frame merging maintains the following simple invariant: All *but one* unfilled frame is at least 50% full. If so, and if $\frac{M}{Max}$ is much larger than 1, this will yield a guaranteed utilization of almost 50%.

Allocate and deallocate requests are handled (Sikka and Varghese, 2000) with the help of tags added to each word that help identify free memory and allocated blocks. The only additional restriction is that all holes be contained *within* a frame; holes are not allowed to span frames.

Call a frame *flawed* if it is nonempty but is less than 50% utilized. To maintain the invariant, frame merging has one additional pointer to keep track of the current flawed frame, if any. Now, an allocate could cause a previously empty frame to become flawed if the allocation is less than $\frac{Max}{2}$.

Similarly, a deallocate could cause a frame that was filled more than 50% to become less than 50% full. For example, consider a frame that contains two allocated blocks of size 1 and size $Max - 1$ and hence has a utilization of 100%. The utilization could reduce to $\frac{1}{Max}$ if the block of $Max - 1$ is deallocated. This could cause two frames to become flawed, which would violate the invariant.

A simple trick to maintain the invariant is as follows. Assume there is already a flawed frame F and that a new flawed frame, F', appears on the scene. The invariant is maintained by merging the contents

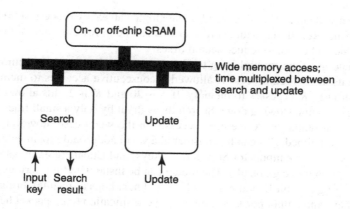

FIGURE 11.17

Model of a lookup chip that does a search in hardware using a common SRAM that could be on or off chip. In some cases, the external memory is cheap low-latency DRAM

of F and F' into F. This is clearly possible because both frames F and F' were less than half full. Note that the only compaction done is *local* and is limited to the two flawed frames, F and F'. Such local compaction leads to fast update times.

The worst-case utilization of frame merging can be improved by increasing the frame size to $kMax$ and by changing the definition of a flawed frame to be one whose utilization is less than $\frac{k}{k+1}$. The scheme described earlier is a special case with $k = 1$. Increasing k improves the utilization, at the cost of increased compaction. More complex allocators with even better performance are described in Sikka and Varghese (2000).

11.14 Fixed Function Lookup-chip models

Classically for Terabit speeds, lookup schemes have been implemented on chips rather than on network processors. We start in Fig. 11.17 by describing a model of a lookup chip that does search and update, and then describe an alternate model for programmable processors such as Intel's (aquired from Barefoot) Tofino-3 (Intel Corporation, 2022). The lookup chip (Fig. 11.17) has a Search and an Update process, both of which access a common memory that is either on or off chip (or both). The Update process allows incremental updates and (potentially) does a memory allocation/deallocation and a small amount of local compaction for every update.

The actual updates can be done either completely on chip, partially in software, or completely in software. If a semiconductor company wishes to sell a lookup chip using a complex update algorithm (e.g., for compressed schemes), it may be wiser also to provide an update algorithm in hardware. If the lookup chip is part of a forwarding engine, however, it may be simpler to relegate the update process completely to a separate CPU on the line card.

The external memory could be SRAM as in Fig. 11.17 but is more likely to be cheaper DRAM today. Each access to external memory can be fairly wide if needed, even up to 1000 bits. This is quite feasible today using a wide bus. The search and update logic can easily process 1000 bits in parallel in one memory cycle time. Recall that wide word accesses can help, for example, in the tree bitmap and binary search on values schemes, to reduce search times.

Search and Update use time multiplexing to share access to the common memory that stores the lookup database. Thus the Search process is allowed S consecutive accesses to memory, and then the Update process is allowed K accesses to memory. If S is 20 and K is 2, this allows Update to steal a few cycles from Search while slowing down Search throughput by only a small fraction. Note that this increases the latency of Search by K memory accesses in the worst case; however, since the Search process is likely to be pipelined, this can be considered a small additional pipeline delay.

The chip has pins to receive inputs for Search (e.g., keys) and Update (e.g., update type, key, result) and can return search outputs (e.g., result). The model can be instantiated for various types of lookups, including IP lookups (e.g., 32-bit IP addresses as keys and next hops as results), bridge lookups (48-bit MAC addresses as keys and output ports as results), and classification (e.g., packet headers as keys and matching rules as results).

Each addition or deletion of a key can result in a call to deallocate a block and to allocate a different-size block. Each allocate request can be in any range from 1 to Max memory words. There is a total of M words that can be allocated. The actual memory can be either off chip, on chip, or both. Clearly, even off-chip solutions will cache the first levels of any lookup tree on chip. On-chip memory is attractive because of its speed and cost. Unfortunately, on-chip memory is limited by current processes which makes it difficult to support databases of 1 million prefixes without external memory, whether DRAM or SRAM.

Internally, the chip is typically heavily pipelined. The lookup data structure is partitioned into several pieces, each of which is concurrently worked on by separate stages of logic. Thus the internal SRAM will likely be broken into several smaller SRAMs that can be accessed independently by each pipeline stage.

There is a problem (Sikka and Varghese, 2000) with statically partitioning SRAM between pipeline stages, because memory needs for each stage can vary as prefixes are inserted and deleted. One possible solution is to break the single SRAM into a fairly large number of smaller SRAMs that can be dynamically allocated to the stages via a partial crossbar switch. However, designing such a crossbar at very high speeds is not easy although such an approach was used in the Procket router (Chung et al., 2004).

All the schemes described in this chapter can be pipelined because they are all fundamentally based on trees. All nodes at the same depth in a tree can be allocated to the same pipeline stage.

11.15 Programmable Lookup Chips and P4

Many routers use fixed function lookup chip models similar to those in the last section, where a limited amount of programmability can be done in firmware. For example, for the wide area Arista 7500R3/7800R3 and 7280R3 routers that scale to more than 2.5 million routes, their documentation (Arista Corporation, 2010) states that "internally FlexRoute uses an algorithmic approach to performing lookups".

By contrast, in recent years, chips, such as Intel's Tofino-3 (Intel Corporation, 2022), have emerged that have a fairly large amount of TCAM and are programmable using higher level languages such as

P4. We will explore P4 and the use of CAMs briefly in this section. For example, Intel's Aurora 710, based on Intel Tofino 3.2T switching silicon, claims (Intel Corporation, 2022) to allow data centers to increase the IP routing table size to 1.2M. Further, the TCAM is distributed among a set of physical stages that can be programmed using P4.

The Tofino-3 is an example of what is called the Reconfigurable Match Table (RMT) (Bosshart et al., 2013) approach to programmable network processors. Briefly, the RMT approach is a generalization of the fixed function chip described in the last section which is internally pipelined, and where each stage has access to on-chip SRAM and is devoted to a single function. By contrast, in the RMT architecture the chip internally has a large number (say 32) of stages that are *anonymous* (not devoted to any function) and *programmable* (they can be programmed to perform basic functions on packet headers). Further, each stage has both RAM and CAM. In fact, the CAM in say the Tofino-3 is so plentiful that it can support a large number of routes without any further algorithmic approaches.

As a packet flows through the RMT chip, each packet header is streamed through the stages with successive packet headers following in lockstep to keep the pipeline full. While the SRAM and the CAM pages are divided among the physical stages, a single logical stage of processing (e.g., a level of processing in a tree) can get more memory by being allocated more physical stages.

Each physical stage can be programmed not just in firmware by internal experts but by *network operators* in the field using a higher language called P4 (though our experience is that P4 programming is also somewhat esoteric). This field-programmability is similar to the programmability offered by Field Programmable Gate Arrays (FPGAs). Unlike FPGAs, chips like Tofino-3 are much faster. They gain speed, however, by offering limited programmabilty, using the P4 language that we now explore.

11.15.1 The P4 language

P4 (P4 Open Source Programming Language) is a high-level language for "programming protocol-independent packet processors". P4's versatility and flexibility change the way network functions are implemented at high speeds. P4 offers:

1. *Reconfigurability*: Even after the P4 program is deployed to a reconfigurable hardware router, an operator can modify the programs in the field as desired, unlike traditional fixed function ASICs.
2. *Protocol independence*: The P4 language can specify how the processor deals with packet headers, regardless of what protocols are used. In particular, while P4 can support IP headers it is not limited to IP. It thus generalizes the SDN approach by allowing custom headers and not just programmable routes.
3. *Target independence:* The same P4 program can be deployed to a variety of hardware, such as CPUs, FPGAs, and programmable processors such as Tofino-3.

P4 needs to allow reconfigurability and yet allow Terabit implementations that are as fast as the ones implemented using custom ASICs in the past. Traditional FPGAs are fully reconfigurable but at least an order of magnitude slower than custom ASICs. P4 resolves this quandary by allowing *limited reconfigurability* that suffices for network implementations.

P4 does this by first *allowing new headers* to be defined using a programmable parser. If, for example, an organization wants to add a new security tag (say STAG) between the Ethernet and IPv4 headers, P4 allows the operator to define the STAG length and fields, and place it between the Ethernet and IPv4 headers. Second, P4 defines a way to *process new headers* where each header is processed by a Table, which can be indexed either by exact matching or with wildcarded bits (thus abstracting across exact match, longest matching prefix and ACL lookup). In a running example, the STAG field could be processed by an exact match table that drops certain values of the STAG that are in the table.

Finally, P4 requires specifying *a control flow graph that chains together the processing of tables* to describe the overall processing of a packet based on its header fields. Thus in the above example, the Control Flow Graph would specify that the header is processed by the STAG table after Ethernet, after which the header is sent to the IPv4 lookup table.

In summary, a P4 program has three major parts: a header specification for parsing, a specification of the tables used to process headers, and a control flow graph that describes the "main" program which specifies how control flows between tables.

What makes P4 attractive is, as we said earlier, the RMT (Bosshart et al., 2013) architecture that provides a set of generic match-action stages arranged in a linear pipeline. The wires between stages are also short unlike traditional FPGA interconnects. Each stage is furnished with a sufficient amount of CAM and RAM and multiple parallel processors. The programmer or compiler can then assign multiple physical pipeline stages (or even a fraction of a stage) to logical tables defined in the control flow graph.

Note that P4 only offers limited reconfurability. Some examples of things that cannot be programmed by P4 include queueing disciplines (the Tofino-3, does, however offer a palette of queue disciplines), stateful processing (e.g., NAT) and content processing (e.g., Intrusion detection, detecting content signatures). A great deal of recent research has appeared to tackle some of those issues. For example, packet transactions (Sivaraman et al., 2016b) attempts to allow programmable stateful processing and schemes like PIFO (Sivaraman et al., 2016a) attempt to allow programmable queue disciplines. We will consider these schemes in the chapter on packet scheduling.

Despite these limitations, P4 appears to be popular. Some important use cases are as follows. First, simply reallocating resoures can be useful. In a core router there is more need for forwarding tables and less for ACLs, while the reverse is true for an edge router. Today's vendors make distinct hardware products for each; instead a single P4 router can simply be programmed to provide specific routers for various market segments. Second, adding new headers is often very time consuming. For example, VXLAN (Mahalingam et al., 2020) took years to be added to custom ASICs; but this could be done in a few hours on a P4 router. Finally, there are new applications such as measurement and security that could be programmed in enterprise-specific ways. We will consider some of these in the chapters on measurement and security.

11.15.2 IP Lookups in the P4 Model

At first glance, chips like the Tofino-3 that use the RMT model trivialize IP lookup because they have plenty of CAM. However, the amount of CAM in these chips do not scale to wide area databases. Could we do better by combining algorithmic methods with TCAM?

For instance, MashUp (Rios and Varghese, 2022) is a a "mash up" of algorithmic and hardware techniques that uses a tree of TCAM and SRAM blocks. While a tree of CAMs has been used for reducing power consumption or update costs (e.g., CoolCAM (Zane et al., 2003) and TreeCAM (Vamanan and Vijaykumar, 2011)), MashUp focuses instead on reducing TCAM bits. It can also easily be implemented in modern reconfigurable pipeline chips such as Tofino-3 (Intel Corporation). As a consequence, MashUp can extend the reach of chips like Tofino-3 to the backbone IPv4 and IPv6 databases, or to much larger data centers than is possible using today's solution of a single logical TCAM.

Mashup is based on a technique called "tiling trees". In other words, Mashup takes into account the internal grain sizes of TCAMs when building a lookup tree. Note that TCAMs come in units, with a grain size of W (width) by D (depth) like memory pages. The Tofino-3, for example, has $W = 44$ and $D = 512$. Each unit TCAM or block in Tofino-3 can do a longest match on up to 512 prefixes of up to 44 bits (any of which can be the wilcard *) in a single clock cycle. For example, to fit the current IPv6 database size of 150,000 prefixes of up to 64 bits, the straightforward approach is to stitch together 2 TCAM blocks horizontally (64<88) and 300 of these pairs vertically (150,00/512 is approximately 300).

By contrast, MashUp builds a tree of TCAM blocks starting with a root which can fit (in other words is "tiled") into a TCAM block. This breaks up the bit-by-bit branching tree (trie) of prefixes into subtrees which we can recursively tile. To pick the tree level at which to define the root TCAM, observe that the tree has pointers, which represent "overhead" not present in a single logical CAM.

The first idea is to reduce pointer overhead by cutting the trie into subtries at heights (which they call *lean lengths*) where the number of downstream pointers are small. For example, the paper (Rios and Varghese, 2022) shows that for a public wide area IPv6 database, the pointer overhead is only 0.41% of total database size at height 20 but rises to 6.84% at height 32.

The second idea is to reduce the wasted space of tiled subtrees by packing up to D subtrees in a single TCAM block. Because the remaining prefix bits may repeat across different subtrees, this requires adding a disambiguating tag of $\log_2 D$ bits. Despite this additional cost, packing ensures that any wasted space (which can be as large as a unit TCAM) in the last block is amortized over D subtrees. In other words, Mashup packs subtrees into a single TCAM block to reduce internal fragmentation.

The third idea is to do a "currency exchange" where "nearly full" subtrees are replaced by SRAM pages in a process the authors call "RAM hybridization". Since SRAM cannot do variable length matching, this must be remedied by "expanding" variable length prefixes to the maximum length prefix in the subtree. Hybridization allows currency "arbitrage" because SRAM pages are cheaper and more plentiful than TCAM blocks (3 to 1 in Tofino-3).

The Mashup paper shows results for IPv4 database sizes of 900k prefixes using all three techniques: lean lengths, tag aggregation and RAM hybridization. A four stage tree with strides of 16-4-4-8 reduces TCAM bits by $7\times$ compared to the straightforward solution of using a single logical CAM, at the cost of around 1000 SRAM pages, which is much less than the RAM required for an all RAM solution. More details can be found in the Mashup paper (Rios and Varghese, 2022).

11.16 Conclusions

It is important to gain some perspective after the large number of isolated lookup variants described in this chapter. Thus we conclude with a summary of the state of the art in lookups, and a survey of the common principles used in their design.

State of the Art in Lookups: Lookup schemes are coming under severe pressure in core routers as both table sizes (up to 1 million prefixes) and speed (several Terabits of aggregate throughput) ratchet upwards. MPLS, once thought to be a way to finesse lookups, is now mostly used to avoid packet classification for traffic engineering purposes. CAMs are nibbling away at even the core router space with chips like Tofino-3, but still do not scale to wide area database sizes (though techniques like Mashup Rios and Varghese (2022) can remedy that). Thus many core router vendors such as Arista (Arista Corporation, 2010) still use and design algorithmic schemes for lookups based on RAM.

For hardware schemes without CAM at Terabit speeds in the core, Tree Bitmap still seems appropriate even after so many years. However, there may be patents that restrict the use of Tree bitmap. This may make other bitmap schemes such as Poptrie (Asai and Ohara, 2015) attractive. Tree bitmap was used in Cisco's CRS-1 Router. On the other hand, ideas based on simplified SAIL (Yang et al., 2014) (as described earlier) may be appropriate for hardware settings that use cheap and plentiful off-chip DRAM.

For data centers and enterprise networks, there seems to be adequate CAM in chips like the Tofino-3, especially when leveraged (as in schemes like Mashup (Rios and Varghese, 2022)) to reduce power and TCAM bits.

For software implementations, the DXR scheme (Zec et al., 2012) seems to be the best approach today especially in the context of Network Function Virtualization (NFV). The underlying binary-search-on-ranges scheme allows efficient multithreading whose throughput scales with the number of cores and fits into the L1 cache. It is also unencumbered by patents.

Finally, binary search on prefix lengths is attractive because of its scaling properties to large address lengths. Unfortunately, its use of hashing makes it hard to guarantee lookup times. It is, however, used by a few vendors in software implementations. It may be a contender in the future as IPv6 becomes more dominant.

The bottom line is that algorithmic solutions together with pipelining can scale with link speeds as long as SRAM speeds scale to match packet arrival times. All the schemes studied in this chapter can be pipelined to provide one lookup per memory access time. The choice between CAMs and algorithmic schemes will continue to be hard to quantify and will probably be made on an ad hoc basis for each product.

Fundamentally, if compressed trie schemes can use less than 32 bits per prefix, compressed tries can use fewer transistors and less power than CAMs. This is because in a CAM the lookup logic is distributed in each of N memory *cells*, whereas in an algorithmic solution the lookup logic, albeit more complicated, is distributed among a small, constant number of *stages*. A careful VLSI scaling analysis of these two approaches would be very useful.

Underlying Principles: Although this is a chapter about lookups and thinking about lookups requires paying attention to current market trends, it is important not to forget that this is a book about underlying principles. It is plausible that routers in the misty future may use all-optical switches and all-optical processing, even for lookups. In that case, the specific algorithms described in this chapter may be discarded; but perhaps the underlying design principles will remain.

All of the schemes described in this chapter start with the algorithmic principle of divide and conquer (divide by bits in the address, address ranges, or prefix lengths) but gain efficiency by other principles. First, most schemes use precomputation, which trades slower insert/delete times for fast search times. The schemes also exploit hardware features such as wide memories, leverage fast and slow memories, trade memory for time, and optimize the degrees of freedom in a given design. Table 11.1 summarizes some of the schemes and the principles used in them. Many of them also use what we could call *information-preserving transformations*. For example, replacing a sequence of one-way branches with a text string, or representing a prefix as a start and end of range.

Finally, this chapter cannot hope to do justice to all the interesting IP lookup schemes that have been published in the academic and patent literature. You can look it up.

11.17 **Exercises**

1. **Caching Prefixes:** Suppose we have the prefixes 10*, 100*, and 1001*. Hugh Hopeful would like to cache prefixes instead of entire 32-bit addresses. Hugh's scheme keeps a set of prefixes in the cache (fast memory), in addition to the complete set of prefixes in slow memory. Hugh's scheme first does a best-matching-prefix search in the cache; if a matching prefix is found, the next hop of the prefix is used. If no matching prefix is found, a best-matching-prefix search is done for the entire database and the resulting prefix cached. Periodically, prefixes that have not been matched for a while are flushed from the cache. Alyssa P. Hacker quickly gives Hugh a counterexample to show him that his scheme is flawed and that caching prefixes are tricky (if not impossible). Can you?

2. **Encoding Prefixes in a Constant Length:** We said in the text that encoding prefixes like 10*, 100*, and 1000* in a fixed length could not be done by padding prefixes with zeroes. It clearly can be done by padding with zeroes and adding an encoding of the prefix length. We want to study a more efficient method.

   - How many possible prefixes on 32 bits can there be?
   - Show how to encode all such prefixes using a fixed length of 33 bits. Make sure that 10*, 100*, and 1000* encode to different values.
   - Can you use this fixed-length encoding of prefixes to have the multiple hash tables used in Section 11.11 be packed into a single hash table? Why might this help to decrease the chances of hash collisions for a given memory size?

3. **Quantifying the Benefits of Compressing One-Way Branches:**

   - For a unibit trie that does not compress one-way branches, show that the maximum number of trie nodes can be $O(N \cdot W)$, where N is the number of prefixes and W is the maximum prefix length. (*Hint*: Generate a trie that uses $\log_2 N$ levels to generate N nodes, and then hang a long string of $N - W$ nodes from each of the N nodes.)
   - Show that a unibit trie with text strings to compress one-way branches can have at most $2N$ trie nodes and $2N$ text strings.
   - Extend your analysis to multibit trie nodes with a fixed stride. How would you implement text string compression in such tries?

4. **Controlled Prefix Expansion:** Code up an efficient algorithm that expands a set of prefixes to any target set of lengths $L_1, \ldots, L_k$. Check your algorithm using the sample database of Fig. 11.6. What is the complexity of your algorithm?

5. **Optimal Variable-Stride Trie:** Prove that the varied-stride trie of Fig. 11.8 is optimal for a trie height of 2. Use the recursive formulation shown in the text.

6. **Reducing Memory References in Lulea:** The naive approach to counting bits shown in Fig. 11.13 should take three memory references (to access *numSet*, to read the appropriate chunk of the bitmap, and to access the compressed trie node for the actual information.) Show how to use **P4a** to combine the first two accesses into a single access.

7. **Next Node versus Leaf Pushing in Lulea:** Before we applied Lulea compression, we first leaf pushed the expanded trie of Fig. 11.7. The motivation was to make every entry either a pointer or a prefix but not both. Suppose we have a special prefix entry at the top of every trie node; if any

entry in a trie node has pointer p and prefix P, we push P to the top of the node pointed to by p. Thus we would push the prefix P8 in the 100 entry of the root of Fig. 11.7 to the top of the rightmost trie node.

- We cited leaf pushing as one of the reasons for slow insertion times in the Lulea scheme. Does next-node pushing allow incremental insertion for the Lulea scheme?
- How would you modify trie search to take into account the fact that prefixes can be stored at the top of (potentially large) trie nodes? How would this increase the search time (in memory accesses) of the Lulea scheme?

8. **CAM Node Compression:** Instead of using the Lulea scheme for compression, we could just store all the prefixes within a trie node without expansion. If we use small trie nodes (3- or 4-bit strides), a chip can potentially read all the entries in a node and internally do a comparison to find the best-matching prefix within the node. Describe the details of such a scheme.

9. **Tree Bitmap Algorithm:** The tree bitmap algorithm described in the text requires rooting through the internal prefix bitmap to decide if there was a matching prefix at a trie node N before moving on. This requires a greater access width (to access the internal prefix bitmaps) and more time. Consider adding state to the next node in the search path (**P12**) and one more final memory access to avoid this overhead.

10. **Multicolumn Binary Search:** In Chapter 4 we saw how to efficiently use binary search when the identifiers were wide. Explain how to combine this idea with that of binary search on prefixes explained in this chapter in order to do IPv6 lookups (up to 128-bit prefixes). How does this scheme compare with the other schemes in terms of lookup performance for IPv6?

11. **Binary Search with Fast Incremental Updates:** (This is difficult.) Find a way to remove all the problems of updates to binary search. The key problem is that if a large prefix range R contains lots of disjoint prefix ranges $R_1, \ldots R_k$, then the spaces between the ranges R_k must be precomputed to map to R. If we now add a new prefix range, R', that is contained in R but still contains R_1 through R_k, then all the spaces between the ranges R_k must be changed to map to the new range, R'. Since k can be $O(n)$, this could lead to a $O(n)$ update. Try to avoid this problem by storing the binary search database as a tree and storing information about precomputed prefixes that cover the space between ranges as high as possible in the tree, as opposed to storing in the leaves. Details can be found in Warkhede et al. (2001).

12. **Counterexamples for Binary Search on Prefix Lengths:** Even in industry, it is often useful to show by counterexample that worst cases can actually exist. This ensures that we are not doing unnecessary work, and it also silences people who say that the worst case will never be too bad. Imagine that Hugh Hopeful is working for the same startup building an IP lookup chip. The company is now considering using binary search on prefix lengths.

- Suppose we use only markers and no precomputation. This would make insertion a lot faster. Hugh Hopeful suggests that backtracking can only lead to a logarithmic number of extra accesses. Find an example that leads to linear time.
- Hugh Hopeful finds that in practice real databases add only 25% extra marker storage, much less than the $\log_2 W$ multiplicative factor that we claimed. This is important because he would like to boast of a larger number of prefixes that his chip can handle for the given amount of memory. Give a worst-case example to show that we can add $\log_2 W$ entries per marker.

13. **Rope Search:** Binary search on prefix lengths can be improved by what is called *rope search* in Waldvogel et al. (1997). If we ever get a match with some entry M at length m, we only search further among the set of lengths corresponding to prefixes that are extensions of M. The basic technique we studied earlier will continue to search among all lengths greater than m in the current set of lengths R. However, many of the lengths $l > m$ may not have a prefix that is an extension of M. Thus this optimization can result in more than halving the set of possible lengths on each match. It may not help the worst case, but it can considerably help the average case. Try to work out the details of such a scheme. In particular, a naive approach would keep a list of all potentially matching lengths ($O(W)$ space, where W is the length of an address) with each prefix. Find a way to reduce the state kept with each marker to $O(\log W)$. Details can be found in Waldvogel et al. (1997).

14. **Invariant for Binary Search on Prefix Ranges:** Designing and proving algorithms that correct via invariants is a useful technique even in network algorithmics. The standard invariant for ordinary binary search when searching for key K is: "K is not in the table, or K is in the current range R." Standard binary search starts with R equal to the entire table and constantly halves the range while maintaining the invariant. Find a similar invariant for binary search on prefix ranges.

15. **Semiperfect Hashing:** Hardware chips can fetch up to 1000 bits at a time using wide buses. Exploit this observation to allow up to X collisions in each hash table entry, where the X colliding entries are stored at adjacent locations. Code up a perfect hashing implementation (of 1000 IP addresses using a set of random hash functions), and compare the amount of memory needed with an implementation based on semiperfect hashing.

16. **Removing Redundancies in Lookup Tables:** Besides the use of compressed structures, another technique to reduce the size of IP lookup tables (especially when the tables are stored in on-chip SRAM) is to remove redundancy. One simple example of redundancy is when a prefix P is longer than a prefix P' and they both have the same next hop. Which prefix can be removed from the table? Can you think of other examples of removing redundancy? How would you implement such compression? Draves et al. (1999) describe a dynamic programming algorithm for compression, but even simpler alternatives can be effective.

17. **Alternative SAIL implementation:** Since there are 4 cases considered in the description of SAIL, the basic SAIL algorithm uses pivot pushing and an extra lookup to the netx hop array at the pivot level to manage with a bitmap (that has only 1 bit and hence 2 possibilities for each bit). Suppose we use 2 bits for each possible prefix P at the pivot length. Can we avoid pivot pushing? What are the tradeoffs in terms of on-chip memory, speed of lookup and insertion costs.

18. **Implementing Lookups in P4:** Go to https://github.com/p4lang/ and download the latest P4 compiler and behavioral model and Mininet if necessary. Implement the DXR, SAIL, Tree bitmap, and Mashup Algorithms and compare them. Can CAM be used to simplify or make more efficient the SAIL and DXR algorithms? Compare these algorithms with respect to a P4 implementation both for IPv4 and IPv6.

19. **Implementing Tries for Best Matching Prefix:** (Due to V. Srinivasan.) The problem is to use tries to implement a file name completion routine in C or C++, similar to ones found in many shells. Given a unique prefix, the query should return the entire string. For example, with the words *angle*, *epsilon*, and *eagle*: Search(a) should return *angle*, Search(e) should return "No unique completion," Search(ea), Search(eag), etc. should return *eagle*; and Search(b) should return "No matching entries found." Assume all lowercase alphabets. To obtain an index into a trie array, use:

```
index= charVariable - 'a'.
```

The following definition of a trie node may be helpful.

```
\#defineALPHA26
structTRIENODE
{
intcompletionStatus;
charcompletion[MAXLEN];
structTRIENODE*next[ALPHA];
}
```

Can other techniques discussed in the text (e.g., binary search) be applied to this problem? Are insertion costs significant?

Packet classification

A classification is a definition comprising a system of definitions.
—**Friedrich von Schlegel**

Traditionally, the post office forwards messages based on the destination address in each letter. Thus all letters to Timbuctoo were forwarded in exactly the same way at each post office. However, to gain additional revenue, the post office introduced *service differentiation* between ordinary mail, priority mail, and express mail. Thus forwarding at the post office is now a function of the destination address and the traffic class. Further, with the specter of terrorist threats and criminal activity, forwarding could even be based on the source address, with special screening for suspicious sources.

In exactly the same way, routers have evolved from traditional destination-based forwarding devices to what are called *packet classification routers*. In modern routers, the route and resources allocated to a packet are determined by the destination address as well as other header fields of the packet, such as the source address and TCP/UDP port numbers.

Packet classification unifies the forwarding functions required by firewalls, resource reservations, QoS routing, unicast routing, and multicast routing. In classification, the forwarding database of a router consists of a potentially large number of rules on key header fields. A given packet header can match multiple rules. So each rule is given a cost, and the packet is forwarded using the *least-cost matching rule*.

The world has changed significantly since the first edition, but most of the changes relevant to packet classification are a subset of the changes described at the start of Chapter 11 on IP lookups. These are the significant use of IPv6 (which complicates packet classification), the increasing use of Software Defined Networks (SDN) and hypervisor switches (Pfaff et al., 2015) to do flexible forwarding using packet classification instead of simpler IP lookups, and the emergence of Network Function Virtualization (NFV) which requires software solutions to packet classification. We are grateful to Balajee Vamanan for helping us with more recent work in packet classification. Despite these technological changes, the essential ideas have remained.

This chapter is organized as follows. The packet classification problem is motivated in Section 12.1. The classification problem is formulated precisely in Section 12.2, and the metrics used to evaluate rule schemes are described in Section 12.3. Section 12.4 presents simple schemes such as linear search, tuple space search and TCAMs. Section 12.5 begins the discussion of more efficient schemes by describing an efficient scheme called *grid of tries* that works only for rules specifying values of only two fields. Section 12.6 transitions to general rule sets by describing a set of insights into the classification problem, including the use of a geometric viewpoint.

Section 12.7 begins the transition to algorithms for the general case with a simple idea to extend 2D schemes. A general approach based on divide-and-conquer is described in Section 12.8. This is followed

Network Algorithmics. https://doi.org/10.1016/B978-0-12-809927-8.00019-1

Table 12.1 Summary of the principles used in the classification algorithms described in this chapter.

Number	Principle	Lookup technique
P12	Add marker state	Rectangle and tuple search
P2a	Precompute filter info	
P15	Use Dest and SRC tries	Grid of tries
P2a	Precompute switch pointers	
P15	Divide-and-conquer by first doing field lookups	Bit vector, pruned tuple, cross-producting
P12, 2a		
P11	Exploit lack of general ranges	Multiple 2D planes
P4a	Exploit bitmap memory locality	Bit vector scheme
P11	Exploit small number of prefixes that match any field	Pruned tuple
P11a, 4a	Exploit cross product locality	On-demand cross product
P1	Avoid redundant cross products	Equivalent cross-producting

by three very different examples of algorithms based on divide-and-conquer: simple and aggregated bit vector linear search (Section 12.9), cross-producting (Section 12.10), and RFC, or equivalenced cross-producting (Section 12.11). Section 12.12 presents the most promising of the current algorithmic approaches, an approach based on decision trees.

This chapter will continue to exhibit the set of principles introduced in Chapter 3, as summarized in Table 12.1. The chapter will also illustrate three general problem-solving strategies: solving simpler problems first before solving a complex problem, collecting different viewpoints, and exploiting the structure of input data sets.

Quick reference guide

The most important lookup algorithms for an implementor today are as follows. If memory is not an issue, the fastest scheme is one called recursive flow classification (RFC), described in Section 12.11. If memory is an issue, a simple scheme that works well for classifiers up to around 5000 rules is the Lucent bit vector scheme (Section 12.9). For larger classifiers, the best trade-off between speed and memory is provided by decision tree schemes, such as HyperCuts and EffiCuts (Section 12.12). For software settings which require fast updates as in Hypervisor switches, then a good solution is Tuple Space Search and the improvements implemented in Open Vswitch (Pfaff et al., 2015). Unfortunately, all these algorithms are based on heuristics and cannot guarantee performance on all databases. If guaranteed performance is required for more than two field classifiers, there is no alternative but to consider hardware schemes such as ternary CAMs.

12.1 Why packet classification?

Packet forwarding based on a longest-matching-prefix lookup of destination IP addresses is fairly well understood, with both algorithmic and CAM-based solutions in the market. Using basic variants of tries and some pipelining (see Chapter 11), it is fairly easy to perform one packet lookup every memory access time.

Unfortunately, the Internet is becoming more complex because of its use for mission-critical functions executed by organizations. Organizations desire that their critical activities not be subverted either by high traffic sent by other organizations (they require QoS guarantees) or by malicious intruders (they require security guarantees). Both QoS and security guarantees require a finer discrimination of packets, based on fields other than the destination. This is called *packet classification*. To quote John McQuillan (1997):

> Routing has traditionally been based solely on destination host numbers. In the future it will also be based on source host or even source users, as well as destination URLs (universal resource locators) and specific business policies. . . . Thus, in the future, you may be sent on one path when you casually browse the Web for CNN headlines. And you may be routed an entirely different way when you go to your corporate Web site to enter monthly sales figures, even though the two sites might be hosted by the same facility at the same location. . . . An order entry form may get very low latency, while other sections get normal service. And then there are Web sites comprised of different servers in different locations. Future routers and switches will have to use class of service and QoS to determine the paths to particular Web pages for particular end users. All this requires the use of layers 4, 5, and above.

This (now standard) vision of forwarding is called *packet classification*. It is also sometimes called *layer 4 switching*, because routing decisions can be based on headers available at layer 4 or higher in the OSI architecture. Examples of other fields a router may need to examine include source addresses (to forbid or provide different service to some source networks), port fields (to discriminate between traffic types, such as Napster and E-mail), and even TCP flags (to distinguish between externally and internally initiated connections). Besides security and QoS, other functions that require classification include network address translation (NAT), metering, traffic shaping, policing, and monitoring.

Several variants of packet classification have already established themselves on the Internet. First, many routers implement *firewalls* (Cheswick and Bellovin, 1995) at trust boundaries, such as the entry and exit points of a corporate network. A firewall database consists of a series of packet rules that implement security policies. A typical policy may be to allow remote login from within the corporation but to disallow it from outside the corporation.

Second, the need for predictable and guaranteed service has led to proposals for reservation protocols, such as DiffServ (Blake et al., 1998), that reserve bandwidth between a source and a destination. Third, the cries for routing based on traffic type have become more strident recently—for instance, the need to route Web traffic between Site 1 and Site 2 on, say, Route A and other traffic on, say, Route B. Fig. 12.1 illustrates some of these examples.

Classifiers historically evolved from firewalls, which were placed at the edges of networks to filter out unwanted packets. Such databases are generally small, containing 10–500 rules, and can be handled by ad hoc methods. However, with the DiffServ movement, there is potential for classifiers that could support 100,000 rules for DiffServ and policing applications at edge routers.

While large classifiers are anticipated for edge routers to enforce QoS via DiffServ, it is perhaps surprising that even within the core, fairly large (e.g., 2000-rule) classifiers are commonly used for security. While these core router classifiers are nowhere near the anticipated size of edge router classifiers, there seems no reason why they should not continue to grow beyond the sizes reported in this book. For example, many of the rules appear to be denying traffic from a specified subnetwork outside

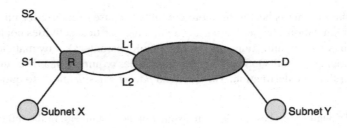

DATABASE AT ROUTER R

To	From	Traffic type	Forwarding directive
D	S1	Video	Forward via L1
*	S2	*	Drop all traffic
Y	X	*	Reserve 50 Mbps

FIGURE 12.1

Example of rules that provide traffic-sensitive routing, a firewall rule, and resource reservation. The first rule routes video traffic from S1 to D via L1; not shown is the default routing to D, which is via L2. The second rule blocks traffic from an experimental site, S2, from accidentally leaving the site. The third rule reserves 50 Mbps of traffic from an internal network X to an external network Y, implemented perhaps by forwarding such traffic to a special outbound queue that receives special scheduling guarantees; here X and Y are prefixes.

the ISP to a server (or subnetwork) within the ISP. Thus, new offending sources could be discovered and new servers could be added that need protection. In fact, we speculate that one reason why core router classifiers are not even bigger is that most core router implementations slow down (and do not guarantee true wire speed forwarding) as classifier sizes increase.

Third, after the emergence of SDN and virtualization, packet classification has also become a key component of software switches especially in hypervisors (Pfaff et al., 2015). The use of server virtualization has resulted in most data center and many enterprise networks becoming virtual networks that connect virtual ports corresponding to virtual machines. Further, these virtual networks may be reconfigured rapidly as virtual machines migrate. For example, Open VSwitch allows the switch to be reprogrammed at rapid rates using an Open Flow controller (Pfaff et al., 2015).

12.2 Packet-classification problem

Traditionally, the rules for classifying a message are called *rules* and the packet-classification problem is to determine the lowest-cost matching rule for each incoming message at a router.

Assume that the information relevant to a lookup is contained in K distinct *header fields* in each message. These header fields are denoted $H[1], H[2], \ldots, H[K]$, where each field is a string of bits.

For instance, the relevant fields for an IPv4 packet could be the destination address (32 bits), the source address (32 bits), the protocol field (8 bits), the destination port (16 bits), the source port (16 bits), and TCP flags (8 bits). The number of relevant TCP flags is limited, and so the protocol and TCP flags are combined into one field—for example, TCP-ACK can be used to mean a TCP packet with the ACK bit set.[1] Other relevant TCP flags can be represented similarly; UDP packets are represented by $H[3] = UDP$.

Thus, the combination $(D, S, \text{TCP-ACK}, 63, 125)$ denotes the header of an IP packet with destination D, source S, protocol TCP, destination port 63, source port 125, and the ACK bit set.

The *classifier*, or *rule database*, router consists of a finite set of rules, $R_1, R_2, \ldots, R_N$. Each rule is a combination of K values, one for each header field. Each field in a rule is allowed three kinds of matches: exact match, prefix match, and range match. In an *exact match*, the header field of the packet should exactly match the rule field—for instance, this is useful for protocol and flag fields. In a *prefix match*, the rule field should be a prefix of the header field—this could be useful for blocking access from a certain subnetwork. In a *range match*, the header values should lie in the range specified by the rule—this can be useful for specifying port number ranges.

Each rule R_i has an associated directive $disp_i$, which specifies how to forward the packet matching this rule. The directive specifies if the packet should be blocked. If the packet is to be forwarded, the directive specifies the outgoing link to which the packet is sent and, perhaps, also a queue within that link if the message belongs to a flow with bandwidth guarantees.

A packet P is said to *match* a rule R if each field of P matches the corresponding field of R—the match type is implicit in the specification of the field. For instance, if the destination field is specified as 1010∗, then it requires a prefix match; if the protocol field is UDP, then it requires an exact match; if the port field is a range, such as 1024–1100, then it requires a range match. For instance, let $R = (1010*, *, TCP, 1024\text{--}1080, *)$ be a rule, with $disp = block$. Then, a packet with header $(10101\ldots111, 11110\ldots000, \text{TCP}, 1050, 3)$ matches R and is therefore blocked. The packet $(10110\ldots000, 11110\ldots000, \text{TCP}, 80, 3)$, on the other hand, doesn't match R.

Since a packet may match multiple rules in the database, each rule R in the database is associated with a nonnegative number, $cost(R)$. Ambiguity is avoided by returning the least-cost rule matching the packet's header. The cost function generalizes the implicit precedence rules that are used in practice to choose between multiple matching rules. In firewall applications or Cisco ACLs, for instance, rules are placed in the database in a specific linear order, where each rule takes precedence over a subsequent rule. Thus, the goal there is to find the *first* matching rule. Of course, the same effect can be achieved by making $cost(R)$ equal to the position of rule R in the database.

As an example of a rule database, consider the topology and firewall database (Cheswick and Bellovin, 1995) shown in Fig. 12.2, where a screened subnet configuration interposes between a company subnetwork (shown on top left) and the rest of the Internet (including hackers). There is a so-called bastion host M within the company that mediates all access to and from the external world. M serves as the mail gateway and also provides external name server access. TI, TO are network time protocol (NTP) sources, where TI is internal to the company and TO is external. S is the address of the secondary name server, which is external to the company.

---

[1] TCP flags are important for packet classification because the first packet in a connection does not have the ACK bit set, while the others do. This allows a simple rule to block TCP connections initiated from the outside while allowing responses to internally initiated connections.

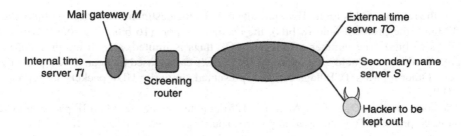

Destination	Source	Destination port	Source port	Flags	Comments
M	*	25	*	*	Allow inbound mail
M	*	53	*	UDP	Allow DNS access
M	S	53	*	*	Secondary access
M	*	23	*	*	Incoming telnet
TI	TO	123	123	UDP	NTP time info
*	Net	*	*	*	Outgoing packets
Net	*	*	*	TCP ack	Return ACKs OK
*	*	*	*	*	Block everything!

FIGURE 12.2

The top half of the figure shows the topology of a small company; the bottom half shows a sample firewall database for this company as described in the book by Cheswick and Bellovin (1995). The *block* flags are not shown in the figure; the first seven rules have *block* = *false* (i.e., allow) and the last rule has *block* = *true* (i.e., block). We assume that all the addresses within the company subnetwork (shown on top left) start with the prefix *Net*, including *M* and *TI*.

Clearly, the site manager wishes to allow communication from within the network to TO and *S* and yet wishes to block hackers. The database of rules shown at the bottom of Fig. 12.2 implements this intention. Terse explanations of each rule are shown on the right of each rule. Assume that all addresses of machines within the company's network start with the CIDR prefix *Net*. Thus *M* and TI both match the prefix *Net*. All packets matching any of the first seven rules are allowed; the remaining (last rule) are dropped by the screening router. A more general firewall could arbitrarily interleave rules that allow packets with rules that drop packets.

As an example, consider a packet sent to *M* from *S* with UDP destination port equal to 53. This packet matches Rules 2, 3, and 8 but must be allowed through because the first matching rule is Rule 2.

Note that this description uses *N* for the number of rules and *K* for the number of packet fields. *K* is sometimes called the *number of dimensions*, for reasons that will become clearer in Section 12.6.

12.3 Requirements and metrics

The requirements for rule matching are similar to those for IP lookups (Chapter 11). We wish to do packet classification at wire speed for minimum-size packets, and thus speed is the dominant metric. To allow the database to fit in high-speed memory, it is useful to reduce the amount of memory needed. For most firewall databases, insertion speed is not an issue because rules are rarely changed.

However, this is not true for *dynamic* or *stateful* packet rules. This capability is useful, for example, for handling UDP traffic. Because UDP headers do not contain an ACK bit that can be used to determine whether a packet is the bellwether packet of a connection, the screening router cannot tell the difference between the first packet sent from the outside to an internal server (which it may want to block) and a response sent to a UDP request to an internal client (which it may want to pass). The solution used in some products is to have the outgoing request packet dynamically trigger the insertion of a rule (which has addresses and ports that match the request) that allows the inbound response to be passed. This requires very fast update times, a third metric.

Besides stateful firewalls, Software-defined Networking (SDN) may also require frequent rule insertions. For instance, reactive SDN controllers add a new rule wherever new traffic starts. Rule updates could become more frequent as network management becomes more agile and programmatic.

12.4 Simple solutions

There are six simple solutions that are often used or considered: linear search, tuple space search, caching, demultiplexing algorithms, MPLS, and content-addressable memories (CAMs). While CAMs have difficult hardware design issues, they effectively represent a parallelization of the simplest algorithmic approach: linear search.

12.4.1 Linear search

Some older firewall implementations do a linear search of the database and keep track of the best-matching rule. Linear search is reasonable for small rule sizes but is extremely slow for large rule sets. For example, a core router that does linear search among a rule set of 2000 rules (used at the time of writing by some ISPs) will considerably degrade its forwarding performance below wire speed.

12.4.2 Tuple space search

A simple improvement of linear search is a simple generalization of IP lookups using hash tables where prefixes were partitioned by length, and all prefixes of the same length are placed in a common hash table. While this requires 32 memory accesses in the worst case for IPv4, recall that the previous chapter described a major improvement, binary search on prefix lengths that could perform IPv4 lookups in $\log_2 32 = 5$ memory accesses.

While the use of binary search does not generalize from IP lookups to packet classification as far as we know, the idea of using linear search on hash tables does and was first called *tuple space search* (*TSS*) by Srinivasan et al. (1998). Consider a simple packet classifier with four rules on IPv4 Destination (D) and Source (S) fields. Ignoring the directive fields, assume that R_1 must match $D = 01*$, $S = 10*$;

second, R_2 must match $D = 10*$, $S = 00*$; third, R_3 must match $D = 0*$, $S = 1*$; finally, R_4 must match $D = 1*$, $S = 0*$.

While there are four rules, there are only 2 combinations of specified lengths or tuples in the table: the tuple $(2, 2)$ (length two specified in source and destination fields as in R_1 and R_2), and the tuple $(1, 1)$ (length 1 specified in source and destination fields as in R_3 and R_4). Thus the key idea is to place all rules with the same tuple in a common hash table and do a linear search across all hash tables corresponding to valid tuples. Each hash table is indexed by a key formed by concatenating the number of bits in each field specified by the tuple. For example, the hash table corresponding to tuple $(2, 2)$ is indexed by a key formed by concatenating the first two bits of the Destination IP address and the first two bits of the Source IP address of the packet to be classified. Note that one cannot stop after a successful match because later tuples could have a lower cost match.

In this simple example, tuple search requires only two memory accesses (assuming each hash table takes one memory access to search) while linear search takes 4 memory access. However, if each tuple has 1000's of rules in the corresponding hash table, tuple space search can be 1000 times faster. However, the worst case number of tuples can still be very large. For example, even for IPv4 and considering only source and destination fields, the number of tuples (length combinations) can be as bad as $32 * 32 = 1024$.

While there are more efficient schemes such as decision trees that are described later, tuple space search has some important advantages. First, it has very fast update times because the time taken to add (or delete) a new rule is $O(1)$: we simply insert or delete the rule from the hash table corresponding to its length tuple. Second, the memory required is $O(n)$ where n is the number of rules. Third, tuple space search easily generalizes to adding new fields as may be required in Software Defined Networks. Perhaps for this reason, tuple space search is used in Open vSwitch (Pfaff et al., 2015) because in a virtualized network new rules can be added several times every second (Pfaff et al., 2015).

The actual use of Tuple Space search in Open vSwitch is much cleverer with several clever heuristics to reduce the average lookup time, an important metric for software switches unlike hardware switches. Two important ideas that speed up the average case in Open vSwitch (Pfaff et al., 2015) are the use of caching and tuple priority sorting. We will discuss caching below, but priority sorting is a way of stopping tuple search early by remembering the highest priority flow associated with each tuple hash table. The details can be found in (Pfaff et al., 2015).

12.4.3 Caching

Some implementations even cache the result of the search keyed against the whole header. There are two problems with this scheme. First, the cache hit rate of caching full IP addresses in the backbones is often small. Early studies show a hit rate of at most 80%–90% (Partridge, 1996; Newman et al., 1997). Part of the problem is Web accesses and other flows that send only a small number of packets; if a Web session sends just five packets to the same address, then the cache hit rate is 80%. Since caching full headers takes a lot more memory, this should have an even worse hit rate (for the same amount of cache memory).

Second, even with a 90% hit rate cache, a slow linear search of the rule space will result in poor performance.[2] For example, suppose that a search of the cache costs 100 nanoseconds (one memory

---

[2] This is an application of a famous principle in computer architecture called *Amdahl's law*.

access) and that a linear search of 10,000 rules costs 1,000,000 nanoseconds = 1 millisecond (one memory access per rule). Then the average search time with a cache hit rate of 90% is still 0.1 millisecond, which is very slow.

However, caching could be combined with some of the fast algorithms in this chapter to improve the expected search time even further. An investigation of the use of caching for classification can be found in Xu et al. (2000). As a more recent example, Open vSwitch (Pfaff et al., 2015) combines Tuple Space search with caching in clever ways. In particular, the Open vSwitch implementation does caching not of full IP and TCP headers of a TCP connection (which they call microflows) but instead for larger aggregates (that they call macroflows). Macroflow caching requires some more complexity to handle correctly (Pfaff et al., 2015).

12.4.4 Demultiplexing algorithms

Chapter 8 describes the use of packet rules for demultiplexing and algorithms such as Pathfinder, Berkeley packet filter, and dynamic path finder. Can't these existing solutions simply be reused? It is important to realize that the two problems are similar but subtly different.

The first packet-classification scheme that avoids a linear search through the set of rules is Pathfinder (Bailey et al., 1994). However, Pathfinder allows wildcards to occur only at the end of a rule. For instance, $(D, S, *, *, *)$ is allowed, but not $(D, *, Prot, *, SourcePort)$. With this restriction, all rules can be merged into a generalized trie—with hash tables replacing array nodes—and rule lookup can be done in time proportional to the number of packet fields. DPF (Engler and Kaashoek, 1996) uses the Pathfinder idea of merging rules into a trie but adds the idea of using dynamic code generation for extra performance. However, it is unclear how to handle intermixed wildcards and specified fields, such as $(D, *, Prot, *, SourcePort)$, using these schemes.

Because packet classification allows more general rules, the Pathfinder idea of using a trie does not work well. There does exist a simple trie scheme (set-pruning tries; see Section 12.5.1) to perform a lookup in time $O(M)$, where M is the number of packet fields. Such schemes are described in Decasper et al. (1998) and Malan and Jahanian (1998). Unfortunately, such schemes require $\Theta(N^K)$ storage, where K is the number of packet fields and N is the number of rules. Thus such schemes are not scalable for large databases. By contrast, some of the schemes we will describe require only $O(NM)$ storage.

12.4.5 Passing labels

Recall from Chapter 11 that one way to finesse lookups is to pass a label from a previous-hop router to a next-hop router. One of the most prominent examples of such a technology is multiprotocol label switching (MPLS) (IETF MPLS Charter, 1997). While IP lookups have been able to keep pace with wire speeds, the difficulties of algorithmic approaches to packet classification have ensured an important niche for MPLS. Refer to Chapter 11 for a description of tag switching and MPLS.

Today MPLS is useful mostly for traffic engineering. For example, if Web traffic between two sites A and B is to be routed along a special path, a label-switched path is set up between the two sites. Before traffic leaves site A, a router does packet classification and maps the Web traffic into an MPLS header. Core routers examine only the label in the header until the traffic reaches B, at which point the MPLS header is removed.

The gain from the MPLS header is that the intermediate routers do not have to repeat the packet-classification effort expended at the edge router; simple table lookup suffices. The DiffServ (Blake et al., 1998) proposal for QoS is actually similar in this sense. Classification is done at the edges to mark packets that deserve special quality of service. The only difference is that the classification information is used to mark the Type of Service (TOS) bits in the IP header, as opposed to an MPLS label. Both are examples of Principle **P10**, passing hints in protocol headers.

Despite MPLS and DiffServ, core routers still do classification at the very highest speeds. This is largely motivated by security concerns, for which it may be infeasible to rely on label switching. For example, Singh et al. (2004a) describe a number of core router classifiers, the largest of which contained 2000 rules.

12.4.6 Content-addressable memories

Recall from Chapter 11 that a CAM is a content-addressable memory, where the first cell that matches a data item will be returned using a parallel lookup in hardware. A ternary CAM allows each bit of data to be either a 0, a 1, or a wildcard. Clearly, ternary CAMs can be used for rule matching as well as for prefix matching. However, the CAMs must provide wide lengths—for example, the combination of the IPv4 destination, source, and two port fields is 96 bits.

Because of problems with algorithmic solutions described in the remainder of this chapter, there is a general belief that hardware solutions such as ternary CAMs are needed for core routers, despite the problems (Gupta and McKeown, 2001) of ternary CAMs. There are, however, several reasons to consider algorithmic alternatives to ternary CAMs, which were presented in Chapter 11.

Recall that these reasons include the smaller density and larger power of CAMs versus SRAMs and the difficulty of integrating forwarding logic with the CAM. These problems remain valid when considering CAMs for classification. An additional issue that arises is the *rule multiplication* caused by ranges. In CAM solutions, each range has to be replaced by a potentially large number of prefixes, thus causing extra entries. Some algorithmic solutions can handle ranges in rules without converting ranges to rules.

These arguments are strengthened by the fact that several CAM vendors have also considered algorithmic solutions, motivated by some of the difficulties with CAMs. While better CAM cell designs that reduce density and power requirements may emerge, it is still important to understand the corresponding advantages and disadvantages of algorithmic solutions. The remainder of the chapter is devoted to this topic. We will return to combinations of TCAMs and Algorithmic methods to get the best of both worlds at the end of the chapter.

12.5 Two-dimensional schemes

A useful problem-solving technique is first to solve a simpler version of a complex problem such as packet classification and to use the insight gained to solve the more complex problem. Since packet classification with just *one* field has been solved in Chapter 11, the next simplest problem is *two-dimensional* packet classification.

Two-dimensional rules may be useful in their own right. This is because large backbone routers may have a large number of destination–source rules to handle virtual private networks and multicast

Rule	Destination	Source
R_1	0*	10*
R_2	0*	01*
R_3	0*	1*
R_4	00*	1*
R_5	00*	11*
R_6	10*	1*
R_7	*	00*

FIGURE 12.3

An example with seven destination–source rules.

forwarding and to keep track of traffic between subnets. Further, as we will see, there is a heuristic observation that reduces the general case to the two-dimensional case.

Since there are only three distinct approaches to one-dimensional prefix matching—using tries, binary search on prefix lengths, and binary search on ranges—it is worth looking for generalizations of each of these distinct approaches. All three generalizations exist. However, this chapter will describe only the most efficient of these (the generalization of tries) in this section.

The appropriate generalization of standard prefix tries to two dimensions is called the *grid of tries*. The main idea will be explained using an example database of seven destination–source rules, shown in Fig. 12.3. We arrive at the final solution by first considering two naive variants.

12.5.1 Fast searching using set-pruning tries

Consider the two-dimensional rule set in Fig. 12.3. The simplest idea is first to build a trie on the destination prefixes in the database and then to hang a number of source tries off the leaves of the destination trie. Fig. 12.4 illustrates the construction for the rules in Fig. 12.3. Each valid prefix in the destination trie points to a trie containing some source prefixes. The question is: Which source prefixes should be stored in the source trie corresponding to each destination prefix?

For instance, consider $D = 00*$. Both rules R_4 and R_5 have this destination prefix, and so the trie at D clearly needs to store the corresponding source prefixes 1* and 11*. But storing only these source prefixes is insufficient. This is because the destination prefix 0* in rules R_1, R_2, and R_3 also matches any destination that D matches. In fact, the wildcard destination prefix * of R_7 also matches whatever D matches. This suggests that the source trie at $D = 00$ must contain the source prefixes for $\{R_1, R_2, R_3, R_4, R_5, R_7\}$, because these are the set of rules *whose destination is a prefix of D*.

Fig. 12.4 shows a schematic representation of this data structure for the database of Fig. 12.3. Note that $S1$ denotes the source prefix of rule R_1, $S2$ of rule R_2, and so on. Thus each prefix D in the destination trie *prunes* the set of rules from the entire set of rules down to the set of rules compatible

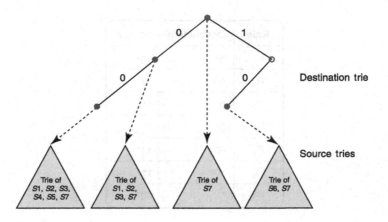

FIGURE 12.4

The set-pruning trie data structure in two dimensions corresponding to the database of Fig. 12.3. Destination trie is a trie for the destination prefixes. The nodes corresponding to a valid destination prefix in the database are shown as filled circles; others are shown as empty circle. Each valid destination prefix D has a pointer to a trie containing the source prefixes that belong to rules whose destination field is a prefix of D.

with D. The same idea can be extended to more than two fields, with each field value in the path pruning the set of rules further.

In this trie of tries, the search algorithm first matches the destination of the header in the destination trie. This yields the longest match on the destination prefix. The search algorithm then traverses the associated source trie to find the longest source match. While searching the source trie, the algorithms keep track of the lowest-cost matching rule. Since all rules that have a matching destination prefix are stored in the source trie being searched, the algorithm finds the correct least-cost rule. This is the basic idea behind set-pruning trees (Decasper et al., 1998).

Unfortunately, this simple extension of tries from one to two dimensions has a memory-explosion problem. The problem arises because a source prefix can occur in multiple tries. In Fig. 12.4 for instance, the source prefixes $S1$, $S2$, $S3$ appear in the source trie associated with $D = 00*$ as well as the trie associated with $D = 0*$.

How bad can this replication get? A worst-case example forcing roughly N^2 memory is created using the set of rules shown in Fig. 12.5. The problem is that since the destination prefix $*$ matches any destination header, each of the $N/2$ source prefixes is replicated $N/2$ times, one for each destination prefix. The example (see exercises) can be extended to show a $O(N^K)$ bound for general set-pruning tries in K dimensions.

While set-pruning tries do not scale to large classifiers, the natural extension to more than two fields has been used in Decasper et al. (1998) as part of a router toolkit, and in Malan and Jahanian (1998) as part of a flexible monitoring system. The performance of set-pruning tries is also studied in Qiu et al. (2001). One interesting optimization introduced in Decasper et al. (1998) and Malan and Jahanian (1998) is to avoid obvious waste (**P1**) when two subtries $S1$ and $S2$ have exactly the same contents. In this case, one can replace the pointers to $S1$ and $S2$ with a pointer to a common subtrie, S. This changes the structure from a tree to a directed acyclic graph (DAG). The DAG optimization can greatly reduce

Rule	Destination	Source
R_1	D1	*
R_2	D2	*
	⋮	
$R_{N/2}$	$D_{N/2}$	*
$R_{N/2+1}$	*	S_1
$R_{N/2+2}$	*	S_2
	⋮	
R_N	*	S_N

FIGURE 12.5

An example forcing $N^2/2$ memory for two-dimensional set-pruning trees. Similar examples, which apply to a number of other simple schemes, can be used to show $O(N^K)$ storage for K-dimensional rules.

storage for set-pruning tries (see Qiu et al., 2001 for other, related optimizations) and can be used to implement small classifiers, say, up to 100 rules, in software.

12.5.2 Reducing memory using backtracking

The previous scheme pays in memory in order to reduce search time. The dual idea is to pay with time in order to reduce memory. In order to avoid the memory blowup of the simple trie scheme, observe that rules associated with a destination prefix D are copied into the source trie of D' whenever D' is a prefix of D. For instance, in Fig. 12.4, the prefix $D = 00*$ has two rules associated with it: R_4 and R_5. The other rules, R_1, R_2, R_3, are copied into D's trie because their destination field $0*$ is a prefix of D.

The copying can be avoided by having each destination prefix D point to a source trie that stores the rules whose destination field is *exactly* D. This requires modifying the search strategy as follows: Instead of just searching the source trie for the best-matching destination prefix D, the search algorithm must now search the source tries associated with all *ancestors* of D.

In order to search for the least-cost rule, the algorithm first traverses the destination trie and finds the longest destination prefix D' matching the header. The algorithm then searches the source trie of D' and updates the least-cost matching rule. Unlike set-pruning tries, however, the search algorithm is not finished at this point.

Instead, the search algorithm must now work its way back up the destination trie and search the source trie associated with every prefix of D' that points to a nonempty source trie.[3]

---

[3] Note that backtracking search can actually search the source tries corresponding to destination prefixes in any order; this particular order was used only to motivate the grid-of-tries scheme. Another search order that minimizes the state required for backtracking is described in Qiu et al. (2001).

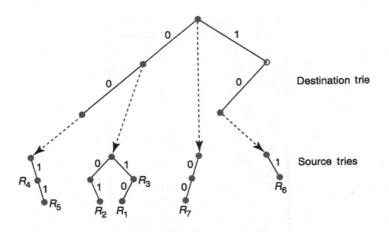

FIGURE 12.6

Avoiding the memory blowup by storing each rule in exactly one trie.

Since each rule now is stored exactly once, the memory requirement for the new structure is $O(NW)$, which is a significant improvement over the previous scheme. Unfortunately, the lookup cost for backtracking is worse than for set-pruning tries: In the worst case, the lookup costs $\Theta(W^2)$, where W is the maximum number of bits specified in the destination or source fields.

The $\Theta(W^2)$ bound on the search cost follows from the observation that, in the worst case, the algorithm may end up searching W source tries, each at the cost of $O(W)$, for a total of $O(W^2)$ time. For $W = 32$ and using 1-bit tries, this is 1024 memory accesses. Even using 4-bit tries, this scheme requires 64 memory accesses.

While backtracking can be very slow in the worst case, it turns out that all classification algorithms exhibit pathological worst-case behavior. For databases encountered in practice, backtracking can work very well. Qiu et al. (2001) describe experimental results using backtracking and also describe potential hardware implementations on pipelined processors.

12.5.3 The best of both worlds: grid of tries

The two naive variants of two-dimensional tries pay either a large price in memory (set-pruning tries) or a large price in time (backtracking search). However, a careful examination of backtracking search reveals obvious waste (**P1**), which can be avoided using precomputation (**P2a**).

To see the wasted time in backtracking search, consider matching the packet with destination address 001 and source address 001 in Fig. 12.6. The search in the destination trie gives $D = 00$ as the best match. So the backtracking algorithm starts its search for the matching source prefix in the associated source trie, which contains rules R_4 and R_5. However, the search immediately fails, since the first bit of the source is 0. Next, backtracking search backs up along the destination trie and *restarts* the search in the source trie of $D = 0*$, the parent of $00*$.

But backing up the trie is a waste because if the search fails after searching destination bits 00 and source bit 0, then any matching rule must be shorter in the destination (e.g., 0) and must contain all the

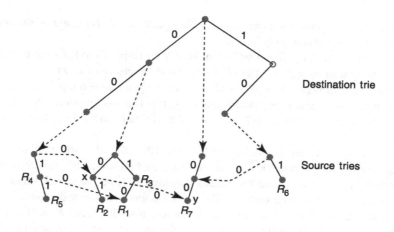

FIGURE 12.7

Improving the search cost with the use of switch pointers.

source bits searched so far, *including* the failed bit. Thus backing up to the source trie of $D = 0*$ and then traversing the source bit 0 to the parent of R_2 in Fig. 12.6 (as done in backtracking search) is a waste.

The algorithm could predict that this sequence of bits would be traversed when it first failed in the source trie of $D = 00$. This motivates a simple idea: Why not jump directly to the parent of R_2 from the failure point in the source trie of $D = 00*$?

Thus in the new scheme (Fig. 12.7), for each failure point in a source trie, the trie-building algorithm *precomputes* what we call a *switch pointer*. Switch pointers allow search to jump directly to the next possible source trie that can contain a matching rule. Thus in Fig. 12.7, notice that the source trie containing R_4 and R_5 has a dashed line labeled with 0 that points to a node x in the source trie containing $\{R_1, R_2, R_3\}$. All the dashed lines between source tries in Fig. 12.7 are switch pointers. Please distinguish the dashed switch pointers from the dotted lines that connect the destination and source tries.

Now consider again the same search for the packet with destination address 001 and source address 001 in Fig. 12.7. As before, the search in the destination trie gives $D = 00$ as the best match. Search fails in the corresponding source trie (containing R_4 and R_5) because the source trie contains a path only if the first source bit is a 1. However, in Fig. 12.7, instead of failing and backtracking, the algorithm follows the switch pointer labeled 0 directly to node x. It then continues matching from node x, without skipping a beat, using the remaining bits of the source.

Since the next bit of the source is a 0, the search in Fig. 12.7 fails again. The search algorithm once again follows the switch pointer labeled 0 and jumps to node y of the third source trie (associated with the destination prefix *). Effectively, the switch pointers allow skipping over all rules in the next ancestor source trie whose source fields are shorter than the current source match. This in turn improves the search complexity from $O(W^2)$ to $O(W)$.

It may help to define *switch pointers* more precisely. Call a destination string D' an *ancestor* of D if D' is a *prefix* of D. Call D' the *lowest ancestor* of D if D' is the *longest* prefix of D in the destination trie. Let $T(D)$ denote the source trie pointed to by D. Recall that $T(D)$ contains the source fields of exactly those rules whose destination field is D.

Let u be a node in $T(D)$ that *fails* on bit 0; that is, if u corresponds to the source prefix s, then the trie $T(D)$ has no string starting with $s0$. Let D'' be the *lowest* ancestor of D whose source trie contains a source string *starting with prefix s0*, say, at node v. Then we place a switch pointer at node u pointing to node v. If no such node v exists, the switch pointer is nil. The switch pointer for failure on bit 1 is defined similarly. For instance, in Fig. 12.7, the node labeled x fails on bit 0 and has a switch pointer to the node labeled y.

As a second example, consider the packet header $(00*, 10*)$. Search starts with the first source trie, pointed to by the destination trie node $00*$. After matching the first source bit, 1, search encounters rule R_4. But then search fails on the second bit. Search therefore follows the switch pointer, which leads to the node in the second trie labeled with R_1. The switch pointers at the node containing R_1 are both nil, and so search terminates. Note, however, that search has missed the rule $R_3 = (0*, 1*)$, which also matches the packet header. While in this case R_3 has a higher cost than R_1, in general, the overlooked rule could have a lower cost.

Such problems can be avoided by having each node in a source trie maintain a variable *storedRule*. Specifically, a node v with destination prefix D and source prefix S stores in *storedRule*(v) the least-cost rule whose destination field is a prefix of D and whose source field is a prefix of S. With this precomputation, the node labeled with R_1 in Fig. 12.7 would store information about R_3 instead of R_1 if R_3 had a lower cost than R_1.

Finally, here is an argument that the search cost in the final scheme is at most $2W$. The time to find the best destination prefix is at most W. The remainder of the time is spent traversing the source tries. However, in each step, the length of the match on the source field increases by 1—either by traversing further down in the same trie or by following a switch pointer to an ancestral trie. Since the maximum length of the source prefixes is W, the total time spent in searching the source tries is also W. The memory requirement is $O(NW)$, since each of the N rules is stored only once, and each rule requires $O(W)$ space.

Note that k-bit tries (Chapter 11) can be used in place of 1-bit tries by expanding each destination or source prefix to the next multiple of k. For instance, suppose $k = 2$. Then, in the example of Fig. 12.7, the destination prefix $0*$ of rules R_1, R_2, R_3 is expanded to 00 and 01. The source prefixes of R_3, R_4, R_6 are expanded to 10 and 11. Using k-bit expansion, a single prefix can expand to 2^{k-1} prefixes. The total memory requirement grows from $2NW$ to $NW2^k/k$, and so the memory increases by the factor $2^{k-1}/k$. On the other hand, the depth of the trie reduces to W/k, and so the total lookup time becomes $O(W/k)$.

The bottom line is that by using multibit tries, the time to search for the best matching rule in an arbitrarily large two-dimensional database is effectively the time for two IP lookups.

Just as the grid of tries represents a generalization of familiar trie search for prefix matching, there is a corresponding generalization of binary search on prefix lengths (Chapter 11) that searches a database of two field rules in $2W$ hashes, where W is the length of the larger of the two fields. This is a big gap from the $\log W$ time required for prefix matching using binary search on prefix lengths. In the special case where the rules do not overlap, the search time reduces even further to $\log_2 W$, as shown in Suri et al. (2001). While these results are interesting theoretically, they seem to have less relevance to real routers, mostly because of the difficulties of implementing hashing in hardware.

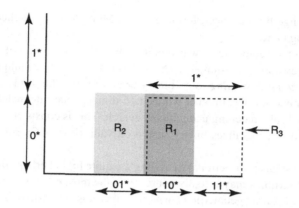

FIGURE 12.8

Geometric view of the first three rules, R_1, R_2, R_3, in the rule database of Fig. 12.3. For example, the rule $R_1 = 0*$, $10*$ is the box whose projection on the destination axis is the range corresponding to $0*$ and whose projection on the source axis is the range corresponding to $10*$. Note that because $R_3 = 0*$, $1*$ has the same destination range as R_1 and a source range that strictly includes the range of R_1, the dashed box, R_3, contains the box R_1.

12.6 Approaches to general rule sets

So far this chapter has concentrated on the special case of rules on just two header fields. Before moving to algorithms for rules with more than two fields, this section brings together some insights that inform the algorithms in later sections. Section 12.6.1 describes a geometric view of classification that provides visual insight into the problem. Section 12.6.2 utilizes the geometric viewpoint to obtain bounds on the fundamental difficulty of packet classification in the general case. Section 12.6.3 describes several observations about real rule sets that can be exploited to provide efficient algorithms that will be described in subsequent sections.

12.6.1 Geometric view of classification

A second problem-solving technique that is useful is to collect different viewpoints for the same problem. This section describes a *geometric* view of classification that was introduced by Lakshman and Stidialis (1998) and independently by Adisheshu (1998).

Recall from Chapter 11 that we can view a 32-bit prefix like $00*$ as a range of addresses from $000...00$ to $001...11$ on the number line from 0 to 2^{32}. If prefixes correspond to *line segments* geometrically, two-dimensional rules correspond to rectangles (Fig. 12.8), three-dimensional rules to cubes, and so on. A given packet header is a point. The problem of packet classification reduces to finding the lowest-cost box that contains the given point.

Fig. 12.8 shows the geometric view of the first three two-dimensional rules in Fig. 12.3. Destination addresses are represented on the y-axis and source addresses on the x-axis. In the figure, some sample prefix ranges are marked off on each axis. For example, the two halves of the y-axis are the prefix ranges $0*$ and $1*$. Similarly, the x-axis is divided into the four prefix ranges $00*$, $01*$, $10*$, and $11*$. To draw the box for a rule like $R_1 = 0*$, $10*$, draw the $0*$ range on the y-axis and the $10*$ range on the *x*-axis, and extend the range lines to meet, forming a box. Multiple-rule matches, such as R_1 and R_2, correspond to overlapping boxes.

The first advantage of the geometric view is that it enables the application of algorithms from computational geometry. For example, Lakshman and Stidialis (1998) adapt a technique from computational geometry known as *fractional cascading* to do binary search for two-field rule matching in $O(\log N)$ time, where N is the number of rules. In other words, two-dimensional rule matching is asymptotically as fast as one-dimensional rule matching using binary search. This is consistent with the results for the grid of tries. The result also generalizes binary search on values for prefix searching as described in Chapter 11.

Unfortunately, the constants for fractional cascading are quite high. Perhaps this suggests that adapting existing geometric algorithms may actually not result in the most efficient algorithms. However, the second and main advantage of the geometric *viewpoint* is that it is suggestive and useful.

For example, the geometric view provides a useful metric, the number of disjoint (i.e., nonintersecting) *classification regions*. Since rules can overlap, this is not the number of rules. In two dimensions, for example, with N rules, one can create N^2 classification regions by having $N/2$ rules that correspond geometrically to horizontal strips together with $N/2$ rules that correspond geometrically to vertical strips. The intersection of the $N/2$ horizontal strips with the $N/2$ vertical strips creates $O(N^2)$ disjoint classification regions. For example, the database in Fig. 12.5 has this property. Similar constructions can be used to generate $O(N^K)$ regions for K-dimensional rules.

As a second example, the database of Fig. 12.8 has four classification regions: the rule R_1, the rule R_2, the points in R_3 not contained in R_1, and all points not contained in R_1, R_2, or R_3. We will use the number of classification regions later to characterize the complexity of a given classifier or rule database.

12.6.2 Beyond two dimensions: the bad news

The success of the grid of tries may make us optimistic about generalizing to larger dimensions. Unfortunately, this optimism is misplaced; either the search time or the storage blows up exponentially with the number of dimensions K for $K > 2$.

Using the geometric viewpoint just described, it is easy to adapt a lower bound from computational geometry. Thus, it is known that general multidimensional range searching over N ranges in K dimensions requires $\Omega((\log N)^{K-1})$ worst-case time if the memory is limited to about linear size (Chazelle, 1990a,b) or requires $O(N^K)$ size memory. While $\log N$ could be reasonable (say, 10 memory accesses), $\log^4 N$ ($K = 5$ in the case of packet classification over source IP, destination IP, source port number, destination port number, and protocol) will be very large (say, 10,000 memory accesses). Notice that this lower bound is consistent with solutions for the two-dimensional cases that take linear storage but are as fast as $O(\log N)$.

The lower bound implies that for perfectly general rule sets, *algorithmic approaches to classification require either a large amount of memory or a large amount of time*. Unfortunately, classification at high speeds, especially for core routers, requires the use of limited and expensive SRAM. Thus the lower bound seems to imply that content address memories are required for reasonably sized classifiers (say, 10,000 rules) that must be searched at high speeds (e.g., OC-768 speeds).

12.6.3 Beyond two dimensions: the good news

The previous subsection may have left the reader wondering whether there is any hope left for algorithmic approaches to packet classification in the general case. Fortunately, real databases have more *structure*, which can be exploited to efficiently solve multidimensional packet classification using algorithmic techniques.

The *good* news about packet classification can be articulated using four observations. Subsequent sections describe a series of heuristic algorithms, all of which do very badly in the worst case but quite well on databases that satisfy one or more of the assumptions.

The expected case can be characterized using four observations drawn from a set of firewall databases studied in Srinivasan et al. (1998) and Gupta and McKeown (1999a) (and not from publically available lookup tables as in the previous chapter). The first is identical to an observation made in Chapter 11 and repeated here. The observations are numbered starting from *O2* to be consistent with observation *O1* made in the lookup chapter.

O2: *Prefix containment is rare.* It is somewhat rare to have prefixes that are prefixes of other prefixes, as, for example, the prefixes 00* and 0001*. In fact, the maximum number of prefixes of a given prefix in lookup tables and classifiers is seven.

O3: *Many fields are not general ranges.* For the destination and source port fields, most rules contain either specific port numbers (e.g., port 80 for Web traffic), the wildcard range (i.e., *), or the port ranges that separate server ports from client ports (1024 or greater and less than 1024). The protocol field is limited to either the wildcard or (more commonly) TCP, UDP. This field also rarely contains protocols such as IGMP and ICMP. While other TCP fields are sometimes referred to, the most common reference is to the ACK bit.

O4: *The number of disjoint classification regions is small.* This is perhaps the most interesting observation. Harking back to the geometric view, the lower bounds in Chazelle (1990a) depend partly on the worst-case possibility of creating N^K classification regions using N rules. Such rules require either N^K space or a large search time. However, Gupta and McKeown (1999a), after an extensive survey of 8000 rule databases, show that the number of classification regions is much smaller than the worst case. Instead of being exponential in the number of dimensions, the number of classification regions is linear in N, with a small constant.

O5: *Source–Destination matching:* In Singh et al. (2004b), several core router classifiers used by real ISPs are analyzed and the following interesting observation is made. Almost all packets match at most five distinct source–destination values found in the classifier. No packet matched more than 20 distinct source–destination pairs. This is a somewhat more refined observation than *O4* because it says that the number of classification regions is small, even when projected only to the source and destination fields. By "small," we mean that the number of regions grows much more slowly than N, the size of the classifier.

12.7 Extending two-dimensional schemes

The simplest general scheme uses observation *O5* to trivially extend any efficient 2D scheme to multiple dimensions. A number of algorithms simply use linear search to search through all possible rules. These scales well in storage but poorly in time. The source–destination matching observation leads to a very

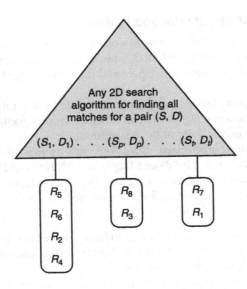

FIGURE 12.9

Extending two-dimensional schemes.

simple idea depicted in Fig. 12.9. Use source–destination address matching to reduce linear searching to just the rules corresponding to source–destination prefix pairs in the database that match the given packet header. Alternately, one can use source-destination matching to reduce power in TCAMs as in SmartPC (Ma and Banerjee, 2012) as we will see later.

By observation $O5$, at most 20 rules match any packet when considering only the source and destination fields. Thus pruning based on source–destination fields will reduce the number of rules to be searched to less than 20, compared to searching the entire database. For example, Singh et al. (2004a) describe a database with 2800 rules used by a large ISP.

Thus in Fig. 12.9 the general idea is to use any efficient two-dimensional matching scheme to find *all* distinct source–destination prefix pairs $(S_1, D_1) \ldots (S_t, D_t)$ that match a header. For each distinct pair (S_i, D_i), there is a linear array or list with all rules that contain (S_i, D_i) in the source and destination fields. Thus in the figure, the algorithm has to traverse the list at (S_1, D_1), searching through all the rules for R_5, R_6, R_2, and R_4. Then the algorithm moves on to consider the lists at (S_2, D_2), and so on.

This structure has two important advantages:

- Each rule is represented only once without replication. However, one may wish to replicate rules to reduce search times even further.
- The port range specifications stay as ranges in the individual lists without the associated blowup associated with range translation in, say, CAMs.

Since the grid-of-tries implementation described earlier is one of the most efficient two-dimensional schemes in the literature, it is natural to instantiate this general schema by using a grid of tries as the two-dimensional algorithm in Fig. 12.9.

Unfortunately, it turns out that there is a delicacy about extending the grid of tries. In the grid of tries, whenever one rule, R, is at least as specific in all fields as a second rule, R', rule R' precomputes its matching directive to be that of R if R is the lower cost of the two rules. This allows the traversal through the grid of tries to safely skip rule R when encountering rule R'. While this works correctly with two-field rules, it requires some further modifications to handle the general case.

One solution, equivalent to precomputing rule costs, is to precompute the list for R' to include all the list elements for R. Unfortunately, this approach can increase storage because each rule is no longer represented exactly once. A more sophisticated solution, called the *extended grid of tries* (EGT) and described in Singh et al. (2004b), is based on extra traversals beyond the standard grid of tries.

The performance of EGT can be described as follows.

Assumption: The extension of two-dimensional schemes depends critically on observation $O5$.

Performance: The scheme takes at least one grid-of-tries traversal plus the time to linearly search c rules, where c is the constant embodied in observation $O5$. Assuming linear storage, the search performance can increase (Singh et al., 2004b) by an additive factor representing the time to search for less specific rules. The addition of a new rule R requires only rebuilding of the individual two-dimensional structure of which R is a part. Thus rule update should be fairly fast.

12.8 Using divide-and-conquer

The next three schemes (bit vector linear search, on-demand cross-producting, and equivalenced cross-producting) all exploit the simple algorithmic idea (**P15**) of divide-and-conquer. Divide-and-conquer refers to dividing a problem into simpler pieces and then efficiently combining the answers to the pieces. We briefly motivate a skeletal framework of this approach in this section. The next three sections will flesh out specific instantiations of this framework.

Chapter 11 has already outlined techniques to do lookups on individual fields. Given this background, the common idea in all three divide-and-conquer algorithms is the following. Start by slicing the rule database into columns, with the ith column storing all distinct prefixes (or ranges) in field i. Then, given a packet P, determine the best-matching prefix (or narrowest-enclosing range) for each of its fields separately. Finally, combine the results of the best-matching-prefix lookups on individual fields. The main problem, of course, lies in finding an efficient method for combining the lookup of individual fields into a single compound lookup.

All the divide-and-conquer algorithms conceptually start by slicing the database of Fig. 12.2 into individual prefix fields. In the sliced columns, from now on, we will sometimes refer to the wildcard character * by the string *default*. Recall that the mail gateway M and internal NTP agent TI are full IP addresses that lie within the prefix range of *Net*. The sliced database corresponding to Fig. 12.2 is shown in Fig. 12.10.

Clearly, any divide-and-conquer algorithm starts by doing an individual lookup in each column and then combines the results. The next three sections show that each of the three schemes returns different results with lookup and follows different strategies to combine the individual field results, despite using the same sliced database shown in Fig. 12.10.

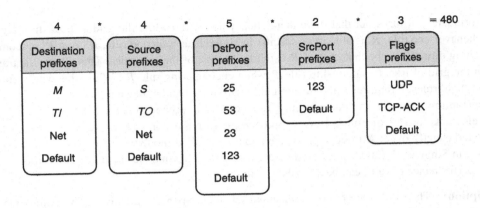

FIGURE 12.10

The database of Fig. 12.2 "sliced" into columns where each column contains the set of prefixes corresponding to a particular field.

12.9 Bit vector linear search

Consider doing a match in one of the individual columns in Fig. 12.10, say, the destination address field, and finding a bit string S as the longest match. Clearly, this lookup result eliminates any rules that *do not* match S in this field. Then the search algorithm can do a linear search in the set of all remaining rules that match S. The logical extension is to perform individual matches in each field; each field match will prune away a number of rules, leaving a remaining set. The search algorithm needs to search only the *intersection* of the remaining sets obtained by each field lookup.

This would clearly be a good heuristic for optimizing the average case if the remaining sets are typically small. However, one can guarantee performance even in the worst case (to some extent) by representing the remaining sets as bitmaps and by using wide memories to retrieve a large number of set members in a single memory access (**P4a**, exploit locality).

In more detail, as in Section 12.8, divide-and-conquer is used to slice the database, as in Fig. 12.10. However, in addition with each possible value M of field i, the algorithm stores the set of rules $S(M)$ that match M in field i as a bit vector. This is easy to do when building the sliced table. The algorithm that builds the data structure scans through the rules linearly to obtain the rules that match M using the match rule (e.g., exact, prefix, or range) specified for the field.

For example, Fig. 12.11 shows the sliced database of Fig. 12.10 together with bit vectors for each sliced field value. The bit vector has 8 bits, one corresponding to each of the eight possible rules in Fig. 12.2. Bit j is set for value M in field i if value M matches Rule j in field i.

Consider the destination prefix field and the first value M in Fig. 12.11. If we compare it to Fig. 12.2, we see that the first four rules specify M in this field. The fifth rule specifies TI (which does not match M), and the sixth and eighth rules specify a wildcard (which matches M). Finally, the seventh rule specifies the prefix Net (which matches M, because Net is assumed to be the prefix of the company network in which M is the mail gateway). Thus the bitmap for M is 11110111, where the only bit not set is the fifth bit. This is because the fifth rule has TI, which does not match M.

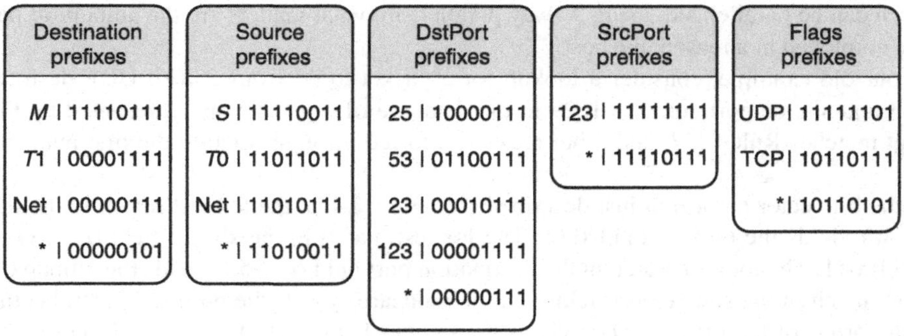

Destination prefixes	Source prefixes	DstPort prefixes	SrcPort prefixes	Flags prefixes
M | 11110111	*S* | 11110011	25 | 10000111	123 | 11111111	UDP| 11111101
*T*1 | 00001111	*T*0 | 11011011	53 | 01100111	* | 11110111	TCP| 10110111
Net | 00000111	Net | 11010111	23 | 00010111		*| 10110101
* | 00000101	* | 11010011	123 | 00001111		
		* | 00000111		

FIGURE 12.11

The sliced database of Fig. 12.10 together with bit vectors for every possible sliced value. The bit vector has 8 bits, one corresponding to each of the eight possible rules in Fig. 12.2. Bit j is set for value M in field i if value M matches Rule j in field i.

When a packet header arrives with fields $H[1]\ldots H[K]$, the search algorithm first performs a longest-matching-prefix lookup in each field i to obtain matches M_i and the corresponding set $S(M_i)$ of matching rules. The search algorithm then proceeds to compute the intersection of all the sets $S(M_i)$ and returns the lowest-cost element in the intersection set.

But if rules are arranged in nondecreasing order of cost and all sets are bitmaps, then the intersection set is the AND of all K bitmaps. Finally, the lowest-cost element corresponds to the index of the first bit set in the intersection bitmap. But, the reader may object, since there are N rules, the intersected bitmaps are N bits long. Hence, computing the AND requires $O(N)$ operations. So the algorithm is effectively doing a linear search after slicing and doing individual field matches. Why not do simple linear search instead?

The reason is subtle and requires a good grasp of models and metrics. Basically, the preceding argument above is correct but ignores the large constant-factor improvement that is possible using bitmaps. Thus computing the AND of K bit vectors and searching the intersection bit vector is still an $O(K \cdot N)$ operation; however, the constants are much lower than doing naive linear search because we are dealing with bitmaps. Wide memories (**P4a**) can be used to make these operations quite cheap, even for a large number of rules.

This is because the cost in memory accesses for these bit operations is $N \cdot (K + 1)/W$ memory accesses, where W is the width of a memory access. Even with W = 32, this brings down the number of memory accesses by a factor of 32. A specialized hardware classification chip can do much better. Using wide memories and wide buses (the bus width is often the limiting factor), a chip can easily achieve W = 1000 with today's technology. As technology scales, one can expect even larger memory widths.

For example, using W = 1000 and $k = 5$ fields, the number of memory accesses for 5000 rules is $5000 * 6/1000 = 30$. Using 10-nanosecond SRAM, this allows a rule lookup in 300 nanoseconds, which is sufficient to process minimum-size (40-byte) packets at wire speed on a gigabit link. By using K-fold parallelism, the further factor of $K + 1$ can be removed, allowing 30,000 rules. Of course, even linear search can be parallelized, using N-way parallelism; what matters are the amount of parallelism that can be employed at a reasonable cost.

Using our old example, consider a lookup for a packet to M from S with UDP destination port equal to 53 and source port equal to 1029 in the database of Fig. 12.2, as represented by Fig. 12.11. This packet matches Rules 2, 3, and 8 but must be allowed through because the first matching rule is Rule 2.

Using the bit vector algorithm just described (see Fig. 12.11), the longest match in the destination field (i.e., M) yields the bitmap 11110111. The longest match in the source field (i.e., S) yields the bitmap 11110011. The longest match in the destination port field (i.e., 53) yields the bitmap 01100111. The longest match in the source port field (i.e., the wildcard) yields the bitmap 11110111; the longest match in the protocol field (i.e., UDP) yields the bitmap 11111101. The AND of the five bitmaps is 01100001. This bitmap corresponds to matching Rules 2, 3, and 8. The index of the first bit set is 2. This corresponds to the second rule, which is indeed the correct match.

The bit vector algorithm was described in detail in Lakshman and Stidialis (1998) and also in a few lines in a paper on network monitoring (Malan and Jahanian, 1998). The first paper (Lakshman and Stidialis, 1998) also describes some trade-offs between search time and memory. A later paper (Baboescu and Varghese, 2001) shows how to add more state for speed (**P12**) by using summary bits. For every W bits in a bitmap, the summary is the OR of the bits. The main intuition is that if, say, W^2 bits are zero, this can be ascertained by checking W summary bits.

The bit vector scheme is a good one for moderate-size databases. However, since the heart of the algorithm relies on linear search, it cannot scale to both very large databases and very high speeds.

The performance of this scheme can be described as follows.

Assumption: The number of rules will stay reasonably small or will grow only in proportion to increases in bus width and parallelism made possible by technology improvements.

Performance: The number of memory accesses is $N \cdot (K + 1)/W$ plus the number of memory accesses for K longest-matching-prefix or narrowest-range operations. The memory required is that for the K individual field matches (see schemes in Chapter 11) plus potentially $N^2 K$ bits. Recall that N is the number of rules, K is the number of fields, and W is the width of a memory access. Updating rules is slow and generally requires rebuilding the entire database.

12.10 Cross-producting

This section describes a crude scheme called cross-producting (Srinivasan et al., 1998). In the next section, we describe a crucial refinement we call *equivalenced cross-producting* (but called RFC by the authors (Gupta and McKeown, 1999a)) that makes cross-producting more feasible. The top of each column in Fig. 12.10 indicates the number of elements in the column. Consider a 5-tuple, formed by taking one value from each column. Call this a *cross product*. Altogether, there are $4 * 4 * 5 * 2 * 3 = 480$ possible cross products. Some sample cross products are shown in Fig. 12.12. Considering the destination field to be most significant and the flags field to be least significant, and pretending that values increase down a column, cross products can be ordered from the smallest to the largest, as in any number system.

A key insight into the utility of cross products is as follows.

Number	Cross product	Matching rule
1	*M, S*, 25, 123, UDP	Rule 1
2	*M, S*, 25, 123, TCP-ACK	Rule 1
3	*M, S*, 25, 123, *default*	Rule 1
4	*M, S*, 25, *default*, UDP	Rule 1
5	*M, S*, 25, *default*, TCP-ACK	Rule 1
6	*M, S*, 25, *default*, *default*	Rule 1
⋮	⋮　⋮　⋮　⋮	⋮
479	*default, default, default, default*, TCP-ACK	Rule 8
480	*default, default, default, default, default*	Rule 8

FIGURE 12.12

A sample of the cross products obtained by cross-producting the individual prefix tables of Fig. 12.10.

Given a packet header H, if the longest-matching-prefix operation for each field $H[i]$ is concatenated to form a cross product C, then the least-cost rule matching H is identical to the least-cost rule matching C.

Suppose this were not true. Since each field in C is a prefix of the corresponding field in H, every rule that matches C also matches H. Thus the only case in which H has a different matching rule is if there is some rule R that matches H but not C. This implies that there is some field i such that $R[i]$ is a prefix of $H[i]$ but not of $C[i]$, where $C[i]$ is the contribution of field i to cross product C. But since $C[i]$ is a prefix of $H[i]$, this can happen only if $R[i]$ is longer than $C[i]$. But that contradicts the fact that $C[i]$ is the longest-matching prefix in column/field i.

Thus, the basic cross-producting algorithm (Srinivasan et al., 1998) builds a table of all possible cross products and *precomputes* the least-cost rule matching each cross product. This is shown in Fig. 12.12. Then, given a packet header, the search algorithm can determine the least-cost matching rule for the packet by performing K longest-matching-prefix operations, together with a single hash lookup of the cross-product table. In hardware, each of the K prefix lookups can be done in parallel.

Using our example, consider matching a packet with header $(M, S, \text{UDP}, 53, 57)$ in the database of Fig. 12.2. The cross product obtained by performing best-matching prefixes on individual fields is $(M, S, \text{UDP}, 53, default)$. It is easy to check that the precomputed rule for this cross product is Rule 2—although Rules 3 and 8 also match the cross product, Rule 2 has the least cost.

The naive cross-producting algorithm suffers from a memory explosion problem: In the worst case, the cross-product table can have N^K entries, where N is the number of rules and K is the number of fields. Thus, even for moderate values, say, $N = 100$ and $K = 5$, the table size can reach 10^{10}, which is prohibitively large.

One idea to reduce memory is to build the cross products on demand (**P2b**, lazy evaluation) (Srinivasan et al., 1998): Instead of building the complete cross-product table at the start, the algorithm incrementally adds entries to the table. The prefix tables for each field are built as before, but the cross-product table is initially empty. When a packet header H arrives, the search algorithm performs longest-matching prefixes on the individual fields to compute a cross-product term C.

If the cross-product table has an entry for C, then of course the associated rule is returned. However, if there is no entry for C in the cross-product table, the search algorithm finds the best-matching rule for C (possibly using a linear search of the database) and inserts that entry into the cross-product table. Of course, any subsequent packets with cross product C will yield fast lookups.

On-demand cross-producting can improve both the building time of the data structure and its storage cost. In fact, the algorithm can treat the cross-product table as a cache and remove all cross products that have not been used recently. Caching based on cross products can be more effective than full header caching because a single cross product can represent multiple headers (see Exercises). However, a more radical improvement of cross-producting comes from the next idea, which essentially aggregates cross products into a much smaller number of equivalence classes.

12.11 Equivalenced cross-producting

Gupta and McKeown (1999a) have invented a scheme called *recursive flow classification* (RFC), which is an improved form of cross-producting that significantly compresses the cross-product table, at a slight extra expense in search time. We prefer to call their scheme *equivalenced cross-producting,* for the following reason. The scheme works by building larger cross products from smaller cross products; the main idea is to place the smaller cross products into equivalence classes before combining them to form larger cross products. This equivalencing of partial cross products considerably reduces memory requirements, because several original cross-product terms map into the same equivalence class.

Recall that in simple cross-producting when a header H arrives, the individual field matches are immediately concatenated to form a cross product that is then looked up in a cross-product table. By contrast, equivalenced cross-producting builds the final cross product in several pairwise combining steps instead of in one fell swoop.

For example, one could form the destination–source cross product and separately form the destination port–source port cross product. Then, a third step can be used to combine these two cross products into a cross product on the first four fields, say, C'. A fourth step is then needed to combine C' with the protocol field to form the final cross product, C. The actual combining sequence is defined by a combining tree, which can be chosen to reduce overall memory.

Just forming the final cross product in several pairwise steps does not reduce memory below N^K. What does reduce memory is the observation that when two partial cross products are combined, many of these pairs are equivalent: Geometrically, they correspond to the same region of space; algebraically, they have the same set of compatible rules.

Thus the main trick is to give each class a class number and to form the larger cross products using the *class numbers* instead of the original matches. Since the algebraic view is easier for computation, we will describe an example of equivalencing using the first two columns of Fig. 12.10 under the algebraic view.

Destination–source prefix pairs	Rule bitmap	Class number
M, S	11110011	C1
M, T0	11010011	C2
M, Net	11010111	C3
M, *	11010011	C2
T1, S	00000011	C4
T1, T0	00001011	C5
T1, Net	00000111	C6
T1, *	00000011	C4
Net, S	00000011	C4
Net, T0	00000011	C4
Net, Net	00000111	C6
Net, *	00000011	C4
*, S	00000001	C7
*, T0	00000001	C7
*, Net	00000101	C8
*, *	00000001	C7

FIGURE 12.13

Forming the partial cross products of the first two columns in Fig. 12.10 and then assigning these cross products into the same equivalence class if they have the same rule set (rule bitmap). Notice that 16 partial cross products form only eight classes.

Fig. 12.13 shows the partial cross products formed by only the destination and source columns in Fig. 12.10. For each pair (e.g., M, S), we compute the set of rules that are compatible with such a pair of matches exactly, as in the bit vector linear search scheme. In fact, we can find the bit vector of any pair, such as M, S, by taking the intersection of the rule bitmaps for M and S in Fig. 12.11. Thus from Fig. 12.11, since the rule bitmap for M is 11110111 and the bitmap for S is 11110011, the intersection bitmap for M, S is 11110011, as shown in Fig. 12.13.

Doing this for each possible pair, we soon see that several bitmaps repeat themselves. For example, M, TO, and $M, *$ (second and fourth entries in Fig. 12.13) have the same bitmap. Two rules that have the same bitmap are assigned to the same equivalence class, and each class is given a class number. Thus in Fig. 12.13, the classes are numbered starting with 1; the table-building algorithm increments

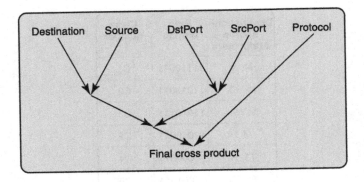

FIGURE 12.14

The combining tree used in the example.

the class number whenever it encounters a new bitmap. Thus, there are only eight distinct class numbers, compared to 16 possible cross products, because there are only eight distinct bitmaps.

Now assume we combine the two port columns to form six classes from 10 possible cross products. When we combine the port pairs with the destination–source pairs, we combine all possible combinations of the destination–source and port pair class numbers and not the original field matches. Thus after combining all four columns, we get $6 * 8 = 48$ cross products. Note that in Fig. 12.10, naive cross-producting will form $4 * 4 * 5 * 2 = 160$ cross products from the first four columns. Thus we have saved a factor of nearly 3 in memory.

Of course, we do not stop here. After combining the destination–source and port pair class numbers, we equivalence them again using the same technique. When combining class number C with class number C', the bitmap for C, C' is the intersection of the bitmaps for C and C'. Once again, pairs with identical bitmaps are equivalenced into groups. After this is done, the final cross product is formed by combining the classes corresponding to the first four columns with the matches in the fifth column.

Our example combined fields 1 and 2, then fields 3 and 4, and then the first four and finally combined in the fifth (Fig. 12.14). Clearly, other pairings are possible, as defined by a binary tree with the fields as nodes and edges representing pairwise combining steps. One could choose the optimal combining tree to reduce memory.

The search process is similar to cross-producting, except the cross products are calculated pairwise (just as they are built) using the same tree. Each pairwise combining uses the two class numbers as input into a table that outputs the class number of the combination. Finally, the class number of the root of the tree is looked up in a table to yield the best-matching rule. Since each class has the same set of matching rules, it is easy to precompute the lowest-cost matching rule for the final classes. Note that the search process does not need to access the rule bitmaps, as is needed for the bit vector linear search scheme. The bitmaps are used only to *build* the structure.

Clearly, each pairwise combining step can take $O(N^2)$ memory because there can be N distinct field values in each field. However, the total memory falls very short of the N^K worst-case memory for real rule databases. To see why this might be the case, we return to the geometric view.

Using a survey of 8000 rule databases, Gupta and McKeown (1999a) observe that all databases studied have only $O(N)$ classification regions, instead of the N^K worst-case number of classification regions. It is not hard to see that when the number of classification regions is N^K, then the number of cross products in the equivalenced scheme and in the naive scheme is also N^K.

But when the number of classification regions is linear, equivalenced cross-producting can do better. However, it is possible to construct counterexamples where the number of classification regions is linear, but equivalenced cross-producting takes exponential memory. Despite such potentially pathological cases, the performance of RFC can be summarized as follows.

Assumption: There is a series of subspaces of the complete rule space (as embodied by nodes in the combining tree) that all have a linear number of classification regions. Note that this is stronger than *O4* and even *O5*. For example, if we combine two fields i and j first, we require that this intermediate two-dimensional subspace have a linear number of regions.

Performance: The memory required is $O(N^2) * T$, where T is the number of nodes in the combining tree. The sequential performance (in terms of time) is $O(T)$ memory accesses, but the time required in a parallel implementation can be $O(1)$ because the tree can be pipelined. Note that the $O(N^2)$ memory is still very large in practice and would preclude the use of SRAM-based solutions.

12.12 Decision tree approaches

This chapter ends with a description of a very simple scheme that performs well in practice, better even than RFC and comparable to or better than the extended grid of tries. This scheme was introduced by Woo (2000). A similar idea, with range tests replacing bit tests, was independently described by Gupta and McKeown (1999b).

The basic idea is extremely close to the simple set-pruning tries described in Section 12.5.1, with the addition of some important degrees of freedom. Recall that set-pruning tries work one field at a time; thus in Fig. 12.7, the algorithm tests *all* the bits for the destination address before testing *all* the bits for the source address. The extension to multiple fields in Decasper et al. (1998) similarly tests all the bits of one field before moving on to another field. The set-pruning trie can be seen as an instance of a general decision tree.

Clearly, an obvious degree of freedom (**P13**) not considered in set-pruning tries is to arbitrarily interleave the bit tests for all fields. Thus the root of the trie could test for (say) bit 15 of the source field; if the bit is 0, this could lead to a node that tests for, say, bit 22 of the port number field. Clearly, there is an exponential number of such decision trees. The schemes in Woo (2000) and Gupta and McKeown (1999b) build the final decision tree using *local optimization* decisions at each node to choose the next bit to test. A simple criterion used in Gupta and McKeown (1999b) is to balance storage and time.

A second important degree of freedom considered in Woo (2000) is to use multiple decision trees. For example, for examples such as Fig. 12.5, it may help to place all the rules with wildcards in the source field in one tree and the remainder in a second tree. While this can increase overall search time, it can greatly reduce storage.

A third degree of freedom exploited in both Woo (2000) and Gupta and McKeown (1999b) is to allow a small amount of linear searching after traversing the decision tree. This is similar to the common strategy of using an insert. Consider a decision tree with 10,000 leaves where each leaf is associated with one of four rules. While it may be possible to distinguish these four rules by lengthening the decision tree in height, this lengthened decision tree could add 40,000 extra nodes of storage.

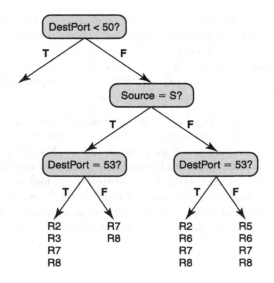

FIGURE 12.15

The HiCuts data structure is essentially a range tree that has pointers corresponding to some ranges of some dimension variable with linear search at the end.

Thus, in balancing storage with time, it may be better to settle for a small amount of linear searching (e.g., among one of four possible rules) at the end of tree search. Intuitively, this can help because the storage of a tree can increase exponentially with its height. Reducing the height by employing some linear search can greatly reduce storage.

The hierarchical cuttings (HiCuts) scheme described in Gupta and McKeown (1999b) is similar in spirit to that in Woo (2000) but uses range checks instead of bit tests at each node of the decision tree. Range checks are slightly more general than bit tests because a range check such as $10 < D < 35$ for a destination address D cannot be emulated by a bit test. A range test (cut) can be viewed geometrically in two dimensions as a line in either dimension that splits the space into half; in general, each range cut is a hyperplane.

In what follows, we describe HiCuts in more detail using an example. The HiCuts local optimization criterion works well when tested on real core router classifiers.

Fig. 12.15 shows a fragment of a HiCuts decision tree on the database of Fig. 12.2. The nodes contain range comparisons on values of any specified fields, and the edges are labeled **True** or **False**. Thus the root node tests whether the destination port field is less than 50. The fragment follows the case only when this test is false. Notice in Fig. 12.2 that this branch eliminates $R1$ (i.e., Rule 1) and $R4$, because these rules contain port numbers 25 and 23, respectively.

The next test checks whether the source address is equal to that of the secondary name server S in Fig. 12.2. If this test evaluates to true, then $R5$ is eliminated (because it contains TO), and so is $R6$ (because it contains Net and because S does not belong to the internal prefix Net). This leads to a second test on the destination port field. If the value is not 53, the only possible rules that can match are $R7$ and $R8$.

Thus on a packet header in which the destination port is 123 and the source is S, the search algorithm takes the right branch at the root, the left branch at the next node, and a right branch at the final node. At this point, the packet header is compared to rules $R7$ and $R8$ using linear search. Note that, unlike set pruning trees, the HiCuts decision tree of Fig. 12.15 uses ranges, interleaves the range checks between the destination port and source fields, and uses linear searching.

Of course, the real trick is to find a way to build an efficient decision tree that minimizes the worst-case height and yet has reasonable storage. Rather than consider the general optimization problem, which is NP-complete, HiCuts (Gupta and McKeown, 1999b) uses a more restricted heuristic based on the repeated application of the following greedy strategy.

- *Pick a field:* The HiCuts paper suggests first picking a field to cut on at each stage based on the number of distinct field values in that field. For example, in Fig. 12.15, this heuristic would pick the destination port field.
- *Pick the number of cuts:* For each field, rather than just pick one range check as in Fig. 12.15, one can pick k ranges or cuts. Of course, these can be implemented as separate range checks, as in Fig. 12.15. To choose k, the algorithm suggested in Gupta and McKeown (1999a) is to keep doubling k and to stop when the storage caused by the k cuts exceeds a prespecified threshold.

Several details are needed to actually implement this somewhat general framework. Assuming the cuts or ranges are equally spaced, the storage cost of k cuts on a field is estimated by counting the sum of the rules assigned to each of the k cuts. Clearly, cuts that cause rule replication will have a large storage estimate. The threshold that defines acceptable storage is a constant (called *spfac*, for space factor) times the number of rules at the node. The intent is to keep the storage linear in the number of rules up to a tunable constant factor.

Finally, the process stops when all decision tree leaves have no more than *binth* (bin threshold) rules. *binth* controls the amount of linear searching at the end of tree search.

The HiCuts paper (Gupta and McKeown, 1999b) mentions the use of the DAG optimization. A more novel optimization, described in Woo (2000) and Gupta and McKeown (1999b), is to eliminate a rule, R, that completely overlaps another rule, R', at a node but has a higher cost. There are also several further degrees of freedom (**P13**) left unexplored in Gupta and McKeown (1999b) and Woo (2000): unequal-size cuts at each node, more sophisticated strategies that pick more than field at a time, and linear searching at nodes other than the leaves.

HiCuts has inspired several follow-up papers that make improvements to the basic idea. First, in HyperCuts (Singh et al., 2004a) the decision tree approach is taken a step further by allowing the use of several cuts in a single step. If the cuts in each dimension are a power of two as well, lookup can be done in a single step via multidimensional array indexing. Once again this is an extra degree of freedom (**P13**) being exploited. Because each cut is now a general hypercube, the scheme is called *HyperCuts*. HyperCuts works significantly faster than HiCuts on many real databases (Singh et al., 2004a).

Finally, Efficuts (Vamanan et al., 2010) adds another degree of freedom by using what they call "equidense cuts": the cuts are not of equal size but instead distribute the child pointers evenly among cuts. They do this by selectively merging equal size cuts in HyperCuts to save memory. Of course, the tradeoff is that lookup is slightly slower because simple array indexing can no longer work. To further reduce redundancy in the data structure, EffiCuts exploits the degree of freedom first considered in Woo (2000) to create mutually exclusive sets of rules and creates multiple decision trees for each such set, with different heuristics to achieve a good trade-off between number of trees (lookup time) and storage (redundancy).

Using a publicly available benchmark of synthetic and other classifiers called ClassBench (Taylor and Turner, 2007), the authors show that for comparable performance EffiCuts needs 57 times less memory than HyperCuts and 4-8 times less power than a TCAM. The last experiment is notable because unlike earlier papers that informally claimed that algorithmic schemes used less power than TCAMs, this is one of the few papers to *quantify* the comparison using a hardware model called CACTI (Wilton and Jouppi, 1996) to model CAM and RAM. However, the benchmarks used (Taylor and Turner, 2007) are mostly synthetic ones; thus a more modern benchmark of real classifiers would be ideal to compare all these schemes.

HiCuts, HyperCuts, and Efficuts all use manually created heuristics to build decision trees – in other words, to decide how to partition rules among multiple trees and how to perform cuts at each node in a tree. A later paper, NeuroCuts (Liang et al., 2019), further advances the state-of-the-art in decision trees by using Reinforcement Learning. First, note that using a neural network for classification, is problematic because a neural classification network cannot guarantee correct results (the answers are correct only with high probability). Further, neural networks are resource intensive, making it hard to guarantee results in time to forward a packet. Instead, NeuroCuts uses deep Reinforcement Learning to *build* efficient decision tree, pushing the cost of the neural network to the time when new rules are added to the classifier.

Thus, while previous approaches attempt to heuristically meet performance objective (e.g., reduce storage), Reinforcement Learning explicitly maximizes the given performance objective. Fortunately, the learning time to evaluate a large number of models, which is one of main drawbacks of RL, is not very high for packet classification. Using synthetic workloads generated using ClassBench, the authors (Liang et al., 2019) show that NeuroCuts outperforms existing hand-tuned decisions in both classification time and memory footprint. More specifically, NeuroCuts improves median classification time by 18%, and reduces both time and memory usage by up to a factor of 3.

In conclusion, the decision tree approach described by (Woo, 2000), (Gupta and McKeown, 1999b), (Singh et al., 2004a), (Vamanan et al., 2010) and (Liang et al., 2019) is best viewed as a framework that encompasses a number of potential algorithms. However, experimental evidence (Singh et al., 2004a; Vamanan et al., 2010) shows that this approach works well in practice. The performance of this scheme can be summarized as follows.

Assumption: The scheme assumes there is a sufficient number of distinct fields to make reasonable cuts without much storage replication. This rather general observation needs to be sharpened.

Performance: The memory required can be kept to roughly linear in the number of rules using various heuristics. The tree can be of relatively small height if it is reasonably balanced. Search can easily be pipelined to allow $O(1)$ lookup times. Finally, the updates are likely to be slow if sophisticated heuristics are used to build the decision tree.

12.13 Hybrid algorithms

Based on the earlier descriptions of the various algorithms it should be clear that different algorithms (and even technlogies like CAMs) can do well for different databases. Thus it is natural to consider

Hybrid Schemes. For example, CAMs are fast but use a great deal of power and updates can be slow for rules with ranges. Can TCAMs be combined with algorithmic schemes to get some of the advantages of both schemes? We now sample a few of these ideas:

Combining TCAMs and Algorithmic Schemes: SmartPC (Ma and Banerjee, 2012) reduces the power consumption of TCAMs by pre-classifying a packet on two header fields, source and destination IP addresses. The packet is only sent to TCAM if there is a match, thus only a small portion of TCAM needs to be activated. The authors show that SmartPC reduces average power by about 90% on real and synthetic classifiers. SAX-PAC (Kogan et al., 2014) exploits order independence to reduce the cost (lookup time or memory) of adding additional range or prefix fields using a hybrid software and TCAM-based approach. The order independent rules are implemented in software using linear memory and logarithmic worst case lookup time, whereas the rest of the rules are in TCAM. The paper shows that on real-life classifiers from Cisco Systems, about 90% of rules are handled in software and only the remaining 10% of rules need to be stored in TCAM.

TreeCAM (Vamanan and Vijaykumar, 2011) is a hybrid decision tree and TCAM-based approach for improving the update complexity (not power) of decision trees without sacrificing lookup performance. TreeCAM employs two versions of decision trees: a coarse version with a few thousand rules per leaf achieves efficient lookups and a fine version with a few tens of rules per leaf reduces update effort. Note that many of the papers that combine TCAM and algorithmic schemes are quite feasible to implement with the advent of pipelined programmable hardware architectures like the Tofino-3 (Intel Corporation, 2022) that have stages that contain both RAM and CAM.

Other combinations: HybridCuts (Li and Li, 2013) uses a combination of decomposition and decision-tree techniques to improve both storage and performance. HybridCuts uses memory comparable to EffiCuts, but outperforms EffiCuts in terms of memory accesses without the added lookup complexity in each node. Finally, CutTSS (Li et al., 2020) combines the good update performance of tuple space search with the quick lookup time of Decision Trees. The CutTSS paper (Li et al., 2020) also has pointers to other more recent papers in packet classification.

12.14 Conclusions

This chapter describes several algorithms for packet classification at gigabit speeds. The grid of tries provides a two-dimensional classification algorithm that is fast and scalable. All the remaining schemes require exploiting some assumptions about real rule databases to avoid the geometric lower bound. While much progress has been made, it is important to reduce the number of such assumptions required for classification and to validate these assumptions extensively.

At the time of writing, decision tree approaches (Woo, 2000; Gupta and McKeown, 1999b; Singh et al., 2004a; Vamanan et al., 2010) and the extended grid of tries method (Singh et al., 2004b) appear to be the most attractive algorithmic schemes for hardware. While the latter depends on each packet's matching only a small number of source–destination prefixes, it is still difficult to characterize what assumptions or parameters influence the performance of decision tree approaches. For software settings, Tuple Space Search (Srinivasan et al., 1998) is attractive, especially when fast updates are required. Caching and early stopping can be used to improve average lookup times (Pfaff et al., 2015).

Of the other general schemes, the bit vector scheme is suitable for hardware implementation for a modest number of rules (say, up to 10,000). Equivalenced cross-producting seems to scale to roughly the same number of rules as the Lucent scheme but perhaps can be improved to lower its memory consumption.

The author and his students have placed code for many of the algorithms described in this chapter on a publicly available Web site (Singh et al., 2004a). Packet classification has stagnated because of the lack of standard comparisons and freely available code. Readers are encouraged to experiment with and contribute to this code base.

Although the schemes described in this chapter require some algorithmic thinking, they make heavy use of the other principles we have stressed. The two-dimensional scheme makes heavy use of precomputation; the Lucent scheme uses memory locality to turn what is essentially linear search into a fast scheme for moderate rule sizes; all the other schemes rely on some expected-case assumption about the structure of rules, such as the lack of general ranges and the small number of classification regions. Table 12.1 summarizes the schemes and the principles used in them.

Because the best-matching prefix is a special case of the lowest-cost matching rule, it is not surprising that rule search schemes are generalizations of prefix search schemes. Thus, the grid of tries and set-pruning tries generalize trie schemes for prefix matching. Multidimensional range-matching schemes generalize prefix-matching schemes based on range matching. Tuple search generalizes binary search on hash tables. While cross-producting is not a generalization of an existing prefix-matching scheme, it can also be specialized for prefix lookups.

The high-level message of this chapter is as follows. Applications such as QoS routing, firewalls, virtual private networks, and DiffServ require a more flexible form of forwarding based on multiple header fields. The techniques in this chapter indicate that such forwarding flexibility can go together with high performance using algorithmic solutions without relying on ternary CAMs.

Returning to the quote at the start of this chapter, it should be easy to see how packet classification gets its name if the word *definition* is replaced with *rule*. Notice that classification in the sciences also encompasses overlapping definitions: Men belong to both the mammal and *Homo sapiens* categories. However, it is hard to imagine a biological analog of the concept of a lowest-cost matching rule, or the requirement to classify species several million times a second!

12.15 Exercises

1. **Range to Prefix Mappings:** CAMs require the use of prefix ranges, but many rules use general ranges. Describe an algorithm that converts an arbitrary range on, say, 16-bit port number fields to a logarithmic number of prefix ranges. Describe the prefix ranges produced by the arbitrary but common range of greater than 1024. Given a rule R with arbitrary range specifications on port numbers, what is the worst-case number of CAM entries required to represent R? Solutions to this problem are discussed in Srinivasan et al. (1998, 1999).

2. **Worst-Case Storage for Set-Pruning Tries:** Generalize the example of Fig. 12.5 to K fields to show that storage in set-pruning-trie approaches can be as bad as $O(N^k/k)$.

3. **Improvements to the Grid of Tries:** In the grid of tries, the only role played by the destination trie is in determining the longest-matching destination prefix. Show how to use other lookup techniques to obtain a total search time of $(\log W + W)$ for the destination–source rules instead of $2W$.

4. **Reasoning about the Correctness of the Grid of Tries:** Given any source and destination IP address pair (o, d), let S be the set of nodes (destination-source rules) that (o, d) matches with. A

node α in S is called a *skyline point* if there is no other node (rule) in S whose source and destination prefixes are both no shorter than those of node α. Now solve the following two subproblems. First, prove that the grid of tries algorithm guarantees to traverse all skyline points in S. Second, explain why this guarantee, in combination with the pre-computation of the stored rule for each node, is sufficient to guarantee the correctness of the grid of tries algorithm.

5. **Aggregate Bit Vector Search:** Use 3-bit summaries in Fig. 12.11 and determine the improvement in the worst-case time by adding summaries, and compare it to the increase in storage for using summaries. Details of the algorithm, if needed, can be found in Baboescu and Varghese (2001).

6. **Aggregate Bit Vector Storage:** The use of summary bits appears to increase storage. Show, however, a simple modification in which the use of aggregates can reduce storage if the bit vectors contain large strings of zeroes. Describe the modifications to the search process to achieve this compression. Does it slow down search?

7. **On-Demand Cross-Producting:** Consider the database of Fig. 12.2, and imagine a series of Web accesses from an internal site to the external network. Suppose the external destinations accessed are $D_1, \ldots, D_M$. How many cache terms will these headers produce in the case of full header caching versus on-demand cross-producting?

8. **Equivalenced Cross-Producting:** Why do the fifth and eighth entries in Fig. 12.13 have the same bitmaps? Check your answer two ways, first by intersecting the corresponding bitmaps for the two fields from Fig. 12.11 and then by arguing directly that they match the same set of rules.

9. **Combining Trees for RFC:** The equivalenced cross-producting idea in RFC leaves unspecified how to choose a combining tree. One technique is to compute all possible combining trees and then to pick the tree with the smallest storage. Describe an algorithm based on dynamic programming to find the optimal tree. Compare the running times of the two algorithms.

10. **Reducing Rule Databases Using Redundancy:** If a smaller prefix has the same next hop as a longer prefix, the longer prefix can be removed from an IP lookup table. Find similar techniques to spot redundancies in classifiers. Compare your ideas with the techniques described in Gupta and McKeown (1999a). Note that as in the case of IP lookups, such techniques to remove redundancy are orthogonal to the classification scheme chosen and can be implemented in a separate preprocessing step.

11. **Generalizing Linear Searching in HiCuts:** In HiCuts, all the linear lists are at the leaves. However, a rule with all wildcarded entries will be replicated at all leaves. This suggests that such rules be placed once in a linear list at the *root* of the HiCuts tree. Generalizing, one could place linear lists at any node to reduce storage. Describe a bottom-up algorithm that starts with the base HiCuts decision tree and then hoists rules to nodes higher up in the tree to reduce storage. Try to do so with minimal impact on the search time.

Switching

I'd rather fight than switch.
—**Tareyton Cigarettes ad, quoted by *Bartlett's***

In the early years of telephones the telephone operator helped knit together the social fabric of a community. If John wanted to talk to Martha, John would call the operator and ask for Martha; the operator would then manually plug a wire into a patch panel that connected John's telephone to Martha's. The switchboard, of course, allowed *parallel* connections between disjoint pairs. James could talk to Mary at the same time that John and Martha conversed. However, each new call could be delayed for a brief period while the operator finished putting through the previous call.

When transistors were invented at Bell Labs, the fact that each transistor was basically a voltage-controlled switch was immediately exploited to manufacture all-electronic telephone switches using an array of transistors. The telephone operator was then relegated to functions that required human intervention, such as making collect calls. The use of electronics greatly increased the speed and reliability of telephone switches.

A router is basically an automated post office for packets. Recall that we are using the word *router* in a generic sense to refer to a general interconnection device, such as a gateway or a SAN switch. Returning to the familiar model of a router in Fig. 13.1, recall that in essence a router is a box that switches packets from input links to output links. The lookup process (**B1** in Fig. 13.1) that determines which output link a packet will be switched to was described in Chapter 11. The packet scheduling done at the outbound link (**B3** in Fig. 13.1) is described in Chapter 14. However, the guts of a router remain its internal switching system (**B2** in Fig. 13.1), which is discussed in this chapter.

This chapter is organized as follows. Section 13.1 compares router switches to telephone switches. Section 13.2 details the simplicity and limitations of a shared memory switch. Section 13.3 describes router evolution, from shared buses to crossbars. Section 13.4 presents a simple matching algorithm for a crossbar scheduler that was used in DEC's first GigaSwitch product. Section 13.5 describes a fundamental problem with DEC's first GigaSwitch and other input-queued switches, called *head-of-line (HOL) blocking*, which occurs when packets waiting for a busy output delay packets waiting for idle outputs. Section 13.6 covers the knockout switch, which avoids HOL blocking, at the cost of some complexity, by queuing packets at the output.

Section 13.7 introduces the now standard solution approach to HOL blocking called virtual output queueing (VOQ). The VOQ approach however leads to the problem of computing bipartite matchings, introduced in Section 13.8, which is much more sophisticated and challenging than that in the case of GigaSwitch. Section 13.9 presents the first such bipartite matching algorithm called PIM. PIM is a randomized algorithm that retains the simplicity of input queuing; this scheme was deployed in DEC's second GigaSwitch product. Section 13.10 describes iSLIP, a scheme that appears to emulate PIM, but

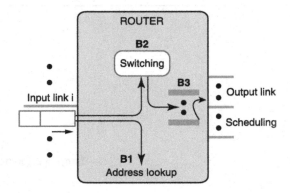

FIGURE 13.1

Router model.

without the use of randomization. iSLIP is found in a number of router products, including the Cisco GSR.

Neither PIM nor its derandomized version iSLIP can achieve close to 100% throughput under all traffic patterns. In addition, if implemented as a centralized algorithm, both PIM and its derandomized version iSLIP have a fairly high time complexity of $O(N \log^2 N)$, where N is the number of input and output ports. Section 13.11 introduces an incremental learning-based approach to computing bipartite matchings, which is taken by the four algorithms we describe next: sample-and-compare SERENA, QPS, and Sliding-Window QPS (SW-QPS). Section 13.12 describes an extremely simple centralized algorithm, called sample-and-compare, that can provably achieve 100% throughput and has a lower time complexity of $O(N)$. Its delay performance under heavy loads, however, is poor. Section 13.13 describes an improved algorithm called SERENA that, like sample-and-compare, also can achieve 100% throughput and has $O(N)$ time complexity, but has much better delay performance under heavy loads than sample-and-compare. SERENA is only a slight modification of sample-and-compare that replaces the "compare" operation with a "merge" operation. Section 13.14 introduces a new sampling strategy called queue-proportional sampling (QPS), that, if used to replace the "sample" operation in SERENA or to generate a starter matching for iSLIP, can further improve their delay performances. Using QPS, an input port can, in $O(1)$ time, sample and propose to match with an output port, with a probability that is proportional to the number of packets (currently in the queue of the input port) destined for that output port. The data structure that enables this $O(1)$ time complexity is described in Section 13.15. The pursuit for better monolithic bipartite matching algorithms culminates in a late-breaking parallel iterative algorithm called sliding-window QPS (SW-QPS), to be described in Section 13.16, that achieves overall better throughput and delay performances than iLSIP, yet has only a $O(1)$ time complexity per input or output port. Finally, in Section 13.17, we describe the Combined Input and Output Queueing (CIOQ) proposal that advocates combining switching with packet scheduling for providing QoS guarantees.

As various hurdles exist for existing monolithic switching schemes to scale to a large number of ports, Section 13.18 describes two approaches to that end. Each achieves the scalability objective by reducing a different switching cost. One reduces the overall size of the switch circuitry through the use of more space-efficient switch fabrics than a monolithic crossbar, such as the Clos and the Benes fabrics. The other, called load-balanced switching (LBS), reduces the algorithmic cost of matching computation to virtually zero, as it requires no such computation at all. However, it does so by using two crossbars instead of one.

Section 13.19 shows how to scale switches to faster link speeds by using bit-slice parallelism and by using shorter fabric links as implemented in the Avici TSR.

The literature on switching is vast, and this chapter can hardly claim to be representative. In the first edition, this section mostly covers switch designs that had been built, analyzed in the literature, and actually used in the networking industry. They include DEC's GigaSwitch, Cisco's GSR, Juniper's T-series, and Avici's TSR. In this edition, we have added several new switching schemes that emerged after the early 2000s, such as SERENA, QPS, SW-QPS, and the LBS algorithms. With these updates, we believe this section now strikes a better balance between the practical and the theoretical issues that arise in designing switch fabrics for high-speed routers.

The switching techniques described in this chapter (and the corresponding principles invoked) are summarized in Table 13.1.

Quick reference guide

Many of the switching algorithms described in this chapter have actually been built. However, for an implementor doing a quick first reading, we suggest first reviewing the iSLIP algorithm, which is implemented in the Cisco GSR (Section 13.10). While iSLIP works very well for moderate-sized switch fabrics, Section 13.18 describes solutions that scale to large switches, including the Clos fabric used by Juniper Networks. Sections 13.14 through 13.16 describe a mind-blowing new technology, called Queue-Propotional Sampling (QPS) and Sliding-Window QPS (SW-QPS), that will make us rethink how switching should be implemented in the future.

13.1 Router versus telephone switches

Given our initial analogy to telephone switches, it is worthwhile outlining the major similarities and differences between telephone and router switches. Early routers used a simple bus to connect input and output links. A bus (Chapter 2) is a wire that allows only one input to send to one output at a time. Today, however, almost every core router uses an internal crossbar that allows disjoint link pairs to communicate in parallel, to increase effective throughput. Once again, the electronics plays the role of the operator, activating transistor switches that connect input links to output links.

In telephony a phone connection typically lasts for seconds if not for minutes. However, in Internet switches each connection lasts for the duration of a single packet. This is 8 nanoseconds for a 40-byte packet at 40 Gbps. Recall that caches cannot be relied upon to finesse lookups because of the rarity of large trains of packets to the same destination. Similarly, it is unlikely that two consecutive packets at a switch input port are destined to the same output port. This makes it hard to amortize the switching overhead over multiple packets.

Thus to operate at wire speed, the switching system must decide (i.e., compute) which input and output links should be matched in a minimum packet arrival time. This makes the control portion of an Internet switch (that sets up connections) much harder to build than a telephone switch. To simplify the

Table 13.1 Principles used in the various switches studied in this chapter.

Number	Principle	Switch
P5b	Widen memory access for bandwidths	Datapath
P13	Distribute queue control via tickets	GigaSwitch
P5a	Schedule outputs and hunt groups in parallel	
P11	Optimize for at most $k < N$ output contention	Knockout
P15	Use tree of randomized concentrators for fairness	
P3	Relax output buffer specification	
P13	Use per-output input queues	AN-2
P14	N^2 communication feasible for small N	
P15	Use randomized iterative matching	
P14	PPEs for round-robin fairness feasible for small N	iSLIP
P3	Relax specification of grant-accept dependency	
P3a	Trade certainty for time	Sample-and-compare
P12a	Compute matching incrementally from the recently used matching	SERENA
P14	Use bitmaps	FFA in SW-QPS
P15	Use a three-stage Clos network to reduce costs	Juniper T640
P3b	Randomize load distribution to reduce k from $2n$ to n	
P15	Use a $(\log N)$-stage Benes network to reduce costs	Growth fabric
P3a	Use fast randomized routing scheme	
P15	Use a copy-twice multicast and binary tree	
P13	Lay out grid using short wires	Avici TSR

problem, most routers internally segment variable-sized packets into fixed-sized cells before sending to the switch fabric. Mathematically, the switching component of a router reduces to solving a bipartite matching problem: the router must match, in a fixed cell arrival time (time slot), input links with output links to the maximum extent, the precise meaning of which will be elaborated in Section 13.8. While "good" algorithms for bipartite matching are well known to run in milliseconds, solving the same problem every 8 nanoseconds at 40 Gbps requires some systems thinking.

For example, the solutions described in this chapter will trade accuracy for time (**P3b**), use hardware parallelism (**P5**) and randomization (**P3a**), and exploit the fact that typical switches have 32–64 ports to build fast priority queue operations using bitmaps (**P14**).

13.2 Shared-memory switches

Before describing bus- and crossbar-based switches, it is helpful to consider one of the simplest switch implementations, based on shared memory. Packets are read into a memory from the input links and read out of memory to the appropriate output links. Such designs have been used as part of time slot interchange switches in telephony for years. They also work well for networking for small switches.

The main problem is memory bandwidth. If the chip takes in eight input links and has eight output links, the chip must read and write each packet or cell once. Thus the memory has to run at 16 times the speed of each link. Up to a point, this can be solved by using a wide memory-access width. The idea is that the bits come in serially on an input link and are accumulated into an input shift register. When a whole cell has been accumulated, the cell can be loaded into the cell-wide memory. Later they can be read out into the output shift register of the corresponding link and be shifted out onto the output link.

The Datapath switch design (Kanakia, 1999; Keshav, 1997) uses a central memory of 4K cells, which clearly does not provide adequate buffering. However, this memory can easily be implemented on-chip and augmented using flow control and off-chip packet buffers. Unfortunately, shared-memory designs such as this do not scale beyond cell-wide memories because minimum-size packets can be at most one cell in size. A switch that gets several minimum-size packets to different destinations can pack several such packets in a single word, but it cannot rely on reading them out at the same time.

Despite this, shared-memory switches can be quite simple for small numbers of ports. A great advantage of shared-memory switches is that they can be memory and power optimal because data is moved in and out of memory only once. Fabric- or crossbar-based switches, which are described in the remainder of this chapter, almost invariably require buffering packets *twice*, potentially doubling memory costs and power costs. It may even be possible to extend the shared-memory idea to larger switches via the randomized DRAM interleaving ideas described in Section 13.19.3.

13.3 Router history: from buses to crossbars

Router switches have evolved from the simplest shared-medium (bus or memory) switches, shown in part A of Fig. 13.2, to the more modern crossbar switches, shown in part D of Fig. 13.2. A line card in a router or switch contains the interface logic for a data link, such as a fiber-optic line or an Ethernet. The earliest switches connected all the line cards internally via a high-speed bus (analogous to an internal local area network) on which only one pair of line cards can communicate at a time. Thus if Line Card 1 is sending a packet to Line Card 2, no other pair of line cards can communicate.

What is worse, in more ancient routers and switches, the forwarding decision was relegated to a shared, general-purpose CPU. General-purpose CPUs allow for simpler and easily changeable forwarding software. However, general-purpose CPUs were often slow because of the extra levels of interpretation of general-purpose instructions. They also lacked the ability to control real-time constraints on packet processing because of nondeterminism due to mechanisms such as caches. Note also that each packet traverses the bus twice, once to go to the CPU and once to go from the CPU to the destination. This is because the CPU is on a separate card reachable only via the bus.

Because the CPU was a bottleneck, a natural extension was the addition of a group of shared CPUs for forwarding, any of which can forward a packet. For example, one CPU can forward packets from Line Cards 1 through 3, the second from Line Cards 4 through 6, and so on. This increases the overall throughput or reduces the performance requirement on each individual CPU, potentially leading to a lower-cost design. However, without care it can lead to packet misordering, which is undesirable.

Despite this, the bus remains a bottleneck. A single shared bus has speed limitations because of the number of different sources and destinations that a single shared bus has to handle. These sources and destinations add extra electrical loading that slows down signal rise times and ultimately the speed of

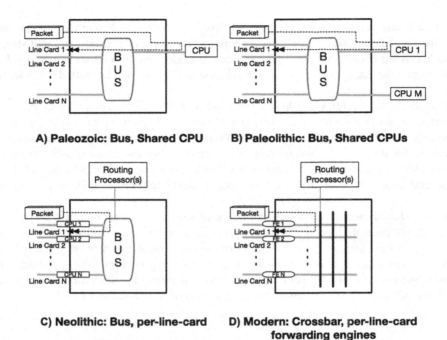

A) Paleozoic: Bus, Shared CPU   **B) Paleolithic: Bus, Shared CPUs**

C) Neolithic: Bus, per-line-card   **D) Modern: Crossbar, per-line-card forwarding engines**

FIGURE 13.2

Evolution of network switches, from shared-bus switches with a shared CPU to crossbar switches with a dedicated forwarding engine per line card.

sending bits on the bus. Other electrical effects include those caused by multiple connectors (from each line card) and reflections on the line (McKeown, 1997).

The classical way to get around this bottleneck is to use a crossbar switch, as shown in Fig. 13.2(D). A crossbar switch essentially has a set of $2N$ parallel buses, one bus per source line card and one bus per destination line card. If one thinks of the source buses as being horizontal and the destination buses as being vertical, the matrix of buses forms what is called a *crossbar*.

Potentially, this provides an N-fold speedup over a single bus because, in the best case, all N buses will be used in parallel at the same time to transfer data, instead of a single bus. Of course, to get this speedup requires finding N disjoint source–destination pairs at each time slot. Trying to get close to this bound is the major scheduling problem studied in this chapter.

Although they do not necessarily go together, another design change that accompanied crossbar switches designed between 1995 and 2002 is the use of special-purpose integrated circuits (ASICs) as forwarding engines instead of general-purpose CPUs. These forwarding engines are typically faster (because they are designed specifically to process Internet packets) and cheaper than general-purpose CPUs. Two disadvantages of such forwarding engines include design costs for each such ASIC and the lack of programmability (which makes changes in the field difficult or impossible). These problems have again led to proposals for faster, but yet programmable, network processors (see Chapter 2).

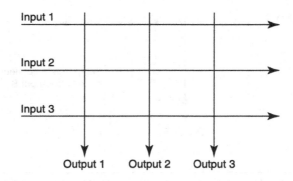

FIGURE 13.3

Basic crossbar switch.

13.4 The take-a-ticket crossbar scheduler

The simplest crossbar is an array of N input buses and N output buses, as shown in Fig. 13.3. Thus if line card R wishes to send data to line card S, input bus R must be connected to output bus S. The simplest way to make this connection is via a "pass" transistor, as shown in Fig. 13.4. For every pair of input and output buses, such as R and S, there is a transistor that when turned on connects the two buses. Such a connection is known as a *crosspoint*. Notice that a crossbar with N inputs and N outputs has N^2 crosspoints, each of which needs a control line from the scheduler to turn it on or off.

While N^2 crosspoints seem large, easy VLSI implementation via transistors makes pin counts, card connector technologies, etc., still more limiting factors in building large switches. Thus most routers and switches built before 2002 use simple crossbar-switch backplanes to support 16–32 ports. Notice that multicast is trivially achieved by connecting input bus R to all the output buses that wish to receive from R. However, scheduling multicast is tricky.

In practice, only older crossbar designs use pass transistors. This is because the overall capacitance (Chapter 2) grows very large as the number of ports increases. This in turn increases the delay to send a signal, which becomes an issue at higher speeds. Modern implementations often use large multiplexer trees per output or tristate buffers (Alleyne, 2002; Turner, 2002). Higher-performance systems even pipeline the data flowing through the crossbar using some memory (i.e., a gate) at the crosspoints.

Thus the design of a modern crossbar switch is actually quite tricky and requires careful attention to physical-layer considerations. However, crossbar-design issues will be ignored in this chapter to concentrate on the algorithmic issues related to switch scheduling. But, what should scheduling guarantee?

For correctness, the control logic must ensure that every output bus is connected to at most one input bus (to prevent inputs from mixing). However, for performance, the logic must also maximize the number of line-card pairs that communicate in parallel. While the ideal parallelism is achieved if all N output buses are busy at the same time, in practice parallelism is limited by two factors. First, there may be no data for certain output line cards. Second, two or more input line cards may wish to send data to the same output line card. Since only one input can win at a time, this limits data throughput if the other "losing" input cannot send data.

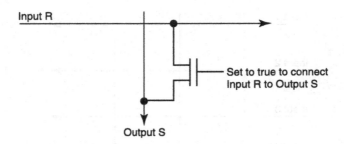

Input R

Set to true to connect
Input R to Output S

Output S

FIGURE 13.4

Connecting input from Line Card R to Line Card S by turning the pass transistor connecting the two buses. Modern crossbars replace this simplistic design by multiplexer trees to reduce capacitance.

Thus despite extensive parallelism, the major contention occurs at the output port. How can contention for output ports be resolved while maximizing parallelism? A simple and elegant scheduling scheme for this purpose was first invented and used in DEC's GigaSwitch. An example of the operation of the so-called "take-a-ticket" algorithm (Souza et al., 1994) used there is given in Fig. 13.5.

The basic idea is that each output line card S essentially maintains a distributed queue for all input line cards R waiting to send to S. The queue for S is actually stored at the input line card itself (instead of being at S) using a simple ticket number mechanism like that at some deli counters. If line card R wants to send a packet to line card S, it first makes a request over a separate control bus to S; S then provides a queue number back to R over the control bus. The queue number is the number of R's position in the output queue for S.

R then monitors the control bus; whenever S finishes accepting a new packet, S sends the current queue number it is serving on the control bus. When R notices that its number is being "served," R places its packet on the input data bus for R. At the same time, S ensures that the R–S crosspoint is turned on.

To see this algorithm in action, consider Fig. 13.5, where, on the top frame, input line card A has three packets destined to outputs 1, 2, and 3, respectively. B has three similar packets destined for the same outputs, while C has packets destined for outputs 1, 3, and 4. Assume the packets have the same size in this example (though this is not necessary for the take-a-ticket algorithm to work).

Each input port works only on the packet at the head of its queue. Thus the algorithm begins with each input sending a request, via a control bus, to the output port for which the packet at the head of its input queue is destined. Thus in the example each input sends a request to output port 1 for permission to send a packet.

In general, a ticket number is a small integer that wraps around and is given out in order of arrival, as in a deli. In this case assume that A's request arrived first on the serial control bus, followed by B, followed by C, though the top left diagram makes it appear that the requests are sent concurrently. Since output port 1 can service only one packet at a time, it serializes the requests, returning $T1$ to A, $T2$ to B, and $T3$ to C.

Thus in the middle diagram of the top row, output port 1 also broadcasts the current ticket number it is serving ($T1$) on another control bus. When A sees it has a matching number for input 1, in the diagram on the top right, A then connects its input bus to the output bus of 1 and sends its packet on

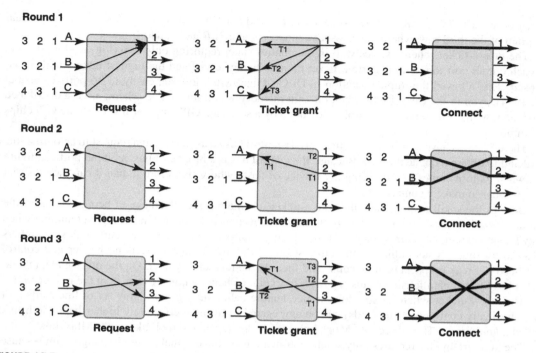

FIGURE 13.5

In the take-a-ticket scheduling mechanism all input ports have a *single* input queue that is labeled with the output port number for which each packet is destined. Thus on the top frame, inputs *A*, *B*, and *C* send requests to output port 1. Output port 1 (top, middle) gives the first number to *A*, the second to *B*, etc., and these numbers are used to serialize access to output ports.

its input bus. Thus by the end of the topmost row of diagrams, *A* has sent the packet at the head of its input queue to output port 1. Unfortunately, all the other input ports, *B* and *C*, are stuck waiting to get a matching ticket number from output port 1.

The second row in Fig. 13.5 starts with *A* sending a request for the packet that is now at the head of its queue to output port 2; *A* is returned a ticket number, *T*1, for port 2.[1] In the middle diagram of the second row port 1 announces that it is ready for *T*2, and port 2 announces it is ready for ticket *T*1. This result is in the rightmost diagram of the second row, where *A* is connected to port 2 and *B* is connected to port 1, and the corresponding packets are transferred.

The third row of diagrams in Fig. 13.5 starts similarly with *A* and *B* sending a request for ports 3 and 2, respectively. Note that poor *C* is still stuck waiting for its ticket number, *T*3, which it obtained two iterations ago, to be announced by output port 1. Thus *C* makes no more requests until the packet at the head of its queue is served. *A* is returned *T*1 for port 3, and *B* is returned *T*2 for port 2. Then

---

[1] Although not shown in the pictures, a ticket should really be considered a pair of numbers, a ticket number and the output port number, so the same ticket number used at different output ports should cause no confusion at input ports.

port 1 broadcasts $T3$ (finally!), port 2 broadcasts $T2$, and port 3 broadcasts $T1$. This results in the final diagram of the third row, where the crossbar connects A and 3, B and 2, and C and 1.

The take-a-ticket scheme scales well in the control state, requiring only two ($\log_2 N$)-bit counters at each output port to store the current ticket number being served and the highest ticket number dispensed. This allowed the implementation in DEC's GigaSwitch to scale easily to 36 ports (Souza et al., 1994), even in the early 1990s when on-chip memory was limited. The scheme used a distributed scheduler, with each output port's arbitration done by a so-called GPI chip per line card; the GPI chips communicate via a control bus.

The GPI chips have to arbitrate for the (serial) control bus so as to present a request to an output line card and to obtain a queue number. Because the control bus is a broadcast bus, an input port can figure out when its turn comes by observing the service of those who were before it, and it can then instruct the crossbar to make a connection.

Besides the small control state, the take-a-ticket scheme has the advantage of being able to handle variable-sized packets directly. Output ports can asynchronously broadcast the next ticket number when they finish receiving the current packet; different output ports can broadcast their current ticket numbers at arbitrary times. Thus unlike all the other schemes described later, there is no header and control overhead to break up packets into "cells" and then do the reassembly later. On the other hand, take-a-ticket has limited parallelism because of *HOL blocking*, a phenomenon we look at in the next section.

The take-a-ticket scheme also allows a nice feature called *hunt groups*. Any set of line cards (not just physically contiguous line cards) can be aggregated to form an effectively higher-bandwidth link called a *hunt group*. Thus three 100-Mbps links can be aggregated to look like a 300-Mbps link.

The hunt group idea requires only small modifications to the original scheduling algorithm because each of the GPI chips in the group can observe each other's messages on the control bus and thus keep local copies of the (common) ticket number consistent. The next packet destined for the group is served by the first free output port in the hunt group, much as in a delicatessen with multiple servers. While basic hunt groups can cause reordering of packets sent to different links, a small modification allows packets from one input to be sent to only one output port in a hunt group via a simple deterministic hash. This modification avoids reordering, at the cost of reduced parallelism.

Since the GigaSwitch was a bridge, it had to handle LAN multicast. Because the take-a-ticket scheduling mechanism uses distributed scheduling via separate GPI chips per output, it is hard to coordinate all schedulers to ensure that every output port is free. Furthermore, waiting for all ports to have a free ticket for a multicast packet would result in blocking some ports that were ready to service the packet early, wasting throughput. Hence, multicast was handled by a central processor in software and was thus accorded "second-class" status.

13.5 Head-of-line blocking

Forgetting about the internal mechanics of Fig. 13.5, observe that there were nine potential transmission opportunities in three iterations (three input ports and three iterations), but, after the connection depicted in the diagram at the bottom right, there is one packet in B's queue and two in C's queue. Thus only six of potentially nine packets have been sent, thereby taking limited advantage of parallelism.

This focus on only input–output behavior is sketched in Fig. 13.6. The figure shows the packets sent in each packet time at each output port. Each output port has an associated timeline labeled with the

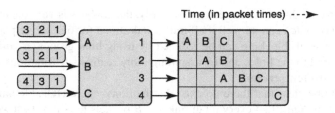

FIGURE 13.6

Example of HOL blocking caused by schemes like take-a-ticket. For each output port, a horizontal time scale is drawn labeled with the input port that sent a packet to that output port during the corresponding time period or a blank mark if there is none. Note the large number of blanks, showing potentially wasted opportunities that limit parallelism.

input port that sent a packet during the corresponding time period, with a blank if there is none. Note also that this picture continues the example started in Fig. 13.5 for three more iterations, until all input queues are empty.

It is easy to see from the righthand diagram in Fig. 13.6 that only roughly half of the transmission opportunities (more precisely, 9 out of 24) are used. Now, of course, no algorithm can do better for certain scenarios. However, other algorithms, such as iSLIP (see Fig. 13.10 in Section 13.10) can extract more parallel opportunities and finish the same nine packets in four iterations instead of six.

In the first iteration of Fig. 13.6 all inputs have packets waiting for output 1. Since only one (i.e., A) can send a packet to output 1 at a time, the entire queue at B (and C) is stuck waiting for A to complete. Since the entire queue is held hostage by the progress of the head of the queue, or line, this is called *head-of-line* blocking. iSLIP and PIM get around this limitation by allowing packets behind a blocked packet to make progress (for example, the packet destined for output port 2 in the input queue at B can be sent to output port 2 in iteration 1 of Fig. 13.6) at the cost of a more complex scheduling algorithm.

The loss of throughput caused by HOL blocking can be analytically captured using a simple uniform-traffic model. Assume that the head of each input queue has a packet destined for each of N outputs with probability $1/N$. Thus if two or more input ports send to the same output port, all but one input are blocked. The entire throughput of the other inputs is "lost" due to HOL blocking.

More precisely, assume equal-sized packets and one initial trial where a random process draws a destination port at each input port uniformly from 1 to N. Instead of focusing on input ports, let us focus on the probability that an output port O is idle. This is simply the probability that *none* of the N input ports chooses O. Since each input port does not choose O with probability $1 - 1/N$, the probability that all N of them will not choose O is $(1 - 1/N)^N$. This expression rapidly converges to $1/e$. Thus the probability that O is busy is $1 - 1/e$, which is 0.63. Thus the throughput of the switch is not $N * B$, which is what it could be ideally if all N output links are busy operating at B bits per second. Instead, it is 63% of this maximum value because 37% of the links are idle.

This analysis is simplistic and (incorrectly) assumes that each iteration is independent. In reality packets picked in one iteration that are not sent must be attempted in the next iteration (without another random coin toss to select the destination). A classic analysis (Karol et al., 1987) that removes the independent-trials assumption shows that the actual utilization is slightly worse and is closer to 58.6%.

But, are uniform-traffic distributions realistic? Clearly, the analysis is very dependent on the traffic distribution because no switch can do well if all traffic is destined for one server port. Simple analyses show that the effect of HOL blocking can be reduced by using hunt groups, by using speedup in the crossbar fabric compared to the links, and by assuming more realistic distributions in which a number of clients send traffic to a few servers.

However, it should be clear that there do exist distributions where HOL blocking can cause great damage to throughput. Imagine that every input link has B packets to port 1, followed by B packets to port 2, and so on, and finally B packets to port N. The same distribution of input packets is present in all input ports. Thus, clearly, when scheduling the group of initial packets to port 1, essentially HOL blocking will limit the switch to sending only one packet per input each time. Thus the switch reduces to $1/N$ of its possible throughput if B is large enough. On the other hand, we will see that switches that use VOQs (defined later in this chapter) can, in the same situations, achieve nearly 100% throughput. This is because in such schemes, each block of B packets stays in separate queues at each input.

13.6 Avoiding HOL blocking via output queuing

When HOL blocking was discovered, there was a slew of papers that proposed *output* queuing in place of *input* queuing to avoid HOL blocking. Suppose that packets can somehow be sent to an output port without any queuing at the input. Then, it is impossible for packet P destined for a busy output port to block another packet behind it. This is because packet P is sent off to the queue at the output port, where it can only block packets sent to the same output port.

The simplest way to do this would be to run the fabric N times faster than the input links. Then, even if all N inputs send to the same output in a given time slot, all N cells can be sent through the fabric to be queued at the output. Thus pure output queuing requires an N-fold speedup within the fabric. This can be expensive or infeasible.

A practical implementation of output queuing was provided by the knockout-switch design (Yeh et al., 1987). Suppose that receiving N cells to the same destination in any time slot is rare and that the expected number is k, which is much smaller than N. Then, the expected case can be optimized (**P11**) by designing the fabric links to run k times as fast as an input link, instead of N. This is a big savings within the fabric. It can be realized with hardware parallelism (**P5**) by using k parallel buses.

Unlike the take-a-ticket scheme, all the remaining schemes in this chapter, including the knockout scheme, rely on breaking up packets into fixed-sized cells. For the rest of the chapter, cells will be used in place of packets, always understanding that there must be an initial stage where packets are broken into cells and then reassembled at the output port.

Besides a faster switch, the knockout scheme needs an output queue that accepts cells k times faster than the speed of the output link. A naive design that uses this simple specification can be built using a fast FIFO but would be expensive. Also, the faster FIFO is overkill because clearly the buffer cannot sustain a long-term imbalance between its input and output speeds. Thus the buffer specification can be relaxed (**P3**) to allow it to handle only short periods, in which cells arrive k times as fast as they are being taken out. This can be handled by memory interleaving and k parallel memories. A distributor (that does run k times as fast) sprays arriving cells into k memories in round-robin order, and departing cells are read out in the same order.

Finally, the design has to fairly handle the case where the expected case is violated and $N > k$ cells get sent to the same output at the same time. The easiest way to understand the general solution is first to understand three simpler cases.

Two contenders, one winner: In the simplest case of $k = 1$ and $N = 2$ the arbiter must choose one cell fairly from two choices. This can be done by building a primitive 2-by-2 switching element, called a *concentrator*, that randomly picks a winner and a loser. The winner output is the cell that is chosen. The loser output is useful for the general case, in which several primitive 2-by-2 concentrators are combined.

Many contenders, one winner: Now, consider when $k = 1$ (only one cell can be accepted) and $N > 2$ (there are more than two cells that the arbiter must choose fairly from). A simple strategy uses divide-and-conquer (**P15**, efficient data structures) to create a *knockout tree* of 2-by-2 concentrators. As in the first round of a tennis tournament, the cells are paired up using $N/2$ copies of the basic 2-by-2 concentrator, each representing a tennis match. This forms the bottom level of the tree. The winners of the first round are sent to a second round of $N/4$ concentrators, and so on. The "tournament" ends with a final, in which the root concentrator chooses a winner. Notice that the loser outputs of each concentrator are still ignored.

Many contenders, more than one winner: Finally, consider the general case where k cells must be chosen from N possible cells for arbitrary values of k and N. A simple idea is to create k separate knockout trees to calculate the first k winners. However, to be fair, the losers of knockout trees for earlier trees have to be sent to the knockout trees for the subsequent places. This is why the basic 2-by-2 knockout concentrator has two outputs, one for the winner and one for the loser, and not just one for the winner. Loser outputs are routed to the trees for later positions.

Notice that, if one had to choose four cells from among eight choices, the simplest design would assign the eight choices (in pairs) to four 2-by-2 knockout concentrators. This logic will pick four winners, the desired quantity. While this logic is certainly much simpler than using four separate knockout trees, it can be very unfair. For example, suppose two very heavy traffic sources, $S1$ and $S2$, happen to be paired up, while another heavy source, $S3$, is paired up with a light source. In this case $S1$ and $S2$ would get roughly half the traffic that $S3$ obtains. It is to avoid these devious examples of unfairness that the knockout logic uses k separate trees, one for each position.

The naive way to implement the trees is to *begin* running the logic for the Position j tree strictly after all the logic for the Position $j - 1$ tree has been *completed*. This ensures that all eligible losers have been collected. A faster implementation trick is explored in the exercises. It is to be hoped that this design should convince you that fairness is hard to implement correctly. This is a theme that will be explored again in the discussion of iSLIP.

While the knockout switch is important to understand because of the techniques it introduced, it is complex to implement and makes assumptions about traffic distributions. These assumptions are untrue for real topologies in which more than k clients frequently gang up to concurrently send to a popular server. More importantly, researchers devised relatively simple ways to combat HOL blocking *without* going to output queuing.

13.7 Avoiding HOL blocking via virtual output queuing

One such solution approach that has sustained the test of time is VOQ (Tamir and Frazier, 1988). In fact, it was proposed earlier than most of the output queueing solutions described in the previous section. The VOQ approach is to reconsider input queuing but retrofit it to avoid HOL blocking. It does so by allowing an input port to schedule not just the head of its input queue but also other cells, which can make progress when the head is blocked. At first glance, this looks very hard. There could be a hundred thousand cells in each queue; attempting to maintain even 1 bit of scheduling state for each cell will take too much memory to store and process.

However, the first significant observation is that cells in each input port queue can be destined for only N possible output ports. Suppose cell $P1$ is before cell $P2$ in input queue X and that both $P1$ and $P2$ are destined for the same output queue Y. Then, to preserve FIFO behavior, $P1$ must be scheduled before $P2$ anyway. Thus there is no point in attempting to schedule $P2$ before $P1$ is done. Thus obvious waste can be avoided (**P1**) by not scheduling any cells *other than the first cell sent to every distinct output port*.

The idea of the VOQ approach is to exploit a degree of freedom (**P13**) and to decompose the single input queue of Fig. 13.5 into *a separate input queue per output* at each input port in Fig. 13.7. These are called *virtual output queues*. Notice that the top left diagram of Fig. 13.7 contains the same input cells as in Fig. 13.6, except now they are placed in separate VOQs.

With the concept of VOQ introduced, we face a new computational problem in switching. Whereas an input port with a single (combined) packet queue should always be paired (if at all) with the output port for which its HOL packet is destined, an input port with N VOQs has up to N pairing options and has to decide on one of them. More generally, the switch with N input ports and N output ports has to decide, out of its N^2 VOQs (N per input port), which N of them (or less) to serve in a time slot.

As we will explain next, in a crossbar switch, to make such a pairing decision involves computing a bipartite matching, which has been known since 1970s to be a nontrivial computational problem in general. Indeed, the general bipartite matching algorithms are too computationally expensive for large and fast switches (i.e., where N is large and a time slot is short). This is perhaps a reason why the VOQ approach was not widely adopted until a decade or so after it was first proposed, when computationally efficient bipartite matching algorithms designed specifically for switching, such as PIM (Anderson et al., 1993) and iSLIP (McKeown, 1999), were discovered.

13.8 Input-queued switching as a bipartite matching problem

We can formulate the problem of scheduling a crossbar as a bipartite matching problem as follows. An $N \times N$ input-queued crossbar can be modeled as a weighted complete bipartite graph, of which the two disjoint vertex sets are the N input ports and the N output ports, respectively. In this bipartite graph there is an edge between any input port i and any output port j, which corresponds to the VOQ at input port i that buffers packets destined for output port j. The weight of this edge is defined as the length of (i.e., the number of cells buffered at) this VOQ. A set of such edges constitutes a *valid crossbar schedule*, or a *matching*, if any two of them do not share a common vertex. The weight of a matching is the total weight of all the edges belonging to it (i.e., the total length of all corresponding VOQs).

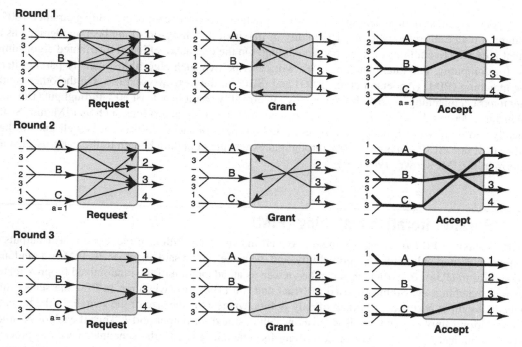

FIGURE 13.7

The parallel iterative matching (PIM) scheme works by having all inputs send requests in *parallel* to all outputs they wish to reach. PIM then uses randomization to do fair matching such that outputs that receive multiple requests pick a random input, and inputs that receive multiple grants randomly pick an output to send to. This three-round process can then be iterated to *improve* the size of the matching.

Three types of matchings play important roles in crossbar scheduling problems: (1) maximal matchings; (2) maximum matchings; and (3) maximum weighted matchings (MWMs). A matching S is called a *maximal matching* if it is no longer a matching when any edge that has nonzero weight and is not in S is added to it. A matching with the largest possible number of edges of nonzero weights is called a *maximum matching* or *maximum cardinality matching*. Neither maximal matchings nor maximum matchings take into account the weights of edges, whereas *maximum weighted matchings* do. A maximum weighted matching is one that has the largest total weight among all matchings. In the switching context (where all edge weights are nonnegative) any maximum matching or maximum weighted matching is also a maximal matching, but neither converse is generally true.

Although crossbar scheduling using MWM (for every time slot) can provably guarantee 100% throughput under all traffic patterns (McKeown et al., 1999; Tassiulas and Ephremides, 1992), and empirically achieve very low queueing delays (McKeown et al., 1999), the state-of-the-art serial MWM algorithm has a very high computational complexity of $O(N^{2.5} \log W)$ (Duan and Su, 2012), where W is the maximum possible weight (length) of an edge (VOQ). By the same measure, maximum matching is an even "rawer deal": it has a slightly lower time complexity of $O(N^{2.5})$ (Hopcroft and Karp,

1973), yet using maximum matchings as crossbar schedules generally cannot provably guarantee 100% throughput under all traffic patterns. The family of maximal matchings has long been recognized as a special cost-effective family for crossbar scheduling. On the one hand, efficient distributed algorithms exist for computing maximal matchings. We will describe two such algorithms, namely parallel iterative matching (PIM) (Anderson et al., 1993) and iSLIP, in the next two sections. On the other hand, using maximal matchings as crossbar schedules can provably result in at least 50% throughput (Dai and Prabhakar, 2000) under all traffic patterns, and maximal matching algorithms such as PIM and iSLIP typically can deliver much better empirical throughput performances. All said, it is well known that neither PIM nor iSLIP can attain 100% throughput except under certain benign traffic patterns such as uniform traffic (McKeown, 1999).

13.9 Parallel iterative matching (PIM)

Strictly speaking, PIM is an approximate maximal matching algorithm in the sense that it outputs a maximal matching only with high probability, and the same can be said about iSLIP. PIM is a randomized algorithm (**P3a**). In particular, it can be viewed as an adaptation of the randomized (approximate) maximal matching algorithm proposed in Israel and Itai (1986) to switching. In PIM the scheduling needs of any input port takes a bitmap of only N bits, where N is the size of the switch. In the bitmap, a 1 in position i implies that there is at least one cell destined for output port i. Thus if each of N input ports communicates an N-bit vector describing its scheduling needs, the scheduler needs to process only N^2 bits. For small $N \leq 32$, this is not many bits to communicate via control buses or to store in control memories.

The communicating of requests is indicated in the top left diagram of Fig. 13.7 by showing a line sent from each input port to each output port for which it has a nonempty VOQ. Notice A does not have a line to port 4 because it has no cell for port 4. Notice also that input port C sends a request for the cell destined for output port 4 in input port C, while the same cell is the last cell in input queue C in the single-input-queue scenario of Fig. 13.5.

What is still required is a scheduling algorithm that matches resources to needs. Although the scheduling algorithm is clever, it is the author's opinion that the real breakthrough was observing that, using VOQs, input-queue scheduling without HOL blocking is feasible to think about. To keep the example in Fig. 13.7 corresponding to Fig. 13.5, assume that every packet in the scenario of Fig. 13.5 is converted into a single cell in Fig. 13.7.

To motivate the scheduling algorithm used in PIM, observe that on the top left diagram of Fig. 13.7, output port 1 gets three requests from A, B, and C but can service only one in the next slot. A simple way to choose between requests is to choose randomly (**P3a**). Thus in the *Grant* phase (top middle diagram of Fig. 13.7) output port 1 chooses B randomly. Similarly, assume that port 2 randomly chooses A (from A and B), port 3 randomly chooses A (from A, B, and C), and finally port 4 chooses its only requester, C.

However, resolving output-port contention is insufficient because there is also input-port contention. Two output ports can randomly grant to the same input port, which must choose exactly one to send a cell to. For example, on the top middle diagram of Fig. 13.7 A has an embarrassment of riches by getting grants from outputs 2 and 3. Thus a third, *Accept*, phase is necessary, in which each input port chooses an output port randomly (since randomization was used in the Grant phase, why not use it again?).

Thus in the top right diagram of Fig. 13.7, A randomly chooses port 2. B and C have no choice and choose ports 1 and 4, respectively. Crossbar connections are made, and the packets from A to port 2, B to port 1, and C to port 4 are transferred. While in this case, the corresponding match found happened to be a maximal matching, in some cases the random choices may result in a matching that is not maximal. For example, in the unlikely event that ports 1, 2, and 3, all choose A, and the matching size will only be of size 2.

In such cases although not shown in the figure, it may be worthwhile for the algorithm to mask out all matched inputs and outputs and iterate more times (for the same forthcoming time slot). If the matching on the current iteration is not maximal, a further iteration will improve the size of the matching by at least 1. Note that subsequent iterations cannot worsen the match because existing matchings are preserved across iterations. While the worst-case time to reach a maximal matching for N inputs is N iterations, a simple argument shows that the expected number of matchings is closer to log N. The DEC AN-2 implementation (Anderson et al., 1993) used three iterations for a 30-port switch.

Our example in Fig. 13.7, however, uses only one iteration for each match (matching). The middle row shows the second match for the second time slot, in which, for example, A and C both ask for port 1 (but not B because the B-to-1 cell was sent in the last time slot). Port 1 randomly chooses C, and the final match is A, 3, B, 2, and C, 1. The third row shows the third match, this time of size 2. At the end of the third match, only the cell destined for port 3 in input queue B is not sent. Thus in four time slots (of which the fourth time slot is sparsely used and could have been used to send more traffic) all the traffic is sent. This is clearly more efficient than the take-a-ticket example of Fig. 13.5.

13.10 **Avoiding randomization with iSLIP**

Parallel iterative matching was a seminal scheme because it introduced the idea that pretty-good bipartite matchings can be computed at reasonable computation and hardware costs with clever parallelization. Once that was done, just as was the case when Roger Bannister first ran the mile in under four minutes, others could make further improvements. But, PIM has two potential problems. First, it uses randomization, and it may be hard to produce a reasonable source of random numbers at very high speeds.[2] Second, it requires a logarithmic number of iterations to attain maximal matches. Given that each of a logarithmic number of iterations takes three phases and that the entire matching decision must be made within a minimum packet arrival time, it would be better to have a matching scheme that comes close to maximal matchings in just one or two iterations.

iSLIP is a very popular and influential scheme that essentially "derandomizes" PIM and also achieves very close to maximal matches after just one or two iterations. The basic idea is extremely simple. When an input port or an output port in PIM experiences multiple requests, it chooses a "winning" request uniformly at random, for the sake of fairness. Whereas Ethernet provides fairness with randomness, token rings do so using a round-robin pointer implemented by a rotating token.

---

[2] One can argue that schemes like RED require randomness at routers, anyway. However, a poor-quality source of random numbers in an RED implementation will be less noticeable than poor-quality random numbers within a switch fabric.

Similarly, iSLIP provides fairness by choosing the next winner among multiple contenders in round-robin fashion using a rotating pointer. While the round-robin pointers can be initially synchronized and cause something akin to HOL blocking, they tend to break free and result in maximal matchings over the long run, at least as measured in simulation. Thus the subtlety in iSLIP is not the use of round-robin pointers but the apparent lack of long-term synchronization among N such pointers running concurrently.

More precisely, each output (respectively input) maintains a pointer g initially set to the first input (respectively output) port. When an output has to choose between multiple input requests, it chooses the lowest input number that is equal to or greater than g. Similarly, when an input port has to choose between multiple output-port requests, it chooses the lowest output-port number that is equal to or greater than a, where a is the pointer of the input port. If an output port is matched to an input port X, then the output-port pointer is incremented to the first port number greater than X in circular order (i.e., g becomes $X + 1$, unless X was the last port, in which case g wraps around to the first port number).

This simple device of a "rotating priority" assures that each resource (output port, input port) is shared reasonably fairly across all contenders at the cost of $2N$ extra $\log_2 N$ pointers, in addition to the N^2 scheduling state needed on every iteration.

Figs. 13.8 and 13.9 show the same scenario as in Fig. 13.7 (and Fig. 13.5), but using a two-iteration iSLIP. Since each row is an iteration of a match, each match is shown using two rows. Thus the three rows of Fig. 13.8 show the first 1.5 matches of the scenario. Similarly, Fig. 13.9 shows the remaining 1.5 matches.

The upper left diagram of Fig. 13.8 is identical to Fig. 13.7, in that each input port sends requests to each output port for which it has a cell destined. However, one difference is that each output port has a so-called *grant* pointer g, which is initialized for all outputs to be A. Similarly, each input has a so-called *accept* pointer called a, which is initialized for all inputs to 1.

The determinism of iSLIP causes a divergence immediately in the Grant phase. Compare the upper middle of Fig. 13.8 with the upper middle of Fig. 13.7. For example, when output 1 receives requests from all three input ports, it grants to A because A is the smallest input greater than or equal to $g_1 = A$. By contrast, in Fig. 13.7 port 1 randomly chooses input port B. At this stage, the determinism of iSLIP seems a real disadvantage because A has sent requests to both output ports 3 and 4. Because 3 and 4 also have grant pointers $g_3 = g_4 = A$, ports 3 and 4 grant to A as well, ignoring the claims of B and C. As before, since C is the lone requester for port 4, C gets the grant from 4.

When the popular A gets three grants back from ports 1, 2, and 3, A accepts 1. This is because port 1 is the first output equal to greater than A's accept pointer, a_A, which was equal to 1. Similarly C chooses 4. Having done so, A increments a_A to 2, and C increments a_C to 1 (1 greater than 4 in circular order is 1). Only at this stage does output 1 increment its grant pointer, g_1, to B (1 greater than the last successful grant) and port 4 similarly increments to A (1 greater than C in circular order).

Note that, although ports 2 and 3 gave grants to A, they do not increment their grant pointers because A spurned their grants. If they did, it would be possible to construct a scenario where output ports keep incrementing their grant pointer beyond some input port I after unsuccessful grants, thereby continually starving input port I. Note also that the match is only of size 2; thus unlike Fig. 13.7, this iSLIP scenario can be improved by a second iteration, shown in the second row of Fig. 13.8. Notice that, at the end of the first iteration, the matched inputs and outputs are not connected by solid lines (denoting data transfer), as shown at the top right of Fig. 13.7. This data transfer will await the end of the final (in this case second) iteration.

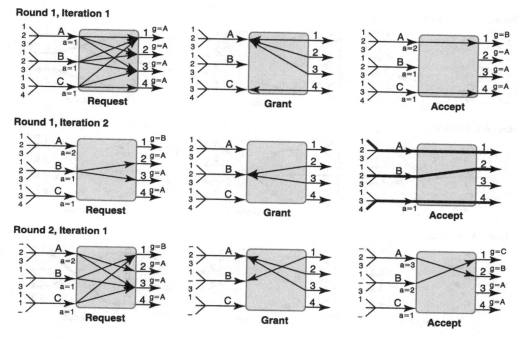

FIGURE 13.8

One-and-a-half rounds of a sample iSLIP scenario.

The second iteration (middle row of Fig. 13.8) starts with only inputs unmatched on previous iterations (i.e., *B*) requesting and only to hitherto unmatched outputs. Thus *B* requests to 2 and 3 (and not to 1, although *B* has a cell destined for 1 as well). Both 2 and 3 grant *B*, and *B* chooses 2 (the lowest one that is greater than or equal to its accept pointer of 1). One might think that *B* should increment its accept pointer to 3 (1 plus the last accepted, which was 2). However, to avoid starvation, iSLIP *does not* increment pointers on iterations other than the first, for reasons that will be explained.

Thus even after *B* is connected to 2, 2's grant pointer remains at *A*, and *B*'s accept pointer remains at 1. Since this is the final iteration, all matched pairs, including pairs, such as *A*, 1, matched in prior iterations, are all connected and data transfer (solid lines) occurs.

The third row provides some insight into how the initial synchronization of grant-and-accept pointers gets broken. Because only one output port has granted to *A*, that port (i.e., 1) gets to move on and this time to provide priority to ports beyond *A*. Thus even if *A* had a second packet destined for 1 (which it does not in this example), 1 would still grant to *B*.

The remaining rows in Figs. 13.8 and 13.9 should be examined carefully by the reader to check for the updating rules for the grant-and-accept pointers and to check which packets are switched at each round. The bottom line is that by, the end of the third row of Fig. 13.9, the only cell that remains to be switched is the cell from *B* to 3. This can clearly be done in a fourth time slot.

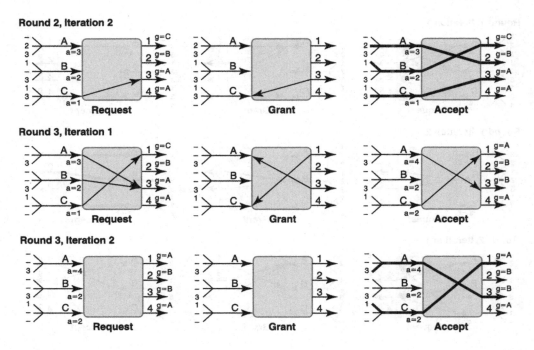

FIGURE 13.9

Last one-and-a-half rounds of the sample iSLIP scenario shown in Fig. 13.8.

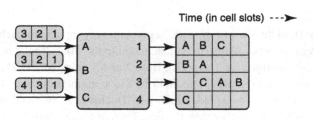

FIGURE 13.10

How iSLIP avoids HOL blocking to increase throughput in the scenario of Fig. 13.6.

Fig. 13.10 shows a summary of the final scheduling (abstracted from the internal mechanics) of the iSLIP scenario and should be compared in terms of scheduling density with Fig. 13.6. While these are just isolated examples, they do suggest that iSLIP (and similarly PIM) tends to waste fewer slots by avoiding HOL blocking and computing pretty-good bipartite matchings. Note that both iSLIP and PIM finish the same input backlog in four time slots, as opposed to six.

Note also that, when we compare Fig. 13.8 with Fig. 13.7, iSLIP looks worse than PIM because it requires two iterations per match for iSLIP to achieve the same match sizes as PIM does using one iteration per match. However, this is more illustrative of the startup penalty that iSLIP pays rather than a long-term penalty. In practice, as soon as the iSLIP pointers desynchronize, iSLIP does very well with just one iteration, and some commercial implementations use just one iteration: iSLIP is extremely popular.

One might summarize iSLIP as PIM with the randomization replaced by round-robin scheduling of input and output pointers. However, this characterization misses two subtle aspects of iSLIP.

- **Grant pointers are incremented only in the third phase, after a grant is accepted:** Intuitively, if O grants to an input port I, there is no guarantee that I will accept. Thus if O were to increment its grant pointer beyond I, it can cause traffic from I to O to be persistently starved. What is even worse, McKeown et al. (1997) show that this simplistic round-robin scheme reduces the throughput to just 63% (for Bernoulli arrivals) because the pointers tend to synchronize and move in lockstep.
- **All pointers are incremented only after the first iteration accept is granted:** Once again, this rule prevents starvation, but the scenario is more subtle, which the exercises will ask you to figure out.

Thus matches on iterations other than the first in iSLIP are considered a "bonus" that boosts throughput without being counted against a port's quota.

13.10.1 iSLIP implementation notes

The heart of the hardware implementation of iSLIP is an arbiter that chooses between N requests (encoded as a bitmap) to find the first one greater than, or equal to, a fixed pointer. This is what in Chapter 2 is called a *programmable priority encoder*; that chapter also described an efficient implementation that is nearly as fast as a priority encoder. Switch scheduling can be done by one such grant arbiter for every output port (to arbitrate requests) and one accept arbiter for every input port (to arbitrate between grants). Priorities and multicast are retrofitted into the basic structure by adding a filter on the inputs before it reaches the arbiter; for example, a priority filter zeroes out all requests except those at the highest-priority level.

Although, in principle, the unicast schedulers can be designed using a separate chip per port, the state is sufficiently small to be handled by a single scheduler chip with control wires coming in from and going out to each of the ports. Also, the multicast algorithm requires a shared multicast pointer per priority level, which also implies a centralized scheduler. Centralization, however, implies a delay, or latency, to send requests and decisions from the port line cards to and from the central scheduler.

To tolerate this latency, the scheduler (Gupta and McKeown, 1999b) works on a pipeline of m cells (eight in Tiny Tera) from each VOQ and n cells (five in Tiny Tera) from each multicast queue. This in turn implies that each line card in the Tiny Tera must communicate 3 bits per unicast VOQ denoting the size of the VOQ, up to a maximum of 8. With 32 outputs and four priority levels, each input port has to send 384 bits of unicast information. Each line card also communicates the fanout (32 bits per fanout) for each of five multicast packets in each of four priority levels, leading to 640 bits. The 32×1024 total bits of input information is stored in on-chip SRAM. However, for higher speed, the information about the heads of each queue (smaller state, for example, only 1 bit per unicast VOQ) is stored in faster but less dense flip-flops.

Now consider handling multiple iterations. Note that the request phase occurs only on the first iteration and needs to be modified only on each iteration by masking off matched inputs. Thus K

iterations appear to take at least $2K$ time steps because the grant-and-accept steps of each iteration take one time step. At first glance, the architecture appears to specify that the *grant* phase of iteration $k + 1$ be started after the accept phase of iteration k. This is because one needs to know whether an input port I has been accepted in iteration k so as to avoid doing a grant for such an input in iteration $k + 1$.

What makes partial pipelining possible is a simple observation (Gupta and McKeown, 1999b): if input I receives *any* grant in iteration k, then I must accept exactly one and so be unavailable in iteration $k + 1$. Thus the implementation specification can be relaxed (**P3**) to allow the grant phase of iteration $k + 1$ to start immediately after the grant phase of iteration k, thus overlapping with the accept phase of iteration k. To do so, we simply use the OR of all the grants to input I (at the end of iteration k) to mask out all of I's requests (in iteration $k + 1$).

This reduces the overall completion time by nearly a factor of two time steps for k iterations, from $2k$ to $k + 1$. For example, the Tiny Tera iSLIP implementation (Gupta and McKeown, 1999b) does three iterations of iSLIP in 51 nanoseconds (roughly OC-192 speeds) using a clock speed of 175 MHz; given that each clock cycle is roughly 5.7 nanoseconds, iSLIP has roughly nine clock cycles to complete. Since each grant and accept step takes two clock cycles, the pipelining is crucial for being able to handle three iterations in nine clock cycles; the naive iteration technique would have taken at least 12 clock cycles.

13.11 Computing near-optimal matchings via learning

Recall from Section 13.8 that a heavy matching, such as maximum weighted matching (MWM), is generally a good matching in terms of throughput and delay performances. In most bipartite matching algorithms for switching, such as PIM and iSLIP described earlier, the computation of the crossbar schedule (matching) for each time slot is done from scratch, or in other words, oblivious of earlier computations. This might sound computationally wasteful (**P1**). For example, a heavy matching computed in the previous time slot typically remains heavy in the current time slot since, in the previous time slot, there can be at most N departures, but possibly close to N arrivals under a heavy load. Intuitively, if we can somehow learn the heavy edges from the matching used in the previous time slot, we may be able to compute a new heavy matching incrementally (**P12a**) with a much lower time complexity than to compute it from scratch. Indeed we can do just that with a family of adaptive algorithms that we will describe in the next few sections.

Besides the bipartite matching used in the previous time slot, there are other things an adaptive algorithm can learn from earlier computations to help compute a good new matching faster. For example, an intelligent adaptive algorithm can develop and maintain "situational awareness" of the weights of all N^2 edges (VOQs) gradually over many past time slots, which can help the algorithm make quick, yet wise, matching decisions, as will be shown in Section 13.14. In the next few sections we assume there is an equal number N of input ports and output ports and that an edge is allowed to have weight 0 (i.e., with the corresponding VOQ being empty). Under both assumptions, a maximum matching (defined in Section 13.8) always contains N edges and is necessarily a full matching. Hence, we use the term full matching instead throughout this section to avoid any confusion.

13.12 Sample-and-compare: a stunningly simple adaptive algorithm

We start with the adaptive algorithm proposed in Tassiulas (1998), which we call sample-and-compare. This algorithm is stunningly simple: at each time slot t, sample a (uniform) random matching (**P3a**) denoted as $R(t)$, compare its weight to that of the matching $S(t-1)$ used in the previous time slot, and use the heavier matching as $S(t)$ (i.e., for the current time slot t). Compared to the MWM algorithm, the sample-and-compare algorithm has a much lower computational complexity of $O(N)$. Amazingly, just like MWM, sample-and-compare can provably attain 100% throughput under all traffic patterns. However, its delay performance is poor under heavy load, as explained by the following queueing dynamics it experiences under heavy load.

It can be shown that the current (i.e., at time t) normalized throughput of a switching algorithm is roughly equal to the weight of $S(t)$ as a fraction of that of MWM at time t. In particular, for any switching algorithm to attain 100% throughput like sample-and-compare does, the weight of $S(t)$ has to eventually be very close to that of MWM. However, since only with a tiny probability can a (uniform) random matching $R(t)$ have a large enough weight to exceed that of $S(t-1)$ (that is already quite large), the rate at which $R(t)$ can "gain enough weight" under sample-and-compare to approach that of MWM is extremely slow. Hence, the weight of $S(t)$ can be much smaller than that of MWM for a long time, during which the throughput of the switch is much smaller than 100%, and as a consequence, the weights of the edges (VOQ lengths) become very large under a heavy load. This explains the poor delay performance of sample-and-compare. When (almost) all edge weights become gigantic, however, the weight of a random matching $R(t)$ starts to have a decent probability of beating that of $S(t-1)$, and the weight of $S(t)$ starts to approach that of MWM much more rapidly. This explains why sample-and-compare can attain 100% throughput at last.

13.13 SERENA: an improved adaptive algorithm

SERENA is the best among the several adaptive algorithms proposed in Shah et al. (2002b); Giaccone et al. (2003). It has the same algorithmic framework and $O(N)$ computational complexity as sample-and-compare, yet delivers much better delay performance. Just like sample-and-compare, SERENA also derives $S(t)$ from $S(t-1)$ and a random matching $R(t)$. However, there are two key differences that make it work much better than sample-and-compare. The first difference is that in SERENA $R(t)$ is not in general a uniform random matching as in sample-and-compare, but is derived from the set of packet arrivals at time t. This difference results in a statistically heavier $R(t)$ than a uniform random matching. The second difference is that, through a MERGE procedure, SERENA picks heavy edges for $S(t)$ from both $R(t)$ and $S(t-1)$ so that the weight of $S(t)$ can be larger than those of both $R(t)$ and $S(t-1)$. This difference allows $S(t)$ to "gain weight" much faster in SERENA than in sample-and-compare. Next, we describe how $R(t)$ is derived from the packet arrivals and how the MERGE procedure works.

13.13.1 Derive $R(t)$ from the arrival graph

In SERENA the random matching $R(t)$ is derived from the *arrival graph* $A(t)$ defined as follows: an edge (I_i, O_j) belongs to $A(t)$ if and only if there is a packet arrival to the corresponding VOQ during

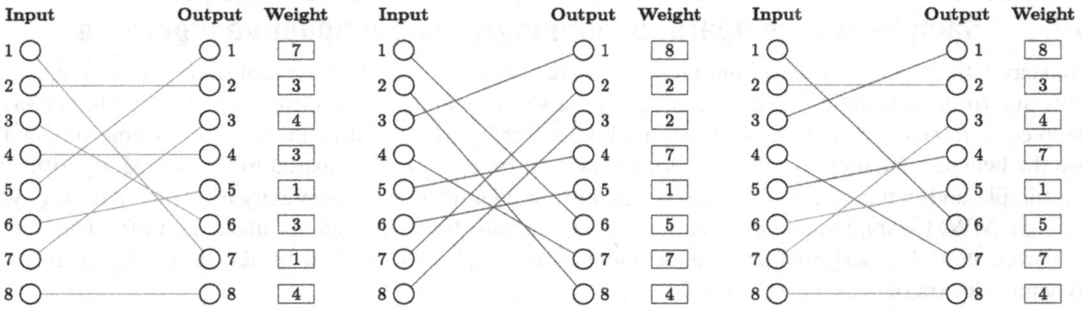

Input	Output	Weight	Input	Output	Weight	Input	Output	Weight
1	1	7	1	1	8	1	1	8
2	2	3	2	2	2	2	2	3
3	3	4	3	3	2	3	3	4
4	4	3	4	4	7	4	4	7
5	5	1	5	5	1	5	5	1
6	6	3	6	6	5	6	6	5
7	7	1	7	7	7	7	7	7
8	8	4	8	8	4	8	8	4

FIGURE 13.11

Illustrate MERGE procedure by an example. The three subfigures are referred to as (a), (b), and (c).

time slot t. Note that $A(t)$ is not necessarily a matching because more than one input ports could have a packet arrival (i.e., edge) destined for the same output port at time slot t. Hence, in this case, each output port prunes all such edges incident upon it except the one with the heaviest weight (with ties broken randomly). The pruned graph, denoted as $A'(t)$, is now a matching.

This matching $A'(t)$, which is typically partial, is then randomly populated into a full matching $R(t)$ by pairing the yet unmatched input ports with the yet unmatched output ports in a round-robin manner. This pairing operation clearly has $O(N)$ computational complexity. Deriving $R(t)$ from $A(t)$ in SERENA is better than generating $R(t)$ from scratch in sample-and-compare in two different ways. First, it allows SERENA to tap into the randomness naturally contained in the packet arrival process, making it cheaper to implement since "man-made" randomness incurs a computational cost, as explained in Section 13.10. Second, as explained in Shah et al. (2002b); Giaccone et al. (2003), some packet arrivals go to heavily backlogged VOQs, and hence $R(t)$ derived from $A(t)$ often has a larger weight than a uniform random matching.

13.13.2 Merge $R(t)$ with $S(t-1)$

We now describe the MERGE procedure that allows SERENA to pick heavy edges for $S(t)$ from both $R(t)$ and $S(t-1)$. To do so with the best clarity, we need to color-code and orient the edges of $R(t)$ and $S(t-1)$, as in Giaccone et al. (2003), as follows. We color all edges in $R(t)$ red and all edges in $S(t-1)$ green, and hence, in the sequel, rename $R(t)$ to S_r ("r" for red) and $S(t-1)$ to S_g ("g" for green) to emphasize the coloring. *We drop the henceforth unnecessary term t here with the implicit understanding that the focus is on the MERGE procedure at time slot t.* We also orient all edges in S_r as pointing from input ports (i.e., I) to output port (i.e., O) and all edges in S_g as pointing from output ports to input ports. We use notations $S_r(I \to O)$ and $S_g(O \to I)$ to emphasize this orientation when necessary in the sequel. Finally, we drop the term t from $S(t)$ and denote the final outcome of the MERGE procedure as S. An example pair of thus-oriented full matchings $S_r(I \to O)$ and $S_g(O \to I)$, over an 8×8 crossbar, are shown in Fig. 13.11(b) and Fig. 13.11(a), respectively.

We now describe how the two color-coded oriented full matchings $S_r(I \to O)$ and $S_g(O \to I)$ are merged to produce the final full matching S. The MERGE procedure consists of two steps. The first

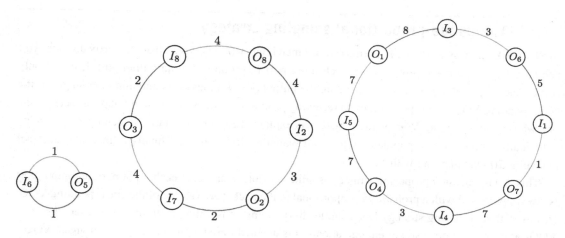

FIGURE 13.12

Cycles.

step is to simply union the two full matchings, viewed as two subgraphs of the complete bipartite graph $G(I \bigcup O)$, into one that we call the *union graph* and denote as $S_r(I \rightarrow O) \bigcup S_g(O \rightarrow I)$ (or $S_r \bigcup S_g$ in short). In other words, the union graph $S_r(I \rightarrow O) \bigcup S_g(O \rightarrow I)$ contains the directed edges in both $S_r(I \rightarrow O)$ and $S_g(O \rightarrow I)$.

It is a mathematical fact that any such union graph can be decomposed into disjoint directed cycles (Giaccone et al., 2003). Furthermore, each directed cycle, starting from an input port I_i and going back to itself, is an alternating path between a red edge in S_r and a green edge in S_g, and hence contains equal numbers of red edges and green edges. In other words, this cycle consists of a red submatching of S_r and a green submatching of S_g. Then in the second step, for each directed cycle, the MERGE procedure compares the weight of the red submatching (i.e., the total weight of the red edges in the cycle), with that of the green submatching, and includes the heavier submatching in the final merged matching S.

To illustrate the MERGE procedure by an example, Fig. 13.12 shows the union graph of the two full matchings shown in Fig. 13.11(a) and (B), respectively. The union graph contains three disjoint directed cycles that consist of two, six, and eight edges, respectively. In each cycle we pick the heavier submatching and the resulting merged matching is shown in Fig. 13.11(c). For example, in the third cycle, the submatching $\{(I_3, O_1), (I_5, O_4), (I_4, O_7), (I_1, O_6)\}$, which has a total weight of $8 + 7 + 7 + 5 = 27$, is heavier than the other submatching, which has a total weight of $7 + 3 + 1 + 3 = 14$. Hence, it is chosen to be a part of the final matching. The standard centralized algorithm for implementing the MERGE procedure is to linearly traverse every cycle once, by following the directed edges in the cycle, to obtain the weights of the green and the red submatchings that comprise the cycle (Giaccone et al., 2003). Clearly, this algorithm has a computational complexity of $O(N)$.

13.14 **The queue-proportional sampling strategy**

In SERENA, the way a (typically partial) starter matching $A'(t)$ is derived from the arrival graph $A(t)$ can be viewed as a *proposing process*: each input port i "proposes" to an output port j, if and only if the edge (i, j) belongs to $A(t)$, by sending the output port j a message containing the length of the corresponding VOQ; an output port, upon receiving proposals from one or more input ports, accepts the one whose corresponding VOQ is the longest. As explained earlier, this starter matching $A'(t)$, which is typically partial, is then populated into a full matching $R(t)$, and it is finally refined into the final matching $S(t)$ via merging with $S(t-1)$.

This $A(t)$-generated proposing strategy is quite sensible because, at each input port, an output port is always proposed with a probability proportional to the packet arrival rate of the corresponding VOQ. However, this proposing strategy has a subtle shortcoming: it is oblivious to the current lengths of N VOQs at each input port, so not enough attention is devoted to reducing the lengths of longest VOQs. For example, a VOQ with many packets but without recent arrivals, which could happen under bursty traffic, will mostly be denied service until it has new arrivals.

In Gong et al. (2017) researchers proposed a data structure that allows the switch to constantly maintain a keen "situational awareness" of the lengths of its N^2 VOQs. This data structure supports, in constant (i.e., $O(1)$) time, an operation called *queue-proportional sampling* that generates an excellent starter matching. It was shown in Gong et al. (2017) that SERENA, when using the QPS-generated starter matching instead (called QPS-SERENA), has better delay performances than when using the $A(t)$-generated starter matching. In addition, just like SERENA, QPS-SERENA can also attain 100% throughput under all traffic patterns.

Furthermore, scheduling algorithms that start from "scratch" (i.e., an empty matching), such as iS-LIP, may also benefit significantly from QPS by instead starting from a QPS-generated starter matching. It was shown in Gong et al. (2017) that iSLIP, when using a QPS-generated starter matching instead (called QPS-iSLIP), attains higher throughputs and better delay performances than iSLIP under various traffic patterns.

The QPS proposing strategy, at any input port, is extremely simple to state: the input port proposes to an output port with a probability proportional to the length of the corresponding VOQ. QPS's name comes from the fact that the output port proposed to by any input port is sampled, out of all N output ports, using the queue-proportional distribution at the input port.

We will shortly describe a data structure and algorithm that can perform a QPS operation (at an input port) in $O(1)$ time. The constant time complexity of the QPS operation may be surprising to readers since even to "read" the lengths of all N VOQs at an input port takes $O(N)$ time. However, a short explanation of this "paradox" is that the QPS operation really only needs to track the small number of changes in the lengths of these N VOQs, caused by packet arrivals to and departures from the input port during a time slot. This is exactly what the QPS data structure does: gain constant situational awareness via learning incrementally (**P12a**) over time rather than in one shot.

13.15 QPS implementation

We now describe the data structure and algorithm that allows an input port to sample a VOQ in the queue-proportional manner, and, if needed, to remove the HOL packet of any VOQ (for receiving switching service), both with $O(1)$ (per port) computational complexity.

13.15.1 The QPS algorithm

This algorithm consists of two steps. In the first step we sample a packet, out of all packets currently queued at the input port, uniformly at random. Specifically, if there are a total of m packets across all N VOQs at the input port, each packet is sampled with probability $1/m$. With such uniform sampling, the jth VOQ that has length m_j will have one of the packets sampled with probability m_j/m. This is precisely the QPS behavior.

Suppose a packet is thus sampled. A part of the second step is to find out which VOQ this packet belongs to so that the input port can propose to the corresponding output port with its queue length. However, more effort is still required. Since all switching algorithms serve packets in a VOQ strictly in the FIFO order, if this proposal is successful (i.e., accepted by the output port), and the input and output port pair is eventually a part of the final matching, the HOL packet of this VOQ, which may or may not be the sampled packet, needs to be located and serviced. Hence, the other part of the second step is to locate the HOL packet of this VOQ.

Before going into the details, we list two other basic operations that this data structure needs also to support. The first operation is that any new incoming packet must be recorded in the data structure so that it is logically "added to the end of the VOQ that it belongs to." The second operation is that, when the scheduling algorithm eventually decides to pair the input port with a different output port than was proposed to, which could happen due to either the proposal being rejected or the initially accepted proposal being overridden by the scheduling algorithm (e.g., during SERENA's MERGE operation in the case of QPS-SERENA), the HOL packet of the (new) corresponding VOQ needs to be located and removed for receiving the switching service. Both operations can be supported with $O(1)$ complexity, as will be shown next.

13.15.2 The QPS data structure

We show that the two steps of the QPS proposing strategy can be performed in $O(1)$ time, at any input port, via a main and an auxiliary data structures, that are the same for all input ports. Fig. 13.13(A) and (B) present the data structures, *at a single input port*, before and after the HOL packet of its jth VOQ is chosen for (switching) service. The top half and bottom half of the figures show the main and the auxiliary data structures, respectively.

The main data structure. The main data structure is an array of N records, corresponding to the N VOQs at the input port. Each record j (i.e., array entry j) is associated with a linked list that corresponds to (pointers to) packets queued at a VOQ in the order they arrived, starting with the HOL packet. Each node in the linked list contains two pointers encoded as "$\langle letter \rangle$" (e.g., A); one points to the actual packet (e.g., packet A) in the packet buffer (not shown in the figure) and the other to the corresponding entry (e.g., entry A) in the auxiliary data structure, which we refer to as a *back pointer*.

For simplicity Fig. 13.13 shows only record j (corresponding to VOQ j). Each record contains a head and tail pointers that point to the head node and the tail node of the linked list, respectively. The

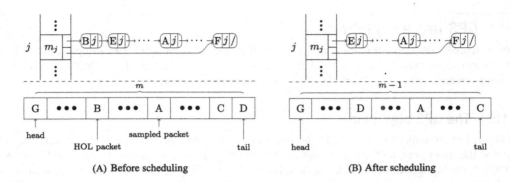

(A) Before scheduling   (B) After scheduling

FIGURE 13.13

Illustrating the action of the QPS data structures on a single-input port. (Adapted from Gong et al., 2017.)

head pointer is needed for locating and for removing the head node (i.e., the HOL packet) in $O(1)$ time; it is also needed for locating and replacing the array entry that corresponds to the HOL packet in the auxiliary data structure. The tail pointer is needed for inserting a newly arrived packet to the "end of the VOQ" (i.e., the first basic operation) in $O(1)$ time.

The auxiliary data structure. The bottom half of Fig. 13.13 shows the auxiliary data structure used for performing the sampling. Suppose there are a total of m packets queued across all N VOQs at the input port. The auxiliary data structure is simply an array of m entries, each of which is a pointer that points to a distinct (packet) node (e.g., node A) in one of the N linked lists in the main data structure.

Despite arrivals and departures of packets over time, the auxiliary data structure always occupies a contiguous block of array entries, the boundaries of which are identified by a head and a tail pointer as shown in the bottom half of Fig. 13.13. This contiguity allows an array entry (packet) to be sampled uniformly at random in $O(1)$ time, an aforementioned key step of QPS. Hence, this contiguity needs to be maintained in the event of packet arrivals and departures. The case of a packet arrival is easier: the entry corresponding to the new packet is inserted after the current tail position, and the tail pointer updated. The case of a packet departure is only slightly trickier: if the departing packet leaves a "hole" in the block, the tail entry is moved to fill this hole, and the tail pointer updated.

In the case of a packet departure the (packet) node in the main data structure that is pointed to by the former tail entry (now moved to "fill the hole") needs to have its *back pointer* updated to the offset of the former hole, where the former tail entry is now. This is clearly an $O(1)$ procedure. A similar procedure can be used to support the second basic operation in $O(1)$ time.

An illustrative example. To see how the main and the auxiliary data structures work together to facilitate QPS, consider the example shown in Fig. 13.13 where the packet A was sampled out of m packets in the auxiliary data structure. However, it is not the HOL packet, so its destination (output) port (i.e., VOQ identifier) is checked, which turns out to be j. By accessing the jth record in the main data structure that corresponds to VOQ j, the HOL packet is found to be packet B. Now, the input port proposes to match with output port j. If the proposal is accepted by, and the input port is eventually matched to, output port j, packet B will depart (for output port j) in the current time slot. The head pointer in the jth record of the main data structure is updated to (point to) E, the new HOL packet. These changes are captured in Fig. 13.13(B). These operations, including the search for the HOL packet and the updates to both data structures, all take $O(1)$ time.

13.16 Small-batch QPS and sliding-window QPS

In this section, we describe a late-breaking input-queued switching algorithm called sliding-window queue-proportional sampling (Meng et al., 2020). SW-QPS improves upon a parallel batch switching algorithm called small-batch queue-proportional sampling (SB-QPS) that was also proposed in Meng et al. (2020). It was shown in Meng et al. (2020) that, compared to other batch switching algorithms such as Aggarwal et al. (2003); Neely et al. (2007); Wang et al. (2018), SB-QPS significantly reduces the batch size without sacrificing the throughput performance and hence has much lower delay when traffic load is light to moderate. It also achieves the lowest possible time complexity of $O(1)$ per matching computation per port, via parallelization, using the QPS data structure and algorithm we have just described. SW-QPS retains and enhances all benefits of SB-QPS and reduces the batching delay to zero via a novel switching framework called sliding-window switching.

To compute each matching, SW-QPS runs only a single iteration, as compared to $O(\log N)$ iterations needed by iSLIP in theory. Each SW-QPS iteration is also "cheaper" than an iSLIP iteration in two aspects. First, the time complexity of each SW-QPS iteration, to be explained next, is $O(1)$, whereas each iSLIP iteration is $O(\log N)$ in theory using the *programmable priority encoder* described in Section 2.2.3. Second, whereas an input port sends out only a single request in each SW-QPS iteration, it sends out in general $O(N)$ requests (to every output port whose corresponding VOQ is nonempty) in each iSLIP iteration. Despite being much "cheaper," SW-QPS achieves overall better throughput and delay performance than iSLIP, as shown in Meng et al. (2020).

13.16.1 Batch switching algorithms

Since SB-QPS is a batch switching algorithm (Aggarwal et al., 2003; Neely et al., 2007; Wang et al., 2018), we first provide some background on batch switching. Unlike in a regular switching algorithm, where a matching decision is computed for every time slot, in a batch-switching algorithm, multiple (say T) consecutive time slots are grouped as a batch and these T matching decisions are batch-computed (**P2c**). Hence, in a batch-switching algorithm, each of the T matchings being computed in a batch has a period of T time slots to find opportunities to have the quality of the matching improved by the underlying bipartite matching algorithm, whereas, in a regular switching algorithm, each matching has only a single time slot to find such opportunities. As a result, a batch-switching algorithm can usually produce matchings of higher quality than a regular switching algorithm using the same underlying bipartite matching algorithm. However, the flip side of the coin is that all batch-switching algorithms suffer an average batching delay of at least $T/2$ time slots since any packet belonging to the current batch has to wait till at least the beginning of the next batch to be switched. A key contribution of SB-QPS, described next, is to make this T much smaller than in all other batch-switching algorithms, for attaining a similar or better throughput performance.

As just explained, in a batch-switching algorithm, the T matchings for a batch of T future time slots are batch-computed. These T matchings form a joint calendar (schedule) of the N output ports that can be encoded as a $T \times N$ table with TN cells in it, as illustrated by an example shown in Fig. 13.14. Each column corresponds to the calendar of an output port and each row a time slot. The content of the cell at

	O_1	O_2	$\cdots$	O_N
1	I_3	I_7	$\cdots$	I_1
2	I_5	$-$	$\cdots$	I_3
$\vdots$	$\vdots$	$\vdots$	$\ddots$	$\vdots$
T	$-$	I_5	$\cdots$	I_2

FIGURE 13.14

A joint calendar. "$-$" means unmatched. (Adapted from Meng et al., 2020.)

the intersection of the tth row and the jth column is the input port that O_j is to pair with during the tth time slot in this batch. Hence, each cell also corresponds to an edge (between the input and the output port pair) and each row also corresponds to a matching (under computation for the corresponding time slot). In the example shown in Section 13.14 output port O_1 is to pair with I_3 during the first time slot (in this batch), I_5 during the second time slot, and is unmatched during the Tth time slot.

13.16.2 The SB-QPS algorithm

SB-QPS is a batch-switching algorithm that uses a small constant batch size T independent of N. SB-QPS is a parallel iterative algorithm: the input and output ports run T QPS-like iterations (request–accept message exchanges) to collaboratively pack the joint calendar. The operation of each iteration is extremely simple: Input ports request for cells in the joint calendar, and output ports accept or reject the requests. More precisely, each iteration of SB-QPS, like that of QPS (Gong et al., 2017), consists of two phases: a proposing phase and an accepting phase.

Proposing Phase. In this phase like in QPS, each input port i proposes to an output port j with a probability proportional to the length of the corresponding VOQ. The content of the proposal (say from i to j) in SB-QPS, however, is slightly different than that in QPS. In QPS the proposal contains only the VOQ length information, whereas, in SB-QPS, it also contains the following availability information (of input port i): out of the T time slots in the batch, what (time slots) are still available for input port i to pair with an output port? The time complexity of this QPS operation, carried out using the data structure described in the previous section, is $O(1)$ per input port.

Accepting Phase. In SB-QPS the accepting phase at an output port is quite different than that in QPS. Whereas the latter allows at most one proposal to be accepted at any output port, the former allows an output port to accept multiple (up to T) proposals (as each output port has up to T cells in its calendar to be filled). The operations at output port j depend on the number of proposals it receives. If output port j receives exactly one proposal from an input port (say input port i), it tries to accommodate this proposal using an accepting strategy called *First Fit Accepting* (FFA) (Meng et al., 2020). The FFA strategy is to match in this case input port i and output port j at the earliest time slot (in the batch of T time slots) during which both are still available (for pairing); if they have "schedule conflicts" over all T time slots, this proposal is rejected. If output port j receives proposals from multiple input ports, then it first sorts (with ties broken arbitrarily) these proposals in a descending order according to their corresponding VOQ lengths, and then it tries to accept each of them using the FFA strategy. It

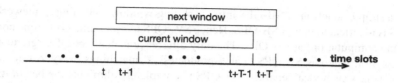

FIGURE 13.15

Sliding-window switching.(Adapted from Meng et al., 2020.)

was shown in Meng et al. (2020) that, when T is not too large (say $T \leq 64$), this FFA operation can be performed in one CPU cycle using a bitmap encoding (**P14**) of (a port's availability during) these T time slots, and the Find First One (FFO) instruction (to be described further in Section 14.14) available on modern CPUs.

The time complexity of SB-QPS is $O(T)$ per input or output port for the joint calendar consisting of T matchings, since SB-QPS runs T iterations and each iteration has $O(1)$ time complexity per input or output port. Hence, the time complexity for computing each matching is $O(1)$ per input or output port.

13.16.3 The SW-QPS algorithm

The only difference between SW-QPS and SB-QPS is that SW-QPS changes the batch-switching operation of SB-QPS to a sliding-window switching operation. Sliding-window switching combines regular switching with batch switching and achieves the better of both worlds, as follows. On the one hand, during each time slot, under a sliding-window switching operation, there are T matchings under computation, just like under a batch-switching operation. Each such matching has had or will have a window of T time slots to find opportunities to have its quality improved by the underlying bipartite matching algorithm before it "graduates."

On the other hand, under a sliding-window switching operation, the "windows of opportunities" of these T matchings are staggered so that one matching ("class") is output ("graduated") every time slot. This matching is to be used as the crossbar configuration for the current time slot. In this respect it behaves like a regular switching algorithm and hence completely eliminates the batching delay of batch switching. More specifically, at the beginning of time slot t, the most senior matching ("class") in the window was added ("enrolled") to the window at the end of time slot $t - T - 1$ and is to "graduate" at the beginning of time slot t so its "window of opportunity" (to have its quality improved) is $[t - T, t - 1]$. The "window of opportunity" for the second most senior matching is $[t - T + 1, t]$ and so on. At the end of time slot t, a "freshman class" (an empty matching) is "enrolled" and scheduled to "graduate" at time slot $t + T + 1$ in the future.

Fig. 13.15 shows how the sliding window evolves from time slot t to time slot $t + 1$. In Fig. 13.15 each interval along the timeline corresponds to a "class." As shown there, at the beginning of time slot t, the current window contains "classes of years" (matchings-under-computation to be used as crossbar schedules for time slots) $t, t + 1, \cdots$, and $t + T - 1$. Then, at the beginning of time slot $t + 1$, the current window slides right by 1 (time slot), and the new window contains "classes of years" $t + 1$, $t + 2, \cdots$, and $t + T$ because the "class of year t" just graduated and the "class of year $t + T$" was just "enrolled."

SW-QPS is a simple adaption of SB-QPS into the sliding-window switching framework. Each iteration of SW-QPS is identical to that of SB-QPS. Hence SW-QPS has the same $O(1)$ time complexity (per port per matching computation) as SB-QPS. The only difference is that SW-QPS "graduates" a matching in every time slot, whereas SB-QPS "batch-graduates" T matchings every T time slots. Clearly, this "graduating a class each year" enables SW-QPS to completely eliminate the batching delay.

SW-QPS inherits the FFA (first fit accepting) strategy of SB-QPS that is to arrange for an input-output pairing – hence, the switching of a packet between the pair – at the earliest mutually available time slot. In other words, an incoming packet is always "advanced to the most senior class that it can fit in schedule-wise" so that it can "graduate" at the earliest "year" possible. This greedy strategy further reduces the queuing delay of a packet, as shown in Meng et al. (2020).

13.17 Combined input and output queueing

A switch architecture called Combined Input and Output Queueing (CIOQ) was studied in late 1990s and early 2000s (Prabhakar and McKeown, 1997) (Stoica and Zhang, 1998) (Chuang et al., 1999) (Iyer et al., 2002) (Yang and Zheng, 2003) (Giaccone et al., 2004) (Firoozshahian et al., 2007). CIOQ was motivated by the need to provide Quality of Service (QoS) guarantees via performing packet scheduling (topic of the next chapter) at output ports. In CIOQ, packets are queued at both input and output ports, which gives the architecture its name. The design objective of CIOQ is to fully emulate the effect of output queueing, as far as the packet scheduling at output ports is concerned, without paying for the aforementioned high cost (of N-fold speedup at the output ports as explained in Section 13.6) of output queueing.

We now elaborate on the concept of "full emulation". For an output-queued switch to provide a certain QoS guarantee, each output port j needs to enforce a certain packet scheduling policy $\mathcal{P}$ (common to all output ports) among the N Virtual Input Queues (VIQs) at output port j, where the ith VIQ (at output port j) holds all the packets that arrived from input port i. In an output-queued switch, given any packet arrival instance, $\mathcal{P}$ completely determines the service order of these packets, since each packet can "fly" directly to its output port upon arrival without any delay as guaranteed by an output-queued switch. A switch is said to fully emulate output queueing if, given any packet arrival instance, it produces exactly the same packet service order as an output-queued switch, no matter what $\mathcal{P}$ is used by both switches (at the output ports for packet scheduling).

A CIOQ switch is very different than an input-queued switch in that the former computes a very different matching than the latter. In a CIOQ switch, the matching between input and output ports at any given time (cycle) is decided based on the deadlines or priority scores assigned to the HOL packets of the N^2 VOQs or VIQs by $\mathcal{P}$; and a matching π thus computed must be a stable matching (Gale and Shapley, 1962) in the sense there does not exist a pair of input and output ports that both prefer (to pair with) each other (according to these deadlines or priority scores) to their current pairing under π. In contrast, no crossbar scheduling algorithms described in the previous sections for an input-queued switch has anything to do with such a $\mathcal{P}$, or computes a stable matching.

The CIOQ technology has never taken off, likely because its cost is high in two aspects. First, CIOQ scheduling algorithms generally have a high time complexity of $O(N^2)$ (per cycle) since these N^2 deadlines or priority scores need to be somehow sorted out for a stable matching to be computed (Gale and Shapley, 1962). Second, they can only guarantee 50% throughput (Chuang et al., 1999) (Dai and

Prabhakar, 2000). Hence the cost here is that a 2-fold speedup at the output ports is needed for providing the QoS guarantees (for which $\mathcal{P}$ is used). An interesting perspective on why CIOQ did not take off was explained in Firoozshahian et al. (2007) and Prabhakar (2009).

CIOQ likely will never take off for the following reason. As explained earlier, we already have excellent input-queued switching algorithms such as SW-QPS that can deliver excellent throughput and delay performances at very low costs. We can simply use such an algorithm for switching (packets from input ports to output ports) and then enforce $\mathcal{P}$ at the output ports. When the load is not too high, the queueing delay (due to switching) of any packet at the corresponding input port should be small, so that with overwhelming probability it will arrive at its destination output port by the deadline dictated by $\mathcal{P}$. This way, we can reap almost the full benefit of CIOQ (the QoS guarantees provided by $\mathcal{P}$) without paying for its high cost.

13.18 Scaling to larger and faster switches

As various hurdles exist for existing switching schemes to scale to a large number of ports and higher per-port speeds, Section 13.18 describes two approaches to that end. Both approaches achieve the two scalability objectives by reducing one or both of the two major switching costs, namely, the overall size of the switch circuitry and the time complexity of the bipartite matching computation. The first approach, based on the principle of divide and conquer (**P15**), reduces the overall size of the switch circuitry through the use of more space-efficient switch fabrics than a monolithic crossbar, such as the Clos fabric (Section 13.18.3) and the Benes fabric (Section 13.18.4). The other, called Load-Balanced Switching (LBS), reduces the algorithmic cost of bipartite matching computation to virtually zero. However, it does so by using two large crossbars instead of one.

So far, this chapter has concentrated on fairly small switches that suffice to build up to a 32-port router. Most Internet routers deployed up to the time of writing have been in this category, sometimes for good reasons. For instance, building wiring codes tend to limit the number of offices that can be served from a wiring closet. Thus switches for local area networks (Simcoe and Pei, 1994) located in wiring closets tend to be well served with small port sizes.

However, the telephone network has generally employed a few very large switches that can switch 1000–10,000 lines. Employing larger switches tends to eliminate switch-to-switch links, reducing overall latency and increasing the number of switch ports available for users (as opposed to being used to connect to other switches). Thus while a number of researchers (e.g., Turner, 1997 and Chaney et al., 1997) have argued for such large switches, there was little large-scale industrial support for such large switches until recently.

There are three recent trends that favor the design of large switches.

1. **DWDM:** The use of dense wavelength-division multiplexing (DWDM) to effectively bundle multiple wavelengths on optical links in the core will effectively increase the number of logical links that must be switched by core routers.
2. **Fiber to the home:** There is a good chance that in the near future, even homes and offices will be wired directly with fiber that goes to a large central office–type switch.
3. **Modular, multichassis routers:** There is increasing interest in deploying router clusters that consist of a set of routers interconnected by a high-speed network. For example, many network access

points connect up routers via an FDDI link or by a GigaSwitch (see Section 13.4). Router clusters, or *multichassis* routers as they are sometimes called, are becoming increasingly interesting because they allow *incremental growth*, as explained later.

The typical lifetime of a core router is estimated (Semeria and Gredler, 2001) to be 18–24 months, after which traffic increases often cause ISPs to throw away older-generation routers and wheel in new ones. Multichassis routers can extend the lifetime of a core router to five years or more, by allowing ISPs to start small and then to add routers to the cluster according to traffic needs.

In the early 2000s Juniper Networks led the pack by announcing its T-series routers, which allow up to 16 single-chassis routers (each of which has up to 16 ports) to be assembled via a fabric into what is effectively a 256-port router. At the heart of the multichassis system is a scalable 256-by-256 switching system. Also in the early 2000s Cisco Networks announced its own version, the CRS-1 Router.

13.18.1 Measuring switch cost

Before studying switch scaling, it helps to understand the most important cost metrics of a switch. We identify two key cost metrics: the number of crosspoints in the crossbar and the complexities of the matching algorithm. They correspond to the complexities of the crossbar hardware and software, respectively.

Metric #1: the number of crosspoints

In the early days of telephone switching, crosspoints were electromagnetic switches, and thus the N^2 crosspoints of a crossbar were a major cost. Even today, this is a major cost for very large switches of size 1000. But, because crosspoints can be thought of as just transistors, they take up very little space on a VLSI die.[3]

The real limits for electronic switches are pin limits on ICs. For example, given current pin limits of around 1000, of which a large number of pins must be devoted to other factors, such as power and ground, even a single bit slice of a 500-by-500 switch is impossible to package in a single chip. Of course, one could multiplex several crossbar inputs on a single pin, but that would slow down the speed of each input to half the I/O speed possible on a pin.

Thus while the crossbar does indeed require N^2 crosspoints (and this indeed does matter for large enough N), for values of N up to 200, much of the crosspoint complexity is contained within chips. Thus one places the largest crossbar one can implement within a chip and then one interconnects these chips to form a larger switch. Thus the dominant cost of the composite switch is the cost of the pins and the number of links between chips. Since these last two are related (most of the pins are for input and output links), the total number of pins is a reasonable cost measure. More refined cost measures take into account the type of pins (backplane, chip, board, etc.) because they have different costs.

Other factors that limit the building of large monolithic crossbar switches are the capacitive loading on the buses, scheduler complexity, and issues of rack space and power. First, if one tries to build a 256-by-256 switch using the crossbar approach of 256 input and output buses, the loading will probably result in not meeting the speed requirements for the buses. Second, note that some centralized algorithms, such as iSLIP, that require N^2 bits of scheduling state will not scale well to large N.

---

[3] However, over time, the number of crosspoints again may begin to matter for optical switches!

Third, many routers are limited by availability requirements to placing only a few (or often one) ports in a line card. Similarly, for power and other reasons, there are often strict requirements on the number of line cards that can be placed in a rack. Thus a router with a large port count is likely to be limited by packaging requirements to use a multirack, multichassis solution consisting of several smaller fabrics connected together to form a larger composite router.

Metric #2: the complexity of matching computation

Another cost to consider in scaling the switch sizes is the computational complexity of the matching computations involved. As shown earlier, the total time complexity of computing a good crossbar schedule (bipartite matching) is at least $O(N)$ (in the case of SERENA) and can go all the way up to $O(N^{2.5} \log W)$ (in the case of MWM), for a switch with N input/output ports. Hence, when the size N of a switch grows larger and larger, it becomes increasingly difficult to compute schedules for its underlying (monolithic) crossbar at line rates (say a packet every eight nanoseconds). This time complexity challenge, coupled with the need to reduce the number of crosspoints as explained previously, has naturally led researchers and the industry to the following divide-and-conquer approach (**P15**).

13.18.2 A divide-and-conquer approach to building large switches

The divide-and-conquer approach is to build a large switch as an interconnection network of smaller switches. As a result, the time complexity of matching computations in each smaller switch becomes small enough to handle at line rates, and, as we will elaborate next, the number of crosspoints is also significantly reduced due to its $O(N^2)$ scaling. In the following subsections we describe one such divide-and-conquer solution and briefly mention another that were actually adopted in real network products in the dot.com era (the end of the 1990s to the early 2000s). The first solution was inspired by, and based on, the Clos networks proposed originally for the circuit switching in a telephone network. The second solution was adapted from a classical solution for interconnection networks, for parallel processing.

Here, we highlight an important fact about these two solutions that was not mentioned in the first edition of the book. The original ideas of both solutions solve a different problem than that of switching in our definition so far. In both original applications, namely circuit switching (in a telephone network) and interconnection network for parallel processors, which "input port" should be paired with which "output port" at any moment is never in doubt and requires no computation. In a telephone network the established phone sessions uniquely define the matchings between inputs and outputs; in an interconnection network this pairing (of communicating processors at any moment) is dictated by the parallel algorithm running on it. In both solutions the computation problem is, given a desired pairing between the inputs and the outputs in the giant (virtual) switch, to arrive at the configurations of the small (physical) switches that realize such a matching.

This computation problem is clearly different from the crossbar scheduling problem we have so far formulated, which is precisely to compute such a pairing. This computation problem, however, is not necessarily in the strict sense a simpler one because of the more stringent constraints that go with it in the original applications. For example, one such constraint is that all these small switches have no buffer, and as a result, the two paths taken by any two distinct input-output port pairs have to be disjoint (i.e., cannot share an intermediate node or link) or, equivalently, the large switch has to be nonblocking (to be defined in Section 13.18.3). In contrast, in the packet switching problem, the input ports are assumed to have adequate amounts of buffers and do not impose such a constraint.

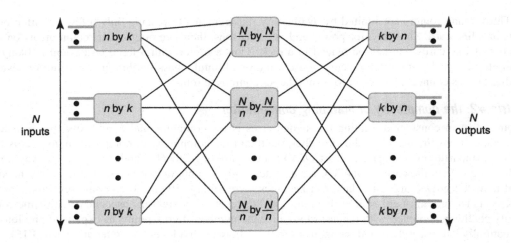

FIGURE 13.16

Three-stage Clos network.

In Sections 13.18.3 and 13.18.4 we will explain both solutions in terms of how they facilitate a known matching between the input and the output ports of the large crossbar, just like in the first edition of the book. In Section 13.18.3 we will describe how to adapt one of them, namely the Clos network, for the packet switching problem. More specifically, we will describe a possible way of constructing a large packet switch using a Clos network of small packet switches with buffers.

13.18.3 Clos networks for medium-sized routers

Despite the lack of current focus on crosspoints in VLSI technology, our survey of scalable fabrics for routers begins by looking at the historically earliest proposal for a scalable switch fabric. Charles Clos first proposed his idea in 1955 to reduce the expense of electromechanical switching in telephone switches. Fortunately, the design also reduces the number of components and links required to connect up a number of smaller switches. It is thus useful in a present-day context. Specifically, a Clos network appears to be used in the Juniper Networks T-series multichassis router product, introduced 47 years later, in 2002.

The basic Clos network uses a simple divide-and-conquer (**P15**) approach to reducing crosspoints by switching in three stages, as shown in Fig. 13.16. The first stage divides the N total inputs into groups of n inputs each, and each group of n inputs is switched to the second stage by a small (n-by-k) switch. Thus there are N/n "small" switches in the first stage.

The second stage consists of k switches, each of which is an N/n-by-N/n switch. Each of the k outputs of each first-stage switch is connected in order to all the k second-stage switches. More precisely, output j of switch i in the first stage is connected to input i of switch j in the second stage. The third stage is a mirror reversal of the first stage, and the interconnections between the second and third stages are also the mirror reversal of those between the first and second stages. The view from outputs leftward to the middle stage is the same as the view from inputs to the middle stage. More precisely, each of the N/n outputs of the first stage is connected in order to the inputs of the third stage.

A switch is said to be *nonblocking* if, whenever the input and output are free, a connection can be made through the switch using free resources. Thus a crossbar is always nonblocking by selecting the crosspoint corresponding to the input–output pair, which is never used for any other pair. On the other hand, in Fig. 13.16 every input switch has only k connections to the middle stage, and every middle stage has only one path to any particular switch in the third stage. Thus for small k, it is easily possible to block a new connection because there is no path from an input I to a middle-stage switch that has a free line to an output O.

Clos networks in telephony

Clos's insight was to see that, if $k \geq 2n - 1$, then the resulting Clos network could indeed simulate a crossbar (i.e., is nonblocking), while still reducing the number of crosspoints to be $5.6N\sqrt{N}$ instead of N^2. This can be big savings for large N. Of course, to achieve this crosspoint reduction, the Clos network has increased latency by two extra stages of switching delay, but that is often acceptable.

The proof of Clos's theorem is easy to see from Fig. 13.17. If a hitherto-idle input i wishes to be connected to an idle output o, then consider the first-stage switch S that I is connected to. There can be at most $n - 1$ other inputs in S that are busy (S is an n-by-k switch). These $n - 1$ busy input links of S can be connected to at most $n - 1$ middle-stage switches.

Similarly, focusing on output o, consider the last-stage switch T that o is connected to. Then, T can have at most $n - 1$ other outputs that are busy, and each of these outputs can be connected via at most $n - 1$ middle-stage switches. Since both S and T are connected to k middle-stage switches, if $k \geq 2n - 1$, then it is always possible to find a middle-stage switch M that has a free input link to connect to S and a free output link to connect to T. Since S and T are assumed to be crossbars or otherwise nonblocking switches, it is always possible to connect i to the corresponding input link to M and to connect the corresponding output link of M to o.

If $k = 2n - 1$ and n is set to its optimal value of $\sqrt{N/2}$, then the number of crosspoints (summed across all smaller switches in Fig. 13.16) becomes $5.6N\sqrt{N}$. For example, for $N = 512$, this reduces the number of crosspoints from 4.2 million for a crossbar to 516,096 for a three-stage Clos switch. Larger telephone switches, such as the No. 1. ESS, which can handle 65,000 inputs, use an eight-stage switch for further reductions in crosspoint size.

Reducing the size of the middle stage

On the other hand, for networking using VLSI switches, what is important is the total number of switches and the number of links interconnecting switches. Recall that the largest possible switches are fabricated in VLSI and that their cost is a constant, regardless of their crosspoint size. Juniper Networks, for example, uses a Clos network to form effectively a 256-by-256 multichassis router by connecting sixteen 16×16 T-series routers in the first stage.

Using a standard Clos network for a fully populated multichassis router would require 16 routers in the first stage, 16 in the third stage, and $k = 2 * 16 - 1 = 31$ switches in the middle stage. Clearly, Juniper can (and does) reduce the cost of this configuration by setting $k = n$. Thus the Juniper multichassis router requires only 16 switches in the middle stage. This is exactly the construction of a large $m \times m$ switch using $3\sqrt{m}$ small switches, each of the size $\sqrt{m} \times \sqrt{m}$ that we mentioned earlier.

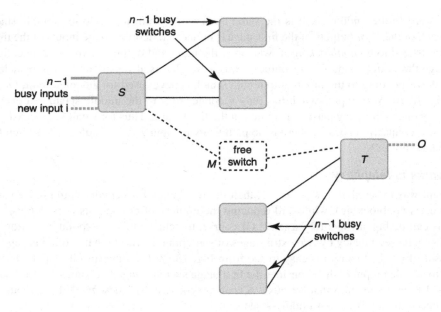

FIGURE 13.17

Proof that a Clos network with $k = 2n - 1$ is nonblocking.

What happens to a Clos network when k reduces from $2n - 1$ to n? If $k = n$, the Clos network is no longer nonblocking. Instead, the Clos network becomes what is called *rearrangeably nonblocking*. In other words, the new input i can be connected to o as long as it's possible to rearrange some of the existing connections between inputs and outputs to use different middle-stage switches. A proof and possible switching algorithm is described in Appendix A. It can be safely skipped by readers uninterested in the theory.

The bottom line behind all the math in Section A.3.1 in Appendix A is as follows. First, $k = n$ is clearly much more economical than $k = 2n - 1$ because it reduces the number of middle-layer switches by a factor of two. However, while the Clos network is rearrangeably nonblocking, deterministic edge-coloring algorithms for switch scheduling appear at this time to be quite complex. Second, the matching proof for telephone calls assumes that all calls appear at the inputs at the same time; when a new call arrives, existing calls have to be potentially rearranged to fit the new routes.

Clos networks and multichassis routers

Whereas the Clos network is required to be nonblocking or at least rearrangeably nonblocking for it to be used for a telephone network, there is no such requirement for it to be used for a multichassis router (i.e., a packet switch), due to a key difference between the two applications: a telephone switch has no buffer, whereas a (small) packet switch does. Roughly speaking, requiring a Clos network to be nonblocking, or rearrangeably nonblocking, equates to requiring it to achieve perfect load-balance among the intermediate switches during every time slot, which is necessary where there is no buffering.

Where there is buffering, however, this load-balance needs only to be statistically perfect, a notion that we will make precise next.

We now construct a large switch that is perfectly load-balanced statistically, using a three-stage Clos network of small switches with buffers. In this construction we make $k = n$ as previously explained, so that there are n switches in each stage. Since $N = n^2$, in this case, we have pieced together an $N \times N$ switch using $3\sqrt{N}$ switches of size $\sqrt{N} \times \sqrt{N}$. For example, when $N = 1024$, we use only 96 switches of size 32×32 to build a giant 1024×1024 switch. We will show that, in this three-stage Clos network, there is no need to compute matchings (every time slot) for this giant 1024×1024 bipartite graph. Instead, each small switch computes matchings for its 32×32 bipartite graph, which is much easier computationally.

In this three-stage Clos network statistically perfect load-balancing can be achieved using the following simple randomized strategy. In this strategy each switch in the first stage statistically evenly distributes all its incoming packets to all n switches in the second stage. Then, at each switch in the second stage, every incoming packet has to be forwarded to the third stage switch where the destination output port is located. This will not cause load imbalance at the second stage since it can be shown that, if every switch in the first stage does a perfect job of statistical load-balancing, then, at each switch in the second stage, there is a statistically equal amount of traffic destined for every output port of it. For a similar reason, there will be no load imbalance at the third stage.

Then, how can every switch in the first stage do a perfect job of statistical load-balancing? This can be achieved by the following simple and intuitive scheme, with a caveat that will be explained shortly. We describe only the operations of a single switch at the first level because operations at any other switch are identical; in this switch we consider only the operations at a single-input port, as operations at other input ports are identical. The scheme is, for every incoming packet, this input port simply forwards it to an output port, and correspondingly a switch at the second level, that is chosen uniformly at random.

The caveat with this scheme is that, because load balancing is performed on a packet-by-packet basis (i.e., at the packet level), two consecutive packets that belong to the same TCP flow may go through two different switches at the second stage and experience different queueing delays. As a result, they may depart from the (same) switch at the third stage and arrive at their destination out of order. Such out-of-order packet arrivals could unnecessarily decrease the throughput of the TCP flow since the TCP clients (on both ends) can mistakenly interpret them as an indication of packet losses caused by network congestion, and respond accordingly (e.g., by reducing the size of congestion window). This was generally not an issue in the dot.com era, when the average data rate provided to a TCP flow was typically quite low (typically tens to hundreds of Kbps), which would not be much further reduced by this packet reorder problem. Indeed, it appears that Juniper adopted a similar packet-level load balancing scheme in the early 2000s, although it's not possible to be sure about what Juniper actually did because their documentation is (probably intentionally) vague.

In recent years, three-stage Clos networks have mostly been used instead to build a large data center network (which can be viewed as a giant switch) (Loukissas et al., 2008; Cao et al., 2013; Ghorbani et al., 2017; Zhao et al., 2019). However, as the data rates of TCP flows nowadays are much higher, especially in a data center network, this packet-reorder problem can no longer be ignored. Hence, all recent packet-based load-balancing solutions for three-stage Clos networks have to either eliminate or mitigate this packet reorder problem. For example, in Ghorbani et al. (2017) the built-in packet re-sequencing capability of modern NICs at end hosts is cleverly exploited to keep the percentage of out-of-order packets to a minimum.

An alternative load-balancing approach, known as TCP hashing (Keslassy, 2004), does not have this packet reorder problem. In this approach all packets belonging to the same TCP flow must take the same path (i.e., links and switches) through the Clos network. At each input port of a switch at the first level, this can be achieved by hashing on the TCP flow identifier (source and destination IP addresses, source and destination ports, and protocol identification) of every incoming packet to obtain a value between 1 and N, which corresponds to the output port of this switch to which this packet should be forwarded. However, while eliminating the packet-reorder problem, TCP hashing can lead to severe load-imbalance. For example, all packets in an elephant flow, which travel the same path, will congest the links and switches along the path. Hence, recently, in an LBS scheme (to be described in Section 13.18.5) called safe randomized switching (SRS) (Yang et al., 2017b), the TCP hashing approach was enhanced with two safety mechanisms to effectively mitigate this load-imbalance problem.

13.18.4 Benes networks for larger routers

Just as the No. 1. ESS telephone switch switches 65,000 input links, Turner (1997); Chaney et al. (1997) has made an eloquent case that the Internet should (at least eventually) be built of a few large routers instead of several smaller routers. Such topologies can reduce the wasted links for router-to-router connections between smaller routers and thus reduce cost; they can also reduce the worst-case end-to-path length, reducing latency and improving user response times.

Essentially, a Clos network has roughly $N\sqrt{N}$ scaling in terms of crosspoint complexity using just three stages. This trade-off and general algorithmic experience (**P15**) suggest that one should be able to get $N \log N$ crosspoint complexity, while increasing the switch depth to $\log N$. Such switching networks are indeed possible and have been known for years in theory, in telephony, and in the parallel computing industry. Alternatives, such as Butterfly, Delta, Banyan, and Hypercube networks, are well-known contenders.

While the subject is vast, this chapter concentrates only on the Delta and Benes networks. Similar networks are used in many implementations. For example, the Washington University Gigabit switch (Chaney et al., 1997) uses a Benes network, which can be thought of as two copies of a Delta network. Section A.4 in Appendix A outlines the (often small) differences between Delta networks and others of the same ilk.

In the following, we describe Delta and Benes networks only in the historical contexts of theory, telephony, and parallel computing, where switches have no or little buffers. We will explain that, in such contexts, the network designs need to address the congestion issues caused by pathological load patterns. In the router context where the (small) switches have adequate amounts of buffers, however, the buffers further alleviate such issues in a similar way as they do in the Clos network, which we have explained in Section 13.18.3.

The Delta networks

The easiest way to understand a Delta network is recursively. Imagine that there are N inputs on the left and that this problem is to be reduced to the problem of building two smaller ($N/2$)-size Delta networks. To help in this reduction, assume a first stage of 2-by-2 switches. A simple scheme (Fig. 13.18) is to inspect the output that every input wishes to speak to. If the output is in the upper half (MSB of output

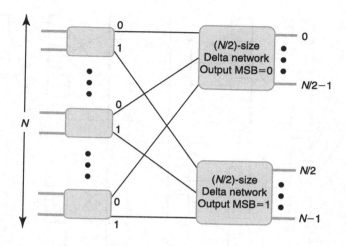

FIGURE 13.18

Constructing a Delta network recursively by reducing the problem of constructing an N-input Delta network to the problem of constructing two ($N/2$)-input Delta networks.

is 0), then the input is routed to the upper $N/2$ Delta Network; if the output is in the lower half (i.e., MSB = 1), the input is routed to the lower $N/2$ Delta network.

To economize on the first stage of two-input switches, group the inputs into consecutive pairs, each of which shares a two-input switch, as in Fig. 13.18. Thus if the two input cells in a pair are going to different output halves, they can be switched in parallel; otherwise, one will be switched and the other is either dropped or buffered. Of course, the same process can be repeated recursively for both of the smaller ($N/2$)-size Delta networks, breaking them up into a layer of 2-by-2 switches followed by four $N/4$ switches, and so on. The complete expansion of a Delta network is shown in the first half of Fig. 13.19. Notice how the recursive construction in Fig. 13.18 can be seen in the connections between the first and second stages in Fig. 13.19.

Thus to reduce the problem to 2×2 switches takes $\log N$ stages; since each stage has $N/2$ crosspoints, the binary Delta network has $N \log N$ crosspoint and link complexity. Clearly, we can also construct a Delta network by using d-by-d switches in the first stage and breaking up the initial network into d Delta networks of size N/d each. This reduces the number of stages to $\log_d N$ and link complexity to $n \log_d N$. Given VLSI costs, it is cheaper to construct a switching chip with as large a value of d as possible to reduce link costs.

The Delta network, as do many of its close relatives (see Section A.4) such as the Banyan and the Butterfly, has a nice property called the *self-routing* property. For a binary Delta network, one can find the unique path from a given input to a given output $o = o_1, o_2, \ldots, o_s$ expressed in binary by following the link corresponding to the value of o_i in stage i. This should be clear from Fig. 13.18, where we use the MSB at the first stage, the second bit at the second stage, and so on. For $d \geq 2$, write the output address as a radix-d number, and follow successive digits in a similar fashion.

An interesting property that one can intuitively see in Fig. 13.18 is that the Delta network is reversible. It is possible to trace a path from an output to an input by following bits of the input in the

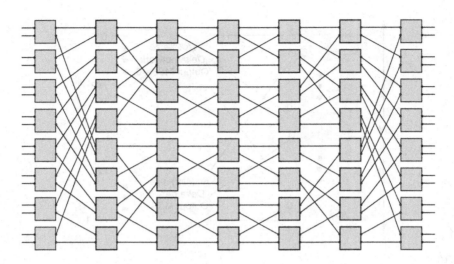

FIGURE 13.19

The first half is a Delta network (Fig. 13.18), and the second half is a mirror-reversed Delta network. The first half distributes load and the second routes.

same way. Thus in Fig. 13.18 notice that, in going from outputs to inputs, the next-to-last bit of the input selects between two consecutive first-stage switches, and the last bit selects the input. This reversibility property is important because it allows the use of a mirror-reversed version of the Delta (see the second half of Fig. 13.19) with similar properties as the original Delta.

One problem with the Delta network is congestion. Since there is a unique path from each input to each output, the Delta network is emphatically not a permutation network. For example, if each successive pair of inputs wishes to send a cell to the same output half, only half of the cells can proceed to the second stage; if this repeats, only a quarter can proceed to the third stage; and so on. Thus there are combinations of output requests for which the Delta network throughput can reduce to that of one link, as opposed to N links.

Clearly, one way to make the Delta network less susceptible to congestion for arbitrary permutations of input requests is to add more paths between an input and an output. Generalizing the ideas in a Clos network (Fig. 13.16), one can construct a *Benes network* (Fig. 13.19) that consists of two $(\log N)$-depth networks: the left half is a standard Delta network, and the right half is a mirror-reversed Delta network. Look at the right half backwards, going left from the outputs: notice that the connections from the last stage to the next-to-last stage are identical to those between the first and second stages.

One can also visualize a Benes network recursively (**P15**) by extending Fig. 13.18 by adding a third stage of 2-by-2 switches and by connecting these third stages to the two $(N/2)$-sized networks in the middle, in the same way as the first-stage switches are connected to the two middle $(N/2)$-sized networks (Fig. 13.20). Observe that this recursion can be used to directly create Fig. 13.19 without creating two separate Delta networks.

Observe the similarity between the recursive version of the Benes network in Fig. 13.20 and the Clos network of Fig. 13.16. This similarity can be exploited to prove that the *Benes* can route any

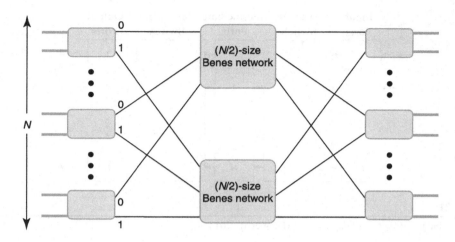

FIGURE 13.20

Recursively constructing a Benes network.

permutation of output requests in a manner similar to our proof (see the earlier box) of the rearrangeably nonblocking property of a Clos network.

In each of two iterations start by doing a perfect matching between the first and last stages of Fig. 13.20, as before, and pick one of the two middle switches. However, rather than stopping here as in the Clos proof, the algorithm must recursively follow the same routing procedure in the $(N/2)$-sized Benes network. Alternatively, the whole process can be formulated using edge coloring. The final message is that it is possible to perfectly route arbitrary permutations in a Benes network; however, doing so is fairly complex and is unlikely to be accomplished cheaply in a minimum packet arrival time.

However, recall the earlier argument that a randomized strategy works well, in an expected sense, for Clos networks instead of a more complex and deterministic edge-coloring scheme. Analogous to picking a random middle switch in the Clos network, returning to Fig. 13.19, one can pick a random destination for each cell in the first half. One can then route from the random intermediate destination to the actual cell destination (using reverse Delta routing) in the second half. The roots of this idea of using random intermediate destinations go back to Valiant (Valiant, 1990), who first used it to route in a (single-copy) hypercube.

As in the case of a Clos network using a random choice of middle switches, it can be shown that (in an expected sense) no internal link gets congested as long as no input or output link is congested. Intuitively, the load-splitting half takes all the traffic destined for any output link from any input and spreads it evenly over all the N output links of the first half of Fig. 13.19. In the second half because of the mirror-image structure, all the traffic of the link fans is back to the destined output links.

For example, consider the upper link coming into the first switch in the last stage of Fig. 13.19. An important claim is that this upper link will carry half of the traffic to output link 1. This is because this upper link carries all the traffic destined for output link 1 from the top half of the input nodes in the route-and-copy network (mirror-reversed Delta). And, by the load-splitting property of the distribute

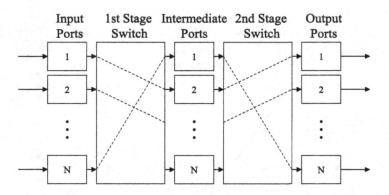

FIGURE 13.21

Generic load-balanced switch. (Adapted from (Ding et al., 2014).)

network (the first half of the Delta network), this is half of the traffic destined for output link 1. Similarly, it is possible to argue that the upper link carries half the traffic going to output link 2. Thus if output links 1 and 2 are not saturated, neither will the upper link to switch 1 in the last stage be. One can make a similar argument for any internal link in the second half.

13.18.5 Load-balanced switching

LBS (Chang et al., 2002a,b; Ding et al., 2014; Jaramillo et al., 2008; Keslassy, 2004; Lin and Keslassy, 2010; Yang et al., 2017a,b), first introduced by Chang et al. (2002a,b), and later further developed by others (e.g. Ding et al., 2014; Jaramillo et al., 2008; Keslassy, 2004; Lin and Keslassy, 2010; Yang et al., 2017a), is another approach to scaling to larger and faster switches. It does so by removing one of the two aforementioned major hurdles to scaling: whereas in a Clos network, bipartite matching computations are still needed in each small switch, in LBS they are completely avoided.

LBS architectures build upon the idea of Valiant load balancing (Leslie, 1982), which predated the design of any IP switch or router. They rely on two switching stages for routing packets. Fig. 13.21 shows a diagram of a generic two-stage load-balanced switch. The first switching stage connects the first stage of input ports to the center stage of intermediate ports, and the second switching stage connects the center stage of intermediate ports to the final stage of output ports. Each switching stage executes a predetermined periodic sequence (hence, no bipartite matching computations are needed!) of connection patterns such that each input is connected to each output of a switching stage $\frac{1}{N}$th of the time.

A typical connection pattern for LBS is the cyclic shifts. For example, the following is a standard cyclic-shift connection pattern that is easy to understand and verify. The first switching fabric executes a periodic "increasing" sequence of matchings: at any time slot t, each input port i is connected to the intermediate port $(i + t) \mod N$. It has been shown in Chang et al. (2002a) that, when the traffic arrival process satisfies certain mild stationarity conditions, this periodic sequence of matchings can spread the incoming traffic very evenly across all intermediate ports. The second switching fabric, on the other hand, will execute a periodic "decreasing" sequence of matchings: at any time slot t, each intermediate port i is connected to the output port $(i - t) \mod N$.

Although the basic load-balanced switch originally proposed in Chang et al. (2002a) is capable of achieving 100% throughput, it has a serious problem that packet departures can be badly out of order. In the basic load-balanced switch consecutive packets at an input port are spread to all N intermediate ports upon arrival. Packets going through different intermediate ports may encounter *different queueing delays*. Thus some of these packets may arrive at their output ports out-of-order. This is detrimental to Internet traffic since the widely used TCP transport protocol falsely regards out-of-order packets as indications of congestion and packet loss. Therefore a number of solutions (Ding et al., 2014; Yang et al., 2017a,b) have been proposed to address this problem.

13.19 Scaling to faster link speeds

The preceding section focused on how switches can scale in *size*. This section studies how switches can scale in *speed*. Now, it may be that the speeds of individual fiber channels level off at some point. Many pundits said in the late 1990s that fundamental SRAM and optical limits would limit individual fiber channels to OC-768 speeds. The capacity of fiber would then be used to produce more individual channels (e.g., using multiple wavelengths) rather than higher-speed individual channels. The use of more channels would then affect switching only in terms of increasing port count and can be handled using the techniques of the previous section.

This prediction has been mostly correct for the past 20 years: at the time of writing, OC-768 (40 Gbps) is still the highest link speed that is widely used, although (Ethernet) products with 100 Gbps link speeds are available. However, the lessons of history should teach us that it is certainly possible for individual applications to increase their speed needs and for technology surprisingly to keep pace by producing faster link speeds that increase from 100 Gbps today to 1 Tbps in, say, 20 years. Thus it is worthwhile to look for techniques to scale switches in speed. There are three common techniques: *bit slicing*, the use of *short links*, and the use of *randomized memory sharing*.

13.19.1 Using bit slicing for higher-speed fabrics

The simplest way to cope with link speed increases is to use a faster clock rate to run the switching electronics. Unfortunately, optical speeds increase exponentially, while ASIC clock rates increase only at around 10% per year. However, by Moore's law, the number of transistors placed on a chip doubles every 18–24 months without a cost increase. Thus the simplest way to cope with link speed increases is to use *parallelism*.

Suppose it were possible to build a crossbar where every link has speed S. Then, to handle links of speed kS for some constant k, a design could use k crossbar "slices." For every group of k bits coming from a link, one bit each is sent to each crossbar slice. Thus each slice sees a reduced link speed of $kS/k = S$ and thus can be feasibly implemented. Of course, this implies that the reassembly logic can scale in speed.

If the bits are distributed to slices in a deterministic fashion (i.e., bit 1 of the first cell goes to slice 1, bit 2 to slice 2, etc.), the reassembly logic can be simplified because it knows on which slice to expect the next bit. However, care must be taken to avoid synchronization errors. The scheduler can make the same decision for all slices, making the scheduler easy to build.

The Juniper T-series (Semeria and Gredler, 2001) uses four active switch fabric planes (i.e., slices). It also uses a fifth plane as a hot-standby for redundancy. Since each plane uses a request–grant mechanism, if a grant does not return within a timeout, a plane failure can be detected. At this point, only the cells in transit within the failed plane are lost, the failed plane is swapped out for maintenance, and the standby plane is swapped in.

While little discussed so far, redundancy and fault tolerance are crucial for large switch designs because more is at stake. If a small, 8-port router fails, only a few users are affected. But a large, 256-port-by-256-port router must work nearly always, with internal redundancy, masking out faults. This is because external redundancy, in terms of a second such router, is too expensive. Most ISPs require core routers to be NEBS (Network Equipment Building System) (NEBS, 2002) compliant. Typically, large routers are expected to have at most five minutes of downtime in a year.

13.19.2 Using short links for higher-speed fabrics

One feature of interconnection networks ignored so far is the physical length of the links used between stages. Links come in various forms, from serial links between chips to backplane traces, to cable connections between different line cards. Intuitively, the length matters because long wires increase delay and decrease bit rate, unless compensated for using more expensive signaling technology, such as optical signaling.

A look at the Delta and Clos networks shows that these networks use at least a few long wires between stages, whose length scales as $O(N)$. There are, however, interconnect networks that can be packaged with uniformly short wires. These are the so-called low-dimensional mesh networks. Such mesh networks have a checkered history in parallel computing, being used by Cray and Intel supercomputers.

The simplest low-dimensional mesh is the 1D torus, which is basically a line of nodes in which the last node is also connected to the first node to form a logical ring (Fig. 13.22). A 2D torus is basically a two-dimensional grid of nodes where the last node in each row or column is also connected to the first node in the same row or column. A 3D torus is the same idea extended to a three-dimensional grid.

Even a 1D torus, which is logically a ring, appears to have one long wire that connects the first and last nodes (Fig. 13.22). However, a clever way to amortize this long line length across all nodes is to use a simple degree of freedom (**P13**) and to lay out the first half of the nodes on the forward path of the ring (Fig. 13.22) and the second half on the reverse path. While the length of the A-to-B wire may have doubled, there are no long wires. The same idea can be extended for 2D and 3D toruses by repeating this idea across rows and columns.

Like a Butterfly or Delta network, the problem with a 1D torus, however, is that it suffers from congestion because there are only two paths between two inputs. It also suffers from high latency because some pairs of nodes have to travel $O(N/2)$ hops. The congestion and latency problems are relieved by using a 3D torus. For example, in a 3D torus that is 8-by-8-by-8, an average message can choose (Dally, 2002) between 90 paths of six hops each.

The Avici TSR Router (Dally, 2002) is an example of a router built using a 3D torus. It can handle up to 560 line cards, and the use of short wires allows it to be packaged very neatly. A 260-line-card configuration can be packaged *without any cables* by connecting only adjacent backplanes using

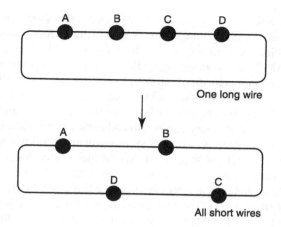

FIGURE 13.22

How a 1D torus can be packaged physically using short wires.

jumpers. The 560-line-card version uses one set of short cables between two rows of racks (Dally, 2002).

Besides the use of short links, the 3D mesh offers a large number of alternate paths for fault tolerance and the ability to be incrementally upgraded with minimal extra cost. By contrast, some interconnection networks tend to require scaling in powers of two.

13.19.3 Memory scaling using randomization

In all the switches seen so far packets have to be stored in buffers during periods of congestion. The standard rule of thumb is for routers to have one RTT (Roundtrip Time) worth of buffering to allow congestion-control algorithms to slow down without causing packet loss. While it may be possible to get around this limit using better higher-level congestion-control algorithms, it appears that the combination of TCP and RED (random early detection) today requires this amount of buffering. Using 200 msec as a conservative estimate for round-trip delay, a two-terabit router must have 0.4 terabit's worth of packet buffers. Thus as link speeds increase and assuming no congestion-control innovations, the memory needs will also increase.

Consider an input-buffered switch and packets coming in at OC-768 speeds. Thus a minimum-size packet arrives every 8 nanoseconds and will require at least two accesses to memory: the first to store the packet and the second to read it out for transmission through the fabric. Given that the fastest DRAM available at the time of writing has a cycle time of 50 nanoseconds, it is clear that the only way to meet the memory bandwidth needs using DRAM would be to use a wider memory word.

Unfortunately, one cannot use a wider memory word size than that of a minimum-size packet because it is not possible to guarantee that the next packet will be read out at the same time. One could use SRAMs (at 4 nanoseconds cycle times at the time of writing, this should be just adequate), but then one would have to pay a cost premium of anywhere from a factor of four to a factor of 10.[4]

One way out of this dilemma is to use parallel banks of DRAMs. It is possible to keep up with link speeds using 12 DRAM banks working in parallel, each with a 40-byte access width. Intuitively, this seems plausible. For any input stream of packets, send the first packet to DRAM 1, the second to DRAM 2, etc. Unfortunately, because of QoS and scheduling algorithms, it is not clear in which order packets will be read out. Thus it may be that during some period of time, all the packets are read out from a few DRAMs only, causing memory bandwidth contention and eventual packet loss.

Such memory contention problems are familiar to computer architects when using interleaved memory. For example, if an array is laid out sequentially across memory banks, it is possible that accesses that are spaced a certain stride apart (e.g., column accesses) may all hit the same bank. One potentially clever way out of the contention problem is to steal a leaf from the designers of the CYDRA-2 stride-insensitive memory (Rau, 1991). Their idea was to *pseudorandomly interleave* storage requests to memory such that with high probability any access pattern (other than to the same word) would not cause hot spots. Indeed, techniques of performing such stride-insensitive or even adversary-resistant randomized memory interleaving have been proposed in several recent papers (Lin et al., 2009; Wang et al., 2010; Zhao et al., 2009).

In the router context instead of sending packet 1 to DRAM 1 and so on, one would send each packet to a randomly selected DRAM. Of course, as with all randomized interleaving schemes (see the earlier Clos and Benes sections), reassembly gets more complicated, with the states having to be kept (in SRAM?) to resequence these packets.

13.20 Conclusions

This chapter has surveyed techniques for building switches, from small shared-memory switches to input-queued switches used in the Cisco GSR, to larger, more scalable switch fabrics used in the Juniper T130 and Avici TSR Routers.

Since this is a book about algorithmics, it is important to focus on the techniques and not get lost in the mass of product names. These are summarized in Table 13.1. Fundamentally, the major idea in PIM and iSLIP is to realize that, by using VOQs, one can feasibly (with $O(N^2)$ bits in total or O(N) bits in per-port communication complexity) communicate all the desired communication patterns to avoid HOL blocking. These schemes go further and show that maximal matching can be done in $N \log N$ time using randomization (PIM) or approximately (iSLIP) using round-robin pointers per port for fairness. Here we assume this randomization and the round-robin pointer mechanism can be performed with $O(1)$ time complexity using hardware such as the priority encoder described in Section 2.2.2.

While $N \log N$ is a large number, by showing that this can be done in parallel by each of N ports, the time reduces to $\log N$ (in PIM) and to a small constant (in iSLIP). Given that $\log N$ is small, even this delay can be pipelined away to run in a minimum packet time. The fundamental lesson is that even algorithms that appear complex, such as matching, can, with randomization and hardware parallelism, be made to run in a minimum packet time. Further scaling in speed can be done using bit slices.

---

[4] The cost premium of DRAM versus SRAM is hard to pin down because DRAM prices sometimes fall dramatically.

Compared to PIM and iSLIP, SW-QPS is a mind-blowing result. Its per-port time complexity is strictly $O(1)$ without using any hardware support. Its per-port communication complexity is also $O(1)$, as compared to $O(N)$ in the cases of PIM and iSLIP. Yet, it delivers overall better throughput and delay performance than iSLIP. It achieves all these by exploiting all relevant algorithmics techniques to the fullest extent: randomization, hardware parallelism, and extreme pipelining (which the sliding-window technique can arguably be viewed as).

Larger port counts can also be handled by algorithmic techniques based on the divide-and-conquer approach. An understanding of the actual costs of switching shows that even a simple three-stage Clos switch works well for port sizes up to 256. However, for larger switch sizes, the Benes network, with its combination of ($2\log N$) depth Delta networks, is better suited for the job. The main issue in both these scalable fabrics is scheduling. And, in both cases, as in PIM, a complex deterministic algorithm is finessed using simple randomization. In both the Clos and Benes networks the essential similarity of structure allows the use of an initial randomized load-balancing step followed by deterministic path selection from the randomized intermediate destination.

Similar ideas are also used to reduce memory needs by either picking a random intermediate line card or a random choice of DRAM bank to send a given packet (cell) to. The knockout switch uses trees of randomized 2-by-2 concentrators to provide k-out-of-N fairness. Thus randomization is a surprisingly important idea in switch implementations.

It is interesting to note that almost every new switch idea described in this chapter has led to the creation of a company. For example, Kanakia worked on shared-memory switches at Bell Labs and then left to found Torrent. Juniper seems to have been started with Sindhu's idea for a new fabric based, perhaps, on the use of staging via a random intermediate line card. McKeown founded Abrizio after the success of iSLIP. Growth Networks was started by Turner, Parulkar, and Cox to commercialize Turner's Benes switch idea, and it was later sold to Cisco. Dally took his ideas for deadlock-free routing on low-dimensional meshes and moved them successfully from Cray Computers to Avici's TSR.

Thus, if you, dear reader, have an idea for a new folded Banyan or an inverted Clos, you, too, may be the founder of the next great thing in networking. Perhaps some venture capitalist will soon be meeting you in a coffee shop in Silicon Valley to make you an offer you cannot refuse.

In conclusion for a router designer it's better to switch than to fight, with the difficulties of designing a high-speed bus.

13.21 Exercises

1. **Take-a-Ticket State Machine:** Draw a state machine for take-a-ticket. Describe the state machine using pseudocode, with a state machine for each sender and each receiver. Extend the state machine to handle hunt groups.
2. **Knockout Implementation:** There are dependencies between the knockout trees. The simplest implementation passes all the losers from the Position $j-1$ tree to the Position j tree. This would take $k \log N$ gate delays because each tree takes $\log N$ gate delays. Find a way to pipeline this process such that Tree j begins to work on each batch of losers as they are determined by Tree $j-1$, as opposed to waiting for all losers to be determined. Draw your implementation using 2-by-2 concentrators as your building block and estimate the worst-case delay in concentrator delays.

3. **PIM unfairness:** In the knockout example using just one tree can lead to unfairness; a collection of locally fair decisions can lead to global unfairness. Surprisingly, PIM can also lead to some form of unfairness (but not to persistent starvation). Consider a 2-by-2 switch, where input 1 has unlimited traffic to outputs 1 and 2, and input 2 has unlimited traffic to output 1.

   • Show that, on average, input 1 will get two grants from outputs 2 and 1 for half the cell slots and one grant (for output 2 only) for the remaining cell slots. What fraction of output 2's link should input 1 receive?
   • Infer, based on the preceding fraction of output 1's bandwidth, what input 1 receives on average versus input 2. Is this fair?

4. **Motivating the iSLIP Pointer Increment Rule:** The following is one unfairness scenario if pointers in iSLIP are incremented incorrectly. For example, suppose in Fig. 13.10 that input port A always has traffic to output ports 1, 2, and 3, whose grant pointers are initialized to A. Suppose also that input ports B and C also always have traffic to 2. Thus initially A, B, and C all grant to 1, which chooses A. In the second iteration since input port 2 has traffic to B, 2 and B are matched.

   • Suppose B increments its grant pointer to 3 based on this second iteration match. Between which port pairs can traffic be continually starved if this scenario persists?
   • How does iSLIP prevent this scenario?

5. **Clos Proof Revisited:** The Clos proof is based on a reduction that looks and is simple. However, until you try a few twists that do not work, you may not appreciate its simplicity. In our reduction each iteration routed n pairs, one per input stage, using just one middle switch. Suppose instead that any set of middle switches is used that had free input and output links. Show, by counterexample, why the reduction does not work.

6. **Benes Switch Load-Balancing Proof:** In the Benes switch the chapter argued that any link one hop from the output cannot be overloaded, assuming perfect load balancing at the first stage. It is helpful to work out with some simple cases to provide intuition before turning, if needed, to the proof provided in Turner (1997).

   • Repeat the same proof for links one hop away from the network, but this time for a two-copy network. Does the proof change for a three-copy network?
   • Repeat all the proofs for links two hops away. Do you see a pattern that can now be stated algebraically (Turner, 1997)?

7. **Avici TSR and 3D Grid Layout:** It seems a good bet that layout and packaging will be increasingly important as switches scale up in speeds. Extend the layout drawing in Fig. 13.22 for a 1D torus to a 2D and a 3D torus. Then, read Dally (2002) to learn how the Avici TSR packages its 3D mesh in a box.

8. **Switching Using iSLIP:** As shown in Fig. 13.23, the switch is the same as shown in Fig. 13.8. However, the inputs and the starting values of accept–grant pointers are different. You need to show intermediate steps like in Figs. 13.8 and 13.9.

   • Please draw a cell transmission timing chart like Fig. 13.10.
   • Please write down the values of grant and accept pointers **after** the transmission of all these cells.

FIGURE 13.23

Switching using iSLIP.

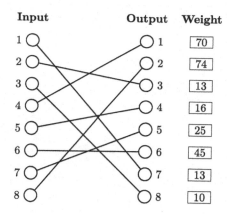

FIGURE 13.24

$R(t)$.

9. Switching Using SERENA: Assume an 8×8 crossbar is being scheduled. At a time slot t, the new random matching $R(t)$ (derived from the arrival graph) and the matching $S(t-1)$ used during the previous time slot, including the weight of each edge in both matchings, are shown in Figs. 13.24 and 13.25 respectively. Please draw or specify the matching $S(t)$ that results from MERGING $R(t)$ with $S(t-1)$.

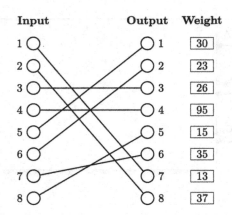

FIGURE 13.25

$S(t-1)$.

Scheduling packets

14

A schedule defends from chaos and whim.
—Annie Dillard

From arranging vacations to making appointments, we are constantly *scheduling* activities. A busy router is no exception. Routers must schedule the handling of routing updates, management queries, and, of course, data packets. Data packets must be scheduled in real time by the forwarding processors within each line card. This chapter concentrates on the efficient scheduling of data packets, while allowing certain classes of data packets to receive different services from other classes.

Returning to our picture of a router (Fig. 14.1), recall that packets enter on input links and are looked up using the address lookup component. Address lookup provides an output-link number, and the packet is switched to the output link by the switching system. Once the packet arrives at the output port, the packet could be placed in a FIFO (first in, first out) queue. If congestion occurs and the output link buffers fill up, packets arriving at the tail of the queue are dropped. Many routers use such a default output-link scheduling mechanism, often referred to as *FIFO with tail-drop*.

However, there are certainly other options. First, we could place packets in multiple queues based on packet headers and schedule these output queues according to some scheduling policy. There are several policies, such as priority and round-robin, that can schedule packets in a different order than FIFO. Second, even if we had a single queue, we need not always drop from the tail when buffers overflow; we can, surprisingly, even drop a packet when the packet buffer is not full.

Packet scheduling can be used to provide (to a flow of packets) so-called *quality of service* (QoS) guarantees on measures such as delay and bandwidth. We will see that QoS requires packet scheduling together with some form of reservations at routers. We will only briefly sketch some reservation schemes, such as those underlying RSVP (Boyle, 1997) and DiffServ (Blake et al., 1998), and we refer the reader to the specifications for more details. This is because the other parts of the QoS picture, such as handling reservations, can be handled out-of-band at a slower rate by a control processor in the router. Since this book concentrates on implementation bottlenecks, this chapter focuses on packet scheduling.

We will briefly examine the motivation for some popular scheduling choices. More importantly, we will use our principles to look for efficient implementations. Since packet scheduling is done in the real-time path, as is switching and lookup, it is crucial that scheduling decisions can be made in the minimum interpacket times because links scale to OC-768 (40-gigabit) speeds and higher.

This chapter is organized as follows. Section 14.1 presents the motivation for providing QoS guarantees. Section 14.2 describes random early detection (RED) schemes, which are better suited to TCP congestion control than tail-drop. Section 14.3 describes a fair queueing technique called Approximate

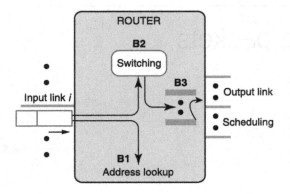

FIGURE 14.1

Router model: This chapter concentrates on the third bottleneck, **B3**, scheduling of data packets.

Fair Dropping (AFD) that has a similarly low time complexity as RED, yet a similarly good QoS guarantee as Deficit Round Robin. Section 14.4 offers a simple scheme to limit the bandwidth and burstiness of a flow, and Section 14.5 describes a basic priority scheme. Section 14.6 provides a brief introduction to reservation protocols. Section 14.7 presents simple techniques to apportion the available link bandwidth among competing flows. The section also briefly describes how the accompanying reservations for flow bandwidths can be made. Section 14.8 provides an introduction to how one can provide good delay guarantees for a flow at the cost of sorting packet deadlines in real time.

Sections 14.9 through Section 14.14 begin a technical description of how to ensure both delay bounds and fairness, culminating in Quick Fair Queuing that is implemented in the Linux kernel. These sections can be skipped by more practical readers who may want to skip to Section 14.14. Section 14.9 introduces generalized processor sharing (GPS), the fairest possible scheduling policy. Although the GPS policy is not practically implementable, a key component of it called GPS clock tracking is. This implementation is described in Section 14.12. GPS clock tracking lies at the heart of implementing weighted fair queueing (WFQ) and worst-case fair weighted-fair queueing (WF^{2}Q), two practically implementable packet scheduling policies that are almost as fair as GPS. They are described in Section 14.10 and Section 14.11, respectively. Section 14.14 describes Quick Fair Queuing (QFQ), a packet scheduling algorithm that provides a QoS guarantee similar to WF^{2}Q, yet has an implementation complexity comparable to DRR.

Finally, Section 14.15 describes two research proposals towards making packet scheduling programmable in switches and routers: PIFO in Section 14.15.1 and UPS in Section 14.15.2. Section 14.16 describe several scalable schedulers that are able to schedule a large number of flows with little or no state.

The packet-scheduling techniques described in this chapter (and the corresponding principles involved) are summarized in Table 14.1.

Quick reference guide

The most important scheduling algorithms that an Internet router must implement are RED (Section 14.2), token buckets (Section 14.4), priority queueing (Section 14.5), deficit round-robin (DRR) (Section 14.7.3), and DiffServ (for DiffServ, consult only the relevant portion of Section 14.16). Other interconnect devices, such as SAN switches and gateways, are not required to implement RED; however, implementing some form of QoS, such as DRR or token buckets, in such devices is also a good idea. Cisco routers also implement Approximate Fair Dropping (Section 14.3) as a cheaper alternative to DRR. Finally, Quick Fair Queuing (QFQ), described in Section 14.14, provides comparable implementation complexity to DRR but has much better delay bounds; it was incorporated into the Linux kernel.

Table 14.1 Summary of packet-scheduling techniques used in this chapter and the corresponding principles.

Number	Principle	Scheduling technique
P7	Use power of two parameters	RED
P3	Use policing, not shaping	Token bucket policing
P3	Focus on bandwidth only	DRR
P12	Maintain list of active queues	
P7	Use large enough quanta	
P3a	Aggregate by hashing flows	SFQ
P3c	Shift work to edge routers	DiffServ
P10	Incrementally compute interest vector	
P10	Pass class in TOS field	Core stateless
P2b	clean up lazily	GPS clock tracking using shape data structure
P15	use augmented data structure	
P3b	schedule among groups using DRR	QFQ
P14	use bucket sorting, bitmaps	
P4c	use built-in instruction	

14.1 Motivation for quality of service

We will be assigning packets flows to queues and sometimes trying to give guarantees to flows. Though we have used the term earlier, we repeat the definition of a *packet flow*. A flow is a stream of packets that traverses the same route from the source to the destination and that requires the same grade of service at each router or gateway in the path. In addition, a flow must be identifiable using fields in a packet header; these fields are typically drawn from the transport, routing, and data link headers only.

The notion of a flow is general and applies to datagram networks (e.g., IP, OSI) and virtual circuit networks (e.g., X.25, ATM). For example, in a virtual circuit network a flow could be identified by a virtual circuit identifier, or VCI. On the other hand, on the Internet a flow could be identified by all packets (1) with a destination address that matches subnet A, (2) with a source address that matches subnet B, and (3) that contain mail traffic, where mail traffic is identified by having either source or destination port numbers equal to 25. We assume that packet classification (Chapter 12) can be used to efficiently identify flows.

Why create complexity in going beyond FIFO with tail-drop? The following needs are arranged roughly in order of importance:

- **Router Support for Congestion:** With link speeds barely catching up with exponentially increasing demand, it is often possible to have congestion on the Internet. Most traffic is based on TCP, which has mechanisms to react to congestion. However, with router support, it is possible to improve the reaction of TCP sources to congestion, improving the overall throughput of sources.
- **Fair Sharing of Links Among Competing Flows:** With tail-drop routers, customers have noticed that during a period of a backup across the network, important Telnet and e-mail connections freeze. This is because the backup packets grab all the buffers at an output in some router, locking out the other flows at that output link.
- **Providing QoS Guarantees to Flows:** A more precise form of fair sharing is to guarantee bandwidths to a flow. For example, an ISP may wish to guarantee a customer 10 Mbps of bandwidth as part of a virtual private network connecting customer sites. A more difficult task is to guarantee the delay through a router for a flow such as a video flow. Live video will not work well if the network delay is not bounded.

None of these needs should be surprising when one looks at a time-sharing operating system (OS), such as UNIX or Windows NT. Clearly, in times of overload the OS must decide which load to shed; the OS often time-shares among a group of competing jobs for fairness; finally, some OSs provide delay guarantees for the scheduling of certain real-time jobs, such as playing a movie.

14.2 Random early detection

RED is a packet-scheduling algorithm implemented in most modern routers, even at the highest speeds, that has become a de facto standard. In a nutshell a RED router monitors the average output-queue length; when this goes beyond a threshold, it randomly drops arriving packets with a certain probability, *even though there may be space to buffer the packet.* The dropped packet acts as a signal to the source to slow down early, preventing a large number of dropped packets later.

To understand RED, we must review the Internet-congestion-control algorithm. The top of Fig. 14.2 shows a network connecting source S and destination D. Imagine the network had links with a capacity of 1 Mbps and that a file transfer can occur at 1 Mbps. Now suppose the middle link is replaced by a faster, 10-Mbps link. Surely it can't make things worse, can it? Well, in the old days of the Internet it did. Packets arrived at a 10-Mbps rate at the second router, which could only forward packets at 1 Mbps; this caused a flood of dropped packets, which led to slow retransmissions. This resulted in a very low throughput for the file transfer.

Fortunately, the dominant Internet transport protocol, TCP, added a mechanism called *TCP congestion control*, which is depicted in Fig. 14.2. The source maintains a window of size W, which is the number of packets the source will send without an acknowledgment. Controlling window size controls the source rate because the source is limited to a rate of W packets in a trip delay to the destination. As shown in Fig. 14.2, a TCP source starts W at 1. Assuming no dropped packets, the source increases its

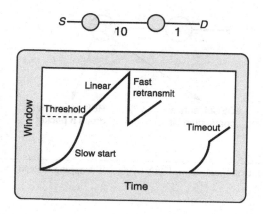

FIGURE 14.2

An illustration of TCP congestion control as a prelude to RED.

window size exponentially, doubling every round-trip delay until W reaches a threshold. After this, the source increases W linearly.

If there is a single dropped packet (this can be inferred from a number of acknowledgments with the same number), the "gap" is repaired by retransmitting only the dropped packet; this is called *fast retransmit*. In this special case the source detects some congestion and reduces its window size to half the original size (Fig. 14.2) and then starts trying to increase again. If several packets are lost, the only way for the source to recover is by having a slow, 200 milliseconds timer expire. In this case the source infers more drastic congestion and restarts the window size at 1, as shown in Fig. 14.2.

For example, with tail-drop routers, the example network shown at the top of Fig. 14.2 will probably have the source ramp up until it drops some packets and then return to a window size of 1 and start again. Despite this oscillation, the average throughput of the source is quite good because the retransmissions rarely occur as compared to the example without congestion control. However, wouldn't it be nicer if the source could drop to half the maximum at each cycle (instead of 1) and avoid expensive timeouts (200 msec) completely? The use of a RED router makes this more likely.

The main idea in a RED (Floyd and Jacobson, 1993) router (Fig. 14.3) is to have the router detect congestion *early*, before all its buffers are exhausted, and to warn the source. The simplest scheme, called the *DECbit scheme* (Ramakrishnan and Jain, 1990), would have the router send a "congestion experienced" bit to the source when its average queue size goes beyond a threshold. Since there is no room for such a bit in current IPv4 headers, RED routers simply drop a packet with some small probability. This makes it more likely that a flow causing congestion will drop just a single packet, which can be recovered by the more efficient fast retransmit instead of a drastic timeout.[1]

---

[1] But, what of sources that do not use TCP and use UDP? Since the majority of traffic is TCP, RED is still useful; the RED drops also motivate UDP applications to add TCP-like congestion, a subject of active research. A more potent question is whether RED helps small packet flows, such as Web traffic, which account for a large percentage of Internet traffic.

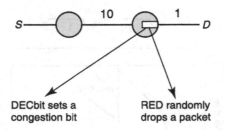

FIGURE 14.3

RED is an early warning system that operates *implicitly* by packet dropping instead of *explicitly* by sending a bit as in the DECbit scheme.

The implementation of RED is more complex than it seems. First, we need to calculate the output-queue size using a weighted average with weight w. Assuming that each arriving packet uses the queue size it sees as a sample, the average queue length is calculated by adding $(1 - w)$ times the old average queue size to w times the new sample. In other words, if w is small, even if the sample is large, it only increases the average queue size by a small amount. The average queue size changes slowly as a result and needs a large number of samples to change value appreciably. This is done deliberately to detect congestion on the order of round-trip delays (100 milliseconds) rather than instantaneous congestion that can come and go. However, we can avoid unnecessary generality (**P7**) by allowing the w to be only a reciprocal of a power of 2; a typical value is $1/512$. There is a small loss in tunability compared to allowing arbitrary values of w. However, the implementation is more efficient because the multiplications reduce to easy bit shifting.

However, there's further complexity to contend with. The drop probability is calculated using the function shown in Fig. 14.4. When the average queue size is below a minimum threshold, the drop probability is zero; it then increases linearly to a maximum drop probability at the maximum threshold; beyond this all packets are dropped. Once again, we can remove unnecessary generality (**P7**) and use appropriate values, such as MaxThreshold being twice MinThreshold and MaxP a power of 2. Then the interpolation can be done with two shifts and a subtract.

But wait, there's more. The version of RED so far is likely to drop more than one packet in a burst of closely spaced packets for a source. To make this less likely and fast retransmit more likely to work, the probability calculated earlier is scaled by a function that depends on the number of packets queued (see Peterson and Davy, 2000 for a pithy explanation) since the last drop. This makes the probability increase with the number of nondropped packets, making closely spaced drops less likely.

But wait, there's even more. There is also the possibility of adding different thresholds for different types of traffic; for example, bursty traffic may need a larger minimum threshold. Cisco has introduced *weighted RED*, where the thresholds can vary depending on the TOS bits in the IP header. Finally, there is the thorny problem of generating a random number at a router. This can be done by grabbing bits from some seemingly random register on the router; a possible example is the low-order bits of a clock that runs faster than packet arrivals. The net result is that RED, which seems easy, takes some care in practice, especially at gigabit speeds. Nevertheless, RED is quite feasible and is almost a requirement for routers being built today.

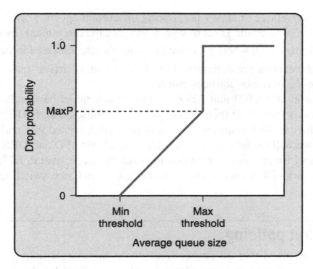

$$AverageQ = (1 - W)*AverageQ + (W*SampleQsize)$$

FIGURE 14.4

Calculating drop probabilities using RED thresholds.

14.3 Approximate fair dropping

One may rightly argue that RED is an admission-control rather than a packet scheduling algorithm, in that the router simply transmits all packets admitted by (i.e., not dropped by) RED in the FIFO order. Later in this chapter, we will focus on real packet scheduling algorithms that decide on an appropriate transmission order among packets belonging to multiple competing classes or flows, that leads to a fair bandwidth allocation. Compared to these real packet scheduling algorithms, RED and its variants (e.g., weighted RED currently used by Cisco routers) incur less computational and system overheads, but do a worse job of fair bandwidth allocation among competing flows. There is really nothing wrong with this tradeoff: RED and its variants were originally designed for congestion control only, and that it can achieve some degree of fair bandwidth allocation is arguably already a bonus. Hence, it was a pleasant surprise when a technique called approximate fair dropping (AFD) (Pan et al., 2008) was proposed that has similar computational and system overheads as RED, yet provides a level of fair bandwidth allocation that is comparable to some such real packet scheduling algorithms, such as Deficit Round Robin (DRR) that we will describe in Section 14.7.2.

As explained earlier, weighted RED also performs differential dropping per traffic class (or flow). However, weighted RED cannot be configured to induce a target allocation of the link bandwidth (say according to a certain fairness criteria) accurately, as shown in Pan et al. (2008). In comparison, AFD provides a level of bandwidth allocation that is almost as fine-grained and accurate as DRR, as also shown in Pan et al. (2008). The key idea of AFD is very simple. The time is divided into epochs that are a few RTTs in length. The router measures and estimates the traffic arrival rate of each class during the current epoch, for the purpose of setting the dropping rate for each class during the next epoch.

Suppose the estimated arrival rate of class i is r_i during the current epoch. Then, during the next epoch, the dropping rate D_i for class i traffic is set in such a way that the discounted (by dropping) arrival rate $r_i(1 - D_i)$ is equal to $\min(r_i, r_i^f)$, where r_i^f is the fair sending rate allocated to flow i. The fair sending rates (r_i^f)'s for all traffic classes are determined by the (estimated) arrival rates of all classes and the link bandwidth r, using the max-min fairness criteria.

It was shown in Pan et al. (2008) that AFD can induce any target bandwidth allocation almost as accurately as DRR. To this end, AFD incurs less systems overheads than DRR: AFD does not require extra packet buffers whereas DRR requires packets to be demultiplexed into and buffered at per-class or per-flow queues, as we will explain in Section 14.7.2; and both AFD and DRR incur the same $O(1)$ computational complexity for processing an incoming packet. Hence, overall AFD offers a bigger bang for the buck than DRR. Both DRR and AFD are currently used in Cisco switch and router products.

14.4 Token bucket policing

So far with RED, we assumed that all packets are placed in a single output queue; the RED drop decision is taken at the input of this queue. Can we add any form of bandwidth guarantees for flows that are placed in a common queue without segregation? For example, many customers require limiting the rate of traffic for a flow. More specifically, an ISP may want to limit NEWS traffic in its network to no more than 1 Mbps. A second example is where UDP traffic is flowing from the router to a slow remote line. Since UDP sources currently do not react to congestion, congestion downstream can be avoided by having a manager limit the UDP traffic to be smaller than the remote line speed. Fortunately, these examples of bandwidth limiting can easily be accomplished by a technique called *token bucket policing*, which uses only a single queue and a counter per flow.

Token bucket policing is a simple derivative of another idea, called *token bucket shaping*. Token bucket shaping (Turner, 1986) is a simple way to limit the burstiness of a flow by limiting its average rate and also its maximum burst size. For example, a flow could be limited to sending at a long-term average of 100 Kbps but could be allowed to send 4 KB as fast as it wants. Since most applications are bursty, it helps to allow *some* burstiness. Downstream nodes are helped by leaky bucket shaping because bursts contribute directly to short-term congestion and packet loss. The implementation is shown conceptually in Fig. 14.5.

Imagine that one has a bucket per flow that fills with "tokens" at the specified average rate of R per second. The bucket size, however, is limited to the specified burst size of B tokens. Thus when the bucket is full, all incoming tokens are dropped. When packets arrive for a flow, they are allowed out only if the bucket contains a number of tokens equal to the size of packet in bits. If not, the packet is queued until sufficient tokens arrive. Since there can be at most B tokens, a burst is limited to at most B bits, followed by a more steady rate of R bits per second. This can easily be implemented using a counter and a timer per flow; the timer is used to increment the counter, and the counter is limited never to grow beyond B. When packets are sent out, the counter is decremented.

Unfortunately, token bucket shaping would require different queues for each flow because some flows may have temporarily run out of tokens and have to wait, while other, later-arriving packets may belong to flows that have accumulated tokens. If one wishes to limit oneself to a single queue, a simpler technique is to limit oneself (**P3**, relax system requirements) to a token bucket policer. The idea would be simply to drop any packet that arrives to find the token bucket empty. In other words, a policer is

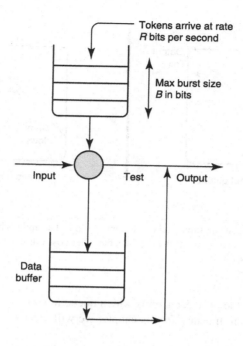

FIGURE 14.5

Conceptual picture of token bucket shaping and policing.

a shaper without the buffer shown in Fig. 14.5. A policer needs only a counter and a timer per flow, which is simple to implement at high speeds using the efficient timer implementations of Chapter 7.

14.5 Multiple outbound queues and priority

So far, we have limited ourselves to one single queue for all outbound packets, as shown on the left of Fig. 14.6. RED or token bucket policing (or both) can be used to decide whether to drop packets before they are placed on this queue. We now transition to examine scheduling disciplines that are possible with multiple queues. This is shown on the right of Fig. 14.6.

First, note that we now need to demultiplex packets based on packet headers to identify which outbound queue to place a packet on. This can be done using the packet-classification techniques described in Chapter 12 or simpler techniques based on inspecting the TOS bits in the IP header. Second, note that we can still implement RED and token bucket policing by dropping packets before they are placed on the appropriate outbound queue.

Third, note that we now have a new problem. If multiple queues have packets to send, we have to decide which queue to service next, and when. If we limit ourselves to *work-conserving* schemes[2]

---
[2] Token bucket shaping is a commonly used example of a scheduling discipline that is not work conserving.

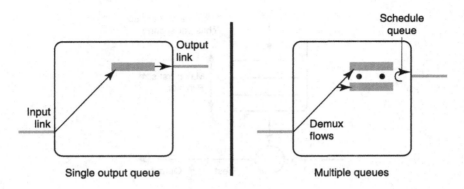

FIGURE 14.6

A single outbound queue (left) versus multiple outbound queues (right). Disciplines based on dropping (such as RED and policing) can be implemented with a single queue, but other possibilities, such as round-robin and priority, are possible with multiple queues.

that never idle the link, then the only decision is which queue to service next when the current packet transmission on the output link finishes. In this chapter we will indeed focus on the work-conserving schemes.

As the simplest example of a multiple queue-scheduling discipline, consider *strict priority*. For example, imagine two outbound queues, one for premium service and one for other packets. Imagine that packets are demultiplexed to these two queues based on a bit in the IP TOS field. In strict priority, we will always service a queue with higher priority before one with lower priority as long as there is a packet in the higher-priority queue.

14.6 A quick detour into reservation protocols

This chapter focuses on packet-scheduling mechanisms. However, before we go deeper into scheduling queues, it may help to see the big picture. Thus we briefly discuss reservation protocols that actually set up the parameters that control scheduling. While we do so to make this chapter self-contained, the reader should refer to the original sources (e.g., Boyle, 1997) for a more detailed description.

First, note that reservations are crucial for any form of absolute performance guarantee for flows passing through a router. Consider an ISP router with a 100-Mbs output link. If the ISP wishes to provide some customer flows with a 10-Mbps-bandwidth guarantee, it clearly cannot provide this guarantee to more than 10 flows. It follows that there must be some mechanism to request the router for bandwidth guarantees for a given flow. Clearly, the router must do *admission control* and be prepared to reject further requests if further requests are beyond its capacity.

Thus if we define QoS as the provision of performance guarantees for flows, it can be said that QoS requires reservation mechanisms and admission control (to limit the set of flows we provide QoS to) together with scheduling (to enforce performance guarantees for the selected flows). *Quality of service* is a sufficiently vague term, and the implied performance guarantees can refer to the bandwidth, delay, or even a variation in delay.

One way to make reservations is for a manager to make reservations for each router in the path of a flow. However, this is tedious and would require the work to be done each time the route of the flow changes and whenever the application that requires reservations is stopped and restarted. One standard that has been proposed is the Resource Reservation Protocol (RSVP) (Boyle, 1997), which allows applications to make reservations.

This protocol works in the context of a multicast tree between a sender and a set of receivers (and works for one receiver). The idea is that the sender sends a periodic PATH message along the tree that allows routers and receivers to know in which direction the sender is. Then, each receiver that wants a reservation of some resource (say, bandwidth) sends a Resource Reservation Protocol (RSV) message up to the next router in the path. Each router accepts the RSV message if the reservation is feasible, merges the RSV messages of all receivers, and then sends it to its parent router. This continues until all reservations have been set up or failure notifications are sent back. Reservations are timed out periodically, so RSV messages must be sent periodically if a receiver wishes to maintain its reservation.

While RSVP appears simple from this description, it has a number of tricky issues. First, it can allow reservations across multiple senders and can include multiple modes of sharing. For shared reservations, it improves scalability by allowing reservations to be merged; for example, for a set of receivers that want differing bandwidths on the same link for the same conference, we can make a single reservation for the maximum of all requests. Finally, we have to deal with the possibility that the requests of a subset of receivers are too large but that the remaining subset can be accommodated. This is handled by creating *blockade* state in the routers. The resulting specification is quite complex.

14.7 Providing bandwidth guarantees

Given that reservations can be set up at routers for a subset of flows, we now return to the problem of schedulers to enforce these reservations. We will concentrate on bandwidth reservations only in this section and consider reservations for delay in the next section. We will start with a metaphor in Section 14.7.1 that illustrates the problems; we move on to describe a solution in Section 14.7.2.

14.7.1 The parochial parcel service

To illustrate the issues, let us consider the story of a hypothetical parcel service called the Parochial Parcel Service, depicted in Fig. 14.7. Two customers, called Jones and Smith, use the parcel service to send their parcels by truck to the next city.

In the beginning all parcels were kept in a *single* queue at the loading dock, as seen in Fig. 14.8. Unfortunately, it so happened that the loading dock was limited in size. It also happened that during busy periods Jones would send all his parcels just a little before Smith sent his. The result was that, when Smith's parcels arrived during busy periods, they were refused; Smith was asked to retry some other time.

To solve this unfairness problem, the Parochial Parcel Service decided to use two queues before the loading dock, one for Jones and one for Smith. When times were busy, some space was left for Smith's queue. The queues were serviced in round-robin order. Unfortunately, even this did not work too well

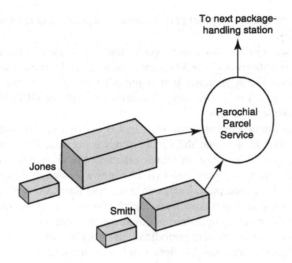

FIGURE 14.7

A hypothetical parcel service.

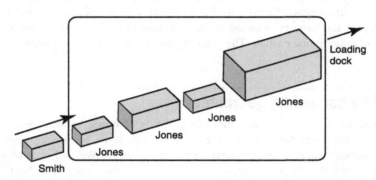

FIGURE 14.8

A FIFO queue for loading parcels that is, unfortunately, hogged by Jones.

because the evil Jones (see Fig. 14.9) cleverly used packages that were consistently larger than those of Smith. Since two large packages of Jones could contain seven of Smith's packages, the net result was that Jones could get 3.5 times the service of Smith during busy periods. Thus Smith was happier, but he was still unhappy.

Another idea that the Parochial Parcel Service briefly toyed with was actually to cut parcels into slices, such as unit cubes, that take a standard time to service. Then, the company could service a slice at a time for each customer. They called this *slice-by-slice round-robin*. When initial field trials produced bitter customer complaints, the Parochial Parcel Service decided they *couldn't* physically cut packages up into slices. However, they realized they *could* calculate the time at which a package will

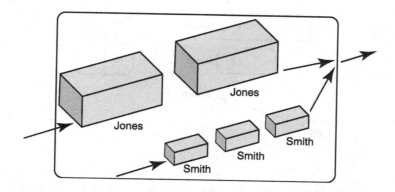

FIGURE 14.9

Two queues and round-robin make Smith happier ... but not completely happy.

leave in an *imaginary* slice-by-slice system. They could then service packages in the order they would have left in the imaginary system. Such a system will indeed be fair for any combination of packet (oops, package) sizes.

Unfortunately, simulating the imaginary system is like performing a discrete event simulation in real time. At the very least, this requires keeping the time stamps at which each head package of each queue will depart and picking the earliest such timestamp to service next; thus the amount of time it takes for this selection (using priority queues) is logarithmic in the number of queues. This must be done whenever a package is sent.

Worse, when a new queue becomes active, potentially all the time stamps have to change. This is shown in Fig. 14.10. Jones has a package at the head of his queue that is due to depart at time 12; Smith has a package due to depart at time 8. Now, imagine that Brown introduces a packet. Since Brown's package must be scanned once for every three slices scanned in the imaginary slice-by-slice system, the speed of Smith and Jones has gone down from a speed of one in every two slices to one in every three slices. This potentially means that the arrival of Brown can cause *every* time stamp to be updated, an operation whose complexity is *linear* in the number of flows.

14.7.2 Deficit round-robin

What was all this stuff about a parcel service about? Clearly, parcels correspond to packets, the parcel office to a router, and loading docks to outbound links. More importantly, the seemingly facetious slice-by-slice round-robin corresponds to a seminal idea, called *bit-by-bit round-robin* or the DKS (Demers, Keshav, and Shenker) scheme (Demers et al., 1989). Simulated bit-by-bit round-robin provides provably fair bandwidth distribution and some remarkably tight delay bounds; unfortunately, it is hard to implement at gigabit speeds. A considerable improvement to bit-by-bit round-robin is proposed in the paper by Stiliadis and Varma (1996b), which shows how to reduce the linear overhead of the DKS scheme to the purely logarithmic overhead of sorting. Sorting can be done at high speeds with hardware multiway heaps; however, it is still more complex than deficit round-robin for bandwidth guarantees.

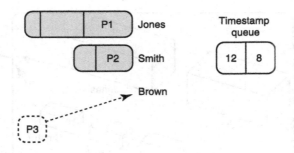

FIGURE 14.10

Brown's entry causes the time stamp of Jones and Smith to change. In general, when a new flow becomes active, the overhead is linear in the number of flows.

Now, while bit-by-bit round-robin provides both bandwidth guarantees and delay bounds, our first observation is that many applications can benefit from just bandwidth guarantees. Thus an interesting question is whether there is a simpler algorithm that can merely provide bandwidth guarantees. We are, of course, relaxing system requirements to pave the way for a more efficient implementation, as suggested by **P3**.

If we are only interested in bandwidth guarantees and would like a constant-time algorithm, a natural point of departure is round-robin. So we ask ourselves: can we retain the efficiency of round-robin and yet add a little state to correct for the unfairness of examples such as Fig. 14.9?

A banking analogy motivates the solution. Each flow is given a *quantum*, which is like a periodic salary that gets credited to the flow's bank account on every round-robin cycle. As with most bank accounts, a flow cannot spend (i.e., send packets of the corresponding size) more than is contained in its account; the algorithm does not allow bank accounts to be overdrawn. However, perfectly naturally, the balance remains in the account for possible spending in the next period. Thus any possible unfairness in a round is compensated for in subsequent rounds, leading to long-term fairness.

More precisely, for each flow i, the algorithm keeps a quantum size Q_i and a deficit counter D_i. The larger the quantum size assigned to a flow, the larger the share of the bandwidth it receives. On each round-robin scan, the algorithm will service as many packets as possible for flow i with a size of less than $Q_i + D_i$. If packets remain in flow i's queue, the algorithm stores the "deficit," or remainder, in D_i for the next opportunity. It is easy to prove that the algorithm is fair in the long term for any combination of packet sizes and that it takes only a few more instructions to implement than round-robin.

Consider the example illustrated in Figs. 14.11 and 14.12. We assume that the *quantum* size of all flows is 500 and that there are four flows. In Fig. 14.11 the round-robin pointer points to the queue of $F1$; the algorithm adds the quantum size to the deficit counter of $F1$, which is now at 500. Thus $F1$ has sufficient funds to send the packet at the head of its queue of size 200 but not the second packet of size 750. Thus the remainder (300) is left in $F1$'s deficit account, and the algorithm skips to $F2$, leaving the picture shown in Fig. 14.12.

Thus in the second round the algorithm will send the packet at the head of $F2$'s queue (leaving a deficit of 0), the packet at the head of $F3$'s queue (leaving a deficit of 400), and the packet at the head of $F4$'s queue (leaving a deficit of 320). It then returns to $F1$'s queue. $F1$'s deficit counter now goes up to 800; this reflects a past account balance of 300 plus a fresh deposit of 500. The algorithm then sends

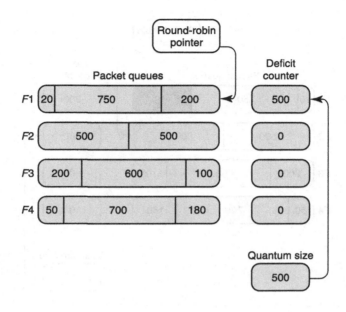

FIGURE 14.11

Deficit round-robin: at the start, all the *deficit* variables are initialized to zero. The round-robin pointer points to the top of the active list. When the first queue is serviced, the *quantum* value of 500 is added to the *deficit* value. The remainder after servicing the queue is left in the *deficit* variable.

the packet of size 750 and the packet of size 20. Assume that no more packets arrive to $F1$'s queue than are shown in Fig. 14.12. Thus since the $F1$ queue is empty, the algorithm skips to $F2$.

Curiously, when skipping to $F2$, the algorithm does not leave behind the deficit of $800 - 750 - 20 = 30$ in $F1$'s queue. Instead, it zeroes out $F1$'s deficit counter. Thus the deficit counter is a somewhat curious bank account that is zeroed unless the account holder can prove a "need" in terms of a nonempty queue. Perhaps this is analogous to a welfare account.

14.7.3 Implementation and extensions of deficit round-robin

As described, DRR (Deficit Round Robin) has one major implementation problem. The algorithm may visit a number of queues that have no packets to send. This would be very wasteful if the number of possible queues is much larger than the number of active queues. However, there is a simple way to avoid idle skipping of inactive queues by adding redundant state for speed (**P12**).

More precisely, the algorithm maintains an auxiliary queue, *ActiveList*, which is a list of indices of queues that contain at least one packet. In the example $F1$, which was at the head of *ActiveList*, is removed from *ActiveList* after its last packet is serviced. If $F1$'s packet queue were nonempty, the algorithm would place $F1$ at the tail of *ActiveList* and keep track of any unused deficit. Notice that this prevents a flow from getting quantum added to its account while the flow is idle.

Note that DRR shares bandwidth among flows in proportion to quantum sizes. For example, suppose there are three flows, $F1$, $F2$, and $F3$, with respective quantum sizes 2, 2, and 3, which have

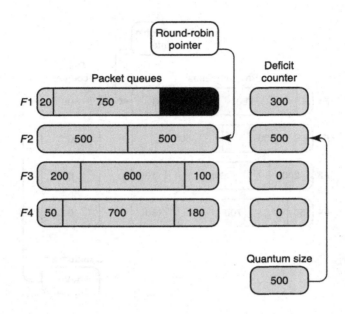

FIGURE 14.12

Deficit round-robin (2): after sending out a packet of size 200, $F1$'s queue had 300 bytes of its quantum left. It could not use it in the current round, since the next packet in the queue is 750 bytes. Therefore the amount 300 will carry over to the next round when it can send packets of size totaling 300 (deficit from previous round) + 500 (quantum).

reservations. Then, if all three are active, $F2$ should get a fraction $\frac{2}{2+2+3} = 2/7$ of the output-link bandwidth. If, for example, $F3$ is idle, then $F2$ is guaranteed the fraction $\frac{2}{2+2} = 1/2$ of the output-link bandwidth. In all cases a flow is guaranteed a *minimum bandwidth*, measured over the period that the flow is active, that is proportional to the ratio of its quantum size to the sum of the quantum sizes of all reservations.

How efficient is the algorithm? The cost to dequeue a packet is a constant number of instructions, as long as each flow's quantum is greater than a maximum-size packet. This ensures that a packet is sent every time a queue is visited. For example, if the quantum size of a flow is 1, the algorithm would have to visit a queue 100 times to send a packet of size 100. Thus if the maximum packet size is 1500 and flow $F1$ is to receive twice the bandwidth as flow $F2$, we may arrange for the quantum of $F1$ to be 3000 and the quantum of $F2$ to be 1500. Once again, in terms of our principles, we note that avoiding the generality (**P7**) of arbitrary quantum settings allows a more efficient implementation.

Extensions of deficit round-robin

We now consider two extensions of DRR: hierarchical DRR and DRR with a single priority queue.

Hierarchical deficit round-robin

An interesting model for bandwidth sharing is introduced in the so-called *class-based queuing (CBQ)* scheme (Floyd and Jacobson, 1995). The idea is to specify a hierarchy of users that can share an output

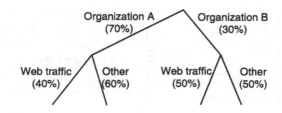

FIGURE 14.13

Example of a class-based queuing specification for bandwidth sharing.

link. For example, a transatlantic link may be shared by two organizations in proportion to the amount each pays for the link. Consider two organizations, A and B, who respectively pay 70% and 30% of the cost of a link and so wish to have assured bandwidth shares in that ratio. However, within organization A there are two main traffic types: Web users and others. Organization A wishes to limit Web traffic to get only 40% of A's share of the traffic when other traffic from A is present. Similarly, B wishes video traffic to take no more than 50% of the total traffic when other traffic from B is present (Fig. 14.13).

Suppose at a given instant organization A's traffic is only Web traffic and organization B has both video and other traffic. Then A's Web traffic should get all of A's share of the bandwidth (say, 0.7 Mbps of a 1-Mbps link); B's video traffic should get 50% of the remaining share, which is 0.15 Mbps. If other traffic for A comes on the scene, then the share of A's Web traffic should fall to $0.7 \times 0.4 = 0.28$ Mbps. CBQ is easy to implement using a *hierarchical* DRR scheduler for each node in the CBQ tree. For example, we would use a DRR scheduler to divide traffic between A and B. When A's queue gets visited, we run the DRR scheduler for A's traffic, which then visits the Web queue and the other traffic queue and serves them in proportion to their quanta.

Deficit round-robin plus priority

A simple idea implemented by Cisco Systems (and called Modified DRR, or MDRR) is to combine DRR with priority to allow minimal delay for voice over IP. The idea, depicted in Fig. 14.14, allows up to eight flow queues for a router. A packet is placed in a queue based on bits in the IP TOS fields called the IP *precedence* bits. However, queue 1 is a special queue typically reserved for voice over IP. There are two modes: in the first mode queue 1 is given strict priority over the other queues. Thus in the figure we would serve all three of queue 1's packets before alternating between queues 2 and 3. On the other hand, in alternating priority mode queue 1 visits alternate with visits to a DRR scan of the remaining queues. Thus in this mode we would first serve queue 1, then queue 2, then queue 1, then queue 3, etc.

14.8 Schedulers that provide delay guarantees

So far, we have considered only schedulers that provide bandwidth guarantees across multiple queues. Our only exception is MDRR, which is an ad hoc solution. We now consider providing delay bounds. The situation is analogous to a number of chefs sharing an oven, as shown in Fig. 14.15. The frozen-food chef (analogous to, say, FTP traffic) cares more about throughput and less about delay; the regular

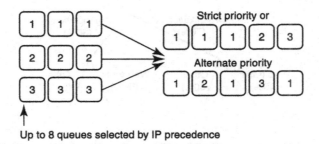

FIGURE 14.14

Cisco's MDRR scheme.

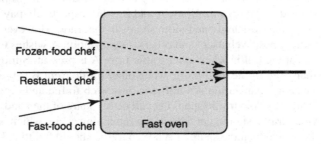

FIGURE 14.15

Three types of chefs sharing an oven, among whom only the fast-food chef needs bounded delay.

chef (analogous to, say, SSH traffic) cares about delay, but for the fast-food chef (analogous to voice or real-time video traffic) a small delay is critical for business.

In practice, most routers implement some form of throughput sharing using algorithms such as DRR. However, almost no commercial router implements schedulers that guarantee delay bounds. The result is that real-time video (e.g., for remote surgery) may not work well at all times. This may be unacceptable for commercial use. One answer to this problem is to have heavily underutilized links and to employ ad hoc schemes like MDRR. This may work if bandwidth becomes plentiful. However, traffic does go up to compensate for increased bandwidth; witness the spurt in traffic due to Netflix, for instance.

In theory, the simulated bit-by-bit round-robin algorithm (Demers et al., 1989) that we have already mentioned guarantees isolation and delay bounds. Thus it was used as the basis for the IntServ proposal as a scheduler that could integrate video, voice, and data. However, bit-by-bit round-robin, also called generalized processor sharing and to be described next in detail, is unrealistic because it would require (relatively) expensive context switching after each bit of service.

WFQ, also called packetized generalized processor sharing (PGPS) in Parekh and Gallager (1993) and to be described in Section 14.10, provides a close approximation to GPS. WFQ does not have the issue of expensive context switching and is hence realistic since its scheduling is packet-by-packet, not bit-by-bit. However, as will be shown in Section 14.10, WFQ depends subtly on GPS in the following manner: the (scheduling) policy statement of WFQ contains references to the *GPS virtual finish times* of packets, and hence its implementation requires *tracking of GPS clock;*. Both concepts will be defined in Section 14.9.4.

For decades it was widely believed that GPS clock tracking operation required a prohibitively high computational complexity of $O(n)$ per packet (Parekh and Gallager, 1993; Bennett and Zhang, 1996a; Stiliadis and Varma, 1996b,a; Bennett and Zhang, 1997; Chao and Guo, 2001), where n is the number of concurrent flows. For this reason, WFQ was always been considered impractical; consequently, several WFQ approximation schemes (e.g., Zhang, 1991; Bennett and Zhang, 1996a, 1997; Cobb et al., 1996; Stiliadis and Varma, 1996b; Suri et al., 1997) have been proposed to reduce this complexity to $O(\log n)$ per packet, all at a cost of GPS tracking errors. However, it is now known that the worst-case computational complexity of GPS tracking can indeed be bounded by $O(\log n)$ per packet using an augmented data structure proposed in Valente (2004). With this, the complexity of WFQ can also be bounded by $O(\log n)$ per packet, making WFQ arguably as computationally efficient as WFQ approximation schemes.

The next sections (Sections 14.9 through Section 14.14) begin a more rigorous explanation of why providing delay bounds together with fairness is challenging. While it is hard to appreciate the innovation behind Quick Fair Queuing (Section 14.14) without these preliminaries, implementors less interested in the theoretical foundations may wish to skip to Section 14.14.

14.9 Generalized processor sharing

The perfect service discipline to provide delay and fairness guarantees is GPS (Keshav et al., 1990; Parekh and Gallager, 1993), which we earlier described as the "simulated bit-by-bit round-robin" algorithm. In a GPS scheduler all backlogged flows are served simultaneously in a weighted fashion as follows. In a link of rate r served by a GPS scheduler each flow F_i is assigned a weight ϕ_i. Each backlogged flow F_i at every moment t is served simultaneously at rate $r_i = r\phi_i / (\sum_{j \in B(t)} \phi_j)$, where $B(t)$ is the set of flows that are backlogged at time t.

14.9.1 A simple example

It helps to explain the GPS scheduler and the related concepts using the following simple example. We consider a packet scheduling instance in which there are three flows, namely $F1$, $F2$, and $F3$, with equal weight 1. Assume they share a link with service rate of 1-bit per second. The jth packet of flow i is denoted $p_{i,j}$. Its arrival time and length (in bits) are denoted as $a_{i,j}$ and $l_{i,j}$, respectively. Let $a_{1,1} = a_{2,1} = a_{3,1} = 0$, $a_{1,2} = a_{2,2} = a_{3,2} = 3$, and $a_{3,3} = 4$. Let $l_{1,1} = 7$, $l_{1,2} = 1$, $l_{2,1} = 5$, $l_{2,2} = 4$, $l_{3,1} = 3$, $l_{3,2} = 1$, and $l_{3,3} = 6$.

The service schedule of this instance, represented as a *GPS graph*, is shown in Fig. 14.16. Each rectangle corresponds to a packet, and each row (of rectangles) corresponds to a flow. The height of each row corresponds to the weight of the corresponding flow. All rows have the same height since all flows have weight 1. The length of each packet is equal to the area and equivalently the length in this case (since all rectangles have the same height) of the corresponding rectangle. For example, as shown in Fig. 14.16, row 3 contains three rectangles of lengths 3, 1, and 6, respectively. They correspond to the three packets $p_{3,1}$, $p_{3,2}$, and $p_{3,3}$ in $F3$.

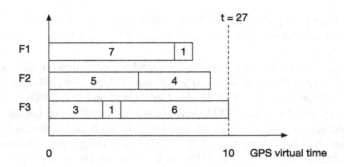

FIGURE 14.16

GPS graph of a simple packet arrival instance.

Under GPS all three flows start receiving service, each at rate 1/3 bits per second, at time 0, since the first packets of all three flows arrive at the same time 0. The x-axis of the GPS graph corresponds to the virtual time, defined as the number of bits of service rendered by GPS to backlogged flows. For example, in Fig. 14.16, at virtual time 7 (bits), 7 bits of service have been rendered to all three flows. Clearly, the real time corresponding to virtual time 7 (bits) is 21 (seconds), since a total of 21 (bits) of service is rendered to the three flows during the virtual time interval $[0, 7]$ (bits) at the assumed link rate of $r = 1$ bit per second.

14.9.2 Recursive definition of GPS virtual start and finish times

Although GPS cannot be used directly as a realistic scheduler as explained earlier, some concepts associated with GPS are important in specifying, reasoning about, and implementing realistic schedulers, such as WFQ, WF^{2}Q (Bennett and Zhang, 1996a), and WFQ+ (Bennett and Zhang, 1997). One such concept is the *GPS virtual finish time* of a packet $p_{i,k}$, defined as the virtual time when this packet finishes service under GPS and denoted as $f_{i,k}$. For example, in Fig. 14.16 the GPS virtual finish time of packet $p_{3,2}$ is 4 (bits). Similarly, the GPS virtual start time of a packet $p_{i,k}$ is defined as the virtual time at which the packet starts to receive service under GPS and denoted as $s_{i,k}$. For example, the GPS virtual start time of $p_{3,2}$ is 3. In general, the virtual start and the virtual finish times of any packet can be computed from the following simple recursive formulae:

$$s_{i,k} = max\{f_{i,k-1}, V(a_{i,k})\}, \tag{14.1}$$

$$f_{i,k} = s_{i,k} + \frac{l_{i,k}}{\phi_i}. \tag{14.2}$$

Here, $V(a_{i,k})$ is the virtual time that corresponds to $a_{i,k}$, the real arrival time of $p_{i,k}$. For example, when packet $p_{3,2}$ arrives at time $a_{3,2} = 3$, the corresponding virtual time $V(3) = \frac{1}{3}$ because there are three backlogged flows sharing GPS service during the real time interval $[0, 1]$, and each receives $\frac{1}{3}$ bits of service. As stated in (14.1), the virtual start time of the packet $p_{i,k}$ is defined as the larger of $f_{i,k-1}$, the virtual finish time of its previous packet $p_{i,k-1}$, and $V(a_{i,k})$. This is because, per GPS policy, a packet $p_{i,k}$ cannot start receiving service under GPS until $p_{i,k-1}$, the previous packet in the same flow, finishes service under GPS. Since in each GPS round flow F_i receives ϕ_i bits of service, the GPS virtual finish time is $\frac{l_{i,k}}{\phi_i}$ bits later than the GPS virtual start time, which is precisely Formula (14.2). Formulae (14.1) and (14.2) imply the following fact.

Fact 1. The virtual start and the virtual finish times of a packet are finalized as soon as the packet arrives. In particular, they neither depend on nor change with, future packet arrivals.

For example, when packet $p_{3,3}$ arrives at real time 4 (seconds), its virtual start time $s_{3,3}$ and virtual finish time $f_{3,3}$, are known to be 4 (bits) and 10, respectively, and they remain unchanged even if a new flow were to arrive to share the link bandwidth with the three existing flows shortly after real time 4 (say at real time 5). Since the x-axis corresponds to virtual times in a GPS graph, another way to state this constancy of virtual start and finish times is that the start and the end positions of existing packets (rectangles) in a GPS graph do not change with future packet arrivals.

In contrast, the expected real finish time of a packet could change with future packet arrivals; this fact was mentioned in Section 14.7.1 in the Parochial Parcel Service example. For this reason, it is not not known for certain until the "finish" event actually happens. For example, at time 0^+, the *expected* real finish time of packet $p_{1,1}$ is 15 because, at the moment, the packet queue contains only three packets $p_{1,1}$, $p_{2,1}$, and $p_{3,1}$ whose lengths are 7, 5, and 3 bits, respectively, and it would take the GPS scheduler 15 seconds to finish serving $p_{1,1}$, the longest among the three. However, at time 3^+, its expected real finish time becomes 18 due to the arrival of $p_{1,2}$, $p_{2,2}$, and $p_{3,2}$ at real time 3, and becomes 21 due to the arrival of $p_{3,3}$ at real time 4. Furthermore, we do not know for certain that the real finish time of $p_{1,1}$ is indeed 21 until its virtual finish time 7 (known for certain since real time 0^+) has passed at real time 21. More generally, the real time corresponding to any future virtual time is not known for certain until the (real and virtual) time occurs. This fact makes the task of tracking the GPS clock much trickier, as will be shown in Section 14.9.4.

As shown in Formula (14.1), when a packet $p_{i,k}$ arrives at real time $a_{i,k}$, we need to obtain the corresponding virtual time $V(a_{i,k})$. In other words, we need to compute the virtual time whose corresponding real time is equal to $a_{i,k}$.

This virtual-to-real mapping is mathematically well-defined, or in other words does not suffer from the "not finalized until the time has come" issue described earlier because here this mapping is performed after this packet has already arrived (at time $a_{i,k}$). However, the computation involved in this mapping, which is the bulk of the aforementioned GPS clock tracking task, is no easy matter, as we elaborate in Section 14.9.4.

Although this computation seems straightforward in Fig. 14.16, it is not when the scheduling instance is less "friendly". In the next section we will present a packet scheduling instance that is not really larger than that in Fig. 14.16, but is a bit more contrived. Even in this fairly simple instance, GPS clock tracking becomes more complex.

14.9.3 Another packet arrival scenario

The following scenario was used in the aforementioned work that presented an algorithm for tracking the GPS clock at a worst-case computational complexity of $O(\log n)$. It is different from the previous simple scenario in two important aspects. First, all flows do not have the same weight. Second, whereas the packets in the same flow are "back-to-back" and leave no "gaps" in the GPS graph of the previous instance, there is a hole in this scenario. Now, when a new flow arrives at real time t, determining the corresponding virtual time $V(t)$ is no longer straightforward.

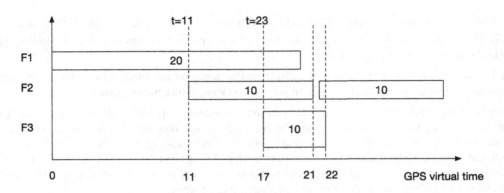

FIGURE 14.17

GPS graph of a more complicated instance.

More precisely, consider a packet scheduling scenario in which there are three flows, namely $F1$, $F2$, and $F3$, with weights 1, 1, and 2, respectively. They share a link again with service rate of $r = 1$ bit per second. The terms $p_{i,j}$, $a_{i,j}$ and $l_{i,j}$ are similarly defined as before. The packet arrival instance consists of $p_{1,1}$ with $a_{1,1} = 0$ and $l_{1,1} = 20$, $p_{2,1}$ with $a_{2,1} = 11$ and $l_{2,1} = 10$, $p_{3,1}$ with $a_{3,1} = 23$ and $l_{2,1} = 10$, and finally $p_{2,2}$ with $a_{2,2} = 39$ and $l_{2,2} = 10$.

The GPS graph of this instance is shown in Fig. 14.17. The GPS virtual start and finish times of the first packet $p_{1,1}$ are straightforward to compute: $s_{1,1} = 0$ and $f_{1,1} = 20$. Those of later packets need some reasoning. For the second packet $p_{2,1}$, its virtual start time $s_{2,1}$ is 11 since $F1$, being the only active flow during the real time interval $[0, 11]$, gets 11 bits of service in the meantime. Its virtual finish time $f_{2,1}$ is $s_{2,1} + l_{2,1}/\phi_2 = 21$. When packet $p_{3,1}$ arrives at $t = 23$, the corresponding virtual time $V(23)$ is 17 because $F1$ and $F2$ are both active during the real time interval $[11, 23]$, and each receives 6 bits of service under GPS. Hence, $s_{3,1} = 17$, and since F3 has weight 2 (so the height of packet $p_{3,1}$ is twice as large as other packets), $f_{3,1} = s_{3,1} + l_{3,1}/\phi_3 = 17 + 10/2 = 22$.

With this example explained, we are now ready to specify the evolution of the virtual time exactly. Let t_i, $i = 0, 1, 2, \cdots$, be the ith real time when a *past* (i.e., earlier than the current time t) event happened that resulted in a change to the set of backlogged flows; note that we emphasize the word "past" here since, at any real time $t = \eta$, the image of the function $V(t)$ is finalized only for the real time interval $[0, \eta]$. There are two types of such events. The first type is when a previously unbacklogged flow becomes backlogged due to a new packet arrival (from this flow). For example, such an event happens when packet $p_{3,1}$ arrives in Fig. 14.17.

In Fig. 14.16, however, the arrival of packet $p_{1,2}$ at real time 3 does not cause such an event since packets $p_{1,1}$ and $p_{1,2}$ are "back-to-back" (i.e., there is no gap in between) in the GPS graph and the total weight of the backlogged flows remains unchanged. The second type of event is when a previously backlogged flow becomes unbacklogged. For example, in Fig. 14.17 such an event happens when packet $p_{1,1}$ finishes service under GPS at real time 35.

With this definition of t_i, it is clear that $t_0 < t_1 < t_2 < \cdots$. The GPS virtual time $V(t)$, as a function of real time t, is calculated as (14.3) and (14.4) as follows.

$$V(t_0) = 0, \tag{14.3}$$

$$V(t_{i-1} + \tau) = V(t_{i-1}) + \frac{\tau}{\sum_{j \in B(t_{i-1})} \phi_j}, \tag{14.4}$$

$$0 \leq \tau \leq t_i - t_{i-1}, \quad i = 1, 2, 3, \cdots$$

We now "prove by induction" that the definition of $V(\cdot)$ in (14.4) is consistent with that of virtual time, as just stated. Assume the value of $V(t_{i-1})$ is equal to the virtual time corresponding to real time t_{i-1}. Then, during interval $[t_{i-1}, t_i]$, the total weight of the backlogged flows is $\sum_{j \in B(t_{i-1})} \phi_j$. Since $t_{i-1} + \tau \in [t_{i-1}, t_i]$ for any $0 \leq \tau \leq t_i - t_{i-1}$, we obtain (14.4) by the definition of the GPS policy (as bit-by-bit round-robin).

14.9.4 Tracking the GPS clock

When $p_{2,2}$ arrives at real time $t = 39$, we need to compute the corresponding virtual time $V(39)$. In Fig. 14.17 we "show" that this virtual time is "after" $f_{2,1} = 21$, but "before" $f_{3,1} = 22$. In practice, such "before-and-after" relationships have to be determined before the value of $V(39)$ can. One way to compute such "before-or-after" relationships is to proactively compute and maintain the expected real finish time of the last packet in each backlogged flow, as illustrated by the following example.

Example. In Fig. 14.17 at real time $t = 23^+$, the expected real finish times corresponding to the virtual finish times $f_{1,1} = 20$, $f_{2,1} = 21$, and $f_{3,1} = 22$ are $V^{-1}(20) = 23 + (20 - 17) * 4 = 35$, $V^{-1}(21) = 35 + (21 - 20) * 3 = 38$, and $V^{-1}(22) = 38 + (22 - 21) * 2 = 40$, respectively. Note the multiplicative terms 4, 3, and 2 are the values of $\sum_{j \in B(t_{i-1})} \phi_j$ (the total weight of the backlogged flows) during the intervals $[17, 20]$, $[20, 21]$, and $[21, 22]$, respectively. As $a_{2,2} = 39$ is between $V^{-1}(21) = 38$ and $V^{-1}(22) = 40$, we know that $V(39) = 21 + (39 - 38)/2 = 21.5$ (since $V^{-1}(21) = 38$ and the total weight during real time interval $[38, 39]$ is 2).

This example also highlights an important fact mentioned earlier. That is, the tracking of the GPS clock consists of two intertwined types of tasks. The first is to evaluate $V^{-1}(v)$ (i.e., to compute the real time given a virtual time) and the second to evaluate $V(t)$ (i.e., to compute the virtual time given a *past* real time). Each type is dependent on the other. For example, in the instance shown in Fig. 14.17, to evaluate $V(39)$, we need to evaluate $V^{-1}(21)$. But to obtain this virtual finish time 21 (of packet $p_{2,1}$), we need to evaluate $V(11) = 11$ (when packet $p_{2,1}$ arrives at real time $t = 11$).

Due to this interdependence, although only the GPS virtual finish times (of packets) are used in the policy statements of WFQ and WF^{2}Q, as will be shown in Sections 14.10 and 14.11, respectively, perhaps ironically the key difficulty in implementing both policies comes from a dilemma that arises in computing the expected future real time (assuming no new flow would arrive before this future time) corresponding to a future virtual (finish) time, as will be explained next.

While both types of GPS clock tracking tasks can be accomplished by proactively computing and maintaining the expected real finish times as shown in the previous example, the cost of doing so however is a very high worst-case computational complexity of $O(n)$ per packet. This is because, if (the first packet of) a new flow arrives, all precomputed real finish times will change and need to be recomputed, and there can be $O(n)$ of them. Indeed, proactively computing the real finish times was suggested in Parekh and Gallager (1993) as the algorithm for tracking the GPS clock as an integral part of the WFQ algorithm. Most later papers cited (Parekh and Gallager, 1993) for the perceived complexity of $O(n)$ per packet for performing WFQ.

However, precomputing all (expected) real finish times here is arguably a "self-inflicted wound." Rather, it appears that we need only to precompute the earliest one among them for tracking the GPS clock (**P2b**). For instance, in the previous example, when $p_{3,1}$ arrives at real time 23, we need only to precompute $V^{-1}(20) = 35$, the real time corresponding to the earliest among the three GPS virtual finish times just described ($f_{1,1} = 20$, $f_{2,1} = 21$, and $f_{3,1} = 22$). Then, it is not until this real time $t = 35$ that the expected real finish time of the next packet (corresponding to $f_{2,1} = 21$) needs to be precomputed as $V^{-1}(21) = 38$. Finally, it is not until $t = 38$ that the expected real finish time of the last packet (corresponding to $f_{3,1} = 22$) needs to be precomputed as $V^{-1}(22) = 40$.

Indeed, in an idealized systems implementation, the scheduler (process) can be put to sleep with a timer (see Chapter 7) set to wake it up at the next earliest expected GPS real finish time. We illustrate such a timer-based implementation using the same instance. After some "cleanup" (defined next) computations (to arrive at $V^{-1}(20) = 35$ among others) at $t = 23$, the scheduler goes to sleep, and a timer is set to wake it up at $t = 35$ as calculated. Then, at $t = 35$, the scheduler that is awoken by the timer performs the following processing: it changes the total weight of the backlogged flows from 4 to 3 (as $F1$ is no longer backlogged after $t = 35$), computes the next real time to wake the scheduler up (which is $V^{-1}(21) = 38$ as just calculated), and sets the next wake-up time to $t = 38$. We refer to this scheduled operation of adjusting the total weight and scheduling the next wake-up time as cleanup, since each such operation corresponds to the necessary maintenance associated with the departure of a previously backlogged flow.

Once the scheduler wakes up again at real time $t = 38$, the cleanup operation needs to change the total weight of backlogged flows from 3 to 2 (as F2 becomes unbacklogged afterward) and sets the wake-up timer to $V^{-1}(22) = 40$. This time, however, the scheduler does not wake up at real time $t = 40$ as scheduled. Instead, at time $t = 39$, the scheduler gets a "rude awakening" from the arrival of packet $p_{3,2}$. When this happens, the scheduler computes $V(39) = 21 + (39 - 38)/2 = 21.5$, the total weight is adjusted to 3 (as F2 becomes backlogged again), and the next wake-up time is changed to $t = 39 + (22 - 21.5) * 3 = 40.5$ (from $t = 40$ previously). Note that there is a tiny gap between packets $p_{2,1}$ and $p_{2,2}$. This is because $p_{2,1}$ finishes service under GPS at real time $t = 38$ and $p_{2,2}$ won't arrive until real time $t = 39$.

With this idealized timer-based implementation, the time complexity of each cleanup operation, including that of computing the next (real) expected wakeup time (which could change due to "rude awakening") and adjusting the total weight of backlogged flows, is $O(1)$, as shown in the previous instance. In addition, we can maintain the GPS virtual finish times of the last packets of backlogged flows in a balanced priority queue, such as a heap or a balanced binary tree, so that the next earliest expected GPS virtual finish time can be obtained (by calling the ExtractMin() method) in $O(\log n)$ time. For example, in the previous instance, at time 23^+, the priority queue contains three nodes keyed by virtual finish times 20, 21, and 22, respectively. Therefore the total computational complexity of tracking the GPS clock is $O(\log n)$ per packet in theory.

However, for this $O(1)$ cleanup algorithm to work in practice, its operation has to closely follow the progress of (current) time in the following sense: when the current time is t, the cleanup operations for all past events must be finished before t since otherwise we cannot compute $V(\cdot)$ in $O(1)$ in the event of a "rude awakening" (such as that at real time $t = 39$ in the previous example). However, it could happen that a large number (say $O(n)$) of such events that require cleanups could happen within a tiny time interval (see an example of that in Zhao and Xu (2004)). In this case we have to perform $O(n)$ cleanup operations, with a total time complexity of $O(n)$, in a short time. Hence, the worse-case time complexity in practice remains $O(n)$ per packet, just as in the case of precomputing all GPS real finish times.

This inconsistency between theory and practice was first elaborated in details in Zhao and Xu (2004). Shortly afterward, this inconsistency was resolved by the aforementioned GPS clock tracking work (Valente, 2004), in which a data structure and algorithm was proposed that strikes a nice tradeoff between theory and the practice. With this new solution, each cleanup operation has a higher time complexity of $O(\log n)$ (than $O(1)$), but the worst-case time complexity of computing $V(\cdot)$ in the event of a "rude awakening" is also capped at $O(\log n)$. As a result, this new solution allows the worst-case time complexity of both WFQ and WF^{2}Q algorithms to be capped at $O(\log n)$ per packet.

14.10 Weighted fair queueing

In this section and the next we distinguish a packet-scheduling policy from a packet-scheduling algorithm, just as we distinguish policy from the mechanism in the OSs literature. This distinction will become clearer once we show how succinctly the WFQ policy can be stated and how hard it is to do the same for the WFQ algorithm.

We now describe WFQ (Parekh and Gallager, 1993), the aforementioned packet-by-packet work-conserving scheduling policy that closely approximates the GPS policy. To state the WFQ policy, it suffices to specify the service order of packets during a busy period because, for all work-conserving scheduling policies, their busy periods are identical (and hence not ambiguous) given any packet arrival instance. Also due to the work-conserving nature of WFQ, it suffices to specify which packet should be chosen for transmission next, when the current packet finishes transmission, since idling (between serving two consecutive packets) is not allowed in a work-conserving policy. With the concept of GPS virtual finish time defined, the WFQ policy on "who is (to be serviced) next" can be succinctly stated as follows:

Among all packets currently in the queue, pick the one with the earliest GPS virtual finish time to serve next.

We highlight a subtle property of the WFQ policy. The policy remains the same if we replace the term "virtual finish time" with "expected real finish time" (when the "who is next" decision has to be made) in its statement. This is because it is not hard to show that, for any pair of real times $\tau_1 \leq \tau_2$, their corresponding virtual times satisfy $V(\tau_1) \leq V(\tau_2)$: thus, sorting based on virtual finish times is the same as sorting based on real finish times. However, the policy statement after this replacement is bad from an implementation point of view. This is because (as explained earlier) the real time that corresponds to a future virtual time v is not finalized until v arrives. In contrast, the virtual finish time of a packet is determined as soon as the packet arrives and will not change afterward, as stated in Fact 1 in Section 14.9.2.

To illustrate how WFQ policy works and to give readers intuition on how it should be implemented, we use WFQ to schedule the packet arrival instance shown in Fig. 14.16. It is not hard to check that the resulting service order is $p_{3,1}$, $p_{3,2}$, $p_{2,2}$, $p_{1,1}$, $p_{1,2}$, $p_{2,2}$, and $p_{3,3}$.

WFQ is considered a close approximation to GPS: it has been proven (e.g., in Parekh and Gallager, 1993) that, given any packet arrival instance, the real finish time of each packet under WFQ scheduling, minus that under GPS scheduling, is upper-bounded by the amount of time it takes to service a maximum-size packet at the full link rate r. For example, in the packet arrival instance, it is not hard to verify that, for each of the seven packets, this difference is always upper-bounded by $7/1 = 7$, where 7 is the maximum packet size and $r = 1$ is the link rate.

Next, we briefly discuss the WFQ algorithm, the implementation of the WFQ policy. The WFQ algorithm consists of two parts. The first part is the tracking of GPS clock, through which the GPS virtual finish time of each packet can be determined. The second part is to have the GPS virtual finish times of all packets currently in queue stored in a balanced priority queue data structure such as a heap, so that "who is next" can be determined by making an ExtractMin() method call, which has $O(\log n)$ time complexity per call (packet). Since the second part is straightforward, we only describe how to implement the first part, GPS clock tracking, in detail in Section 14.12.

14.11 Worst-case fair weighed fair queueing

In this section we describe another scheduling policy called worst-case fair WFQ or WF^{2}Q in short (Bennett and Zhang, 1996b). WF^{2}Q is a modification of WFQ to improve its fairness. We have just shown that, under WFQ, any packet cannot finish service much later than it would under GPS. However, the former could lead the latter by a considerable amount. Due to this potential large lead in the short-term, there can be significant unfairness in serving different flows, as we will show using an example taken from the WF^{2}Q paper (Bennett and Zhang, 1996b).

In this example there are 11 flows denoted as $F1$, $F2$, ..., $F11$. Among them flows $F1$, $F2$, ..., $F10$ each has weight 1, and flow $F11$ has weight 10. With this weight assignment, flows $F1$, $F2$, ..., $F10$ get 50% of the link rate, and flow $F11$ gets the other 50%. Flows $F1$, $F2$, ..., $F10$ each has a packet arrival at (real) time 0, whereas flow $F11$ has 10 packet arrivals at (real) times 0, 0.1, 0.2, ..., 0.9, respectively. All packets have the same length of 1 bit and the service rate of the link is 1 bit per second. The GPS graph of this packet arrival instance is shown in Fig. 14.18.

Under WFQ the service order of the packets will be $p_{11,1}$, $p_{11,2}$, ..., $p_{11,10}$, $p_{1,1}$, $p_{2,1}$, ..., $p_{10,1}$. In other words, under WFQ, $F11$ gets all its 10 packets served before all other 10 flows have their 10 packets. Although this is consistent with the intended 50/50 rate allocation, the manner this allocation is made sounds very unfair: F11 gets the entirety of its 50% allocation before all the other 10 flows get any. Another way to look at this unfairness is that the packet $p_{11,10}$ has a real finish time of 20 under GPS but a real finish time of 10 under WFQ, so the former leads the latter by 10.

This lead time can grow as $O(nL)$, where n ($n = 11$ here) is the total number of flows and L ($L = 1$ here) is the maximum packet length, since for any n, we can create a packet arrival instance like that shown in Fig. 14.18, in which one flow (like $F11$ here) get 50% bandwidth and the other $n - 1$ flows (like $F1$, $F2$, ..., $F10$ here) share the remaining 50% equally. For a certain scheduling policy, the maximum amount by which the real finish time of any packet under the policy can either lead or lag behind that under GPS is called T-WFI (Bennett and Zhang, 1996b) of the policy, where T stands for (real finish) time and WFI stands for weighted fair index. Using this definition, we can say that the T-WFI of WFQ is $O(nL)$.

As WFQ is already a close approximation to GPS, readers might wonder if we can design a much fairer packet scheduling policy than WFQ at all. Quite surprisingly, the answer is yes, and the solution is WF^{2}Q. It was shown in Bennett and Zhang (1996b) that WF^{2}Q has the smallest (best) possible T-WFI of $O(L)$ (that does not grow with n). The WF^{2}Q policy can be succinctly stated as follows.

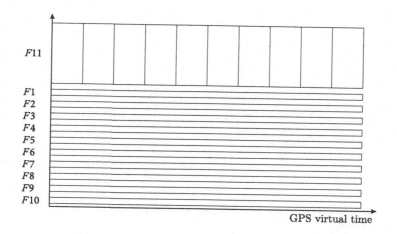

FIGURE 14.18

A motivating example for WF^{2}Q.

Among all eligible packets currently in the queue, pick the one with the earliest GPS virtual finish time to serve next.

WF^{2}Q is only slightly different than WFQ in that "who is next" is picked only from those that are eligible in the packet queue. At any time t, a packet is said to be eligible if and only if it should have started service under GPS at t. Using the same packet arrival instance, we now show that WF^{2}Q policy results in a much fairer service schedule given the packet arrival instance shown in Fig. 14.18.

At time 0, packet $p_{11,1}$ is the first to receive service under WF^{2}Q because it is eligible at time 0 (since its GPS start time is 0). The real time becomes 1 when $p_{11,1}$ finishes service. However, unlike in the schedule under WFQ, packet $p_{11,2}$ cannot receive service next because, at this moment (real time 1), the corresponding virtual time is only 0.05, but the GPS virtual start time of $p_{11,2}$ is 0.1 (so it is not eligible yet). Hence, $p_{1,1}$ is serviced next (assuming flow ID is used for tiebreaking).

When $p_{1,1}$ finishes service at real time 2, $p_{11,2}$ becomes eligible because the corresponding virtual time is 0.1, and is hence serviced next. By this reasoning, the service order for the rest of the packets is $p_{2,1}$, $p_{11,3}$, $p_{3,1}$, ..., $p_{11,10}$, $p_{10,1}$. In other words, the service alternates between $F11$ and the other 10 flows. This schedule is much fairer because it can be shown (e.g., in Bennett and Zhang (1996b)) that, for any packet, its real finish time under WFQ neither lags behind nor leads that under GPS by more than L/r, the amount of time needed to service a maximum size packet.

14.12 The data structure and algorithm for efficient GPS clock tracking

As explained earlier, the tracking of the GPS clock boils down to exactly computing the corresponding virtual time $V(t)$ given a real time t as input. An augmented data structure called *shape data structure* was proposed in Valente (2004) to perform this computation with a worst-case time complexity of $O(\log n)$ per packet (**P15**). To more clearly describe the shape data structure and its companion algo-

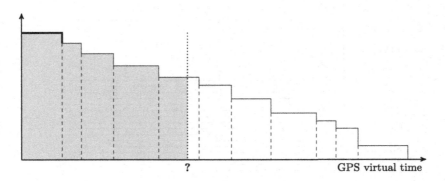

FIGURE 14.19

Data structure (before arrival).

rithm, we convert this problem to a much cleaner computation problem that is provably equivalent. In the latter problem we need to answer a query concerning a staircase like the one shown in Fig. 14.19.

14.12.1 The staircase query problem

In this staircase the values of the run (width) and the rise (height) of each step are precisely known, and the x-coordinate of the leftmost vertical line is assumed to be 0. For example, the run and the rise of the first step are highlighted in bold in Fig. 14.19. Our computation problem is that, given any $t > 0$ as input, we need to find the x-coordinate, say v, of a vertical line such that the area between the 0-line and the v-line "under the staircase" is t, as shown in Fig. 14.19. One requirement is that the proposed solution should have a low worst-case time complexity of $O(\log n)$ per query, where n is the number of steps in the staircase.

With the computation problem thus specified, we expect most readers to be able to come up with such a solution in minutes. For example, for each vertical line along the edge of a step, say with x-coordinate v_i, we first precompute (**P3b**) the area between the 0-line and the v_i-line and store them in a balanced priority queue. Then, given any t, we can perform a binary search over these areas to find the corresponding v in $O(\log n)$ time.

This computation problem becomes much more challenging when the following three requirements are imposed. As we will explain shortly, from time to time, a new step may be "inserted into" the staircase based on the x-coordinate of its right edge. For example, in Fig. 14.20 a new step is inserted between two previously consecutive steps in Fig. 14.19. The first requirement is that the proposed solution has to be able to still answer the query in $O(\log n)$ time in the face of such insertions.

Note the precomputation-based solution won't work in $O(\log n)$ time any more because every precomputed area value changes with the insertion of the new step, and updating them all takes $O(n)$ time. Hence, a different data structure and algorithm is needed, and the second requirement is that the time complexity of updating this data structure, in the event of the insertion of a step, is also $O(\log n)$. We will also show shortly that, from time to time, the leftmost step of the staircase needs to be removed, and this data structure needs to be updated to properly account for the removal. The third and last requirement is that the cost of this update has to be also bounded at $O(\log n)$.

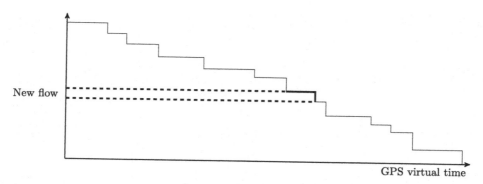

FIGURE 14.20

Data structure (after arrival).

Standard priority-queue data structure finds it hard to satisfy all three requirements. Intuitively, the first requirement and the two latter requirements require objects in the priority queue to be organized (i.e., represented and sorted) in two very different ways. However, there is a family of specialized data structures that can deal with two (but not three or more) conflicting requirements as in this case. This family, called augmented data structures (Cormen et al., 2009, Chapter 14), is described next.

14.12.2 Augmented data structures

An augmented data structure, denoted as $\mathcal{A}$, builds on a conventional data structure such as a binary search tree, which we call a base data structure and denote as $\mathcal{B}$. In $\mathcal{B}$ there is usually a set of logic invariants $\mathcal{I}_\mathcal{B}$ associated with its data fields that need to be maintained when $\mathcal{B}$ is updated, using function calls (or methods in object-oriented programming terms) of $\mathcal{B}$. For example, when a new node is to be *inserted* into a binary search tree, the point of insertion needs to be found (through a binary tree search), and some other nodes may have to shifted up or down in the tree (called rotations in the algorithm literature (Cormen et al., 2009)), so that the following invariant is maintained: when nodes are listed in the in-order traversal order, the values of their search keys are monotonically increasing.

An augmented data structure $\mathcal{A}$ usually contains several new data fields that are not a part of the underlying base data structure $\mathcal{B}$. There are logical invariants associated with these new data fields, which we denote as $\mathcal{I}_{\mathcal{A}\backslash\mathcal{B}}$, that need to be maintained when $\mathcal{A}$ is updated. However, since the methods of $\mathcal{B}$ were programmed without the knowledge of these new data fields, they generally "have no respect for" $\mathcal{I}_{\mathcal{A}\backslash\mathcal{B}}$ in the sense that, when called, these methods will likely destroy $\mathcal{I}_{\mathcal{A}\backslash\mathcal{B}}$. For example, as we will show in the next subsection, when insertions and deletions happen to an AVL tree (Adel'son-Vel'skii and Landis, 1962) serving as the base data structure, the resulting rotations will damage the invariants associated with the new data fields in the augmented data structure that builds on it. Hence, in programming an augmented data structure $\mathcal{A}$, we usually have to modify the implementations of some methods inherited from $\mathcal{B}$, to repair the damage to $\mathcal{I}_{\mathcal{A}\backslash\mathcal{B}}$ caused by these methods.

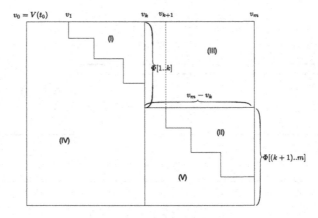

(a) The shape data structure.

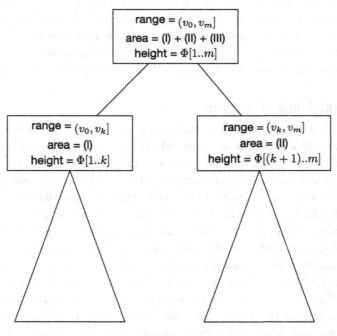

(b) Valente tree.

FIGURE 14.21

Shape vis-a-vis Tree.

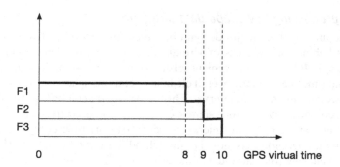

FIGURE 14.22

The "staircase" representation of the GPS graph shown in Fig. 14.16.

14.12.3 The "shape" data structure

In this section we focus on the design of the shape data structure proposed in Valente (2004) for tracking the GPS clock. We first translate the GPS clock tracking problem into the aforementioned "binary search-over-staircase" problem and then describe how the shape data structure solves the latter.

The staircase representation of GPS graph

The aforementioned staircase corresponds to a certain representation of the GPS graph at a certain real time t. This representation is different than that used in Figs. 14.16–14.18 in three different ways. First, we sort the order, from top to bottom, of the backlogged flows (at time t) according to the GPS virtual finish time of the last packet in each flow (at time t). Second, we leave no vertical space between any two "neighboring" flows, and hence the virtual finish times (sorted in increasing order), together with the horizontal boundaries of these flows, form the contour of a staircase. Third, we omit all vertical boundaries of neighboring packets in the same flow so that each flow looks like a "seamless slab" in the graph. This omission is technically sound because these boundaries have no algorithmic significance in the GPS clock tracking.

We illustrate such a staircase GPS graph representation in Fig. 14.22, with the staircase (contour) highlighted in bold. This graph corresponds to the GPS graph, at time $t = 3$ (after all seven packets have arrived), of the packet arrival instance shown in Fig. 14.16. Flow $F1$, whose last packet has the earliest GPS virtual finish time of 8, is the first "slab" at the top. It is followed by $F2$ and $F3$, whose GPS virtual finish times are 9 and 10, respectively.

The staircase representation of the GPS graph allows us to "visualize" the flaw in the aforementioned timer-based $O(1)$-complexity solution to GPS clock tracking as follows. In any GPS graph representation the line of current virtual time (i.e., virtual timeline) moves from left to right. The flawed algorithm requires the leftmost step of the staircase to be removed, as a part of the aforementioned cleanup operation, as soon as the virtual timeline has moved to the right of the vertical edge ("rise") of the step. In other words, the cleanup operation has to "walk down the stairs" as fast as the virtual timeline moves. However, this requirement is problematic since a section of the staircase can be "precipitous" with as many as $O(n)$ "tiny runs" that correspond to the aforementioned case of a tiny time interval containing GPS finish times of the last packets of many backlogged flows.

"Staircase query processing" by shape data structure

The shape data structure has three major design objectives. The first objective is to allow the cleanup operation to lag far behind the progress of virtual timeline when needed, so that each cleanup can be done, using Principle **P2b**, "at a convenient leisure time" (i.e., not under constant pressure by the progress of the virtual timeline), and the overall cleanup operation incurs only $O(\log n)$ worst-case time complexity in practice during any time interval. This objective, if achieved, would directly address the flaw of having to "race down a precipitous staircase." The second objective is to allow each evaluation of $V(t)$ (due to a "rude awakening" at time t) to incur $O(\log n)$ time complexity in the worst-case despite that the cleanup operation may now lag far behind the virtual timeline. The third objective is to allow a newly arrived flow (that caused a "rude awakening") to have the GPS virtual finish time of its first (which is at the moment also its last) packet inserted into the shape data structure in at most $O(\log n)$ time. This operation corresponds to the aforementioned insertion of a new step (slab) into the staircase as shown in Fig. 14.20. These three objectives correspond to the three aforementioned requirements imposed on the "query over the staircase" computation problem, respectively.

We are now close to finish translating the GPS clock tracking problem to the aforementioned "query over the staircase" computation problem with the three requirements. The staircase in the latter problem is precisely the staircase representation of the GPS graph in the former, at a real time t when the corresponding virtual time $V(t)$ needs to be computed. Each step in the staircase corresponds to a flow, its height, the weight of the flow, and its x-coordinate the GPS virtual finish time of the last packet in the flow. Those flows before the virtual timeline $V(t)$ are no longer backlogged whereas those after are backlogged at real time t.

Suppose this staircase contains m steps (flows) whose x-coordinates (virtual times) in the increasing order are $v_1 < v_2 < \cdots < v_m$, as shown in Fig. 14.21(a). We further assume that the previous packet arrival ("rude awakening") to any new flow happens at time t_0, and the corresponding virtual time $v_0 = V(t_0)$ is smaller than v_1, the earliest GPS finish time in the graph; this assumption will be relaxed after we describe the shape data structure. With this assumption, v_0 is the x-coordinate of the left edge of the staircase, as shown in Fig. 14.21(a). This assumption has the following subtle implication: every flow, say the ith flow (step) from the top in the GPS graph (staircase), was or is backlogged between v_0 and v_i. In other words, the entire area under the staircase is "solid" (i.e., without a gap in it). As a result, the area under the staircase between the virtual timelines v_0 and $V(t)$ is equal to $t - t_0$. Therefore our problem of computing $V(t)$ is equivalent to the "query over the staircase" problem above (with $t_0 = 0$ and $v_0 = V(t_0) = 0$).

As mentioned earlier, the shape data structure is an augmented data structure. Its base data structure is a balanced search tree, such as AVL (Adel'son-Vel'skii and Landis, 1962) or Red-Black (Cormen et al., 2009), with one special stipulation: all keys are stored in the leaf nodes only. It is widely known that this stipulation can be accommodated without increasing the asymptotic computational complexity of (any method of) the data structure. For example, in a B+ tree (Elmasri and Navathe, 2010), all keys are stored at the leaf nodes at the tree. For the staircase shown in Fig. 14.21(a), the tree contains exactly m leaf nodes and the keys contained in these leaf nodes are exactly these m values. More precisely, if we perform an in-order traversal of the tree and "print" only the keys of the leaf nodes, the output would be exactly $v_1, v_2, v_3, \ldots, v_m$.

In lieu of a key each internal node keeps track of the smallest and the largest key values, or in other words, the range of the key values in the subtree rooted by it. This range of information serves two purposes. First, in the absence of keys, internal nodes rely on this information to carry out binary searches. For example, in the case of the insertion of a new leaf node with a certain key value, which will be described in the next subsection, such range information guides the search down the tree to the appropriate leaf position to insert. Second, the width of such a range, or more precisely the difference between the two key values, is used for calculating an important quantity called area that is an additional (w.r.t. the base data structure) data field of the augmented data structure. Since only leaf nodes contain keys, the algorithmic steps for maintaining the balance of the tree, such as various rotation operations (e.g., RR, RL, LR, LL rotations in an AVL tree), need to be suitably modified as in say B+ trees.

Detailed data structure design

We now describe the shape data structure. We do so recursively, since its base data structure, a balanced binary search tree, is best explained recursively. The shape data structure, corresponding to the staircase shown in Fig. 14.21(a), is shown in Fig. 14.21(b) with the details of the two top levels expanded and the rest abbreviated. As explained earlier, the (entire) tree rooted by L_0 contains m leaf nodes with key values $v_1, v_2, v_3, \cdots, v_m$, respectively. Hence the (key) range of the root node L_0 is $(v_0, v_m]$ with v_k as the "middle" point of the range. This v_k is roughly the "would-have-been" middle point in the following sense: Had this tree been a usual binary balanced search tree in which every node, internal or leaf, is associated with a key value, the root node L_0 would have been associated with the key value v_k, or something "close" in the rank order (e.g., v_{k-2}).

We now proceed to the next level of the tree. The range of its left child node L_1 is $(v_0, v_k]$, and hence the left subtree contains k leaf nodes with key values $v_1, v_2, ..., v_k$. The range of its right child node L_2 is $(v_k, v_m]$, and hence the right subtree contains $m - k$ leaf nodes with key values $v_{k+1}, v_{k+2}, ..., v_m$. We do not name a middle point for either range since there are no such details in Fig. 14.21(b) anyway. With this middle point field, the binary search over the binary search tree is straightforward: compare the search key with the middle point (e.g., v_k at L_0), and then continue the search in either the left or the right subtree accordingly.

Now, we describe the three "augmentation" data fields in the shape data structure. To do so, we first describe a specific objective we would like to achieve. The union of the solid-line-enclosed regions (IV) and (V) corresponds to the shape information maintained at the root. We want to know if its area is smaller or larger than $t - t_0$, the amount of real time that has elapsed since the last time the function $V(\cdot)$ is evaluated (at time t_0); the "equal to" case is trivial so we ignore it here and in the subsequent discussions. The search shall continue in the left subtree in the case of "smaller than," and in the right subtree otherwise. While it may sound natural to include the quantity (IV) + (V) as a new data field, from a data structure and algorithm design point of view, this quantity is hard to maintain in event of the insertion or deletion of a leaf node. Instead, we maintain two other quantities from which this quantity can be readily (i.e., in $O(1)$ time) calculated. One such quantity is the area of the solid-line-enclosed region (I), which is denoted ΔW in the original paper (Valente, 2004). The other is the height of the staircase, which is the total weight of flows $F1, F2, ..., Fk$ and hence is denoted as $\Phi[1..m]$ ($\triangleq \sum_{i=1}^{m} \Phi_i$) in Fig. 14.21(b). With a slight abuse of notation, we denote the area of region (IV) also as (IV), and the area of region (I) also as (I), and so on. With this notational abuse, the relationship between these three quantities ((IV), $\Phi[1..m]$, and (I)) is $(IV) = (v_k - v_0) * \Phi[1..m] - (I)$.

The values of the base data structure field (key) *range* and the two augmented data structure fields *area* and *height*, for the tree nodes L_0, L_1, and L_2, are shown in Fig. 14.21(b). The area associated with the root node is $L_0.area = (I) + (II) + (III)$. This area is used to calculate the area (VI) + (V), which $t - t_0$ should be compared against first (before it is compared against (IV) if at all). Its (key) range is $(v_0, v_m]$ (with v_k as the "middle point") as just explained, and the height of is area is clearly $\Phi[1..m]$. The values of these three fields in its left child L_1 are $L_1.area = (I)$, $L_1.range = (v_0, v_k]$, and $L_1.height = \Phi[1..k] \triangleq \sum_{i=1}^{k} \Phi_i$. Those in its right child L_2 are $L_2.area = (II)$, $L_2.range = (v_k, v_m]$, and $L_2.height = \Phi[(k+1)..m] \triangleq \sum_{i=k+1}^{m} \Phi_i$. It is not hard to check that the three fields values of L_0, L_1, and L_2 satisfy the following three equations:

$$L_0.area = L_1.area + L_2.area + |L_2.range| * L_1.height, \tag{14.5}$$

$$L_0.height = L_1.height + L_2.height, \tag{14.6}$$

$$L_0.range = L_1.range \bigcup L_2.range. \tag{14.7}$$

More generally, for any node and its two children, the values of these three fields in the trio satisfy the three equations above. (The first equation corresponds to "Theorem 1" in Valente (2004) with "area" replaced by "δW.") These three equations are precisely the set of logic invariants to be satisfied by the additional data fields of the augmented data structure. When "=" (equal) is replaced by ":=" in these three equations, the three resulting assignment commands can be used for repairing any damage to these invariants by certain "destructive" method calls to the base data structure, such as node insertions and deletions. Such an "easy repair" explains why we should maintain areas (I), (II), and (III) instead of areas (IV) and (V) in the augmented data structure.

In presenting the augmented data structure (the three additional data fields) and the associated invariants, we pick a representation that is most convenient and provides the best possible clarity. This representation, however, is awkward when we design and describe the "query over the staircase" algorithm that runs on it. For example, with this representation, the algorithm starts at the root by checking whether $t - t_0 < |L_0.range| * L_0.height - L_0.area$. If so, it proceeds to the left child L_1 and checks whether $t - t_0 < |L_1.range| * L_0.height - L_1.area$. If the answer is no (and equality is ruled out), then the algorithm has to proceed to the sibling node L_2 (by backtracking first to the parent node L_0) and then to $L_1's$ left child for the next (binary search) comparison, which is awkward (but not flawed since the time complexity of the binary search remains $O(\log n)$). Hence, to facilitate a clean algorithm design, we let a parent node "lease" (cache) the values, in both its children, of these three data fields so that the second comparison above can be performed at L_0 instead of at L_1. With this "leasing," the binary search here can proceed in the usual way of traveling down from the root to a leaf without "going up" (backtracking).

The left edge of the staircase corresponds to the GPS finish time of the (last) packet whose flow record was deleted from the shape data structure during the most recent cleanup operation. How the logic invariant of the shape (augmented) data structure is repaired in the event of such a cleanup will be discussed shortly. So far, we assume that $v_0 < v_1$ so that the binary search (for the $V(t)$ line) starts from exactly the left edge of the staircase. In practice, we almost certainly would encounter the situation of $v_0 > v_1$, since as explained earlier, the very purpose of the shape data structure is to allow the timeline of the cleanup to lag far behind the $V(t)$ line (and hence the time t_0 at which the function $V(\cdot)$ was last evaluated).

We now describe the second situation of $v_0 > v_1$ (we still have $v_1 < v_2 < ... < v_m$), as shown in Fig. 14.23. To tackle this situation, we need to make two changes to the algorithm logic. First, we replace every occurrence of v_0 in the range fields (of the tree nodes) with $v_c = V(t_c)$, where v_c and t_c are the virtual and the real times of the last cleanup operation, respectively. For example, the range of L_0 is now $(v_c, v_m]$ instead of $(v_0, v_m]$. Second, the algorithmic logic is extended in the following

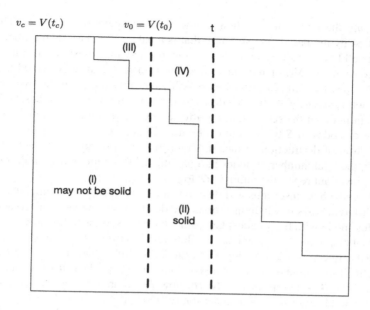

FIGURE 14.23

Data structure (after arrival).

manner: The algorithm shall not only map t to $V(t)$ "upon request" but also output the value of the area (III) + (IV) in Fig. 14.23. Hence, our "induction hypothesis" is that this logic held true at time t_0, i.e., the algorithm output both $v_0 = V(t_0)$ and the value of area (III) at time t_0. Based on this "induction hypothesis," we now show how the revised algorithm delivers the extended logic (of outputting both $V(t)$ and (III) + (IV) at time t).

Recall that we can query the shape data structure that encodes this staircase for the line $V(t)$ such that the area under the staircase between $V(t_c)$ and $V(t)$ is equal to (I) + (II). Since the staircase is solid to the right of the $V(t_0)$ line (because there was no new flow arrival between t_0 and t), we have $(II) = t - t_0$. However, the area of (I) is not necessarily equal to $t_0 - t_c$ because the area under the staircase between t_c and t_0 is not necessarily solid. Instead, the area of (I) can be calculated as the area of the enclosing rectangle $((v_0 - v_c) * \Phi[1..m])$ minus (III), where (III) is known thanks to the "induction hypothesis." Hence, our algorithm is to query the staircase for the virtual timeline v such that the area below the staircase between v_c and v is $(v_0 - v_c) * \Phi[1..m] - (III) + t - t_0$. As just explained, the shape data structure can handle this query because it corresponds to the first situation. This v is the value of $V(t)$ that we are looking for. Once we obtain the value of $V(t)$, the area of (IV) can be calculated as $(V(t) - v_0) * \Phi[1..m] - (t - t_0)$. Now, we have obtained the value of (III) + (IV) as promised, so the "induction proof" is complete.

Invariant maintenance under insertions and deletions

In this section we first describe the two method calls that would destroy the invariant of the augmented data fields, namely an insertion or deletion of a flow record, and how to repair the invariant. We then describe how the GPS clocking tracking operation would trigger the two method calls.

We describe only the insertion operation, as the deletion operation is similar. The insertion of a node is handled first by the based data structure that is a balanced binary search tree. Note that in our special case where all keys are stored at the leaves, the inserted node must be a leaf node. In a balanced binary search tree such as AVL or red-black insertion of a new leaf node would trigger a series of rotations (e.g., of types LL, LR, RL, and RR in AVL) that first travel up the tree and then possibly travel down (but not necessarily all the way down to another leaf). This would destroy the invariants of the augmented data fields in the set of nodes S affected by the rotations and the path from the lowest common ancestor of nodes in S to the root of the tree. Hence we need to repair this invariant for all nodes along this "trail of destruction." Since it is known that, in balanced tree data structures such as AVL or red-black, the total number of nodes in S and the height of the tree are both $O(\log n)$, the time complexity of the invariant repair operation is $O(\log n)$.

Finally, we describe how insertions and deletions are triggered by GPS clock tracking operations. There are three different ways in which insertions and deletions can happen. First, each cleanup operation results in a leaf node with the smallest key value that corresponds to the lower-leftmost leaf in the binary search tree being deleted. Second, a new flow arrival at time t, as shown in Fig. 14.20, would result in a "staircase query" for computing $V(t)$, the GPS virtual start time of the first packet of this flow. Its GPS virtual finish time needs to be inserted into the shape data structure. Third, a new packet arrival, say $p_{i,k+1}$ (the $(k+1)$th packet in the ith flow F_i) to an existing (i.e., currently backlogged) flow F_i at time t, would result in both an insertion (of the leaf node keyed by $f_{i,k+1}$, the GPS virtual finish time of $p_{i,k+1}$) and a deletion (of the leaf node keyed by $f_{i,k}$, the GPS virtual finish time of the previous packet $p_{i,k}$), in addition to a "staircase query" for computing $V(t)$. Note that in this case we must have $V(t) < f_{i,k}$ since otherwise F_i is not backlogged at time t.

We note that, in real-world operations, the WFQ scheduler can usually "get away with" not performing any cleanup operation for the following reason. The utilization level of the link to be scheduled is usually much less than 100%. In this case a busy period (of the combined queue for the link) is usually not very long in duration, and hence the number of leaf nodes in the binary search tree is not going to be large enough to start causing trouble (e.g., exceed the available memory or make the tree "too tall"). Then, "throwing away" (e.g., by making "memset" + "free" systems calls) the whole augmented data structure at the end of a busy period will do the trick. Conceivably, this "laid back" approach to cleanup can considerably reduce cleanup time in real-world operations.

14.13 Implementing WFQ and WF²Q

It was shown in Valente (2004) that the shape data structure alone is sufficient for implementing WFQ. However, WF²Q is even harder to implement than WFQ because, in addition to tracking the GPS clock and sorting the GPS virtual finish times, its implementation has to somehow maintain the set of eligible packets. It was shown in Valente (2004) that another augmented data structure and algorithm, proposed in Stoica and Abdel-Wahab (1995) for implementing a different scheduling policy called Earliest Eligible Virtual Deadline First (EEVDF), can be used to carry out each WF²Q operation, namely to find the (next) eligible packet that has the lowest GPS virtual finish time, in $O(\log n)$ time in the worst case. The WF²Q implementation proposed in Valente (2004) contains both a shape data structure and an EEVDF data structure. Each arriving packet is first processed by the shape data structure to obtain its virtual start and finish times as described above, and then inserted into the EEVDF data structure for

EEVDF scheduling; the virtual start and finish times of this packet are regarded as the eligible time and the deadline respectively, for EEVDF scheduling. We summarize this data structure and algorithm into an exercise problem in Section 14.18.

14.14 Quick fair queueing (QFQ)

Recall from Section 14.11 that the WF^{2}Q scheduling algorithm can closely approximate the GPS scheduler with the smallest possible T-WFI (the maximum amount by which the real finish time of any packet under a certain policy can either lead or lag behind that under GPS, as defined in Section 14.11) of $O(L)$. It does so with time complexity $O(\log n)$ using the sophisticated data structures described in Section 14.12 (for tracking GPS clock and sorting GPS virtual finish times) and Section 14.13 (for checking eligibility). In this section, we describe a scheduling algorithm called QFQ (Quick Fair Queuing) that can achieve nearly the same T-WFI as WF^{2}Q, yet has a time complexity of only $O(1)$.

14.14.1 Fair round robin (FRR) algorithm

To be fair, QFQ is not the first scheduling algorithm to be nearly as fair as WF^{2}Q yet have $O(1)$ time complexity. Fair Round Robin (FRR) (Yuan et al., 2009) is the first such algorithm. In the following, we describe FRR first, since QFQ builds and improves on FRR. The design of FRR is based on the following insight: It is computationally much easier to schedule n flows with equal or similar weights than that with very different weights (that can differ from one another by $O(n)$ times such as that in the example shown in Fig. 14.18). This insight can be seen from the following two facts: (1) When all flows have the same weight or similar weights, the T-WFI of even a round robin scheduler (that has $O(1)$ time complexity) such as DRR does not grow with n; (2) when flows have very different weights however, the T-WFI of even the WFQ (that has $O(\log n)$ time complexity) grows linearly with n as shown in Section 14.11.

Based on this insight, the idea of FRR is to bundle flows into groups such that in each group, the weights of flows are similar. The grouping is done in the following "exponential" manner: Each flow F_k belongs to the group $i = \lceil \log_C \phi_k \rceil$, where ϕ_k is the weight of F_k. Here C is a parameter that controls the tradeoff between the time complexity of FRR and the service guarantees FRR provides; larger C leads to fewer number of groups and hence better time complexity, but also to worse QoS guarantees (more specifically worse delay bounds). C is typically set to an integer value such as 2. For convenience of presentation, we assume C = 2 in the sequel. In this case, in each group, weights of flows can differ by at most 2 times. One effect of this grouping is that the number of groups, which we denote as G, is independent of n, or in other words is $O(1)$ with respect to n. It is not hard to show that $G = \lceil \log_C (\phi_{max}/\phi_{min}) \rceil$ where ϕ_{max} and ϕ_{min} are the maximum and the minimum weight of a flow, respectively. When $C = 2$, we have $G \leq 64$ under all conceivable use cases.

After bundling flows into groups, FRR takes the following two-tiered approach towards cost-effective packet scheduling: It performs fine-grained scheduling among groups and coarse-grained scheduling among flows within a group (**P3b**) as follows. FRR views each group (of flows) as a super flow, and serves these G super flows using a variant of WF^{2}Q. This variant, which has a time complexity of $O(G \log G)$, is more computationally expensive than the vanilla WF^{2}Q (whose time complexity is $O(\log G)$), since in this (FRR's) use case (of WF^{2}Q) the weight of a group can change dynamically (say when a constituent flow of a group becomes newly backlogged) whereas in a standard use case, the weight of a flow never changes; however, since G is small ($G \leq 64$ as explained above), $O(G \log G)$ is technically still $O(1)$. Note such fine-grained scheduling among groups (using this WF^{2}Q variant) is necessary for FRR to achieve good fairness, since (the constituent flows of) different super flows can have very different weights, and using a coarse-grained scheduler among them can result in a poor T-WFI that grows linearly with n as explained above.

Once FRR picks a group for service, it picks the HOL packet of one of the flows belonging to the group for service according to a round-robin order using an extended form of DRR; note even a round-robin scheduler can achieve good fairness when scheduling flows within a group, since these flows have similar weights by design. Using this two-tiered approach, FRR achieves excellent overall fairness yet has a low time complexity that is technically $O(1)$.

14.14.2 How QFQ improves upon FRR

QFQ improves upon FRR by reducing its technically $O(1)$ (actually $O(G \log G)$) time complexity to true $O(1)$, or in other words getting rid of its dependence on G, through three modifications. The first modification is that it makes use of an approximate virtual time function $V(t)$ proposed in what was called WF^{2}Q+ (Bennett and Zhang, 1996a). WF^{2}Q+ is pretty much the same algorithm as WF^{2}Q except that its $V(t)$ only approximately tracks the GPS clock (whereas that of WF^{2}Q does so exactly). This approximation, combined with the third modification to be described shortly, allows the WF^{2}Q+ clock to be tracked with true $O(1)$ (independent of both n and G) time complexity. The tradeoff (**P3b**) is that its fairness guarantee, as measured by T-WFI, is slightly worse than that of WF^{2}Q.

The second modification is that it assigns a flow F_k to a group based not only on its weight ϕ_k, but also on its maximum packet size L_k. More precisely, it assigns a flow F_k to flow group i, where $i = \lceil \log_2(L_k/\phi_k) \rceil$ (with base $C = 2$). It was shown in Checconi et al. (2013) that the use of WF^{2}Q+ clock with this modification leads to the following nice property of QFQ that is key to its true $O(1)$ time complexity: The difference between the WF^{2}Q+ virtual finish times of the HOL packets of any two flows in the system is bounded by a small universal constant δ, no matter what the traffic arrival pattern is. A weaker version of this property is called the Globally Bounded Timestamp (GBT) property in Bennett and Zhang (1996a).

The third modification is that for the purpose of sorting (the WF^{2}Q+ virtual finish times of HOL packets), in each group i, the WF^{2}Q+ virtual finish times are rounded to the multiples of a certain unit value σ_i. For each group index i, the value of σ_i is defined to be 2^i (bits). With this σ_i-integral rounding, the rounded WF^{2}Q+ virtual finish time of any HOL packet can only take a small number of possible values thanks to the GBT property described above. Hence the sorting of rounded WF^{2}Q+ virtual finish times (to decide which flow shall have its HOL packet transmitted) within any group can be done in $O(1)$ time using bucket sorting (**P14**). In the rest of this section, we drop the qualifier "rounded WF^{2}Q+" with the understanding that all virtual finish and start times referred to below has this qualifier.

For any flow F_k that belongs to a group i^*, its maximum normalized packet length L_k/ϕ_k is less than $2\sigma_{i^*}$ as a result of how we assign flows to groups as described above. This property in turn guarantees that the virtual finish time of any packet is no later than its virtual start time by more than $2\sigma_i$. For each group i, define $s^{(i)}$ to be the earliest virtual start time among all flows (their HOL packets) in group i. This $s^{(i)}$ is called the virtual start time of group i, and the corresponding packet is called the HOL packet of group i. Let $f^{(i)}$ be the virtual finish time of this HOL packet. To achieve $O(1)$ time complexity, QFQ makes the following simplifying assumption: $f^{(i)}$ is assumed to be $s^{(i)} + 2\sigma_i$. Arguably, this assumption is a bit unfair for the HOL packet of a group i if the length of this packet is much smaller than the maximum packet length of the flow this packet belongs to. However, the overall degradation of fairness due to this assumption is typically small (**P3b**), since within each group, packets are still served in the order of their actual virtual finish times.

The QFQ scheduling policy can now be precisely stated as follows: Whenever the link becomes idle, the QFQ policy picks, among the eligible groups (those that should have started service under the WF^{2}Q+ clock), the group that has the earliest virtual finish time to service next. Intuitively, as in the implementation of the WF^{2}Q policy, a scheduling algorithm that implements the QFQ policy needs to do both the sorting (of virtual finish times) and the eligibility checks.

The QFQ algorithm manages to do both checks in $O(1)$ time. The key idea is to partition (at any time) the (set of) G groups into four subsets according to whether a group is ready (R) to receive service or blocked (B), and whether a group is eligible (E) or ineligible (I), with invariants maintained for these four subsets (at any time). Since $G \leq 64$, we can represent these G groups by $G \leq 64$ different locations; hence each subset (of these G groups) can be encoded as a 64-bit-long bitmap (**P14**), with the value of each bit indicating whether or not the corresponding group is in the subset. With these invariants maintained at all times, the QFQ algorithm boils down to performing the following basic operation, a few times, per scheduling or maintenance event: identify the group with the smallest index in one of these four subsets. But this is equivalent to "finding first one" (FFO, mentioned in Section 13.16) in the 64-bit integer (bitmap) that encodes the subset. Since most modern CPUs have a built-in FFO instruction (**P4c**) that completes in one clock cycle, the QFQ algorithm can process each scheduling or maintenance event in a few clock cycles. For a scheduling event, after the QFQ algorithm identifies the group with the smallest index (using FFO), it identifies the flow within this group that has the smallest virtual finish time again in true $O(1)$ time using bucket sorting.

The first subset is the ER (eligible and ready) subset. Whenever the QFQ algorithm picks the next group to service it picks from this subset. Two invariants are maintained for ER at any time t. First, it contains the "right" group, say group i^*, to pick (at time t) in the sense group i^* both is eligible and has the earliest virtual finish time among all eligible groups. Second, the virtual finish times of all groups in ER are sorted by their group indices in the following sense: For any $i_1, i_2 \in$ ER and $i_1 < i_2$, the virtual finish time of group i_1 is no later than that of group i_2. With these two invariants, to find the "right" group, the QFQ algorithm needs only to perform FFO on the 64-bit-long ER bitmap.

However, without additional "magic", apparently something is wrong with the second invariant: There can certainly be an eligible group whose index is smaller than i^*, and in this case FFO would not locate the "right" group i^*. The ingenious idea of QFQ is to block all such groups, and push them to the second subset, named EB (eligible and blocked). Compared to the ER subset, the EB subset does not contain the "right" group i^*, satisfies the second invariant above as proven in Checconi et al. (2013) (in Theorem 5). The other two subsets are IB (ineligible and blocked) and IR (ineligible and ready). It was shown in Checconi et al. (2013) that groups in IB$\bigcup$IR satisfy two invariants: (1) The virtual start times of these groups are sorted by their group indices; and (2) The virtual finish times of these groups are sorted by their group indices. Note (1) and (2) can both be true simultaneously since we assume $f^{(i)} = s^{(i)} + 2\sigma_i$ as explained above.

Conceivably, as time evolves, a group needs to move from one subset to another, and each such move corresponds to an aforementioned maintenance event. As shown in Checconi et al. (2013), there are four types of moves: (1) IB→IR; (2) IR→ER; (3) IB→EB; and (4) EB→ER. The QFQ algorithm has two remarkable properties: (1) All four invariants concerning these four subsets can be maintained in the event of any such move, and (2) the maintenance cost (time complexity) of each such move is true $O(1)$ (as it involves mostly a FFO operation). As shown in Checconi et al. (2013), both properties result from (1) the the assumption that $f^{(i)} = s^{(i)} + 2\sigma_i$; (2) the aforementioned GBT property; and (3) the grouping rule $i = \lceil \log_2(L_k/\phi_k) \rceil$. Due to its true $O(1)$ time complexity and excellent QoS guarantee (that is close to that of WF²Q), the QFQ algorithm has been integrated into the Linux kernel (QFQ source code in Linux Kernels, 2012).

14.15 Towards programmable packet scheduling

We introduced the concept of programmable switches and routers in Section 11.15 in the context of programmable IP lookups and P4. As mentioned in Section 11.15, P4 currently does not currently support programmable queueing disciplines (i.e., packet scheduling policies), but considerable research effort has been expended towards this goal. In this section, we introduce the concept of programmable packet scheduling and describe two representative research proposals.

14.15.1 Push-In First-Out (PIFO) framework

Under the PIFO framework Sivaraman et al. (2016a), packet scheduling is programmable in the sense that several different packet scheduling algorithms can be instantiated from a template via picking different parameter values. For example, a data center network equipped with switches supporting such a programmable capability can allow network operators to instantiate a supported packet scheduling algorithm best suited for the network.

The PIFO framework can support both work-conserving and non-work-conserving packet scheduling algorithms. However, since the former is the focus of this chapter, in the rest of this section we consider only the former and omit the qualifier "work-conserving" with the implicit understanding that we are only referring to work-conserving algorithms. The design of PIFO is based on the observation that a packet scheduling algorithm needs to make only one decision concerning packet arrivals: *In what order* should existing packets (those currently in the packet queue) be served? For many algorithms, this decision can be made when a packet is enqueued in the following sense. For any two exiting packets, the relative order in which they should be served will not change with any future packet arrivals. For example, this is the case in WFQ, since the QPS virtual finish time of any packet is determined as soon as the packet has arrived. Not all work-conserving algorithms have this invariant property though. For example, although the WF²Q algorithm is work-conserving (see exercise problem 10 in Section 14.18), it does not have this invariant property (see exercise problem 11 in Section 14.18).

This invariant property is important, with respect to programmability, because a packet scheduling algorithm having this property can be implemented using an abstract data structure called a push-in first-out (PIFO) queue (Sivaraman et al., 2016a). A PIFO is a priority queue that allows elements to be pushed to an arbitrary relative position based on an element's rank, but always dequeues from the head. In the context of packet scheduling using a work-conserving algorithm, this rank is a timestamp indicating the priority of a packet relative to other packets. For example, in WFQ the timestamp of a packet is its GPS virtual finish time. Hence, in this context, a PIFO is precisely a standard priority queue. However, the term PIFO is used (rather than call it a priority queue) for three reasons. First, in the context of packet scheduling, PIFO is more than just an abstract data structure: It also embodies the aforementioned invariant property that the service order of existing packets do not change with future packet arrivals. Second, as explained in Sivaraman et al. (2016a), for non-work-conserving algorithms that have this invariant property, a PIFO is a calendar queue instead. Third, the term PIFO was first introduced in Chuang et al. (1999) for describing the proposed combined input and output queueing (CIOQ) switching algorithm (described in Section 13.17), in which PIFO means only this invariant property (but not the data structure). In the sequel, we refer to a work-conserving packet scheduling algorithm that has this property as PIFO-compatible.

For each supported PIFO-compatible algorithm, there is only one parameter to be specified under this programmable packet scheduling framework: a callback procedure that assigns a timestamp to each packet right upon its arrival. Such a callback procedure is called *scheduling transaction* in Sivaraman et al. (2016b). For example, the scheduling transaction in WFQ can be implemented using the efficient GPS clock tracking algorithm (Valente, 2004) described in Section 14.12. For another example, the scheduling transaction in FIFO (first in first out) is trivial: The timestamp of a packet is simply the arrival time of the packet. It was shown in Sivaraman et al. (2016a) that this programmable packet scheduling framework supports, besides WFQ and FIFO, several other well-known algorithms (including those that are non-work-conserving) such as Token Bucket Filtering (described in Section 14.4), Hierarchical Packet Fair Queueing (aka. WF^{2}Q+) (Bennett and Zhang, 1996a), Least-Slack Time-First (Leung, 1989), the Rate Controlled Service Disciplines (Zhang and Ferrari, 1994), and fine-grained priority scheduling (e.g., Shortest Job First).

14.15.2 Universal packet scheduler

Programmable packet scheduling implies that when the switch packet scheduling algorithm changes for say a new bandwidth allocation criterion, the switch must be reprogrammed. However, reprogramming switches frequently can disrupt the high-speed operations of a production network. The Universal Packet Scheduler paper (Mittal et al., 2015) studied whether a change in the fairness criteria necessarily requires switch reprogramming. Does there exist a universal packet scheduler S that can emulate (called *replay*) the bandwidth allocation behavior of any packet scheduling algorithm? If the answer to this question is yes, then we need to program only S on programmable switches once and for all, and never need to reprogram it thereafter.

To provide a short introduction to the concept of a universal packet scheduler, we have to introduce some terms and notation. Consider a network of routers connected by links, with a boundary comprised of ingress and egress routers. Every router uses a certain packet scheduling algorithm for scheduling packets along its output links, and different routers may use different packet scheduling algorithms. We denote the set of packet scheduling algorithms these routers use as $\{A_\alpha\}$ in the sense router α uses algorithm A_α. Consider a packet arrival instance $\{(p, i(p), path(p)) | p \in P\}$ to the ingress routers, where P is a set of packets, $i(p)$ is the arrival time of p to an ingress router, and $path(p)$ is the path p takes through the network to the egress router. Let $o(p)$ be the departure time of p (from the network), or when p leaves the corresponding egress router. Then $\{(path(p), i(p), o(p)) | p \in P\}$ is called a schedule.

Suppose we now use another set of packet scheduling algorithms $\{A'_\alpha\}$ on these routers, and the resulting schedule given the same packet arrival instance is $\{(path(p), i(p), o'(p))|p \in P\}$ where $o'(p)$ is the departure time of p under $\{A'_\alpha\}$. In Mittal et al. (2015), $\{A'_\alpha\}$ is said to *replay* $\{A_\alpha\}$ if $o'(p) \leq o(p)$ for all $p \in P$. A universal packet scheduler is one that, when used by all routers, can be "manipulated" to replay any *viable schedule*, defined as one that can be produced by a certain $\{A_\alpha\}$. Here, information used to "manipulate" a universal packet scheduler is limited to header values commonly used for packet scheduling such as a priority value or a timestamp. For example, a packet p is not allowed to have a "full route schedule" in the header that specifies the departure deadlines of p from every hop along $path(p)$.

The following theoretical results were shown in Mittal et al. (2015). First, under some mild and commonsense assumptions, no universal packet scheduler can exist in general. Second, if for every packet $p \in P$ there are at most two congestion points along its path, then it is possible to manipulate the Least Slack Time First (LSTF) algorithm (Leung, 1989) into a universal packet scheduler, where the manipulation is to assign the appropriate slack (in the schedule) value in its packet header at the ingress point. A congestion point is a node (router) where a packet has to wait for its turn to be transmitted. Third, if there can be at most one congestion point along the path of every packet, then the simple priority scheduling algorithm can also be manipulated into a universal packet scheduler, where the manipulation is to assign each packet p an appropriate priority value. Finally, if there can be three more congestion points along the path of a packet, then again no universal packet scheduler can exist. The second and the third results can be useful in practice, since in both data center and wide-area networks, typically there can be at most two congestion points along each path: the ingress router and the egress router.

14.16 Scalable fair queuing

Using multiple queues for each flow, we have seen that: (1) A constant-time algorithm (DRR) can provide bandwidth guarantees for QoS even using software and (2) a logarithmic time-overhead algorithm can provide bandwidth and delay guarantees; further, the logarithmic overhead can be made negligible using extra hardware to implement a priority queue. Thus it would seem that QoS is easy to implement in routers ranging from small edge routers to the bigger backbone (core) routers.

Unfortunately, even very old studies by Thompson et al. (1997) of backbone routers show there to be around 250,000 concurrent flows. With increasing traffic, we expect this number to grow to a million and possibly larger as Internet speed and traffic increase. Keeping state for a million flows can be a difficult task in backbone routers. If the state is kept in SRAM, the amount of memory required can be expensive; if the state is kept in DRAM, state lookup could be slow.

More cogently, advocates of Internet scaling and aggregation point out that Internet routing currently uses only around 1,000,000 prefixes for over a billion nodes. Why should QoS require so much state when none of the other components of IP do? In particular, while the QoS state *may* be manageable today, it might represent a serious threat to the scaling of the Internet. Just as prefixes aggregate routes for multiple IP addresses, is there a way to aggregate flow state?

Aggregation implies that backbone routers will treat groups of flows in identical fashion. Aggregation requires that: (1) It must be reasonable for the members of the aggregated group to be treated identically and (2) there must be an efficient mapping from packet headers to aggregation groups. For example, in the case of IP routing: (1) A prefix aggregates a number of addresses that share the same output link, often because they are in the same relative geographic area, and (2) the longest matching prefix provides an efficient mapping from destination addresses in headers to the appropriate prefix.

There are three interesting proposals to provide aggregated QoS, which we describe briefly: random aggregation (stochastic fair queueing (SFQ)); aggregation at the network edge (DiffServ); and aggregation at the network edge together with efficient policing of misbehaving flows (core stateless fair queuing).

14.16.1 Random aggregation

The idea behind SFQ (McKenney, 1991) is to employ Principle **P3a** by trading certainty in fairness for reduced state. In this proposal backbone routers keep a fixed set of flow queues that is affordable, say, 125,000, on which they do, say, DRR. When packets arrive, some set of packet fields (say, destination, source, and the destination and source ports for TCP and UDP traffic) are hashed to a flow queue. Thus assuming that a flow is defined by the set of fields used for hashing, a given flow will always be hashed to the same flow queue. Thus with 250,000 concurrent flows and 125,000 flow queues, roughly 2 flows will share the same flow queue or hash bucket.

Stochastic fair queuing has two disadvantages. First, different backbone routers can hash flows into different groups because routers need to be able to change their hash function if the hash distributes unevenly. Second, SFQ does not allow some flows to be treated differently (either locally within one router or globally across routers) from other flows, a crucial feature for QoS. Thus SFQ only provides some sort of scalable and uniform bandwidth fairness.

14.16.2 Edge aggregation

The three ideas behind the DiffServ proposal (Blake et al., 1998) are: relaxing system requirements (**P3**) by aggregating flows into classes at the cost of a reduced ability to discriminate between flows; shifting the mapping to classes from core routers to edge routers (**P3c**, shifting computation in space); and passing the aggregate class information from the edge to core routers in the IP header (**P10**, passing hints in protocol headers).

Thus edge routers aggregate flows into classes and mark the packet class by using a standardized value in the IP TOS field. The IP type-of-service (TOS) field was meant for some such use, but it was never standardized; vendors such as Cisco used it within their networks to denote traffic classes, such as voice over IP, but there was no standard definition of traffic classes. The DiffServ group generalizes and standardizes such vendor behavior, reserving values for classes that are being standardized. One class being discussed is so-called *expedited service*, in which a certain bandwidth is reserved for the class. Another is *assured service*, which is given a lower drop probability for RED in output queues.

However, the key point is that backbone routers have a much easier job in DiffServ. First, they map flows to classes based on a small number of field values in a single TOS field. Second, the backbone router has to manage only a small number of queues, mostly one for each class and sometimes one for each subclass within a class; for example, assured service currently specifies three levels of service within the class. Edge routers, though, have to map flows to classes based on ACL-like rules and examination of possibly the entire header. This is, however, a good trade-off because edge routers operate at slower speeds.

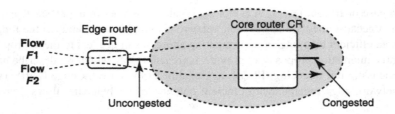

FIGURE 14.24

If flows $F1$ and $F2$ are aggregated by the time they reach the core router CR, how can the core router realize that $F1$ is oversubscribing without keeping state for each (unaggregated) flow?

14.16.3 Edge aggregation with policing

Using edge aggregation, two flows (say, $F1$ and $F2$) that have reserved bandwidth (say, B_1 and B_2, respectively) could be aggregated into a class that has nominally reserved some bandwidth, which is $B \geq B_1 + B_2$ for all flows in the class. Consider Fig. 14.24. Suppose $F1$ decides to oversubscribe and to send at a rate greater than B. The edge router ER in Fig. 14.24 may currently have sufficient bandwidth to allow all packets of flow $F1$ and $F2$ through. Unfortunately, when this aggregated class reaches the backbone (core) router CR, suppose the core router is limited in bandwidth and must drop packets. Ideally, CR should only drop oversubscribed flows like $F1$ and let all of $F2$'s packets through.

How, though, can CR tell which flows are oversubscribed? It could do so by keeping state for all flows passing through, but that would defeat scaling. A clever idea, called *core-stateless fair queuing* (Stoica et al., 1998), makes the observation that the edge router ER has sufficient information to distinguish the oversubscribed flows. Thus ER can, using Principle **P10**, pass information in packet headers to CR.

How, though, should CR handle oversubscribed flows? Dropping all such marked packets may be too severe. If there is enough bandwidth for some oversubscribed flows, it seems reasonable for CR to drop in proportion to the degree a flow is oversubscribed. Thus ER should pass a value in the packet header of a flow that is proportional to the degree a flow is oversubscribed. To implement this idea, CR can drop randomly (**P3a**), with a drop probability that is proportional to the degree of oversubscription. While this has some error probability, it is close enough. Most importantly, random dropping can be implemented without CR keeping any state per flow. In effect, CR is implementing RED, but with the drop probability computed based on a packet header field set by an edge router.

While core-stateless is a nice idea, we note that unlike SFQ (which can be implemented in isolation without cooperation between routers) and DiffServ (which has mustered sufficient support for its standardized use of the TOS field), core-stateless fair queuing is, as of now, only a research proposal (Stoica et al., 1998).

14.17 Summary

In this chapter we attacked another major implementation bottleneck for a router: scheduling data packets to reduce the effects of congestion and to provide fairness and QoS guarantees to certain flows. We worked our way upward from schemes, such as RED, that provide congestion feedback to schemes that provide QoS guarantees in terms of bandwidth and delay. We also studied how to scale the QoS state to core routers using aggregation techniques such as DiffServ.

A real router will often have to choose various *combinations* of these individual schemes. Many routers today offer RED, Approximate Fair Dropping (AFD), token bucket policing, and multiple queues and DRR. However, the major point is that all these schemes, with the exception of the schemes that provide delay bounds, can be implemented efficiently.

Even schemes that provide excellent delay bounds can be implemented fairly efficiently. For example, we have shown that both WFQ and WF^{2}Q can provide excellent delay bounds with only $O(\log N)$ time complexity (per packet), using a sophisticated shape data structure described in Section 14.12. Furthermore, Quick Fair Queueing (QFQ) described in Section 14.14 can provide similar delay bounds with $O(1)$ time complexity. A number of combination schemes can also be implemented efficiently using the principles we have outlined. The exercises explore some of these combinations.

To make this chapter self-contained, we devoted a great deal of the discussion to explanations of topics, such as congestion control and resource reservation, that are really peripheral to the main business of this book. What we really care about is the use of our principles to attack scheduling bottlenecks. Lest that be forgotten, we remind you as always, of the summary, in Table 14.1 of the techniques used in this chapter and the corresponding principles.

14.18 Exercises

1. Consider what happens if there are large variations in the reserved bandwidths of flows, for example, $F1$ with a rate of 1000 and $F2, \ldots, Fn$ with a rate of 1. Assuming that all flows have the same minimum packet size, show that flow $F1$ can be locked out for a long period.
2. Consider the simple idea of sending one packet for each queue with an enabled quantum for each round in DRR. In other words, we interleave the packets sent in various queues during a DRR round rather than finishing a quantum's worth for every flow. Describe how to implement this efficiently.
3. Work out the details of implementing a hierarchical DRR scheme.
4. Suppose an implementation wishes to combine DRR with token bucket shaping also on the queues. How can the implementation ensure that it skips empty queues (a DRR scan should not visit a queue that has no token bucket credits)?
5. Describe how to efficiently combine DRR with multiple levels of priority. In other words, there are several levels of priority; within each level of priority, the algorithm runs DRR.
6. Suppose that the required bandwidths of flows vary by an order of magnitude in DRR. What fairness problems can result? Suggest a simple fix that provides better short-term fairness without requiring sorting.
7. We consider a packet scheduling scenario in which there are three flows (denoted as $F1$, $F2$, and $F3$) with equal weights. The jth packet of F_i is denoted $p_{i,j}$. Its arrival time and length (in bits) are denoted as $a_{i,j}$ and $l_{i,j}$, respectively. Let $a_{1,1} = a_{2,1} = a_{3,1} = 0$. Let $a_{1,2} = a_{2,2} = a_{3,2} = 1$ and $a_{1,3} = a_{3,3} = 2$. Let $l_{1,1} = 2$, $l_{1,2} = 3$, $l_{1,3} = 6$, $l_{2,1} = 6$, $l_{2,2} = 3$, $l_{3,1} = 3$, $l_{3,2} = 1$, and $l_{3,3} = 6$. Suppose the service rate of the link is 1 bit per second. Then

(a) What is the GPS finish time of each packet?

   (b)   What is the service order of these packets under WFQ?

   (c)   What is the service order of these packets under WF^{2}Q?

   (d)   What is the service order of these packets under DRR when the quantum size is 3 bits?

8. Reuse distance (Bennett and Kruskal, 1975) is a heavily studied concept in computer architecture and programming languages. Given a sequence of memory references (addresses accessed during the execution of a computer program), the reuse distance of a memory reference (say, to memory address a) is the number of distinct memory references that have happened between the previous reference to a and this reference. For example, suppose the list of memory references is a, b, c, b, c, a. Then the reuse distance between the two consecutive references to a is 2, since only two distinct addresses, namely b and c, are referenced in between. Please design and implement in C++/C an augmented data structure that, given as input a long list of memory references (by a program), allows a companion algorithm to compute, for each memory access, its reuse distance in $O(\log N)$ time, where N is the number of distinct addresses in the list. (Hint: This augmented data structure subsumes one for implementing dynamic order statistics, which is the sole topic of Section 14.1 in Cormen et al. (2009). Reading and understanding that section will make this problem much easier to tackle.)

9. As mentioned in Section 14.13, an augmented data structure and algorithm was proposed in Stoica and Abdel-Wahab (1995) for implementing the Earliest Eligible Virtual Deadline First (EEVDF) scheduling policy, in a computationally efficient manner. The EEVDF policy is used to schedule tasks in a system for service. Each task has a virtual deadline, that like a virtual time, is determined when this task arrives (to the system), and its value does not change thereafter. Each task also has a virtual eligible time t_e (that is also determined when the task arrives) in the sense when the current virtual time is at least t_e this task is eligible for service. The EEVDF policy is that, whenever the server becomes idle (right after finishing serving the current task), the scheduler needs to pick, among the eligible tasks (as determined by their eligible times), the one with the earliest virtual deadline for service. Now, please design an augmented data structure that can carry out the following three operations (and hence implements the EEVDF policy), all in $O(\log n)$ time, where n is the number of tasks in the system.

- **Insertion.** When a new task arrives with a virtual eligible time and a virtual deadline, this method is called to insert the task into the data structure.
- **Searching.** This method, with the current virtual time as its argument, is called when the scheduler selects the next task for service. This method shall return, among the eligible tasks, the one with the earliest virtual deadline.
- **Deletion.** This method is called to delete a task after the server finishes serving the task.

Note in both insertion and deletion, rebalancing the base data structure (and correspondingly repairing the invariants of the augmented data structure) is necessary for guaranteeing $O(\log n)$ time complexity in the worse case. The design of this augmented data structure is much simpler than that of the shape data structure, so please refrain from reading Stoica and Abdel-Wahab (1995) while working on this problem.

10. Prove that the WF^{2}Q packet scheduling policy is work-conserving.

11. Construct a counterexample to show that the WF^{2}Q packet scheduling policy is not PIFO-compatible.

Routers as distributed systems

Come now and let us reason together.
—Isaiah 1:18, The Bible

Distributed systems are clearly evil things. They are subject to a lack of synchrony, a lack of assurance, and a lack of trust. Thus in a distributed system, the time to receive messages can vary widely; messages can be lost and servers can crash, and when a message does arrive, it could even contain a virus. In Lamport's well-known words a distributed system is "one in which the failure of a computer you didn't even know existed can render your own computer unusable."

Of course, the main reason to use a distributed system is that people are distributed. It would perhaps be unreasonable to pack every computer on the Internet into an efficiency apartment in upper Manhattan. But a router? Behind the gleaming metallic cage and the flashing lights, surely there lies an orderly world of synchrony, assurance, and trust.

On the contrary, this chapter argues that, as routers (recall *routers* include general interconnect devices such as also switches and gateways) get faster, the delay between router components increases in importance when compared to message-transmission times. The delay across links connecting router components can also vary significantly. Finally, availability requirements make it infeasible to deal with component failures by crashing the entire router. With the exception of trust, trust arguably exists between router components, a router *is* a distributed system. Thus within a router, it makes sense to use techniques developed to design reliable distributed systems.

To support this thesis, this chapter considers four sample phenomena that commonly occur within most high-performance interconnect devices, flow control, striping across links, striping across DRAMs, and asynchronous data structure updates. In each case the desire for performance leads to intuitively plausible schemes. However, the combination of failure and asynchrony can lead to subtle interactions.

Thus a second thesis of this chapter is that the use of distributed algorithms within routers requires careful analysis to ensure reliable operation. While this is trite advice for protocol designers (who ignore it anyway), it may be slightly more novel in the context of a router's internal microcosm.

The chapter is organized as follows. Section 15.1 motivates the need for flow control on long chip-to-chip links and describes solutions that are simpler than, say, transmission control protocol's (TCP) window flow control. Section 15.2 motivates the need for internal striping across links and fabrics to gain throughput and presents solutions that restore packet ordering after striping. Section 15.3 motivates the need for further internal striping across DRAMs at high packet rates. Section 15.4 details the difficulties of performing asynchronous updates on data structures that run concurrently with search operations.

Network Algorithmics. https://doi.org/10.1016/B978-0-12-809927-8.00022-1

Table 15.1 Principles used in the various distributed systems techniques (for use within a router) discussed in this chapter.

Number	Principle	Used in
P1	Avoid waste caused by partitioned buffers	Internal flow control
P13	Exploit degrees of freedom by decoupling logical from physical reception	Internal striping
P5c	Make fast buffers out of banks of DRAM with a DRAM cache	Distributed Memory
P3	Relax binary search requirements to allow duplicate key values	Binary search update

The techniques described in this chapter (and the corresponding principles invoked) are summarized in Table 15.1.

In all four examples in this chapter the focus is not merely on performance but also on the use of design and reasoning techniques from distributed algorithms to produce solutions that gain performance without sacrificing reliability. The techniques used to gain reliability include periodic synchronization of key invariants and centralizing asynchronous computation to avoid race conditions. Counterexamples are also given to show how easily the desire to gain performance can lead, without care, to obscure failure modes that are hard to debug.

The sample of internal distributed algorithms presented in this chapter is necessarily incomplete. An important omission is the use of failure detectors to detect and swap out failed boards, switching fabrics, and power supplies.

Quick reference guide

It is important for an implementor to learn how to make link flow control reliable, as described in Section 15.1.2. Implementors are increasingly turning to striping within networking devices. Solutions for link striping are described in Section 15.2. Solutions for striping across DRAMs while maintaining guarantees are described in Section 15.3.

15.1 Internal flow control

As noted in Chapter 13, packaging technology and switch size are forcing switches to expand beyond single racks. These multichassis systems interconnect various components with serial links that span relatively large distances of 5–20 m. At the speed of light, a 20-m link contributes a round-trip link delay of 60 nanoseconds. On the other hand, at OC-768 speeds, a 40-byte minimum-size packet takes 8 nanoseconds to transmit. Thus eight packets can be simultaneously in transit on such a link.

What is worse, link signals propagate slower than the speed of light; also, there are other delays, such as serialization delay, that make the number of cells that can be in flight on a single link even larger. This is quite similar to a stream of packets in flight on a transatlantic link. A single router is now a miniature Internet.

TCP and other transport protocols already solve the problem of *flow control*. If the receiver has finite buffers, sender flow control ensures that any packet sent by the sender has a buffer available when

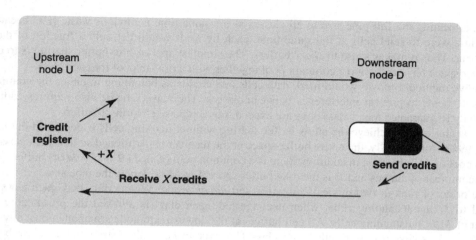

FIGURE 15.1

Basic credit-based flow control.

it arrives at the receiver. Chip-to-chip links also require flow control. It is considered bad form to drop packets or cells (we will use cells in what follows) within a router for reasons other than output-link congestion.

It is possible to reuse directly the TCP flow control mechanisms between chips. But, TCP is complex to implement. Disentangling mechanisms, TCP is complex because it does error control *and* flow control, both using sequence numbers. However, within a chip-to-chip link, errors on the link are rare enough for recovery to be relegated to the original source computer. Thus it is possible to apply fairly recent work on flow control (Kung et al., 1994; Ozveren et al., 1994) that is not intertwined with error control.

Fig. 15.1 depicts a simple credit flow control mechanism (Ozveren et al., 1994) for a chip-to-chip link within a router. The sender keeps a credit register (CR) that is initialized to the number of buffers allocated at the receiver. The sender sends cells only when the CR is positive and decrements the CR after a cell is sent. At the receiving chip, whenever a cell is removed from the buffer, the receiver sends a credit to the sender. Finally, when a credit message arrives, the sender increments the CR.

15.1.1 Improving performance

In Fig. 15.1 if the number of buffers allocated is greater than the product of the line speed and the round-trip delay (called the *pipe size*), then transfers can run at the full link speed.

One problem in real routers is that there are often several different traffic classes that share the link. One way to accommodate all classes is to strictly partition destination buffers among classes. This can be wasteful because it requires allocating the pipe size (say, 10 cell buffers) to each class. For a large number of classes, the number of cell buffers will grow alarmingly, potentially pushing the amount of on-chip SRAM required beyond feasible limits. Recall that field-programmable gate arrays (FPGAs) especially have smaller on-chip SRAM limits.

But, allocating the full pipe size to all classes at the same time is obvious waste (**P1**) because, if every class were to send cells at the same time, each by itself would get only a fraction of the link throughput. Thus it makes sense to *share* buffers. The simplest approach to buffer sharing is to divide the buffer space physically into a common pool together with a private pool for each class.

A naive method to do so would mark data cells and credits as belonging to either the common or the private pools to prevent interference between classes. The naive scheme also requires additional complexity to guarantee that a class does not exceed, say, a pipe size worth of buffers.

An elegant way to achieve the allow buffer sharing without marking cells is described in Ozveren et al. (1994). Conceptually, the entire buffer space at the receiver is partitioned so that each class has a private pool of Min buffers; in addition, there is a common pool of size $(B - N * Min)$ buffers, where N is the number of classes and B is the total buffer space. Let Max denote the pipe size.

The protocol runs in two modes: *congested* and *uncongested*. When congested, each class is restricted to Min outstanding cells; when uncongested, each class is allowed the presumably larger amount of Max outstanding cells. All cell buffers at the downstream node are anonymous; any buffer can be assigned to the incoming cells of any class. However, by carefully restricting transitions between the two modes, we can allow buffer sharing while preventing deadlock and cell loss.

To enforce the separation between private pools *without* marking cells, the sender keeps track of the total number of outstanding cells S, which is the number of cells sent minus the number of credits received. Each class i also keeps track of a corresponding counter S_i, which is the number of cells outstanding for class i. When $S < N \cdot Min$ (i.e., the private pools are in no danger of depletion), then the protocol is said to be uncongested, and every class i can send as long as $S_i \le Max$.

However, when $S \ge N \cdot Min$, the link is said to be congested, and each class is restricted to a smaller limit by ensuring that $S_i \le Min$. Intuitively, this buffer-sharing protocol performs as follows. Under a light load, when there are only a few classes active, each active class gets Max buffers and goes as fast as it possibly can. Finally, during a continuous period of heavy loading when all classes are active, each class is still guaranteed Min buffers.

Hysteresis can be added to prevent oscillation between the two modes. It is also possible to extend the idea of *buffer sharing* for credit-based flow control to *rate sharing* for rate-based flow control using, say, leaky buckets (Chapter 14).

15.1.2 Rescuing reliability

The protocol sketched in the last subsection uses limited receiver SRAM buffers very efficiently but is not robust to failures. Before understanding how to make the more elaborate flow control protocol robust against failures, it is wiser to start with the simpler credit protocol portrayed in Fig. 15.1.

Intuitively, the protocol in Fig. 15.1 is like transferring money between two banks: the "banks" are the sender and the receiver, and both credits and cells count as "money." It is easy to see that, in the absence of errors, the total "money" in the system is conserved. More formally, let CR be the credit register, M the number of cells in transit from sender to receiver, C the number of credits in transit in the other direction, and Q the number of cell buffers that are occupied at the receiver.

Then, it is easy to see that (assuming proper initialization and that no cells or credits are lost on the link), the protocol maintains the following property at any instant: $CR + M + Q + C = B$, where B is the total buffer space at the receiver. The relationship is called an *invariant* because it holds at all times when the protocol works correctly. It is the job of protocol initialization to *establish* the invariant and the job of fault tolerance mechanisms to *maintain* the invariant.

If this invariant is maintained at all times, then the system will never drop cells because the number of cells in transit plus the number of stored cells is never more than the number of buffers allocated.

There are two potential problems with a simple hop-by-hop flow control scheme. First, if initialization is not done correctly, then the sender can have too many credits, which can lead to cells being dropped. Second, credits or cells for a class can be lost due to link errors. Even chip-to-chip links are not immune from infrequent bit errors; at high link speeds, such errors can occur several times an hour. This second problem can lead to a slowdown or deadlock.

Many implementors can be incorrectly persuaded that these problems can be fixed by simple mechanisms. One immediate response is to argue that these cases won't happen or will happen rarely. Second, one can attempt to fix the second problem by using a timer to detect possible deadlock. Unfortunately, it is difficult to distinguish deadlock from the receiver's removing cells very slowly. What is worse, the entire link can slow down to a crawl, causing router performance to fall; the result will be hard to debug.

The problems can probably be cured by a router reset, but this is a Draconian solution. Instead, consider the following resynchronization scheme. For clarity, the scheme is presented using a series of refinements depicted in Fig. 15.2.

In the simplest synchronization scheme (Scheme 1, Fig. 15.2) assume that the protocol periodically sends a specially marked cell called a *marker*. Until the marker returns, the sender stops sending data cells. At the receiver, the *marker flows through the buffer before being sent back to the upstream node*. It is easy to see that after the marker returns, it has "flushed" the pipe of all cells and credits. Thus at the point the marker returns, the protocol can set the CR to the maximum value (B). Scheme 1 is simple but requires the sender to be idled periodically to do resynchronization.

So, Scheme 2 (Fig. 15.2) augments Scheme 1 by allowing the sender to send cells after the marker has been sent; however, the sender keeps track of the cells sent since the marker was launched in a register, say, CSM (for "cells sent since marker"). When the marker returns, the sender adjusts the correction to take into account the cells sent since the marker was launched and so sets $CR = B - CSM$.

The major flaw in Scheme 2 is the inability to bound the delay that it takes the marker to go through the queue at the receiver. This causes two problems. First, it makes it hard to bound how long the scheme takes to correct itself. Second, to make the marker scheme itself reliable, the sender must periodically retransmit the marker. Without a bound on the marker round-trip delay, the sender could retransmit too early, making it hard to match a marker response to a marker request without additional complexity in terms of sequence numbers.

To bound the marker round-trip delay, Scheme 3 (Fig. 15.2) lets the marker bypass the receiver queue and "reflect back" immediately. However, this requires the marker to return with the number of free cell buffers F in the receiver at the instant the marker was received. Then, when the marker returns, the sender sets the credit register $CR = F - CSM$.

The marker scheme is a special instance of a classical distributed systems technique called a *snapshot*. Informally, a snapshot is a distributed audit that produces a consistent state of a distributed system. Our marker-based snapshot is slightly different from the classical snapshot described in Chandy and Lamport (1985). The important point, however, is that snapshots can be used to detect incorrect states of any distributed algorithm and can be efficiently implemented in a two-node subsystem to make any such protocol robust. In particular, the same technique can be used (Ozveren et al., 1994) to make the fancier flow control of Section 15.1.1 equally robust.

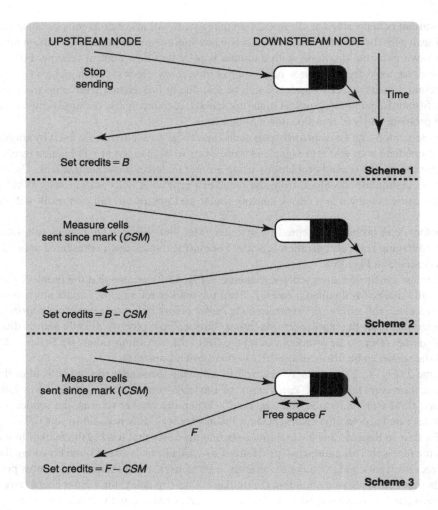

FIGURE 15.2

Three steps to a marker algorithm.

In particular, the marker protocol makes the credit-update protocol *self-stabilizing*, i.e., it can recover from arbitrary errors, including link errors, and also hardware errors that corrupt registers. This is an extreme form of fault tolerance that can greatly improve the reliability of subsystems without sacrificing performance.

In summary, the general technique for a two-node system is to write down the protocol invariants and then to design a periodic snapshot to verify and, if necessary, correct the invariants. Further techniques for protocols that work on more than two nodes are described in Awerbuch et al. (1991); they are based on decomposing, when possible, multinode protocols into two-node subsystems and repeating the snapshot idea.

An alternative technique for making a two-node credit protocol fault tolerant is the FCVC idea of Kung et al. (1994), which is explored in the exercises. The main idea is to use absolute packet numbers instead of incremental updates; with this modification, the protocol can be made robust by the technique of periodically resending the control state on the two links without the use of a snapshot.

15.2 Internal Link Striping

Flow control within routers is motivated by the twin forces of increasingly large interconnect length and increasing speeds. On the other hand, internal link striping within a router is motivated by slow interconnect speeds. If serial lines are not fast enough, a designer may resort to striping cells internally across multiple serial links.

Besides serial link striping, designers often resort to striping across slow DRAM banks (as we will see in the next section) to gain memory bandwidth, and across switch fabrics, to scale scheduling algorithms like iSLIP. We saw these trends in Chapter 13. In each case the designer distributes cells across multiple copies of a slow resource, called a *channel*.

In most applications the delay across each channel is variable; there is some large skew between the fastest and slowest times to send a packet on each channel. Thus the goals of a good striping algorithm are FIFO delivery in the face of arbitrary skew, routers should not reorder packets because of internal mechanisms, and robustness in the face of link bit errors.

To understand why this combination of goals may be difficult, consider round-robin striping. The sender sends packets in round-robin order on the channels. Round-robin, however, does not provide FIFO delivery without packet modification. The channels may have varying skews, and so the physical arrival of packets at the receiver may differ from their logical ordering. Without sequencing information, packets may be persistently misordered.

Round-robin schemes can be made to guarantee FIFO delivery by adding a packet sequence number that can be used to resequence packets at the receiver. However, many implementations would prefer not to add a sequence number because it adds to cell overhead and reduces the effective throughput of the router.

15.2.1 Improving performance

To gain ordering without the expense of sequence numbers, the main idea is to exploit a hidden degree of freedom (**P13**) by decoupling *physical reception* from *logical reception*. Physical reception is subject to skew-induced misordering. Logical reception eliminates misordering by using buffering and by having the receiver remove cells using the same algorithm as the sender.

For example, suppose the sender stripes cells in round-robin order using a round-robin pointer that walks through the sending channels. Thus cell A is sent on Channel 1, after which the round-robin pointer at the sender is incremented to 2. The next cell, B, is sent on Channel 2, and so on.

The receiver buffers received cells but does not dequeue a cell when it arrives. Instead, the receiver *also* maintains a round-robin pointer that is initialized to Channel 1. The receiver waits at Channel 1 to receive a cell; when a cell arrives, that cell is dequeued, and the receiver moves on to wait for Channel 2. Thus if skew causes cell B (that was sent on Channel 2 after cell A was sent on Channel 1) to arrive before cell 1, the receiver will not dequeue cell B before cell A. Instead, the receiver will wait for cell

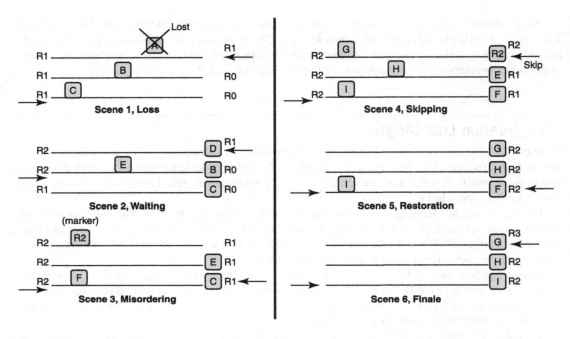

FIGURE 15.3

Misordering and recovery: a play in six scenes. The final output at the receiver is D, B, C, E, F, G, H, I, and synchronization is achieved after the logical reception of E.

A to arrive; after dequeuing cell A, the receiver will move on to Channel 2, where it will dequeue the waiting cell, B.

15.2.2 Rescuing reliability

Synchronization between sender and receiver can be lost due to the loss of a single cell. In the round-robin example shown earlier if cell A is lost in a large stream of cells sent over three links (Fig. 15.3), the receiver will deliver the packet sequence D, B, C, G, E, F, ...and permanently reorder cells.

For switch fabrics and some links, one may be able to assume that cell loss is very rare (say, once a year). Still, such an assumption should make the designer queasy, especially if one loss can cause permanent damage from that point on. To prevent permanent damage after a single cell loss, the sender must periodically resynchronize with the receiver.

To do so, define a *round* as a sequence of visits to consecutive channels before returning to the starting channel. In each round, the sender sends data over all channels. Similarly, in each round, the receiver receives data from all channels. To enable resynchronization, the sender maintains the round number (initialized to $R0$) of all channels, and so does the receiver.

Thus in Fig. 15.3 after sending A, B, and C, all the sender channel numbers are at $R1$. However, only channel 1 at the receiver is at $R1$, while the other channels are at $R0$ because the second and third channels have not been visited in the first round-robin scan at the receiver. When the round-robin pointer increments to a channel at the sender or receiver, the corresponding round number is incremented.

Effectively, round numbers can be considered to be implicit per-channel sequence numbers. Thus A can be considered to have sequence number $R1$, the next cell, D, sent on Channel 1 can be considered to have sequence number $R2$, etc.

Thus in Scene 2 of Fig. 15.3 the sender has marched on to send D on Channel 1 and E on Channel 2. The receiver is still waiting for a cell on Channel 1, which it finally receives. At this point, the play shifts to Scene 3, where the receiver outputs D and B (in that order) and moves to Channel 3, where it eventually receives cell C.

Basically, the misordering problem in Scene 2 is caused by the receiver's dequeuing a cell sent in Round $R2$ (i.e., D) in Round $R1$ at the receiver. This suggests a simple strategy to synchronize the round numbers in channels: periodically, the sender should send its current round number on each channel to the receiver. To reduce overhead, such a *marker* cell should be sent after hundreds of data cells are sent, at the cost of having potentially hundreds of cells misordered after a loss.

Because brevity is the soul of wit, the play in Fig. 15.3 assumes a marker is sent after D on Channel 1; the sending of markers on other channels is not shown. Thus in Scene 3 notice that a marker is sent on Channel 1 with the current round number, $R2$, at the sender.

In Scene 4 the receiver has output D, B, and C, in that order, and is now waiting for Channel 1 again. At this point, the marker containing $R2$ arrives.

A marker is processed at the receiver only when the marker is at the head of the buffer and the round-robin pointer is at the corresponding channel. Processing is done by the following four rules. (1) If the round number in the marker is strictly greater than the current receiver round number, the marker has arrived too early; the round-robin pointer is incremented; (2) if the round numbers are equal, any subsequent cells will have higher round numbers; thus the round-robin pointer is incremented, and the marker is also removed (but not sent to the output).

(3) If the round number in the marker is 1 less than the current channel round number, this is the normal error-free case; the subsequent cell will have the right round number. In this case the marker is removed, but the round-robin pointer at the receiver is *not* incremented. And last, (4) if the round number in the marker is $k > 1$ less than the current channel round number, a serious error (other than cell loss) has occurred and the sender and receiver should reinitialize.

Thus in Scene 4 Rule 2 applies: the marker is destroyed and the round-robin pointer incremented. At this point, it is easy to see that the sender and receiver are now in perfect synchronization because, for each channel at the receiver, the round number when that channel is reached is equal to the round number of the next cell. Thus the play ends with E's being (correctly) dequeued in Scene 4, then F in Scene 5, and finally G in Scene 6. Order is restored; morality is vindicated.

Thus the augmented load-balancing algorithm recovers from errors very quickly (time between sending the marker plus a one-way propagation delay). The general technique underlying the method of Fig. 15.3 is to detect state inconsistency on each channel by periodically sending a marker one way.

One-way sending of periodic state (unlike, say, Fig. 15.2) suffices for load balancing and also for the FCVC protocol (see Exercises) because the invariants of the protocol are one-way. A one-way invariant is an invariant that involves only variables at the two nodes and one link. By contrast, the flow control protocol of Fig. 15.1 has an invariant that uses variables on both links.

Periodic sending of state has been advocated as a technique for building reliable Internet protocols, together with timing out state that has not been refreshed for a specified period (Clark, 1988). While this is a powerful technique, the example of Fig. 15.1 shows that perhaps the soft state approach, at least as currently expressed, works only if the protocol invariants are one-way.

For load balancing, besides the one-way invariants on each channel that relate sender and receiver round numbers, there is also a global invariant that ensures that, assuming no packet loss, channel round numbers never differ by more than 1. This node invariant is enforced, after a violation due to loss, by skipping at the receiver.

Even in the case when sequence numbers can be added to cells, logical reception can help simplify the resequencing implementation. Some resequencers use fast parallel hardware sorting circuits to re-assemble packets. If logical reception is used, this circuitry is overkill. Logical reception is adequate for the expected case, and a slow scan looking for a matching sequence number is sufficient in the rare error case. Recall that, on chip-to-chip links, errors should be very rare. Notice that, if sequence numbers are added, FIFO delivery is guaranteed, unlike the protocol of Fig. 15.3.

15.3 **Distributed Memory**

So far in this book, we have ignored the problem of *building* packet buffers. The following section is based on Chapter 7 of Sundar Iyer's PhD Thesis (Sundar, 2008). The reader should consult the thesis for more details.

Packet buffers are an important part of the hardware of a router for three reasons: size and ubiquity and Quality of Service. First, the size of packet buffers has been increasing as speeds increase. The classic rule of thumb is that a switch should buffer $RTT \times R$ bits to account for congestion (where RTT is the average round-trip time for TCP flows passing through the router. Assuming a coast to coast delay of around 250 msec, a 100 Gb/s interface requires 25 Gb of memory, within the capacity of commodity DRAMs, but much larger than high-speed SRAMs. Iyer's thesis (Sundar, 2008) claims that at the time of writing, buffering was responsible for almost 40% of all memory consumed by high speed routers/switches. There is reason to believe that the situation is only worse today.

Second, packet buffers are ubiquitous in routers. Iyer's thesis (Sundar, 2008) gives several examples of where buffers are used. Two important examples are at the input to the VOQs in an input buffered switch (because of contention for output ports), and at the output port (because of congestion on the output link). There are, however, many other places in real routers including reordering buffers when packets are striped across the fabric as seen in the previous section, and multicast replication buffers.

Third, router buffering is complicated by Quality of Service (QoS) as we have seen earlier. Routers used by service providers, such as the Cisco GSR 12000 router maintain about 2,000 queues per line card, while edge routers such as the Juniper E-series provide as many as 64,000 queues for fine-grained QoS (Sundar, 2008).

The principal problem with router buffers today is that as soon as the link speed exceeds 10 Gb/s, a miniumum size 40-byte packet arrives within 32 ns. This implies that every 16 ns a packet needs to be written to or read from memory (recall a packet must be written and stored, and read out to be sent out). If one uses a single standard DRAM with a 50-ns access time, this is impossible. Similarly, the use of SRAMs of this capacity is much too expensive and power hungry.

A possible approach is to design new DRAMs with smaller access times. The access time of a DRAM depends on its geometry. One can theoretically make DRAMs faster by designing it internally with smaller banks creating even DRAMs with (say) 20 nsec access times. Unfortunately, this approach does not scale as speeds increase. Further, the extra bank overhead requires significantly larger chip area, and leads to an unacceptable area versus cost tradeoff. This is true especially in a world where router memory is a very small portion of the overall DRAM market, which is dominated today by the stringent cost pressures of computer memory.

15.3.1 Improving performance

Just as in the previous section, where we striped packets across links when the links were bottlenecks, many router manufacturers routinely stripe packets across DRAMs within routers. This appears simple: when packets arrive, they are written into any DRAM not currently being written to. When a packet leaves, it is read from DRAM, if and only if its DRAM is free. Note that DRAM protocols allow some limited pipelining of reads or writes to a different bank within the same DRAM, even if the DRAM itself has not fully completed the previous read or write requests from those different banks within the same DRAM.

Unfortunately, while this may work well most of the time or when the system is lightly loaded, it can work very badly at high loads and for certain access patterns. Some vendors attempt to make such cases unlikely by adding some speedup, but the approach remains statistical and hard to characterize.

If worst-case performance is required, especially in situations where there are stringent QoS constraints, then such an approach is not correct. In particular, there are several testing firms that can uncover such flaws in a router. We need a middle way between the correct but expensive solution of using all SRAM buffers, and the statistical but incorrect solution of striping across DRAM banks.

A pipelined memory system was proposed in Wang et al. (2010) that can provide robust performance in the following sense. This memory system, when receiving a read or write request at time t, guarantees to complete the request at exactly time $t + \Delta$ (where Δ is a constant delay), with an overwhelming probability (say $1 - 10^{-25}$) under arbitrary memory read or write patterns including the worst case; it can accommodate a request every SRAM cycle, so it has the same throughput as SRAM. This statistical guarantee was rigorously proven using worse-case large deviation theory. This memory system is general-purpose: It can not only support router packet buffers, but also other router or firewall functions such as the storage, access, and maintenance of network flow state. This memory system has a shortcoming though: The fixed delay Δ can be over 1000 SRAM cycles long, or more than several microseconds long, which is a bit too high for today's routers and switches. In comparison, the memory system proposed in Iyer's thesis provides a tight absolute (not statistical) delay guarantee when used specifically for router packet buffers. It does so by exploiting the specific memory access patterns of router packet buffers (**P7**).

15.3.2 Rescuing reliability

The solution advocated in Iyer's thesis (and first explained in a seminal paper (Sundar et al., 2008)) is to use SRAM as a cache front-end to an array of DRAM banks. Using clever algorithms and the "staging SRAM," it is possible to provably emulate the behavior of a single large SRAM.

Of course, this is very similar to the use of an SRAM cache for measurement counters we will study later in the measurement chapter (Section 16.2). This is not surprising because both ideas are described in Iyer's thesis (Sundar, 2008). However, in that idea the *low order* bits of each counter are stored in an SRAM cache and the *high order* bits of each counter are stored in DRAM. In this idea, some portion of the *head* and *tail* of each queue are stored in SRAM (for fast read out of packets, and for acceptance into a buffer queue respectively) but the vast majority of *intermediate* packets not in the head or tail are stored in DRAM.

To make this idea more precise, however, requires more work. First, we must define the *size* of the head and tail queues and show that these numbers are small in comparison to the queue size. Second, and most importantly, we must define *algorithms* that decide which packets are read in from SRAM tail cache to DRAM (on the input side) and which packets are read out from DRAM to SRAM head cache (on the output side).

To define the sizes of the head and tail caches required for various algorithms (with different trade-offs), we need the following notation (Sundar, 2008). First, it seems clear that the ratio between DRAM and SRAM speeds is a fundamental parameter. If the DRAM access time is 50 nsec and the SRAM access time is 5 nsec, then $10 = 50/5$ packets can arrive to the SRAM during a single DRAM write. Thus if the memory works in cells of say 64 bytes in length, the cache block (which is also the block size to be read from and written to DRAM) must be at least 640 bytes. This ratio of DRAM to SRAM memory speeds expressed in memory units is the first fundamental parameter b.

The second fundamental parameter is the number of queues Q. Clearly, the more the queues, the more the possible backlog between SRAM and DRAM. In the worst case, small packets can arrive to each queue while waiting for a DRAM write. Note that it is possible to do only a single DRAM write per queue; one cannot batch packets across queues as one can within the same queue. Batching packets from different queues is in principle possible with complex pointer management when writing to DRAM. Unfortunately, this defeats the purpose when one reads from DRAM. A read block from DRAM would now contain data from different queues in varying sizes, and such "scatter gather" reads cannot cater to the differing per-queue speeds required for dynamic and unpredictable read access patterns.

The tail cache is the easiest to understand. Intuitively, the controller gathers up to b bytes per queue in a tail cache and writes to DRAM in a single larger DRAM block write when possible. Thus a tail queue size of Qb makes sense. On the other hand, the head cache is more complex, since the controller has to deal with adversarial read patterns from any queue, and there are a combinatorially large number of such patterns.

Surprisingly, if the head cache is slightly larger (proportional to $Qb \log Q$), the algorithm can guarantee worst case performance with no starvation at the head cache regardless of which queue is asked for (assuming, of course, there is data for that queue). Intuitively, again, one might think of something similar to an earliest deadline first algorithm (but the proof of the worst case bound of $Qb \log Q$ still requires insight). The idea is to replenish from DRAM the head cache with the smallest amount of bytes first because the adversary may pick on that queue next. The thesis calls this the "most deficited queue first" algorithm. The actual notion of a deficit is more subtle because of possible pipelining. However, ignoring pipelining one can think of the queue with the most deficit to be the queue with the least number of bytes.

The thesis (Sundar, 2008) and paper (Sundar et al., 2008) also show a series of subtler algorithms that account for pipelining between DRAM and SRAM, and tradeoff head cache memory for latency. The general idea is to reduce the amount of head cache maintained on a per queue basis, if one is prepared to tolerate a larger read latency. A larger read latency allows the algorithm to "look ahead" into the future queue read patterns and get a better idea of the queues that should be serviced, taking into account both the current size of the queues in the SRAM head cache and the future request pattern.

Further, if it is known that queues do not behave completely adversarially, the head cache size can be reduced further.

The distributed memory algorithms described in this section have had a large impact. They were first commercialized in a startup called Nemo founded by Iyer and McKeown. After Nemo was acquired by Cisco, it began to considerably impact Cisco routers. By some estimates in Iyer's thesis Sundar (2008) distributed memory within Cisco alone is used by several million chips per year in over 7 product lines, saving hundreds of millions of dollars per year by replacing SRAM with cheap off-chip DRAM, while allowing queue sizes in the thousands. While the more complex algorithms were used rarely, the simple most deficited queue algorithm was used in the vast majority of Cisco head cache implementations. For the tail cache, the simple dynamically allocated cache of size Qb was universally used.

Besides the memory savings, other advantages include reduced power, reduced pins on ASICs (to deal with multiple memories), and better utiilization. The better utilization comes from the batching into blocks of b. A surprising side effect is to eliminate the thorny problem of what happens when 65 byte packets are sent when the internal SRAM cell size is 64 bytes. Such memory fragmentation becomes less of an issue when a stream of 65 byte packets are batched in a tail cache of size $b = 640$ bytes (say). A second subtle advantage is that these provably worst case queues eliminate packet drops: this is crucial for example in the storage market (Sundar, 2008), as well as other applications whose QoS requirements require strict bounded latency.

15.4 Asynchronous updates

Atomic updates that work concurrently with fast search operations are a necessary part of all the incremental algorithms in Chapters 11 and 10. For example, assume that trie node X points to node Z. Often, inserting a prefix requires adding a new node Y so that X points to Y and Y points to Z. Since packets are arriving concurrently at wire speed, the update process must minimally block the search process. The simplest way to do this without locks is to first build Y completely to point to Z and then, in a single atomic write, swing the pointer at X to point to Y.

In general, however, there are many delicacies in such designs, especially when faced with complications such as pipelining. To illustrate the potential pitfalls and the power of correct reasoning, consider the following example taken from the first bridge implementation.

In the first bridge product studied in Chapter 10 the bridge used binary search. Imagine we had a long list of distinct keys $B, C, D, E, \ldots$ and with all the free space after the last (greatest key). Consider the problem of adding a new entry, say, A. There are two standard ways to handle this.

The first is to mimic the atomic update techniques of databases and keep to two copies of the binary search table. When A is inserted, search works on the old copy, while A is inserted into a second copy. Then, in one atomic operation update flips a pointer (which the chip uses to identify the table to be searched) to the second copy.

However, this doubles the storage needed, especially if memory is SRAM, and is expensive. Hence, many designers prefer a second option: create a hole for A by moving all elements B and greater one position downward.

15.4.1 Improving performance

To reduce memory needs, update must work on the same binary search table on which search works. To insert element A in, say, Fig. 15.4, update must move the elements B, C, and D one element down.

If the update and search designers are different, the normal specification for the update designer is always to ensure that the search process sees a consistent binary search table consisting of *distinct* keys. It appears to be very hard to meet this specification without allowing any search to take place until a complete update has terminated. Since an update can take a long time for a bridge database with 32,000 elements, this is unacceptable.

Thus one could consider relaxing the specification (**P3**) to allow a consistent binary search table that contains *duplicates* of key values. After all, as long as the table is sorted, the presence of two or more keys with the same value cannot affect the correctness of binary search.

Thus the creation of a hole for A in Fig. 15.4 is accomplished by creating two entries for D, then two entries for C, and then two entries for B, each with a single write to the table. In the last step A is written in place of the first copy of B.

To keep the binary search chip simple (see Chapter 10), a route processor was responsible for updates while the chip worked on searches. The table was stored in a separate off-chip memory; all three devices (memory, processor, and chip) can communicate with each other via a common bus. Abstractly, separate search and update processes are concurrently making access to memory. Using locks to mediate access to the memory is infeasible because of the consequent slowdown of memory.

Given that the new specification allows duplicates, it is tempting to get away with the simplest atomicity in terms of reads and writes to memory. Search reads the memory and update reads and writes; the memory operations of search and update can arbitrarily interleave. Some implementors may assume that, because binary search can work correctly even with duplicates, this is sufficient.

Unfortunately, this does not work, as shown in Fig. 15.4.[1] At the start of the scenario (leftmost picture), only B, C, and D are in the first, second, and third table entries. The fourth entry is free. A search for B begins with the second entry; a comparison with C indicates that binary search should move to the top half, which consists of only entry 1.

Next, search is delayed while update begins to go through the process of inserting A by writing duplicates from the bottom up. By the time update is finished, B has moved down to the second entry. When search finishes up by examining the first entry, it finds A and concludes (wrongly) that B is not in the table.

A simple attempt at reasoning correctly exposes this sort of counterexample directly. The standard invariant for binary search is that either the element being searched for (e.g., B) is in the current binary search range or B is not in the table. The problem is that an update can destroy this invariant by moving the element searched for outside the current range.

In the bridge application the only consequence of this failure is that a packet arriving at a known destination may get flooded to all ports. This will worsen performance only slightly but is unlikely to be noticed by external users!

---

[1] This example is due to Cristi Estan.

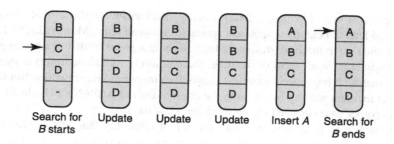

FIGURE 15.4

Concurrent search and update to a binary tree can lead to incorrect search results. A binary search for B fails, although B is in the table. This is because B moves out of the search range during an update that occurs in between search steps.

15.4.2 Rescuing reliability

A panic reaction to the counterexample of Fig. 15.4 might be to jettison single-copy update and retreat to the safety of two copies. However, all the counterexample demonstrates is that a search must complete without intervening update operations. If so, the binary search invariants hold and correctness follows. The counterexample *does not* imply the converse: that an entire update must complete without intervening search operations. The converse property is restrictive and would considerably slow down search.

There are simple ways to ensure that a search completes without intervening updates. The first is to change the architectural model, algorithmics, after all, is the art of changing the problem to fit our limited ingenuity, so that all update writes are centralized through the search chip. When update wishes to perform a write, it posts the write to search and waits for an acknowledgment. After finishing its current search cycle, search does the required write and sends an acknowledgment. Search can then work on the next search task.

A second way, more consonant with the bridge implementation, is to observe that the route processor does packet forwarding. The route processor asks the chip to do search, and it waits for a few microseconds to get the answer. Finally, the route processor does updates only when no packets are being forwarded and hence no searches are in progress. Thus an update can be interrupted by a search, but not vice versa.

The final solution relies on search tolerating duplicates, and it avoids locking by changing the model to centralize updates and searches. Note that centralizing updates are insufficient by itself (without also relaxing the specification to allow duplicates) because this would require performing a complete update without intervening searches.

15.5 Conclusions

The routing protocol BGP (Border Gateway Protocol) controls the backbone of the Internet. In the last few years careful scrutiny of BGP has uncovered several subtle flaws. Incompatible policies can lead to routing loops (Varadhan et al., 2000), and attempts to make Internal BGP scale using route reflectors also lead to loops (Griffin and Wilfong, 2002). Finally, mechanisms to thwart instability by damping flapping routes can lead to penalizing innocent routes for up to an hour (Mao et al., 2002).

While credit must go to the BGP designers for designing a protocol that deals with great diversity while making the Internet work most of the time, there is surely some discomfort at these findings. It is often asserted that such bugs rarely manifest themselves inoperational networks. But there may be a Three Mile Island incident waiting for us, as in the crash of the old ARPANET (Perlman, 1992), where a single unlikely corner case capsized the network for a few days.

Even worse, there may be a slow, insidious erosion of reliability that gets masked by transparent recovery mechanisms. Routers restart, TCPs retransmit, and applications retry. Thus failures in protocols and router implementations may only manifest themselves in terms of slow response times, frozen screens, and rebooting computers.

Jeff Raskin said: "Imagine if every Thursday your shoes exploded if you tied them the usual way. This happens to us all of the time with computers, and nobody thinks of complaining." Given our tolerance for pain when dealing with networks and computers, a lack of reliability ultimately translates into a decline in user productivity.

The examples in this chapter fit this thesis. In each case incorrect distributed algorithm design leads to productivity erosion, not Titanic failures. Flow control deadlocks can be masked by router reboots, and cell loss can be masked by TCP retransmits. Failure to preserve ordering within an internal striping algorithm leads to TCP performance degradation, but not to loss. Failure to consider all cases in DRAM striping can lead to adversarial access patterns where queues are starved and packets are lost, though such packets can be retransmitted. Finally, incorrect binary search table updates lead only to increased packet flooding. But together, the nickels and dimes of every reboot, retransmission, performance loss, and unnecessary flood can add up to significant losses.

Thus this chapter is a plea for care in the design of protocols *between* routers and also *within* routers. In the quest for performance that has characterized the rest of the book this chapter is a lonely plea for rigor. While full proofs may be infeasible, even sketching key invariants and using informal arguments can help find obscure failure modes. Perhaps, if we reason together, routers can become as comfortable and free of surprises as an ordinary pair of shoes.

15.6 Exercises

1. **FCVC flow control protocol:** The FCVC flow control protocol of Kung et al. (1994) provides an important alternative to the credit protocols described in Section 15.1. In the FCVC protocol, shown in Fig. 15.5, the sender keeps a count of cells sent H, while the receiver keeps a count of cells received R and cells dequeued D. The receiver periodically sends its current value of D, which is stored at the sender as estimate L. The sender is allowed to send if $H - L > Max$. More importantly, if the sender periodically sends H to the receiver, the receiver can deal with errors due to cell loss.

   - Assume cells are lost and that the sender periodically sends H to the receiver. How can the receiver use the values of H and R to detect how many cells have been lost?
   - How can the receiver use this estimate of cell loss to fix D and so correct the sender?

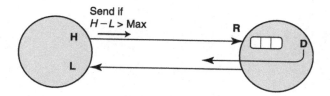

FIGURE 15.5

The FCVC protocol uses a count H of cells sent by the sender and an estimated L of the cells dequeued at the receiver; flow control is achieved by limiting the difference between H and L. More importantly, the use of absolute packet numbers instead of incremental credits allows the periodic sending of counts to fix errors due to cell loss.

- Can this protocol be made self-stabilizing without using the full machinery of a snapshot and reset?
- Compare the general features of this method of achieving reliability to the method used in the load-balancing algorithm described in the chapter.

2. **Load balancing with variable-sized packets:** Load balancing within a router is typically at the granularity of cells. However, load balancing across routers is often at the granularity of (variable-sized) packets. Thus simple round-robin striping may not balance load equally because all the large packets may be sent on one link and the small ones on another. Modify the load-balancing algorithm without sequence numbers (using ideas suggested by the deficit round-robin (DRR) algorithm described in Chapter 14) to balance the load evenly, even while striping variable-sized packets. Extend the fault-tolerance machinery to also handle this case.

3. **Concurrent compaction and search:** In many lookup applications, routers must use available on-chip SRAM efficiently and may have to compact memory periodically to avoid filling up memory with unusably small amounts of free space. Imagine a sequence of N trie nodes of size-4 words that are laid out contiguously in SRAM memory, after which there is a hole of size-2 words. As a fundamental operation in compaction, the update algorithm needs to move the sequence of N nodes two words to the right to fill the hole. Unfortunately, moving a node two steps to the right can overwrite itself and its neighbor. Find a technique for doing compaction for updating with minimal disruption to a concurrent search process. Assume that, when a node X is moved, there is at most one other node Y that points to X and that the update process has a fast technique for finding Y given X (see Chapter 11). Use this method to find a way to compact a sequence of trie nodes arbitrarily laid out in memory into a configuration where all the free space is at one end of memory and there are no "holes" between nodes. Of course, the catch is that the algorithm should work without locking out a concurrent search process for more than one write operation every K search operations, as in the bridge binary search example.

Endgame

Daring ideas are like chessmen moved forward. They may be beaten, but they may start a winning game.
—Goethe

We didn't lose the game; we just ran out of time.
—Vince Lombardi

The last part of the book applies network algorithmics to the emerging fields of security and measurement. As the Internet matures, we believe that good abstractions for security and measurement will be key to well-engineered networks. While the problems (e.g., detecting a denial-of-service (DoS) attack at a high-speed router) seem hard, some remarkable ideas have been proposed. The final chapter reaches closure by distilling the underlying unities behind the many different techniques surveyed in this book and by surveying the future of network algorithmics.

PART

4

Endgame

Measuring network traffic

16

Not everything that is counted counts, and not everything that counts can be counted.
—**Albert Einstein**

Every graduate with a business degree knows that the task of optimizing an organization or process begins with *measurement*. Once the bottlenecks in a supply chain are identified and the major cost factors are outlined, improvements can be targeted. The situation is no different in computer networks. For example, in service provider networks packet counting and logging provide powerful tools for the following.

Capacity Planning: Internet service providers (ISPs) need to determine the traffic matrix or the traffic between all source and destination subnets they connect. This knowledge can be used on short time scales (say, hours) to perform traffic engineering by reconfiguring optical switches; it can also be used on longer time scales (say, months) to upgrade link capacity.

Accounting: Internet service providers implement complex service-level agreements (SLAs) with customers and peers. Simple accounting arrangements based on overall traffic can easily be monitored by a single counter; however, more sophisticated agreements based on traffic type require a counter per traffic type. Packet counters can also be used to decide peering relationships. Suppose ISP *A* is currently sending packets to ISP *C* via ISP *B* and is considering directly connecting (peering) with *B*; a rational way for *A* to decide is to count the traffic destined to prefixes corresponding to *B*.

Traffic Analysis: Many network managers monitor the relative ratio of one packet type to another. For example, a spike in peer-to-peer traffic may require rate limiting. A spike in ICMP messages may indicate a Smurf attack.

Once causes—such as links that are unstable or have excessive traffic—are identified, network operators can take action by a variety of means. Thus measurement is crucial not just to characterize the network but to better engineer its behavior.

There are several control mechanisms that network operators currently have at their disposal. For example, operators can tweak Open Shortest Path First (OSPF) link weights and BGP policy to spread the load, can set up circuit-switched paths to avoid hot spots, and can simply buy new equipment. This chapter focuses only on network changes that address the measurement problem—i.e., changes that make a network more *observable*. However, we recognize that making a network more *controllable*, for instance, by adding more tuning knobs, is an equally important problem we do not address here.

Despite its importance, traffic measurement, at first glance, does not appear to offer any great challenges or have much intellectual appeal. As with mopping a floor or washing dishes, traffic measurement appears to be a necessary but mundane chore.

Network Algorithmics. https://doi.org/10.1016/B978-0-12-809927-8.00024-5

The goal of this chapter is to argue the contrary: that measurement at high speeds is difficult because of resource limitations and lack of built-in support; that the problems will only grow worse as ISPs abandon their current generation of links for even faster ones; and that algorithmics can provide exciting alternatives to the measurement quandary by focusing on how measurements will ultimately be used. To develop this theme, it is worth understanding right away why the general problem of measurement is hard and why even the specific problem of packet counting can be difficult.

This chapter is organized as follows. Section 16.1 describes the challenges involved in measurement. Section 16.2 shows how to reduce the required width of an SRAM counter using a DRAM backing-store and introduces two different schemes, both of which are deterministic algorithms, for that purpose. Section 16.3 describes a randomized algorithm for the same purpose that is much simpler and much more SRAM-efficient. These three counter schemes all implement passive counters, in which counters need to handle increments, but not read accesses, in real time.

Section 16.4 describes an SRAM-efficient scheme called BRICK for maintaining active counters that need to handle both in real time. In network measurement applications each counter is associated with a traffic flow, and the value of the counter is a special and very simple type of state information associated with the flow. Section 16.5 describes an extension of BRICK for efficiently maintaining general state information for many traffic flows.

Section 16.6 details a different technique for reducing counter widths by using randomized counting, which trades accuracy for counter width. Section 16.7 presents a different approach to reducing the number of counters required (as opposed to the width) by keeping track of counters only above a threshold. Section 16.8 shows how to reduce the number of counters even further for some applications by counting only the number of distinct flows.

Techniques in prior sections require computation on every packet. Section 16.9 takes a different tack by describing the sampled NetFlow technique for reducing packet processing; in NetFlow only a random subset of packets is processed to produce either a log or an aggregated set of counters. Section 16.10 shows how to reduce the overhead of shipping NetFlow records to managers. Section 16.11 explains how to replace the independent sampling method of NetFlow with a consistent sampling technique in all routers that allow packet trajectories to be traced.

The next three sections of the chapter move to a higher-level view of measurement. In Section 16.12 we describe a solution to the accounting problem. This problem is of great interest to ISPs, and the solution method is in the best tradition of the systems approach advocated throughout this book. In Section 16.13 we describe a solution to the traffic matrix problem using the same concerted systems approach. Section 16.14 presents a very different approach to measurement, called *passive* measurement, that treats the network as a black box. It includes an example of the use of passive measurement to compute the loss rate to a Web server.

The last six sections of this chapter provide a small sample of a fascinating new algorithmic tool to network measurement that has been developed mostly in the new millennium: data streaming and sketching algorithms (Muthukrishnan, 2005). These algorithms can, among other things, generate more informative and hence better traffic logs for a variety of measurement tasks. Section 16.15 provides a brief introduction to the data streaming model and the design objectives of data streaming algorithms. Section 16.16 revisits the counting of the number of distinct flows from a new data-streaming perspective. One such data-streaming algorithm, called min-hash sketch, leads to an unexpected solution to a classical database problem called associative-rule mining.

With this new perspective Section 16.17 revisits the elephant or heavy-hitter detection problem introduced in Section 16.7. Section 16.18 describes a data-streaming algorithm for estimating the distribution of flow sizes in a high-speed link. Finally, Section 16.19 describes the celebrated Tug-of-War (ToW) algorithm for estimating the second moment of a data stream. This algorithm was introduced in a seminal paper on data streaming, for which the authors, Noga Alon, Phillip Gibbons, Yossi Matias, and Mario Szegedy, received the 2019 ACM Paris Kanellakis Theory and Practice Award.

The implementation techniques for the measurement primitives described in this chapter (and the corresponding principles used) are summarized in Table 16.1.

Quick reference guide

Section 16.2 may be of interest to a network device implementor seeking to implement a large number of counters at high speeds. Section 16.3 describes a hybrid SRAM/DRAM scheme for efficiently maintaining a large number of passive counters that has been used in Huawei router products since 2010. Section 16.4 describes an SRAM-efficient scheme for maintaining a large number of active counters. Section 16.5 describes an extension of BRICK for efficiently maintaining general state information for many traffic flows. Section 16.8 describes a useful mechanism for quickly counting the list of distinct identifiers in a stream of received packets without keeping large hash tables. Section 16.12 presents a solution proposed by Juniper Networks for accounting. Section 16.13 covers inferring traffic matrices and is useful for implementors building tools for monitoring ISPs.

Table 16.1 Principles used in the implementation of the measurement primitives discussed in this chapter.

Number	Principle	Used in
P5c	Low-order counter bits in SRAM, all bits in DRAM	LCF algorithm
P15	Update only counters above threshold	LR algorithm
P3b	Randomized counting	Morris algorithm
P3a	Multiple hashed counters to detect heavy flows	Multistage filters
P3b	Flow counting by hashing flows to bitmaps	Multiresolution bitmap
P3a	Packet sampling to collect representative logs	Sampled NetFlow
P3a	Sampling flows proportional to size	Sampled charging
P3	Aggregating prefixes into buckets	Juniper's DCU
P4	Routing protocol helps color prefixes	
P4	Using TCP semantics for measurement	Sting
P3a	Allow counter updates to be missed occasionally	RS algorithm
P7	Optimize for a restricted access pattern	BRICK
P4c	Use built-in instructions	

16.1 Why measurement is hard

Unlike the telephone network, where observability and controllability were built into the design, the very simplicity of the successful Internet service model has made it difficult to observe (Duffield and

Grossglauser, 2000). In particular, there appears to be a great semantic distance between what users (e.g., ISPs) want to know and what the network provides. In this tussle (Clark et al., 2002) between user needs and the data generated by the network, users respond by distorting (Clark et al., 2002) existing network features to obtain the desired data.

For example, Traceroute uses the TTL field in an admittedly clever but distorted way, and the Path MTU discovery mechanism is similar. Tools like Sting (1999) use TCP in an even more baroque fashion to yield end-to-end measures. Even tools that make more conventional use of network features to populate traffic matrices (e.g., Feldmann et al., 2000; Zhang et al., 2003) bridge the semantic gap by correlating vast amounts of spatially separated data and possibly inconsistent configuration information. All this is clever, but it may not be engineering.[1] Perhaps much of this complexity could be removed by providing measurement features directly in the network.

One of the fundamental tools of measurement is *counting*: counting the number of packets or events of a given type. It is instructive to realize that even packet counting is hard, as we show next.

16.1.1 Why counting is hard

Legacy routers provide only per-interface counters that can be read by the management protocol SNMP. Such counters count only the aggregate of all counters going on an interface and make it difficult to estimate traffic AS–AS matrices that are needed for traffic engineering. They can also be used only for crude forms of accounting, as opposed to more sophisticated forms of accounting that count by traffic type (e.g., real-time traffic may be charged higher) and destination (some destinations may be routed through a more expensive upstream provider).

Thus, vendors have introduced filter-based accounting, which enables customers to count traffic that matches a rule specifying a predicate on packet header values. Similarly, Cisco provides NetFlow-based accounting (Cisco netflow, 2001b), where sampled packets can be logged for later analysis, and 5-tuples can be aggregated and counted on the router. Cisco also provides Express Forwarding commands, which allow per-prefix counters (Cisco, 2001a).

Per-interface counters can easily be implemented because there are only a few counters per interface, which can be stored in chip registers. However, doing filter-based or per-prefix counters is more challenging because of the following.

- **Many counters:** Given that even current routers support 500,000 prefixes and that future routers may have a million prefixes, a router potentially needs to support millions of real-time counters.
- **Multiple counters per packet:** A single packet may result in updating more than one counter, such as a flow counter and a per-prefix counter.
- **High speeds:** Line rates have been increasing from OC-192 (10 Gbps) to OC-768 (40 Gbps). Thus each counter matched by a packet must be read and written in the time taken to receive a packet at line speeds.
- **Large widths:** As line speeds get higher, even 32-bit counters overflow quickly. To prevent the overhead of frequent polling, most vendors now provide 64-bit counters.

One million counters of 64 bits each require a total of 64 Mbits of memory, while two counters of 64 bits each every 8 nanoseconds require 16 Gbps of memory bandwidth. The memory-bandwidth

---

[1] Recall the comment by hardened battle veterans about the heroic Charge of the Light Brigade: "It is beautiful, but is it war?"

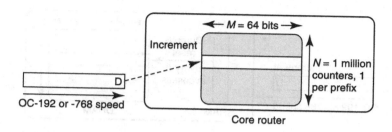

FIGURE 16.1

Basic model for packet counting at high speeds using a large-width counter for each of a large number of flows.

needs require the use of SRAM, but the large amount of memory needed makes SRAM of this size too expensive. Thus, maintaining counters or packet logs at wire speeds is as challenging as other packet-processing tasks, such as classification and scheduling; it is the focus of much of this chapter.

In summary, this section argues that: (i) packet counters and logs are important for network monitoring and analysis; and (ii) naive implementations of packet counting and logs require potentially infeasible amounts of fast memory. The remainder of this chapter describes the use of algorithmics to reduce the amount of fast memory and processing needed to implement counters and logs.

16.2 Reducing SRAM width using DRAM backing store

The next few sections ignore the general measurement problem and concentrate on the specific problem of packet counting. The simplest way to implement packet counting is shown in Fig. 16.1. One SRAM location is used for each of, say, 1 million 64-bit counters. When a packet arrives, the corresponding flow counter (say, based on the destination) is incremented.

Given that such large amounts of SRAM are expensive and infeasible, is it required? If a packet arrives, say, every 8 nanoseconds, some SRAM counter must be accessed, as opposed to, say, 40 nanoseconds DRAM. However, intuitively keeping a *full* 64-bit SRAM location is an obvious waste (**P1**).

Instead, the best hardware features of DRAM and SRAM can be combined (**P5c**). DRAM is currently roughly two orders of magnitude cheaper costly. On the other hand, DRAM is slow. This is exactly analogous to the memory hierarchy in a computer. The analogy suggests that DRAM and SRAM can be combined to provide a solution that is both cheap and fast.

Observe that, if the router keeps a 64-bit DRAM backing location for each counter and a much smaller width (say, 12 bits) for each SRAM counter, then the counter system will be accurate *as long as every SRAM counter is backed up (i.e., flushed) to DRAM before the smaller SRAM counter overflows.* This scheme is depicted in Fig. 16.2. What is missing, however, is a good algorithm (**P15**) for deciding when and how to flush SRAM counters.

Assume that the chip maintaining counters is allowed to dump some SRAM counter to DRAM every b SRAM accesses. b is chosen to be large enough that b SRAM access times correspond to 1 DRAM access time. In other words, b is the ratio of DRAM access speed to SRAM access speed. In terms of the smallest SRAM width required, Shah et al. (2002a) show that, *under this algorithmic framework of "pick-a-counter-to-flush,"* the conditionally *optimal* counter-management algorithm is to flush the

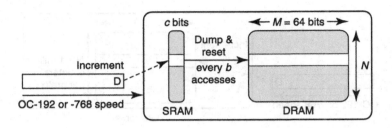

FIGURE 16.2

Using large DRAM counters as a backing store for small SRAM counters, reducing overall cost. For correctness, an SRAM counter must be flushed to DRAM before it overflows.

largest SRAM counter. With this strategy, Shah et al. (2002a) show that the SRAM counter width c can be significantly smaller than M, the width of a DRAM counter.

More precisely, they show that $2^c \approx \frac{\log b(N-1)}{\log(b/(b-1))}$, where N is the total number of counters. Note that this means that the SRAM counter width grows approximately as $\log \log bN$ since $b/(b-1)$ can be ignored for large b. For example, with three 64-bit counters, every 8 nanoseconds (OC-768) for N equal to a million requires only 8 Mbit of 2.5 microseconds SRAM with 51.2 microseconds DRAM. Note that in this case the value of b is $51.2/2.5 \approx 21$.

The bottom line is that the naive method would have required 192 Mbit of SRAM compared to 8 Mbit, a factor of 24 savings in expensive SRAM. Overall, this provides roughly a factor of 24 savings in cost since DRAM is roughly two orders of magnitude cheaper than SRAM.

But this begs the question: How do the chip processing counters find the largest counter? Bhagwan and Lin (2000) describe an implementation of a pipelined heap structure that can determine the largest value at a fairly high expense in hardware complexity and space. Their heap structure requires pointers of size $\log_2 N$ for each counter just to identify the counter to be evicted. Unfortunately, $\log_2 N$ additional bits per counter can be large (20 for $N = 1$ million) and can defeat the overall goal that was to reduce the required SRAM bits from 64 to say 10.

The need for a pointer per heap value seems hard to avoid. This is because the counters must be in a fixed place to be updated when packets arrive, but values in a heap must keep moving to maintain the heap property. On the other hand, when the largest value arrives at the top of the heap, one has to correlate it to the counter index to reset the appropriate counter and to banish its contents to DRAM. Notice also that all values in the heap, including pointers and values, must be in SRAM for speed.

The following LR algorithm (Ramabhadran and Varghese, 2003) simplifies the largest count first (LCF) algorithm of Shah et al. (2002a) and is easier to implement. Let j be the index of the counter with the largest value among the counters incremented in the last cycle of b updates to SRAM. Ties may be broken arbitrarily. If $c_j \geq b$, the algorithm updates counter c_j to DRAM. If $c_j < b$, the algorithm updates any counter with value at least b to DRAM. If no such counter exists, $LR(T)$ updates counter C_j to DRAM.

It can be shown that LR (Ramabhadran and Varghese, 2003) is also conditionally optimal (within the "pick-a-counter-to-flush" algorithmic framework) and produces SRAM counter width c, which is equal to that of LCF. The maintaining of all counters above the threshold b can be done using a size-N bitmap in which a 1 implies that the corresponding position has a counter no less than b.

This leaf structure can be augmented with a simple tree that maintains the position of the first 1 (see the end-of-chapter exercises). The tree can be easily pipelined for speed, and only roughly 2 bits per counter are required for this additional data structure; thus c is increased from its optimal value, say, x to $x + 2$, a reasonable cost.

Thus, the final LR algorithm is a better algorithm (**P15**) and one that is easier to implement, provides a new data structure to efficiently find the first bit set in a bitmap (**P15**), and adds pipelining hardware (**P5**) to gain speed.

The overall approach could be considered superficially similar to the usual use of the memory hierarchy, in which a faster memory acts as a cache for a slower memory. However, unlike a conventional cache, this design ensures *worst-case* performance and not *expected* case performance. The goals of the two algorithms are also different: Counter management stores an entry for *all* items but seeks to reduce the width of cache entries, while standard caching stores full widths for only *some* frequent items.

16.3 A randomized counter scheme

Both LCF and LR are deterministic algorithms and both guarantee that no counter update will be lost. However, in most real-world network measurement operations, missing some counter updates "occasionally" (say once a few billion years) is acceptable (**P3**). This has motivated Zhao et al. to design a randomized algorithm (**P3a**) that is better than both LCF and LR in virtually all aspects (Zhao et al., 2006b). We call this algorithm RS (random seeding) for reasons that will become clear shortly. RS can be proved to be unconditionally (among all possible schemes and not restricted to the "pick-a-counter-to-flush" framework) near-optimal in terms of SRAM consumption, yet has very simple control logic. RS has been used on Huawei router products since 2010.

With the same assumption (that the SRAM/DRAM speed difference $b \approx 21$), RS requires only $5 + \epsilon$ bits per counter, where each SRAM counter consumes 5 bits and its control logic consumes ϵ bits per counter. Here, ϵ is typically a small number (e.g., 0.01). Clearly, in this case 5 bits per counter is the absolute minimum for any algorithm/scheme since using 4 bits per counter would necessarily lead to one DRAM access every 16 SRAM accesses, which would exceed the DRAM bandwidth (as $b \approx 21$). More generally, it can be shown that this absolute minimum is $\lceil \log_2(b + 1) \rceil$.

Note that reducing the SRAM counter size from 8 to 5 bits per counter is $2^{8-5} = 8$ times harder since overflows from an SRAM counter happen 8 times faster with the smaller overflow threshold (2^5 as compared to 2^8), requiring the "flushing" mechanism to operate 8 times more efficiently. Fortunately, this improvement in the efficiency of RS is achieved with a simple counter-flushing technique that costs only a small fraction of bits per counter, as compared to 20 bits per counter in LCF and 2 bits per counter in LR.

Like LCF and LR, the performance (in terms of not losing a counter update) guarantee of RS is still worst case in nature in the sense that this guarantee holds under all possible sequences of counter indices (to increment). Unlike LCF and LR, however, the guarantee is not with probability 1: With an extremely small yet nonzero probability, RS may miss some increments to the counters.

However, in practice, this probability can be made so small that even if a router operates continuously for billions of years, the probability that a single loss of increment happens is less than one in a billion. Note that router software/hardware failures and other unexpected or catastrophic events (e.g., earthquakes) that may disable a router happen with a probability many orders of magnitude higher.

In a nutshell, RS works as follows. Each logical counter is represented by a 5-bit counter in SRAM, backed up by a 64-bit counter in DRAM. Increments to a logical counter happen first to its 5-bit SRAM counter until it reaches the overflow value 32, at which point the value of this SRAM counter (i.e., 32) needs to be flushed to the corresponding DRAM counter. Since updates to DRAM counters take much longer (more specifically $b = 21$ times) than to SRAM counters, multiple SRAM counters may overflow during the time it takes to update just one DRAM counter.

In RS the solution is to maintain in SRAM a small FIFO buffer between the SRAM counters and the DRAM counters to temporarily hold the "flush requests" that need to be made to the DRAM in the future. With the parameter settings in this case ($b = 21$ and $c = 5$), this FIFO buffer, viewed as a simple queueing system with births (arrivals of new flush-to-DRAM requests) and deaths (completed flushings of overflowed counters to DRAM), has a moderate load factor (birth rate divided by death rate) of only $b/32 \approx 65.6\%$ (where $32 = 2^5$).

Hence, intuition from queueing theory suggests that only a small buffer is needed to ensure that this FIFO queue does not overflow with overwhelming probability. However, while this intuition is correct "in the average case" (i.e., when the arrival process is "smooth"), it is not in the worst case, as we elaborate next.

Let $A[1..N]$ and $B[1..N]$ be the SRAM array and the DRAM counter array, respectively. Simply setting $A[i]$ and $B[i]$, $i = 1, 2, ..., N$, to 0 at the beginning of a measurement (counting) interval is a standard way of assigning initial values. However, it would not work well in this scheme for the following reason. In the worst case, an adversary (not in the context of security or cryptography) could choose the sequence of the indices of the counters to be increased to be $1, 2, ..., N, 1, 2, ..., N, ...$ (the repetition of the subsequence "$1, 2, 3, ..., N$" over and over).

At the end of the 31st repetition, the values of $A[i]$, $i = 1, 2, ..., N$, will all become 31. Then, during the next repetition, $A[i]$, $i = 1, 2, ..., N$ will overflow one by one after each increment, resulting in a "burst arrival" of $O(N)$ flushing-to-DRAM requests to the FIFO queue. The FIFO queue has to be made very large (in fact, much larger than the SRAM counter array A) to be able to accommodate this burst, which would defeat the very purpose of combining DRAM and SRAM (that is, to save SRAM).

This example shows that, in this queueing system, the arrival rate can far exceed the departure rate for an extended period of time in the worst case, even when the aforementioned necessary condition (for stability) $21 < 2^5$ is met. However, from queuing theory, we know such a situation cannot happen when the arrival process is "smooth". Hence, a key innovation of RS is to guarantee that the arrival process (of the counter overflows) is fairly smooth, even in the worst case, through a simple randomization of seed SRAM counter values as follows.

Each SRAM counter $A[i]$ is assigned a random seed value uniformly distributed over $\{0, 1, 2, ..., 31\}$. We need to somehow remember this seed value since it should be subtracted from the observed counter value at the end of a measurement (counting) interval. This is achieved by setting the initial value of $B[i]$ to $-A[i]$, for $i = 1, 2, ..., N$.

Using large deviation theory, Zhao et al. (2006b) shows that a small FIFO buffer (say a few hundred slots) is large enough to ensure that the probability for it to be filled up by flush requests (so that an arriving flushing request would be tail-dropped) is vanishingly small, even when there are millions of counters and the sequence of counters to be incremented is arbitrary. Here, each slot holds a counter index to be flushed, which is usually shorter than 4 bytes. This translates into the aforementioned ϵ bits per counter when the cost of hundreds of buffer slots is amortized over millions of counters.

We conclude this section using a numerical example from Zhao et al. (2006b). Let there be $N = 1$ million counters. The measurement epoch is set to $n = 10^{12}$ (1 trillion) cycles with one counter increment per cycle. This interval is a bit over two hours long if we assume each cycle is 8 anosecond long as before. The SRAM/DRAM speed difference b is assumed to be 12 and, correspondingly, the number of bits per SRAM counter is set to $c = 4$, the minimum that is needed (since $2^3 < 12$).

With this parameter setting, the load factor of the FIFO queue is $12/16 = 75\%$, a bit larger than $21/32 \approx 65.6\%$ in the earlier parameter setting. Suppose there are 300 slots in the FIFO buffer, which costs 6000 bits (each index is 20 bits since N is 1 million) or $\epsilon = 0.006$ bits per counter. Under these parameter settings, the probability for the FIFO queue to become full is less than 2.4×10^{-14}. This translates into the FIFO queue dropping a flushing request every 10.57 billion years!

16.4 **Maintain active counters using BRICK**

In all three DRAM backing-store schemes described, namely LCF, LR, and RS, whereas incrementing a counter can happen at the SRAM speed, reading a counter can happen only at the DRAM speed. Therefore, they only solve the problem of so-called *passive counters* in which full counter values in general do not need to be read out frequently (say not until the end of a measurement interval). Indeed, the designs of all three schemes exploit this restricted access pattern (**P7**) to the fullest extent.

16.4.1 **Motivation and design objectives**

While passive counters are good enough for many network monitoring applications, a number of other applications require the maintenance of *active counters*, in which the values of counters need to be read out as frequently as they are incremented, typically on a per packet basis. In many network data-streaming algorithms (Cormode and Muthukrishnan, 2005; Estan and Varghese, 2002; Krishnamurthy et al., 2003; Kumar et al., 2004b; Zhang et al., 2004; Zhao et al., 2005), upon the arrival of each packet, values need to be read out from some counters to decide on actions that need to be taken; we will provide a brief introduction to network data streaming and sketching in Section 16.15.

A paper on approximate active counters (Stanojevic, 2007) identifies several other data-streaming algorithms that need to maintain active counters, including multistage filters for elephant detection (Estan and Varghese, 2002) and online hierarchical heavy hitter identification (Zhang et al., 2004). All these data-streaming algorithms that use exact active counters implement them as full-size SRAM counters. An efficient solution for exact active counters can significantly reduce SRAM cost for all such applications, as we will show next.

BRICK (Bucketized Rank Index Counter) (Hua et al., 2008b) is an early solution to the problem of efficiently maintaining exact active counters. BRICK allows extremely fast read *and* increment (by 1) accesses at on-chip SRAM speeds, yet is much more SRAM-efficient than the naive solution of maintaining full-size SRAM counters, in the following sense.

Suppose at the end of a measurement interval, the sum of the values of all N counters in the array, which is equal to the total number of increments during the interval, is M. When the naive solution is used, every SRAM counter has to be at least $\lceil \log_2 M \rceil$ bits long since, in the worst case, all the M increments can hit this counter. When BRICK is used, however, the average size of each SRAM counter only needs to be slightly larger than $\lceil \log_2(M/N) \rceil$ bits, the minimum length needed to encode

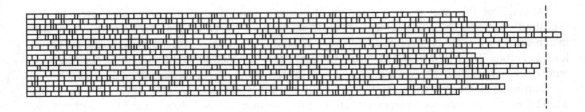

FIGURE 16.3

BRICK wall (conceptual baseline scheme) (Hua et al., 2008b).

the average counter value M/N. Hence, roughly speaking, BRICK pays the average cost (**P11**), not the worst-case cost.

We emphasize that the average cost $\lceil \log_2(M/N) \rceil$ can be much smaller than the worst-case cost $\lceil \log_2 M \rceil$. For example, let the total counts be $M = 15$ million and the number of counters be $N = 1$ million. In this case, the average cost $\lceil \log_2(M/N) \rceil$ is only 4 bits, but the worst-case cost $\lceil \log_2 M \rceil$ is 24 bits, which is six times larger.

16.4.2 Overview of BRICK

The base idea of BRICK is intuitive and is based on a very familiar networking concept: statistical multiplexing. The idea is to first bundle groups of a fixed number (say 64) of counters, which is randomly selected from the array, into buckets; then just enough bits are allocated to each counter in the sense that, if its current value is C_i, $\lfloor \log_2 C_i \rfloor + 1$ bits are allocated for storing the value. Therefore, counters inside a bucket have variable widths.

Suppose the mean width of a counter averaged over the entire array is γ. By the law of large numbers, the total widths of counters in most of the buckets will be fairly close to γ multiplied by the number of counters per bucket. Depicting each counter as a "brick," as shown in Fig. 16.3, a section of the "brick wall" illustrates the effect of statistical multiplexing, where each horizontal layer of bricks (consisting of 64 of them) corresponds to a bucket and the length of bricks corresponds to the real counter widths encoding flow sizes in a real-world Internet packet trace (the USC trace used in Hua et al. (2008b)).

As can be seen in this figure, when the bucket size is set to be slightly longer than 64γ (the vertical dashed line), the probability of the total widths of the bricks overflowing over this line is quite small; among the 20 buckets shown, only 1 of them has an overflow. Although overflowed buckets need to be handled separately and will cost more memory, this probability can be made small so that the overall overflow cost is small and bounded. Therefore, the memory consumption of BRICK only needs to be slightly larger than 64γ per bucket, which is the optimal size (per bucket).

This baseline approach is hard to implement in hardware in practice for two primary reasons. First, the application (employing the active counter array) has to be able to randomly access (i.e., jump to) any counter with ease. Since counters are of variable sizes, we have to store, for each counter, its index within the bucket. Note that being able to randomly access is different from being able to delimit all these counters. The latter can be solved with much less overhead using prefix-free coding (e.g.,

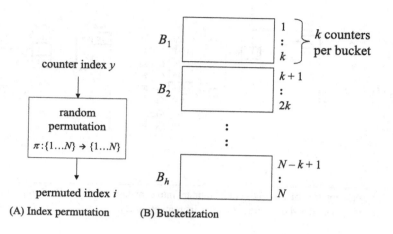

FIGURE 16.4

Randomly bundling counters into buckets.

Huffman coding) of the counter values. But, in this case, to access the ith counter in a bucket, one has to scan through the first $i - 1$ counters (and, hence, very slowly). Second, when the ith counter (brick) in a bucket grows, counters $i + 1, i + 2,..., 64$ will have to be shifted.

BRICK addresses these two difficulties with slightly more SRAM. It allows for very efficient read and expansion (for increments that increase the width of a counter such as from 15 to 16). The operations involved in reading and updating this data structure (based on the idea of *rank indexing*) not only are simple for ASIC implementations but also are supported in modern processors through built-in instructions (**P4c**) such as `shift` and `popcount` (Intel 64 and IA-32, 2007; AMD, 2007) so that software implementation is efficient. For example, current generations of 64-bit ×86 processors have the `popcount` instruction built-in (Intel 64 and IA-32, 2007; AMD, 2007), which is named "__builtin_pop-count" and recognized by the GCC compiler on Linux.

16.4.3 Detailed design

Fig. 16.4 depicts the ideas of randomization and bucketization. In particular, as depicted in Fig. 16.4(A), to access the yth counter, a pseudorandom permutation function $\pi : \{1...N\} \to \{1...N\}$ is first applied to the index y to obtain a permuted index i. This pseudorandom permutation function in practice can be as simple as reversing the bits of y. The corresponding counter C_i can then be found in the ℓth bucket B_ℓ, where $\ell = \lceil i/k \rceil$ and k is the number of counters per bucket. The bucket structure is depicted in Fig. 16.4(B). Unless otherwise noted, when we refer to the ith counter C_i, we will assume i is already the result of a random permutation.

Partition into subcounters

As we explained before, the baseline bucketing scheme does not allow for efficient read and increment (by 1) accesses. In BRICK, a multi-level partitioning scheme is designed to address this problem as follows. The worst-case counter width L is divided into p parts, which we refer to as "subcoun-

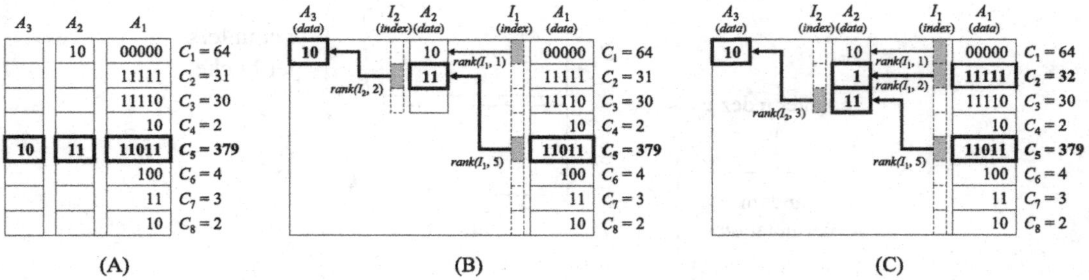

FIGURE 16.5

(A) Within a bucket, segmentation of variable-width counters into subcounter arrays. (B) Compact representation of variable-width counters. (C) Updated data structure after incrementing C_2.

ters". The jth subcounter, $j \in [1, p]$ (from the least significant bits to the most significant bits) has w_j bits, such that $0 < w_j \le L$ and $\sum_{j=1}^{p} w_j = L$. To save space, for each counter, BRICK maintains just enough of its subcounters to hold its current value. In other words, counters with values no more than $2^{w_1+w_2+\cdots+w_i}$ will not have its $(i+1)$th, ..., pth subcounters stored in BRICK. For example, if $w_1 = 5$, any counter with a value less than $2^5 = 32$ will only be allocated a memory entry for its first subcounter. Consider the example shown in Fig. 16.5(A) with $k = 8$ counters in a bucket. Only C_1 and C_5 require more than their first subcounters. Such an on-demand allocation requires us to link together all subcounters of a counter, which we achieve using a simple and memory-efficient bitmap indexing scheme called *rank indexing*. Rank indexing enables efficient lookup and efficient expansion (when counter values exceed certain thresholds after increments), which will be discussed in detail next.

Each bucket contains p subcounter arrays $A_1, A_2, \ldots, A_p$ to store the 1st, 2nd, ..., pth sub-counters (as needed) of all k counters in the bucket. How many entries should be allocated for each array A_i, denoted as k_i, turns out to be a nontrivial statistical optimization problem. On the one hand, to save memory, we would like to make $k_2, k_3, \ldots, k_p$ (k_1 is fixed as k) as small as possible. On the other hand, when we encounter the unlucky situation that we need to exceed any of these limits (say for a certain d, we have more than k_d counters in a bucket that have values larger than or equal to $2^{w_1+w_2+\cdots+w_{i-1}}$), then we will have a "bucket overflow" that would require that all counters inside the bucket be relocated to an additional array of full-size buckets with fixed worst-case width L for each counter. Given the high cost of storing a duplicate bucket in the full-size array, we would like to choose larger $k_2, \ldots, k_p$ to make this probability as small as possible. For the example shown in Fig. 16.5(B), the allocation for A_1, A_2, and A_3 are $k_1 = k = 8$, $k_2 = 3$, and $k_3 = 1$, respectively. Observe that the number of entries is decreasing exponentially as we go to the higher subcounter arrays. In Hua et al. (2008b) extremely tight tail bounds were developed on the overflow probability that can be used to guide the choosing of parameters $\{k_i\}_{2 \le i \le p}$ and $\{w_i\}_{1 \le i \le p-1}$ to achieve near-optimal tradeoffs between these two conflicting issues and minimize the overall memory consumption.

Indexing for efficiently locating a counter

A key innovation in the BRICK data structure is an indexing scheme that allows for the efficient identification of the locations of the subcounters across the different subcounter arrays for some counter C_i. In particular, for C_i, its d subcounters $C_{i,1}, \ldots, C_{i,d}$ are spread across $A_1, \ldots, A_d$ at locations

$a_{i,1}, \ldots, a_{i,d}$, respectively (i.e., $C_{i,j} = A_j[a_{i,j}]$). For example, as shown in Fig. 16.5(B), C_5 is spread across $A_3[1] = 10$, $A_2[2] = 11$, and $A_1[5] = 11011$.

An index bitmap I is maintained for each bucket. I is divided into $p - 1$ parts, $I_1, \ldots, I_{p-1}$, with a one-to-one correspondence to the subcounter arrays $A_1, \ldots, A_{p-1}$, respectively. Each part I_j is a bitmap with k_j bits, $I_j[1], \ldots, I_j[k_j]$, one bit $I_j[a]$ for each entry $A_j[a]$ in A_j. Each $I_j[a]$ is used to determine if the counter stored in $A_j[a]$ has expanded beyond the jth subcounter array. I_j is also used to compute the index location of C_i in the next subcounter array A_{j+1}. Because a counter cannot expand beyond the last sub-counter array, there is no need for an index bitmap component for the most significant subcounter array A_p. For example, consider the entries $A_1[1]$ and $A_1[5]$ where the corresponding counter has expanded beyond A_1. This is indicated by having the corresponding bit positions $I_1[1]$ and $I_1[5]$ set to 1, as shown in shaded boxes in Fig. 16.5(B). All remaining bit positions in I_1 are set to 0, as shown in clear boxes.

For each counter that has expanded beyond A_1, an arrow is shown in Fig. 16.5(B) that links a subcounter in A_1 with the corresponding subcounter entry in A_2. For example, for C_5, its subcounter entry $A_1[5]$ in A_1 is linked to the subcounter entry $A_2[2]$ in A_2. Rather than expending memory to store these links explicitly, which could vanish savings gained by reduced counter widths, we *dynamically* compute the location of a subcounter in the next subcounter array A_{j+1} based on the current bitmap I_j. In this way no memory space is needed to store link pointers. This dynamic computation can be readily determined using an operation called rank(s, j), which returns the number of ones only in the range $s[1] \ldots s[j]$ in the bit-string s (similar to the rank operator defined in Jacobson (1989)). The rank operator in turn can be efficiently computed in software using the aforementioned popcount(s) instruction, which returns the number of ones in the bit-string s.

Handling increments

The increment operation is also based on the traversal of subcounters using rank indexing. We will first describe the basic idea by means of an example. Consider the counter C_2 in Fig. 16.5(B). Its count is 31, which can be encoded in just the subcounter array A_1 with $C_{2,1} = 11111$. Suppose we want to increment C_2. We first increment its first subcounter component $C_{2,1} = 11111$, which results in $C_{2,1} = 00000$ with a *carry propagation* to the next level. This is depicted in Fig. 16.5(C).

This carry propagation triggers the increment of the next subcounter component $C_{2,2}$. The location of $C_{2,2}$ can be determined using rank indexing (i.e. rank$(I_1, 2) = 2$). However, the location of $A_2[2]$ was previously occupied by counter C_5. To maintain *rank ordering*, we have to *shift* the entries in A_2 down by one to free up the location $A_2[2]$. This is achieved by applying an operation called varshift(s, j, c), which performs a right shift on the substring starting at bit-position j by c bits (with vacant bits filled by zeros). The varshift operator can be readily implemented in most processors by means of shift and bitwise logical instructions.

16.5 **Extending BRICK for maintaining associated states**

The approach of combining randomized bundling and rank indexing has also been used for a similar but different application: memory- and computation-efficient storage and lookup of exact or approximate states associated with flow labels. The resulting scheme is called Rank Indexed Hashing (RIH) (Hua et al., 2008a). In Section 10.3.3 we have already described a hash-table-based scheme that can be adapted

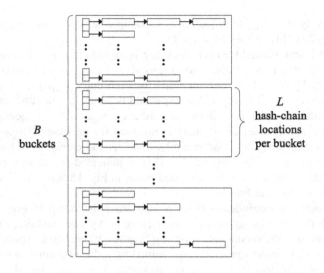

FIGURE 16.6

Buckets and hash-chain locations.

for maintaining such states: d-Left hashing (Broder and Mitzenmacher, 2001). Compared to d-Left, RIH is more memory-efficient and, by taking advantage of built-in CPU instructions such as `popcount`, is similarly computationally efficient, as shown in Hua et al. (2008a).

The design of RIH is based on the same two key ideas as that of BRICK: randomized bundling and rank-indexed chaining. Hence, we provide only a brief description, in this new context, of both innovations using a few figures. Conceptually, the starting point of RIH is a conventional chaining-based hash-table scheme. As also shown in Fig. 16.6 its first key idea is to randomly bundle a decent number of hash buckets (with chaining) together so that the number of hash nodes in each bundle (called hash-chain locations in Hua et al. (2008a)) is not far from the average number statistically, like that is shown in Fig. 16.3 (the "BRICK wall"). In this way we only need to allocate a fixed amount of memory that is slightly more than the average amount to each "hash bundle" to satisfy its resource needs with high probability.

In a chaining-based hash table maintaining a 32- or 64-bit pointer for each hash node is costly, especially when the hash key and the associated state are both short in length, which, as shown in Hua et al. (2008a), can happen in practice. In Fig. 16.7(A) the fingerprints are 7 bits long; the associated state is not shown in Fig. 16.7(A) to better convey the main idea. The second key idea of RIH, illustrated in Fig. 16.7, is a rank indexing method, similar to that in BRICK, that allows us to efficiently realize *dynamic chaining* without storing and paying the large cost of full-size pointers.

Instead, like subcounters that comprise a counter in BRICK, consecutive hash nodes in a bucket are linked together using single-bit "rank index pointers," as shown in Fig. 16.7(B). However, whereas in BRICK sub-counters of a counter can have various lengths, in RIH each hash node, including the signature (the hash value of the flow label by a different hash function than that for the hash table oper-tion) and the associated state, has the same length. This allows us to "collapse" all hash nodes into one pile and the corresponding single-bit "rank index pointers" into another, as illustrated in Fig. 16.7(C).

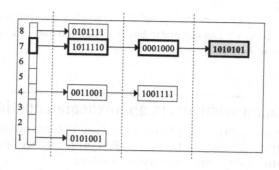

(A) A bucket.

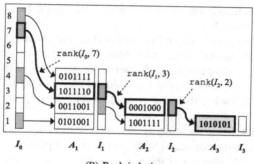

(B) Rank-indexing.

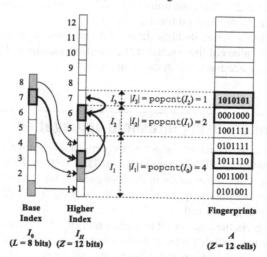

(C) Packed bucket organization.

FIGURE 16.7

Rank-indexed hashing.

Such a collapse facilitates more efficient storage of these contents and pointers and faster read access to them. Finally, like in BRICK, we can accommodate the insertion and deletion of hash nodes in RIH in a computationally efficient manner.

16.6 Reducing counter width using approximate counting

The DRAM backing-store approach trades reduced counter widths for more processing and complexity. A second approach is to trade accuracy and certainty (**P3a, b**) for reduced counter widths. For many applications described earlier, approximate counters may suffice.

The basic idea is as follows. If we increment a b-bit counter only with probability $1/c$, then, when the counter saturates, the expected number of counted events is $2^b \cdot c$. Thus a b-bit randomized counter can count c times more events than a deterministic version. But, once the notion of approximate counting is accepted, it is possible to do better.

Notice that, in the basic idea, the standard deviation (i.e., the expected value of the counter error) is a few c's, which is small at counter values $\gg c$. Morris's idea for randomized counting is to notice that, for higher counter values, one can tolerate higher absolute values of the error. For example, if the standard deviation is equal to the counter, the real value is likely to be within half to twice the value determined by the counter. Allowing the error to scale with counter values in turn allows a smaller counter width.

To achieve this, Morris's scheme increments a counter with *nonconstant probability that depends on counter value*, so the expected error scales with counter size. Specifically, the algorithm increments a counter with probability $1/2^x$, where x is the value of the counter. At the end, a counter value of x represents an expected value of 2^x. Thus, the number of bits required for such a counter is $\log \log Max$, where Max is the maximum value required for the counter.

While this is an interesting scheme, its high standard deviation and the need to pick accurate small numbers, especially for high values of the counter, are clear disadvantages. Approximate counting is an example of using **P3b**, trading accuracy for storage (and time).

16.7 Reducing counters using threshold aggregation

The last two schemes reduce the *width* of the SRAM counter table shown in Fig. 16.1. The next two approaches reduce the *height* of the SRAM counter table. They rely on the quote from Einstein (which opened the chapter) that not all the information in the final counter table may be useful to an application, at least for some applications. Effectively, by relaxing the specification (**P3**), the number of counters that need to be maintained can be reduced.

One simple way to compress the counter table is shown in Fig. 16.8. The idea is to pick a threshold, say, 0.1% of the traffic, that can possibly be sent in the measurement interval and to keep counters only for such "large" flows. Since, by definition, there can be at most 1000 such flows, the final table reduces to 1000 flow ID, counter pairs, which can be indexed using a CAM. Note that small CAMs are perfectly feasible at high speed.

This form of compression is reasonable for applications that only want counters above a threshold. For example, just as most cell phone plans charge a fixed price up to a threshold and a usage-based fee

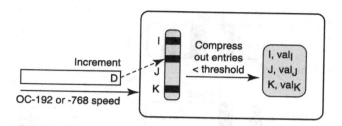

FIGURE 16.8

Using threshold compression to reduce the number of counters stored.

beyond the threshold, a router may only wish to keep track of the traffic sent by large flows. All other flows are charged a fixed price. Similarly, ISPs wishing to reroute traffic hot spots or detect attacks are only interested in large, "elephant" flows and not the "mice."

However, this idea gives rise to a technical problem. How can a chip detect the elephants above the threshold without keeping track of all flows? The simplest approach would be to keep a counter for all flows, as in Fig. 16.1, to determine which flows are above the threshold. However, doing so does not save any memory.

A trick (Estan and Varghese, 2002) to directly compute the elephants together with the traffic sent by each elephant is shown in Fig. 16.9. The building blocks are hash stages that operate in parallel. First, consider how the filter operates if it had only one stage. A stage is a table of counters indexed by a hash function computed on a packet flow ID; all counters in the table are initialized to 0 at the start of a measurement interval.

When a packet comes in, a hash on its flow ID is computed and the size of the packet is added to the corresponding counter. Since all packets belonging to the same flow hash to the same counter, if a flow F sends more than threshold T, F's counter will exceed the threshold. If we add to the flow memory all packets that hash to counters of T or more, we are guaranteed to identify all the large flows (no false negatives).

Unfortunately, since the number of counters we can afford is significantly smaller than the number of flows, many flows will map to the same counter. This can cause false positives in two ways: First, small flows can map to counters that hold large flows and get added to flow memory; second, several small flows can hash to the same counter and add up to a number larger than the threshold.

To reduce this large number of false positives, the algorithm uses multiple stages. Each stage (Fig. 16.9) uses an *independent* hash function. Only the packets that map to counters of T or more at *all* stages get added to the flow memory. For example, in Fig. 16.9, if a packet with a flow ID F arrives that hashes to counters 3, 1, and 7, respectively, at the three stages, F will pass the filter (counters that are over the threshold are shown darkened).

On the other hand, a flow G that hashes to counters 7, 5, and 4 will not pass the filter because the second-stage counter is not over the threshold. Effectively, the multiple stages attenuate the probability of false positives exponentially in the number of stages. This is shown by the following simple analysis.

Assume a 100-MB/sec link with 100,000 flows. We want to identify the flows above 1% of the link during a 1-second measurement interval. Assume each stage has 1000 buckets and a threshold of 1 MB. Let's see what the probability is for a flow sending 100 KB to pass the filter. For this flow to pass one stage, the other flows need to add up to 1 MB − 100 KB = 900 KB.

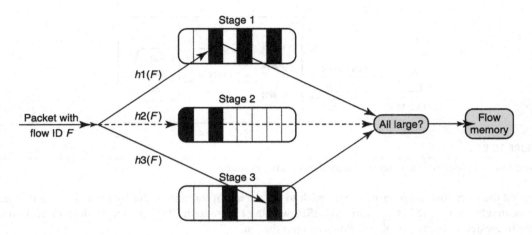

FIGURE 16.9

In a parallel multistage filter, a packet with a flow ID F is hashed using hash function $h1$ into a Stage 1 hash table, $h2$ into a Stage 2 hash table, etc. Each of the hash buckets contains a counter that is incremented by the packet size. If *all* the hash bucket counters are above the threshold (shown bolded), then flow F is passed to the flow memory for more careful observation.

There are at most $99,900/900 = 111$ such buckets out of the 1000 at each stage. Therefore, the probability of passing one stage is at most 11.1%. With four independent stages, the probability that a small flow no larger than 100 KB passes all four stages is the *product* of the individual stage probabilities, which is at most $1.52 * 10^{-4}$.

Note the potential scalability of the scheme. If the number of flows increases to one million, we simply add a fifth hash stage to get the same effect. Thus, to handle 100,000 flows requires roughly 4000 counters and a flow memory of approximately 100 memory locations; to handle one million flows requires roughly 5000 counters and the same size of flow memory. This is logarithmic scaling.

The number of memory accesses at packet arrival time performed by the filter is exactly one read and one write per stage. If the number of stages is small enough, this is affordable, even at high speeds, since the memory accesses can be performed in parallel, especially in chip implementation. A simple optimization called *conservative update* (see the exercises) can improve the performance of multistage filtering even further. Multistage filters can be seen as an application of Principle **P3a**, trading certainty (allowing some false positives and false negatives) for time and storage.

16.8 Reducing counters using flow counting

A second way to reduce the number of counters even further, beyond even threshold compression, is to realize that many applications do not even require identifying flows above a threshold. Some only need a *count* of the number of flows. For example, the Snort (www.snort.org) intrusion-detection tool detects port scans by counting all the distinct destinations sent to by a given source and warning if this amount is over a threshold.

On the other hand, to detect a denial-of-service attack, one might want to count the number of sources sending to a destination because many such attacks use multiple forged addresses. In both examples it suffices to count flows, where a flow identifier is a destination (port scan) or a source (denial of service).

A naive method to count source-destination pairs would be to keep a counter together with a hash table (such as Fig. 16.1, except without the counter) that stores all the distinct 64-bit source–destination address pairs seen thus far. When a packet arrives with source and destination addresses S, D, the algorithm searches the hash table for S, D; if there is no match, the counter is incremented, and S, D is added to the hash table. Unfortunately, this solution takes too much memory.

An algorithm called HyperLogLog (Flajolet and Martin, 1985) can considerably reduce the memory needed by the naive solution at the cost of some accuracy in counting flows. The intuition behind probabilistic counting is to compute a metric of how uncommon a certain pattern within a flow ID is. It then keeps track of the degree of "uncommonness" across all packets seen. If the algorithm sees very uncommon patterns, the algorithm concludes it saw a large number of flows.

More precisely, for each packet seen, the algorithm computes a hash function on the flow ID. It then counts the number of *consecutive zeroes*, starting from the least significant position of the hash result; this is the measure of uncommonness used. The algorithm keeps track of X, i.e., the largest number of consecutive zeroes seen (starting from the least significant position) in the hashed flow ID values of all packets seen so far.

At the end of the interval, the algorithm converts X, the largest number of trailing zeroes seen, into an estimate 2^X for the number of flows. Intuitively, if the stream contains two distinct flows, on average one flow will have the least significant bit of its hashed value equal to zero; if the stream contains eight flows, on average, one flow will have the last three bits of its hashed value equal to zero, and so on.

Note that hashing is essential for two reasons. First, implementing the algorithm directly on the sequence of flow IDs itself could make the algorithm susceptible to flow ID assignments where the traffic stream contains a flow ID F with many trailing zeroes. If F is in the traffic stream, then even if the stream has only a few flows, the algorithm without hashing will wrongly report a large number of flows. Notice that adding multiple copies of the same flow ID to the stream will not change the algorithm's final result because all copies hash to the same value.

A second reason for hashing is that accuracy can be boosted using multiple independent hash functions. The basic idea with one hash function can guarantee at most 50% accuracy. By using N-independent hash functions in parallel to compute N separate estimates of X, probabilistic counting greatly reduces the error of its final estimate. It does so by keeping the average value of X (as a floating-point number, not an integer) and then computing 2^X. Better algorithms for networking purposes are described in Estan et al. (2002).

The bottom line is that a chip can count approximately the number of flows with small error but with much less memory than required to track all flows. The computation of each hash function can be done in parallel. Flow counting can be seen as an application of Principle **P3b**, trading accuracy in the estimate for low storage and time.

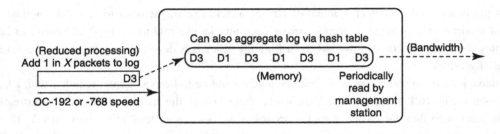

FIGURE 16.10

Using sampling to reduce packet processing while maintaining a packet log for later analysis.

16.9 Reducing processing using sampled NetFlow

So far, we have restricted ourselves to packet counting. However, several applications might require packet logs. Packet logs are useful for analysts to retrospectively analyze for patterns and attacks.

In networking there are general-purpose traffic measurement systems, such as Cisco's NetFlow (Cisco netflow, 2001b), that report per-flow records for very fine-grained flows, where a flow is identified by a TCP or UDP connection. Unfortunately, the large amount of memory needed to store packet logs requires the use of DRAM to store the logs. Clearly, writing to DRAM on every packet arrival is infeasible for high speeds, just as it was for counter management.

Basic NetFlow has two problems.

1. **Processing Overhead:** Updating the DRAM slows down the forwarding rate.
2. **Collection Overhead:** The amount of data generated by NetFlow can overwhelm the collection server or its network connection. Feldmann et al. (2000) report loss rates of up to 90% using basic NetFlow.

Thus, for example, Cisco recommends the use of sampling (see Fig. 16.10) at speeds above OC-3: Only the sampled packets result in updates to the DRAM flow cache that keeps the per-flow state. For example, sampling 1 in 16 packets or 1 in 1000 packets is common. The advantage is that the DRAM must be written to at most 1 in, say, 16 packets, allowing the DRAM access time to be (say) 16 times slower than a packet arrival time. Sampling introduces considerable inaccuracy in the estimate; this is not a problem for measurements over long periods (errors average out) and if applications do not need exact data.

The data-collection overhead can be alleviated by having the router aggregate the log information into counters (e.g., by source and destination autonomous systems (AS) numbers) as directed by a manager. However, Fang and Peterson (1999) show that even the number of aggregated flows is very large. For example, collecting packet headers for Code Red traffic on a class A network (Moore, 2001) produced 0.5 GB per hour of compressed NetFlow data. Aggregation reduced this data only by a factor of four.

Sampling is an example of using **P3a**, trading certainty for storage (and time), via a randomized pruning algorithm.

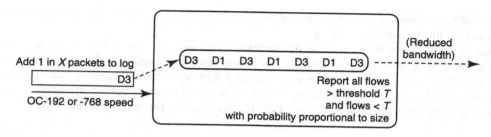

FIGURE 16.11

Using sampled charging to report only all large flows over a threshold and report flows below a threshold with a probability proportional to their size.

16.10 Reducing reporting using sampled charging

A technique called *sampled charging* (Duffield et al., 2001) can be used to reduce the collection overhead of NetFlow, at the cost of further errors. The idea is to start with a NetFlow log that is aggregated by TCP or UDP connections and to reduce the overhead of sending this data to a collection station. The goal is to *reduce collection bandwidth* and processing, as opposed to reducing the size of the router log.

The idea, depicted in Fig. 16.11, is at first glance similar to threshold compression, described in Section 16.7. The router reports only flow above a threshold to the collection station. The only additional twist is that the router also reports a flow with size s that is less than the threshold with a probability proportional to s.

Thus the difference between this idea and simple threshold compression is that the final transmitted bandwidth is still small, but some attention is paid to flows below the threshold as well. Why might this be useful? Suppose all TCP individual connections in the aggregated log are small and below threshold but that 50% of the connections are from subnet A to subnet B.

If the router reported only the connections above threshold, the router would report no flows because no *individual* TCP flow is large. Thus, the collection agency would be unable to determine this unusual pattern in the destination and source addresses of the TCP connections. On the other hand, by reporting flows below threshold with a probability proportional to their size, on average, half the flows the router will report will be from A to B. Thus, the collection station can determine this unusual traffic pattern and take steps (e.g., increase bandwidth between these two) accordingly.

Thus the advantage of sampled charging over simple threshold compression is that it allows the manager to infer potentially interesting traffic patterns that are not decided in advance while still reducing the bandwidth sent to the collection node.

For example, sampled charging could also be used to detect an unusual number of packets sent by Napster using the same data sent to the collection station. Its disadvantage is that it still requires a large DRAM log. The large DRAM log scales poorly in size or accuracy as speeds increase.

On the other hand, threshold compression removes the need for the large DRAM log while directly identifying the large traffic flows. However, unless the manager knew in advance that he was interested in traffic between source and destination subnets, one could not solve the earlier problem. For example, one cannot use a log that is threshold compressed with respect to TCP flows to infer that traffic between a pair of subnets is unusually large. Thus threshold compression has a more compact implementation but is less flexible than sample charging.

More formally, it can be shown that the multistage memory solution in Fig. 16.9 requires $\sqrt{M}$ memory, where M is the memory required by NetFlow or sampled charging for the same relative error. On the other hand, this solution requires more packet processing. Threshold compression is also less flexible than NetFlow and sampled charging in terms of being able to mine traffic patterns after the fact.

Sampled charging is an example of using **P3b**, trading certainty for bandwidth (and time).

16.11 **Correlating measurements using trajectory sampling**

A final technique for *router* measurement is called *trajectory sampling* (Duffield and Grossglauser, 2000). It is orthogonal to the last two techniques and can be combined with them. Recall that in sampled NetFlow and sampled charging, each router *independently* samples a packet. Thus, the set of packets sampled at each router is different even when a set of routers sees the same stream of packets.

The main idea in trajectory sampling is to have routers in a path make *correlated* packet-sampling decisions using a common hash function. Fig. 16.12[2] shows packets entering a router line card. The stream is "tapped" before it goes to the switch fabric. For every packet, a hash function h is used to decide whether the packet will be sampled by comparing the hashed value of the packet to a specified range. If the packet is sampled, a second hash function, g, on the packet is used to store a packet label in a log.

Trajectory sampling enables managers to correlate packets on different links. To ensure this, two more things are necessary. First, all routers must use the same values of g and h. Second, since packets can change header fields from router to router (e.g., TTL is decremented, data link header fields change), the hash functions are applied only to portions of the network packet that are *invariant*. This is achieved by computing the hash on header fields that do not change from hop to hop together with a few bytes of the packet payload.

A packet that is sampled at *one* router will be sampled at *all* routers in the packet's trajectory or path. Thus a manager can use trajectory sampling to see path effects, such as packet looping, packet drops, and multiple shortest paths, that may not be possible to discern using ordinary sampled NetFlow.

In summary, the two differences between trajectory sampling and sampled NetFlow are: (1) the use of a hash function instead of a random number to decide when to sample a packet; and (2) the use of a second hash function on invariant packet content to represent a packet header more compactly.

16.12 **A concerted approach to accounting**

In moving from efficient counter schemes to trajectory sampling, we moved from schemes that required only local support at each router to a scheme (i.e., trajectory sampling) that enlists the cooperation of multiple routers to extract more useful information. We now take this theme a step further by showing the power of concerted schemes that can involve all aspects of the network system (e.g., protocols,

---

[2] The picture is courtesy of Duffield and Grossglauser (2000).

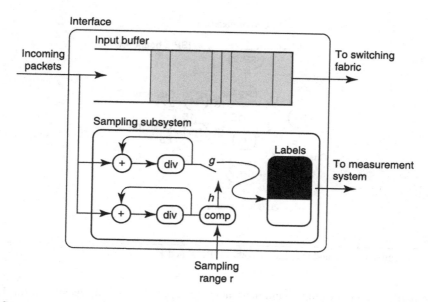

Interface

FIGURE 16.12

Trajectory sampling ensures that all routers sample a packet, or do not, by using the same hash function (as opposed to a random coin) to decide when to sample a packet.

routers) at various time scales (e.g., route computation, forwarding). We provide two examples: an accounting example based on a scheme proposed by Juniper networks (described in this section) and the problem of traffic matrices (described in the next section).

The specific problem being addressed in this section is that of an ISP wishing to collect traffic statistics on traffic sent by a customer to charge the customer based on the type of traffic and the destination of the traffic. Refer to Fig. 16.13, which depicts a small ISP, Z, for the discussion that follows.

In the figure assume that ISP Z wishes to bill Customer A at one rate for all traffic that exits via ISP X and at a different rate for all traffic that exits via ISP Y. One way to do this would be for router $R1$ to keep a separate counter for each prefix that represents traffic sent to that prefix. In the figure $R1$ would have to keep at least 30,000 prefix counters. Not only does this make implementation more complex, but it is also unaligned with the user's need, which will eventually aggregate the 30,000 prefixes into two tariff classes. Further, if routes change rapidly, the prefixes advertised by each ISP may change rapidly, requiring constant updating of this mapping by the tool.

Instead, the Juniper DCU solution (Semeria and Gredler, 2001) has two components.

1. **Class Counters:** Each forwarding table entry has a 16-bit class ID. Each bit in the class ID represents one of 16 classes. Thus if a packet matches prefix P with associated class ID C and C has bits set in bits 3, 6, and 9, then the counters corresponding to all three set bits are incremented. Thus, there are only 16 classes supported, but a single packet can cause multiple class counters to be incremented. The solution aligns with hardware design realities because 16 counters per link is

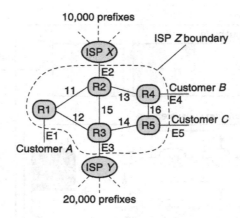

FIGURE 16.13

Example of an ISP with customer and peer links to other ISPs, X and Y.

not much harder than one counter, and incrementing in parallel is easily feasible if the 16 counters are maintained on-chip in a forwarding ASIC. The solution also aligns with real user needs because it cheaply supports the use of up to 16 destination-sensitive[3] counters.

2. **Routing Support:** To attack the problem of changing prefix routes (which would result in the tool's having to constantly map each prefix into a different class), the DCU solution enlists the help of the routing protocol. The idea is that all prefixes advertised by ISP X are given a color (which can be controlled using a simple route policy filter), and prefixes advertised by ISP Y are given a different color. Thus, when a router such as $R1$ gets a route advertisement for prefix P with color c, it automatically assigns prefix P to class c. This small change in the routing protocol greatly reduces the work of the tool.

Juniper also has other schemes (Semeria and Gredler, 2001), including counters based on packet classifiers and counters based on MPLS tunnels. These are slightly more flexible than DCU accounting because they can take into account the source address of a packet in determining its class. But these other schemes do not have the administrative scalability of DCU accounting because they lack routing support.

The DCU accounting scheme is an example of **P4**, leveraging existing system components, and **P3**, relaxing system requirements (e.g., only a small number of aggregate classes).

16.13 Computing traffic matrices

While the DCU solution is useful only for accounting, a generalization of some of the essential ideas can help in solving the *traffic matrix* problem. This is a problem of great interest to many ISPs.

---

[3] It can also be made sensitive to the type of service by also using the DiffServ byte to determine the class.

To define the traffic matrix problem, consider a network (e.g., Z in Fig. 16.13) such as those used by ISPs Sprint and AT&T. The network can be modeled as a graph with links connecting router nodes. Some of the links from a router in ISP Z go to routers belonging to other ISPs ($E2$, $E3$) or customers ($E1$, $E4$, $E5$). Let us call such links *external* links. Although we have lumped them together in Fig. 16.13, external links directed toward the ISP router are called *input* links, and external links directed away from an ISP router are called *output* links.

The traffic matrix of a network enumerates the amount of traffic that was sent (in some arbitrary period, say, a day) between *every* pair of input and output links of the network. For example, the traffic matrix could tell managers of ISP Z in Fig. 16.13 that 60 Mbits of traffic entered during the day from Customer A, of which 20 Mbits exited on the peering link $E2$ to ISP X, and 40 Mbps left on link $E5$ to Customer B.

Network operators find traffic matrices (over various time scales ranging from hours to months) indispensable. They can be used to make more optimal routing decisions (working around suboptimal routing by changing OSPF weights or setting up MPLS tunnels), for knowing when to set up circuit-switched paths (avoiding hot spots), for network diagnosis (understanding causes of congestion), and for provisioning (knowing which links to upgrade on a longer time scale of months).

Unfortunately, existing legacy routers provide only a single aggregate counter (the SNMP link byte counter) of all traffic traversing a link, which aggregates traffic sent between all pairs of input and output links that traverse the link. Inferring the traffic matrix from such data is problematic because there are $O(V^2)$ possible traffic pairs in the matrix (where V is the number of external links), and many sparse networks may have only, say, $O(V)$ links (and hence $O(V)$ counters). Even after knowing how traffic is routed, one has $O(V)$ equations for $O(V^2)$ variables, which makes deterministic inference (of all traffic pairs) impossible. This dilemma has led to two very different solution approaches. We now describe these two existing solutions and a proposed new approach.

16.13.1 Approach 1: Internet tomography

This approach (see Medina et al. (2002); Zhang et al. (2003) for useful reviews of past work) recognizes the impossibility of deterministic inference from SNMP counters cited earlier and instead attempts statistical inference, with some probability of error. At the heart of the inference technique is some model of the underlying traffic distribution (e.g., Gaussian, gravity model) and some statistical (e.g., maximum likelihood) or optimization technique (e.g., quadratic programming (Zhang et al., 2003)[4]).

Early approaches based on Gaussian distributions did very poorly (Medina et al., 2002), but a new approach based on gravity models does much better, at least on the AT&T backbone. The great advantage of tomography is that it works without retrofitting existing routers, and it is also clearly cheap to implement in routers. A possible disadvantage of this method is the potential errors in the method (off by as much as 20% in Zhang et al. (2003)), its sensitivity to routing errors (a single link failure can throw an estimate off by 50%), and its sensitivity to topology.

---

[4] Some authors limit the term *tomography* to the use of statistical models; thus Zhang et al. (2003) refer to their work as *tomogravity*. But this is splitting hairs.

16.13.2 Approach 2: per-prefix counters

Designers of modern routers have considered other systems solutions to the traffic matrix problem based on changes to router implementations and (sometimes) changes to routing protocols (see the DCU scheme described earlier). For example, one solution being designed into some routers built at Cisco (2001a) and some start-ups is to use per-prefix counters. Recall that prefixes are used to aggregate route entries for many millions of Internet addresses into, say, 100,000–150,000 prefixes at the present time.

A router has a forwarding engine for each input line card that contains a copy of the forwarding prefix table. Suppose each prefix P has an associated counter that is incremented (by the number of bytes) for each packet entering the line card that matches P. Then, by pooling the per-prefix counters kept at the routers corresponding to each input link, a tool can reconstruct the traffic matrix. To do so, the tool must associate prefix routes with the corresponding output links using its knowledge of routes computed by a protocol, such as OSPF. In Fig. 16.13, if $R1$ keeps per-prefix counters on traffic entering from link $E1$, it can sum the 10,000 counters corresponding to prefixes advertised by ISP X to find the traffic between Customer A and ISP X.

One advantage of this scheme is that it provides perfect traffic matrices. A second advantage is that it can be used for differential traffic charging based on the destination address, as in the DCU proposal. The two disadvantages are the implementation complexity of maintaining per-prefix counters (and the lack thereof in legacy routers) and the large amount of data that needs to be collected and synthesized from each router to form traffic matrices.

16.13.3 Approach 3: class counters

Our idea is that each prefix is mapped to a small class ID of 8–14 bits (256–16,384 classes) using the forwarding table. When an input packet is matched to a prefix P, the forwarding entry for P maps the packet to a class counter that is incremented. For up to 10,000 counters, the class counters can easily be stored in on-chip SRAM on the forwarding ASIC, allowing the increment to occur internally in parallel with other functions.

For accounting, the DCU proposal (Section 16.12) already suggests that routers use policy filters to color routes by tariff classes and to pass the colors using the routing protocol. These colors can then be used to automatically set class IDs at each router. For the traffic matrix, a similar idea can be used to colorize routes based on the matrix equivalence class (e.g., all prefixes arising from the same external link or network in one class).

How can class counters be used? For example, many ISPs have points of presence (or PoPs) in major cities, and just calculating the aggregate PoP-to-PoP traffic matrix is very valuable (Bhattacharyya et al., 2001). Today, this is done by aggregating the complete router-to-router matrix to find this. This can be done directly by classes by setting each PoP into a separate class. For example, in Fig. 16.13, $R4$ and $R5$ may be part of the same PoP, and thus $E4$ and $E5$ would be mapped to the same class. Measurement data from 2003 (Spring et al., 2002) indicates a great reduction in the number of classes, with 150 counters sufficing to handle the largest ISP.

The class-counter scheme is an example of Principle **P4**, leveraging existing system components. It is also an example of Principle **P3**, relaxing system requirements (e.g., using only a small number of aggregate classes).

16.14 **Sting as an example of passive measurement**

So far, this chapter has dealt exclusively with *router* measurement problems that involve changes to router implementations and to other subsystems, such as routing protocols. While such changes can be achieved with the cooperation of a few dominant router vendors, they do face the difficulty of incremental deployment. By contrast to the schemes already described, passive measurement focuses on the ability to trick a network into providing useful measurement data without changing network internals. The basic idea is to get around the lack of measurement support provided by the Internet protocol suite.

Imagine you are no longer an ISP but a network manager at the Acme Widget Company. An upstart ISP is claiming to provide better service than your existing ISP. You would like to conduct a test to see whether this is true. To do so, you want to determine end-to-end performance measurements from your site to various Web servers across the country, using both ISPs in turn.

The standard solution is to use tools, such as Ping and Traceroute, that are based on sending ICMP messages. The difficulty with these tools is that ISPs regularly filter or rate-limit such messages because of their use by hackers.

An idea that gets around this limitation was introduced by Sting (1999) tool, invented by Stefan Savage. The main idea is to send measurement packets in the clothing of TCP packets; ISPs and Web servers cannot drop or rate-limit such packets without penalizing good clients. Then every protocol mechanism of TCP becomes a degree of freedom (**P13**) for the measurement tool.

Consider the problem of determining the loss probability between a source and a distant Web server. This may be useful to know if most of the traffic is sent in only one direction, as in a video broadcast. Even if Ping were not rate-limited, Ping only provides the combined loss probability in both directions.

The Sting idea to find the loss probability from the source to the server is as follows. The algorithm starts by making a normal TCP connection to the server and sending N data packets to the server in sequence. Acknowledgments are ignored: After all, it's measurements we are after, not data transfer.

After the *data-seeding* stage, the algorithm moves into a second stage, called *hole filling*. Hole filling starts with sending a single data packet with sequence number 1 greater than the last packet sent in the first phase. If an acknowledgment is received, all is well; no data packets were lost.

If not, after sufficient retransmission, the receiver will respond with the highest number, X, received in sequence. The sender tool now sends *only* the segment corresponding to $X + 1$. Eventually, an updated acknowledgment arrives with the next highest received in sequence. The receiver fills in this next hole and marches along until all "holes" are filled. At the end of the second phase, the sender knows exactly which data packets were lost in the first phase and can compute the loss rate.

It is more of a challenge to compute the reverse loss rate because the receiver TCP may batch acknowledgments. However, once it is grasped that the tool is not limited to behaving like a normal TCP connection, all the stops can be loosed. By sending packets out of order in the first phase and a series of bizarre ploys, the receiver is conned into providing the required information.

At this point, the theoretician may shake his head sadly and say, "It's a bunch of tricks. I always knew these network researchers were not quite the thing." Indeed, Sting employs a collection of tricks to compute its particular metrics. But the *idea* of using TCP's venerable protocol mechanisms as a palette for measurement is perhaps an eye-opener. It has influenced later measurement tools, such as TBIT (Padhye and Floyd, 2001) that used the same general idea to measure the extent to which new TCP features were deployed.

Of course, the idea is not limited to TCP but applies to any protocol. Any protocol, including BGP, can be subverted for the purposes of measurement. Philosophically, this is, however, dangerous ground because the tools used by the measurement maven (presumably on the side of the angels) are now the same as used by the hacker (presumably on the dark side). For example, denial-of-service attacks exploit the same inability of a server to discriminate between standard usages of a protocol and adaptations thereof.

While Sting is less of an exercise in efficient implementation than it is an exercise in adding features, it can be regarded as an example of **P4**, leveraging features of existing TCP implementations.

16.15 Generating better traffic logs via data streaming

Most of the measurement and the inference techniques introduced in Sections 16.9–16.11 were designed to work with the traffic logs generated by sampled Cisco NetFlow. In this section we provide a brief introduction to a now-well-established family of algorithms, called data-streaming and sketching algorithms (Muthukrishnan, 2005), that can generate more informative and hence better traffic logs for a variety of measurement tasks. In fact, we have already described one such algorithm in Section 16.8: the HyperLogLog algorithm introduced in Flajolet and Martin (1985) that can be used for counting the number of active flows.

It has been nearly two decades since the contents of this chapter in the first edition of this book were written. During these two decades, the amount and the rate of traffic flowing on the Internet and across data centers has increased by several orders of magnitude. Sampled NetFlow-based techniques alone are no longer adequate for the measurement and the monitoring of current networks for the following reason.

Traditional implementations of such monitoring functions typically involve a search and update to per-flow state (typically organized as a hash table), and this state has to be stored in fast yet expensive SRAM to keep up with the high link speed. However, since this state can be very large (say gigabytes) at high link speeds, storing it in SRAM can be prohibitively expensive. Strategies to alleviate this problem, such as packet sampling, typically result in lower accuracy due to the low sampling rate (e.g., a 1 out of 500 NetFlow sampling rate was used in the mid-2000s at a Tier-1 ISP in the US (Zhao et al., 2006a)) that is necessary to make the sampling operation affordable (Duffield et al., 2003; Hohn and Veitch, 2003; Kumar et al., 2004b) for today's high link rates.

Network data streaming has been recognized as a viable solution for measuring and monitoring high-speed links in large networks (Kumar et al., 2004b). Data streaming is concerned with processing a long stream of data items typically in one pass and using a small working memory to answer a query regarding the stream. The key challenge is to "remember", in a small *working memory* (typically in SRAM), as much information *pertinent to the query* as possible. A network data streaming algorithm typically processes each and every packet passing through a high-speed link, using a small yet well-organized data structure called *sketch*, to measure important network statistics such as flow size distribution.

The design principle of network data-streaming algorithms can be summarized as follows:

Lossy data structure + Bayesian statistics = Accurate streaming (Kumar et al., 2004b).

Its main idea is to first perform data streaming at a very high speed in a small memory to get the streaming results that are lossy. There are two causes for this loss to be inevitable. First, due to the stringent computational complexity requirement of the application (e.g., 8 nanoseconds per packet when processing OC-768 traffic), the streaming algorithm does not have enough processing time to "put the data into the exact place." Second, the streaming algorithm does not have enough space to store all the relevant data. Due to the loss, the streaming result is typically far away from the information we would like to estimate. Bayesian statistics is therefore used to recover information from the streaming result as much as possible.

Data-streaming and sketching algorithms were first proposed as memory-efficient approximate query processing solutions in databases (Alon et al., 1999b). In general, a success is declared if the solution has a small memory footprint that is sublinear with respect to the number of data points in the database. However, data-streaming algorithms for network applications have to possess an additional property: the time complexity of updating the corresponding sketch has to be very low since every packet arrival triggers one or more such updates and the network link rate can be extremely high.

16.16 **Counting the number of distinct flows**

We start with a simple data-streaming algorithm, called the min-hash algorithm or sketch (Cohen, 2016), for counting the number of distinct flows. This problem is equivalent to counting the number of distinct elements in a data stream because we can view each packet as an element identified by its flow identifier (which, as explained earlier, can be a source IP address, a source-destination IP address pair, or a four-tuple). Hence, two different packets are considered two copies of the same element if they belong to the same flow. The min-hash algorithm can be considered a variant of the HyperLogLog algorithm (Flajolet and Martin, 1985) described in Section 16.8. Although it is slightly less cost-effective than HyperLogLog, it is much easier to describe and understand.

16.16.1 **The min-hash algorithm**

The min-hash algorithm, also called min-wise hash in a related but different context of locality-sensitive hashing (Indyk et al., 1997), works as follows. Assume $\mathcal{H}$ is a hash function that maps the ID of an element into a real number uniformly distributed in the open interval $(0, 1)$. The lossy data structure in this case is very simple. For all data items $d_1, d_2, \cdots$ in the data stream, we only maintain, in a variable V, a so-called min-hash value: the minimum among their hash values $\mathcal{H}(d_1), \mathcal{H}(d_2), \cdots$. The actual algorithm is, for each data item d_i, to compare $H(d_i)$ with the value of the min-hash variable V seen so far. The value V is clearly a random variable whose randomness comes from both the hash function $\mathcal{H}$ and the data items $d_1, d_2, \cdots$.

Suppose, after the entire data stream has passed, the value of the min-hash variable is $V = v$. This value v provides a good amount of information concerning the number of distinct elements in the data stream, which we denote as N. Any statistics book that has a section on order statistics (e.g., Section 5.4 in Casella and Berger (2001)) proves that $E[V] = \frac{1}{N+1}$. Hence, $N = \frac{1}{E[V]} - 1$. Replacing $E[V]$ (the first moment of V) by the observed (sample) value v, we obtain an estimator of N, denoted as $\hat{N}$, as

$$\hat{N} \triangleq \frac{1}{v} - 1. \tag{16.1}$$

The manner in which this estimator is obtained, by replacing the first moment of V with a realization of V is called the method of moments in statistics (Casella and Berger, 2001).

Clearly, a single estimator $\hat{N}$ is very noisy and can lead to large estimation errors. To improve on that, we often use a number of, say 25, such estimators that are statistically independent. This can be achieved using 25 different and statistically independent hash functions $\mathcal{H}_1, \mathcal{H}_2, \cdots, \mathcal{H}_{25}$ as follows. Instead of a single min-hash variable V we compute an array $V[1..25]$ of 25 min-hash variables. This array is called a min-hash sketch. Each variable $V[i]$ is generated using the hash function $\mathcal{H}_i$. Suppose their corresponding values are $v[1..25]$ after processing a data stream. Then what would be a good estimator derived from these 25 values?

A good guess is simply to use the average (i.e., the sample mean) of these 25 values in the place of v in Formula (16.1). However, the resulting estimator is not robust since an outlier among them can significantly distort the average. In statistics, the median of means or the mean of medians is often used instead to both achieve low variance and guard against outliers. For example, a median of means estimator in this case can be obtained by organizing these 25 values into a 5×5 matrix, calculating the average of each row, and outputting the median of the 5 averages. In the following, we denote such an estimator as $MM(v[1..25])$ so that we do not have to spell out whether MM stands for median of means or mean of medians. With this notation, an MM estimator is

$$\hat{N} = \frac{1}{MM(v[1..25])} - 1. \tag{16.2}$$

Such an MM-based estimator is frequently used in synthesizing multiple independent observations, such as in Alon et al. (1999b).

Compared to maintaining a hash table, which requires $O(N)$ memory, this data-sketching algorithm requires only 25 or so words of memory, or $O(1)$ memory. It does sacrifice some estimation accuracy, but this can be tolerated in many applications. Since its memory requirement is extremely low, these memory words can be stored in SRAM or even registers to allow for accesses at line rates. Since each $V[i]$ is independent of others, they can be accessed and updated in parallel, at an extra cost.

16.16.2 An extension of min-hash for estimating $|A \bigcup B|$

Now, we describe a slight extension of the min-hash algorithm for solving a different but related counting problem: counting the number of distinct elements in the union of two large sets A and B that are "streaming by," or in other words estimating $|A \bigcup B|$. More precisely, we assume that elements in each set arrive as a data stream (so that the processor can take only a single pass over it), and the two sets (streams) A and B are processed by two different processors. Suppose the streams A and B each is processed using the stated algorithm by the same set of 25 independent hash functions $\mathcal{H}_1, \mathcal{H}_2, \cdots,$ $\mathcal{H}_{25}$, and the resulting arrays are $a[1..25]$ and $b[1..25]$, respectively. The question is whether we can obtain a good estimate of $|A \bigcup B|$ from $a[1..25]$ and $b[1..25]$.

The answer becomes quite obvious when we ask the same question from a different angle. Suppose, using this algorithm, a processor $\hat{N}$ processes the concatenated stream $A||B$, which contains all elements in A followed by all elements in B, and suppose the resulting array is $c[1..25]$. Our question is how $c[1..25]$ is related to $a[1..25]$ and $b[1..25]$. Clearly, for any $1 \leq i \leq 25$, we have $c[i] = min\{a[i], b[i]\}$ because $c[i]$ is the min-hash value (by the hash function $\mathcal{H}_i$) of $A \bigcup B$, which must equal the smaller between $a[i]$, the min-hash value of A, and $b[i]$, the min-hash value of B. Once we obtain $c[1..25]$ this way, we arrive at the following estimator:

$$\widehat{|A \bigcup B|} = \frac{1}{MM(c[1..25])} - 1. \tag{16.3}$$

It will become clear shortly that our "ulterior motive" is to count $|A \bigcap B|$, the number of distinct elements in the intersection of these two sets. However, it is straightforward to obtain the following estimator using the principle of inclusion and exclusion and the fact that the number of elements in a set (here A or B) can be counted exactly (using a single counter):

$$\widehat{|A \bigcap B|} = |A| + |B| - \widehat{|A \bigcup B|}. \tag{16.4}$$

While this extension, in hindsight, may appear like a simple mental exercise for readers, it led to a beautiful solution (Li and Church, 2007), to be described next, to a classical database problem called association rule mining (Agrawal et al., 1993). While this solution may sound like a "low-hanging fruit" after we describe it, it actually eluded discovery for more than a decade (from Agrawal et al. (1993) to Li and Church (2007)).

16.16.3 Application to data mining

In this section, we first state the problem of association rule mining and then explain how to reduce it to the problem just described of estimating $|A \bigcap B|$. Association rule mining (Agrawal et al., 1993) is arguably the most classical and fundamental problem in data mining (Kamber and Han, 2000). It can be best described using the following application. Let us organize the transactions of customers shopping at Walmart as a two-dimensional table shown in Table 16.2. Each column except the 0th corresponds to a type of merchandise (say milk), and each row corresponds to a transaction (made by a customer at the time of checkout). The cell at the intersection of the ith row and jth column takes value 1 if the ith transaction has the jth type of merchandise in it and takes value 0 otherwise. The 0th column contains the customer-transaction identifiers that are distinct for each customer transaction.

Let us say Walmart is interested in finding all pairs of merchandise that are more frequently bought together by customers (say milk and cereal) than if the purchases of these two merchandises are statistically uncorrelated. Such a positive statistical correlation is called an association in the data-mining literature. For example, if roughly 1/2 of the customer transactions contain milk and roughly 1/3 of customer transactions contain cereal, then an association between milk and cereal is established if much more than $1/2 * 1/3 = 1/6$ of the customer transactions contain both milk and cereal.

Given any pair of columns (merchandises), to check if there is an association between them is a straightforward counting problem: to count the number of rows (customer transactions) in which the two corresponding cells both have value 1 (contain both merchandises). This suggests a straightforward but naive algorithm: Do this counting for every pair of columns. However, this naive algorithm is extremely time-consuming if the numbers of rows and columns in the table are both large. For example, suppose Walmart (table) has 50,000 different merchandises (columns) and 1 billion transactions (rows). Then, to do this counting for a pair of columns takes roughly a second on a gigahertz processor. To do this counting for every two columns takes roughly $\binom{50000}{2} \approx 1.25$ billion seconds, which is roughly 39.64 years. Such a slow solution is not going to help with Walmart's business.

Now, we describe a much more efficient solution, based on the algorithm just described for estimating $|\widehat{A \cap B}|$, that can find all associations in two weeks! To do so, we simply convert the counting problem for a pair of columns to the problem of estimating $|\widehat{A \cap B}|$ as follows. For each column of cells in Table 16.2, except the 0th that contains customer-transactions identifiers, we perform the following transformation. If the value of the cell on row i (the ith customer transaction) is 1, we rewrite the value of this cell to α_i, the corresponding customer-transaction identifier; if the value of this cell is 0, we rewrite it to "empty." The resulting table with the cell values rewritten is shown in Table 16.3.

We view each column, except the 0th, in Table 16.3 as a set of customer-transactions identifiers. For example, the "milk" column corresponds to the set of customer transactions, which we denote as A, that contain the purchase of "milk." We have $A = \{\alpha_1, \alpha_3, \alpha_4, \cdots\}$ as shown in Table 16.3. Also, as shown in Table 16.3, the "cereal" column corresponds to the set $\{\alpha_1, \alpha_3, \cdots\}$, which we denote as B. Then, our counting problem is equivalent to the problem of estimating $|A \cap B|$ since $A \cap B$ is precisely the set of customer transactions that contain both milk and cereal.

This conversion naturally suggests the following data-streaming algorithm. The first step of this algorithm is to take a one-pass scan over every column except the 0th. For each column, which corresponds to a set of customer transaction identifiers as just explained, the algorithm processes the set into an array of 25 numbers using the min-hash algorithm described above. Suppose processing each column to obtain a min-hash value (out of a total of 25 min-hash array elements) takes 1 second (1 nanosecond for processing each cell) as just explained, the preprocessing takes 1.25 million seconds, or roughly two weeks, for the 50,000 columns. The second step of the algorithm is, for every pair of columns (sets) say A and B, to estimate $|A \cap B|$ using Formulae (16.3) and (16.4). Suppose processing each such pair takes 50 nanoseconds (2 nanoseconds for each pair of array elements), the total processing time of this step is only $\binom{50000}{2} * 50 * 10^{-9} \approx 62.5$ seconds!

Note that, unlike in network data streaming applications where the constraint of taking only a one-pass scan over the data stream is imposed by the reality of networks, in this association rule mining scenario, this constraint is self-imposed. Since all data items are in the database, the algorithm in theory can scan the database as many times as it wishes. However, doing so comes at a high computational cost (of close to 40 years) that this algorithm rightly avoids.

Table 16.2 The Walmart customer-transaction table before transformation.

Transaction ID	Milk	Cereal	Banana	Apple	...
α_1	1	1	0	1	...
α_2	0	0	1	1	...
α_3	1	1	1	1	...
α_4	1	0	1	1	...
$\vdots$	$\vdots$	$\vdots$	$\vdots$	$\vdots$	$\vdots$

16.16.4 Bitmap sketch: a worthy alternative to min-hash

Another technique for counting F_0 is the bitmap sketch, invented in Whang et al. (1990) for database applications. It requires more space than the min-hash sketch but has a much lower update time for

Table 16.3 The Walmart customer-transaction table after transformation.					
Transaction ID	Milk	Cereal	Banana	Apple	⋯
α_1	α_1	α_1		α_1	⋯
α_2			α_2	α_2	⋯
α_3	α_3	α_3	α_3	α_3	⋯
α_4	α_4		α_4	α_4	⋯
⋮	⋮	⋮	⋮	⋮	⋰

the same estimation accuracy. The bitmap sketch is extremely simple: an array of bits (bitmap) $A[1..n]$ initialized to all zero and a hash function h whose range is $\{1, 2, \cdots, n\}$. For each new data item d, the bit indexed by the hash value $h(d)$ in A is set to 1. Let n_0 be the number of bits in A that remain 0 at the end of a measurement epoch. Suppose $n_0 \neq 0$. The estimator for F_0 is simply $n \log(n/n_0)$, where the "log" here is the natural logarithm. When $n_0 = 0$, however, it implies that F_0 is too large for the array A (of size n) to estimate accurately. Using a simple coupon-collector analysis, it can be shown that F_0 needs to be at least $n \log n$ for $n_0 = 0$ with high probability. For this reason, a bitmap of size n (bits) is large enough for accurately estimating F_0 of magnitude $O(n)$, as long as the constant factor in the Big-O is small (say, no more than 2 or 3).

If F_0 is close to or exceeds $n \log n$, then most, if not all, of the bits in the bitmap are set to 1. In this case accurate estimation of F_0 is no longer possible from this bitmap. To cope with this problem, a standard technique is sampling. Sampling works best when we know the approximate range of F_0 value, in which case we choose a sampling rate p such that $pF_0 = O(n)$ with a small constant factor. Note that the sampling has to be done consistently in the sense that, if an element is sampled earlier, then a repetition of this element later in the stream must also be sampled. This consistency requirement suggests the following hashed sampling similar to that used in trajectory sampling (Duffield and Gross-glauser, 2000) (described in Section 16.11): Fix a uniform hash function g (unrelated to the other hash function h) whose range is $(0, 1)$; any data item d is sampled and "inserted" into the bitmap if and only if $g(d) < p$.

In this hashed sampling scheme, there are two sources of estimation errors. The first source is hash collisions, each of which happens when two or more distinct elements are hashed to the same bit location. When n, the size of the bitmap, is fixed, estimation error caused by hash collisions increases when p increases. The second source is the sampling error, which decreases when p increases. An obvious research question is "how to set the value of p so that the total estimation error caused by both is statistically minimized?" This question was carefully studied and settled in Zhao et al. (2005).

In some network measurement applications, however, we do not know even the rough range of F_0 to set this sampling rate p properly. This case can be solved using the bitmap sketch augmented by a multi-resolution sampling technique as follows. We divide $(0, 1)$, the hash space of g, into $k > 1$ exponentially smaller intervals $(0, 1/2), (1/2, 3/4), (3/4, 7/8), \cdots, (1 - 2^{-k+1}, 1 - 2^{-k})$. We also use k bitmaps, each of size m. For any data item d, if the value of $g(d)$ falls into the first interval $(0, 1/2)$, then we insert it into the first bitmap; if the value of $g(d)$ falls into the second interval $(1/2, 3/4)$, then we insert it into the second bitmap, and so on. This way, roughly $1/2, 1/4, \cdots$, and $1/2^k$ of the F_0 distinct elements are inserted into the first, the second,..., and the kth bitmaps, respectively. If k is large enough (on the order of $\log_2(F_0/n)$), then one of the bitmaps should allow F_0 to be accurately estimated.

This multiresolution technique, first introduced in Fisk and Varghese (2001), has since been used in several network measurement applications, such as estimating flow-size distribution (Kumar et al., 2004a) (described in Section 16.18), EarlyBird (Singh et al., 2004b) (described in Section 17.6), and Carousel (The Lam et al., 2010) (described in Section 17.7), where the appropriate sampling rate is hard to determine beforehand.

16.17 Detection of heavy hitters

In Section 16.7 we already described the problem of detecting "large" flows (those that contain many more packets than others). Such flows are also called elephants or heavy hitters in the networking literature. In the database literature, data items that occur frequently (e.g., merchandise that appears in a large number of customer transactions) are called frequent items or icebergs.

Over the years, many different heavy-hitter detection algorithms have been proposed, such as Misra and Gries (1982); Manku and Motwani (2002); Estan and Varghese (2002); Charikar et al. (2002); and Cormode and Muthukrishnan (2005). Most of them, however, are not suitable for measuring a high-speed network link since, upon the arrival of each new data item, they need to update the values of a fairly large number (say hundreds) of counters. Algorithms suitable for elephant detection and size estimation in high-speed networks include (Estan and Varghese, 2002; Charikar et al., 2002; Cormode and Muthukrishnan, 2005). Among the three, we will only describe the sample-and-hold algorithm (Estan and Varghese, 2002) since it is conceptually the simplest. We also describe a similar technique called ElephantTrap (Lu et al., 2007) that detects elephants but does not track their sizes.

The objective of the sample-and-hold algorithm is to output the identities and the approximate packet counts of the elephants, defined as the flows whose actual packet counts are at least θ (percentage) of the total packet count n in the packet stream. To do so, sample-and-hold requires only $O(1/\theta)$ amount of working memory (in CAM), takes only a one-pass scan over the packet stream, and, for each packet, searches for and updates (if at all) only a single counter. Hence, sample-and-hold can scale to very high link speeds.

The algorithmic logic of sample-and-hold is very simple. The algorithm maintains a small set D of flow entries in CAM. Each flow entry contains a flow identifier and the associated packet counter. The algorithm is, for each incoming packet, to check if its flow identifier is already included in D (which is supported by CAM). If the answer is "yes," then the corresponding packet counter is incremented ("hold"). Otherwise, a new flow entry containing this flow identifier is sampled ("sample") with probability $b/(n\theta)$ and added to D. At the end of a measurement epoch, all items in D with high frequencies are returned as probable heavy hitters. It was shown in Estan and Varghese (2002) that, when D contains b/θ entries, the probability number with which an elephant is not included in D is only e^{-b}.

Most existing elephant-detection algorithms also produce an approximate count of the size of the elephant flows detected. An exception to that is ElephantTrap (Lu et al., 2007). As its name suggests, ElephantTrap is very effective at capturing and "trapping" the identities of elephant flows in a small table. However, ElephantTrap purposefully gives up the capability of accurately tracking their packet (or byte) counts, in exchange for a "streamlined" design that makes the algorithm extremely efficient to implement.

The idea of ElephantTrap is quite similar to that of sample-and-hold. It also samples packets and adds new flows to the flow table. There are, however, two main differences. First, unlike sample-and-hold, which checks every packet against the cached flow table, ElephantTrap samples a certain percentage of packets and only checks them against the cached flow table (sampled increments).

Second, unlike sample-and-hold, which only increments and never decrements the values of (flow size) counters, ElephantTrap gradually cycles around the cached flow table and halves their values (exponential decay). Flow-table entries with counter values lower than a certain threshold are eligible for eviction to make room for a new flow. Due to the sampled increments and the exponential decay, the size of a flow can no longer be inferred accurately from the corresponding counter value. ElephantTrap, developed and nicknamed "ETrap" (Cisco Systems Inc., 2017; Ronad, 2019) by Cisco, has been used for intelligent buffering and scheduling on the Cisco Nexus 9000 Series Switch products.

16.18 Estimation of flow-size distribution

Counting the number of distinct elements or detecting heavy hitters are among the simplest and arguably the easiest objectives to achieve in network data streaming. In this section we describe a data-streaming algorithm for achieving a much more sophisticated objective: the estimation of flow size distribution.

The problem of estimating flow size distribution on a high-speed link is another network measurement problem that has received considerable attention (Duffield et al., 2003; Hohn and Veitch, 2003; Duffield et al., 2001, 2002; Estan and Varghese, 2002; Estan et al., 2002). In this problem, given an arbitrary flow size s, we are interested in knowing the number of flows that contain s packets within a monitoring interval. In other words we would like to know how the total traffic volume splits into flows of different sizes. An estimate of the flow distribution contains knowledge about the number of flows for all possible flow sizes, including elephants (large flows), "kangaroos/rabbits" (medium flows), and "mice" (small flows).

16.18.1 Motivation

Flow-size distribution information can be useful in a number of applications in network measurement and monitoring. First, flow-size distribution information may allow Internet service providers to infer the usage pattern of their networks, such as the approximate number of users with dial-up or broadband access. Such information on usage patterns can be important for the purpose of pricing, billing, infrastructure engineering, and resource planning. In addition, network operators may also infer the type of applications that are running over a network link without looking into the details of traffic, such as how many customers are using streaming music, streaming video, and voice over IP. Over the years, more and more network applications have become recognizable through flow-distribution information.

Second, flow-size distribution information can help locally detect the existence of an event that causes the transition of the global network dynamics from one mode to another. An example of such mode transition is a sudden increase in the number of large flows (i.e., elephants) in a link. Possible events that may cause this include link failure or route flapping. Merely looking at the total load of the link may not detect such a transition since this link could be consistently heavily used anyway.

Third, flow-size distribution information may also help us detect various types of Internet security attacks, such as DDoS and Internet worms. In the case of DDoS attacks, if the attackers are using spoofed IP addresses, we will observe a significant increase in flows of size 1. In the case of Internet worms, we may suddenly find a large number of flows of a particular size in Internet links around the same time if the worm is a naive one that does not change in size. Also, the historical flow-distribution information stored at various links may help us study its evolution over time.

16.18.2 A data streaming algorithm solution

As explained earlier in Section 16.15, a naive solution to this problem is to use a hash table of per-flow counters to keep track of all active flows, but the naive solution cannot scale to high link speeds at a reasonable cost. Another possible approach (Duffield et al., 2003) is to sample a small percentage of packets and then infer the flow distribution from the sampled traffic. The algorithm proposed in Duffield et al. (2003) may well be the best algorithm in getting as much information as possible from the sampled data. However, its accuracy is limited by the typically low sampling rate (e.g., 0.2%) required to make the sampling operation affordable. The work by Hohn and Veitch (2003) has provided theoretical insights into the limitation of inferring flow distribution from sampled traffic.

A data-streaming algorithm was proposed in Kumar et al. (2004a) for providing very accurate estimates of flow-size distribution. The algorithm uses a very simple lossy data structure: a large array of passive counters. Upon the arrival of a packet at the router, its flow label is hashed to generate an index into this array, and the counter at this index is incremented by 1. Collisions due to hashing might cause two or more flow labels to be hashed to the same indices. Counters at such an index would contain the total number of packets belonging to all of the flows colliding into this index. There is no explicit mechanism to handle collisions because any such mechanism would impose additional processing and storage overheads that are unsustainable at high speeds.

The online streaming process is simple: Each packet arrival results in only a hashing operation and a counter increment. This streamlined (pun intended) design allows the online streaming process to operate at speeds as high as OC-768 without missing any packets. Furthermore, since during the online streaming phase the counters only need to be incremented (by 1), it suffices to use an array of passive counters. Such a counter array can be very cost-effectively implemented using a DRAM backing-store scheme such as RS (Zhao et al., 2006b) (described in Section 16.3).

The data structure is lossy in the sense that, due to collision in hashing, sizes of multiple flows may be accumulated in the same counter. Therefore, the raw information obtained from the counters can be far away from the actual flow distribution. This algorithm then uses Bayesian statistical methods such as expectation–maximization (EM) to infer the most likely flow-size distribution that results in the observed counter values after collision.

For achieving high accuracy, the number of counters used needs to be on the same order as the number of active flows $O(N)$ in a measurement epoch. Hence, its space requirement is linear with respect to N rather than sublinear as desired. However, since the constant factor is very small, this cost is still modest even for very high-speed links and is justifiable since the flow-size distribution subsumes and contains much more information than other statistics of traffic. Indeed, we will show in the next few sections that, when the objective is a simple function of this distribution, the space requirement can become much smaller.

16.19 The Tug-of-War algorithm for estimating F_2

In this section we describe a data-streaming algorithm for estimating a certain statistic of the flow size distribution: the second frequency moment of a data stream that is commonly denoted as F_2. Let $\mathcal{L}$ be the set of identifiers of flows that have at least one packet arrival during the measurement epoch. Let c_l denote the frequency of (number of packets in) the flow l during the epoch. The multiset $\{c_l | l \in \mathcal{L}\}$ is precisely the flow-size distribution. The second frequency moment (F_2) of this (traffic) data stream is defined as $F_2 \triangleq \sum_{l \in \mathcal{L}} c_l^2$.

F_2 is an important statistic of a data stream. It was shown in Alon et al. (1999b) that, in databases, the size of the self-join of a table with itself can be expressed as F_2 of the records (rows) in the table viewed as a data stream. In the networking context, the F_2 of a traffic data stream measures how skewed the traffic volume is toward the large flows. For example, as shown in Zhao et al. (2010), the F_2 becomes extremely large when the traffic volume is heavily concentrated in a small number of elephant flows, due to the squaring effect (of c_l^2 for large c_l terms).

A well-known solution to the problem of estimating the F_2 of a data stream is the Tug-of-War (ToW) algorithm (Alon et al., 1999b). This algorithm is easy to explain in the network data stream context. As in the min-hash algorithm, we need a small number of counters, each of which is associated with a hash function. For ease of presentation, we only describe, upon the arrival of a packet whose flow identifier is l, how the algorithm updates a single counter C_1 according to an associated hash function $\mathcal{H}_1(\cdot)$. This $\mathcal{H}_1$ maps any flow identifier to a random variable that takes the values 1 and -1, each with probability 0.5. The value of C_1 is set to 0 at the beginning of the measurement epoch. The update rule of the ToW algorithm for counter C_1 is extremely simple: $C_1 := C_1 + \mathcal{H}_1(l)$.

As in the min-hash algorithm, at the end of the measurement epoch, we need to estimate the F_2 of the data stream from the value of C_1. The estimator here is again extremely simple: the square of the value of C_1. Note that the final value of C_1 is $\sum_{l \in \mathcal{L}} c_l * \mathcal{H}_1(l)$. It was proven in Alon et al. (1999a) that, as long as the hash function $\mathcal{H}_1$ is two-way independent, we have $E[C_1^2] = \sum_{l \in \mathcal{L}} c_l^2 = F_2$. Hence, roughly speaking, the ToW algorithm has "modulated" the value of F_2 into the distribution of the random variable C_1, and this value can be "demodulated" by measuring $E[C_1^2]$. In statistics terms, C_1^2 is an unbiased estimator of F_2.

Here, a hash function $\mathcal{H}(\cdot)$ is said to be two-way independent, if, for any $l_1 \neq l_2$, the random variables $\mathcal{H}(l_1)$ and $\mathcal{H}(l_2)$ are mutually independent; the concept of 4-way independent is similarly defined. To reason about the accuracy of this estimator, however, knowing only that it is unbiased is not enough. In addition we need to know its variance. It was proven in Alon et al. (1999a) that, if the hash function $\mathcal{H}_1$ is four-way independent, then the variance of the estimator can be bounded by $2(F_2)^2$.

This variance bound is still quite large, and hence a single counter and estimator is clearly not enough. As in the min-hash algorithm, when multiple estimators $C_1^2, C_2^2, \cdots, C_k^2$ are used, the final estimator is the median of means, which we denote as $MM(C_1^2, C_2^2, \cdots, C_k^2)$ as before. Now, the question is how many such counters (and hash functions) are enough? It was shown in Alon et al. (1999a) that, to guarantee an ϵ relative error approximation (of F_2) with a probability at least $1 - \delta$, we need $k = \log(1/\delta)/\epsilon^2$ counters. Clearly, the number of counters needed here is a constant with respect to the number of active flows N, unlike in the case of the data-streaming algorithm for estimating the flow-size distribution where $O(N)$ counters are generally needed. In general, for any integer $p > 0$, we can define the pth moment of the data stream as $\sum_{l \in \mathcal{L}} c_l^p$. However, the cost of estimating F_p when

$p \geq 3$, in terms of space complexity, however, is very high (more precisely at least $O(N^{1-(2/p)})$ as shown in Alon et al. (1999a)).

Another salient feature of the ToW sketch is that it is summable in the following sense. Let A and B be two disjoint data streams. Let $C(A)$ and $C(B)$ be the respective ToW counter values resulting from processing A and B using the same hash function $\mathcal{H}$. Clearly, the ToW counter value resulting from processing $A \bigcup B$ is precisely $C(A) + C(B)$. Hence, $(C(A) + C(B))^2$ is an unbiased estimator of $||A \bigcup B||_2$, the F_2 of the union of two streams. Similarly, the ToW sketch is "differentiable" in the sense that $(C(A) - C(B))^2$ is an unbiased estimator of $||A - B||_2$, the F_2 of their difference.

The need for a sketch to be summable and "differentiable" is motivated by the theory and the applications of distributed data streaming (Feigenbaum et al., 2003). Today's Internet applications often generate and collect a massive amount of data at many distributed locations. For example, an ISP (Internet Service Provider) security monitoring application may require that packet traces be collected at hundreds (or even thousands) of ingress and egress routers, and the amount of data collected at each router can be on the order of several terabytes.

From time to time, various types of queries need to be performed over the union of these data sets. For example, in this ISP security monitoring application, we may need to query the union of packet trace data sets at all ingress and egress points to look for globally frequent signatures that may correspond to certain Internet worms. Given the gigantic and evolving nature of these physically distributed data sets, it is usually infeasible to ship all the data to a single location for centralized query processing, due to the prohibitively high communication cost. Therefore, how to execute various types of (approximate) queries over the union of distributed data sets without physically merging them together has received considerable research attention in the past two decades.

Next, we describe a distributed data-streaming problem that has been studied extensively, and its summable sketch solution, as an example. The problem is to detect global heavy hitters or *icebergs*, which are data elements whose aggregate frequency across all these data sets exceeds a prespecified threshold. The hardness of this problem arises from the fact that a global iceberg may be finely distributed across all the measurement points so that it does not appear large at any one location. For example, in security scenarios an adversary may conceal the presence of the iceberg by spreading it thinly across many different nodes. This precludes the possibility of using a naive algorithm that simply reports locally frequent elements. On the other hand, it would be prohibitively expensive for every node to send records for every small fragment to the central server.

In Zhao et al. (2010), a data-streaming algorithm solution, based on the ToW sketch, was proposed for the problem of detecting global icebergs. Its key idea is to compute the F_2 of the union of the data streams by exploiting the summability of the ToW sketch. The F_2 value is intuitively a good indicator of global iceberg existence/nonexistence because of its "squaring effect" that significantly magnifies the skewness of the data (if any). For example, a global iceberg item that is 100 times larger than a noniceberg item contributes $100^2 = 10\,000$ times more to the total F_2 value!

16.20 Conclusion

This chapter was written to convince the reader that measurement is an exciting field of endeavor. Many years ago, the advice to an ambitious youngster was, "Go West, young man" because the East was (supposedly) played out.

Similarly, it may be that protocol *design* is played out while protocol *measurement* is not. After all, TCP and IP have been cast in stone these many years; despite some confusion as to its parentage, the Internet could only be invented once. Reinventing the Internet is even harder if one follows the fate of the next-generation Internet proposal. But there will always be new ways to understand and measure the Internet, especially using techniques that depend on minimal cooperation.

The first part of the chapter focused on the problems of the most basic measurement issue at high speeds: packet counting. This is a real problem faced by every high-speed-router vendor because they deal, on the one hand, with increasing ISP demands for observability and, on the other hand, with hardware limitations. Algorithmics can help by clever uses of memories (**P5c**), by changing the specification to focus only on large counters or flow counts (**P3**), by unusual uses of sampling (**P3a**), and finally by determining real user needs to reduce the space of counters required by aggregation for accounting or traffic matrices (**P7**). Table 16.1 presents a summary of the techniques used in this chapter, together with the major principles involved.

The chapter concluded with an excursion into the field of passive measurement with an updated section that describes the remarkable progress of data streaming algorithms since the first edition of the book. Unlike all the other schemes described in this chapter, passive measurement schemes do not require implementation or protocol changes and hence are likely to continue to be a useful source of measurement data. Thus, it seems fitting to end this chapter with Savage's summary of the main idea behind Sting: "Stop thinking of a protocol as a protocol. Think of it as ... an opportunity."

16.21 **Exercises**

1. **Using DRAM-Backed up Counters:** This chapter described only the implementation of packet counting, not byte counting. Suggest extensions to byte counting.
2. **Finding the First Set Bit:** Using the techniques and assumptions stated in Chapter 2, find a fast parallel implementation of the find-first-bit-set operation for a large (say, of length 1 million) bit vector in the context of the counter-management algorithm described in the text.
3. **Conservative Update of Multistage Hash Counting:** In the multistage filter there is obvious waste (**P1**) in the way counters are incremented. Supposes a flow F, of size 2, hashes into three buckets whose counters are 15, 16, and 40. The naive method increases the counters to 17, 18, and 42. However, to avoid false negatives, it suffices to increase only the smallest counter to 17 and to ensure that all other counters are at least as large. Thus, with this more conservative update strategy (Estan and Varghese, 2002), the counters become 17, 17, and 40. Argue why this optimization does not cause false negatives and can only improve the false-positive rate.
4. **Trajectory Sampling:** Extend trajectory sampling to the case where different routers wish to have the flexibility to store a different number of packet labels because of different storage capabilities. Describe a mechanism that accommodates this and how this affects the potential uses for trajectory sampling.
5. **Passive Measurement and Denial of Service:** In SYN flooding attacks, an attack sends TCP SYN packets to a destination D it wishes to attack using a series of fictitious source addresses. When D replies to the (often) fictitious host, these packets are not replied to. Thus D accumulates a backlog of connections that are "half-open" and eventually refuses to accept new connections. Assume you are working at a university and you have an unused Class A address space. How might you use

this address space to infer denial-of-service attacks going on to various destinations on the Internet? Assume that attackers pick fake source addresses randomly from the 32-bit address space. More details for the curious reader can be found in Moore et al. (2001).

6. **Association Rule Mining Using Min-Hash:** Let R_1 be the min-hash value after every element in the multiset $\{A, B, A, C, D, K, A, B, L, G, A, L, H, B\}$ is processed. Let R_2 be the min-hash value after every element in the multiset $\{A, C, K, C, H, K, X, Y, Z\}$ has been processed. Here, we assume that a uniform hash function h with range $(0, 1)$ is used in obtaining both R_1 and R_2. Answer the following three questions.
   a. What is $E[R_1]$, the expectation of the random variable R_1?
   b. What is $E[R_2]$?
   c. What is $E[MIN\{R_1, R_2\}]$?
7. **Association Rule Mining:** Explain how to extend the min-hash-based solution for mining three-way associations (e.g., milk–cereal–banana).

Network security

17

Hacking is an exciting and sometimes scary phenomenon, depending on which side of the
battlements you happen to be standing.

—**Marcus J. Ranum**

From denial-of-service to Smurf attacks, hackers that perpetrate exploits have captured both the imagination of the public and the ire of victims. There is some reason for indignation and ire. A survey by the Computer Security Institute placed the cost of computer intrusions at an average of $970,000 per company in 2000.

Thus there is a growing market for *intrusion detection*, a field that consists of detecting and reacting to attacks. A 2020 report says that the Intrusion detection market is was USD 4.57 billion in 2020 and is forecasted to reach USD 9.04 billion by 2028 (Fior Markets, 2020). Further, the report says that roughly half this market is for network intrusion detection, the topic of this chapter.

Yet the capabilities of current intrusion detection systems are widely accepted as inadequate, particularly in the context of growing threats and capabilities. The first problem with some current systems are that they are slow; but the bigger problem is that they have a high false-positive rate. As a result of these deficiencies, intrusion detection serves primarily a monitoring and audit function rather than as a real-time component of a protection architecture on par with firewalls and encryption.

However, many vendors have introduced *real-time* intrusion detection systems. If intrusion detection systems can work in real time with only a small fraction of false positives, they can actually be used to *respond* to attacks by either deflecting the attack or tracing the perpetrators.

Intrusion detection systems (IDSs) have been studied in many forms since Denning's classic statistical analysis of host intrusions (Denning, 1987). Today, IDS techniques are usually classified as either *signature detection* or *anomaly detection*. Signature detection is based on matching events to the signatures of known attacks.

In contrast, anomaly detection, based on statistical or learning theory techniques, identifies aberrant events, whether known to be malicious or not. As a result, anomaly detection can potentially detect new types of attacks that signature-based systems will miss. Unfortunately, anomaly detection systems are prone to falsely identifying events as malicious. Thus this chapter does *not* address anomaly-based methods.

Meanwhile, signature-based systems are highly popular due to their relatively simple implementation and their ability to detect commonly used attack tools. The lightweight detection system Snort (Roesch, 1999) is one of the more popular examples because of its free availability and efficiency.

Network Algorithmics. https://doi.org/10.1016/B978-0-12-809927-8.00025-7

Given the growing importance of real-time intrusion detection, intrusion detection furnishes a rich source of packet patterns that can benefit from network algorithmics. Thus this chapter samples three important subtasks that arise in the context of intrusion detection. The first is an *analysis* subtask, string matching, which is a key bottleneck in popular signature-based systems such as Snort. The second is a *response* subtask, traceback, which is of growing importance given the ability of intruders to use forged source addresses. The third is an *analysis* subtask to detect the onset of a new worm (e.g., Code Red) without prior knowledge.

These three subtasks only scratch the surface of a vast area that needs to be explored. They were chosen to provide an indication of the richness of the problem space and to outline some potentially powerful tools, such as Bloom filters and Aho–Corasick trees, that may be useful in more general contexts. Worm detection was also chosen to showcase how mechanisms studied earlier in the book can be combined in powerful ways.

This chapter is organized as follows. The first few sections explore solutions to the important problem of searching for suspicious strings in packet payloads. Current implementations of intrusion detection systems such as Snort (www.snort.org) do multiple passes through the packet to search for each string. Section 17.1.1 describes the Aho–Corasick algorithm for searching for multiple strings in one pass using a trie with backpointers. Section 17.1.2 describes a generalization of the classical Boyer–Moore algorithm, which can sometimes act faster by skipping more bits in a packet.

Section 17.2 shows how to approach an even harder problem, searching for *approximate* string matches. The section introduces two powerful ideas: min-wise hashing and random projections. This section suggests that even complex tasks such as approximate string matching can plausibly be implemented at wire speeds.

Section 17.3 marks a transition to the problem of responding to an attack by introducing the IP traceback problem. It also presents a seminal solution using probabilistic packet marking. Section 17.4 offers a second solution, which uses packet logs and no packet modifications; the logs are implemented efficiently using an important technique called a *Bloom filter*. While these traceback solutions are unlikely to become deployed when compared to more recent standards, they introduce a significant problem and invoke important techniques that could be useful in other contexts.

Section 17.5 explains how algorithmic techniques can be used to extract automatically the strings used by intrusion detection systems such as Snort. In other words, instead of having these strings be installed manually by security analysts, could a system automatically extract the suspicious strings? We ground the discussion in the context of detecting worm attack payloads. Such techniques have since been known as automatic worm fingerprinting. Section 17.6 describes an early automatic worm fingerprinting system called EarlyBird and the network algorithmics techniques it uses to scale to high link and system speeds. Section 17.7 describes Carousel, a network algorithmics solution for another network security problem that looks deceptively simple but is in fact challenging when the solution has to scale to high link and system speeds.

The implementation techniques for security primitives described in this chapter (and the corresponding principles) are summarized in Table 17.1.

Quick reference guide

Sections 17.1.1 and 17.1.2 show how to speed up searching for *multiple* strings in packet payloads, a fundamental operation for a signature-based IDS. The Aho–Corasick algorithm of Section 17.1.1 can easily be implemented in hardware. While the traceback ideas in Section 17.4 are unlikely to be useful in the near future, the section introduces an important data structure, called a Bloom filter, for representing sets and also describes a hardware implementation. Bloom filters have found a variety of uses and should be part of the implementor's bag of tricks. Section 17.5 explains how signatures for attacks can be *automatically* computed (i.e., fingerprinted), reducing the delay and difficulty required to have humans generate signatures. Section 17.6 describes EarlyBird, an early system that learns worm fingerprints. Section 17.7 describes Carousel.

Table 17.1 Principles used in the implementation of the various security primitives discussed in this chapter.

Number	Principle	Used in
P15	Integrated string matching using Aho–Corasick	Snort
P3a, 5a	Approximate string match using min-wise hashing	Altavista
P3a	Path reconstruction using probabilistic marking	Edge sampling
P3a	Efficient packet logging via Bloom filters	SPIE
P7, P3a	Worm detection by detecting frequent content	EarlyBird
P12a	Compute incrementally	
P2a	Precompute $x^2, x^3, \ldots,$ and x^q	
P14	Use bitmap-based counting	

17.1 Searching for multiple strings in packet payloads

The first few sections tackle a problem of detecting an attack by searching for suspicious strings in payloads. A large number of attacks can be detected by their use of such strings. For example, packets that attempt to execute the Perl interpreter have *perl.exe* in their payload. For example, the arachNIDS database (Max Vision, 2001) of vulnerabilities contains the following description.

> An attempt was made to execute perl.exe. If the Perl interpreter is available to Web clients, it can be used to execute arbitrary commands on the Web server. This can be used to break into the server, obtain sensitive information, and potentially compromise the availability of the Web server and the machine it runs on. Many Web server administrators inadvertently place copies of the Perl interpreter into their Web server script directories. If perl is executable from the cgi directory, then an attacker can execute arbitrary commands on the Web server.

This observation has led to a commonly used technique to detect attacks in so-called signature-based intrusion detection systems such as Snort. The idea is that a router or monitor has a set of rules, much like the classifiers in Chapter 12. However, the Snort rules go beyond classifiers by allowing a 5-tuple rule specifying the type of packet (e.g., port number equal to Web traffic) *plus* an arbitrary string that can *appear anywhere in the packet payload.*

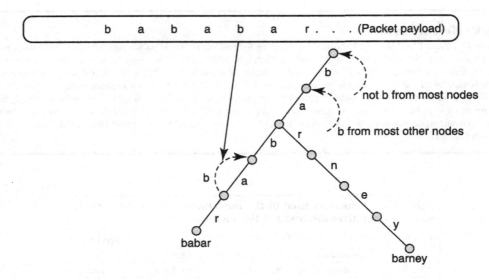

FIGURE 17.1

The Aho–Corasick algorithm builds an alphabetical trie on the set of strings to be searched for. A search for the string "barney" can be found by following the "b" pointer at the root, the "a" pointer at the next node, etc. More interestingly, the trie is augmented with failure pointers that prevent restarting at the top of the trie when failure occurs and a new attempt is made to match, shifting one position to the right.

Thus the Snort rule for the attempt to execute perl.exe will specify the protocol (TCP) and destination port (80 for Web) as well as the string "perl.exe" occurring anywhere in the payload. If a packet matches this rule, an alert is generated. Snort has 300 such augmented rules, with 300 possible strings to search for.

Early versions of Snort do string search by matching each packet against each Snort rule in turn. For each rule that matches in the classifier part, Snort runs a Boyer–Moore search on the corresponding string, potentially doing several string searches per packet. Since each scan through a packet is expensive, a natural question is: can one search for all possible strings in one pass through packet?

There are two algorithms that can be used for this purpose: the Aho–Corasick algorithm (Aho and Corasick, 1975) and a modified algorithm due to Commentz-Walter (1979), which we describe next.

17.1.1 Integrated string matching using Aho–Corasick

Chapter 11 used a trie to search for matching prefixes. Clearly, a trie can also be used to search for a string that starts at a known position in a packet. Thus Fig. 17.1 contains a trie built on the set of two strings "babar" and "barney"; both are well-known characters in children's literature. Unlike in Chapter 11, the trie is built on characters and not on arbitrary groups of bits. The characters in the text to be searched are used to follow pointers through the trie until a leaf string is found or until failure occurs.

The hard part, however, is looking for strings that can start anywhere in a packet payload. The naivest approach would be to assume the string starts at byte 1 of the payload and then traverse the trie. Then if a failure occurs, one could start again at the top of trie with the character that starts at byte 2.

However, if packet bytes form several "near misses" with target strings, then for each possible starting position, the search can traverse close to the height of the trie. Thus if the payload has L bytes and the trie has maximum height h, the algorithm can take $L \cdot h$ memory references.

For example, when searching for "babar" in the packet payload shown in Fig. 17.1, the algorithm jogs merrily down the trie until it reaches the node corresponding to the second "a" in "babar." At that point, the next packet byte is a "b" and not the "r" required to make progress in the trie. The naive approach would be to back up to the start of the trie and start the trie search again from the second byte "a" in the packet.

However, it is not hard to see that backing up to the top is obvious waste (**P1**) because the packet bytes examined so far in the search for "babab" have "bab" as a suffix, which is a prefix of "babar." Thus rather than back up to the top, one can precompute (much as in a grid of tries; see Chapter 12) a failure pointer corresponding to the failing "b" that allows the search to go directly to the node corresponding to path "bab" in the trie, as shown by the leftmost dotted arc in Fig. 17.1.

Thus rather than have the fifth byte (a "b") lead to a null pointer, as it would in a normal trie, it contains a failure pointer that points back up the trie. Search now proceeds directly from this node using the sixth byte "a" (as opposed to the second byte) and leads after seven bytes to "babar."

Search is easy to do in hardware after the trie is precomputed. This is not hard to believe because the trie with failure pointers essentially forms a state machine. The Aho–Corasick algorithm has some complexity that ensues when one of the search strings, R, is a suffix of another search string, S. However, in the security context this can be avoided by relaxing the specification (**P3**). One can remove string S from the trie and later check whether the packet matched R or S.

Another concern is the potentially large number of pointers (256) in the Aho–Corasick trie. This can make it difficult to fit a trie for a large set of strings in cache (in software) or in SRAM (in hardware). One alternative is to use, say, Lulea-style encoding (Chapter 11) to compress the trie nodes.

17.1.2 Integrated string matching using Boyer–Moore

The exercises at the end of Chapter 3 suggest that the famous Boyer–Moore (Boyer and Moore, 1977) algorithm for *single*-string matching can be derived by realizing that there is an interesting degree of freedom that can be exploited (**P13**) in string matching: one can equally well start comparing the text and the target string from the last character as from the first.

Thus in Fig. 17.2 the search starts with the fifth character of the packet, a "b," and matches it to the fifth character of, say, "babar" (shown below the packet), an "r." When this fails, one of the heuristics in the Boyer–Moore algorithm is to shift the search template of "babar" two characters to the right to match the rightmost occurrence of "b" in the template.[1] Boyer–Moore's claim to fame is that in practice it skips over a large number of characters, unlike, say, the Aho–Corasick algorithm.

To generalize Boyer–Moore to multiple strings, imagine that the algorithm concurrently compares the fifth character in the packet to the fifth character, "e," in the other string, "barney" (shown above

---

[1] There is a second heuristic in Boyer–Moore (Cormen et al., 1990), but studies have shown that this simple Horspool variation works best in practice.

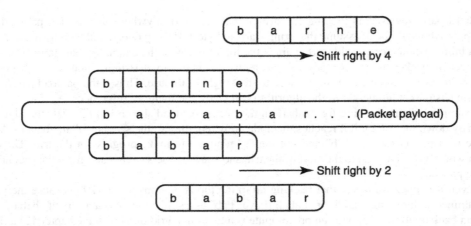

FIGURE 17.2

Integrated Boyer–Moore by shifting a character.

the packet). If one were only doing Boyer–Moore with "barney," the "barney" search template would be shifted right by four characters to match the only "b" in barney.

When doing a search for both "barney" and "babar" concurrently, the obvious idea is to shift the search template by the smallest shift proposed by any string being compared for. Thus in this example we shift the template by two characters and do a comparison next with the seventh character in the packet.

Doing a concurrent comparison with the last character in all the search strings may seem inefficient. This can be taken care of as follows. First, chop off all characters in all search strings beyond L, the shortest search string. Thus in Fig. 17.2 L is 5 and "barney" is chopped down to "barne" to align in length with "babar."

Having aligned all search string fragments to the same length, now build a trie starting *backward* from the last character in the chopped strings. Thus in the example of Fig. 17.2 the root node of the trie would have an "e" pointer pointing toward "barne" and an "r" pointer pointing towards "babar." Thus comparing concurrently requires using only the current packet character to index into the trie node.

On success, the backward trie keeps being traversed. On failure, the amount to be shifted is precomputed in the failure pointer. Finally, even if a backward search through the trie navigates successfully to a leaf, the fact that the ends may have been chopped off requires an epilogue, in terms of checking that the chopped-off characters also match. For reasonably small sets of strings, this method does better than Aho–Corasick.

The generalized Boyer–Moore was proposed by Commentz-Walter (1979). The application to intrusion detection was proposed concurrently by Coit et al. (2001) and Fisk and Varghese (2001). The Fisk implementation (Fisk and Varghese, 2001) was ported to Snort at one stage.

Unfortunately, the performance improvement of using either Aho–Corasick or the integrated Boyer–Moore is minimal because many real traces (Coit et al., 2001; Fisk and Varghese, 2001) have only a few packets that match a large number of strings, enabling the naive method to do well. In fact, the new

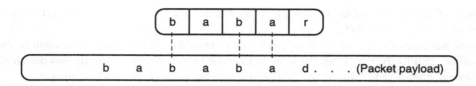

FIGURE 17.3

Checking for matching with a random projection of the target string "babar" allows the detecting of similar strings with substitution errors in the payload.

algorithms add somewhat more overhead due to slightly increased code complexity, which can exhibit cache effects, as shown in Chapter 3.

While the code as it currently stands needs further improvement, it is clear that at least the Aho–Corasick version does produce a large improvement for *worst-case* traces, which may be crucial for a hardware implementation. The use of Aho–Corasick and integrated Boyer–Moore can be considered straightforward applications of efficient data structures (**P15**).

17.2 Approximate string matching

This section briefly considers an even harder problem, that of approximately detecting strings in payloads. Thus instead of settling for an exact match or a prefix match, the specification now allows a few errors in the match. For example, with one insertion, "p-erl.exe" should match "perl.exe," where the intruder may have added a character.

While the security implications of using the mechanisms described next need much more thought, the mechanisms themselves are powerful and should be part of the arsenal of designers of detection mechanisms.

The first simple idea can handle substitution errors. A *substitution error* is a replacement of one or more characters with others. For example, "parl.exe" can be obtained from "perl.exe" by substituting "a" for "e." One way to handle this is to search not for the complete string but for one or more random projections of the original string.

For example, in Fig. 17.3 instead of searching for "babar" one could search for the first, third, and fourth characters in "babar." Thus the misspelled string "babad" will still be found. Of course, this particular projection will not find a misspelled string such as "rabad." To make it hard for an adversary, the scheme in general can use a small set of such random projections. This simple idea is generalized greatly in a set of papers on *locality-sensitive hashing* (e.g., Indyk et al., 1997).

Interestingly, the use of random projections may make it hard to efficiently shift one character to the right. One alternative is to replace the random projections with deterministic projections. For example, if one replaces every string by its two halves and places each half in an Aho–Corasick trie, then any one substitution error will be caught without slowing down the Aho–Corasick processing. However, the final efficiency will depend on the number of false alarms.

The simplest random projection idea, described earlier, does not work with insertions or deletions that can displace every character one or more steps to the left or right. One simple and powerful way of detecting whether two or more sets of characters, say, "abcef" and "abfecd," are similar is by computing their *resemblance* (Broder, 1998).

The resemblance of two sets of characters is the ratio of the size of their intersection to the size of their union. Intuitively, the higher the resemblance, the higher the similarity. By this definition, the resemblance of "abcef" and "abfecd" is 5/6 because they have five characters in common.

Unfortunately, resemblance per se does not take into account order, so "abcef" completely resembles "fecab." One way to fix this is to rewrite the sets with order numbers attached so that "abcef" becomes "1a2b3c4e5f" while "fecab" now becomes "1f2e3c4a5b." The resemblance, using pairs of characters as set elements instead of characters, is now nil. Another method that captures order in a more relaxed manner is to use shingles (Broder, 1998) by forming the two sets to be compared using as elements all possible substrings of size k of the two sets.

Resemblance is a nice idea, but it also needs a fast implementation. A naive implementation requires sorting both sets, which is expensive and takes large storage. Broder's idea (Broder, 1998) is to quickly compare the two sets by computing a random (**P3a**, trade certainty for time) permutation on two sets. For example, the most practical permutation function on integers of size at most $m - 1$ is to compute $P(X) = ax + b \bmod m$, for random values of a and b and prime values of the modulus m.

For example, consider the two sets of integers $\{1, 3, 5\}$ and $\{1, 7, 3\}$. Using the random permutation $\{3 \text{ x} + 5 \bmod 11\}$, the two sets become permuted to $\{8, 3, 9\}$ and $\{8, 4, 3\}$. Notice that the minimum values of the two randomly permuted sets (i.e., 3) are the same.

Intuitively, it is easy to see that the higher the resemblance of the two sets, the higher the chance that a random permutation of the two sets will have the same minimum. Formally, this is because the two permuted sets will have the same minimum if and only if they contain the same element that gets mapped to the minimum in the permuted set. Since an ideal random permutation makes it equally likely for any element to be the minimum after permutation, the more elements the two sets have in common, the higher the probability that the two minimums match.

More precisely, the probability that two minimums match is equal to the resemblance. Thus one way to compute the resemblance of two sets is to use some number of random permutations (say, 16) and compute all 16 random permutations of the two sets. The fraction of these 16 permutations in which the two minimums match is a good estimate of the resemblance.

This idea was used by Broder (1998) to detect the similarity of Web documents. However, it is also quite feasible to implement at high link speeds. The chip must maintain, say, 16 registers to keep the current minimum using each of the 16 random hash functions. When a new character is read, the logic permutes the new character according to each of the 16 functions in parallel. Each of the 16 hash results is compared in parallel with the corresponding register, and the register value is replaced if the new value is smaller.

At the end, the 16 computed minima are compared in parallel against the 16 minima for the target set to compute a bitmap, where a bit is set for positions in which there is equality. Finally, the number of set bits is counted and divided by the size of the bitmap by shifting left by 4 bits. If the resemblance is over some specified threshold, some further processing is done.

Once again, the moral of this section is not that computing the resemblance is the solution to all problems (or in fact to any specific problem at this moment) but that fairly complex functions can be computed in hardware using multiple hash functions, randomization, and parallelism. Such solutions exhibit the interplay of Principles **P5** (use parallel memories) and Principle **P3a** (use randomization).

17.3 IP traceback via probabilistic marking

This section transitions from the problem of *detecting* an attack to *responding* to an attack. Response could involve a variety of tasks, from determining the source of the attack to stopping the attack by adding some checks at incoming routers.

The next two sections concentrate on *traceback*, an important aspect of response, given the ability of attackers to use forged IP source addresses. To understand the traceback problem it helps first to understand a canonical denial-of-service (DOS) attack that motivates the problem.

In one version of a DOS attack, called *SYN flooding*, Wily Harry Hacker wakes up one morning looking for fun and games and decides to attack CNN. To do so, he makes his computer fire off a large number of TCP connection requests to the CNN server, each with a different forged source address. The CNN server sends back a response to each request R and places R in a pending connection queue.

Assuming the source addresses do not exist or are not online, there is no response. This effect can be ensured by using random source addresses and by periodically resending connection requests. Eventually the server's pending-connection queue fills up. This denies service to innocent users like you who wish to read CNN news because the server can no longer accept connection requests.

Assume that each such DOS attack has a traffic signature (e.g., too many TCP connection requests) that can be used to detect the onset of an attack. Given that it is difficult to shut off a public server, one way to respond to this attack is to trace such a DOS back to the originating source point despite the use of fake source addresses. This is the IP traceback problem.

The first and simplest systems approach (**P3**, relax system requirements) is to finesse the problem completely using help from routers. Observe that when Harry Hacker sitting in an IP subnetwork with prefix S sends a packet with fake source address H, the first router on the path can detect this fact if H does not match S. This would imply that Harry's packet cannot disguise its subnetworks, and offending packets can be traced at least to the right subnetwork.

There are two difficulties with this approach. First, it requires that edge routers do more processing with the source address. Second, it requires trusting edge routers to do this processing, which may be difficult to ensure if Harry Hacker has already compromised his ISP. There is little incentive for a local ISP to slow down performance with extra checks to prevent DOS attacks to a remote ISP.

A second and cruder systems approach is to have managers that detect an attack call their ISP, say, A. ISP A monitors traffic for a while and realizes these packets are coming from prior-hop ISP B, who is then called. B then traces the packets back to the prior-hop provider and so on until the path is traced. This is the solution used currently.

A better solution than *manual* tracing would be *automatic* tracing of the packet back to the source. Assume one can modify routers for now. Then packet tracing can be trivially achieved by having each router in the path of a packet P write its router IP address in sequence into P's header. However, given common route lengths of 10, this would be a large overhead (40 bytes for 10 router IDs), especially for minimum-size acknowledgments. Besides the overhead, there is the problem of modifying IP headers to add fields for path tracing. It may be easier to steal a small number of unused message bits.

This leads to the following problem. Assuming router modifications are possible, find a way to trace the path of an attack by marking as few bits as possible in a packet's header.

For a single-packet attack, this is very difficult in an information theoretic sense. Clearly, it is impossible to construct a path of 10 32-bit router IDs from, say, a 2-byte mark in a packet. One can't make a silk purse from a sow's ear.

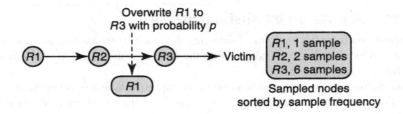

FIGURE 17.4

Reconstructing an attack path by having each router stamp its ID independently, with probability p, into a single node ID field. The receiver reconstructs order by sorting, assuming that closer routers will produce more samples.

However, in the systems context one can optimize the expected case (**P11**), since most interesting attacks consist of hundreds of packets at least. Assuming they are all coming from the same physical source, the victim can shift the path computation over time (**P2**) by making each mark contribute a piece of the path information.

Let's start by assuming a single 32-bit field in a packet that can hold a single router ID. How are the routers on the path to synchronize access the field so that each router ID gets a chance, over a stream of packets, to place its ID in the field?

A naive solution is shown in Fig. 17.4. The basic idea is that each router independently writes its ID into a *single* node ID field in the packet with probability p, possibly overwriting a previous router's ID. Thus in Fig. 17.4 the packet already has $R1$ in it and can be overwritten by $R3$ to $R1$ with probability p.

The hope, however, is that over a large sequence of packets from the attacker to the victim, every router ID in the path will get chance to place its ID without being overwritten. Finally, the victim can sort the received IDs by the number of samples. Intuitively, the nodes closer to the victim should have more samples, but one has to allow for random variation.

The two problems with this naive approach are that too many samples (i.e., attack packets) are needed to deal with random variation in inferring order. Also, the attacker, knowing this scheme, can place malicious marks in the packet to fool the reconstruction scheme into believing that fictitious nodes are close to the victim because they receive extra marks.

To foil this threat, p must be large, say, 0.51. But in this case the number of packets required to receive the router IDs far away from the victim becomes very large. For example, with $p = 0.5$ and a path of length $L = 15$, the number of packets required is the reciprocal of the probability that the router furthest from the victim sends a mark that survives. This is $p(1 - p)^{L-1} = 2^{-15}$, because it requires the furthest router to put a mark and the remaining $L - 1$ routers not to. Thus the average number of packets for this to happen is $\frac{1}{2^{-15}} = 32\,000$. Attacks have a number of packets, but not necessarily this many.

The straightforward lesson from the naive solution is that randomization is good for synchronization (to allow routers to independently synchronize access to the single node ID field) but not to reconstruct order. The simplest solution to this problem is to use a hop count (the attacker can initialize each packet with a different TTL (time-to-live), making the TTL hard to use) as well as a node ID. But a hop count by itself can be confusing if there are multiple attacks going on. Clearly a mark of node X with hop count 2 may correspond to a different attack path from a mark of node Y with hop count 1.

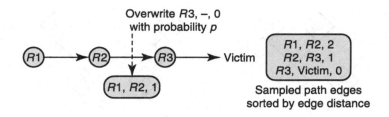

FIGURE 17.5

Edge sampling improves on node sampling by sampling edges and not nodes. This allows trivial order reconstruction based on edge distance and not sample frequency.

The solution provided in the seminal paper (Savage et al., 2000) avoids the aliasing due to hop counts by conceptually starting with a pair of consecutive node IDs and a hop count to form a triple (R, S, h), as shown in Fig. 17.5.

When a router R receives a packet with triple (X, Y, h), R generates a random number between 0 and 1. If the number is less than the sampling probability p, router R writes its own ID into the mark triple, rewriting it as $(R, -, 0)$, where the "$-$" character indicates that the next router in the path has still to be determined. If the random number is greater than p, then R must maintain the integrity of the previously written mark. If $h = 0$, R writes R to the second field because R is the next router after the writer of the mark. Finally, if the random number is greater than p, R increments h.

It should be clear that by assuming that every edge gets sampled once, the victim can reconstruct the path. Note also that the attacker can only add fictitious nodes to the start of the path. But how many packets are required to find all edges? Given that ordering is explicit, one can use arbitrary values of p.

In particular, if p is approximately $1/L$, where L is the path length to the furthest router, the probability we computed before of the furthest router sending an edge mark that survives becomes $p(1-p)^{L-1} \approx p/(1-p)e$, where e is the base of natural logarithms. For example, for $p = 1/25$, this is roughly $1/70$, which is fairly large compared to the earlier attempt.

What is even nicer is that if we choose $p = 1/50$ based on the largest path lengths encountered in practice on the Internet (say, 50), the probability does not grow much smaller, even for much smaller path lengths. This makes it easy to reconstruct the path with hundreds of packets as opposed to thousands.

Finally, one can get rid of obvious waste (**P1**) and avoid the need for two node IDs by storing only the Exclusive-OR of the two fields in a single field. Working backward from the last router ID known to the victim, one can Exclusive-OR with the previous edge mark to get the next router in the path, and so on. Finally, by viewing each node as consisting of a sequence of a number of "pseudonodes," each with a small fragment (say, 8 bits) of the node's ID, one can reduce the mark length to around 16 bits total.

17.4 IP traceback via logging

A problem with the edge-sampling approach of the previous section is that it requires changes to the IP header to update marks and does not work for single-packet attacks like the Teardrop attack. The

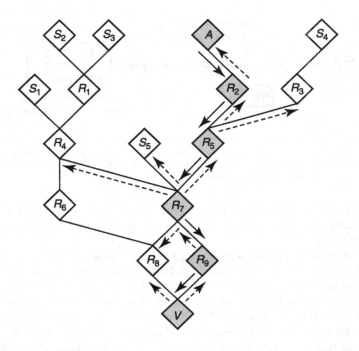

FIGURE 17.6

Using a packet log to trace an attack packet P backward from the victim V to the attacker A by having the currently traced node ask all its neighbors (the dotted lines) if they have seen P (solid line).

following approach, traceback via logging (Snoeren et al., 2001), avoids both problems by adding more storage at routers to maintain a compressed packet log.

As motivations, neither of the difficulties the logging approach gets around is very compelling. This is because the logging approach still requires modifying router forwarding, even though it requires no header modification. This is due to the difficulty of convincing vendors (who have already committed forwarding paths to silicon) and ISPs (who wish to preserve equipment for, say, 5 years) to make changes. Similarly, single-packet attacks are not very common and can often be filtered directly by routers.

However, the idea of maintaining compressed searchable packet logs may be useful as a general building block. It could be used, more generally, for, say, a network monitor that wishes to maintain such logs for forensics after attacks. But even more importantly, it introduces an important technique called *Bloom filters*.

Given an efficient packet log at each router, the high-level idea for traceback is shown in Fig. 17.6. The victim V first detects an attack packet P; it then queries all its neighboring routers, say, R_8 and R_9, to see whether any of them have P in their log of recently sent packets. When R_9 replies in the affirmative, the search moves on to R_9, who asks its sole neighbor, R_7. Then R_7 asks its neighbors R_5 and R_4, and the search moves backward to A.

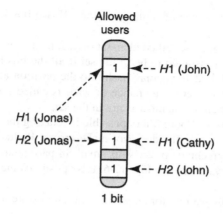

Allowed
users

Is Jonas an allowed user?

FIGURE 17.7

A Bloom filter represents a set element by setting k bits in a bitmap using k independent hash functions applied to the element. Thus the element John sets the second (using $H1$) and next-to-last (using $H2$) bits. When searching for Jonas, Jonas is considered a member of the set only if all bit positions hashed to by Jonas have set bits.

The simplest way to implement a log is to reuse one of the techniques in trajectory sampling (Chapter 16). Instead of logging a packet, we log a 32-bit hash of invariant content (i.e., exclude fields that change from hop to hop, such as the TTL) of the packet. However, 32 bits per packet for all the packets sent in the last 10 minutes is still huge at 10 Gbps. Bloom filters, described next, allow a large reduction to around 5 bits per packet.

17.4.1 Bloom filters

Start by observing that querying either a packet log or a table of allowed users is a *set membership query*, which is easily implemented by a hash table. For example, in a different security context, if John and Cathy are allowed users and we wish to check if Jonas is an allowed user, we can use a hash table that stores John and Cathy's IDs but not Jonas.

Checking for Jonas requires hashing Jonas's ID into the hash table and following any lists at that entry. To handle collisions, each hash table entry must contain a list of IDs of all users that hash into that bucket. This requires at least W bits per allowed user, where W is the length of each user ID. In general, to implement a hash table for a set of identifiers requires at least W bits per identifier, where W is the length of the smallest identifier.

Bloom filters (Bloom, 1970), shown in Fig. 17.7, allow one to reduce the amount of memory for set membership to a few bits per set element. The idea is to keep a bitmap of size, say, $5N$, where N is the number of set elements. Before elements are inserted, all bits in the bitmap are cleared.

For each element in the set, its ID is hashed using k independent hash functions (two in Fig. 17.7, $H1$ and $H2$) to determine bit positions in the bitmap to set. Thus in the case of a set of valid users in Fig. 17.7 ID John hashes into the second and next-to-last bit positions. ID Cathy hashes into one position in the middle and also into one of John's positions. If two IDs hash to the same position, the bit remains set.

Finally, when searching to see if a specified element (say, Jonas) is in the set, Jonas is hashed using all the *k* hash functions. Jonas is assumed to be in the set if all the bits hashed into by Jonas are set. Of course, there is some chance that Jonas may hash into the position already set by, say, Cathy and one by John (see Fig. 17.7). Thus there is a chance of what is called a *false positive*: answering the membership query positively when the member is not in the set.

Notice that the trick that makes Bloom filters possible is relaxing the specification (**P3**). A normal hash table, which requires *W* bits per ID, does not make errors! Reducing to 5 bits per ID requires allowing errors; however, the percentage of errors is small. In particular, if there is an attack tree and set elements are hashed packet values, as in Fig. 17.6, false positives mean only occasionally barking up the wrong tree branch(es).

More precisely, the false-positive rate for an *m*-size bitmap to store *n* members using *k* hash functions is

$$\left(1 - (1 - 1/m)^{kn}\right)^k \approx \left(1 - e^{-kn/m}\right)^k$$

The equation is not as complicated as it may appear: $(1 - 1/m)^{kn}$ is the probability that any bit is *not* set, given *n* elements that each hashes *k* times to any of *m* bit positions. Finally, to get a false positive, all of the *k* bit positions hashed onto by the ID that causes a false positive must be set.

Using this equation, it is easy to see that for $k = 3$ (three independent hash functions) and 5 bits per member ($m/n = 5$), the false-positive rate is roughly 1%. The false-positive rate can be improved up to a point by using more hash functions and by increasing the bitmap size.

17.4.2 Bloom filter implementation of packet logging

The Bloom filter implementation of packet logging in the SPIE system is shown in Fig. 17.8 (the picture is courtesy of Sanchez et al. (2001)). Each line card calculates a 32-bit hash digest of the packet and places it in a FIFO queue. To save costs, several line cards share, via a RAM multiplexer, a fast SRAM containing the Bloom filter bitmap.

As in the case of counters in Chapter 16, one can combine the best features of SRAM and DRAM to reduce expense. One needs to use SRAM for fast front-end *random access* to the bitmap. Unfortunately, the expense of SRAM would allow storing only a small number of packets. To allow a larger amount, the Bloom filter bitmaps in SRAM are periodically read out to a large DRAM ring buffer. Because these are no longer random writes to bits, the write to DRAM can be written in DRAM pages or rows, which provide sufficient memory bandwidth.

17.4.3 Scale to higher link speeds

When the link speeds continue to grow faster, a router cannot even afford to record a full Bloom filter for every packet. It can however afford to record either a full Bloom filter for a small percentage of packets or a "tiny fraction" of a Bloom filter for every packet. For example, when the SRAM budget is only 0.4 bits (hash functions) per packet and each full Bloom filter is 12 bits (hash functions), a router can record a full Bloom filter for only 3.3% of the packets. In this case the traceback by logging scheme described above would not work. For example, if two neighboring routers along an attack path sample

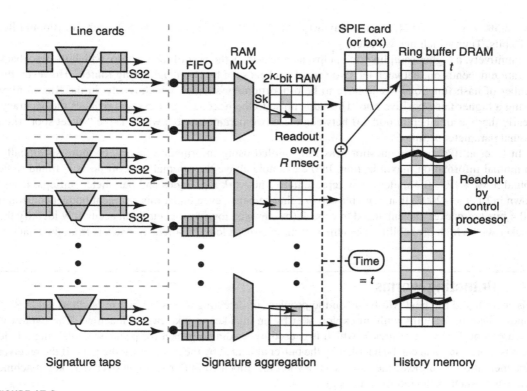

FIGURE 17.8

Hardware implementation of packet logging using Bloom filters. Note the use of two-level memory: SRAM for random read-modify-writes and DRAM for large row writes.

packets independently uniformly at random each at such a low sampling rate, an attack packet seen by one router is likely not seen by the other, making it hard to trace back even this single step.

In Li et al. (2004) two significant enhancements are made to this scheme to make it perform well in this more challenging environment. The first enhancement is a correlated sampling scheme called One-Bit Random Marking and Sampling (ORMS), which is similar to that in trajectory sampling in spirit but is more sophisticated to make it adversary-proof (necessary for this security application). This idea can improve the correlation factor between the two sets of packets sampled (for Bloom filter logging) at two neighboring routers to over 50%; in contrast, independent uniform random sampling by the two neighboring routers would result in a correlation factor of only 3.3% in the example above. Intuitively, a higher correlation factor between packets sampled by two neighboring routers makes it easier to trace back to an attacker.

The second enhancement is to fully develop the optimization theory concerning the optimal tradeoff point between the sampling rate and the "size" of each full Bloom filter. Again suppose the budget is 0.4 bits per packet, as in the example above. For example, since $5\% \times 8 = 0.4$, one possible way to use this budget is to sample 5% of the packets and let each full Bloom filter be 8 bits (hash functions); but since $2.5\% \times 16$ is also 0.4, another way is to sample 2.5% of the packets, and let each full Bloom filter be 16 bits. Then which one is better?

Intuitively, a higher sampling rate helps, as it increases the size of the overlap, which the traceback operation depends on, between the two sets of packets seen by two neighboring routers. However, the number of hash functions would have to be proportionally smaller, which results in the Bloom filter having a higher false-positive rate. This adds noise to the traceback process and reduces the accuracy. Clearly there is an inherent tradeoff between these two parameters, but where is the "sweet spot" (i.e., optimal parameter setting)?

In Li et al. (2004) this question was fully settled using information theory, or more specifically, via mutual information maximization. In the example above the optimal tradeoff point is found to be around $3.3\% * 12 = 0.4$ under a few representative network topologies and parameter settings. It was shown in Li et al. (2004) that, with these two enhancements, even under this stringent budget constraint of 0.4 bits per packet, the enhanced traceback (by sampled logging) scheme can accurately identify the attacker with a high probability when the victim receives at least hundreds of packets from the attacker.

17.5 Detecting worms

This section and the next two focus on the problem of detecting worms. A worm (such as Code Red, Nimda, Slammer) begins with an exploit sent by an attacker to take over a machine. The exploit is typically a buffer overflow attack, which is caused by sending a packet (or packets) containing a field that has more data than can be handled by the buffer allocated by the receiver for the field. If the receiver implementation is careless, the extra data beyond the allocated buffer size can overwrite key machine parameters, such as the return address on the stack.

Thus with some effort, a buffer overflow can allow the attacking machine to run code on the attacked machine. The new code then picks several random IP addresses[2] and sends similar packets to these new victims. Even if only a small fraction of IP addresses respond to these attacks, the worm spreads rapidly.

Current worm detection technology is both *retroactive* (i.e., only after a new worm is first detected and analyzed by a human, a process that can take days, can the containment process be initiated) and *manual* (i.e., requires human intervention to identify the signature of a new worm). Such technology is exemplified by Code Red and Slammer, which took days of human effort to identify, following which containment strategies were applied in the form of turning off ports, applying patches, and doing signature-based filtering in routers and intrusion detection systems.

There are difficulties with these current technologies.

1. *Slow Response:* There is a proverb that talks about locking the stable door after the horse has escaped. Current technologies fit this paradigm because, by the time the worm containment strategies are initiated, the worm has already infected much of the network.
2. *Constant Effort:* Every new worm requires a major amount of human work to identify, post advisories, and finally take action to contain the worm. Unfortunately, all evidence seems to indicate that

---

[2] By contrast, a *virus* requires user intervention, such as opening an attachment, to take over the user machine. Viruses also typically spread by using known addresses, such as those in the mail address book, rather than random probing.

there is no shortage of new exploits. And worse, simple binary rewriting and other modifications of existing attacks can get around simple signature-based blocking (as in Snort).

Thus there is a pressing need for a new worm detection and containment strategy that is real time (and hence can contain the worm before it can infect a significant fraction of the network) and is able to deal with new worms with a minimum of human intervention (some human intervention is probably unavoidable to at least catalog detected worms, do forensics, and fine-tune automatic mechanisms). In particular, the detection system should be *content agnostic*. The detection system should not rely on external, manually supplied input of worm signatures. Instead, the system should *automatically* extract worm signatures, even for new worms that may arise in the future.

Can network algorithmics speak to this problem? We believe it can. First, we observe that the only way to detect new worms and old worms with the same mechanism is to abstract the basic properties of worms.

As a first approximation, define a worm to have the following abstract features, which are indeed discernible in all the worms we know, even ones with such varying features as Code Red (massive payload, uses TCP, and attacks on the well-known HTTP port) and MS SQL Slammer (minimal payload, uses UDP, and attacks on the lesser-known MS SQL port).

1. *Large Volume of Identical Traffic:* These worms have the property that at least at an intermediate stage (after an initial priming period but before full infection), the volume of traffic (aggregated across all sources and destinations) carrying the worm is a significant fraction of the network bandwidth.
2. *Rising Infection Levels:* The number of infected sources participating in the attack steadily increases.
3. *Random Probing:* An infected source spreads infection by attempting to communicate to random IP addresses at a fixed port to probe for vulnerable services.

Note that detecting all three of these features may be crucial to avoid false positives. For example, a popular mailing list or a flash crowd could have the first feature but not the third.

An algorithmics approach for worm detection would naturally lead to the following detection strategy, which automatically detects each of these abstract features with low memory and small amounts of processing, works with asymmetric flows, and does not use active probing. The high-level mechanisms[3] are:

1. *Identify Large Flows in Real Time with Small Amounts of Memory:* In Section 16.7 we showed how to describe mechanisms to identify flows with large traffic volumes for any definition of a flow (e.g., sources, destinations). A simple twist on this definition is to realize that the content of a packet (or, more efficiently, a hash of the content) can be a valid flow identifier, which by prior work can identify in real time (and with low memory) a high volume of repeated content. An even more specific idea (which distinguishes worms from valid traffic such as peer-to-peer) is to compute a hash based on the content as well as the destination port (which remains invariant for a worm).
2. *Count the Number of Sources:* In Section 16.8 we described mechanisms using simple bitmaps of small size to estimate the number of sources on a link using small amounts of memory and

---

[3] Each of these mechanisms needs to be modulated to handle some special cases, but we prefer to present the main idea untarnished with extraneous details.

processing. These mechanisms can easily be used to count sources corresponding to high traffic volumes identified by the previous mechanism.

3. *Determine Random Probing by Counting the Number of Connection Attempts to Unused Portions of the IP Address:* One could keep a simple compact representation of portions of the IP address space known to be unused. One example is the so-called Bogon list, which lists unused 8-bit prefixes (can be stored as a bitmap of size 256). A second example is a secret space of IP addresses (can be stored as a single prefix) known to an ISP to be unused. A third is a set of unused 32-bit addresses (can be stored as a Bloom filter).

Of course, worm authors could defeat this detection scheme by violating any of these assumptions. For example, a worm author could defeat Assumption 1 by using a very slow infection rate and by mutating content frequently. Assumption 3 could be defeated using addresses known to be used. For each such attack, there are possible countermeasures. More importantly, before the advent of polymorphic worms (defined next), the scheme described was able to detect at least all existing worms we knew of, though they differed greatly in their semantics. In initial experiments at UCSD that led to the EarlyBird system (Singh et al., 2004b), to be described in the next section, we also found very few false positives where the detection mechanisms complained about innocuous traffic.

17.6 EarlyBird system for worm detection

EarlyBird (Singh et al., 2004b) is one of the earliest systems for detecting new worms, whose signatures have never been learned or analyzed, with no or minimum human intervention. A key innovation of EarlyBird is a fingerprinting technique that is among the earliest for the automated extraction of two aforementioned features of a new worm: *large volume of identical traffic* and *large number of sources (IP addresses) sending identical traffic*. More specifically, EarlyBird offers a highly scalable solution to the problem of detecting common substrings in application-layer messages sent by many different source IP addresses. Such a common substring can be a worm suspect, if it appears in a large number of application (layer) messages sent from a large number of sources. Since an application message is often divided into multiple packets for network transmission, we call it an object instead in the rest of this section to distinguish it from a packet.

To motivate the EarlyBird solution, we highlight three major challenges in detecting and fingerprinting a common substring in objects, and describe why simple ideas do not work. The first challenge is that the content of such a common substring is not known in advance and is itself to be learned. As a result, this problem cannot be simply modeled and solved as the aforementioned string matching problem (see Section 17.2), since here we do not have a target string to search for.

The second challenge lies in the fact that, even if we knew the exact target substring, the aforementioned string matching solutions still would not apply. This is because an object containing the substring to be searched for can be packetized into multiple packets and it is usually not certain at which byte position the substring is cut (into packets) for two reasons. First, the typical length of a payload-containing packet varies across different operating systems. Second, since the application-layer header of an object (e.g., SMTP header in an email) can vary in length, the location (relative offset from the first byte of the packet payload) at which the substring appears in an object may vary from one object to another.

The third challenge lies in the fact that a proposed solution has to scan the content of every packet, byte by byte, at the full rate of a high-speed link, for such common substrings. Hence any viable solution has to be simple and take only one quick pass over each packet.

EarlyBird meets all three challenges by combining a few separate ideas. We now "build" the Early-Bird solution up one idea at a time. The design of EarlyBird is based on a key observation that if an n-byte-long worm string $s_1 s_2 \cdots s_n$ appears frequently in network objects, then most of its q-byte-long substrings (called q-grams in the database literature) $s_1 s_2 \cdots s_q$, $s_2 s_3 \cdots s_{q+1}$, $\cdots$, $s_{n-q+1} s_{n-q+2} \cdots s_n$ should also, as long as $q > 0$ is much smaller than the typical length of a payload-containing packet. This is because each packetizing cut of an object into packets will break at most $q - 1$ such q-grams (into two pieces).

Based on this observation, the first idea is to search for one or more q-grams that appear frequently in different packets. Again suppose the content of a packet is $b_1 b_2 \cdots b_n$. The idea is to somehow record the fact that we have seen each of its $n - q + 1$ q-grams once. However, the naive solution of maintaining a hash table of all q-grams seen and their respective counts is not viable, since each such packet can lead to $n - q + 1$ different hash nodes being added to the hash table.

Fortunately, the problem we have at hand is much simpler in two ways. First, here we care only about those q-grams that occur frequently. Hence it boils down to an elephant (heavy hitter) detection problem, for which we have many scalable solutions, including those described in Sections 16.7 and 16.17. Among them, the multistage filter scheme described in Section 16.7 is used as the elephant detection technique in EarlyBird. Here we have applied the principle of avoiding unnecessary generality (**P7**).

Second, we are in general not interested in the exact (byte-by-byte) value of a (frequently occurring) q-gram. Hence, we can hash each q-gram into a fixed-length integer value, which we call a fingerprint, for easier processing. Here, we have applied the principle of trading certainty for time (**P3a**).

We now describe how a multistage filter is used in EarlyBird for detecting frequently occurring q-grams. Recall that a multistage filter, shown in Fig. 16.8, employs $k > 1$ different hash functions and consists of k equal-sized array of counters. The update procedure, or how the multistage filter "records" seeing a q-gram $s_1 s_2 \cdots s_q$ is straightforward: this q-gram is mapped by the k hash functions to k aforementioned fingerprints; each fingerprint is considered an index into the corresponding array of counters and each corresponding counter is incremented by 1.

The (elephant) detection procedure is also straightforward: when incrementing the k counters that correspond to a q-gram, if the algorithm finds that all counter values are larger than a certain threshold, then the packet containing the q-gram is logged for further inspection.

Two challenges remain to be addressed for this elephant detection approach to work in a high-speed network environment. The first challenge is that, since a worm string can be thousands of bytes long, thousands of its q-grams would have to be recorded in the multistage filter and marked as elephants. This would significantly increase the number of counters in each array for the multistage filter to accurately detect elephants (say to have a low false-positive rate). This would make the multistage filter very costly, which, as explained earlier, is typically stored in SRAM. This is also unnecessary and wasteful since, to detect a worm, it suffices to record just one such q-gram.

To address this challenge, EarlyBird samples over the signature space. The idea is to sample each fingerprint value with a small probability. For example, in an implementation of EarlyBird described in Singh et al. (2004b), only fingerprints that end with six 0's are sampled, resulting in a sampling rate of 1/64. With the 1/64 sampling, a TCP packet that contains an application-layer payload (i.e., not a data-less acknowledgment) and is typically hundreds of bytes long still has a high probability of being flagged (for further inspection) at least once, yet the resource consumption is reduced by roughly 64 times compared to that without sampling. For example, for a TCP packet with a 512-byte payload, the probability of not having even a single q-gram of it sampled is only $e^{-8} \approx 0.00034$.

The second challenge is that hashing a q-gram is quite expensive computationally, when q is moderately large (e.g., $q = 40$ bytes is used in Singh et al. (2004b)). Depending on the hash function used, the computational complexity is at least $O(q)$, and usually larger. For example, measurements in Singh et al. (2004b) show that the average computation time for a hash value is a fraction of a microsecond. Doing this for a packet with a 512-byte-long payload would take hundreds of microseconds. In comparison, the typical delay incurred by a router to a packet is on the order of microseconds.

To address the second challenge, EarlyBird makes use of the following insight: the inputs to these hundreds of hashing operations, given a packet content string $s_1 s_2 \cdots s_n$, are not independent of each other. Rather, they are "consecutive" q-grams $s_1 s_2 \cdots s_q$, $s_2 s_3 \cdots s_{q+1}$, $\cdots$, and $s_{n-q+1} s_{n-q+2} \cdots s_n$.

Hence the solution is to use a hash function that is incrementally computable (**P12a**) so that it is computationally much cheaper to compute the hash value of the next q-gram from the hash value of the current q-gram than from scratch. One such hash function is the Rabin fingerprint (Rabin, 1981), defined as follows.

A Rabin fingerprint function f_x is parameterized by a value x that is chosen randomly but fixed after being chosen. This function f_x maps a q-gram $s_1 s_2 ... s_q$ to $s_1 x^{q-1} + s_2 x^{q-2} + \cdots + s_{q-1} x + s_q$. Evaluating this polynomial (of x with s_1, s_2, $\cdots$, s_q as coefficients) from scratch is relatively computationally expensive, as it involves q multiplications and q additions even when using the well-known efficient technique (of rewriting it as $(s_1 x^{q-2} + s_2 x^{q-3} + s_{q-1}) * x + s_q$ and applying the same trick recursively to what is inside the parenthesis).

This function f, however, can be incrementally computed (**P12a**) as follows. It is not hard to check that $f_x(s_2 s_3 \cdots s_{q+1}) = s_2 x^{q-1} + s_3 x^{q-2} + ... + s_q x + s_{q+1} = f_x(s_1 s_2 \cdots s_q) * x - s_1 * x^q + s_{q+1}$. Hence to compute $f_x(s_2 s_3 \cdots s_{q+1})$, based on the value of $f(s_1 s_2 \cdots s_q)$, takes only two multiplications and two additions, assuming the values of x^2, x^3,..., x^q have all been precomputed (**P2a**). This reduces the computation time of all fingerprints except the first one by more than an order of magnitude, as shown in Singh et al. (2004b).

Finally, once a host detects a suspect packet, a q-gram (say α) of which has had its fingerprint $f_x(\alpha)$ flagged by the multistage filter at the host as an elephant, we need to further verify that it is indeed sent by a spreading worm. If it is, then the q-gram α should appear in packets sent by a large number of different infected hosts (source IP addresses) within the network; in EarlyBird (Singh et al., 2004b), this number is called the address dispersion of α. Hence for each suspect packet caught, we need to estimate its address dispersion. In EarlyBird this is done using a bitmap-based counting scheme (**P14**) combined with a multiresolution twist (both described in Section 16.16.4).

17.7 Carousel: scalable logging for intrusion prevention systems

In this section we first describe a network security problem that looks trivial but is in fact challenging because naive solutions can deliver poor performance. We then present a simple solution called Carousel (The Lam et al., 2010) that leverages hashing and sampling in an unusual way.

Consider an application scenario in which an enterprise network containing a large number of hosts is monitored and protected by an intrusion prevention system (IPS). We assume that the IPS, which, by sitting in a strategic position, can "see" all the packets transiting in the network. When a widespread security event happens to this network, the IPS is tasked with logging, to its disk or SSD (solid state drive), every *distinct* IP address involved in this event and a succinct event report associated with the IP address.

One such security event is the infection of many of its hosts by a worm. In this event for each IP address (host) already infected by the worm, the IPS needs to record it along with a packet sent from the host that serves as the evidence (event report). Here for simplicity, we assume that, upon examining the header and the content of a packet, IPS can decide whether the packet is "infectious"; if so, its source IP address needs to be logged. Our goal in this application scenario is to design a scalable solution for the IPS to log all these IP addresses and their associated event reports.

For ease of presentation, in the rest of this section we use this application scenario (of assessing the scale of a worm attack) as the context for formulating our problem. Before we can get to the gist of this problem, however, we need to make two additional assumptions. First, we assume that each infected source (IP address) sends out a large number of packets (trying to infect others).

With this assumption, the naive solution of logging the source (or destination) IP address of every "infectious" packet does not work well, since it can log an infected source many times, which can lead to poor throughput performance, as we will elaborate shortly. In other words, a good solution needs to somehow filter out most of the duplicates and ideally log each infected source only once.

Second, we assume that each infected source is *persistent* in the sense that it will send out "infectious" packets for a relatively long period of time. This is really an "enabling" assumption in the sense that without the assumption, it appears hard, if not impossible, to design an elegant solution to our problem, as we will explain shortly. On the other hand, this assumption is also reasonable for this application for the following reason. The very purpose for logging infected sources is to "neutralize" and if possible remediate such sources. If an infected source has stopped sending packets, it no longer poses a clear and present danger as far as the spreading of this particular (suspected) worm is concerned. In this case, to log its IP address is less important than logging those persistent sources (worm spreaders).

We now make our first attempt at formulating the problem using the data streaming language we have introduced in Section 16.15. Consider a stream of data items, each of which is the source IP address of an infectious packet, that arrive at the IPS at a very high rate. With high probability, each such IP address appears many times (the first additional assumption above) and does so persistently (the second additional assumption above) in the stream. Our problem is for the IPS to gather a near-complete list of such IP addresses after performing one-pass processing of the data stream. This problem is intuitively more difficult than the problem of counting the number of distinct elements (explained in Section 16.16): here we need to write down the list of distinct elements.

Like many other network algorithmics problems, this problem would be trivial if we did not have stringent performance expectations for an ideal solution. In this case our expectations, to be stated next, are reasonable with respect to the resource constraints of the system.

Suppose the total number of such IP addresses is a large number N and the bandwidth of the disk in the IPS is b. Suppose the IPS has certain resource constraints (which we will elaborate shortly) that prevent various clever "smoothing" or "work amortization" tricks (e.g., via caching or buffering in memory) from being used to speed up this logging task. Then intuitively an ideal solution can attain no more than a maximum "throughput" of b, so it would need at least N/b amount of time to log the vast majority of these N identities (at least once). Our problem is to come up with such an ideal solution. Clearly, the aforementioned naive solution of logging the IP addresses of all "infectious" packets without any duplicate filtering has a much poorer throughput performance than the ideal solution, since many IP addresses can each appear in a large number of packets.

We start by explaining the aforementioned "anti-smoothing" resource constraint and why another naive solution does not work under it. A typical, and perhaps expected (by readers who have gone this far in reading this book) constraint is that the amount of memory (say M) that the IPS has available for this logging task is much smaller than that is needed to store all N identifies. This is a reasonable constraint since, for the IPS to scan each and every packet in the network in real-time, this memory has to be SRAM.

Under this constraint, the naive solution of filtering out duplicates via keeping a hash table of all "infectious" IP addresses seen and logged so far does not work because the hash table clearly cannot fit in the memory (SRAM). Although using a Bloom filter instead reduces the memory footprint by roughly an order of magnitude (at the cost of some false positives as explained in Section 17.4.1), the Bloom filter may still be too large to fit in the memory. We call this constraint "anti-smoothing" because without this constraint, IPS can simply gather all distinct IP addresses (and filter out duplicates) in memory and write them to disk at the ideal throughput of b.

Now we are ready to describe Carousel (The Lam et al., 2010), which solves the problem of logging most of the distinct elements while filtering out most of the duplicates. The solution is in fact quite simple. Its basic idea is first divide the IP address space statistically evenly into K subspaces (partitions) so that roughly N/K distinct "infectious" IP addresses fall into each partition.

Then Carousal takes turns ("rotates around") to perform this logging task for each and every partition, one at a time; this rotation gives the scheme its name. When focusing on a partition, Carousal processes each packet whose source IP address falls into the partition using a Bloom filter (to filter out duplicates) and logs most of the roughly N/K distinct elements in this partition. The parameter K is set to be just large enough for the Bloom filter encoding these N/K distinct elements to fit in the amount of memory M available for this logging task.

Once the Bloom filter is close to full (when roughly half or more of its bits are set to 1), the IPS writes these IP addresses to the disk and moves on to the next partition. Such a partitioning can be easily achieved via hashing. It was shown in The Lam et al. (2010) that, when the disk throughput b is the performance bottleneck, Carousel can accomplish this logging mission in roughly N/b seconds, assuming that Carousel commits the list of distinct IP addresses found in the current partition to the disk at the same time as it processes the next partition (using a Bloom filter) in memory.

Note that the assumption made earlier that nearly every such IP address appears persistently (i.e., for a "long enough" period of time) is necessary because it takes Carousel roughly N/b seconds to "rotate around" and "visit" every partition.

The last remaining issue is how to pick the right value for K, the number of partitions. Making K too large leads to an unnecessarily long delay for logging all distinct elements. Making K too small overcrowds the Bloom filter and leads to high false positives, which would result in many IP addresses being misclassified as duplicates and not being logged. A typical solution is an adaptive one: to start with a conservative (larger) K, which is typically a power of 2, and adjust it by halving it when the Bloom filter is found to be underpopulated (when much less than half of its bits have value 1).

17.8 Conclusion

Returning to Marcus Ranum's quote at the start of this chapter, hacking is probably exciting for hackers and scary for network administrators, who are clearly on different sides of the battlements. However, hacking is also an exciting phenomenon for practitioners of network algorithmics, there is just so much to do. Compared to more limited areas, such as accounting and packet lookups, where the basic tasks have been frozen for several years, the creativity and persistence of hackers promise to produce interesting problems for years to come.

In terms of technology currently used, the set string–matching algorithms seem useful and may be ignored by current products. However, other varieties of string matching, such as regular expression matches, are in use. While the approximate matching techniques are somewhat speculative in terms of current applications, past history indicates they may be useful in the future.

Second, the traceback solutions only represent imaginative approaches to the problem. Their requirements for drastic changes to router forwarding make them unlikely to be used for current deployment as compared to techniques that work in the control plane. Despite this pessimistic assessment, the underlying techniques seem much more generally useful.

For example, sampling with a probability inversely proportional to a rough upper bound on the distance is useful for efficiently collecting input from each of a number of participants without explicit coordination. Similarly, Bloom filters are useful to reduce the size of hash tables to 5 bits per entry, at the cost of a small probability of false positives. Given their beauty and potential for high-speed implementation, such techniques should undoubtedly be part of the designer's bag of tricks.

Finally, we described our approach to content-agnostic worm detection using algorithmic techniques. The solution combines existing mechanisms described earlier in this book. While the experimental results on our new method are still preliminary, we hope this example gives the reader some glimpse into the possible applications of algorithmics to the scary and exciting field of network security. Table 17.1 presents a summary of the techniques used in this chapter, together with the major principles involved.

17.9 Exercises

1. **Traceback by edge sampling:** Extend the IP traceback edge-sampling idea to reduce the space required. As described in the text, try to do this by chopping the node ID required in the base scheme into smaller (say, 8-bit) fragments. It may help to consider each of the fragment IDs to be the IDs of four virtual nodes that are housed in a single physical node, thus effectively extending the path and the number of samples needed for reconstruction.

2. **Bloom filters and trajectory sampling:** Can you use Bloom filters to improve the label storage required by trajectory sampling in Chapter 16? Explain.

3. **Sampling and packet logging:** Can you use packet sampling to reduce the amount of memory required by the logging traceback solution? What are the disadvantages and advantages?

4. **Traceback by packet logging:** Why does the implementation in Fig. 17.8 go through the indirection of a hash to 32 bits (as in trajectory sampling) and then to a Bloom filter?

5. **Aho–Corasick as a state machine:** In many applications one may wish to ignore certain padding characters that can be inserted by an intruder to make strings hard to detect. How might you extend Aho–Corasick to ignore these padding characters while searching for suspicious strings?
6. **Resemblance and min-wise hashing:** Generalize the Broder methods to approximately search for multiple strings and return the string with the highest resemblance.
7. **Approximate matching and worm detection:** Could the methods for approximate search generalize to detecting worms that mutate?

Conclusions

18

> *The end of a matter is better than its beginning.*
> —**Ecclesiastes, The Bible**

We began the book by setting up the rules of the network algorithmics game. The second part of the book dealt with server implementations and the third part with router implementations. The fourth and last part of the book dealt with current and future issues in measurement and security.

The book covers a large number of specific techniques and a variety of settings, there are techniques for fast server design versus techniques for fast routers, techniques specific to operating systems versus techniques specific to hardware. While all these topics are part of the spectrum of network algorithmics, there is a risk that the material can appear to degenerate into a patchwork of assorted topics that are not linked together in any coherent way.

Thus as we draw to a close, it is appropriate to try and reach closure by answering the following questions in the next four sections.

- *What has the book been about?* What were the main problems, and how did they arise? What are the main techniques? While endnode and router techniques appear to be different when considered superficially, are there some underlying characteristics that unite these two topics? Can these unities be exploited to suggest some cross-fertilization between these areas? (Section 18.1)
- *What is network algorithmics about?* What is the underlying philosophy behind network algorithmics, and how does it differ from algorithms by themselves? (Section 18.2)
- *Is network algorithmics used in real systems?* Are the techniques in this book exercises in speculation, or are there real systems that use some of these techniques? (Section 18.3)
- *What is the future of network algorithmics?* Are all the interesting problems already solved? Are the techniques studied in this book useful only to understand existing work or to guide new implementations of existing tasks? Or are there always likely to be new problems that will require fresh applications of the principles and techniques described in this book? (Section 18.4)

18.1 What this book has been about

The main problem considered in this book is bridging the performance gap between good network abstractions and fast network hardware. Abstractions, such as modular server code and prefix-based forwarding, make networks more usable, but they also exact a performance penalty when compared to the capacity of raw transmission links, such as optical fiber. The central question tackled in this book is whether we can have our cake and eat it too: retain the usability of the abstractions and yet achieve wire speed performance for the fastest-transmission links.

To make this general assertion more concrete, we review the main contents of this book in two subsections: Section 18.1.1 on endnode algorithmics and Section 18.1.2 on router algorithmics. This initial summary is similar to that found in Chapter 1. However, we go beyond the description in Chapter 1 in Section 18.1.3, where we present the common themes in endnode and router algorithmics and suggest how these unities can potentially be exploited.

18.1.1 Endnode algorithmics

Chapters 5–9 of this book concentrate on endnode algorithmics, especially for servers. Many of the problems tackled under endnode algorithmics involve getting around complexities due to software and structure, in other words, complexities of our own making as opposed to necessarily fundamental complexities. These complexities arise because of the following characteristics of endnodes.

- *Computation Versus Communication:* Endnodes are about general-purpose computing and must handle possible unknown and varied computational demands, from database queries to weather prediction. By contrast, routers are devoted to communication.
- *Vertical Versus Horizontal Integration:* Endnodes are typically horizontally integrated, with one institution building boards, another writing kernel software, and another writing applications. In particular, kernels have to be designed to tolerate unknown and potentially buggy applications to run on top of them. Today, routers are typically vertically integrated, where the hardware and all software are assembled by a single company.
- *Complexity of Computation:* Endnode protocol functions are more complex (application, transport) as compared to the corresponding functions in routers (routing, data link).

As a consequence, endnode software has three important artifacts that seem hard to avoid, each of which contributes to inefficiencies that must be worked around or minimized.

1. *Structure:* Because of the complexity and vastness of endnode software, code is structured and modular to ease software development. In particular, unknown applications are allowed using a standard application programming interface (API) between the core operating system and the unknown application.
2. *Protection:* Because of the need to accommodate unknown applications, there is a need to protect applications from each other and to protect the operating system from applications.
3. *Generality:* Core routines such as buffer allocators and the scheduler are written with the most general use (and the widest variety of applications) in mind and thus are unlikely to be as efficient as special-purpose routines.

In addition, since most endnodes were initially designed in an environment where the endnode communicated with only a few nodes at a time, there is little surprise that when these nodes were retrofitted as servers, a fourth artifact was discovered.

4. *Scalability:* By scalability, we often mean in terms of the number of concurrent connections. A number of operating systems use simple data structures that work well for a few concurrent con-

Bottleneck	Chapter	Cause	Sample Solution
Copying	5	Protection, structure	Passing by reference optimized by caching (IO-Lite)
Context switching	6	Complex scheduling	User-level protocols, event-driven Web servers
System calls	6	Protection, structure	Application device channels
Slow select	6	Scaling with number of clients	Kernel keeps state across calls
Timers	7	Scaling with number of timers	Timing wheels
Demuxing	8	Scaling with number of classifiers	Generalized tries (Pathfinder)
Buffer allocation	9	Generality	Linear buffers
Checksums/ CRCs	9	Generality Scaling with link speeds	Multibit computation
Protocol code	9	Generality	Header prediction

FIGURE 18.1

Endnode bottlenecks covered in this book. Associated with each bottleneck is the chapter in which the material is reviewed, the underlying cause, and one or more sample solutions.

nections but become major bottlenecks in a server environment, where there is a large number of connections.

With this list of four endnode artifacts in mind, Fig. 18.1 reviews the main endnode bottlenecks covered in this book, together with causes and workarounds. This picture is a more detailed version of the corresponding figure in Chapter 1.

18.1.2 Router algorithmics

In router algorithmics, by contrast, the bottlenecks are caused not by structuring artifacts (as in some problems in endnode algorithmics) but by the scaling problems caused by the need for global Internets, together with the fast technological scaling of optical link speeds. Thus the global Internet puts pressure on router algorithmics because of both *population* scaling and *speed* scaling.

For example, simple caches worked fine for route lookups until address diversity and the need for CIDR (both caused by population scaling) forced the use of a fast longest-matching prefix. Also, simple DRAM-based schemes sufficed for prefix lookup (e.g., using expanded tries) until increasing link speeds forced the use of limited SRAM and compressed tries. Unlike endnodes, routers do not have protection issues, because they largely execute one code base. The only variability comes from different packet headers. Hence protection is less of an issue.

With the two main drivers of router algorithmics in mind, Fig. 18.2 reviews the main router bottlenecks covered in this book together with causes and workarounds. This picture is a more detailed version of the corresponding figure in Chapter 1.

Bottleneck	Chapter	Cause	Sample Solution
Prefix lookups	11	CIDR, link speed scaling, Prefix database size scaling	Expanded multibit tries Compressed multibit tries
Packet classification	12	Service differentiation Link speed and size scaling	Decision trees and heuristics Hardware parallelism (CAMs)
Switching	13	Electrical scaling of buses Scaling in bandwidth Head-of-line blocking Scalability in number of ports	Crossbar switches VOQs, fast approximate matches Hierarchical fabrics, randomized resource-contention algorithms
Fair queuing	14	Service differentiation in resource scheduling Link speed scaling Memory scaling	Weighted fair queuing DRR, fast heaps SFQ, DiffServ, Core stateless
Measurement	16	Link speed scaling, number of counters	Low-order bits in SRAM + DRAM Juniper's DCU
Security	17	Scaling in number and intensity of attacks	Traceback with Bloom filters Frequent content-based worm detection

FIGURE 18.2

Router bottlenecks covered in this book. Associated with each bottleneck is the chapter in which the material is reviewed, the underlying cause, and one or more sample solutions.

While we have talked about routers as *the* canonical switching device, many of the techniques discussed in this book apply equally well to any switching device, such as a bridge (Chapter 10 is devoted to lookups in bridges) or a gateway. It also applies to intrusion detection systems, firewalls, and network monitors who do not switch packets but must still work efficiently with packet streams at high speeds.

18.1.3 Toward a synthesis

In his book *The Character of Physical Law*, Richard Feynman argues that we have a need to understand the world in "various hierarchies, or levels." Later, he goes on to say that "all the sciences, and not just the sciences but all the efforts of intellectual kinds, are an endeavor to see the connections of the hierarchies ... and in that way we are gradually understanding this tremendous world of interconnecting hierarchies."

We have divided network algorithmics into two hierarchies: endnode algorithmics and router algorithmics. What are the connections between these two hierarchies? Clearly, we have used the same set of 15 principles to understand and derive techniques in both areas. But are there other unities that can provide insight and suggest new directions?

There are differences between endnode and router algorithmics. Endnodes have large, structured, and general-purpose operating systems that require workarounds to obtain high performance; routers, by contrast, have fairly primitive operating systems (e.g., Cisco IOS) that bear some resemblance to a real-time operating system. Most endnodes' protocol functions are implemented (today) in software, while the critical performance functions in a router are implemented in hardware. Endnodes compute, routers communicate. Thus routers have no file system and no complex process scheduling.

But there are similarities as well between endnode and router algorithmics.

- *Copying* in endnodes is analogous to the data movement orchestrated by *switching* in routers.
- *Demultiplexing* in endnodes is analogous to *classification* in routers.
- *Scheduling* in endnodes is analogous to *fair queuing* in routers.

Other than packet classification, where the analogy is more exact, it may seem that the other correspondences are a little stretched. However, these analogies suggest the following potentially fruitful directions.

1. Switch-based endnode architectures: The analogy between copying and switching, and the clean separation between I/O and computation in a router, suggests that this may also be a good idea for endnodes. More precisely, most routers have a crossbar switch that allows parallel data transfers using dedicated ASICs or processors; packets meant for internal computation are routed to a separate set of processors. While we considered this briefly in Chapter 2, we did not consider very deeply the implications for endnode operating systems.

By dedicating memory bandwidth and processing to I/O streams, the main computational processors can compute without interruptions, system calls, or kernel thread because I/O is essentially serviced and placed in clean form by a set of I/O processors (using separate memory bandwidth that does not interfere with the main processors) for use by the computational processors when they switch computational tasks. With switch-based bus replacements such as Infiniband, and the increasing use of protocol offload engines such as TCP chips, this vision is already realizable. However, while the hardware elements are present, a fundamental restructuring of operating systems is needed to fully realize the potential of this vision as for example in Arrakis (Peter et al., 2015) described in Chapter 6.

2. Generalized endnode packet classification: Although there seems to be a direct correspondence between packet classification in endnodes (Chapter 8) and packet classification in routers (Chapter 12), the endnode problem is simpler because it works only for a constrained set of classifiers, where all the wildcards are at the end. Router classifiers, on the other hand, allow arbitrary classifiers, requiring more complicated algorithmic machineries or CAMs. To be fair, in recent years the packet classifiers in Linux and other operating systems have come closer to the power of routers and in some cases have gone beyond because of their ability to do application level filtering.

3. Fair queuing in endnodes: Fair queuing in routers was originally invented to provide more discriminating treatment to flows in times of overload and (later) to provide quality of service to flows in terms of, say, latency. Both these issues resonate in the endnode environment. For example, the problem of receiver livelock (Chapter 6) requires discriminating between flows during times of overload. The use of early demultiplexing and separate IP queues per flow in lazy receiver processing seems like a first crude step toward fair queuing. Similarly, many endnodes do real-time processing, such as running MPEG players, just as routers have to deal with the real-time constraints of, say, voice-over-IP packets. Thus a reasonable question is whether the work on fair schedulers in the networking community can be useful in an operating system environment. When a sending TCP is scheduling between multiple concurrent connections, could it use a scheduling algorithm such as DRR for better fairness? At a higher level, could a Web server use worst-case weighted fair queuing to provide better delay bounds for certain clients? In recent years the two communities (scheduling in routers and scheduling in endnode) have influenced each other. Today sophisticated endnode scheduling algorithms are implemented in operating systems such as Linux qdisc (Components of Linux Traffic Control, 2022) and Google's carousel (Saeed et al., 2017) described in Chapter 7.

So far, we have suggested that endnodes could learn from router design in overall I/O architecture and operating system design. Routers can potentially learn the following from endnodes.

1. Fundamental Algorithms: Fundamental algorithms for endnodes, such as selection, buffer allocation, CRCs, and timers, are likely to be useful for routers, because the router processor is still an endnode, with very similar issues.

2. More Structured Router Operating Systems: While the internals of router operating systems, such as Cisco's IOS and Juniper's JunOS, are hidden from public scrutiny, there is at least anecdotal evidence that there are major software engineering challenges associated with such systems as time progresses (leading to the need to be compatible with multiple past versions) and as customers ask for special builds. Perhaps routers can benefit from some of the design ideas behind existing operating systems that have stood the test of time.

While protection may be fundamentally unnecessary (no third-party applications running on a router), how should a router operating system be structured for modularity? One approach to building a modular but efficient router operating system can be found in the router plugins system (Decasper et al., 1998) and the Click operating system (Kohler et al., 2000). More modern proposals include Arrakis (Peter et al., 2015) and (Belay et al., 2016).

3. Vertically Integrated Routers: The components of an endnode (applications, operating system, boxes, chips) are often built by separate companies, thus encouraging innovation. The interface between these components is standardized (e.g., the API between applications and operating system), allowing multiple companies to supply new solutions. Why should a similar vision not hold for routers some years from now especially as the vision of Software Defined Networks continues to take hold? Currently, this is more of a business than a technical issue because the dominant vendors do not want to open up the market to competitors. However, this was true in the past for computers and is no longer true; thus there is hope.

We are already seeing router chips being manufactured by semiconductor companies. However, a great aid to progress would be a standardized router operating system that is serious and general enough for production use by several, if not all, router companies.[1] Such a router operating system would have to work across a range of router architectures, just as operating systems span a variety of multiprocessor and disk architectures.

Once this is the case, perhaps there is even a possibility of "applications" that run on routers. This is not as far-fetched as it sounds, because there could be a variety of security and measurement programs that operate on a subset of the packets received by the router. With the appropriate API (and especially if the programs are operating on a logged copy of the router packet stream), such applications could even be farmed out to third-party application developers. It is probably easy to build an environment where

---

[1] Click is somewhat biased toward endnode bus-based routers as opposed to switch-based routers with ASIC support.

a third-party application (working on logged packets) cannot harm the main router functions, such as forwarding and routing.

18.2 What network algorithmics is about

Chapter 1 introduced network algorithmics with the following definition.

Definition. Network algorithmics is the use of an interdisciplinary systems approach, seasoned with algorithmic thinking, to design fast implementations of network processing tasks.

The definition stresses the fact that network algorithmics is interdisciplinary, requires systems thinking, and can sometimes benefit from algorithmic thinking. We review each of these three aspects (interdisciplinary thinking, systems thinking, algorithmic thinking) in turn.

18.2.1 Interdisciplinary thinking

Network algorithmics represents the intersection of several disciplines within computer science that are often taught separately. Endnode algorithmics is a combination of networking, operating systems, computer architecture, and algorithms. Router algorithmics is a combination of networking, hardware design, and algorithms. Fig. 18.3 provides examples of uses of these disciplines that are studied in the book.

For example, in Fig. 18.3 techniques such as header prediction (Chapter 9) require a deep networking knowledge of TCP to optimize the expected case, while internal link striping (Chapter 15) requires knowing how to correctly design a striping protocol. On the other hand, application device channels (Chapter 6) require a careful understanding of the protection issues in operating systems.

Similarly, locality-driven receiver processing requires understanding the architectural function and limitations of the instruction cache. Finally, in router algorithmics it is crucial to understand hardware

Endnode algorithmics

Discipline	Example
Networking	Header prediction (Chapter 6)
Operating systems	Application device channels (Chapter 6)
Computer architecture	Locality-driven receiver processing (Chapter 5)
Algorithms	Timing wheels (Chapter 7)

Router algorithmics

Discipline	Example
Networking	Link striping (Chapter 15)
Hardware design	Switch arbiters (Chapters 2 and 13)
Algorithms	Fast IP lookup (Chapter 11)

FIGURE 18.3

Examples of disciplines used in this book along with sample applications.

design. Arbiters like iSLIP and PIM were designed to allow scheduling decisions in a minimum packet arrival time.

Later in this chapter we argue that other disciplines, such as statistics and learning theory, will also be useful for network algorithmics.

18.2.2 Systems thinking

Systems thinking is embodied by Principles **P1** through **P10**. Principles **P1** through **P5** were described earlier as systems principles. Systems unfold in space and time: in space, through various components (e.g., kernel, application), and in time, through certain key time points (e.g., application initialization time, packet arrival time). Principles **P1** through **P5** ask that a designer expand his or her vision to see the entire system and then to consider moving functions in space and time to gain efficiency.

For example, Principle **P1**, avoiding obvious waste, is a cliché by itself. However, our understanding of systems, in terms of separable and modular hierarchies, often precludes the synoptic eye required to see waste across system hierarchies. For example, the number of wasted copies is apparent only when one broadens one's view to that of a Web server (see I/O-Lite in Chapter 5). Similarly, the opportunities for dynamic code generation in going from Pathfinder to DPF (see Chapter 8) are apparent only when one considers the code required to implement a generic classifier.

Similarly, Principle **P4** asks the designer to be aware of existing system components that can be leveraged. Fbufs (Chapter 5) leverage off the virtual memory subsystem, while timing wheels (Chapter 7) leverage off the existing time-of-day computation to amortize the overhead of stepping through empty buckets. Principle **P4** also asks the designer to be especially aware of the underlying hardware, whether to exploit local access costs (e.g., DRAM pages, cache lines), to trade memory for speed (either by compression, if the underlying memory is SRAM, or by expansion, if memory is DRAM), or to exploit other hardware features (e.g., replacing multiplies by shifts in RED calculations in Chapter 14).

Principle **P5** asks the designer to be even bolder and to consider adding new hardware to the system; this is especially useful in a router context. While this is somewhat vague, Principles **5a** (parallelism via memory interleaving), **P5b** (parallelism via wide words), and **P5c** (combining DRAM and SRAM to improve overall speed and cost) appear to underlie many clever hardware designs to implement router functions. Thus memory interleaving and pipelining can be used to speed up IP lookups (Chapter 11), wide words are used to improve the speed of the Lucent classification scheme (Chapter 12), and DRAM and SRAM can be combined to construct an efficient counter scheme (Chapter 16).

Once the designer sees the system and identifies wasted sequences of operations together with possible components to leverage, the next step is to consider moving functions in time (**P2**) and space (**P3c**). Fig. 18.4 shows examples of endnode algorithmic techniques that move functions between components. Fig. 18.5 shows similar examples for router algorithmics.

Besides moving functions in space, moving functions in time is a key enabler for efficient algorithms. Besides the more conventional approaches of precomputation (**P2a**), lazy evaluation (**P2b**), and batch processing (**P2c**), there are subtler examples of moving functions to different times at which the system is instantiated. For example, in fbufs (Chapter 5), common VM mappings between the application and kernel are calculated when the application first starts up. Application device channels (Chapter 6) have the kernel authorize buffers (on behalf of an application) to the adaptor when the application starts up. Dynamic packet filter (DPF) (Chapter 8) specializes code when a classifier is updated. Tag switching (Chapter 11) moves the work of computing labels from packet-forwarding time to route-computation time.

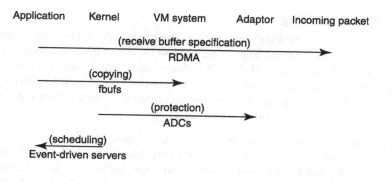

FIGURE 18.4

Endnode algorithmics: examples of moving functions in space.

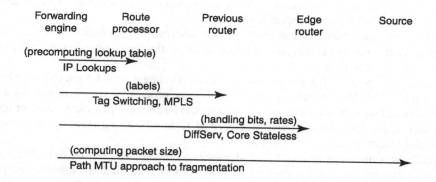

FIGURE 18.5

Router algorithmics: examples of moving functions in space.

Finally, Principles **P6** through **P10** concern the use of alternative system structuring techniques to remove inefficiencies. **P6** suggests considering specialized routines or alternative interfaces; for example, Chapter 6 suggests that event-driven APIs may be more efficient than the state-based interface of the *select()* call. **P7** suggests designing interfaces to avoid unnecessary generality; for example, in Chapter 5 fbufs map the fbuf pages into the same locations in all processes, avoiding the need for a further mapping when moving between processes. **P8** suggests avoiding being unduly influenced by reference implementations; for example, in Chapter 9 naive reference implementations of checksums have poor performance.

Principles **P9** and **P10** suggest keeping existing interfaces but adding extra information to interfaces (**P9**) or packet headers (**P10**). For example, efficiently reimplementing the *select()* call (Chapter 6) requires passing information between the protocol module and the select module. Passing information in packet headers, on the other hand, has a huge array of examples, including RDMA (Chapter 5), MPLS (Chapter 11), DiffServ, and core stateless fair queuing (Chapter 14).

18.2.3 Algorithmic thinking

Algorithmic thinking refers to thinking about networking bottlenecks the way algorithm designers approach problems. Overall, algorithmic approaches are less important than other systems approaches, as embodied by Principles **P1** through **P10**. Also, it is dangerous to blindly reuse existing algorithms.

The first problem that must be confronted in using algorithmic thinking is how to frame the problem that must be solved. By changing the problem, one can often find more effective solutions. Consider the following problem, which we avoided in Chapter 11.

Example (Pipelining and Memory Allocation). A lookup engine is using a trie. The lookup engine must be pipelined for speed. The simplest solution is to pipeline the trie by level. The root is at the first stage, the children of the root are assigned to the second stage, the nodes at height 2 to the third stage, etc. Unfortunately, the memory needs for each stage can vary as prefixes are inserted and deleted. There is the following spectrum of approaches.

- *Centralized memory:* All the processing stages share a single memory. Memory allocation is easy, but the centralized memory becomes a bottleneck.
- *One memory per stage:* Each processing stage has its own memory, minimizing memory contention. However, since the memory is statically allocated at fabrication time, any memory unused by a stage cannot be used by another stage.
- *Dynamically allocate small 1-port memories to stages:* As suggested in Chapter 11, on-chip memory is divided into M SRAMs, which are connected to stage processors via a crossbar. As a processor requires more or less memory, crossbar connections can be changed to allocate more or fewer memories to each stage. This scheme requires a large M to avoid wasting memory, but a large M can lead to high capacitive loads.
- *Dynamically allocate medium-size 2-port memories to stages:* The setting is identical to the last approach, except that each memory is now a 2-port memory that can be allocated to two processors. Using this, it is possible to show that N memories are sufficient for N processors, with almost no memory wastage.
- *Dynamically change the starting point in the pipeline:* In a conventional linear pipeline all lookups start at the first stage and leave at the last. Florin Baboescu has suggested an alternative: Using a lookup table indexed on the first few bits, assign each address to a different first processor in the pipeline. Thus different addresses have different start and end processors. However, this gives considerably more flexibility in allocating memory to processors by changing the assignment of addresses to processors.
- *Pipeline by depth:* Instead of pipelining a tree by height, consider pipelining by depth. All leaves are assigned to the last stage, K, all parents of the leaves to stage $K - 1$, etc.

These approaches represent the interplay between Principles **P13** (optimizing degrees of freedom) and **P5** (add hardware). However, each approach results in a different algorithmic problem! Thus a far more important skill than solving a hard problem is the skill required to frame the right problems that balance overall system needs.

Principles **P11** and **P13** help choose the right problem to solve. The pipelining example shows that choosing the degrees of freedom (**P13**) can change the algorithmic problem solved.

Similarly, Principle **P11**, optimizing the expected case, can sometimes help decide what the right measure is to optimize. This in turn influences the choice of algorithm. For example, simple TCP header prediction (Chapter 9) optimizes the expected case when the next packet is from the same connection and is the next data packet or ack. If this is indeed the expected case, there is no need for fancy connection lookup structures (a simple one-element cache) or fancy structures to deal with sequence number bookkeeping. However, if there are several concurrent connections, as in a server, a hash table may be better for connection lookup. Similarly, if packets routinely arrive out of order, then more fancy sequence number bookkeeping schemes (Thomas et al., 1992) may be needed.

Principle **P12**, adding state for speed, is a simple technique used often in standard algorithmic design. However, it is quite common for just this principle by itself (without fancy additional algorithmic machinery) to help remove systems bottlenecks. For example, the major bottleneck in the *select()* call implementation is the need to repeatedly check for data in network connections known not to be ready. By simply keeping state across calls, this key bottleneck can be removed. By contrast, the bottlenecks caused by the bitmap interface can be removed by algorithmic means, but these are less important.

Having framed the appropriate problem using **P11**, **P12**, and **P13**, Principles **P14** and **P15** can be used to guide the search for solutions.

Principle **P14** asks whether there are any important special cases, such as the use of finite universes, that can be leveraged to derive a more efficient algorithm. For example, the McKenney buffer-stealing algorithm of Chapter 9 provides a fast heap with $O(1)$ operations for the special case when elements to the heap change by at most 1 on each call.

Finally, Principle **P15** asks whether there are algorithmic methods that can be adapted to the system. It is dangerous to blindly adapt existing algorithms because of the following possibilities that can mislead the designer.

- *Wrong Measures:* The measure for most systems implementations is the number of memory accesses and not the number of operations. For example, the fast *ufalloc()* operation uses a selection tree on bitmaps instead of a standard heap, leveraging off the fact that a single read can access W bits, where W is the size of a word. Again, the important measure in many IP lookup algorithms is search speed and not update speed.

- *Asymptotic Complexity:* Asymptotic complexity hides constants that are crucial in systems. When every microsecond counts, surely constant factors are important. Thus the switch matching algorithms in Chapter 13 have much smaller constants than the best bipartite matching algorithms in the literature and hence can be implemented.

- *Incorrect Cost Penalties:* In timing wheels (Chapter 7) a priority heap is implemented using a bucket-sorting data structure. However, the cost of strolling through empty buckets, a severe cost in bucket sort, is unimportant because, on every timer tick, the system clock must be incremented anyway. As a second example, the dynamic programming algorithm to compute optimal lookup strides for multibit tries (Chapter 11) is $O(N * W^2)$, where N is the number of prefixes and W is the address width. While this appears to be quadratic, it is linear in the important term N (100,000 or more) and quadratic in the address width (32 bits, and the term is smaller in practice).

In spite of all these warnings algorithmic methods are useful in networking, ranging from the use of Pathfinder-like tries in Chapter 8 to the use of tries and binary search (suitably modified) in Chapter 11.

18.3 **Network algorithmics and real products**

Many of the algorithms used in this book are found in real products. The following is a quick survey.

Endnode Algorithmics: Zero-copy implementations of network stacks are now quite common (sendmsg, 2022), as are implementations of memory-mapped files; however, more drastic changes, such as IO-Lite are still not in commodity operating systems. The RDMA specification has developed considerably since the first edition. For instance, RDMA is now implemented over commodity Ethernet in ROCE (Guo et al., 2016). Event-driven Web servers are quite common, and many operating systems other than UNIX (such as Windows NT) have fast implementations of *select()* equivalents. The DPDK standard (DPDK, 2018) avoids system calls and copies using ideas similar to ADCs. Google's Carousel (Saeed et al., 2017) uses timing wheels to schedule packets.

Most commercial systems for early demultiplexing still rely on BPF (Berkeley packet filter) (Engler and Kaashoek, 1996), but that is because few systems require so many classifiers that they need the scalability of a Pathfinder or a DPF (dynamic packet filter). Some operating systems use timing wheels, notably Linux and FreeBSD. Linux uses fast buffer-manipulation operations on linear buffers. Fast IP checksum algorithms are common, and so are multibit CRC algorithms in hardware.

Router Algorithmics: Binary search lookup algorithms for bridges were common in products, as were hashing schemes (e.g., Gigaswitch). Multibit trie algorithms for IP lookups are very common; recently, compressed versions, such as the tree bitmap algorithm, have become popular in Cisco's latest CRS-1 router. Classification is often done by CAMs, but Virtual Switches like Open vSwitch (Pfaff et al., 2015) use tuple search and Hypercuts was used in the Cisco CRS-1 router Chapter 12. Distributed memory ideas (Sundar et al., 2008) that combine SRAM and DRAM cleverly to build router buffers are used in Cisco routers.

In some chapters, such as the chapter on switching (Chapter 13), we provided a real product example for every switching scheme (see Table 13.1, for example) described in the first edition. In the second edition, we have added a few switching schemes that are of pedagogical importance, such as Sample-and-compare (Section 13.12), SERENA (Section 13.13), QPS (Section 13.14), and SW-QPS (Section 13.16.3); among them SW-QPS has been patented and may find adoption in future router products due to its simple design and low complexities. In fair queuing DRR, RED, AFD and token buckets are commonly implemented. General weighted fair queuing (WFQ), WF^2Q, virtual clock, and core stateless fair queuing are hardly ever used except for an approximation called Quick Fair Queuing (QFQ) that provides better delay bounds and is available in Linux. However, for pedagogical purpose, we have added the materials describing how WFQ and WF^2Q can be implemented (in Sections 14.12 and 14.13) so that their time complexities are strictly $O(\log n)$ (still considered impractically high) in the worse case.

It is useful to see many of these ideas come together in a complete system. While it is hard to find details of such systems (because of commercial secrecy), the following two large systems pull together ideas in endnode and router algorithmics.

System Example 1: Flash Web server

The Flash (Pai et al., 1999a) Web server was designed at Rice University and undoubtedly served as the inspiration (and initial code base) for a company called iMimic. A version of Flash called Flash-lite uses the following ideas from endnode algorithmics.

- *Fast copies:* Flash-lite uses IO-Lite to avoid redundant copies.
- *Process scheduling:* Flash uses an event-driven server with helper processes to minimize scheduling and maximize concurrency.
- *Fast select:* Flash uses an optimized implementation of the *select()* call.
- *Other optimizations:* Flash caches response headers and file mappings.

System Example 2: Cisco 12000 GSR router

The Cisco GSR (Cisco Systems, 2001c) is a popular gigabit router and uses the following ideas from router algorithmics.

- *Fast IP lookups:* The GSR uses a multibit tree to do IP lookups.
- *Fast switching:* The GSR uses the iSLIP algorithm for fast bipartite matching of VOQs.
- *Fair queuing:* The GSR implements a modified form of DRR called MDRR, where one queue is given priority (e.g., for voice-over-IP). It also implements a sophisticated form of RED called *weighted RED* and token buckets. All these algorithms are implemented in hardware.

18.4 Network algorithmics: back to the future

The preceding three sections of this chapter talked of the past and the present. But are all the ideas played out? Has network algorithmics already been milked to the point where nothing new is left to do? We believe this is not the case. This is because we believe network algorithmics will be enriched in the near future in three ways: new *abstractions* that require new solutions will become popular; new connecting *disciplines* will provide new approaches to existing problems; and new *requirements* will require rethinking existing solutions. We expand on each of these possibilities in turn.

18.4.1 New abstractions

This book dealt with the fast implementation of the standard networking abstractions: TCP sockets at endnodes and IP routing at routers. However, new abstractions are constantly being invented to increase user productivity. While these abstractions make life easier for users, unoptimized implementations of these abstractions can exact a severe performance penalty. But this only creates new opportunities for network algorithmics. Here are some examples of such abstractions.

- *TCP offload engines:* While the book has concentrated on software TCP implementations, movements such as iSCSI have made hardware TCP offload engines more interesting. Doing TCP in hardware and handling worst-case performance at 10 Gbps and even 40 Gbps is very challenging. For example, to do complete offload, the chip must even handle out-of-order packets and packet fragments (see Chapter 9) without appreciable slowdown. TCP Offload has become a reality at speeds like 1 Gbps since the first edition of the book. For example, in Windows Server 2008, TCP Chimney Offload 2022 can relegate the processing of a TCP/IP connection to a network adapter (such as from Broadcome) that includes TCP/IP offload processing.
- *HTML and Web server processing:* There have been a number of papers trying to improve Web server performance that can be considered an application of endnode algorithmics. For example, persistent HTTP (Mogul, 1995) can be considered an application of **P1** to the problem of connection

overhead. A more speculative approach to reduce DNS lookup times in Web accesses by passing hints (**P10**) is described in Chandranmenon and Varghese (2001).

- *Web services:* The notion of Web services, by which a Web page is used to provide a service, is getting increasingly popular. There are a number of protocols that underly Web services, and standard implementations of these services can be slow.
- *CORBA:* The common object request broker architecture is popular but quite slow. Gokhale and Schmidt (1998) apply to the problem four of the principles described in this book (eliminating waste, **P1**, optimizing the expected case, **P11**, passing information between layers, **P9**, and exploiting locality for good cache behavior, **P4a**). They show that such techniques from endnode algorithmics can improve the performance of the SunSoft Inter-Orb protocol by a factor of 2–4.5, depending on the data type. Similar optimizations should be possible in hardware.
- *SSL and other encryption standards:* Many Web servers use the secure socket layer (SSL) for secure transactions. Software implementations of SSL are quite slow.
- *XML processing:* XML is rapidly becoming the *lingua franca* of the Web. Parsing and converting from XML to HTML can be a bottleneck.
- *Measurement and security abstractions:* Currently, SNMP and NetFlow allow very primitive measurement abstractions. The abstraction level can be raised only by a tool that integrates all the raw measurement data. Perhaps in the future routers will have to implement more sophisticated abstractions to help in measurement and security analysis.
- *Sensor networks:* A sensor network may wish to calculate new abstractions to solve such specific problems as finding high concentrations of pollutants and ascertaining the direction of a forest fire.

If history is any guide, every time an existing bottleneck becomes well studied, a new abstraction appears with a new bottleneck. Thus after lookups became well understood, packet classification emerged. After classification came TCP offload; and now SSL and XML are clearly important. Many pundits believe that wire speed security solutions (as implemented in a router or an intrusion detection system) will be required by the year 2006. Thus it seems clear that future abstractions will keep presenting new challenges to network algorithmics.

18.4.2 New connecting disciplines

Earlier we said that a key aspect of network algorithmics is its interdisciplinary nature. Solutions require a knowledge of operating systems, computer architecture, hardware design, networking, and algorithms. We believe the following disciplines will also impinge on network algorithmics very soon.

- *Optics:* Optics has been abstracted away as a link layer technology in this book. Currently, optics provides a way to add extra channels to existing fiber using dense wavelength-division multiplexing. However, optical research has made amazing strides. There are undoubtedly exciting possibilities to rethink router design using some combination of electronics and optics.[2]
- *Network processor architecture:* While this field is still in its infancy as compared to computer architecture, there are surely more imaginative approaches than current approaches that assign packets to

---

[2] Electronics still appears to be required today because of the lack of optical buffers and the difficulty of optical header processing.

one of several processors. One such approach, described many years ago in Sherwood et al. (2003), uses a wide word state machine as a fundamental building block. A more modern approach that uses a pipeline of stages is embodied in the Reconfigurable Match Table architecture (Bosshart et al., 2013) as embodied for instance in Intel's Tofino-3 chip (Intel Corporation, 2022).

- *Learning theory:* The fields of security and measurement are crying out for techniques to pick out interesting patterns from massive traffic data sets. Learning theory and data mining have been used for these purposes in other fields. Rather than simply reusing, say, standard clustering algorithms or standard techniques such as hidden Markov models, the real breakthroughs may belong to those who can find variations of these techniques that can be implemented at high speeds with some loss of accuracy. Similarly, online analytical processing (OLAP) tools may be useful for networking, with twists to fit the networking milieu. An example of a tool that has an OLAP flavor in a unique network setting can be found in Estan et al. (2003). Machine learning is increasingly intersecting with network algorithmics. A modern paper that uses machine learning ideas for packet classification is (Liang et al., 2019).
- *Databases:* The field of databases has a great deal to teach networking in terms of systematic techniques for querying for information. Recently, an even more relevant trend has been the subarea of continuous queries. Techniques developed in databases can be of great utility to algorithmics. The second edition of this book has a new section on streaming algorithms for networks in Chapter 16. Streaming algorithms originated in the database and theory communities. In Section 16.16, we have shown how the networking problem of counting the number of distinct flows is intricately connected to association rule mining, a classical problem in databases and data mining.
- *Statistics:* The field of statistics will be of even more importance in dealing with large data sets. Already, NetFlow and other tools have to resort to sampling. What inferences can safely be made from sampled data? As we have seen in Chapter 16, statistical methods are already used by ISPs to solve the traffic matrix problem from limited SNMP data.

18.4.3 New requirements

Much of this book has focused on processing time as the main metric to be optimized while minimizing dollar cost. Storage was also an important consideration because of limited on-chip storage and the expense of SRAM. However, even minimizing storage was related to speed, in order to maximize the possibility of storing the entire data structure in high-speed storage.

The future may bring new requirements. Two important such requirements are (mechanical) space and power. Space is particularly important in PoPs and hosting centers, because rack space is limited. Thus routers with small form factors are crucial. It may be that optimizing space is mostly a matter of mechanical design together with the use of higher and higher levels of integration. However, engineering routers (and individual sensors in sensor networks) for power may require attention to algorithmics.

Today power per rack is limited to a few kilowatts, and routers that need more power do so by spreading out across multiple racks. Power is a major problem in modern router design. It may be possible to rethink lookup, switching, and fair queuing algorithms in order to minimize power. Such power-conscious designs have already appeared in the computer architecture and operating systems community. It is logical to expect this trend to spread to router design.

18.5 **The inner life of a networking device**

We have tried to summarize in this chapter the major themes of this book in terms of the techniques described and the principles used. We have also tried to argue that network algorithmics is used in real products and is likely to find further application in the future because of new abstractions, new connecting disciplines, and new requirements. While the specific techniques and problems may change, we hope the *principles* involved remain useful.

Besides the fact that network algorithmics is *useful* in building better and faster network devices, we hope this book makes the case that network algorithmics is also *intellectually stimulating*. While it may lack the *depth* of hard problems in theoretical computer science or physics, perhaps what can be most stimulating is the *breadth*, in terms of the disciplines it encompasses.

An endnode, for instance, may appear as a simple processing state machine at the highest level of abstraction. A more detailed inspection would see a Web request packet arriving at a server interface, the interrupt firing, and the protocol code being scheduled via a software interrupt. Even within the protocol code, each line of code has to be fetched, hopefully from the I-cache, and each data item has to go through the VM system (via the TLB hopefully) and the data cache. Finally, the application must get involved via a returned system call and a process-scheduling operation. The request may trigger file system activity and disk activity.

A router similarly has an interesting inner life. Reflecting the macrocosmos of the Internet *outside* the router is a microcosmos *within* the router consisting of major subsystems, such as line cards and the switch fabric, together with striping and flow control across chip-to-chip links.

Network algorithmics seeks to understand these hidden subsystems of the Internet to make the Internet faster. This book is a first attempt to begin understanding, in Feynman's phrase, this "tremendous world of interconnected hierarchies" within routers and endnodes. In furthering this process of understanding and streamlining these hierarchies, there are still home runs to be hit and touchdowns to be scored as the game against networking bottlenecks continues to be played.

Detailed models

This appendix contains further models and information that can be useful for some readers of this book. For example, the protocols section may be useful for hardware designers who wish to work in networking but need a quick self-contained overview of protocols such as TCP and IP to orient themselves. On the other hand, the hardware section provides insights that may be useful for software designers without requiring a great deal of reading. The switch section provides some more details about switching theory.

A.1 TCP and IP

To be self-contained, Section A.1.1 provides a very brief sketch of how transmission control protocol (TCP) operates, and Section A.1.2 briefly describes how IP routing operates.

A.1.1 Transport protocols

When you point your Web browser to www.cs.ucsd.edu, your browser first converts the destination host name (i.e., cs.ucsd.edu) into a 32-bit Internet address, such as 132.239.51.18, by making a request to a local DNS name server (Perlman, 1992); this is akin to dialing directory assistance to find a telephone number. A 32-bit IP address is written in dotted decimal form for convenience; each of the four numbers between dots (e.g., 132) represents the decimal value of a byte. Domain names such as cs.ucsd.edu appear only in user interfaces; the Internet transport and routing protocols deal only with 32-bit Internet addresses.

Networks lose and reorder messages. If a network application cares that all its messages are received in sequence, the application can subcontract the job of reliable delivery to a transport protocol such as TCP. It is the job of TCP to provide the sending and receiving applications with the illusion of two shared data queues in each direction, despite the fact that the sender and receiver machines are separated by a lossy network. Thus whatever the sender application writes to its local TCP send queue should magically appear in the same order at the local TCP receive queue at the receiver, and vice versa.

Since Web browsers care about reliability, the Web browser at sender S (Fig. A.1) first contacts its local TCP with a request to set up a *connection* to the destination application. The destination application is identified by a well-known port number (such as 80 for Web traffic) at the destination IP address. If IP addresses are thought of as telephone numbers, port numbers can be thought of as extension numbers. A connection is the shared state information, such as sequence numbers and timers, at the sender and receiver TCP programs that facilitate reliable delivery.

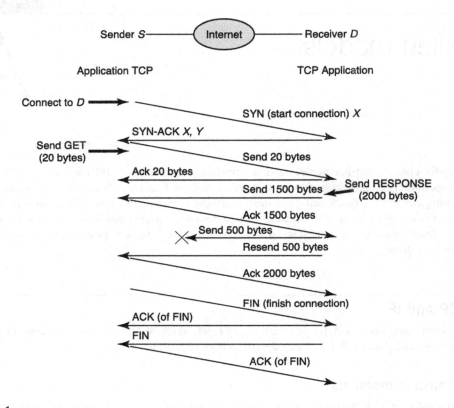

FIGURE A.1

Time–space figure of a possible scenario for a conversation between Web client *S* and Web server *D* as mediated by the reliable transport protocol TCP. Assume that the ack to the SYN-ACK is piggybacked on the 20-byte GET message.

Fig. A.1 is an example of a time–space figure, with time flowing downward and space represented horizontally. A line from *S* to *D* that slopes downward represents the sending of a message from *S* to *D*, which arrives at a later time.

To set up a connection, the sending TCP (Fig. A.1) sends out a request to start the connection, called a SYN message, with a number *X* the sender has not used recently. If all goes well, the destination will send back a SYN-ACK to signify acceptance, along with a number *Y* that the destination has not used before. Only after the SYN-ACK is the first data message sent.

The messages sent between TCPs are called TCP *segments*. Thus to be precise, the following models will refer to TCP segments and to IP packets (often called *datagrams* in IP terminology).

In Fig. A.1 the sender is a Web client, whose first message is a small (say) 20-byte HTTP GET message for the Web page (e.g., index.html) at the destination. To ensure message delivery, TCP will retransmit all segments until it gets an acknowledgment. To ensure that data is delivered in order and to correlate acks with data, each byte of data in a segment carries a sequence number. In TCP only the sequence number of the first byte in a segment is carried explicitly; the sequence numbers of the other bytes are implicit, based on their offset.

When the 20-byte GET message arrives at the receiver, the receiving TCP delivers it to the receiving Web application. The Web server at D may respond with a Web page of (say) 1900 bytes that it writes to the receiver TCP input queue along with an HTTP header of 100 bytes, making a total of 2000 bytes. TCP can choose to break up the 2000-byte data arbitrarily into segments; the example of Fig. A.1 uses two segments of 1500 and 500 bytes.

Assume for variety that the second segment of 500 bytes is lost in the network; this is shown in a time–space picture by a message arrow that does not reach the other end. Since the receiver does not receive an ACK, the receiver retransmits the second segment after a timer expires. Note that ACKs are cumulative: A single ACK acknowledges the byte specified and all previous bytes. Finally, if the sender is done, the sender begins closing the connection with a FIN message that is also asked (if all goes well), and the receiver does the same.

Once the connection is closed with FIN messages, the receiver TCP keeps no sequence number information about the sender application that terminated. But networks can also cause duplicates (because of retransmissions, say) of SYN and DATA segments that appear later and confuse the receiver. This is why the receiver in Fig. A.1 does not believe any data that is in a SYN message until it is validated by receiving a third message containing the unused number Y the receiver picked. If Y is echoed back in a third message, then the initial message is not a delayed duplicate, since Y was not used recently. Note that if the SYN is a retransmission of a previously closed connection, the sender will not echo back Y, because the connection is closed.

This preliminary dance featuring a SYN and a SYN-ACK is called TCP's three-way handshake. It allows TCP to forget about past communication, at the cost of increased latency to send new data. In practice, the validation numbers X and Y do double duty as the initial sequence numbers of the data segments in each direction. This works because sequence numbers need not start at 0 or 1 as long as both sender and receiver use the same initial value.

The TCP sequence numbers are carried in a TCP header contained in each segment. The TCP header contains 16 bits for the destination port (recall that a port is like a telephone extension that helps identify the receiving application), 16 bits for the sending port (analogous to a sending application extension), a 32-bit sequence number for any data contained in the segment, and a 32-bit number acknowledging any data that arrived in the reverse direction. There are also flags that identify segments as being SYN, FIN, etc. A segment also carries a routing header[1] and a link header that changes on every link in the path.

If the application is (say) a videoconferencing application that does not want reliability guarantees, it can choose to use a protocol called UDP (user datagram protocol) instead of TCP. Unlike TCP, UDP does not need acks or retransmissions, because it does not guarantee reliability. Thus the only sensible fields in the UDP header corresponding to the TCP header are the destination and source port numbers. Like ordinary mail versus certified mail, UDP is cheaper in bandwidth and processing but offers no reliability guarantees. For more information about TCP and UDP, Stevens (1994) is highly recommended.

---

[1] The routing header is often called the Internet protocol, or IP, header.

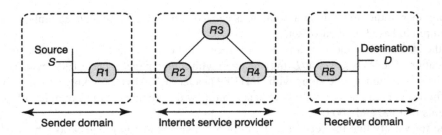

FIGURE A.2

A sample network topology corresponding to the Internet of Fig. A.1.

A.1.2 Routing protocols

Fig. A.2 shows a more detailed view of a plausible network topology between Web client *S* and Web server *D* of Fig. A.1. The source is attached to a local area network such as an Ethernet, to which is also connected a router, *R*1. Routers are the automated post offices of the Internet, which consult the destination address in an Internet message (often called a *packet*) to decide on which output link to forward the message.

In the figure source *S* belongs to an administrative unit (say, a small company) called a *domain*. In this simple example, the domain of *S* consists only of an Ethernet and a router, *R*1, that connects to an Internet service provider (ISP) through router *R*2. Our Internet service provider is also a small outfit, and it consists only of three routers, *R*2, *R*3, and *R*4, connected by fiber-optic communication links. Finally, *R*4 is connected to router *R*5 in *D*'s domain, which leads to the destination, *D*.

Internet routing is broken into two conceptual parts, called *forwarding* and *routing*. First consider forwarding, which explains how packets move from *S* to *D* through intermediate routers.

When *S* sends a TCP packet to *D*, it first places the IP address of *D* in the routing header of the packet and sends it to the neighboring router, *R*1. Forwarding at endnodes such as *S* and *D* is kept simple and consists of sending the packet to an adjoining router. *R*1 realizes it has no information about *D* and so passes it to ISP router *R*2. When it gets to *R*2, *R*2 must choose to send the packet to either *R*3 or *R*4. *R*2 makes its choice based on a forwarding table at *R*2 that specifies (say) that packets to *D* should be sent to R4. Similarly, *R*4 will have a forwarding entry for traffic to *D* that points to *R*5. A description of how forwarding entries are compressed using prefixes can be found in Section 2.3.2. In summary, an Internet packet is forwarded to a destination by following forwarding information about the destination at each router. Each router need not know the complete path to *D*, but only the next hop to get to *D*.

While forwarding must be done at extremely high speeds, the forwarding tables at each router must be built by a routing protocol. For example, if the link from R2 to R4 fails, the routing protocol within the ISP domain should change the forwarding table at *R*2 to forward packets to *D* to *R*3. Typically, each domain uses its own routing protocol to calculate shortest-path routes within the domain. Two main approaches to routing within a domain are *distance vector* and *link state*.

In the distance vector approach exemplified by the protocol RIP (Perlman, 1992), the neighbors of each router periodically exchange distance estimates for each destination network. Thus in Fig. A.2 *R*2 may get a distance estimate of 2 to *D*'s network from *R*3 and a distance estimate of 1 from *R*4. Thus *R*2 picks the shorter-distance neighbor, *R*4, to reach *D*. If the link from *R*2 to *R*4 fails, *R*2 will time-out this link, set its estimate of distance to D through $R4$ to infinity, and then choose the route through $R3$. Unfortunately, distance vector takes a long time to converge when destinations become unreachable (Perlman, 1992).

Link state routing (Perlman, 1992) avoids the convergence problems of distance vector by having each router construct a *link state packet* (LSP) listing its neighbors. In Fig. A.2 for instance, R3's LSP will list its links to $R2$ and $R4$. Each router then broadcasts its LSP to all other routers in the domain using a primitive flooding mechanism; LSP sequence numbers are used to prevent LSPs from circulating forever. When all routers have each other's LSP, every router has a map of the network and can use Dijkstra's algorithm (Perlman, 1992) to calculate shortest-path routes to all destinations. The most common routing protocol used *within* ISP domains is a link state routing protocol called *open shortest path first* (OSPF) (Perlman, 1992).

While shortest-path routing works well within domains, the situation is more complex for routing between domains. Imagine that Fig. A.2 is modified so that the ISP in the middle, say, ISP A, does not have a direct route to D's domain but instead is connected to ISPs C and E, each of which has a path to D's domain. Should ISP A send a packet addressed to D to ISP C or E? Shortest-path routing no longer makes sense because ISPs want to route based on other metrics (e.g., dollar cost) or on policy (e.g., always send data through a major competitor, as in so-called "hot potato" routing).

Thus interdomain routing is a more messy kettle of fish than routing within a domain. The most commonly used interdomain protocol today is called the *border gateway protocol* (BGP) (Stevens, 1998), which uses a gossip mechanism akin to distance vector, except that each route is augmented with the path of domains instead of just the distance. The path ostensibly makes convergence faster than the distance vector and provides information for policy decisions.

To go beyond this brief sketch of routing protocols, the reader is directed to *Interconnections* by Radia Perlman (1992) for insight into routing in general and to *BGP-4* by John Stewart (1999) as the best published textbook on the arcana of BGP.

A.2 Hardware models

For completeness, this section contains some details of hardware models that were skipped in Chapter 2 for the sake of brevity. These detailed models are included in this section to provide a somewhat deeper understanding for software designers.

A.2.1 From transistors to logic gates

The fundamental building block of the most complex network processor is a *transistor* (Fig. A.3). A transistor is a voltage-controlled switch. More precisely, a transistor is a device with three external attachments (Fig. A.3): a gate, a source, and a drain. When an input voltage I is applied to the gate, the source-drain path conducts electricity; when the input voltage is turned off, the source-drain path does not conduct. The output O voltage occurs at the drain. Transistors are physically synthesized on a chip by having a polysilicon path (gate) cross a diffusion path (source-drain) at points governed by a mask.

The simplest logic gate is an *inverter* (also known as a *NOT* gate). This gate is formed (Fig. A.3) by connecting the drain to a power supply and the source to ground (0 volts). The circuit functions as an inverter because when I is a high voltage (i.e., $I = 1$), the transistor turns on, "pulling down" the output to ground (i.e., $O = 0$). On the other hand, when $I = 0$, the transistor turns off, "pulling up" the

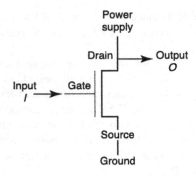

FIGURE A.3

A transistor is a voltage-controlled switch allowing the source-to-drain path to conduct current when the gate voltage is high. An inverter is a transistor whose source is connected to ground and whose drain is connected to a power supply.

output to the power supply (i.e., $O = 1$). Thus an inverter output flips the input bit, implementing the NOT operation. Although omitted in our pictures, real gates also add a resistance in the path to avoid "shorting" the power supply when $I = 1$, by connecting it directly to ground.

The inverter generalizes to a NAND gate (Fig. A.4) of two inputs, I1 and I2, using two transistors whose source-drain paths are connected in series. The output O is pulled down to ground if and only if both transistors are on, which happens if and only if both $I1$ and $I2$ are 1. Similarly, a NOR gate is formed by placing two transistors in parallel.

A.2.2 Timing delays

Fig. A.3 assumes that the output changed instantaneously when the input changed. In practice, when I is turned from 0 to 1, it takes time for the gate to accumulate enough charge to allow the source-drain path to conduct. This is modeled by thinking of the gate input as charging a gate capacitor (C) in series with a resistor (R). If you don't remember what capacitance and resistance are, think of charge as water, voltage as water pressure, capacitance as the size of a container that must be filled with water, and resistance as a form of friction impeding water flow. The larger the container capacity and the larger the friction, the longer the time to fill the container. Formally, the voltage at time t after the input I is set to V is $V(1 - e^{-t/RC})$. The product RC is the charging time constant; within one time constant, the output reaches $1 - 1/e = 63.2\%$ of its final value.

In Fig. A.3 notice also that if I is turned off, output O pulls up to the power supply voltage. But to do so, the output must charge one or more gates to which it is connected, each of which is a resistance and a capacitance (the sum of which is called the *output load*). For instance, in a typical 0.18-micron process,[2] the delay through a single inverter driving an output load of four identical inverters is 60 picoseconds.

---

[2] Semiconductor processes are graded by the smallest gate lengths they can produce. Shrinking process width decreases capacitances and resistances and so increases speed.

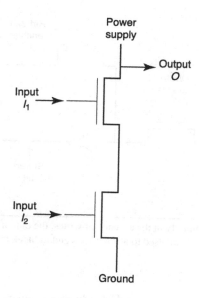

FIGURE A.4

Using two transistors in series to create a NAND gate.

   Charging one input can cause further outputs to charge further inputs, and so on. Thus for a combinatorial function, the delay is the sum of the charging and discharging delays over the worst-case path of transistors. Such path delays must fit within a minimum packet arrival time. Logic designs are simulated to see if they meet timing using approximate analysis as well as accurate circuit models, such as Spice. Good designers have intuition that allows them to create designs that meet timing. A formalization of such intuition is the method of logical effort (Sutherland et al., 1999), which allows a designer to make quick timing estimates. Besides the time to charge capacitors, another source of delay is wire delay.

A.2.3 Hardware design building blocks

This section describes some standard terminology for higher-level building blocks used by hardware designers that can be useful to know.

Programmable logic arrays and programmable array logics

A programmable logic array (PLA) has the generality of a software lookup table but is more compact. Any binary function can be written as the OR of a set of product terms, each of which is the AND of a subset of (possibly complemented) inputs. The PLA thus has all the inputs pass through an AND plane, where the desired product terms are produced by making the appropriate connections. The products are then routed to an OR plane. A designer produces specific functions by making connections within the PLA. A more restrictive but simpler form of PLA is a PAL (programmable array logic).

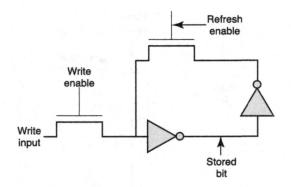

FIGURE A.5

To store the output of an inverter indefinitely in the absence of writes, the output is fed back to the input after a second inversion. Two further transistors are used to allow writes and to block the feedback refresh.

Standard cells

Just as software designers reuse code, so also do hardware designers reuse a repertoire of commonly occurring functions, such as multiplexers and adders.

The functional approach to design is generally embodied in *standard cell* libraries and *gate array* technologies, in which a designer must map his or her specific problem to a set of building blocks offered by the technology. At even higher abstraction levels, designers use synthesis tools to write higher-level language code in Verilog or VHDL for the function they wish to implement. The VHDL code is then synthesized into hardware by commercial tools. The trade-off is reduced design time, at some cost in performance. Since a large fraction of the design is not on the critical path, synthesis can greatly reduce time to market. This section ends with a networking example of the use of reduction for a critical path function.

A.2.4 Memories: the inside scoop

This section briefly describes implementation models for registers, static random access memories (SRAMs), and dynamic RAMs (DRAMs).

Registers

How can a bit be stored such that in the absence of writes and power failures, the bit stays indefinitely? Storing a bit as the output of the inverter shown in Fig. A.3 will not work, because, left to itself, the output will discharge from a high to a low voltage via "parasitic" capacitances. A simple solution is to use *feedback:* in the absence of a write the inverter output can be fed back to the input and "refresh" the output. Of course, an inverter flips the input bit, and so the output must be inverted a second time in the feedback path to get the polarity right, as shown in Fig. A.5. Rather than show the complete inverter (Fig. A.3), a standard triangular icon is used to represent an inverter.

Input to the first transistor must be supplied by the write input when a write is enabled and by the feedback output when a write is disabled. This is accomplished by two more "pass" transistors. The

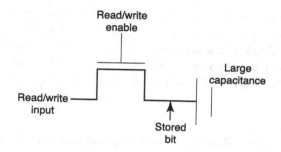

FIGURE A.6

A DRAM cell stores a bit using charge on a capacitor that leaks away slowly and must be refreshed periodically.

pass transistor whose gate is labeled "Refresh Enable" is set to high when a write is disabled, while the pass transistor whose gate is labeled "Write Enable" is set to high when a write is enabled. In practice, refreshes and writes are done only at the periodic pulses of a systemwide signal called a *clock*. Fig. A.5 is called a *flip-flop*.

A *register* is an ordered collection of flip-flops. For example, most modern processors (e.g., the Pentium series) have a collection of 32- or 64-bit on-chip registers. A 32-bit register contains 32 flip-flops, each storing a bit. Access from logic to a register on the same chip is extremely fast, say, 0.5–1 nanosecond. Access to a register off-chip is slightly slower because of the delay to drive larger off-chip loads.

Static RAM

A SRAM contains N registers addressed by $\log N$ address bits A. SRAM is so named because the underlying flip-flops refresh themselves and so are "static." Besides flip-flops, an SRAM needs a decoder that decodes A into a unary value used to select the right register. Accessing an SRAM on-chip is only slightly slower than accessing a register because of the added decode delay. At the time of writing, it was possible to obtain on-chip SRAMs with 0.5 nanoseconds access times. Access times of 1–2 nanoseconds for on-chip SRAM and 5–10 nanoseconds for off-chip SRAM are common. On-chip SRAM is limited to around 64 Mbits today.

Dynamic RAM

The SRAM bit cell of Fig. A.5 requires at least five transistors. Thus SRAM is always less dense or more expensive than memory technology based on DRAM. In Fig. A.6 a DRAM cell uses only a single transistor connected to an output capacitance. The transistor is only used to connect the write input to the output when the write enable signal on the gate is high. The output voltage is stored on the output capacitance, which is significantly larger than the gate capacitance; thus the charge leaks, but slowly. Loss due to leakage is fixed by refreshing the DRAM cell externally within a few milliseconds.

To obtain high densities, DRAMs use "pseudo-three-dimensional trench or stacked capacitors" (Fromm et al., 1997); together with the factor of 5–6 reduction in the number of transistors, a DRAM cell is roughly 16 times smaller than an SRAM cell (Fromm et al., 1997).

The compact design of a DRAM cell has another important side effect: a DRAM cell requires higher latency to read or write than the SRAM cell of Fig. A.5. Intuitively, if the SRAM cell of Fig. A.5

is selected, the power supply quickly drives the output bit line to the appropriate threshold. On the other hand, the capacitor in Fig. A.6 has to drive an output line of higher capacitance. The resulting small voltage swing of a DRAM bit line takes longer to sense reliably. In addition, DRAMs need extra delay for two-stage decoding and for refresh. DRAM refreshes are done automatically by the DRAM controller's periodically enabling RAS for each row R, thereby refreshing all the bits in R.

A.2.5 Chip design

Finally, it may be useful for networking readers to understand how chips for networking functions are designed.

After partitioning functions between chips, the box architect creates a design team for each chip and works with the team to create chip specification. For each block within a chip, logic designers write software register transfer level (RTL) descriptions using a hardware design language such as Verilog or VHDL. Block sizes are estimated and a crude floor plan of the chip is done in preparation for circuit design.

At this stage, there is a fork in the road. In *synthesized* design the designer applies synthesis tools to the RTL code to generate hardware circuits. Synthesis speeds the design process but generally produces slower circuits than custom-designed circuits. If the synthesized circuit does not meet timing (e.g., 8 nsec for OC-768 routers), the designer redoes the synthesis after adding constraints and tweaking parameters. In *custom* design, on the other hand, the designer can design individual gates or drag-and-drop cells from a standard library. If the chip does not meet timing, the designer must change the design (Sutherland et al., 1999). Finally, the chip "tapes out" and is manufactured, and the first yield is inspected.

Even at the highest level, it helps to understand the chip design process. For example, systemwide problems can be solved by repartitioning functions between chips. This is easy when the chip is being specified, is an irritant after RTL is written, and causes blood feuds after the chip has taped out. A second "spin" of a chip is something that any engineering manager would rather work around.

Interconnects, power, and packaging

Chips are connected using either point-to-high connections known as *high-speed serial links*, shared links known as *buses*, or parallel arrays of buses known as *crossbar switches*. Instead of using N^2 point-to-point links to connect N chips, it is cheaper to use a shared bus. A bus is similar to any shared media network, such as an Ethernet, and requires an arbitration protocol often implemented (unlike an Ethernet) using a centralized arbiter. Once a sender has been selected in a time slot, other potential senders must not send any signals. Electrically, this is done by having transmitters use a *tristate* output device that can output a0 or a1 or be in a high-impedance state. In a high-impedance state there is no path through the device to either the power supply or ground. Thus the selected transmitter sends 0's or 1's, while the nonselected transmitters stay in a high-impedance state.

Buses are limited today to around 20 Gb/sec. Thus many routers today use parallel buses in the form of crossbar switches (Chapter 13). A router can be built with a small number of chips, such as a link interface chip, a packet-forwarding chip, memory chips to store lookup state, a crossbar switch, and a queuing chip with associated DRAM memory for packet buffers.

A.3 Switching theory

This section provides some more details about matching algorithms for Clos networks and the dazzling variety of interconnection networks.

A.3.1 Matching algorithms for Clos networks with $k = n$

A Clos network can be proved to be rearrangably nonblocking for $k = n$. The proof uses *Hall's theorem* and the notion of *perfect matchings*. A bipartite graph is a special graph with two sets of nodes I and O; edges are only between a node in I and a node in O. A perfect matching is a subset E of edges in this graph such that every node in I is the endpoint of exactly one edge in E, and every node in O is also the endpoint of exactly one edge in E. A perfect match marries every man in I to every woman in O while respecting monogamy. Hall's theorem states that a necessary and sufficient condition for a perfect matching to exist is that every subset X of I of size d has at least d edges going to d distinct nodes in O.

To apply Hall's theorem to prove the Clos network is nonblocking, we show that any arrangement of N inputs that wish to go to N different outputs can be connected via the Clos network. Use the following iterative algorithm. In each iteration match input switches (set I) to output switches (set O) after ignoring the middle switches. Draw an edge between an input switch i and an output switch o if there is at least one input of i that wishes to send to an output directly reachable through o.

Using this definition of an edge, here is *Claim 1:* every subset X of d input switches in I has edges to at least d output switches in O. Suppose Claim 1 were false. Then the total number of outputs desired by all inputs in X would be strictly less than nd (because each edge to an output switch can correspond to at most n outputs). But this cannot be so, because d input switches with n inputs each must require exactly nd outputs.

Claim 1 and Hall's theorem can be used to conclude that there is a perfect matching between input switches and output switches. Hence the algorithm is to perform this matching after placing back *exactly one* middle switch M. This is possible because every middle switch has a link to every input switch and a link to every output switch. This allows routing one input link in every input switch to one output link in every switch. It also makes unavailable all the n links from each input switch to the middle switch M and all output links from M.

Thus the problem has been reduced from having to route n inputs on each input switch using n middle switches to having to route $n - 1$ inputs per input switch using $n - 1$ middle switches. Thus n iterations are sufficient to route all inputs to all outputs without causing resource conflicts that lead to blocking.

Thus a simple version of this algorithm would take n perfect matches; using the best existing algorithm for perfect matching (Hopcroft and Karp, 1973) takes $O(N^{2.5}/n^{1.5})$ time. A faster approach is via edge coloring; each middle switch is assigned a color, and we color the edges of the demand multigraph between input switches and output switches so that no two edges coming out of a node have the same color.[3] However, edge coloring can be done directly (without n iterations as before) in around $O(N \log N)$ time (Cole and Hopcroft, 1982).

---

[3] Intuitively, each set of edges colored with a single color corresponds to one matching and one middle switch, as in our first algorithm.

A.4 **The interconnection network Zoo**

There is a dazzling variety of ($\log N$)-depth interconnection networks, all based on the same idea of using bits in the output address to steer to the appropriate portion, starting with the most significant bit. For example, one can construct the famous Butterfly network in a very similar way to the recursive construction of the Delta network of Fig. 13.13. In the Delta network all the inputs to the top ($N/2$)-size Delta network come from the 0 outputs of the first stage in order. Thus the 0 output of the first first-stage switch is the first input, the 0 output of the second switch is the second input, etc.

By contrast, in a Butterfly the second input of the upper $N/2$ switch is the 0 output of the middle switch of the first stage (rather than the second switch of the first stage). The 0 output of the second switch is then the third input, while the 0 output of the switch following the middle switch gets the fourth input, etc. Thus the two halves are interleaved in the Butterfly but not in the Delta, forming a classic bowtie or butterfly pattern. However, even with this change, it is still easy to see that the same principle is operative: outputs with MSB 0 go to the top half, while outputs with MSB 1 go to the bottom.

Because the Butterfly can be created from the Delta by renumbering inputs and outputs, the two networks are said to be *isomorphic*. Butterflies were extremely popular in parallel computing (Culler et al., 1999), gaining fame in the BBN Butterfly, though they seem to have lost ground to low-dimensional meshes (see Section 13.19) in recent machines.

There is also a small variant of the Butterfly, called the *Banyan*, that involves pairing the inputs even in the first stage in a more shuffled fashion (the first input pairs with the middle input, etc.) before following Butterfly connections to the second stage. Banyans enjoyed a brief resurgence in the network community when it was noticed that if the outputs for each input are in sorted order, then the Banyan can route without internal blocking. An important such switch was the Sunshine switch (Giacopelli et al., 1991). Since sorting can be achieved using Batcher sorting networks (Cormen et al., 1990), these were called Batcher-Banyan networks. Perhaps because much the same effect can be obtained by randomization in a Benes or Clos network without the complexity of sorting, this approach has not found a niche commercially.

Finally, there is another popular network called the *hypercube*. The networks described so far use d-by-d building block switches, where d is a constant such as 2, *independent* of the size of N. By contrast, hypercubes use switches with $\log N$ links per switch. Each switch is assigned a binary address from 1 to N and is connected to all other switches that differ from it in exactly one bit. Thus in a very similar fashion to traversing a Delta or a Butterfly one can travel from an input switch to an output switch by successively correcting the bits that are different between output and input addresses, in any order. Unfortunately, the $\log N$ link requirement is onerous for large N and can lead to an "impractical number of links per line card" (Semeria, 2002).

References

A Retrospective on SEDA, 2010. http://matt-welsh.blogspot.com/2010/07/retrospective-on-seda.html.

A reworked TCP zero-copy receive API, 2018. https://lwn.net/Articles/754681/.

Adel'son-Vel'skii, G.M., Landis, E.M., 1962. An algorithm for organization of information. Doklady Akademii Nauk 146, 263–266.

Adisheshu, H., 1998. Services for next generation routers. PhD thesis. Washington University Computer Science Department.

Aggarwal, G., Motwani, R., Shah, D., Zhu, A., 2003. Switch scheduling via randomized edge coloring. In: Proceedings of the IEEE FOCS, pp. 502–512.

Agrawal, R., Imielinski, T., Swami, A., 1993. Mining association rules between sets of items in large databases. In: Proceedings of ACM SIGMOD, pp. 207–216.

Aho, A., Corasick, M., 1975. Efficient string matching: an aid to bibliographic search. Communications of the ACM 18 (6), 333–343.

Ahuja, R., Magnanti, T., Orlin, J., 1993. Network Flows. Prentice-Hall.

Albertengo, G., Riccardo, S., 1990. Parallel CRC generation. In: IEEE Micro.

Alleyne, B., 2002. Personal communication.

Alon, N., Matias, Y., Szegedy, M., 1999a. The space complexity of approximating the frequency moments. Journal of Computer and System Sciences 58 (1), 137–143.

Alon, N., Gibbons, P.B., Matias, Y., Szegedy, M., 1999b. Tracking join and self-join sizes in limited storage. In: Proceedings of the ACM SIGACT-SIGMOD-SIGART Symposium on Principles of Database Systems.

AMD, 2007. Software optimization guide for AMD family 10h processors. Available at http://www.amd.com/us-en/assets/content_type/white_papers_and_tech_docs/40546.pdf.

Anderson, T., Owicki, S., Saxe, J., Thacker, C., 1993. High speed switch scheduling for local area networks. ACM Transactions on Computer Systems 11 (4), 319–352.

Arista Corporation, Flex Route Engine White Paper, 2010. https://www.arista.com/assets/data/pdf/Whitepapers/FlexRoute-WP.pdf.

Aron, M., Druschel, P., 1999. Soft timers: efficient microsecond timer support for network processing. In: Proceedings of the 17th Symposium on Operating System Principles (SOSP).

Asai, H., Ohara, Y., 2015. Poptrie: a compressed trie with population count for fast and scalable software IP routing table lookup. In: Proceedings of the 2015 ACM Conference on Special Interest Group on Data Communication. Association for Computing Machinery, pp. 57–70.

Awerbuch, B., Patt-Shamir, B., Varghese, G., 1991. Self-stabilization by local checking and correction. In: Proceedings of the 32nd Annual Symposium of Foundations of Computer Science (FOCS).

Baboescu, F., Varghese, G., 2001. Scalable packet classification. In: Proceedings of ACM SIGCOMM.

Bailey, M., Gopal, B., Pagels, M., Peterson, L., Sarkar, P., 1994. PATHFINDER: a pattern-based packet classifier. In: Proceedings of the First Symposium on Operating Systems Design and Implementation (OSDI), pp. 115–123.

Banga, G., Mogul, J., 1998. Scalable kernel performance for Internet servers under realistic loads. In: Proceedings of the 1998 USENIX Annual Technical Conference. New Orleans, LA.

Banga, G., Mogul, J., Druschel, P., 1999. A scalable and explicit event delivery mechanism for UNIX. In: USENIX Annual Technical Conference, pp. 253–265.

Banks, D., Prudence, M., 1993. A high-performance network architecture for a PA-RISC workstation. IEEE Journal on Selected Areas in Communications.

Barile, I., 2004. I/O multiplexing and scalable socket servers. Dr. Dobbs Journal.

Barroso, L., Marty, M., Patterson, D., Ranganathan, P., 2017. Attack of the killer microseconds. Communications of the ACM 60 (4), 48–54. https://doi.org/10.1145/3015146.

Belazzougui, D., Botelho, F.C., Dietzfelbinger, M., 2009. Hash, displace, and compress. In: Fiat, A., Sanders, P. (Eds.), Algorithms – ESA 2009. Springer Berlin Heidelberg, pp. 682–693.

Belay, A., Prekas, G., Primorac, M., Klimovic, A., Grossman, S., Kozyrakis, C., Bugnion, E., 2016. The IX Operating System: combining low latency, high throughput, and efficiency in a protected dataplane. ACM Transactions on Computer Systems 34 (4), 11. https://doi.org/10.1145/2997641.

Bell, E.T., 1986. Men of Mathematics, reissue edition. Touchstone Books.

Benner, A., 1995. Fibre Channel: Gigabit Communications and I/O for Computer Networks. McGraw-Hill.

Bennett, B.T., Kruskal, V.J., 1975. LRU stack processing. IBM Journal of Research and Development 19 (4), 353–357.

Bennett, J., Zhang, H., 1996a. Hierarchical packet fair queuing algorithms. SIGCOMM Computer Communication Review 26 (4), 143–156. https://doi.org/10.1145/248157.248170.

Bennett, J., Zhang, H., 1996b. wf^2q: worst-case fair weighted fair queuing. In: IEEE INFOCOM'96.

Bennett, J., Zhang, H., 1997. Hierarchical packet fair queuing algorithms. IEEE/ACM Transactions on Networking 5, 675–689.

Bentley, J.L., 1982. Writing Efficient Programs. Prentice Hall.

Bhagwan, R., Lin, W., 2000. Fast and scalable priority queue architecture for high-speed network switches. In: IEEE INFOCOM, pp. 538–547.

Bhattacharyya, S., Diot, C., Jetcheva, J., Taft, N., 2001. Pop-level and access-link traffic dynamics in a tier-1 pop. In: SIGCOMM Internet Measurement Workshop.

Birell, A., et al., 1982. Grapevine: an exercise in distributed computing. Communications of the ACM 25 (4), 202–208.

Blackwell, T., 1996. Speeding up protocols for small messages. In: Proceedings of ACM SIGCOMM.

Blake, S., et al., 1998. An architecture for differentiated services. https://datatracker.ietf.org/doc/html/rfc2475.

Bloom, B.H., 1970. Space/time trade-offs in hash coding with allowable errors. Communications of the ACM 13 (7), 422–426. https://doi.org/10.1145/362686.362692.

Boecking, S., Seidel, V., Vindeby, P., 1995. Channels—a run-time system for multimedia protocols. In: ICCCN.

Boggs, D.R., Mogul, J.C., Kent, C.A., 1988. Measured capacity of an Ethernet: myths and reality. Proceedings ACM SIGCOMM 18, 222–234.

Bosshart, P.W., Gibb, G., Kim, H.-S., Varghese, G., McKeown, N., Izzard, M., Mujica, F.A., Horowitz, M., 2013. Forwarding metamorphosis: fast programmable match-action processing in hardware for SDN. In: Proceedings of the ACM SIGCOMM 2013 Conference on SIGCOMM.

Boyer, R.S., Moore, J.S., 1977. A fast string searching algorithm. Communications of the ACM 20 (10), 762–772.

Boyle, J., 1997. Internet draft: RSVP extensions for CIDR aggregated data flows. In: Internic.

Brakmo, L., Malley, S.O., Peterson, L., 1994. TCP Vegas: New techniques for congestion detection and avoidance. In: Proceedings of ACM SIGCOMM.

Braun, H.W., 1998. Characterizing traffic workload. www.caida.org.

Broder, A., 1998. On the resemblance and containment of documents. In: Sequences'91.

Broder, A., Mitzenmacher, M., 2001. Using multiple hash functions to improve IP lookups. In: Proceedings IEEE Infocom, pp. 1454–1463.

Brustoloni, J., 1999. Interoperation of copy avoidance in network and file I/O. In: Proceedings of IEEE Infocom. New York.

Brustoloni, J., Steenkiste, P., 1996. Effects of buffering semantics on I/O performance. In: Proceedings of the 2nd USENIX Symposium on Operating Systems Design and Implementation.

Build Ultra High-Performance Storage Applications with the Storage Performance Development Kit, 2022. https://spdk.io/.

Buonadonna, P., Geweke, A., Culler, D., 2002. An implementation and analysis of the virtual interface architecture. In: SC98: High Performance Networking and Computing Conference.

Bux, W., Grillo, D., 1985. Flow control in local-area networks of interconnected token rings. IEEE Transactions on Communications COM-33 (10), 1058–1066.

Cai, Q., Chaudhary, S., Vuppalapati, M., Hwang, J., Agarwal, R., 2021. Understanding host network stack overheads. In: Proceedings of the 2021 ACM SIGCOMM 2021 Conference, SIGCOMM '21. Association for Computing Machinery, pp. 65–77.

Cao, J., Xia, R., Yang, P., Guo, C., Lu, G., Yuan, L., Zheng, Y., Wu, H., Xiong, Y., Maltz, D., 2013. Per-packet load-balanced, low-latency routing for clos-based data center networks. In: Proceedings of the Ninth ACM Conference on Emerging Networking Experiments and Technologies, CoNEXT'13. Association for Computing Machinery, New York, NY, pp. 49–60.

Cardwell, N., Cheng, Y, Gunn, S.C., Yeganeh, S.H., Van, J., 2017. BBR: congestion-based congestion control. Communications of the ACM 60 (2), 58–66. https://doi.org/10.1145/3009824.

Carlton, A., 1996. An explanation of the SPECweb96 benchmark. Standard performance evaluation corporation white paper. http://www.specbench.org/.

Casella, G., Berger, R., 2001. Statistical Inference, 2 edition. Duxbury Thomson Learning.

Chandranmenon, G., Varghese, G., 1996. Trading packet headers for packet processing. ACM /IEEE Transactions Networking 17 (1).

Chandranmenon, G., Varghese, G., 1998. Reconsidering fragmentation and reassembly. In: Symposium on Principles of Distributed Computing, pp. 21–29.

Chandranmenon, G., Varghese, G., 2001. Reducing web latencies using precomputed hints. In: Proceedings of IEEE INFOCOM.

Chandy, K.M., Lamport, L., 1985. Distributed snapshots: determining global states of distributed systems. ACM Transactions on Computer Systems 3 (1), 63–75.

Chaney, T., Fingerhut, A., Flucke, M., Turner, J., 1997. Design of a gigabit ATM switch. In: Proceedings of IEEE INFOCOM, pp. 2–11.

Chang, C.-S., Lee, D.-S., Jou, Y.-S., 2002a. Load balanced Birkhoff–von Neumann switches, part I: one-stage buffering. Computer Communications 25 (6), 611–622.

Chang, C.-S., Lee, D.-S., Lien, C.-M., 2002b. Load balanced Birkhoff–von Neumann switches, part II: multi-stage buffering. Computer Communications 25 (6), 623–634.

Chankhunthod, A., Danzig, P., et al., 1996. A hierarchical Internet object cache. In: USENIX Annual Technical Conference, pp. 153–164.

Chao, H.J., Guo, X., 2001. Quality of Service Control in High-Speed Networks. Wiley.

Charikar, M., Chen, K., Farach-Colton, M., 2002. Finding frequent items in data streams. In: ICALP'02: Proceedings of the 29th International Colloquium on Automata, Languages and Programming. Springer-Verlag, London, pp. 693–703.

Chazelle, B., 1990a. Lower bounds for orthogonal range searching, I: the reporting case. Journal of the ACM 37.

Chazelle, B., 1990b. Lower bounds for orthogonal range searching, II: the arithmetic model. Journal of the ACM 37.

Checconi, F., Rizzo, L., Valente, P., 2013. IEEE/ACM transactions on networking. QFQ: Efficient Packet Scheduling With Tight Guarantees 21 (3), 802–816. https://doi.org/10.1109/TNET.2012.2215881.

Chelf, B., 2001. Dynamic memory management. Linux magazine readable at http://www.linux-mag.com/2001-06/compile_03.html.

Chesson, G., 1989. XTP/PE design considerations. In: IFIP Workshop on Protocols for High Speed Networks.

Cheswick, W., Bellovin, S., 1995. Firewalls and Internet Security. Addison-Wesley.

Chiueh, T., Pradhan, P., 1999. High performance IP routing table lookup using CPU caching. In: Proceedings IEEE INFOCOM, pp. 1421–1428.

Choudhury, A., Hahne, E., 1998. Dynamic queue length thresholds for shared-memory packet switches. IEEE/ACM Transactions on Networking 6 (2), 130–140.

Chuang, S.-T., Goel, A., McKeown, N., Prabhakar, B., 1999. Matching output queueing with a combined input/output-queued switch. IEEE Journal on Selected Areas in Communications 17 (6), 1030–1039.

Chung, F., Graham, R., Varghese, G., 2004. Parallelism versus memory allocation in pipelined router forwarding engines. In: Proceedings of the Sixteenth Annual ACM Symposium on Parallelism in Algorithms and Architectures. Association for Computing Machinery, pp. 103–111.

Cisco express forwarding commands, 2001a. http://www.cisco.com.

Cisco netflow, 2001b. http://www.cisco.com/warp/public/732/Tech/netflow.

Cisco Systems, 2001c. Cisco 12000 series Internet routers. http://www.cisco.com/warp/public/cc/pd/rt/12000/tech/index.shtml.

Cisco Systems, Inc., 2017. Intelligent buffer management on Cisco Nexus 9000 Series switches white paper. Technical report. Available at https://www.cisco.com/c/en/us/products/collateral/switches/nexus-9000-series-switches/white-paper-c11-738488.html. (Accessed November 2020).

Clark, D.D., 1985. Structuring of systems using upcalls. In: Proceedings of the 10th ACM Symposium on Operating Systems Principles (SOSP), pp. 171–180.

Clark, D.D., 1988. The design philosophy of the DARPA Internet protocols. In: Proceedings ACM SIGCOMM, pp. 106–114.

Clark, D., Tennenhouse, D., 1990. Architectural considerations for a new generation of protocols. In: Proceedings of ACM SIGCOMM.

Clark, D.D., Jacobson, V., Romkey, J., Salwen, H., 1989. An analysis of TCP processing overhead. IEEE Communications 27 (6), 23–29.

Clark, D., Wroclawski, J., Sollins, K., Braden, R., 2002. Tussle in cyberspace: defining tomorrow's Internet. In: Proceedings ACM SIGCOMM.

Cobb, J., Gouda, M., El Nahas, A., 1996. Time-shift scheduling: fair scheduling of flows in high speed networks. In: Proceedings of ICNP.

Cohen, E., 2016. Minhash sketches: a brief survey. http://www.cohenwang.com/edith/Surveys/minhash.pdf. (Accessed 27 January 2021).

Coit, C., Staniford, S., McAlerney, J., 2001. Towards faster pattern matching for intrusion detection or exceeding the speed of snort. In: Proceedings of the 2nd DARPA Information Survivability Conference and Exposition (DISCEX II).

Cole, R., Hopcroft, J., 1982. On edge coloring bipartite graphs. SIAM Journal of Computation 11, 540–546.

Commentz-Walter, B., 1979. A string matching algorithm fast on the average. In: Proceedings 6th International Colloquium on Automata, Languages and Programming, vol. 71. Springer.

Compaq, Intel, and Microsoft Corporations, 1997. Virtual interface architecture specification. http://www.viaarch.org.

Corbet, J., 2015. Reinventing the timer wheel. https://lwn.net/Articles/646950/.

Components of Linux Traffic Control, 2022. https://tldp.org/HOWTO/Traffic-Control-HOWTO/components.html.

Cormen, T., Leiserson, C., Rivest, R., 1990. Introduction to Algorithms. MIT Press/McGraw-Hill.

Cormen, T.H., Leiserson, C.E., Rivest, R.L., Stein, C., 2009. Introduction to Algorithms, 3rd edition. MIT Press.

Cormode, Graham, Muthukrishnan, S., 2005. An improved data stream summary: the count-min sketch and its applications. Journal of Algorithms 55 (1), 58–75.

Costello, A., Varghese, G., 1998. Redesigning the BSD Callout and timeout facilities. In: Software Practice and Experience.

Cox, A., 1996. Kernel Korner: network buffers and memory management. Linux Journal. www.linuxjournal.com.

Crovella, M., Carter, R., 1995. Dynamic server selection in the Internet. In: Proceedings of HPCS'95.

Culler, D., Singh, J., Gupta, A., 1999. Parallel Computer Architecture: A Hardware/Software Approach. Morgan Kaufman.

Dai, J., Prabhakar, B., 2000. The throughput of data switches with and without speedup. In: Proceedings of the IEEE INFOCOM. Tel Aviv, Israel, pp. 556–564.

Dally, W., 2002. Scalable switching fabrics for Internet routers. In: Avici Networks White Paper. http://www.avici.com/technology/whitepapers.

Dally, W., Chao, L., et al., 1987. Architecture of a message-driven processor. In: Proceedings of the International Symposium on Computer Architecture (ISCA).

Davison, G., 1989. Calendar p's and q's. Communications of the ACM 32 (10), 1241–1242.

Decasper, D., Dittia, Z., Parulkar, G., Plattner, B., 1998. Router plugins: a software architecture for next generation routers. In: Proceedings ACM SIGCOMM.

Degermark, M., Brodnik, A., Carlsson, S., Pink, S., 1997. Small forwarding tables for fast routing lookups. In: Proceedings ACM SIGCOMM, pp. 3–14.

Demers, A., Keshav, S., Shenker, S., 1989. Analysis and simulation of a fair queueing algorithm. ACM SIGCOMM Computer Communication Review 19 (4), 1–12. Proceedings of the Sigcomm'89 Symposium on Communications Architectures and Protocols.

Denning, D., 1987. An intrusion-detection model. IEEE Transactions on Software Engineering 13 (2), 222–232.

Dharmapurikar, S., Krishnamurthy, P., Taylor, D.E., 2003. Longest prefix matching using bloom filters. In: Proceedings of the 2003 Conference on Applications, Technologies, Architectures, and Protocols for Computer Communications. Association for Computing Machinery, pp. 201–212.

Dietzfelbinger, M., Karlin, A., et al., 1988. Dynamic perfect hashing: upper and lower bounds. In: 29th IEEE Symposium on Foundations of Computer Science (FOCS).

Ding, W., Xu, J., Dai, J.G., Song, Y., Bill, L., 2014. Sprinklers: A randomized variable-size striping approach to reordering-free load-balanced switching. In: ACM CoNext, the 10th International Conference on Emerging Networking EXperiments and Technologies. ACM.

Dittia, Z.D., Parulkar, G.M., Cox Jr., J.R., 1997. The APIC approach to high performance network interface design: protected DMA and other techniques. In: Proceedings of IEEE INFOCOM.

Draves, R., King, C., Venkatachary, S., Zill, B., 1999. Constructing optimal IP routing tables. In: Proceedings IEEE INFOCOM.

Druschel, P., Banga, G., 1996. Lazy receiver processing: a network subsystem architecture for server systems. In: Proceedings of the UNIX 2nd OSDI Conference.

Druschel, P., Peterson, L., 1993. Fbufs: A high-bandwidth cross-domain transfer facility. In: Proceedings of the Fourteenth ACM Symposium on Operating System Principles, pp. 189–202.

Druschel, P., Davie, B., Peterson, L., 1994. Experiences with a high-speed network adapter: a software perspective. In: Proceedings ACM SIGCOMM.

Duan, R., Su, H., 2012. A scaling algorithm for maximum weight matching in bipartite graphs. In: Proceedings of the ACM-SIAM SODA, pp. 1413–1424.

Duffield, N., Grossglauser, M., 2000. Trajectory sampling for direct traffic observation. In: Proceedings ACM SIGCOMM, pp. 271–282.

Duffield, N., Lund, C., Thorup, M., 2001. Charging from sampled network usage. In: SIGCOMM Internet Measurement Workshop.

Duffield, N., Lund, C., Thorup, M., 2002. Properties and prediction of flow statistics from sampled packet streams. In: Proceedings of ACM SIGCOMM Internet Measurement Workshop.

Duffield, N., Lund, C., Thorup, M., 2003. Estimating flow distributions from sampled flow statistics. In: Proceedings of ACM SIGCOMM.

DXR: Beyond two billion IPv4 routing lookups per second in software, 2022. http://www.nxlab.fer.hr/dxr/.

Eatherton, W., 1995. Hardware-based Internet protocol prefix lookups. MS thesis. Washington University Electrical Engineering Department.

Eatherton, W., Dittia, Z., Varghese, G., 2004. Tree bitmap: hardware software IP lookups with incremental updates. ACM Computer Communications Review 34 (2), 97–123.

Elmasri, R., Navathe, S., 2010. Fundamentals of Database Systems, 6th edition. Addison-Wesley Publishing Company.

Engler, D., 1996. VCODE: a retargetable, extensible, very fast dynamic code generation system. In: SIGPLAN Conference on Programming Language Design and Implementation, pp. 160–170.

Engler, D., Kaashoek, M.F., 1996. DPF: fast, flexible message demultiplexing using dynamic code generation. In: Proceedings ACM SIGCOMM, pp. 53–59.

Engler, D., Kaashoek, F., O'Toole, J., 1995. Exokernel: an operating system architecture for application-level resource management. In: Symposium on Operating Systems Principles, pp. 251–266.

epoll(7) – Linux manual page, 2022. https://man7.org/linux/man-pages/man7/epoll.7.html.

Estan, C., Varghese, G., 2002. New directions in traffic measurement and accounting. In: Proceedings of ACM SIGCOMM.

Estan, C., Varghese, G., Fisk, M., 2002. Counting the number of active flows on a high speed link. Technical Report 0705. CSE Department, UCSD.

Estan, C., Savage, S., Varghese, G., 2003. Automatically inferring patterns of resource consumption in network traffic. In: Proceedings ACM SIGCOMM.

Fall, K., Pasquale, J., 1993. Exploiting in-kernel data paths to improve I/O throughput and CPU availability. In: USENIX Winter, pp. 327–334.

Fang, W., Peterson, L., 1999. Inter-AS traffic patterns and their implications. In: Proceedings of IEEE GLOBE-COM.

Feigenbaum, J., Kannan, S., Strauss, M.J., Viswanathan, M., 2003. An approximate l1-difference algorithm for massive data streams. SIAM Journal on Computing 32 (1), 131–151.

Feldmann, A., Greenberg, A., et al., 2000. Deriving traffic demands for operational IP networks: methodology and experience. In: Proceedings ACM SIGCOMM, pp. 257–270.

Firoozshahian, A., Manshadi, V., Goel, A., Prabhakar, B., 2007. Efficient, fully local algorithms for CIOQ switches. In: IEEE INFOCOM 2007—26th IEEE International Conference on Computer Communications, pp. 2491–2495.

Fisk, M., Varghese, George, 2001. Fast content-based packet handling for intrusion detection. UCSD Technical Report CS2001-0670.

Flajolet, P., Martin, G., 1985. Probabilistic counting algorithms for data base applications. Journal of Computer and System Sciences 31 (2), 182–209.

Floyd, S., Jacobson, V., 1993. Random early detection gateways for congestion avoidance. In: ACM/IEEE Transactions Networking.

Floyd, S., Jacobson, V., 1995. Link-sharing and resource management models for packet networks. In: ACM/IEEE Transactions Networking.

Floyd, S., Jacobson, V., McCanne, S., Liu, C., Zhang, L., 1995. A reliable multicast framework for light-weight sessions and application level framing. In: Proceedings ACM SIGCOMM.

Floyd, S., Mahdavi, J., Mathis, M., Podolsky, M., Romanow, A., 1999. An extension to the selective acknowledgement (SACK) option for TCP.

Fromm, R., Perissakis, S., Cardwell, N., et al., 1997. The energy efficiency of IRAM architectures. In: International Symposium on Computer Architecture (ISCA 97).

Gale, D., Shapley, L.S., 1962. College admissions and the stability of marriage. The American Mathematical Monthly 69 (1), 9–15.

Gammo, L., Brecht, T., Shukla, A., Pariag, D., 2004. Comparing and evaluating epoll, select, and poll event mechanisms. In: Proceedings of the 6th Annual Ottawa Linux Symposium.

Ghorbani, S., Yang, Z., Brighten Godfrey, P., Ganjali, Y., Drill, A.F., 2017. Micro load balancing for low-latency data center networks. In: Proceedings of the Conference of the ACM Special Interest Group on Data Communication, SIGCOMM'17. Association for Computing Machinery, New York, NY, pp. 225–238.

Giaccone, P., Prabhakar, B., Shah, D., 2003. Randomized scheduling algorithms for high-aggregate bandwidth switches. IEEE Journal on Selected Areas in Communications 21 (4), 546–559.

Giaccone, P., Leonardi, E., Prabhakar, B., Shah, D., 2004. Delay bounds for combined input-output switches with low speedup. Performance Evaluation 55 (1), 113–128. https://doi.org/10.1016/S0166-5316(03)00103-2.

Gleixner, T., Niehaus, D., 2006. Linux HR timers and beyond: transforming the Linux time subsystems. https://www.kernel.org/doc/ols/2006/ols2006v1-pages-333-346.pdf.

Giacopelli, J., et al., 1991. Sunshine: a high performance self-routing packet switch architecture. IEEE Journal on Selected Areas in Communication 9 (8).

Global Intrusion Detection and Prevention Systems Market to Record an Impressive Growth of USD 9.04 Billion by 2028: Fior Markets. https://www.globenewswire.com/news-release/2022/05/10/2440086/0/en/Global-Intrusion-Detection-and-Prevention-Systems-Market-to-Record-an-Impressive-Growth-of-USD-9-04-Billion-by-2028-Fior-Markets.html.

Gokhale, A., Schmidt, D., 1998. Principles for optimizing CORBA Internet inter-ORB protocol performance. In: Hawaiian International Conference on System Sciences.

Gong, L., Tune, P., Liu, L., Yang, S., Xu, J., 2017. Queue-proportional sampling: a better approach to crossbar scheduling for input-queued switches. Proceedings of the ACM SIGMETRICS 1 (1), 3:1–3:33. https://doi.org/10.1145/3084440.

Gonnet, Gaston H., 1981. Expected length of the longest probe sequence in hash code searching. Journal of the ACM 28 (2), 289–304.

Google, IPv6 statistics. https://www.google.com/intl/en/ipv6/statistics.html.

Griffin, T., Wilfong, G., 2002. On the correctness of IBGP configuration. In: Proceedings ACM SIGCOMM, pp. 17–30.

Guo, C., Wu, H., Deng, Z., Soni, G., Ye, J., Padhye, J., Lipshteyn, M., 2016. RDMA over commodity ethernet at scale. In: Proceedings of the 2016 ACM SIGCOMM Conference, SIGCOMM '16. Association for Computing Machinery, pp. 202–215.

Gupta, P., McKeown, N., 1999a. Packet classification on multiple fields. In: Proceedings ACM SIGCOMM, pp. 147–160.

Gupta, P., McKeown, N., 1999b. Designing and implementing a fast crossbar scheduler. IEEE Micro.

Gupta, P., McKeown, N., 2001. Algorithms for packet classification. IEEE Network 15 (2).

Gupta, P., Lin, S., McKeown, N., 1998. Routing lookups in hardware at memory access speeds. In: IEEE INFOCOM.

Han, S., Marshall, S., Chun, B.-G., Ratnasamy, S., 2012. MegaPipe: a new programming interface for scalable network I/O. In: Proceedings of the 10th USENIX Conference on Operating Systems Design and Implementation, OSDI'12. USENIX Association, pp. 135–148.

Hennessey, J., Patterson, D., 1996. Computer Architecture: A Quantitative Approach, 2nd ednition. Morgan Kaufmann.

Hohn, N., Veitch, D., 2003. Inverting sampled traffic. In: Proceedings of ACM SIGCOMM Internet Measurement Conference.

Hopcroft, J., Karp, R., 1973. An $n^{5/2}$ algorithm for maximum matchings in bipartite graphs. SIAM Journal on Computation 2, 225–231.

Horowitz, E., Sahni, S., 1978. Fundamentals of Computer Algorithms. Computer Science Press.

Hua, N., Zhao, H., Lin, B., Xu, J., 2008a. Rank-indexed hashing: a compact construction of bloom filters and variants. In: Proceedings of IEEE International Conference on Network Protocols (ICNP).

Hua, N., Lin, B., Xu, J., Zhao, H., 2008b. Brick: a novel exact active statistics counter architecture. In: Proceedings of ACM/IEEE Symposium on Architectures for Networking and Communications Systems (ANCS). http://doi.acm.org/10.1145/1477942.1477956.

Huggahalli, R., Iyer, R., Tetrick, S., 2005. Direct cache access for high bandwidth network I/O. In: Proceedings of the 32nd Annual International Symposium on Computer Architecture, ISCA '05. IEEE Computer Society, pp. 50–59.

Hutchinson, N.C., Peterson, L.L., 1991. The x-Kernel: an architecture for implementing network protocols. IEEE Transactions on Software Engineering 17 (1), 64–76.

IEEE, 1997. Media access control (mac) bridging of ethernet v2.0 in local area networks. http://standards.ieee.org/reading/ieee/std/lanman/802.1H-1997.pdf.

IETF MPLS Charter, 1997. Multiprotocol label switching. http://www.ietf.org/html-charters/mpls-charter.html.

Indyk, P., Motwani, R., et al., 1997. Locality-preserving hashing in multidimensional spaces. In: Proceedings of the 29th ACM Symposium on Theory of Computing, pp. 618–625.

Infiniband Specification, 2000. Infiniband Architecture Specification.

Infiniband Trade Association, 2001. Infiniband architecture. http://www.infinibandta.org/home.

Information about the TCP Chimney Offload, Receive Side Scaling, and Network Direct Memory Access features in Windows Server 2008. https://learn.microsoft.com/en-us/troubleshoot/windows-server/networking/information-about-tcp-chimney-offload-rss-netdma-feature.

Intel Corporation, Intel Aurora 710 Product datasheet, 2022. https://netbergtw.com/products/aurora-710/.

Intel 64 and IA-32r, 2007. Architectures software developer's manual, vol. 2B. Available at ftp://download.intel.com/technology/architecture/new-instructions-paper.pdf.

Israel, A., Itai, A., 1986. A fast and simple randomized parallel algorithm for maximal matching. Information Processing Letters 22 (2), 77–80.

Iyer, S., Zhang, R., McKeown, N., 2002. Routers with a single stage of buffering. SIGCOMM Computer Communication Review 32 (4), 251–264. https://doi.org/10.1145/964725.633050.

Jacobson, V., 1988. Congestion avoidance and control. In: Proceedings ACM SIGCOMM.

Jacobson, G., 1989. Space-efficient static trees and graphs. In: 30th FOCS, pp. 549–554.

Jacobson, V., 1993. TCP in 30 instructions. In: Message Sent to Comp.Protocols. TCP Newsgroup.

Jaramillo, J.J., Milan, F., Srikant, R., 2008. Padded frames: a novel algorithm for stable scheduling in load-balanced switches. Networking, IEEE/ACM Transactions on Networking 16 (5), 1212–1225.

Kamber, M., Han, J., 2000. Data Management Systems: Data Mining: Concepts and Techniques. Elsevier.

Kanakia, H., 1999. Datapath Switch. In: ATT Bell Labs Internal Memorandum.

Karol, M., Hluchyj, M., Morgan, S., 1987. Input versus output queuing on a space division switch. IEEE Transactions on Communications, 1347–1356.

Kay, J., Pasquale, J., 1993. The importance of non-data touching processing overheads in TCP/IP. In: Proceedings ACM SIGCOMM.

Kent, C.A., Mogul, J.C., 1987. Fragmentation considered harmful. In: Proceedings ACM SIGCOMM.

Keshav, S., 1991. On the efficient implementation of fair queueing. Internetworking: Research and Experience 2, 157–173.

Keshav, S., 1997. Computer Networks: An Engineering Approach. Addison-Wesley.

Keshav, S., Demers, A., Shenker, S., 1990. Analysis and simulation of a fair queueing algorithm. In: Internetworking: Research and Experience, pp. 3–26.

Keslassy, I., 2004. The load-balanced router. PhD thesis. Stanford University.

Knuth, D., 1973. Fundamental Algorithms vol 3: Sorting and Searching. Addison-Wesley.

Kogan, K., Nikolenko, S., Rottenstreich, O., Culhane, W., Eugster, P., 2014. SAX-PAC (scalable and EXpressive PAcket classification). In: Proceedings of the 2014 ACM Conference on SIGCOMM. SIGCOMM '14. Association for Computing Machinery, pp. 15–26.

Kohler, E., Morris, R., et al., 2000. The click modular router. ACM Transactions on Computer Systems.

Krishnamurthy, B., Sen, S., Zhang, Y., Chen, Y., 2003. Sketch-based change detection: methods, evaluation, and applications. In: Proceedings of ACM SIGCOMM IMC.

Kronenberg, N., Levy, H., Strecker, W., 1986. Vaxclusters: a closely-coupled distributed system. ACM Transactions on Computer Systems 4 (2).

Kumar, A., Xu, J., Wang, J., Spatschek, O., Li, L., 2004a. Space-code bloom filter for efficient per-flow traffic measurement. In: Proceedings of IEEE INFOCOM.

Kumar, A., Sung, M., Xu, J., Wang, J., 2004b. Data streaming algorithms for efficient and accurate estimation of flow size distribution. In: Proceedings of the ACM SIGMETRICS.

Kung, H.T., Chapman, A., Blackwell, T., 1994. The FCVC credit based flow control protocol. In: Proceedings of the ACM SIGCOMM.

Kurzweil, R., 2001. What's creativity and who's creative. https://www.closertotruth.com/roundtables/whats-creativity-and-whos-creative.

Labovitz, C., Malan, G., Jahanian, F., 1997. Internet routing instability. In: Proceedings of the ACM SIGCOMM.

Lai, K., Baker, M., 1996. A performance comparison of UNIX operating systems on the Pentium. In: Proceedings of the 1996 USENIX Conference. San Diego.

Lakshman, T.V., Stidialis, D., 1998. High speed policy-based packet forwarding using efficient multi-dimensional range matching. In: Proceedings of the ACM SIGCOMM.

Lampson, B., 1989. Hints for computer system design. In: Proceedings of the 9th ACM Symposium on Operating Systems Principles (SOSP) 1989.

Lampson, B., Srinivasan, V., Varghese, G., 1998. IP lookups using multi-way and multicolumn search. In: Proceedings of IEEE INFOCOM.

Leslie, G. Valiant, 1982. A scheme for fast parallel communication. SIAM Journal on Computing 11 (2), 350–361.

Leung, J.Y.-T., 1989. A new algorithm for scheduling periodic, real-time tasks. Algorithmica 4 (1), 209–219.

Li, P., Church, K.W., 2007. A sketch algorithm for estimating two-way and multi-way associations. Computational Linguistics, p. 2007.

Li, W., Li, X., 2013. HybridCuts: a scheme combining decomposition and cutting for packet classification. In: 2013 IEEE 21st Annual Symposium on High-Performance Interconnects, pp. 41–48.

Li, J., Sung, M., Xu, J., Li, L., May 2004. Large-scale IP traceback in high-speed internet: practical techniques and theoretical foundation. In Proceedings of IEEE Symposium on Security and Privacy.

Li, W., Yang, T., Rottenstreich, O., Li, X., Xie, G., Li, H., Vamanan, B., Li, D., Lin, H., 2020. Tuple space assisted packet classification with high performance on both search and update. IEEE Journal on Selected Areas in Communications 38 (7), 1555–1569.

Liang, E., Zhu, H., Jin, X., Stoica, I., 2019. Neural packet classification. In: Proceedings of the ACM Special Interest Group on Data Communication. SIGCOMM '19. Association for Computing Machinery, pp. 256–269.

Limasset, A., Rizk, G., Chikhi, R., Peterlongo, P., 2017. Fast and scalable minimal perfect hashing for massive key sets. In: 16th International Symposium on Experimental Algorithms, vol. 11, pp. 1–11. hal-01566246.

Lin, B., Keslassy, I., 2010. The concurrent matching switch architecture. IEEE/ACM Transactions on Networking 18 (4), 1330–1343.

Lin, B., Xu, J. (Jim), Hua, N., Wang, H., Zhao, H. (Chuck), 2009. A randomized interleaved DRAM architecture for the maintenance of exact statistics counters. ACM SIGMETRICS Performance Evaluation Review 37 (2), 53–54.

Loukissas, A., Al-Fares, M., Vahdat, A., 2008. A scalable, commodity data center network architecture. In: Proceedings of the ACM SIGCOMM 2008 Conference on Data Communication, SIGCOMM'08. Association for Computing Machinery, New York, NY, pp. 63–74.

Lu, Y., Wang, M., Prabhakar, B., Elephanttrap, F.B., 2007. A low cost device for identifying large flows. In: 15th IEEE Symposium on High-Performance Interconnects, pp. 99–105.

Ma, Y., Banerjee, S., 2012. A smart pre-classifier to reduce power consumption of TCAMs for multi-dimensional packet classification. In: Proceedings of the ACM SIGCOMM 2012 Conference on Applications, Technologies, Architectures, and Protocols for Computer Communication. SIGCOMM '12. Association for Computing Machinery, pp. 335–346.

Maeda, C., Bershad, B., 1993. Protocol service decomposition for high-performance networking. In: Proceedings of the 14th ACM Symposium on Operating Systems Principles (SOSP).

Mahalingam, M., et al., 2020. Virtual eXtensible local area network (VXLAN): a framework for overlaying virtualized layer 2 networks over layer 3 networks. https://datatracker.ietf.org/doc/html/rfc7348.

Malan, G., Jahanian, F., 1998. An extensible probe architecture for network protocol measurement. In: Proceedings of the ACM SIGCOMM.

Maltzahn, C., Richardson, K., Grunwald, D., 1997. Performance issues of enterprise level web proxies. In: Measurement and Modeling of Computer Systems, pp. 13–23.

Manku, G., Motwani, R., 2002. Approximate frequency counts over data streams. In: Proceedings of the 28th International Conference on Very Large Data Bases (VLDB).

Mao, Z., Govindan, R., Varghese, G., Katz, R., 2002. Route flap damping can exacerbate BGP convergence. In: Proceedings of the ACM SIGCOMM, pp. 221–234.

Marty, M., de Kruijf, M., Adriaens, J., Alfeld, C., Bauer, S., Contavalli, C., Dalton, M., Dukkipati, N., Evans, W.C., Gribble, S., Kidd, N., Kononov, R., Kumar, G., Mauer, C., Musick, E., Olson, L., Rubow, E., Ryan, M., Springborn, K., Turner, P., Valancius, V., Wang, X., Vahdat, A., 2019. Snap: a microkernel approach to host networking. In: Proceedings of the 27th ACM Symposium on Operating Systems Principles, SOSP '19. Association for Computing Machinery, pp. 399–413.

Max Vision, 2001. Advanced reference archive of current heuristics for network intrusion detection systems (arach-NIDS). http://www.whitehats.com/ids/.

McCanne, S., 1992. A distributed whiteboard for network conferencing. In: UC Berkeley CS 268 Computer Networks Term Project.

McCanne, S., Jacobson, V., 1993. The BSD packet filter: a new architecture for user-level packet capture. In: USENIX Winter Conference, pp. 259–270.

McKenney, P., 1991. Stochastic fairness queueing. Internetworking: Research and Experience 2, 113–131.

McKeown, N., 1997. A fast switched backplane for a gigabit switched router. Business Communications Review 27 (12).

McKeown, N., 1999. The iSLIP scheduling algorithm for input-queued switches. IEEE/ACM Transactions on Networking 7 (2), 188–201.

McKeown, N., et al., 1997. The tiny tera: a packet switch core. IEEE Micro.

McKeown, N., Mekkittikul, A., Anantharam, V., Walrand, J., 1999. Achieving 100% throughput in an input-queued switch. IEEE Transactions on Communications 47 (8), 1260–1267.

McQuillan, J., 1997. Layer 4 switching. In: Data Communications.

Mead, C., Conway, L., 1980. Introduction to VLSI Systems. Addison Wesley.

Medina, A., Taft, N., et al., 2002. Traffic matrix estimation: existing techniques and new directions. In: Proceedings of the ACM SIGCOMM.

Meng, J., Gong, L., Xu, J., 2020. Sliding-window GPS (SW-GPS): a perfect parallel iterative switching algorithm for input-queued switches. In: Proceedings of IFIP PERFORMANCE. https://dl.acm.org/doi/10.1145/3453953.3453969.

Meiners, C.R., Liu, A.X., Torng, E., 2008. Algorithmic approaches to redesigning TCAM-based systems. https://www.cse.msu.edu/~alexliu/publications/pipeline/sigmetricabstract.pdf.

Misra, J., Gries, D., 1982. Finding repeated elements. Technical report.

Mittal, R., Agarwal, R., Ratnasamy, S., Shenker, S., 2015. Universal packet scheduling. In: Proceedings of the 14th ACM Workshop on Hot Topics in Networks. Association for Computing Machinery.

Mittal, R., Shpiner, A., Panda, A., Zahavi, E., Krishnamurthy, A., Ratnasamy, S., Shenker, S., 2018. Revisiting network support for RDMA. In: Proceedings of the 2018 Conference of the ACM Special Interest Group on Data Communication, SIGCOMM '18. Association for Computing Machinery, pp. 313–326.

Mitzenmacher, M.D., 1996. The power of two choices in randomized load balancing. PhD thesis. University of California at Berkeley.

Mogul, J., 1995. The case for persistent-connection http. In: Proceedings of the ACM SIGCOMM.

Mogul, J., Ramakrishnan, K.K., 1997. Eliminating receive livelock in an interrupt-driven kernel. In: ACM Transactions on Computer Systems, pp. 303–313.

Mogul, J., Rashid, R., Accetta, M., 1987. The packet filter: an efficient mechanism for user-level network code. In: Proceedings of the 11th ACM Symposium on Operating Systems Principles (SOSP), vol. 21, pp. 39–51.

Molinero-Fernandez, P., McKeown, N., 2002. TCP switching exposing circuits to IP. IEEE Microwave Magazine 22 (1), 82–89.

Montazeri, Behnam, Li, Yilong, Alizadeh, Mohammad, Ousterhout, John, Homa, 2018. A Receiver-Driven Low-Latency Transport Protocol Using Network Priorities. In: Proceedings of the 2018 Conference of the ACM Special Interest Group on Data Communication, SIGCOMM '18. Association for Computing Machinery, pp. 221–235.

Moore, D., 2001. CAIDA analysis of code red. Personal conversation. Also see http://www.caida.org/analysis/security/code-red/.

Moore, D., Voelker, G., Savage, S., 2001. Inferring Internet denial-of-service activity. In: Proceedings of the 2001 USENIX Security Symposium.

Mosberger, D., Peterson, L., 1996. Making paths explicit in the Scout operating system. In: Operating Systems Design and Implementation, pp. 153–167.

Mosberger, D., Peterson, L., Bridges, P., O' Malley, S., 1996. Analysis of techniques to improve protocol latency. In: Proceedings of the ACM SIGCOMM.

Motin, A., Italiano, D., 2018. Calloutng: a new infrastructure for for timer facilities in the FreeBSD kernel. https://people.freebsd.org/davide/asia/calloutng.pdf.

Muthukrishnan, S., 2005. Data Streams: Algorithms and Applications at Foundations and Trends in Theoretical Computer Science. NOW Publisher Inc.

Myhrhaug, B., 2001. Sequencing set efficiency. In: Pub. A9, Norwegian Computing Center.

NEBS, 2002. Network equipment building system (NEBS) requirements. http://www.telecordia.com.

Neely, M.J., Modiano, E., Cheng, Y.S., 2007. Logarithmic delay for N × N packet switches under the crossbar constraint. IEEE/ACM Transactions on Networking 15 (3), 657–668.

Newman, P., Minshall, G., Huston, L., 1997. IP switching and Gigabit routers. In: IEEE Communications Magazine.

Nilsson, S., Karlsson, G., 1998. Fast address lookup for Internet routers. In: Proceedings of IEEE Broadband Communications 98.

Network Functions Virtualization (NFV), 2022. https://www.etsi.org/technologies/nfv.

Ousterhout, J., 2021. A Linux Kernel Implementation of the Homa Transport Protocol. In: 2021 USENIX Annual Technical Conference (USENIX ATC 21). USENIX Association, pp. 99–115.

Ousterhout, A., Fried, J., Behrens, J., Belay, A., Balakrishnan, H., 2019. Shenango: achieving high CPU efficiency for latency-sensitive datacenter workloads. In: NSDI'19. USENIX Association, pp. 361–377.

Ozveren, C., Simcoe, R., Varghese, G., 1994. Reliable and efficient hop-by-hop flow control. In: Proceedings of the ACM SIGCOMM.

P4 Open Source Programming Language, 2022. https://p4.org/.

Padhye, J., Floyd, S., 2001. On inferring TCP behavior. In: Proceedings of the ACM SIGCOMM, pp. 271–282.

Pai, V., Druschel, P., Zwaenepoel, W., 1999a. Flash: an efficient and portable Web server. In: Proceedings of the USENIX 1999 Annual Technical Conference.

Pai, V., Druschel, P., Zwaenepoel, W., 1999b. I/O-lite: a unified I/O buffering and caching system. In: Proceedings of the 3rd USENIX Symposium on Operating Systems Design and Implementation.

Pakin, S., Karamcheti, V., Chien, A.A., 1997. Fast messages: efficient, portable communication for workstation clusters and MPPs. In: IEEE Concurrency.

Pan, R., Prabhakar, B., Bonomi, F., Olsen, B., 2008. Approximate fair bandwidth allocation: A method for simple and flexible traffic management. In: 2008 46th Annual Allerton Conference on Communication, Control, and Computing, pp. 1081–1085.

Parekh, A., Gallager, R., 1993. A generalized processor sharing approach to flow control in integrated services networks: the single node case. IEEE/ACM Transactions on Networking 1 (3), 344–357.

Partridge, C., 1993. Gigabit Networking. Addison-Wesley, Reading.

Partridge, C., 1996. Locality and route caches. In: NSF Workshop on Internet Statistics Measurement. San Diego.

Partridge, C., Pink, S., 1993. A faster UDP. IEEE/ACM Transactions on Networking 1 (4).

Partridge, C., Blumenthal, S., Walden, D., 2004. Data networking BBN. In: IEEE Annals of Computing, pp. 56–71.

Parulkar, G., Turner, J., Schmidt, D., 1995. IP over ATM: a new strategy for integrating IP and ATM. In: Proceedings of the ACM SIGCOMM.

Patterson, H., et al., 1995. Informed prefetching and caching. In: Proceedings of the 15th ACM Symposium of Operating Systems Principles (SOSP).

Perlman, R., 1992. Interconnections: Bridges and Routers. Addison Wesley.

Peter, S., Li, J., Zhang, I., Ports, D.R.K., Woos, D., Krishnamurthy, A., Anderson, T., Roscoe, T., 2015. Arrakis: the operating system is the control plane. ACM Transactions on Computer Systems 33 (4), 11. https://doi.org/10.1145/2812806.

Peterson, L., Davy, B., 2000. Computer Networking: A Systems Approach, second edition. Morgan-Kaufman.

Pfaff, B., Pettit, J., Koponen, T., Jackson, E.J., Zhou, A., Rajahalme, J., Gross, J., Wang, A., Stringer, J., Shelar, P., Amidon, K., Casado, M., 2015. The design and implementation of open VSwitch. In: Proceedings of the 12th USENIX Conference on Networked Systems Design and Implementation. NSDI'15, Oakland, CA. USENIX Association, pp. 117–130.

Polya, G., 1957. How to Solve It, 2nd edition. Princeton University Press.

PPCI-SIG Single Root I/O Virtualization, 2018. (SR-IOV) Support in Intel Virtualization Technology for Connectivity. https://www.intel.com/content/dam/doc/white-paper/pci-sig-single-root-io-virtualization-support-in-virtualization-technology-for-connectivity-paper.pdf.

Prabhakar, B., 2009. Scheduling algorithms for CIOQ switches. https://web.stanford.edu/class/ee384m/Handouts/handout9.pdf.

Prabhakar, B., McKeown, N., 1997. On the Speedup Required for Combined Input and Output Queued Switching. Stanford University.

Prekas, G., Kogias, M., Bugnion, E., 2017. ZygOS: achieving low tail latency for microsecond-scale networked tasks. In: Proceedings of the 26th Symposium on Operating Systems Principles, SOSP '17. Association for Computing Machinery, pp. 325–341.

Preparata, F., Shamos, M., 1985. Computational Geometry: An Introduction. Springer-Verlag, New York.

QFQ source code in Linux Kernels. https://github.com/torvalds/linux/blob/master/net/sched/sch_qfq.c.

Qiu, L., Varghese, G., Suri, S., 2001. Fast firewall implementations for software and hardware-based routers. In: Proceedings of the 9th International Conference on Network Protocols (ICNP).

Rabin, M.O., 1981. Fingerprinting by random polynomials. Technical report.

Ramabhadran, S., Varghese, G., 2003. Efficient implementation of a statistics counter architecture. In: Proceedings ACM SIGMETRICS.

Ramakrishnan, K.K., Jain, R., 1990. A binary feedback scheme for congestion avoidance in computer networks. ACM Transactions on Computer Systems.

Rashid, R., Forin, A., Golub, D., Jones, M., Orr, D., Sanzi, R., 1989. Mach: a foundation for open systems (operating systems). In: Proceedings of the Second Workshop on Workstation Operating Systems.

Rau, B., 1991. Pseudo-randomly interleaved memory. In: Proceedings International Symposium on Computer Architecture (ISCA).

RDMA Consortium, 2001. Architectural specifications for RDMA over TCP/IP. http://www.rdmaconsortium.org/home.

Rekhter, Y., Li, T., 1996. An architecture for IP address allocation with CIDR. In: RFC 1518.

Riccardi, F., 2001. Posted note. In: Linux Kernel Archive.

Rijsinghani, A., 1994. Computation of the Internet checksum via incremental update. In: RFC 1624. www.ietf.org/rfc/rfc1624.txt.

Rios, V., Varghese, G., 2022. MashUp: scaling TCAM-based IP lookup to larger databases by tiling trees. https://arxiv.org/abs/2204.09813.

Rizzo, L., Landi, M., 2011. Netmap: memory mapped access to network devices. In: Proceedings of the ACM SIGCOMM 2011 Conference, SIGCOMM '11. In: Association for Computing Machinery, pp. 422–423.

Robson, J.M., 1974. Bounds for some functions concerning dynamic storage allocation. Journal of the Association for Computing Machinery.

Roesch, M., 1999. Snort—lightweight intrusion detection for networks. In: Proceedings of the 13th Systems Administration Conference. USENIX.

Ronad, A., 2019. Troubleshooting QoS on the Nexus9k. Presented at Cisco Live 2019, San Diego, CA. https://www.ciscolive.com/c/dam/r/ciscolive/us/docs/2019/pdf/CTHDCN-2301.pdf. (Accessed November 2020).

Sabnani, K., Netravali, A., 1989. A high speed transport protocol for datagram virtual circuit networks. In: Proceedings of the ACM SIGCOMM.

Saeed, A., Dukkipati, N., Valancius, V., The Lam, V., Contavalli, C., Vahdat, A.C., 2017. Carousel: scalable traffic shaping at end hosts. In: Proceedings of the Conference of the ACM Special Interest Group on Data Communication, SIGCOMM '17. Association for Computing Machinery, pp. 404–417.

Salim, J.H., Olsson, R., Kuznetsov, A., Softnet, B., 2001. Beyond Softnet. In: Proceedings of the 5th Annual Linux Showcase & Conference, vol. 5, ALS '01. USENIX Association, p. 18.

Sanchez, L., Milliken, W., et al., 2001. Hardware support for hash-based IP traceback. In: Proceedings of the 2nd DARPA Information Survivability Conference and Exposition. DISCEX.

Sarwate, D., 1988. Computation of cyclic redundancy checks by table lookup. Communications of the ACM 31 (8).

Satran, J., Smith, D., Meth, K., et al., July 2001. ISCSI. In Internet Draft draft-ietf-ips-iSCSI-07.txt.

Savage, S., Wetherall, D., Karlin, A., Anderson, T., 2000. Practical network support for IP traceback. In: Proceedings of the ACM SIGCOMM, pp. 295–306.

Segmentation Offloads, 2022. https://www.kernel.org/doc/html/latest/networking/segmentation-offloads.html.

sendmsg copy avoidance with MS_ZEROCOPY, 2022. https://legacy.netdevconf.info/2.1/papers/debruijn-msgzerocopy-talk.pdf.

Semeria, C., 2002. T-series routing platforms: system and forwarding architecture. In: Juniper Networks White Paper, Part Number 200027-001.

Semeria, C., Gredler, J., 2001. Juniper networks solutions for network accounting. In: Juniper White Paper, 200010-001.

Shah, D., Gupta, P., 2001. Fast updates on Ternary CAMs for packet lookups and classification. IEEE Micro 21 (1).

Shah, D., Iyer, S., Prabhakar, B., McKeown, N., 2002a. Maintaining statistics counters in router line cards. IEEE Micro.

SHARP, 2019. In-Network Scalable Hierarchical Aggregation and Reduction Protocol. http://www.hpcadvisorycouncil.com/events/2019/swiss-workshop/pdf/020419/G_Bloch_Mellanox_SHARP_02042019.pdf.

Shah, D., Giaccone, P., Prabhakar, B., 2002b. Efficient randomized algorithms for input-queued switch scheduling. IEEE Micro 22 (1), 10–18.

Shannon, C., Moore, D., Claffy, K., 2001. Characteristics of fragmented IP traffic on Internet links. In: ACM SIGCOMM Internet Measurement Workshop.

Sherwood, T., Varghese, G., Calder, B., 2003. A pipelined memory architecture for high throughput network processors. In: International Symposium on Computer Architecture.

Sikka, S., Varghese, G., 2000. Memory efficient state lookups. In: Proceedings of the ACM SIGCOMM.

Simcoe, R., Pei, T., 1994. Perspectives on ATM switch architecture and the influence of traffic pattern assumptions on switch design. In: ACM Computer Communication Review.

Singh, S., Baboescu, F., Varghese, G., 2004a. Packet classification using multidimensional cutting. In: Proceedings ACM SIGCOMM.

Singh, S., Estan, C., Varghese, G., Savage, S., 2004b. Automated worm fingerprinting. In: OSDI.

Sivaraman, A., Subramanian, S., Alizadeh, M., Chole, S., Chuang, S.-T., Agrawal, A., Balakrishnan, H., Edsall, T., Katti, S., McKeown, N., 2016a. Programmable packet scheduling at line rate. In: Proceedings of the 2016 ACM SIGCOMM Conference. Association for Computing Machinery, pp. 44–57.

Sivaraman, A., Cheung, A., Budiu, M., Kim, C., Alizadeh, M., Balakrishnan, H., Varghese, G., McKeown, N., Licking, S., 2016b. Packet transactions: high-level programming for line-rate switches. In: SIGCOMM '16. Association for Computing Machinery, pp. 15–28.

Smith, J., Traw, B., 2001. Technical report. Operating systems support for end-to-end Gbps networking.

Snoeren, A., Partridge, C., et al., 2001. Hash-based IP traceback. In: Proceedings of the ACM SIGCOMM, pp. 295–306.

Snort, 2001. The open source network intrusion detection system. http://www.snort.org/.

Souza, R., Krishnakumar, P., Ozveren, C., Simcoe, R., Spinney, B., Thomas, R., Walsh, R., 1994. GIGAswitch: A high-performance packet switching platform. Digital Technical Journal 6 (1), 9–22.

Spalink, T., Karlin, S., Peterson, L., 2000. Evaluating network processors in IP forwarding. Computer Science Technical Report TR-626-00. Princeton University.

SPEC consortium, 1999. Specweb99 benchmark. http://www.specbench.org/osg/web99/.

Spring, N., Mahajan, R., Wetherall, D., 2002. Measuring ISP topologies using rocketfuel. In: Proceedings of the ACM SIGCOMM.

Srinivasan, V., Varghese, G., 1999. Faster IP lookups using controlled prefix expansion. ACM Transactions on Computer Systems.

Srinivasan, V., Varghese, G., Suri, S., Waldvogel, M., 1998. Fast and scalable layer four switching. Computer Communication Review 28 (4), 191–202.

Srinivasan, V., Suri, S., Varghese, G., 1999. Packet classification using tuple space search. In: Proceedings of the ACM SIGCOMM, pp. 135–146.

Stanojevic, R., 2007. Small active counters. In: Proceedings of IEEE Infocom.

Stevens, W.R., 1994. TCP/IP Illustrated, vol. 1. Addison Wesley.

Stevens, W.R., 1998. UNIX Network Programming. Prentice-Hall.

Stewart, J.W., 1999. BGP-4: Interdomain Routing in the Internet. Addison Wesley.

Stiliadis, D., Varma, A., 1996a. Latency-rate servers: a general model for analysis of traffic scheduling algorithms. In: Proceedings of Infocom'96.

Stiliadis, D., Varma, A., 1996b. Design and analysis of frame-based fair queuing: a new traffic scheduling algorithm for packet switched networks. In: Proceedings of ACM Sigmetrics'96, pp. 104–115.

Sting, S. Savage, 1999. A TCP-based network measurement tool. In: USENIX Symposium on Internet Technologies and Systems.

Stoica, I., Abdel-Wahab, H., 1995. Earliest Eligible Virtual Deadline First: A Flexible and Accurate Mechanism for Proportional Share Resource Allocation. Old Dominion University.

Stoica, I., Zhang, H., 1998. Exact emulation of an output queueing switch by a combined input output queueing switch. In: Sixth IEEE/IFIP International Workshop on Quality of Service, pp. 218–224.

Stoica, I., Shenker, S., Zhang, H., 1998. Core-Stateless Fair Queuing: Achieving approximately fair bandwidth. In: Proceedings of ACM SIGCOMM'98, pp. 118–130.

Stone, J., Partridge, C., 2000. When the CRC and TCP checksum disagree. In: Proceedings of the ACM SIGCOMM, pp. 309–319.

Sundar, I., 2008. Load balancing and parallelism for the internet. PhD Thesis. Stanford University.

Sundar, I., Kompella, R.R., McKeown, N., 2008. Designing packet buffers for router linecards. IEEE/ACM Transactions on Networking 16 (3), 705–717. https://doi.org/10.1109/TNET.2008.923720.

Suri, S., Varghese, G., Chandranmenon, G., 1997. Leap forward virtual clock: a new fair queuing scheme with guaranteed delays and throughput fairness. In: Proceedings of Infocom 97.

Suri, P., Warkhede, S., Varghese, G., 2001. Multiway range trees: Scalable IP lookup with fast updates. In: Globecom.

Sutherland, I., Sproull, R., Harris, D., 1999. Logical Effort, Designing Fast CMOS Circuits. Morgan Kaufmann.

Tamir, Y., Frazier, G.L., 1988. High-performance multi-queue buffers for VLSI communications switches. SIGARCH Computer Architecture News 16 (2), 343–354.

Tanenbaum, A.S., 1981. Computer Networks. Prentice-Hall.

Tanenbaum, A., 1992. Modern Operating Systems. Prentice Hall.

Tassiulas, L., 1998. Linear complexity algorithms for maximum throughput in radio networks and input queued switches. In: Proceedings of the IEEE INFOCOM. San Francisco, CA, pp. 533–539.

Tassiulas, L., Ephremides, A., 1992. Stability properties of constrained queueing systems and scheduling policies for maximum throughput in multihop radio networks. IEEE Transactions on Automatic Control 37 (12), 1936–1948.

Taylor, D.E., Turner, J.S., 2007. ClassBench: a packet classification benchmark. IEEE/ACM Transactions on Networking 15 (3), 499–511.

Thadani, M.N., Khalidi, Y.A., 1995. An efficient zero-copy I/O framework for UNIX. Technical Report SMLI TR-95-39. Sun Microsystems Laboratories, Inc.

The Lam, V., Mitzenmacher, M., Varghese, G., 2010. Carousel: scalable logging for intrusion prevention systems. In: Proceedings of the 7th USENIX Symposium on Networked Systems Design and Implementation. NSDI 2010, April 28–30, 2010. USENIX Association, San Jose, CA, pp. 361–376.

The State of Fibre Channel, 2022. https://fibrechannel.org/state-of-fibre-channel/.

Thekkath, C., Nguyen, T., Moy, E., Lazowska, E., 1993. Implementing network protocols at user level. In: Proceedings ACM SIGCOMM.

Thomas, R., Varghese, G., Harvey, G., Souza, R., 1992. Method for keeping track of sequence numbers in a large space.

Thompson, K., Miller, G., Wilder, R., 1997. Wide-area traffic patterns and characterizations. In: IEEE Network.

Touch, J., Parham, B., 1996. Implementing the Internet checksum in hardware. In: RFC 1936. www.ietf.org/rfc/rfc1936.txt.

Toynbee, A., Caplan, J., 1972. A Study of History, Abridged Version. Oxford University Press.

Turner, J.S., 1986. New directions in communications (or which way to the information age?). IEEE Communications.

Turner, J., 1997. Design of a gigabit ATM switch. In: Proceedings of IEEE INFOCOM.

Turner, J., 2002. Personal communication.

UNH Inter Operability Lab, 2001. FDDI tutorials. http://www.iol.unh.edu/training/fddi.html.

Userspace Networking with DPDK. https://www.linuxjournal.com/content/userspace-networking-dpdk.

Valente, P.o, 2004. Exact GPS simulation with logarithmic complexity, and its application to an optimally fair scheduler. In: Proceedings of the ACM SIGCOMM.

Valiant, L., 1990. A bridging model for parallel computation. Communications of the ACM 33 (8).

Vamanan, B., Vijaykumar, T.N., 2011. TreeCAM: decoupling updates and lookups in packet classification. In: Proceedings of the Seventh COnference on Emerging Networking EXperiments and Technologies. Association for Computing Machinery.

Vamanan, B., Voskuilen, G., Vijaykumar, T.N., 2010. EffiCuts: Optimizing packet classification for memory and throughput. In: Proceedings of the ACM SIGCOMM 2010 Conference. SIGCOMM '10. Association for Computing Machinery, pp. 207–218.

Varadhan, K., Govindan, R., Estrin, D., 2000. Persistent route oscillations in inter-domain routing. Computer Networks 32 (1), 1–16.

Varghese, G., Lauck, A., 1987. Hashed and hierarchical timing wheels: data structures for the efficient implementation of a timer facility. In: Proceedings of the 11th ACM Symposium on Operating Systems Principles (SOSP).

Vaucher, J.G., Duval, P., 1975. A comparison of simulation event list algorithms. In: CACM, vol. 18.

von Eicken, T., Culler, D., et al., 1992a. Active messages: a mechanism for integrated communication and computation. In: 19th International Symposium on Computer Architecture, pp. 256–266.

von Eicken, T., Culler, D., Goldstein, S., Schauser, K., 1992b. Active messages: a mechanism for integrated communication and computation. In: Proceedings of the 19th International Symposium on Computer Architecture (ISCA), pp. 256–266.

von Eicken, T., Basu, A., et al., 1995. U-Net: a user-level network interface for parallel and distributed computing. In: Proceedings of the 15th ACM Symposium on Operating Systems Principles (SOSP).

Waldvogel, M., Varghese, G., Turner, J., Plattner, B., 1997. Scalable high speed IP routing lookups. In: SIGCOMM.

Wang, J., Huang, C., 2000. A high-speed single-phase-clocked CMOS priority encoder. In: IEEE International Symposium on Circuits and Systems.

Wang, H., Zhao, H., Lin, B., Xu, J., 2010. Design and analysis of a robust pipelined memory system. In: 2010 Proceedings of IEEE INFOCOM, pp. 1541–1549.

Wang, L., Ye, T., Lee, T., Hu, W., 2018. A parallel complex coloring algorithm for scheduling of input-queued switches. IEEE Transactions on Parallel and Distributed Systems 29 (7), 1456–1468.

Warkhede, P., Suri, S., Varghese, G., 2001. Multiway range trees: scalable IP lookups with fast updates. In: IEEE Globecom 2001 Internet Symposium.

Web Polygraph Association, 2001. Web polygraph. http://www.web-polygraph.org/.

Welsh, M., Culler, David E., Brewer, Eric A., 2001. SEDA: an architecture for well-conditioned, scalable Internet services. In: Proceedings of the 22nd Symposium on Operating Systems Principles (SOSP), pp. 230–243.

Whang, K., Vander-Zanden, B., Taylor, H., 1990. A linear-time probabilistic counting algorithm for database applications. ACM Transactions on Database Systems.

Wilson, P., 1992. Uniprocessor garbage collection techniques. Lecture Notes in Computer Science, vol. 637. Springer-Verlag.

Wilson, P., Johnstone, M., et al., 1995. Dynamic storage allocation: a survey and critical review. In: Proceedings of the International Workshop on Memory Management. Kinross Scotland (UK).

Wilton, S.J.E., Jouppi, N.P., 1996. CACTI: an enhanced cache access and cycle time model. IEEE Journal of Solid-State Circuits 31 (5), 677–688.

Woo, T., 2000. A modular approach to packet classification: algorithms and results. In: Proceedings IEEE INFO-COM.

Wright, G.R., Stevens, W.R., 1995. TCP/IP Illustrated, vol. 2. Addison-Wesley.

Xu, J., Singhal, M., Degroat, J., 2000. A novel cache architecture to support layer four packet classification at memory access speeds. In: Proceedings IEEE INFOCOM, pp. 1445–1454.

Yang, M., Zheng, S.Q., 2003. An efficient scheduling algorithm for CIOQ switches with space-division multi-plexing expansion. In: INFOCOM 2003. Twenty-Second Annual Joint Conference of the IEEE Computer and Communications, vol. 3. IEEE Societies, pp. 1643–1650.

Yang, T., Xie, G., Li, Y., Fu, Q., Liu, A.X., Li, Q., Mathy, L., 2014. Guarantee IP lookup performance with FIB explosion. Computer Communication Review 44 (4), 39–50. https://doi.org/10.1145/2740070.2626297.

Yang, S., Lin, B., Tune, P., Xu, J., 2017a. A simple re-sequencing load-balanced switch based on analytical packet reordering bounds. In: The 36th Annual IEEE International Conference on Computer Communications (INFO-COM).

Yang, Sen, Lin, Bill, Xu, Jun, 2017b. Safe randomized load-balanced switching by diffusing extra loads. Proceedings of the ACM on Measurement and Analysis of Computing Systems 1 (2), 29:1–29:37.

Yeh, Y., Hluchyj, M., Acampora, A., 1987. The knockout switch: a simple modular architecture for high-performance packet switching. IEEE Journal on Selected Areas in Communications, 1426–1435.

Yuan, X., Duan, Z., Round-Robin, F., 2009. A low complexity packet schduler with proportional and worst-case fairness. IEEE Transactions on Computers 58 (3), 365–379. https://doi.org/10.1109/TC.2008.176.

Zane, F., Narlikar, G., Basu, A., 2003. Coolcams: power-efficient TCAMs for forwarding engines. In: IEEE INFO-COM 2003. Twenty-Second Annual Joint Conference of the IEEE Computer and Communications Societies, vol. 1, pp. 42–52. (IEEE Cat. No. 03CH37428).

Zec, M., Mikuc, M., 2017. Pushing the envelope: beyond two billion IP routing lookups per second on com-modity CPUs. In: 25th International Conference on Software, Telecommunications and Computer Networks (SoftCOM), pp. 1–6.

Zec, M., Rizzo, L., Mikuc, M., 2012. DXR: towards a billion routing lookups per second in software. Computer Communication Review 42 (5), 29–36. https://doi.org/10.1145/2378956.2378961.

Zhang, L., 1991. Virtual clock: a new traffic control algorithm for packet-switched networks. ACM Transactions on Computer Systems.

Zhang, H., Ferrari, D., 1994. Rate-controlled service disciplines. Journal of High Speed Networks 3 (4), 389–412.

Zhang, Y., Roughan, M., Duffield, N., Greenberg, A., 2003. Fast accurate computation of large-scale IP matrices from link loads. In: Proceedings of the ACM SIGMETRICS.

Zhang, Y., Singh, S., Sen, S., Duffield, N., Lund, C., 2004. Online identification of hierarchical heavy hitters: algorithms, evaluation, and application. In: Proceedings of the ACM Internet Measurement Conference (IMC).

Zhao, Q., Xu, J., 2004. On the computational complexity of maintaining GPS clock in packet scheduling. In: Proceedings of IEEE INFOCOM.

Zhao, Q., Kumar, A., Wang, J., Xu, J., 2005. Data streaming algorithms for accurate and efficient measurement of traffic and flow matrices. In: Proceedings of ACM SIGMETRICS.

Zhao, Q., Ge, Z., Wang, J., Xu, J., 2006a. Robust traffic matrix estimation with imperfect information: making use of multiple data sources. In: Proceedings of ACM SIGMETRICS.

Zhao, Q., Xu, J., Liu, Z., 2006b. Design of a novel statistics counter architecture with optimal space and time efficiency. In: Proceedings of ACM SIGMETRICS.

Zhao, H. (Chuck), Wang, H., Lin, B., Xu, J. (Jim), 2009. Design and performance analysis of a DRAM-based statistics counter array architecture. In: Proceedings of the 5th ACM/IEEE Symposium on Architectures for Networking and Communications Systems, ANCS'09. ACM, New York, NY, pp. 84–93.

Zhao, H. (Chuck), Lall, A., Ogihara, M., Xu, J., 2010. Global iceberg detection over distributed data streams. In: Proceedings of IEEE ICDE.

Zhao, S., Wang, R., Zhou, J., Ong, J., Mogul, J.C., Vahdat, A., 2019. Minimal rewiring: efficient live expansion for clos data center networks. In: 16th USENIX Symposium on Networked Systems Design and Implementation (NSDI 19). USENIX Association, Boston, MA, pp. 221–234.

Index

Printed in the United States
by Baker & Taylor Publisher Services